# PUB. 110

# LIST OF LIGHTS

## RADIO AIDS AND FOG SIGNALS

## 2015

## GREENLAND, THE EAST COASTS OF NORTH AND SOUTH AMERICA (EXCLUDING CONTINENTAL U.S.A. EXCEPT THE EAST COAST OF FLORIDA) AND THE WEST INDIES

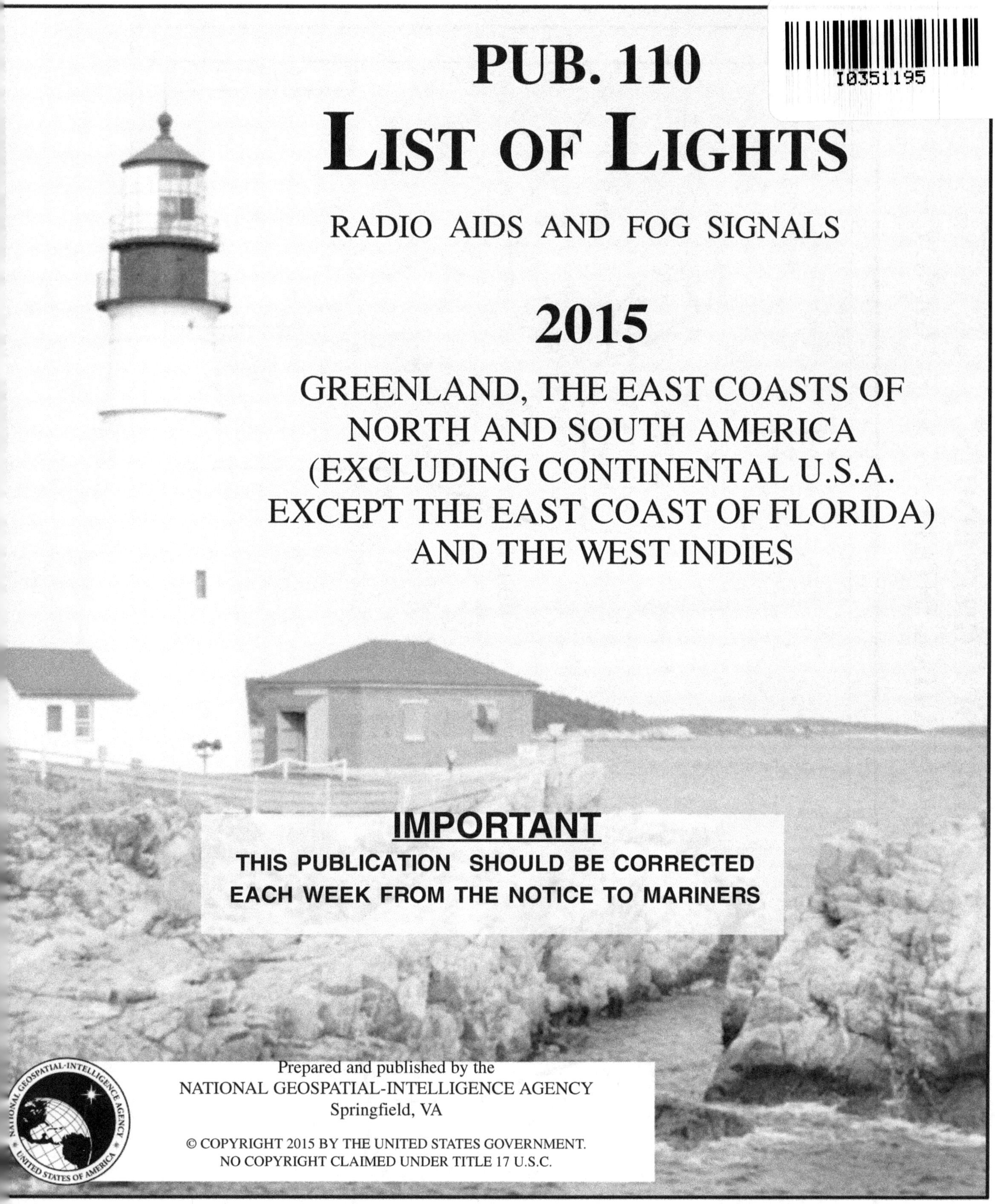

**IMPORTANT**

**THIS PUBLICATION SHOULD BE CORRECTED EACH WEEK FROM THE NOTICE TO MARINERS**

Prepared and published by the
NATIONAL GEOSPATIAL-INTELLIGENCE AGENCY
Springfield, VA



NSN 7642014007534
NGA REF. NO. LLPUB110

# LIST OF LIGHTS LIMITS
# NATIONAL GEOSPATIAL-INTELLIGENCE AGENCY

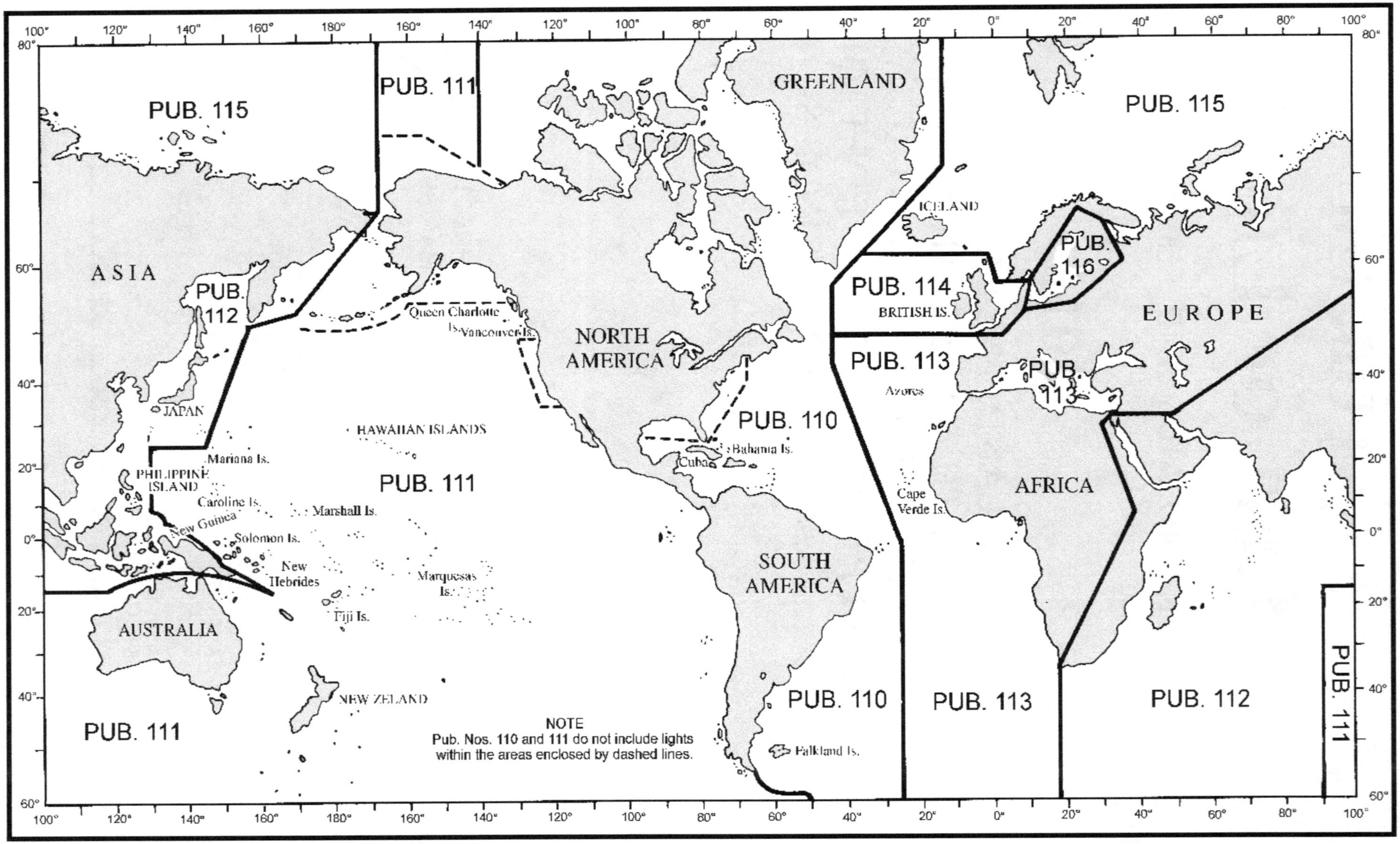

110 **LIGHTS** **ATLANTIC** **2015**

## WARNING ON USE OF FLOATING AIDS TO NAVIGATION TO FIX A NAVIGATIONAL POSITION

The aids to navigation depicted on charts comprise a system consisting of fixed and floating aids with varying degrees of reliability. Therefore, prudent mariners will not rely solely on any single aid to navigation, particularly a floating aid.

The buoy symbol is used to indicate the approximate position of the buoy body and the sinker which secures the buoy to the seabed. The approximate position is used because of practical limitations in positioning and maintaining buoys and their sinkers in precise geographical locations. These limitations include, but are not limited to, inherent imprecisions in position fixing methods, prevailing atmospheric and sea conditions, the slope of and the material making up the seabed, the fact that buoys are moored to sinkers by varying lengths of chain, and the fact that buoy and/or sinker positions are not under continuous surveillance but are normally checked only during periodic maintenance visits which often occur more than a year apart. The position of the buoy body can be expected to shift inside and outside the charting symbol due to the forces of nature. The mariner is also cautioned that buoys are liable to be carried away, shifted, capsized, sunk, etc. Lighted buoys may be extinguished or sound signals may not function as the result of ice or other natural causes, collisions, or other accidents.

For the foregoing reasons, a prudent mariner must not rely completely upon the position or operation of floating aids to navigation, but will also utilize bearings from fixed objects and aids to navigation on shore. Further, a vessel attempting to pass close aboard always risks collision with a yawing buoy or with the obstruction the buoy marks.

## PREFACE

The 2015 edition of Pub. 110, List of Lights, Radio Aids and Fog Signals for Greenland, the East Coasts of North and South America (excluding Continental U.S.A. except the East Coast of Florida), and the West Indies, cancels the previous edition of Pub. 110.

This edition contains information available to the National Geospatial-Intelligence Agency (NGA) up to 28 February 2015, including Notice to Mariners No. 9 of 2015.

A summary of corrections subsequent to the above date will be in Section II of the Notice to Mariners which announced the issuance of this publication.

In the interval between new editions, corrective information affecting this publication will be published in the Notice to Mariners and must be applied in order to keep this publication current.

Nothing in the manner of presentation of information in this publication or in the arrangement of material implies endorsement or acceptance by NGA in matters affecting the status and boundaries of States and Territories.

## RECORD OF CORRECTIONS
## PUBLISHED IN WEEKLY NOTICE TO MARINERS

NOTICE TO MARINERS

| YEAR 2015 | | | | YEAR 2016 | | | |
|---|---|---|---|---|---|---|---|
| 1........ | 14........ | 27........ | 40........ | 1........ | 14........ | 27........ | 40........ |
| 2........ | 15........ | 28........ | 41........ | 2........ | 15........ | 28........ | 41........ |
| 3........ | 16........ | 29........ | 42........ | 3........ | 16........ | 29........ | 42........ |
| 4........ | 17........ | 30........ | 43........ | 4........ | 17........ | 30........ | 43........ |
| 5........ | 18........ | 31........ | 44........ | 5........ | 18........ | 31........ | 44........ |
| 6........ | 19........ | 32........ | 45........ | 6........ | 19........ | 32........ | 45........ |
| 7........ | 20........ | 33........ | 46........ | 7........ | 20........ | 33........ | 46........ |
| 8........ | 21........ | 34........ | 47........ | 8........ | 21........ | 34........ | 47........ |
| 9........ | 22........ | 35........ | 48........ | 9........ | 22........ | 35........ | 48........ |
| 10........ | 23........ | 36........ | 49........ | 10........ | 23........ | 36........ | 49........ |
| 11........ | 24........ | 37........ | 50........ | 11........ | 24........ | 37........ | 50........ |
| 12........ | 25........ | 38........ | 51........ | 12........ | 25........ | 38........ | 51........ |
| 13........ | 26........ | 39........ | 52........ | 13........ | 26........ | 39........ | 52........ |

# TABLE OF CONTENTS

## Section 13
### Brazil


## Section 14
### East Coast of South America
### Including Uruguay, Argentina, Falkland Islands and Straits of Magellan


## Section 15
### Radiobeacons


## Section 16
### Differential GPS Stations

# INTRODUCTION

The National Geospatial-Intelligence Agency publishes a List of Lights, Radio Aids and Fog Signals in seven volumes divided geographically as shown on the index chartlet on the inside front cover of this book. Major fixed and outermost floating aids to navigation, such as sea buoys, safety fairway buoys, traffic separation buoys, etc., are listed. Other floating aids are not generally listed. Storm signals, signal stations, radio direction finders, radiobeacons, RACONs and RAMARKs located at or near lights are found in this List. Radiobeacons are listed in a separate section in the back of this publication.

The date to which this publication has been corrected can be found in the Preface. In the interval between new editions, corrective information affecting this publication will be published in Section II of Notice to Mariners, and must be applied to keep this publication current. All of these corrections should be applied in the appropriate places and their insertion noted in the "Record of Corrections."

Mariners and other users are requested to forward new or corrective information useful in the correction of this publication to:

MARITIME SAFETY OFFICE
N64-SH
NATIONAL GEOSPATIAL-INTELLIGENCE AGENCY
7500 GEOINT DRIVE
SPRINGFIELD VA 22150-7500

# Buoys and Beacons IALA* Buoyage System

Where in force, the IALA System applies to all fixed and floating marks and occasionally lighthouses, sector lights, range marks, lightships and LANBY's (large automatic navigational buoys).

The standard buoy shapes are cylindrical (can), conical, spherical, pillar (including high focal plane) and spar, but variations may occur, for example lightfloats. In the illustrations below, only the standard buoy shapes are used. In the case of fixed beacons (lighted or unlighted), only the shape of the topmark is of navigational significance.

**Lateral Marks** (used in conjunction with a conventional direction of buoyage) are generally for well-defined channels. There are two international Buoyage Regions-A and B-where Lateral marks differ.

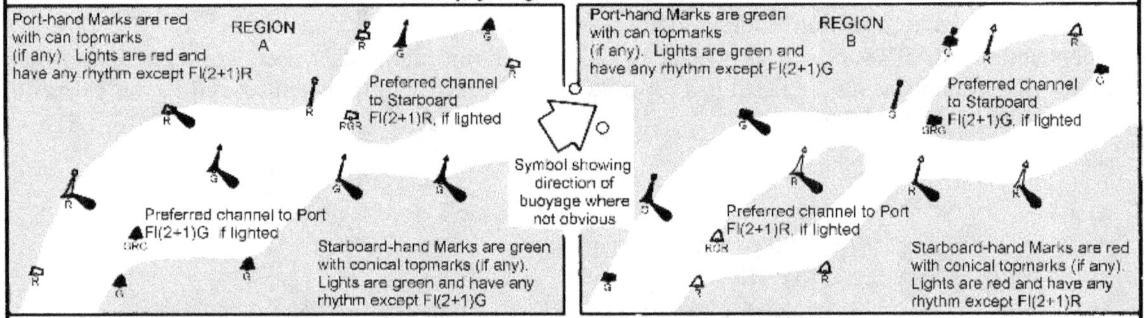


A preferred channel buoy may also be a pillar or a spar. All preferred channel marks have three horizontal bands of color.

All marks other than Lateral Marks are the same in REGIONS A and B

| UNLIGHTED MARKS | LIGHTED MARKS |
|---|---|

**Cardinal Marks** indicating navigable water to the named side of the marks

Topmark 2 black cones

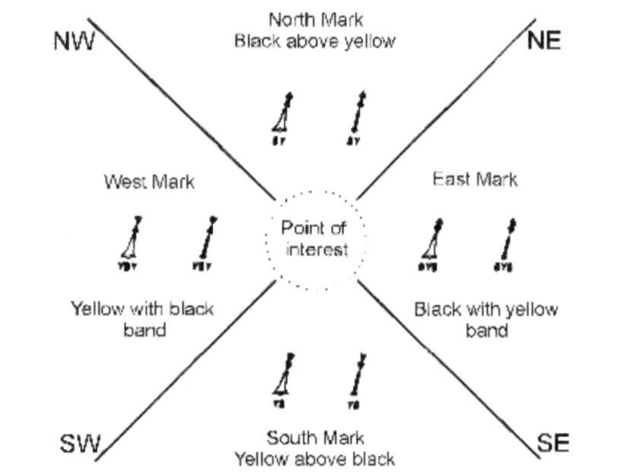


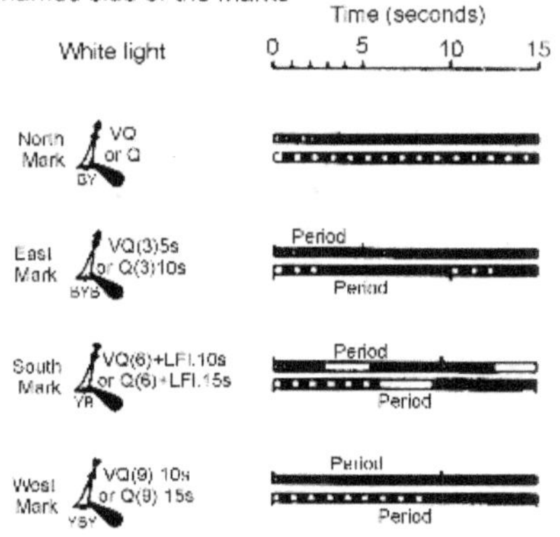


* The same abbreviations are used for lights on spar buoys and beacons. The periods, 5s, 10s and 15s, may not always be charted.

**Isolated Danger Marks,** stationed over dangers with navigable water around them.

Body black with red band (s)
Topmark: 2 black balls

Fl(2) White light

**Safe Water Marks,** such as mid-channel and landfall marks.

Body red and white stripes
Topmark (if any): red ball

White light

**Special Marks,** not primarily to assist navigation but to indicate special features.

Body (shape optional): yellow
Topmark (if any) yellow X

etc

Fl. Y etc Yellow light

BEACONS with IALA System topmarks are charted by upright symbols, eg. (minor beacon) or, on smaller-scale charts:

Beacon towers are charted: (occasionally lighted)

RADAR REFLECTORS on buoys and beacons are not generally charted.

COLOR ABBREVIATIONS under symbols, especially those of spar buoys, may be omitted or may be at variance with symbols shown above.

LIGHTFLOATS: The IALA System is not usually applied to large lightfloats (replacing manned lightships) but may be applied to smaller lightfloats.

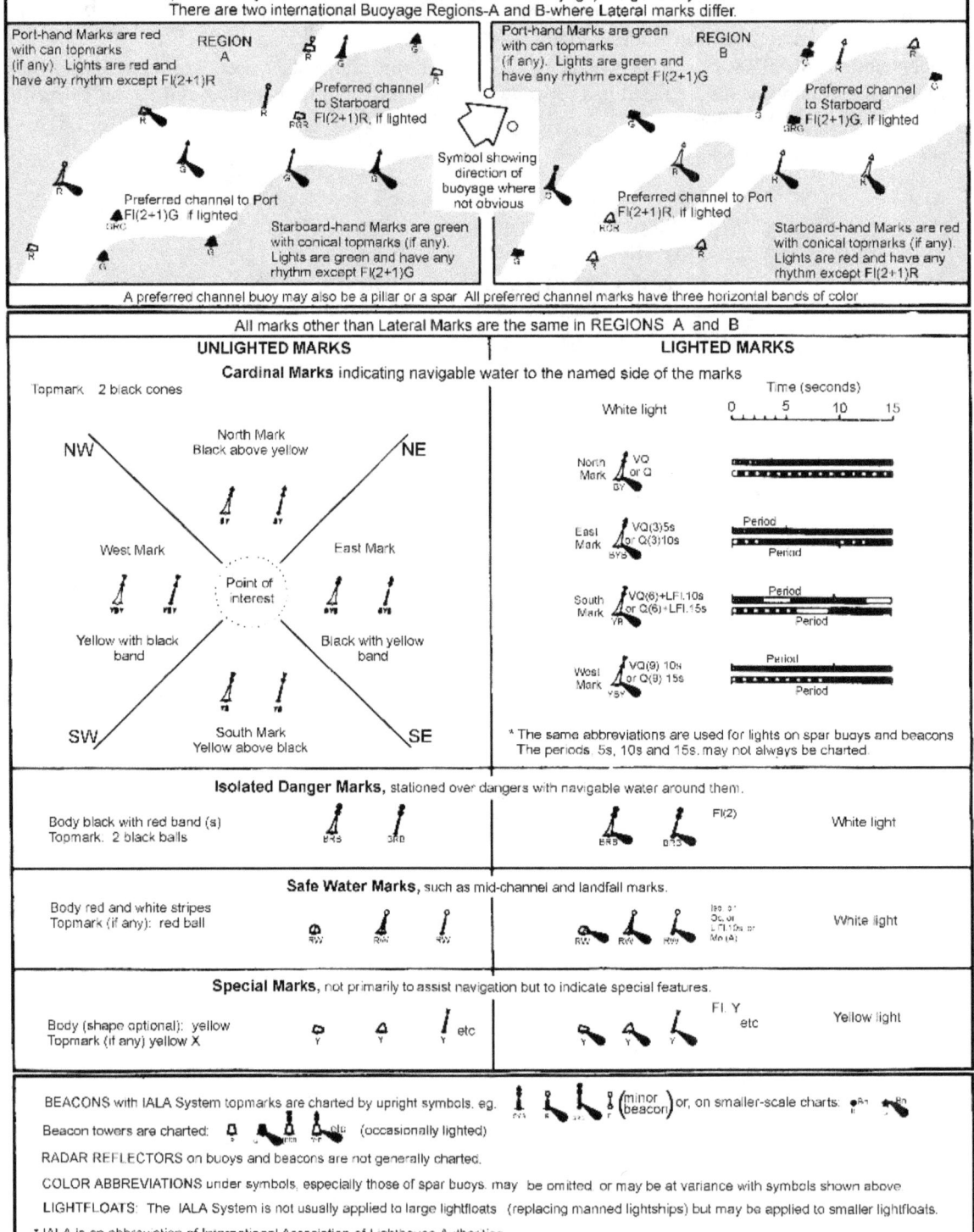

* IALA is an abbreviation of International Association of Lighthouse Authorities

# MARITIME SAFETY WEB SITE

The National Geospatial-Intelligence Agency (NGA) Maritime Safety Web site provides worldwide remote query access to extensive menus of maritime safety information 24 hours a day.

Databases made available for access, query and download include Notice to Mariners, Publications, Broadcast Warnings, Office of Naval Intelligence (ONI) Reports, Anti-Shipping Activity Messages (ASAMs), Arctic Maritime Safety Information (AMSI) Reports, Mobile Offshore Drilling Units (MODUs), Product Catalog and Miscellaneous Products. Publications that are also made available as PDF files include the U.S. Notice to Mariners, U.S. Chart No. 1, The American Practical Navigator (Bowditch), International Code of Signals, Radio Navigational Aids, World Port Index, Distances Between Ports, Sight Reduction Tables for Marine and Air Navigation, Radar Navigation and Maneuvering Board Manual.

The Maritime Safety Web site can be accessed via the NGA Homepage (**www.nga.mil**) under the Products and Services link or directly at **http://msi.nga.mil/NGAPortal/MSI.portal**. Any questions concerning the Maritime Safety Web site should be directed to:

MARITIME SAFETY OFFICE
ATTN: NSS STAFF
N64-SH
NATIONAL GEOSPATIAL-INTELLIGENCE AGENCY
7500 GEOINT DRIVE
SPRINGFIELD, VA 22150-7500

Telephone: (1) 571-557-7103 or DSN 547-7103
E-mail: webmaster_nss@nga.mil

## DESCRIPTION

(Lights, Buoys, RACONs, RAMARKs)

Information is tabulated in eight columns as follows:

*Column 1:* The number assigned to each light, RACON or RAMARK by this Agency. International numbers are listed below this number in italic type and in a cross reference in the back of the book. RACONs and RAMARKs located at a light are listed with the light. Those not located at a light are assigned separate numbers.

*Column 2:* Name and descriptive location of the light or buoy, RACON or RAMARK. A dash (-) or dashes (--) in this column is used to reduce repetition of principal geographic names. This column is intended to describe the location of the navigational aid and to distinguish it from others in proximity. Differences in type indicate the following:

**Bold-faced:** Lights intended for landfall or having a visibility (range) of 15 miles or more.

*Italics:* Floating aids.

*ITALICS CAPITALS:* Lightships and LANBYs.

Roman: All other lights not mentioned above.

*Column 3:* Approximate latitude and longitude of a navigational aid to the nearest tenth of a minute, intended to facilitate chart orientation (use column 2 and the appropriate chart for precise positioning).

*Column 4:* Light, buoy, RACON or RAMARK characteristic (see Characteristics of Lights chart for explanation of lights).

*Column 5:* Height of light in feet (Roman type) equivalent measurement (below) given in meters (Bold-faced type).

*Column 6:* Range. The distance, expressed in nautical miles, that a light can be seen in clear weather or that a RACON or RAMARK can be received.

*Column 7:* Description of the structure and its height in feet.

Note–Stripes are vertical. Bands are horizontal. The use of the term "diagonal stripes" is the exception.

*Column 8:* Remarks–sectors, fog signals, radar reflectors, minor lights close by, radiobeacons, storm signals, signal stations, radio direction finders, and other pertinent information.

Geographic names or their spellings do not necessarily reflect recognition of the political status of an area by the United States Government.

The names of lights may differ from geographic names on charts.

### ABBREVIATIONS

Where the lights of different countries intermingle in the list they are distinguished by the following letters:

| | | | |
|---|---|---|---|
| (A.) | Argentina | (M.) | Mexico |
| (B.) | Belize | (N.) | Netherlands |
| (C.) | Chile | (Nic.) | Nicaragua |
| (Can.) | Canada | (P.) | Panama |
| (Col.) | Colombia | (U.) | Uruguay |
| (C.R.) | Costa Rica | (U.K.) | United Kingdom |
| (F.) | France | (U.S.) | United States |
| (H.) | Haiti | (V.) | Venezuela |

Other abbreviations:

| | |
|---|---|
| Al.—alternating | lt.—lit |
| bl.—blast | Mo.—Morse code |
| Bu.—blue | min.—minute |
| Dir.—directional | obsc.—obscured |
| ec.—eclipsed | Oc.—occulting |
| ev.—every | Or.—orange |
| F.—fixed | Q.—quick flashing |
| Fl.—flashing | R.—red |
| fl.—flash | s.—seconds |
| G.—green | si.—silent |
| horiz.—horizontal | U.Q.—ultra quick flashing |
| intens.—intensified | unintens.—unintensified |
| I.Q.— interrupted quick flashing | vert.—vertical |
| Iso.—isophase | Vi.—violet |
| I.V.Q.—interrupted very quick flashing | vis.—visible |
| Km.— kilometer (0.62137 mile) | V.Q.— very quick flashing |
| L.Fl.—long flashing | W.—white |
| | Y.—yellow |

# CHARACTERISTICS OF LIGHTS

| TYPE | ABBR. | GENERAL DESCRIPTION | ILLUSTRATION |
|---|---|---|---|
| Fixed | F. | A continuous and steady light. |  |
| Occulting | Oc. | The total duration of light in a period is longer than the total duration of darkness and the intervals of darkness (eclipses) are usually of equal duration. Eclipse regularly repeated. |  |
| Group occulting | Oc.(2) | An occulting light for which a group of eclipses, specified in number, is regularly repeated. |  |
| Composite group occulting | Oc.(2+1) | A light similar to a group occulting light except that successive groups in a period have different numbers of eclipses. |  |
| Isophase | Iso. | A light for which all durations of light and darkness are clearly equal. |  |
| Flashing | Fl. | A light for which the total duration of light in a period is shorter than the total duration of darkness and the appearances of light (flashes) are usually of equal duration (at a rate of less than 50 flashes per minute). | 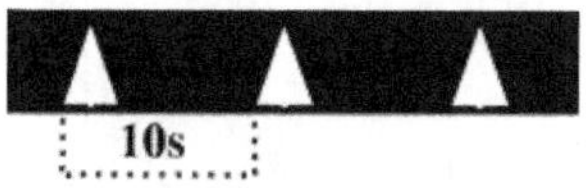 |
| Long flashing | L.Fl. | A single flashing light for which an appearance of light of not less than 2 sec. duration (long flash) is regularly repeated. |  |
| Group flashing | Fl.(3) | A flashing light for which a group of flashes, specified in number, is regularly repeated. |  |
| Composite group flashing | Fl.(2+1) | A light similar to a group flashing light except that successive groups in a period have different numbers of flashes. | 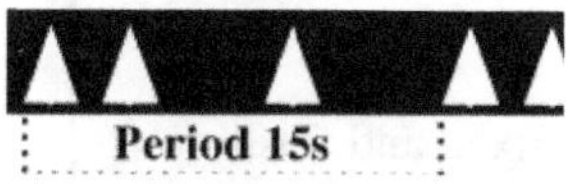 |
| Quick flashing | Q. | A light for which a flash is regularly repeated at a rate of not less than 50 flashes per minute but less than 80 flashes per minute. |  |
| Group quick flashing | Q.(3) | A light for which a specified group of flashes is regularly repeated; flashes are repeated at a rate of not less than 50 flashes per minute but less than 80 flashes per minute. |  |
| | Q.(9) | |  |
| | Q.(6)+L.Fl. | |  |

| TYPE | ABBR. | GENERAL DESCRIPTION | ILLUSTRATION |
|---|---|---|---|
| Interrupted quick flashing | I.Q. | A light for which the sequence of quick flashes is interrupted by regularly repeated eclipses of constant and long duration. |   |
| Very quick flashing | V.Q. | A light for which a flash is regularly repeated at a rate of not less than 80 flashes per minute but less than 160 flashes per minute. |  |
| Group very quick flashing | V.Q.(3) | A light for which a specified group of very quick flashes is regularly repeated. |   |
| | V.Q.(9) | |   |
| | V.Q.(6)+L.Fl. | |   |
| Interrupted very quick flashing | I.V.Q. | A light for which the sequence of very quick flashes is interrupted by regularly repeated eclipses of constant and long duration. |   |
| Ultra quick flashing | U.Q. | A light for which a flash is regularly repeated at a rate of not less than 160 flashes per minute. |  |
| Interrupted ultra quick flashing | I.U.Q. | A light for which the sequence of ultra quick flashes is interrupted by regularly repeated eclipses of constant and long duration. |  |
| Morse code | Mo.(U) | A light for which appearances of light of two clearly different durations are grouped to represent a character or characters in Morse Code. |  |
| Fixed and flashing | F.Fl. | A light for which a fixed light is combined with a flashing light of greater luminous intensity. |   |
| Alternating light | Al. | A light showing different colors alternately. | |

NOTE - Alternating lights may be used in combined form with most of the previous types of lights.

# NOMENCLATURE OF LIGHTS

Lights exhibit a distinctive appearance by which they are recognized, e.g. Fixed, Flashing, Group Flashing, etc. The properties of their appearance, by which they are distinguished, are referred to as the *characteristics* of the light. The principal characteristics are generally the sequence of intervals of light and darkness, and, in some cases, the sequence of colors of light exhibited.

*Fixed lights*-those which exhibit a continuous steady light.

*Rhythmic lights*-those which exhibit a sequence of intervals of light and eclipse (repeated at regular intervals) in a manner described in Chart No. 1 and this volume.

*Alternating lights*-rhythmic lights which exhibit different colors during each sequence.

*Period of a light*-the time occupied by an entire cycle of intervals of light(s) and eclipse(s).

*Range: Meteorological visibility*-the greatest distance at which a black object of suitable dimensions can be seen and recognized against the horizon sky or, in the case of night observations, could be seen and recognized if the general illumination were raised to the normal daylight level.

*Luminous range of a light*-the greatest distance at which a light can be seen merely as a function of its luminous intensity, the meteorological visibility, and the sensitivity of the observer's eyes.

*Nominal range of the light*-the luminous range of a light in a homogeneous atmosphere in which the meteorological visibility is 10 nautical miles.

*Geographical range of a light*-the greatest distance at which a light can be seen as a function of the curvature of the earth, the height of the light source and the height of the observer.

The visibility of a light is usually the distance that it can be seen in clear weather and is expressed in nautical miles. Visibilities listed are values received from foreign sources.

*Range lights*-two or more lights at different elevations, so situated to form a range (leading line) when brought into transit. The light nearest the observer is the *front light* and the one farthest from the observer is the *rear light*. The front light is normally at a lower elevation than the rear light.

*Directional lights*-lights illuminating a sector of very narrow angle and intended to mark a direction to be followed.

*Vertical lights*-Two or more lights disposed vertically or geometrically to form a triangle, square, or other figure. If the individual lights serve different purposes, those of lesser importance are called *Auxiliary lights*.

*Occasional lights*-lights exhibited only when specially needed:

(a) *Tidal lights*-shown at the entrance of a harbor, to indicate tide and tidal current conditions within the harbor.

(b) *Fishing light*-for the use of fishermen and shown when required.

(c) *Private light*-maintained by a private authority for its own purposes. The mariner should exercise special caution when using a private light for general navigation.

*Seasonal lights*-usually shown only during the navigation season or for a lesser time period within that season.

*Articulated lights*-offshore aids to navigation consisting of a length of pipe attached directly to a sinker by means of a pivot or such other device employing the principle of the universal joint. The positional integrity is intermediary between that of a buoy and a fixed aid.

*Aeronautical lights*-lights of high intensity which may be the first lights observed at night from vessels approaching the coast. Those lights situated near the coast are listed in the List of Lights in order that the navigator may be able to obtain more information concerning their description.

These lights are not designed or maintained for marine navigation and they are subject to change without prompt notification.

These lights are indicated in this List by the designation AVIATION LIGHT and are placed in geographical sequence in the body of the text along with lights for surface navigation.

*Aeromarine lights*-marine-type lights for which part of the beam is deflected to an angle of 10 to 15 degrees above the horizon to facilitate use by aircraft.

*Sector limits and arcs of visibility*-these are arranged clockwise and are given from seaward toward the light. Thus, in the diagram, the sectors of the light are defined as: obscured from shore to 302°, red to 358°, green to 052°, white to shore. These are bearings of the light as seen from a vessel crossing the sector lines.

Under some conditions of the atmosphere, white lights may have a reddish hue. The mariner should not judge solely by color where there are sectors but should verify this position by taking a bearing of the light. On either side of the line of demarcation between white and red there is always a small sector of uncertain color, as the edges of a sector of visibility cannot be clearly defined.

When a light is obscured by adjoining land and the arc of visibility is given, the bearing on which the light disappears may vary with the distance from which it is observed. When the light is cut off by a sloping point of land or hill, the light may be seen over a wider arc by a ship farther off than by one closer.

*Bearings*-all bearings are true, measured clockwise from 000°, and given in degrees or degrees and minutes.

Oil drilling and production platforms in *Canadian* waters exhibit a Q.W. light and sound a horn every 20 seconds.

Many of the navigational lights for *Colombia*, *Panama*, *Costa Rica*, *Nicaragua*, and *Guatemala* have been reported as irregular or unreliable.

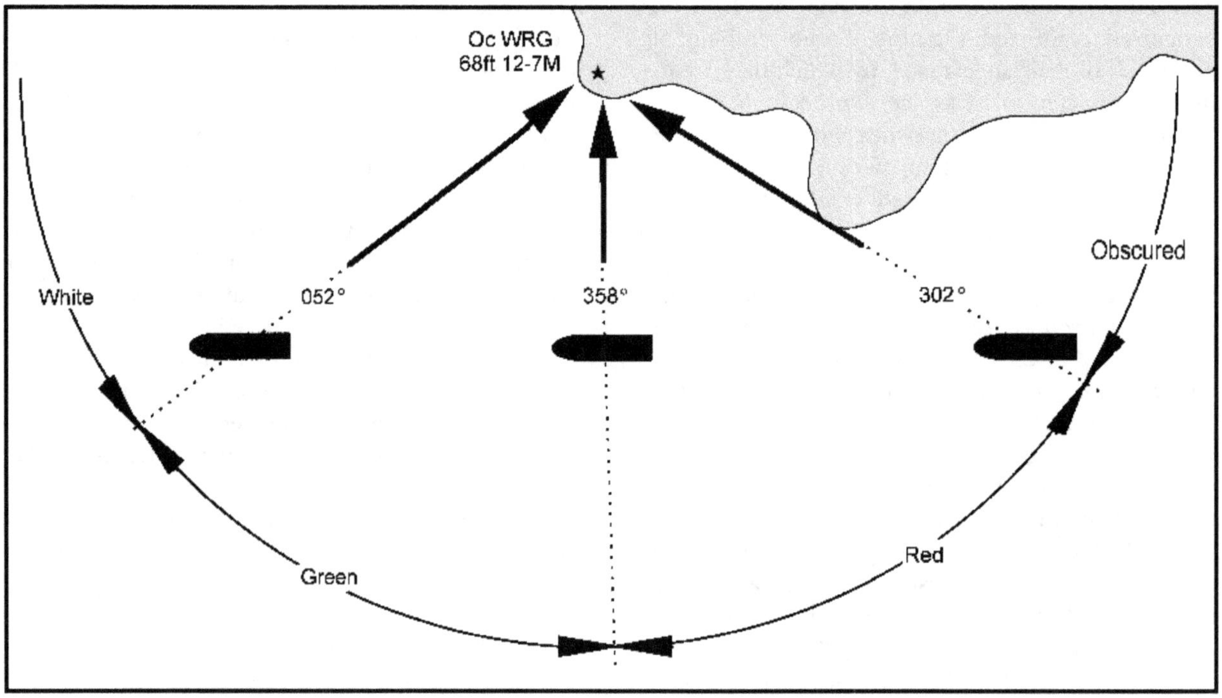
Oc WRG
68ft 12-7M
White
052°
358°
302°
Obscured
Green
Red

## LIGHTSHIPS, SUPERBUOYS, AND OFFSHORE LIGHT STATIONS

Courses should be set to pass all floating aids to navigation with sufficient clearance to avoid the possibility of collision from any cause. Experience shows that floating aids to navigation cannot be safely used as leading marks to be passed close aboard, but should always be left broad off the course, whenever searoom permits.

When approaching a lightship, superbuoy, or a station on a submarine site on radio bearings, the risk of collision will be avoided by insuring that the radio bearing does not remain constant.

Most lightships and large buoys are anchored with a very long scope of chain and, as a result, the radius of their swinging circle is considerable. The charted position is the location of the anchor. Furthermore, under certain conditions of wind and current, they are subject to sudden and unexpected sheers which are certain to hazard a vessel attempting to pass close aboard.

During extremely heavy weather and due to their exposed locations, lightships may be carried off station. The mariner should, therefore, not implicitly rely on a lightship maintaining its precisely charted position during and immediately following severe storms. A lightship known to be off station will secure her light, fog signal, and radiobeacon and fly the International Code signal "LO" signifying "I am not in my correct position."

The lights in the following areas of Canada are shown all year round unless otherwise indicated in column 8: certain lights on the east coast of Newfoundland north of Cape St. Francis; those on the east and south coasts of Newfoundland, from Cape St. Francis to Cape Anguille; those in the Bay of Fundy west of a line joining Quaco Head and Margaretville; those required by vessels or iceboats for winter passage to Prince Edward Island.

All other lights under the control of the Department of Transport are maintained in operation whenever navigation in the vicinity is open. Lights used solely as harbor lights are not exhibited when the harbor is closed, although general navigation may remain open. Fishing lights are maintained only during the fishing season. In any case where there is reasonable doubt whether the light is required, it is kept in operation.

Major light stations which exhibit the main light 24 hours per day are being equipped with an emergency light which is brought into service automatically throughout the hours of darkness in the event of failure of the main light. This emergency light has a standard characteristic of Group Flashing White (6) 15 sec., that is six flashes of 1/2 second duration followed by a period of darkness (eclipse) of 7 seconds. It will normally (on a dark night with a clear atmosphere) be visible at 2 nautical miles. The presence of such emergency lights is shown in column 8.

In the St. Lawrence River and Gulf of St. Lawrence, except as otherwise stated, all lights will be maintained while general navigation is open. If for any exceptional reason it is found desirable to continue certain lights in operation after the close of general navigation, arrangements may be made through the Agency of the Department of Quebec and Charlottetown for notifying such stations as can be reached by telegraph, telephone or radio. Lights at remote and island stations, where communication is not available, will be extinguished after 22 December.

Lights in the St. Lawrence seaway are shown from 1 April to 15 December.

The harbors on the north coast of Prince Edward Island and exposed harbors on the east coast of New Brunswick have sandbars at their mouths, the channels through which are liable to be blocked or shifted by storms. Range lights may be changed without notice being given and it is never safe for mariners without local knowledge to cross the bars.

Oil drilling and production platforms are marked as follows: Q.W. Horn 20sec.

Many of the lights of *Belize*, *Colombia*, *Costa Rica*, *Dominican Republic*, *Guatemala*, *Haiti*, *Honduras*, *Nicaragua*, *Panama*, and *Venezuela* have been reported as irregular or unreliable.

Oil drilling and production platforms off the coast of *Brazil* are marked as follows: F.R. 10M on the masthead and 4 Mo. (U) W. 10M; those in harbors and in inner waters are marked by F.R. and 4 F.W. 5M.

They may occasionally be equipped with Aero radiobeacons.

# FOG SIGNALS

The function of a fog signal in the system of aids to navigation is to warn of danger and to provide the mariner with an audible means of approximating his position relative to the fog signal when the station, or any visual signal which it displays, is obscured from view by atmospheric conditions.

Fog signals depend upon the transmission of sound through air. As aids to navigation, they have certain inherent defects that should be considered. Sound travels through the air in a variable and frequently unpredictable manner.

It has been established that:

fog signals are heard at greatly varying distances and that the distance at which a fog signal can be heard may vary with the bearing of the signal and may be different on different occasions;

under certain conditions of atmosphere, when a fog signal has a combination of high and low tones, it is not unusual for one of the tones to be inaudible. In the case of sirens, which produce a varying tone, portions of the blast may not be heard;

there are occasionally areas close to the signal in which it is wholly inaudible. This is particularly true when the fog signal is screened by intervening land or other obstructions;

fog may exist a short distance from a station and not be observable from it, so that the signal may not be in operation;

even though a fog signal may not be heard from the deck or bridge of a ship when the engines are in motion, it may be heard when the ship is stopped, or from a quiet position. Sometimes it may be heard from aloft though not on deck;

the intensity of the sound emitted by a fog signal may be greater at a distance than in immediate proximity.

All these considerations point to the necessity for the utmost caution when navigating near land in fog. Particular attention should be given to placing lookouts in positions in which the noises in the ship are least likely to interfere with hearing a fog signal. Fog signals are valuable as warnings, but the mariner should not place implicit reliance upon them in navigating his vessel. They should be considered solely as warning devices.

Among the devices in common use as fog signals are:

Radiobeacons which broadcast simple dot-and-dash combinations by means of a transmitter emitting modulated continuous waves;

Diaphones which produce sound by means of a slotted reciprocating piston actuated by compressed air. Blasts may consist of two tones of different pitch, in which case the first part of the blast is high and the last of a low pitch. These alternate pitch signals are called "two-tone;"

Diaphragm horns which produce sound by means of a diaphragm vibrated by compressed air, steam, or electricity. Duplex or triplex horn units of differing pitch produce a chime signal;

Nautophones, electrically operated instruments, each comprising a vibrating diaphragm, fitted with a horn, which emits a high note similar in power and tone to that of the reed;

Reed horns which produce sound by means of a steel reed vibrator by compressed air;

Sirens which produce sound by means of either a disk or a cup-shaped rotor actuated by compressed air or electricity;

Whistles which produce sound by compressed air emitted through a circumferential slot into a cylindrical bell chamber;

Bells which are sounded by means of a hammer actuated by hand, wave motion, by a descending weight, compressed gas, or electricity;

Guns and explosive signals which are produced by firing of explosive charges, the former being discharged from a gun, and the latter being exploded in midair;

Fog Detector Lights—certain light stations, in addition to the main light, are equipped with fog detector lights for automatic detection of fog. These lights sweep back and forth through an area over which the fog watch is necessary, showing a powerful bluish-white flash of about 1 second in duration. The interval between successive flashes will vary with the position of the vessel within the sector. At the limits of the sector the duration of the flash may be considerably longer than 1 second.

Fog detector lights operate continuously.

Standby fog signals are sounded at some of the light and fog signal stations when the main fog signal is inoperative. Some of these standby fog signals are of a different type and characteristic than the main fog signal.

Radiobeacons, RACONs, RAMARKs, and radio direction-finders are mentioned in the List of Lights, but for detailed information, including the synchronization of radio signals and sound signals for distance finding, the navigator should consult Pub. 117, Radio Navigational Aids.

Note—use Chart No. 1 for the complete list of symbols and abbreviations commonly used in presenting the essential characteristics of lights, fog signals, and radio aids found on charts.

# VISIBILITY TABLE

*Table of distances at which objects can be seen at sea according to their respective elevations and the elevation of the eye of the observer*

| Height in Feet | Distance in geographic or nautical miles | Height in feet | Distance in geographic or nautical miles | Height in feet | Distance in geographic or nautical miles | Height in feet | Distance in geographic or nautical miles | Height in feet | Distance in geographic or nautical miles | Height in feet | Distance in geographic or nautical miles |
|---|---|---|---|---|---|---|---|---|---|---|---|
| 1 | 1.2 | 23 | 5.6 | 45 | 7.8 | 135 | 13.6 | 340 | 21.6 | 600 | 28.7 |
| 2 | 1.7 | 24 | 5.7 | 46 | 7.9 | 140 | 13.8 | 350 | 21.9 | 620 | 29.1 |
| 3 | 2.0 | 25 | 5.9 | 47 | 8.0 | 145 | 14.1 | 360 | 22.2 | 640 | 29.5 |
| 4 | 2.3 | 26 | 6.0 | 48 | 8.1 | 150 | 14.3 | 370 | 22.5 | 660 | 30.1 |
| 5 | 2.6 | 27 | 6.1 | 49 | 8.2 | 160 | 14.8 | 380 | 22.8 | 680 | 30.5 |
| 6 | 2.9 | 28 | 6.2 | 50 | 8.3 | 170 | 15.3 | 390 | 23.1 | 700 | 31.0 |
| 7 | 3.1 | 29 | 6.3 | 55 | 8.7 | 180 | 15.7 | 400 | 23.4 | 720 | 31.4 |
| 8 | 3.3 | 30 | 6.4 | 60 | 9.1 | 190 | 16.1 | 410 | 23.7 | 740 | 31.8 |
| 9 | 3.5 | 31 | 6.5 | 65 | 9.4 | 200 | 16.5 | 420 | 24.0 | 760 | 32.3 |
| 10 | 3.7 | 32 | 6.6 | 70 | 9.8 | 210 | 17.0 | 430 | 24.3 | 780 | 32.7 |
| 11 | 3.9 | 33 | 6.7 | 75 | 10.1 | 220 | 17.4 | 440 | 24.5 | 800 | 33.1 |
| 12 | 4.1 | 34 | 6.8 | 80 | 10.5 | 230 | 17.7 | 450 | 24.8 | 820 | 33.5 |
| 13 | 4.2 | 35 | 6.9 | 85 | 10.8 | 240 | 18.1 | 460 | 25.1 | 840 | 33.9 |
| 14 | 4.4 | 36 | 7.0 | 90 | 11.1 | 250 | 18.5 | 470 | 25.4 | 860 | 34.3 |
| 15 | 4.5 | 37 | 7.1 | 95 | 11.4 | 260 | 18.9 | 480 | 25.6 | 880 | 34.7 |
| 16 | 4.7 | 38 | 7.2 | 100 | 11.7 | 270 | 19.2 | 490 | 25.9 | 900 | 35.1 |
| 17 | 4.8 | 39 | 7.3 | 105 | 12.0 | 280 | 19.6 | 500 | 26.2 | 920 | 35.5 |
| 18 | 5.0 | 40 | 7.4 | 110 | 12.3 | 290 | 19.9 | 520 | 26.7 | 940 | 35.9 |
| 19 | 5.1 | 41 | 7.5 | 115 | 12.5 | 300 | 20.3 | 540 | 27.2 | 960 | 36.3 |
| 20 | 5.2 | 42 | 7.6 | 120 | 12.8 | 310 | 20.6 | 560 | 27.7 | 980 | 36.6 |
| 21 | 5.4 | 43 | 7.7 | 125 | 13.1 | 320 | 20.9 | 580 | 28.2 | 1000 | 37.0 |
| 22 | 5.5 | 44 | 7.8 | 130 | 13.3 | 330 | 21.3 | | | | |

**Explanation.**—The line of sight connecting the observer and a distant object is at maximum length tangent with the spherical surface of the sea. It is from this point of tangency that the tabular distances are calculated. The table must accordingly be entered twice to obtain the actual geographic visibility of the object—first with the height of the object, and second with the height of the observer's eye—and the two figures so obtained must be added. Thus, if it is desired to find the maximum distance at which a powerful light may be seen from the bridge of a vessel where the height of eye of the observer is 55 feet above the sea, from the table:

| | Nautical Miles |
|---|---|
| 55 feet height of observer (visible). . . . . . . . . . . . . | 8.7 |
| 200 feet height of light(visible) . . . . . . . . . . . . . . | 16.5 |
| Distance visible . . . . . . . . . . . . . . . . . . . . . . . . . | 25.2 |

## CONVERSION TABLE — FEET TO WHOLE METERS

(FOR HEIGHTS OF LIGHTS)
**1 foot = 0.3048 meter**

| Feet | Meters | Feet | Meters | Feet | Meters | Feet | Meters | Feet | Meters | Feet | Meters |
|---|---|---|---|---|---|---|---|---|---|---|---|
| | | 40 | 12 | 80 | 24 | 120 | 37 | 160 | 49 | 200 | 61 |
| 1 | 0 | 41 | 12 | 81 | 25 | 121 | 37 | 161 | 49 | 300 | 91 |
| 2 | 1 | 42 | 13 | 82 | 25 | 122 | 37 | 162 | 49 | 400 | 122 |
| 3 | 1 | 43 | 13 | 83 | 25 | 123 | 37 | 163 | 50 | 500 | 152 |
| 4 | 1 | 44 | 13 | 84 | 26 | 124 | 38 | 164 | 50 | 600 | 183 |
| 5 | 2 | 45 | 14 | 85 | 26 | 125 | 38 | 165 | 50 | 700 | 213 |
| 6 | 2 | 46 | 14 | 86 | 26 | 126 | 38 | 166 | 51 | 800 | 244 |
| 7 | 2 | 47 | 14 | 87 | 27 | 127 | 39 | 167 | 51 | 900 | 274 |
| 8 | 2 | 48 | 15 | 88 | 27 | 128 | 39 | 168 | 51 | 1000 | 305 |
| 9 | 3 | 49 | 15 | 89 | 27 | 129 | 39 | 169 | 52 | | |
| 10 | 3 | 50 | 15 | 90 | 27 | 130 | 40 | 170 | 52 | | |
| 11 | 3 | 51 | 16 | 91 | 28 | 131 | 40 | 171 | 52 | | |
| 12 | 4 | 52 | 16 | 92 | 28 | 132 | 40 | 172 | 52 | | |
| 13 | 4 | 53 | 16 | 93 | 28 | 133 | 41 | 173 | 53 | | |
| 14 | 4 | 54 | 16 | 94 | 29 | 134 | 41 | 174 | 53 | | |
| 15 | 5 | 55 | 17 | 95 | 29 | 135 | 41 | 175 | 53 | | |
| 16 | 5 | 56 | 17 | 96 | 29 | 136 | 41 | 176 | 54 | | |
| 17 | 5 | 57 | 17 | 97 | 30 | 137 | 42 | 177 | 54 | | |
| 18 | 5 | 58 | 18 | 98 | 30 | 138 | 42 | 178 | 54 | | |
| 19 | 6 | 59 | 18 | 99 | 30 | 139 | 42 | 179 | 55 | | |
| 20 | 6 | 60 | 18 | 100 | 30 | 140 | 43 | 180 | 55 | | |
| 21 | 6 | 61 | 19 | 101 | 31 | 141 | 43 | 181 | 55 | | |
| 22 | 7 | 62 | 19 | 102 | 31 | 142 | 43 | 182 | 55 | | |
| 23 | 7 | 63 | 19 | 103 | 31 | 143 | 44 | 183 | 56 | | |
| 24 | 7 | 64 | 20 | 104 | 32 | 144 | 44 | 184 | 56 | | |
| 25 | 8 | 65 | 20 | 105 | 32 | 145 | 44 | 185 | 56 | | |
| 26 | 8 | 66 | 20 | 106 | 32 | 146 | 45 | 186 | 57 | | |
| 27 | 8 | 67 | 20 | 107 | 33 | 147 | 45 | 187 | 57 | | |
| 28 | 9 | 68 | 21 | 108 | 33 | 148 | 45 | 188 | 57 | | |
| 29 | 9 | 69 | 21 | 109 | 33 | 149 | 45 | 189 | 58 | | |
| 30 | 9 | 70 | 21 | 110 | 34 | 150 | 46 | 190 | 58 | | |
| 31 | 9 | 71 | 22 | 111 | 34 | 151 | 46 | 191 | 58 | | |
| 32 | 10 | 72 | 22 | 112 | 34 | 152 | 46 | 192 | 59 | | |
| 33 | 10 | 73 | 22 | 113 | 34 | 153 | 47 | 193 | 59 | | |
| 34 | 10 | 74 | 23 | 114 | 35 | 154 | 47 | 194 | 59 | | |
| 35 | 11 | 75 | 23 | 115 | 35 | 155 | 47 | 195 | 59 | | |
| 36 | 11 | 76 | 23 | 116 | 35 | 156 | 48 | 196 | 60 | | |
| 37 | 11 | 77 | 23 | 117 | 36 | 157 | 48 | 197 | 60 | | |
| 38 | 12 | 78 | 24 | 118 | 36 | 158 | 48 | 198 | 60 | | |
| 39 | 12 | 79 | 24 | 119 | 36 | 159 | 48 | 199 | 61 | | |

# RADIOBEACONS

## RADIO DIRECTION-FINDER SETS ON SHIPS

Radio direction-finder sets on board ship enable bearings to be taken of transmissions from other ships, aircraft, shore stations, marine radiobeacons, and the coastal stations of the radio communication network. When located in the pilothouse or on the navigating bridge, the direction-finder enables the navigating officer to obtain bearings himself without reference to others and without delay.

Due to the great value of radio bearings, particularly when visibility is poor and when celestial observations cannot be obtained, the radio direction-finder on board ship deserves the same consideration and care as are given to the sextant and compass. It has the following characteristics in common with the two latter navigational instruments: the readings are subject to certain errors; these errors may be reduced by skillful and intelligent operation; the dangers of using erroneous readings may be greatly reduced by the intelligence and good judgment of the mariner. In order to acquire experienced judgment in the operation of the instrument, it is essential that the mariner use it as much as practicable.

Troubles from interference and weak signals are greatly reduced by the use of direction-finders of proper selectivity. The bearings must be corrected for radio deviation as shown by the calibration curve of the set.

### Types of Radiobeacons

1. Directional radiobeacons which transmit radio waves in beams along fixed bearings.
2. Rotating radiobeacons by which a beam of radio waves is resolved in azimuth in a manner similar to the beam of light sent out by rotating lights.
3. Circular radiobeacons which send out waves of approximately uniform strength in all directions so that ships may take radio bearings of them by means of the ship's radio direction-finder sets. This is the most common type of radiobeacon.

To extend the usefulness of marine radiobeacons to ships and aircraft employing automatic radio direction finders, U.S. marine radiobeacons on the Atlantic and Pacific Coasts and Great Lakes have been modified to transmit a continuous carrier signal during the entire radiobeacon operating period with keyed modulation providing the characteristic signal. Unless a beat frequency oscillator is installed, the continuous carrier signals are not audible to the operator of an aural null direction finder. A ten second dash has been included in the characteristic of these radiobeacons, to enable the navigator using a conventional aural null direction finder to refine his bearing. Vessels with direction finders will be able to use the United States radiobeacons located on the Atlantic and Pacific Coasts, and Great Lakes at any time in their assigned sequence.

### Aeronautical Radio Aids

Aeronautical radiobeacons and radio ranges are often used by navigators of marine craft in the same manner as marine radiobeacons are used for determining lines of positions. They are particularly useful along coasts where marine broadcast coverage is inadequate. Aeronautical aids situated inland become less trustworthy, so far as ships are concerned, when high land intervenes between them and the coast. They are established to be of primary usefulness to aircraft, and surface craft should use these aids with caution. Only those aeronautical radiobeacons considered to be of use to the mariner have been selected for inclusion in this publication.

AERONAUTICAL RADIOBEACONS. Like marine radiobeacons, these aids broadcast a characteristic signal on a fixed frequency.

NOTE: The assigned frequency of aeronautical radiobeacons is normally from 200 to 415 kHz while the frequency of marine radiobeacons is normally from 285 to 325 kHz. Aeronautical radiobeacons not within the marine radiobeacon band will not normally be listed in this publication.

The range signals are interrupted at intervals to permit broadcast of the identification signal. In aviation publications the range leg bearings are most often given as magnetic bearings toward the station; in this publication they are given as true bearings toward the station. Unless otherwise stated in the station details, aeronautical radio aids mentioned in this publication transmit continuously.

NOTE: Mariners are advised that changes to and deficiencies in aeronautical radio facilities are not always immediately available to maritime interests and the positions are approximate and listed to the nearest minute only.

### Obligations of Administrations Operating Radiobeacons

The obligations of nations and other administrations operating radiobeacons are given in Article 43 of the Radio Regulations of the International Telecommunication Union, Geneva.

### Accuracy of Bearings Taken Aboard Ship

No exact rules can be given as to the accuracy to be expected in radio bearings taken by a ship as the accuracy depends to a large extent upon the skill of the ship's operator, the condition of the ship's equipment, and the accuracy of the ship's calibration curve. Mariners are urged to obtain this information by taking frequent radio bearings when their ship's position is accurately known and by recording the results. Normally, United States radiobeacons are operated in a group of six, each station in a group using the same frequency and transmitting for one minute in its proper sequence, and operate during all periods, either sequenced or continuously, regardless of weather conditions.

SKILL OF OPERATOR: Skill in the operation of the radio direction-finder can be obtained only by practice and by observing the technical instructions for the set in question. For these reasons the operator should carefully study the instructions issued with the set and should practice taking bearings frequently.

OPERATOR'S ERROR: As the operator obtains bearings by revolving the direction-finder coil until the signal disappears or becomes a minimum, the operator can tell by the size of the arc of silence or of minimum strength approximately how accurately the bearing has been taken. For instance, if the minimum is broad and the residual signal covers about 10° with equal strength, it is doubtful if the bearing can be accurately estimated. On the other hand, if a sharp minimum can be obtained, the operator can determine the bearing to within a half of a degree.

In this connection it should be noted that a properly operating and correctly adjusted direction-finder should in no case produce other than a point or arc of absolute silence. That is, there should be no "residual" signal at the point or arc of observation. The sharpness and completeness of the arc of silence are the best indications of a properly operating direction-finder, and their absence is the best indication of the presence of "night effect."

SUNRISE, SUNSET, OR NIGHT EFFECT: Bearings obtained from about half an hour before sunset to about half an hour after sunrise may be subject to errors due to night effect. On some nights this effect is more pronounced than on others and effect is usually greatest during the hours of twilight. Night effect may be detected by a broadening of the arc of minimum signals and by a fluctuation in the strength of the signals. It may also be indicated by difficulty in obtaining a minimum or by a rapidly shifting minimum. It is sometimes accompanied by an actual shift in the direction of the bearings. If it is essential to obtain a bearing when the night effect is pronounced, several bearings should be taken over a short period of time and an average taken of them.

RADIO DIRECTION FINDER WITHOUT GYRO REPEATERS: The ship's compass must be read as the bearing is taken or an error may be introduced equal to the amount that the ship has yawed in the interval between taking the bearing and reading the compass. Any error in the ship's compass must be applied to the bearing.

RECIPROCAL BEARINGS: In some direction-finder sets, the operator cannot tell from which side of the ship the signals are coming. With these sets the operator shall correct both bearings for their respective deviations and give both corrected bearings to the person who is plotting the bearings on the chart. If the mariner is in doubt as to the side of the ship from which the bearings are coming, this difficulty can usually be solved by having another bearing taken after the ship has steamed a short distance and noting in which direction the bearing is changing.

CALIBRATION: It is essential that the radio direction-finder be accurately calibrated in order that the bearings may be corrected for deviation. While the bearings are being taken, other radio antennas on board must be in the same condition as they were when the calibration was made; movable parts of the ship's superstructure such as booms, davits, wire rigging, etc., must be secured in the positions which they occupied when the direction-finder was calibrated. Unusual cargoes such as large quantities of metals and extraordinary conditions of loading may cause errors.

The direction-finder should be recalibrated after any changes have been made in the set or its surroundings (this includes alterations to or changes in position of antennas, wire rigging, boat davits, booms, etc.) whenever there is reason to believe that the previous calibration has become inaccurate, and also at periodic intervals.

The calibration must be made on approximately the same frequency or frequencies as will be used to take bearings because the deviation for several frequencies is not likely to be the same. It is believed that one calibration curve is satisfactory for the normal radiobeacon frequency (285 to 325 kHz), but the instructions issued by the manufacturer of the particular direction-finder in question should be studied in this connection.

To facilitate the calibration of ship's direction-finders, special arrangements have been made by some services for operation of their radiobeacons at times other than their published schedules. Information as to the arrangements made by the United States stations in this respect is as follow:

Sequenced radiobeacons cannot broadcast at any time other than on their assigned operating minute for the purpose of enabling vessels to calibrate their radio direction finders without causing interference. Special radio direction finder calibration transmitters of short range are operated at certain localities to provide continuous calibration service.

The position given for the antenna is the point from which the radiobeacon signal is emitted.

If it is not practicable to determine the time of calibration sufficiently in advance to contact the district commander, request may be made directly to the stations by means of telephone, telegraph, or a whistle signal consisting of three long blasts; followed by three short blasts. This whistle signal is to be repeated until it is acknowledged by the station through the starting of the transmitter.

The same group of signals should be sounded at the termination of calibration.

The work of the station personnel is not confined to standing watch and there may be times when the whistle request for calibration is not immediately heard, due to the noise from operating station machinery, etc. Usually, a repeated signal not too far from the station will attract attention.

"COMPENSATED" RADIO DIRECTION-FINDERS: Many radio direction-finders are "compensated" and no calibration chart or curve is used. Attention is invited to the fact that such compensation is just as vulnerable as the calibration data due to changes made in the set or its surroundings.

CHECK THE CALIBRATION: The calibration of compensation should be checked frequently by taking bearings when the ship's position is accurately known and the results should be recorded for future reference.

CALIBRATION RADIOBEACONS: In the United States and certain other areas special radiobeacons, primarily for calibrating shipboard direction-finders are in operation. These radiobeacons transmit either continuously during scheduled hours or upon request, as indicated in station details.

COASTAL REFRACTION (OR LAND EFFECT): Errors may occur in bearings taken by ships so located that the line of observation to the radiobeacon passes over land or along the shore line. However, many observations seem to indicate that such errors are negligible when the observing vessel is well out from the shore. Bearings secured entirely over water areas are to be preferred since "land effect" is thus eliminated. Bearings taken at sunset and sunrise are likely to be erratic, and observations taken at these hours should therefore be repeated and checked as may be feasible.

PROGRAM BROADCASTING STATIONS: Before taking bearings on a station broadcasting entertainment programs a mariner should consider that frequency may differ widely from the frequency for which the set is calibrated, that the published location of the station may be that of its studio and not that of its transmitting antenna, that if the station is synchronized with other stations it may be impossible to tell on which station the bearing was taken, and that as the majority of these stations are inland, the coastal refraction may be excessive.

### Station Details

FREQUENCY: The frequency listed is that used by the station in transmitting its "Characteristic Signal." Calling frequencies, if any, will be given under "remarks."

RANGE: In this book the range of radiobeacons is only approximate and is given merely to assist mariners in planning their voyages and to inform them of several radiobeacons they will probably hear first. Frequently, when conditions for radio reception are good, radiobeacons may be heard at greater distances than indicated. The mariner who is at a greater distance than the range indicated should attempt to obtain bearings when necessary, and not assume that the radiobeacon will be unheard beyond its indicated range.

GROUP SEQUENCE: Selected radiobeacons are grouped together on the same operating frequency and are assigned a specific sequence of transmission within this group. This reduces station interference and unnecessary returning.

ANTENNA LEAD-IN: Included in the details of many radiobeacons located at or near light stations is a statement of the distance and bearing of the radiobeacon transmitting antenna from the light tower. Use should be made of this information when calibrating the ship's direction-finding equipment by means of simultaneous visual and radio bearings.

### Plotting Radio Bearings

The procedure for converting radio (great circle) bearings as received by direction-finder equipment aboard ship is identical with that used in converting radio bearings supplied by direction-finder stations on shore and is described in section 100E "Plotting Radio Bearings" of Pub. 117, Radio Navigational Aids.

### Synchronization for Distance Finding

At some radiobeacon stations, sound signals, either submarine or air or both, are synchronized with the radiobeacon signals for distance finding. Ordinarily, the sound signals do not operate during the transmission period of the radio signal in clear weather. The methods in use employ, as a rule, distinctive signals to indicate the point of synchronization, and make use, for determining distance, of the lag of signals traveling through air or water as compared to the practically instantaneous travel of the radio signals.

In the case of some sound signals, a series of short radio dashes is transmitted at intervals following the synchronizing point, so that by counting the number of such short dashes heard after the distinctive radio signal and before hearing the corresponding distinctive sound signal, the observer obtains the distance, in miles equal to the number of dashes counted, from the sound signal apparatus unless stated otherwise.

In the case of other signals, the observer notes the number of seconds intervening between the reception of the distinctive radio signal and the corresponding sound signal and uses a factor to determine distances in miles as follows:

Submarine signals–multiply the observed numbers of seconds by 0.8 or divide by 1.25 distance in nautical miles.

Air signals–multipy the observed number of seconds by 0.18 or divide by 5.5. For more approximate results or for statute miles, multiply the observed number of seconds by 0.2 or divide by 5.

*Tables for finding distance*

| Interval in seconds | Distances in nautical miles from sound signal source | |
|---|---|---|
| | Air | Submarine |
| 1 | 0.18 | 0.8 |
| 2 | 0.36 | 1.6 |
| 3 | 0.54 | 2.4 |
| 4 | 0.72 | 3.2 |
| 5 | 0.90 | 4.0 |
| 6 | 1.08 | 4.8 |
| 7 | 1.26 | 5.6 |
| 8 | 1.44 | 6.4 |
| 9 | 1.62 | 7.2 |
| 10 | 1.80 | 8.0 |
| 20 | 3.60 | 16.0 |
| 30 | 5.40 | 24.0 |
| 40 | 7.20 | |
| 50 | 9.00 | |
| 60 | 10.80 | |

REMARKS: Average speed of sound travel in water is 1 nautical mile in 11/4 seconds.

The speed of sound travel is influenced by a number of conditions making it impracticable to state a factor that will give exact results under all conditions. The results obtained by the methods described may be accepted as being accurate to within 10 percent of the distance.

Methods of synchronizing the signals vary and are described or illustrated in official announcements regarding them. It is essential to note carefully the point of synchronization used so that no error will be made through taking time on the wrong signal or the wrong part of it.

In observing air signals it is usually sufficient to use a watch with second hand, although a stop watch is helpful. For submarine signals where the interval is shorter and a time error correspondingly more important, it is essential that a stop watch or other timing device be used. Where the radiobeacon and submarine signals are not received at the same point on the vessel, means of instant communication between two observers should be available or synchronized stop watches provided for each.

Ships not equipped with a DF receiver can take advantage of the distance-finding feature of a radiobeacon station, if equipped with a radio receiver capable of receiving the transmission. In the case of obtaining distance from a radiobeacon station which is synchronized with a submarine sound signal, the ship must also be equipped with a device for picking up submarine sound signals.

### Rotating Loop Radiobeacon

MODE OF OPERATION:

(1) The radiobeacon consists of a rotating loop transmitter having directional properties by which an observer in a ship can obtain his bearing from the beacon without the use of a direction-finder. Any ordinary receiving set capable of being tuned to the radiobeacon's frequency may be used. The only other equipment required is a reliable stop watch or chronograph with a sweep second hand. Stop watches and clocks with dials graduated in degrees may be used, from which bearings may be read directly without any mathematical calculation.

(2) During each revolution of the beacon, the signals received by the observer will rise and fall in intensity, passing through a maximum and a minimum twice each minute. The positions of minimum intensity, which occur at intervals of thirty seconds from one another, are very sharp and can be accurately observed. These are, therefore, used for navigation purposes.

The beacon may be regarded as having a line or beam of minimum intensity which rotates at a uniform speed of 360° in 1 minute (i.e. 6° in 1 second) based on the true meridian as starting point. Therefore, if the observer can (a) identify the beacon and (b) measure the number of seconds which this minimum beam takes to reach their position starting from the true meridian, this number multiplied by six will give their true bearing from the beacon or its reciprocal.

The signals which enable the beacon to be identified and the bearing to be calculated are described in the following paragraphs:

Signals transmitted by the beacon: Each transmission from the beacon lasts for 4 minutes; the beacon is then silent for 8 minutes, and automatically starts again at the end of the silent period. Each transmission consists of two parts: (a) the identification signal of the station set at a slow speed for the first minute, commencing when the minimum beam is true east and west and followed by a long dash of about 12 seconds duration; (b) the signal group commencing when the minimum beam is approaching the true meridian, and consisting of (i) the north starting signal, which is the letter V followed by two dots (••• – ••); (ii) a long dash of about 12 seconds duration; (iii) the east starting signal, which is the letter B followed by two dots (– ••• ••); and (iv) a long dash for about 42 seconds.

The navigation signals are repeated during the remainder of the transmission and signals cease when the minimum beam is in the east and west position.

## INSTRUCTIONS FOR TAKING BEARINGS

Set stop watch to zero.

Listen for identification signal.

When the first long dash begins (at A on diagram) get ready for the "north signal."

After the "north signal," start stop watch exactly at beginning of long dash (see "00 seconds" on diagram) counting one-two with the two preceding dots, and 3 for the start of the stop watch.

Listen for minimum and note its exact time by stop watch.

NOTE: If stop watch is graduated in degrees note exact angle, which is the bearing.

Multiply number of seconds by 6° for bearing.

Determine whether bearing is direct or reciprocal.

If the "north signal" is faint, use the "east signal," but add 090° to final bearing.

Particular attention is directed to the following:

The stop watch must be started exactly at the beginning of the long dash for each series of observations.

The time of occurrence of the minimum must be read to the nearest fifth of a second.

The bearing obtained will be either the direct bearing or its reciprocal.

When using the east signal, add 090° to obtain bearings from true north.

The beacon is set up on the true meridian, and no correction is required for magnetic variation.

No quadrantal error arises, and no corrections are necessary except as in (c) and (d) above.

(A correction must, of course, be made for convergency; this should be applied as if the beacon were a shore radio direction-finder station.)

A comparatively large error of bearing may occur due to inaccuracy in the stop watch, and to obviate this, observers or navigators should check their stop watches on the beacon station before taking bearings. This can easily be done by checking the time by stop watch of the complete revolution of the beacon transmission. Any error found can then be allowed for.

### Caution

Due to the many factors which enter into the transmission and reception of radio signals, a mariner cannot practically estimate its distance from a radiobeacon either by the strength of the signals received or by the time at which the signals were first heard. Mariners should give this fact careful consideration in approaching radiobeacons. A diagram showing the signals used is given below.

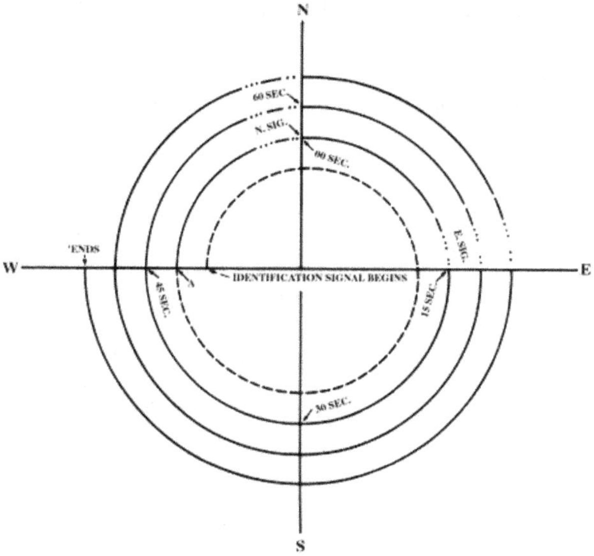


ROTATING RADIOBEACON
SIGNAL DIAGRAM

# DESCRIPTION

(Radiobeacons)

Information is tabulated in eight columns as follows:

*column 1:* The number assigned to each radiobeacon by this Agency.

*column 2:* Name and/or descriptive location of the radiobeacon.

*column 3:* Approximate latitude and longitude of the radiobeacon to the nearest tenth of a minute.

*column 4:* Radiobeacon characteristics. Included in this column are the Morse code, period in seconds, length of transmission and silence time.

*column 5:* Range (approximate) in nautical miles.

*column 6:* Group sequence. Selected radiobeacons are grouped together on the same operating frequency and are assigned a specific sequence of transmission within this group. This reduces station interference and unnecessary return.

*column 7:* Frequency (given in kilohertz) and amplitude modulation (see Table Symbols).

*column 8:* Remarks. Transmission synchronization, type of radiobeacon (marine, aero, etc.), calibration, antenna lead-in, calling frequencies, distance-finding information, service charges, hours of transmission, directional signals and other pertinent information.

ABBREVIATIONS

aero . . . . . . . . . . . . . . . . . . . . . . . . . . . . aeronautical
tr . . . . . . . . . . . . . . . . . . . . . . . . . . . . . transmission
si . . . . . . . . . . . . . . . . . . . . . . . . . . . . . . . . . silence
s . . . . . . . . . . . . . . . . . . . . . . . . . . . . . . . . . seconds
(4) . . . . . . . . . . . . . . . . . . . . . . . . . . . . . . . . 4 times
Transmission is continuous unless otherwise stated.

# TABLE OF SYMBOLS

**LEGEND**

(1) Type of modulation of the main carrier.
(2) Nature of signal(s) modulating the main carrier.
(3) Type of "information" to be transmitted. "Information" does not include information of a constant, unvarying nature such as provided by standard frequency emissions, continuous wave and pulse radars, etc.

**AMPLITUDE MODULATION:**

**N0N**

(1) Emission of an unmodulated carrier.
(2) No modulating signal.
(3) No information transmitted.

**A1A**

(1) Double-sideband.
(2) Single channel containing quantized or digital information without the use of a modulating subcarrier.
(3) Telegraphy (for aural reception).

**A2A**

(1) Double-sideband.
(2) Single channel containing quantized or digital information with the use of a modulating subcarrier.
(3) Telegraphy (for aural reception).

**A3E**

(1) Double-sideband.
(2) Single channel containing analog information.
(3) Telephony (including sound broadcasting).

**R3E**

(1) Single-sideband (reduced or variable level carrier).
(2) Single channel containing analog information.
(3) Telephony (including sound broadcasting).

**B8E**

(1) Independent sidebands.
(2) Two or more channels containing analog information.
(3) Telephony (including sound broadcasting).

**H2A**

(1) Single-sideband (full carrier).
(2) Single channel containing quantized or digital information with the use of a modulating subcarrier.
(3) Telegraphy (for aural reception).

**H3E**

(1) Single-sideband (full carrier).
(2) Single channel containing analog information.
(3) Telephony (including sound broadcasting).

**J3E**

(1) Single-sideband (suppressed carrier).
(2) Single channel containing analog information.
(3) Telephony (including sound broadcasting).

**A3C**

(1) Double-sideband.
(2) Single channel containing analog information.
(3) Facsimile.

**A3F**

(1) Double-sideband.
(2) Single channel containing analog information.
(3) Television (video).

**B7D**

(1) Independent sidebands.
(2) Two or more channels containing quantized or digital information.
(3) Data transmissions, telemetry, telecommand.
Note: With 6 kHz. EDW operation in the bands below 30 MHz allocated exclusively for Maritime Mobile Service (FC, MO).

**FREQUENCY (OR PHASE) MODULATION:**

**F1B**

(1) Frequency modulation.
(2) Single channel containing quantized or digital information without the use of a modulating subcarrier.
(3) Telegraphy (for automatic reception).

**F2A**

(1) Frequency modulation.
(2) Single channel containing quantized or digital information with the use of a modulating subcarrier.
(3) Telegraphy (for aural reception).

**F3E**

(1) Frequency modulation.
(2) Single channel containing analog information.
(3) Telephony (including sound broadcasting).

**F3C**

(1) Frequency modulation.
(2) Single channel containing analog information.
(3) Facsimile.

**F3F**

(1) Frequency modulation.
(2) Single channel containing analog information.
(3) Television (video).

**P1B**

(1) Sequence of unmodulated pulses.
(2) Single channel containing quantized or digital information without the use of a modulating subcarrier.
(3) Telegraphy (for automatic reception).

Pulse Modulation:
GHz = gigahertz
kHz = kilohertz
MHz = megahertz

# DIFFERENTIAL GLOBAL POSITIONING SYSTEM (DGPS)

Differential Global Positioning System (DGPS) is a radio-based navigation system that eliminates errors in a GPS receiver that will allow the accuracy level to be significantly enhanced. DGPS accuracy can be 10 meters or better, compared with 100 meters or better with GPS. This is possible by placing a high-performance GPS receiver (reference station) at a known location. Because the receiver knows its exact location, it can determine the errors in the satellite signals. The satellite measures the ranges to each satellite using the signals received and comparing these measured ranges to the actual ranges calculated from its known position. The total error is the difference between the measured and calculated range. The error data for each tracked satellite is formatted into a correction message and transmitted to GPS users. The correction message format follows the standard established by the Radio Technical Commission for Maritime Services, Special Committee 104 (RTCM-SC104). These differential corrections are then applied to the GPS calculations, thus removing most of the satellite signal error and improving accuracy.

Terms for understanding DGPS:

### DGPS Correction Receiver

A DGPS correction receiver decodes the signals received from a reference site. Data is formatted into a serial RTCM SC104 data stream and provided to the remote GPS receiver. There are many types of DGPS correction receivers.

### GPS Receivers

The GPS receiver measures ranges to each satellite, but before the measurements are used to calculate position, corrections received from the DGPS receiver are applied to the measurements. The position is then calculated using the corrected range measurements providing vastly increased accuracy.

### Modulator

Depending on the transmission format, the modulator encodes the data as necessary for transmission.

### Reference Station

The refrence station GPS receiver knows exactly the position of its antenna, therefore it knows what each satellite range measurement should be. It measures the ranges to each satellite using the received signals just as if it was going to calculate position. The measured ranges are subtracted from the known ranges and the result is range error. The range error values for each satellite are formatted into messages in the RTCM SC104 format and transmitted continuously.

### Transmitter

The transmitter is basically a power amplifier which is connected to an antenna system. The modulated carrier is amplified and driven to the antenna. In the United States Coast Guard system, the transmitter is 250-1000 Watts and operates in the 300Khz frequency range. The amplified signal is radiated via the antenna to remote DGPS receivers for real-time position correction.

# DESCRIPTION

(Differential GPS Stations)

Information is tabulated in eight columns as follows:

*column 1:* The number assigned to each DGPS Station by this Agency.

*column 2:* Name of the DGPS Station

*column 3:* Approximate latitude and longitude of the DGPS Transmitting Station to the nearest tenth of a minute.

*column 4:* Station ID which can be found in the IALA Master list. No two stations have the same ID. **T** denotes the Transmitting Station, **R** denotes the Reference Station.

*column 5:* Range (approximate) in nautical miles.

*column 6:* Frequency in kHz.

*column 7:* Transfer Rate which equates to the baud rate and will be published as a whole number without any additional abbreviations such as "bps" (bits per second)

*column 8:* Remarks. This column contains information about the reference stations and messages types transmitted. GPS Message Type Numbers are 1, 3, 4, 5, 6, 7, 9, 15 and 16. *(Refer to message type descriptions below)*

GPS MESSAGE TYPE NUMBER INDICATORS

| | |
|---|---|
| 1 | Differential GNSS corrections (full set of satellites) |
| 3 | Reference stations parameters |
| 4 | Datum used |
| 5 | Constellation health |
| 6 | Null frame (no information) |
| 7 | Radiobeacons Almanacs |
| 9 | Sub-set differential GNSS corrections |
| 15 | Ionospheric corrections |
| 16 | Special messages |

# Section 1

## Greenland and North Coast of Canada
## Including Labrador, Hudson Bay and Hudson Strait

| (1)<br>No. | (2)<br>Name and Location | (3)<br>Position | (4)<br>Characteristic | (5)<br>Height | (6)<br>Range | (7)<br>Structure | (8)<br>Remarks |
|---|---|---|---|---|---|---|---|
| | **GREENLAND** | | | | | | |
| | ANGMAGSSALIK: | | | | | | |
| 4<br>*L 5000* | -Outer. | 65° 35.5′ N<br>37° 34.1′ W | **Fl.W.**<br>period 5s<br>fl. 1s, ec. 4s | 36<br>**11** | 7 | Yellow pedestal, red band; 7. | |
| 6 | Kulusuk, NW Coast, RACON. | 65° 33.9′ N<br>37° 12.4′ W | **T(−)**<br>period 60s | | | | (3 & 10cm). |
| 8<br>*L 5100* | Prins Christians Sund. | 60° 03.5′ N<br>43° 09.5′ W | **Fl.W.R.G.**<br>period 5s<br>fl. 1s, ec. 4s | 295<br>**90** | W. 14<br>R. 11<br>G. 11 | Orange tower; 15. | W. 000°-180°, R.-255°, G.-263°, W.-288°, R.-295°, G.-000°. |
| | RACON | | **T(−)**<br>period 60s | | | | (3 & 10cm). |
| 12<br>*L 5200* | Frederiksdal Range, front. | 59° 59.0′ N<br>44° 39.9′ W | **Iso.W.**<br>period 2s | 55<br>**17** | 9 | Red pedestal, red triangular daymark point up. | Visible 058°-067°.<br>F.R. on radio mast 440 meters ENE. |
| 16<br>*L 5200.1* | -Rear, 224 meters 063° from front. | 59° 59.1′ N<br>44° 39.7′ W | **Iso.W.**<br>period 4s | 88<br>**27** | 9 | Red tripod, red triangular daymark point down. | Visible 059°-067°. |
| | -RACON | | **O(− − −)**<br>period 60s | | | | (3 & 10cm). |
| 20<br>*L 5204* | Frederiksdal E. Range, front. | 59° 58.9′ N<br>44° 42.8′ W | **Iso.R.**<br>period 2s | 66<br>**20** | 9 | Red pedestal, yellow band; 7. | Visible 281°-289°.<br>Shown 24 hours. |
| 24<br>*L 5204.1* | -Rear, 240 meters 285° from front. | 59° 59.0′ N<br>44° 43.0′ W | **Iso.R.**<br>period 4s | 85<br>**26** | 9 | Red pedestal, yellow band; 13. | Visible 281°-289°.<br>Shown 24 hours. |
| 28<br>*L 5212* | Tateratkasik Range, front. | 60° 03.9′ N<br>45° 08.3′ W | **Iso.W.**<br>period 2s | 56<br>**17** | 9 | Yellow tripod, red band; 20. | F.R. lights on radio mast 4.8 miles S. |
| 32<br>*L 5212.1* | -Rear, 183 meters 091°30′ from front. | 60° 04.0′ N<br>45° 08.6′ W | **Iso.W.**<br>period 4s | 157<br>**48** | 9 | Red pedestal, yellow band. | |
| 36<br>*L 5214* | Tuapait. | 60° 07.3′ N<br>45° 11.0′ W | **Fl.W.R.G.**<br>period 3s<br>fl. 0.8s, ec. 2.2s | 26<br>**8** | W. 7<br>R. 4<br>G. 4 | Yellow pedestal, red band. | W. 001°-008°, R.-184°30′, G.-001°. |
| 38 | Inugsugtalik RACON. | 60° 04.7′ N<br>45° 13.9′ W | **T(−)**<br>period 60s | | | | (3 & 10cm). |
| | NANORTALIK HAVN: | | | | | | |
| 40<br>*L 5216* | -Approach Range, front, on islet. | 60° 08.0′ N<br>45° 14.0′ W | **Iso.W.**<br>period 2s | 26<br>**8** | 9 | Yellow pedestal, red band; 7. | Visible 309°-317°.<br>Shown 24 hours. |
| 44<br>*L 5216.1* | --Rear, 137 meters 313° from front. | 60° 07.9′ N<br>45° 14.1′ W | **Iso.W.**<br>period 4s | 49<br>**15** | 9 | Yellow pedestal, red band; 7. | Visible 309°-317°.<br>Shown 24 hours. |
| 48<br>*L 5215* | -Second Range, front, on Nugarssuk. | 60° 08.0′ N<br>45° 14.0′ W | **Iso.R.**<br>period 4s | 36<br>**11** | 2 | Red framework mast, red triangular daymark point up. | |
| 52<br>*L 5215.1* | --Rear, 192 meters 332° from front. | 60° 08.4′ N<br>45° 14.2′ W | **Iso.R.**<br>period 4s | 59<br>**18** | 2 | Red framework mast, red triangular daymark point down. | |
| 56<br>*L 5221* | -W. Anchorage Range, front. | 60° 08.0′ N<br>45° 15.0′ W | **F.G.** | 23<br>**7** | 2 | Gray framework mast, orange triangular daymark point up; 23. | |
| 60<br>*L 5221.1* | --Rear, 100 meters 310° from front. | 60° 08.5′ N<br>45° 14.7′ W | **F.G.** | 38<br>**12** | 2 | Gray framework mast, orange triangular daymark point down; 23. | |

| (1) No. | (2) Name and Location | (3) Position | (4) Characteristic | (5) Height | (6) Range | (7) Structure | (8) Remarks |
|---|---|---|---|---|---|---|---|
| | | | **GREENLAND** | | | | |
| 64 *L 5222* | -E. Anchorage Range, front. | 60° 08.0′ N 45° 14.0′ W | **F.R.** | 61 **19** | 2 | Gray framework mast, orange triangular daymark point up. | |
| 68 *L 5222.1* | --Rear, 32 meters 010° from front. | 60° 08.5′ N 45° 14.4′ W | **F.R.** | 71 **22** | 2 | Gray framework mast, orange triangular daymark point down. | |
| 72 *L 5217* | -Kolonibugt, at mole, head. | 60° 08.2′ N 45° 14.7′ W | **Iso.G.** period 2s | 13 **4** | | Gray framework mast; 13. | |
| 80 | Iliartalik RACON. | 60° 25.5′ N 45° 39.2′ W | **M(– –)** period 60s | | | | (3 & 10cm). |
| | JULIANEHAB APPROACH: | | | | | | |
| 92 *L 5226* | -Sardlog, W. side. | 60° 32.6′ N 46° 02.1′ W | **Fl.(3)W.R.G.** period 10s fl. 1s, ec. 1s fl. 1s, ec. 1s fl. 1s, ec. 5s | 65 **20** | W. 8 R. 6 G. 6 | Orange tower; 13. | W. 062°-073°, R.-112°, G.-143°, W.-147°, R.-190°, G.-062°. |
| 94 | Paggivik RACON. | 60° 37.5′ N 46° 11.7′ W | **T(–)** period 60s | | | | (3 & 10cm). |
| 96 *L 5228* | Paggisvik (Akia), S. end. | 60° 37.5′ N 46° 11.6′ W | **Fl.(2)W.R.G.** period 10s fl. 1.5s, ec. 1.5s fl. 1.5s, ec. 5.5s | 131 **40** | W. 8 R. 6 G. 6 | Orange tower; 16. | W. 067°-093°, R.-101°, G.-129°, R.-155°, G.-281°, W.-284°, R.-289°, G.-302°, R.-307°, G.-067°. |
| 100 *L 5230* | -Pardlit, E. end. | 60° 41.5′ N 46° 11.9′ W | **Fl.W.R.G.** period 3s fl. 0.8s, ec. 2.2s | 89 **27** | W. 8 R. 6 G. 6 | Red tower, yellow band; 23. | W. 021°30′-036°, R.-180°, G.-260°, W.-267°, R.-319°, G.-021°30′, obscured when bearing 095° and 211°. |
| 104 *L 5232* | -Kilagtoq, NE. end. | 60° 43.9′ N 46° 13.8′ W | **Fl.W.R.G.** period 5s fl. 1s, ec. 4s | 24 **7** | W. 8 R. 5 G. 5 | Orange tower; 13. | G. 047°-137°, W.-141°, R.-227°, G.-317°, W.-324°, R.-047°. |
| 106 | -Simiutaq RACON. | 60° 40.5′ N 46° 33.0′ W | **M(– –)** period 60s | | | | (3 & 10cm). |
| 108 *L 5234* | -Hvide Naes, on point. | 60° 42.3′ N 46° 04.7′ W | **Fl.(2)W.R.G.** period 5s fl. 0.8s, ec. 0.8s fl. 0.8s, ec. 2.8s | 30 **9** | W. 6 R. 4 G. 4 | Red pedestal, yellow band; 6. | W. 062°-067°, R.-180°, G.-062°. Shown 24 hours. |
| 112 *L 5244* | -Breakwater, W. side of entrance, head. | 60° 43.0′ N 46° 02.2′ W | **Fl.R.** period 3s fl. 0.7s, ec. 2.3s | 16 **5** | 1 | White column; 10. | Seasonal. **Radar reflector.** |
| 116 *L 5238* | Julianehab Range, front. | 60° 43.1′ N 46° 02.1′ W | **Iso.R.** period 2s | 82 **25** | 5 | Gray framework mast, red triangular daymark point up; 75. | Visible 280°42′-067°42′. Seasonal. |
| 120 *L 5238.1* | -Rear, 39 meters 350°42′ from front. | 60° 43.1′ N 46° 02.2′ W | **Iso.R.** period 4s | 95 **29** | 5 | Framework mast, red triangular daymark point down; 72. | Visible 280°42′-067°42′. Seasonal. |
| 124 *L 5246* | -NE. Range, front. | 60° 43.1′ N 46° 02.0′ W | **Iso.G.** period 2s | 39 **12** | 5 | White mast, red and white triangular daymark point up; 30. | Visible 318°-098°. Shown 24 hours. Seasonal. |
| 128 *L 5246.1* | --Rear, about 17 meters 028° from front. | 60° 43.1′ N 46° 02.0′ W | **Iso.G.** period 4s | 56 **17** | 5 | White mast, red and white triangular daymark point down; 16. | Visible 318°-098°. Shown 24 hours. Seasonal. |
| 132 *L 5242* | -W. Range, front. | 60° 42.9′ N 46° 02.5′ W | **F.G.** | 39 **12** | | Mast, orange triangular daymark, point up; 20. | Shown 24 hours. Seasonal. |
| 136 *L 5242.1* | --Rear, about 31 meters 305° from front. | 60° 42.9′ N 46° 02.6′ W | **F.G.** | 59 **18** | | Mast, orange triangular daymark point down; 20. | Shown 24 hours. Seasonal. |
| 137 *L 5235* | -Tank installation anchorage Range, front. | 60° 42.8′ N 46° 02.6′ W | **F.R.** | 46 **14** | | Gray framework mast, orange triangular daymark point up; 23. | On request. Occasional. |
| 138 *L 5235.1* | --Rear, 50 meters 013° from front. | 60° 42.8′ N 46° 02.6′ W | **F.R.** | 59 **18** | | Gray framework mast, orange triangular daymark point down; 23. | On request. Occasional. |

| (1) No. | (2) Name and Location | (3) Position | (4) Characteristic | (5) Height | (6) Range | (7) Structure | (8) Remarks |
|---|---|---|---|---|---|---|---|
| | | | **GREENLAND** | | | | |
| 140 *L 5260* | Narssaq Havn Range, front. | 60° 54.6′ N 46° 03.0′ W | **F.G.** | 50 **15** | 5 | Framework mast, red triangular daymark point up; 26. | Visible 260°-080°. |
| 144 *L 5260.1* | -Rear, 34 meters 350° from front. | 60° 54.6′ N 46° 03.0′ W | **F.G.** | 60 **18** | 4 | Framework mast, orange triangular daymark point down; 13. | Visible 260°-080°. |
| 148 *L 5264* | -Anchorage Range, front, E. side of harbor. | 60° 55.0′ N 46° 03.0′ W | **F.G.** | 26 **8** | 2 | Framework mast, triangular daymark point up; 23. | |
| 152 *L 5264.1* | --Rear, 28 meters 072° from front. | 60° 54.4′ N 46° 02.5′ W | **F.G.** | 62 **19** | 2 | Framework mast, triangular daymark point down; 23. | |
| 156 *L 5266* | Brede Fjord, Inugsugtut. | 60° 43.2′ N 46° 59.2′ W | **Fl.(3)W.R.G.** period 10s fl. 1s, ec. 1s fl. 1s, ec. 1s fl. 1s, ec. 5s | 131 **40** | W. 8 R. 6 G. 6 | Orange tower; 16. | W. 059°-080°, R.-106°30′, G.-113°, W.-118°30′, R.-131°, G.-059°. |
| | RACON | | **O(– – –)** period 60s | | | | (3 & 10cm). |
| | ARSUK FJORD: | | | | | | |
| 160 *L 5270* | -Qajartalik Island, SW. part. | 61° 09.8′ N 48° 31.4′ W | **Fl.(2)W.R.G.** period 5s fl. 0.7s, ec. 0.8s fl. 0.7s, ec. 2.8s | 88 **27** | W. 7 R. 4 G. 4 | Red tower, yellow band; 23. | W. 049°-081°, R.-281°, G.-049°. |
| 164 *L 5273.9* | -Napassut Island, W. side. | 61° 06.3′ N 48° 14.3′ W | **Iso.W.R.G.** period 2s | 39 **12** | W. 5 R. 3 G. 3 | Red cabinet, yellow band; 7. | G. 078°-086°, W.-089°, R.-159°, G.-209°, W.-216°, R.-266°30′. |
| 212 *L 5284* | -Gronne Dal, NW. corner of pier. | 61° 14.1′ N 48° 06.1′ W | **F.G.** | 7 **2** | | Post. | Visible 069°-181°30′. Shown 24 hours. |
| 216 *L 5281.9* | ---Front, 60 meters 302° from common rear. | 61° 14.3′ N 48° 06.3′ W | **F.R.** | 82 **25** | | Orange beacon, square daymark; 20. | Visible 055°-061°. Shown 24 hours. |
| 220 *L 5281.91* | ---Common Rear. | 61° 14.3′ N 48° 06.2′ W | **F.R.** | 147 **45** | | Orange beacon, square daymark; 13. | Visible 055°-061°. Shown 24 hours. |
| 224 *L 5282.1* | ---Front, 37 meters 160° from common rear. | 61° 14.3′ N 48° 06.3′ W | **F.G.** | 92 **28** | 3 | Yellow beacon, orange triangular daymark point up; 13. | Shown 24 hours. |
| | FREDERIKSHAB APPROACH: | | | | | | |
| 228 *L 5346* | -Satuarssugssuaq. | 61° 58.0′ N 49° 45.3′ W | **Fl.(3)W.** period 10s fl. 1s, ec. 1s fl. 1s, ec. 1s fl. 1s, ec. 5s | 66 **20** | 7 | Red tower, yellow band; 23. | |
| | -RACON | | **O(– – –)** period 60s | | | | (3 & 10 cm) |
| 232 *L 5348* | -Approach Range, front. | 61° 59.9′ N 49° 40.4′ W | **Q.W.** | 46 **14** | 12 | Framework mast, red triangular daymark point up; 43. | Visible 028°-044°. Obscured locally. |
| 236 *L 5348.1* | --Rear, 357 meters 036° from front. | 62° 00.0′ N 49° 40.2′ W | **Iso.W.** period 4s | 85 **26** | 12 | White framework mast, red triangular daymark point down; 26. | Visible 028°-044°. |
| 248 *L 5400* | Fiskenaes Fjord, entrance portside. | 63° 01.7′ N 50° 49.3′ W | **Fl.W.R.G.** period 3s fl. 0.7s, ec. 2.3s | 66 **20** | W. 7 R. 5 G. 5 | Orange tower; 16. | R. 076°-093°, G.-219°, W.-222°, R.-303°, G.-341°, W.-076°. |
| | HELLEFISKE ISLANDS: | | | | | | |
| 250 | -RACON. | 63° 02.5′ N 51° 00.2′ W | **T(–)** period 60s | | | | (3 & 10cm). |

| (1) No. | (2) Name and Location | (3) Position | (4) Characteristic | (5) Height | (6) Range | (7) Structure | (8) Remarks |
|---|---|---|---|---|---|---|---|

## GREENLAND

| (1) No. | (2) Name and Location | (3) Position | (4) Characteristic | (5) Height | (6) Range | (7) Structure | (8) Remarks |
|---|---|---|---|---|---|---|---|
| | FAERINGEHAVN APPROACH: | | | | | | |
| 252 *L 5500* | -Satut. | 63° 41.9′ N 51° 36.4′ W | **Fl.W.R.G.** period 5s fl. 1s, ec. 4s | 69 **21** | W. 8 R. 4 G. 4 | Red concrete pillar, white lantern; 10. | W. 019°-049°, R.-089°, G.-180°, W.-192°, R.-277°, G.-019°. |
| | -RACON | | **M(– –)** period 60s | | | | (3 & 10 cm). |
| 256 *L 5504* | -Smukke 0. | 63° 41.3′ N 51° 32.6′ W | **Fl.W.R.G.** period 3s fl. 0.8s, ec. 2.2s | 52 **16** | W. 6 R. 3 G. 3 | Red concrete pillar, lantern; 3. | G. 000°-071°, W.-081°, R.-180°, W.-000°. |
| 260 *L 5508* | -Sondre Naes Range, front. | 63° 41.3′ N 51° 32.2′ W | **Iso.W.** period 2s | 26 **8** | 8 | Yellow pedestal, red band; 6. | |
| 264 *L 5508.1* | --Rear, 408 meters 073° from front. | 63° 41.3′ N 51° 31.7′ W | **Iso.W.** period 4s | 62 **19** | 8 | Yellow tripod, red band; 23. | |
| 282 *L 5512* | Kigtorgat, NE. island. | 63° 55.6′ N 51° 35.5′ W | **Fl.W.** period 3s fl. 0.8s, ec. 2.2s | 66 **20** | 4 | Yellow tripod, red band; 19. | Shown 24 hours. |
| 284 *L 5520* | Angissorssuaq Island Range, front. | 63° 58.1′ N 51° 43.7′ W | **Iso.R.** period 2s | 52 **16** | 6 | Red framework mast; 33. | Visible 204°-210°. |
| 288 *L 5520.1* | -Rear, 460 meters 207° from front. | 63° 57.9′ N 51° 43.9′ W | **Iso.R.** period 4s | 98 **30** | 6 | Red pedestal; 7. | Visible 204°-210°. |
| 292 *L 5525* | Tukingassarassuak. | 64° 00.2′ N 51° 41.9′ W | **Fl.W.R.G.** period 3s fl. 0.8s, ec. 2.2s | 39 **12** | W. 5 R. 4 G. 4 | Yellow pedestal, red band; 6. | G. 090°-321°, W.-326°, R.-090°. |
| 294 *L 5531* | Stromstedet Range, front. | 64° 00.8′ N 51° 38.7′ W | **Iso.W.** period 2s | 59 **18** | 9 | Gray framework tower, red rectangular daymark, white stripe; 13. | Visible 176°-192°. |
| 294.1 *L 5531.1* | -Rear, 184° from front. | 64° 00.6′ N 51° 38.7′ W | **Iso.W.** period 4s | 98 **30** | 9 | Gray framework tower, red rectangular daymark, white stripe; 7. | Visible 176°-192°. |
| 296 *L 5530* | Simiuta. | 64° 02.5′ N 51° 38.1′ W | **Fl.G.** period 3s fl. 0.8s, ec. 2.2s | 39 **12** | 4 | Yellow pedestal, red band; 7. | Shown 24 hours. |
| 300 *L 5535* | Serfartorssuag. | 64° 05.6′ N 51° 37.6′ W | **Fl.W.** period 3s fl. 0.8s, ec. 2.2s | 88 **27** | 4 | Yellow tripod, red band; 33. | Shown 24 hours. |
| | GODTHABFJORD: | | | | | | |
| 304 *L 5550* | -Agtorssuit Island, Kookoerne. | 64° 03.2′ N 52° 07.7′ W | **Fl.(2)W.R.G.** period 5s fl. 0.7s, ec. 0.8s fl. 0.7s, ec. 2.8s | 85 **26** | W. 9 R. 6 G. 6 | Red tower, yellow band; 23. | W. 073°-121°, R.-206°, G.-231°, W.-235°, R.-275°, G.-073°. 2 F.R. (vert.) on radio tower 1.7M SE. |
| | -RACON | | **O(– – –)** period 60s | | | | (3 & 10cm). |
| 308 *L 5552* | -Renso. | 64° 07.2′ N 51° 56.9′ W | **Fl.W.** period 5s fl. 1s, ec. 4s | 39 **12** | 10 7 | Yellow hut, red band; 6. | Visible (unintensified) 229°-049°, (intensified) -058°. |
| 312 *L 5554* | -Ships Harbor Approach Range, front. | 64° 09.8′ N 51° 43.1′ W | **Iso.G.** period 2s | 30 **9** | 11 | Yellow hut, red band; 6. | Intensified 056°30′-065°30′. Shown 24 hours. |
| 316 *L 5554.1* | --Rear, 220 meters 061° from front. | 64° 09.9′ N 51° 42.8′ W | **Iso.G.** period 4s | 85 **26** | 11 | Yellow hut, red band; 6. | Visible 053°-069°. Shown 24 hours. |
| 320 *L 5558* | --Entrance, E. | 64° 10.3′ N 51° 42.9′ W | **Fl.W.R.G.** period 3s fl. 0.8s, ec. 2.2s | 39 **12** | 5 | Yellow hut, red band; 6. | G. 268°-015°, W.-025°, R.-132°. |
| 326 *L 5572* | -Malene Bay Range, front. | 64° 10.8′ N 51° 41.4′ W | **Iso.R.** period 2s | 46 **14** | 4 | Framework mast, red triangular daymark, point up; 33. | Visible 265°12′-145°12′. Shown May 1 to Nov. 15. |

| (1) No. | (2) Name and Location | (3) Position | (4) Characteristic | (5) Height | (6) Range | (7) Structure | (8) Remarks |
|---|---|---|---|---|---|---|---|

## GREENLAND

| (1) No. | (2) Name and Location | (3) Position | (4) Characteristic | (5) Height | (6) Range | (7) Structure | (8) Remarks |
|---|---|---|---|---|---|---|---|
| 326.1 *L 5572.1* | --Rear, 145 meters 025°12′ from front. | 64° 10.8′ N 51° 41.3′ W | **Iso.R.** period 4s | 62 **19** | 4 | Framework mast, red triangular daymark, point down; 15. | Visible 265°12′-145°12′. Shown May 1 to Nov. 15. |
| 328 *L 5575* | -AVIATION LIGHT. | 64° 11.3′ N 51° 40.7′ W | **Al.Fl.W.G.** period 5s fl. 0.5s, ec. 4.5s | 325 **99** | W. **19** G. **16** | Control tower; 49. | |
| 332 *L 5580* | Sukkertoppen Approach, Kitdliaraq Islet. | 65° 21.6′ N 52° 50.2′ W | **Fl.(3)W.** period 10s fl. 1s, ec. 1s fl. 1s, ec. 1s fl. 1s, ec. 5s | 69 **21** | 9 | Yellow tower, red band; 23. | |
| | RACON | | **M(– –)** period 60s | | 3 | | (3 & 10cm). |
| 336 *L 5590* | Sukkertoppen, Kirkegaards Naesset Range, front. | 65° 25.4′ N 52° 53.0′ W | **Oc.W.R.G.** period 5s | 98 **30** | W. 7 R. 4 G. 4 | Metal framework tower, yellow top, red roof; 39. | G. 152°-004°30′, W.-011°30′, R.-031°. In line with unlit rear beacon 010°30′. |
| 340 *L 5594* | Sukkertoppen Havn, W. side of harbor. | 65° 24.6′ N 52° 54.3′ W | **Iso.W.R.G.** period 2s | 43 **13** | W. 5 R. 3 G. 3 | Red column, yellow band; 6. | G. 288°-301°42′, W.-310°, R.-321°. |
| 344 *L 5596* | -E. anchorage Range, front. | 65° 25.0′ N 52° 54.0′ W | **F.G.** | 26 **8** | 10 | Mast, orange triangular daymark, point up; 49. | |
| 348 *L 5596.1* | --Rear, 59 meters 030° from front. | 65° 24.8′ N 52° 54.2′ W | **F.G.** | 43 **13** | 10 | Mast, orange triangular daymark, point down; 49. | |
| 352 *L 5598* | -W. anchorage Range, front. | 65° 24.8′ N 52° 54.5′ W | **Iso.R.** period 4s | 82 **25** | 10 | Metal framework tower, orange triangular daymark, point up; 26. | |
| 356 *L 5598.1* | --Rear, about 30 meters 323° from front. | 65° 24.8′ N 52° 54.5′ W | **Iso.R.** period 4s | 92 **28** | 10 | Metal framework tower, orange triangular daymark, point down; 33. | |
| 362 | Kangaamiut RACON. | 65° 49.1′ N 53° 22.9′ W | **O(– – –)** period 60s | | 3 | | |
| 364 *L 5620* | Sondre Stromfjord S. Range, front. | 66° 00.3′ N 53° 31.1′ W | **Iso.W.** period 2s | 26 **8** | 9 | Yellow hut, red band, white rectangular daymark, red border; 8. | Visible 091°-107°. |
| 368 *L 5620.1* | -Rear, 660 meters 099° from front. | 66° 00.2′ N 53° 30.2′ W | **Iso.W.** period 4s | 42 **13** | 10 | Yellow hut, red band, white rectangular daymarks, red border; 7. | Visible 091°-107°. |
| 370 | Qeqertasugssuk RACON. | 66° 00.6′ N 53° 31.6′ W | **T(–)** period 60s | | | | (3 & 10cm). |
| 372 *L 5625* | Sondre Stromfjord, N. Range, front. | 66° 01.5′ N 53° 30.8′ W | **Iso.R.** period 2s | 62 **19** | 10 | Yellow hut, red band; 8. | Visible 048°-064°. |
| 376 *L 5625.1* | -Rear, about 550 meters 056° from front. | 66° 01.7′ N 53° 30.3′ W | **Iso.R.** period 4s | 112 **34** | 10 | Yellow hut, red band; 8. | Visible 048°-064°. |
| 380 *L 5640* | Itivdleg, Qeqertarssuatsiaq. | 66° 30.6′ N 53° 41.8′ W | **Fl.W.R.G.** period 5s fl. 1s, ec. 4s | 138 **42** | W. 8 R. 6 G. 5 | Orange tower; 16. | G. 010°-055°, W.-134°, R.-144°, G.- 172°, W.-177°, R.-185°, G.-230°, W.-240°, R.-010°. |
| 384 *L 5660* | Mollers O (Anatsusok). | 66° 55.5′ N 53° 45.1′ W | **Fl.W.** period 3s fl. 0.8s, ec. 2.2s | 121 **37** | 7 | Yellow tower, red band; 23. | |
| | RACON | | **M(– –)** period 60s | | | | (3 & 10cm). |
| 388 *L 5680* | Praestefjeld Range, front. | 66° 56.9′ N 53° 43.4′ W | **Iso.W.** period 2s | 46 **14** | 8 | Orange hut. | Visible 004°-010°. |
| 392 *L 5680.1* | -Rear, 500 meters 007° from front. | 66° 57.2′ N 53° 43.3′ W | **Iso.W.** period 4s | 92 **28** | 8 | Orange hut. | Visible 004°-010°. |
| 396 *L 5696* | Holsteinborg Entrance Range, front. | 66° 56.6′ N 53° 40.5′ W | **Iso.W.** period 2s | 112 **34** | 9 | Metal framework tower, orange triangular daymark, point up; 66. | Shown 24 hours. |

| (1) No. | (2) Name and Location | (3) Position | (4) Characteristic | (5) Height | (6) Range | (7) Structure | (8) Remarks |
|---|---|---|---|---|---|---|---|
| | | | **GREENLAND** | | | | |
| 400<br>*L 5696.1* | -Rear, 300 meters 092°30′ from front. | 66° 56.6′ N<br>53° 40.1′ W | **Iso.W.**<br>period 4s | 164<br>**50** | 10 | Metal framework tower, orange triangular daymark, point down; 23. | Shown 24 hours. |
| 404<br>*L 5712* | -Lee mole, head. | 66° 56.5′ N<br>53° 41.0′ W | **F.R.** | 13<br>**4** | 3 | Post; 7. | |
| 408<br>*L 5706* | Tommermandsoen, anchorage W. Range, front. | 66° 56.5′ N<br>53° 41.9′ W | **Oc.G.**<br>period 7s<br>lt. 6s, ec. 1s | 59<br>**18** | 3 | Metal framework tower, orange triangular daymark, point up; 13. | |
| 412<br>*L 5706.1* | -Rear, 24 meters 174°30′ from front. | 66° 56.5′ N<br>53° 41.9′ W | **Oc.G.**<br>period 5s<br>lt. 4s, ec. 1s | 69<br>**21** | 3 | Metal framework tower, orange triangular daymark, point down; 19. | |
| 424<br>*L 5718* | Sydbay (Ukivik). | 67° 13.2′ N<br>53° 55.3′ W | **Fl.W.**<br>period 5s<br>fl. 1s, ec. 4s | 295<br>**90** | 6 | Orange tower; 23. | |
| 425<br>*L 5719.1* | Agto Anchorage S. Range, front. | 67° 56.5′ N<br>53° 37.9′ W | **F.G.** | 66<br>**20** | 4 | Gray framework mast, red triangular daymark, point up; 30. | |
| 425.1<br>*L 5719.11* | -Rear, 40 meters 192°48′ from front. | 67° 56.5′ N<br>53° 37.9′ W | **F.G.** | 79<br>**24** | 4 | Gray framework mast, red triangular daymark, point down; 30. | |
| 426<br>*L 5720* | -E. Range, front. | 67° 56.5′ N<br>53° 37.9′ W | **F.R.** | 16<br>**5** | 4 | Green and brown mast, red triangular daymark, point up; 10. | |
| 426.1<br>*L 5720.1* | --Rear, 65 meters 111°36′ from front. | 67° 56.6′ N<br>53° 37.6′ W | **F.R.** | 33<br>**10** | 4 | Green and brown mast, red triangular daymark, point down; 13. | |
| 428<br>*L 5790* | Kangatsiag. | 68° 18.5′ N<br>53° 28.8′ W | **Oc.W.R.G.**<br>period 5s<br>lt. 4s, ec. 1s | 65<br>**20** | W. 7<br>R. 4<br>G. 4 | Framework tower; 26. | W. 103°-108°, R.-140°, G.-103°. |
| 432<br>*L 5791* | -SW. | 68° 18.3′ N<br>53° 29.0′ W | **Fl.R.**<br>period 3s<br>fl. 0.3s, ec. 2.7s | 16<br>**5** | 2 | Concrete base; 5. | |
| 436<br>*L 5800* | -Vester Ejland. | 68° 37.4′ N<br>53° 32.2′ W | **Fl.(2)W.**<br>period 5s<br>fl. 0.7s, ec. 0.8s<br>fl. 0.7s, ec. 2.8s | 148<br>**45** | 7 | Red tower, white band; 23. | |
| | -RACON | | **T(−)**<br>period 60s | | | | (3 & 10cm). |
| 440<br>*L 5840* | -Susanne Oerne, NW. island. | 68° 39.6′ N<br>53° 09.2′ W | **Fl.(3)W.**<br>period 10s<br>fl. 1s, ec. 1s<br>fl. 1s, ec. 1s<br>fl. 1s, ec. 5s | 82<br>**25** | 5 | Red tower, yellow band; 16. | |
| | EGEDESMINDE APPROACH: | | | | | | |
| 444<br>*L 5860* | -Qarajugtoq Range, front. | 68° 42.8′ N<br>52° 58.8′ W | **Iso.W.**<br>period 2s | 26<br>**8** | 8 | Red tower, yellow band; 7. | Visible 048°-054°.<br>Shown Aug. 1 to close of navigation. |
| | | | **Fl.W.R.G.**<br>period 5s<br>fl. 1s, ec. 4s | 26<br>**8** | W. 5<br>R. 2<br>G. 2 | | Shown Aug. 1 to close of navigation. |
| 448<br>*L 5860.1* | --Rear, 890 meters 051° from front. | 68° 43.0′ N<br>52° 57.8′ W | **Iso.W.**<br>period 4s | 69<br>**21** | 8 | Red framework mast and red locker, yellow band; 23. | Visible 048°-054°.<br>Shown Aug. 1 to close of navigation. |
| 456<br>*L 5892* | -Zimmers O. | 68° 45.1′ N<br>52° 47.8′ W | **Fl.W.R.G.**<br>period 3s<br>fl. 0.7s, ec. 2.3s | 59<br>**18** | W. 7<br>R. 4<br>G. 4 | Red tower, yellow band; 16. | G. 326°-040°, W.-056°, R.-109°, G.-171°, W.-212°, R.-326°. |
| 457<br>*L 5891* | -Tipitooq Kangilleq, W. Range, front. | 68° 43.1′ N<br>52° 49.6′ W | **Iso.R.**<br>period 2s | 33<br>**10** | 5 | Gray framework tower, orange triangular daymark, point up. | Visible 074°-114°. |

| (1) No. | (2) Name and Location | (3) Position | (4) Characteristic | (5) Height | (6) Range | (7) Structure | (8) Remarks |
|---|---|---|---|---|---|---|---|
| | | | **GREENLAND** | | | | |
| 457.1 *L 5891.1* | --Rear, 240 meters 094° from front. | 68° 43.0′ N 52° 49.3′ W | **Iso.R.** period 4s | 56 **17** | 5 | Gray framework tower, orange triangular daymark, point down. | Visible 074°-114°. |
| 458 *L 5891.4* | -N. Range, front. | 68° 43.1′ N 52° 49.3′ W | **Iso.G.** period 2s | 56 **17** | 5 | Gray framework tower, orange triangular daymark, point up. | Visible 171°-271°. |
| 458.1 *L 5891.41* | --Rear, 328 meters 191° from front. | 68° 42.9′ N 52° 49.4′ W | **Iso.G.** period 4s | 82 **25** | 5 | Gray framework tower, orange triangular daymark, point down. | Visible 171°-271°. |
| 460 *L 5890* | -Raeveo Range, front. | 68° 42.8′ N 52° 53.4′ W | **Iso.R.** period 2s | 52 **16** | 2 | Mast, red triangular daymark, point up; 16. | Shown Aug. 1 to May 15. |
| 464 *L 5890.1* | --Rear, 82 meters 268° from front. | 68° 42.8′ N 52° 53.6′ W | **Iso.R.** period 4s | 75 **23** | 2 | Mast, red triangular daymark, point down; 16. | Shown Aug. 1 to May 15. |
| | EGEDESMINDE HAVN: | | | | | | |
| 468 *L 5870* | -Entrance Range, front. | 68° 42.6′ N 52° 52.3′ W | **Iso.G.** period 2s | 60 **18** | 4 | White wooden mast, red triangular daymark, point up; 49. | Visible 050°-230°. Shown 24 hours, Aug. 1 to May 15. |
| 472 *L 5870.1* | --Rear, 100 meters 140° from front. | 68° 42.6′ N 52° 52.2′ W | **Iso.G.** period 4s | 98 **30** | 4 | White wooden mast, red triangular daymark, point down; 49. | Visible 050°-230°. Shown 24 hours, Aug. 1 to May 15. |
| 476 *L 5884* | -Naesset, inner harbor Range, front. | 68° 42.5′ N 52° 53.2′ W | **F.R.** | 39 **12** | 1 | Wooden mast, red triangular daymark, point up; 10. | Visible 175°-181°. Shown Aug. 1 to May 15. |
| 480 *L 5884.1* | --Rear, 23 meters 178° from front. | 68° 42.5′ N 52° 53.2′ W | **F.R.** | 51 **16** | 1 | Wooden mast, red triangular daymark, point down; 13. | Visible 175°-181°. Shown Aug. 1 to May 15. |
| 506 | Basiso, RACON. | 68° 50.3′ N 51° 58.6′ W | **M(– –)** period 60s | | | | (3 & 10cm). |
| | DISKO: | | | | | | |
| 508 *L 5918* | **-Udkiggen.** | 69° 13.9′ N 53° 33.3′ W | **Oc.W.R.G.** period 10s lt. 8s, ec. 2s | 131 **40** | W. **15** R. 11 G. 11 | Orange tower; 18. | R. 034°-043°, G.-052°, W.-069°, R.-074°, G.-079°, W.-095°, R.-106°, G.-275°, W.-333°, R.-347°, G.-357°, W.-034°. |
| | -RACON | | **T(–)** period 60s | | | | (3 & 10cm). |
| 512 *L 5920* | -Godhavn Range, front. | 69° 15.2′ N 53° 32.8′ W | **F.G.** | 46 **14** | 3 | Framework mast, red triangular daymark, white border, point up. | Visible 058°-064°. Shown Aug. 1 to Jan. 1. |
| 516 *L 5920.1* | --Rear, 46 meters 061° from front. | 69° 15.2′ N 53° 32.7′ W | **F.G.** | 105 **32** | 3 | Framework mast, red triangular daymark, white border, point down. | Visible 058°-064°. Shown Aug. 1 to Jan. 1. |
| 520 *L 5928* | -Anchorage Range, front. | 69° 15.1′ N 53° 32.9′ W | **F.R.** | 36 **11** | 2 | White mast, red and white triangular daymark, point up; 22. | Visible 357°-117°. Shown 24 hours. |
| 524 *L 5928.1* | --Rear, 61 meters 057° from front. | 69° 15.2′ N 53° 32.8′ W | **F.R.** | 52 **16** | 2 | White mast, red and white triangular daymark, point down; 22. | Visible 357°-117°. Shown 24 hours. |
| | CHRISTIANSHAB: | | | | | | |
| 535 *L 5932* | -Qasigiannguit Range, front. | 68° 49.3′ N 51° 10.9′ W | **Iso.R.** period 2s | 52 **16** | 2 | Mast, red triangular daymark, point up; 23. | Visible 338°30′-098°30′. Shown May to Dec. |
| 536 *L 5932.1* | --Rear, 038°30′ from front. | 68° 49.4′ N 51° 10.7′ W | **Iso.R.** period 4s | 82 **25** | 2 | Mast, red triangular daymark, point down; 23. | Visible 338°30′-098°30′. Shown May to Dec. |
| 538 | Nuugaarsuk, RACON. | 69° 14.1′ N 51° 07.4′ W | **O(– – –)** period 60s | | | | (3 & 10cm). |

| (1) No. | (2) Name and Location | (3) Position | (4) Characteristic | (5) Height | (6) Range | (7) Structure | (8) Remarks |
|---|---|---|---|---|---|---|---|
| | **GREENLAND** | | | | | | |
| 540<br>*L 5940* | Jakobshavn Range, front. | 69° 13.5′ N<br>51° 06.0′ W | **Iso.R.**<br>period 2s | 46<br>**14** | 4 | Mast, red triangular daymark, point up; 33. | Shown 24 hours. |
| 544<br>*L 5940.1* | -Rear, 167 meters 119°36′ from front. | 69° 13.5′ N<br>51° 05.8′ W | **Iso.R.**<br>period 4s | 92<br>**28** | 4 | Mast, red triangular daymark, point down; 24. | Shown 24 hours. |
| 548<br>*L 5942* | -Inner Harbor Range, front. | 69° 13.2′ N<br>51° 05.5′ W | **Iso.G.**<br>period 2s | 144<br>**44** | 4 | Mast, red triangular daymark, point up; 24. | Shown 24 hours. |
| 552<br>*L 5942.1* | --Rear, 149 meters 142°54′ from front. | 69° 13.1′ N<br>51° 05.3′ W | **Iso.G.**<br>period 4s | 171<br>**52** | 4 | Mast, red triangular daymark, point down; 24. | Shown 24 hours. |
| 556<br>*L 5944* | -NE. mole, head. | 69° 13.4′ N<br>51° 05.8′ W | **F.R.** | 7<br>**2** | 2 | Platform. | |
| 560<br>*L 5936* | -Napissaq. | 68° 48.5′ N<br>51° 13.3′ W | **Fl.W.R.G.**<br>period 3s<br>fl. 0.8s, ec. 2.2s | 30<br>**9** | W. 6<br>R. 4<br>G. 4 | Orange tower; 15. | G. 030°-045°, W.-058°, R.-069°, G.-118°, W.-156°, R.-166°, G.-247°, W.-275°, R.-282°. |
| 562<br>*L 5951* | -Forfyr Range, front. | 70° 40.6′ N<br>52° 07.7′ W | **Iso.G.**<br>period 2s | 72<br>**22** | 3 | Framework mast, red triangular daymark, point up; 15. | Shown 24 hours, May to Dec. |
| 566<br>*L 5951.1* | --Rear, 22 meters 312°36′ from front. | 70° 40.6′ N<br>52° 07.7′ W | **Iso.G.**<br>period 4s | 82<br>**25** | 3 | Framework mast, red triangular daymark, point down; 23. | Shown 24 hours, May to Dec. |
| | UPERNAVIK: | | | | | | |
| 580<br>*L 5970* | -Entrance Range, front. | 72° 47.5′ N<br>56° 08.3′ W | **F.R.** | 39<br>**12** | 4 | Mast, red triangular daymark, point up; 33. | Visible 105°36′-111°36′. Shown 24 hours, May 1 to Dec. 31. |
| 584<br>*L 5970.1* | --Rear, 50 meters 108°36′ from front. | 72° 47.4′ N<br>56° 08.8′ W | **F.R.** | 46<br>**14** | 4 | Mast, red triangular daymark, point down; 16. | Visible 105°36′-111°36′. Shown 24 hours, May 1 to Dec. 31. |
| 594 | Hvalo, RACON. | 72° 40.4′ N<br>56° 18.7′ W | **T(–)**<br>period 60s | | | | |
| 596<br>*L 5990* | Thule AVIATION LIGHT. | 76° 31.0′ N<br>68° 48.3′ W | **Al.W.G.** | | | | |
| | **CANADA-HUDSON BAY AND STRAIT** | | | | | | |
| | UNGAVA BAY: | | | | | | |
| 601<br>*H 0058* | -Koksoak River Range, front. | 58° 27.6′ N<br>68° 12.4′ W | **F.G.** | 59<br>**18** | 10 | Square skeleton tower, orange trapezoidal daymark, black stripe; 26. | Seasonal. |
| 601.1<br>*H 0058.1* | --Rear, 614 meters 197°38′ from front. | 58° 27.3′ N<br>68° 12.6′ W | **F.G.** | 130<br>**40** | 13 | Square tower, orange trapezoidal daymark, black stripe; 80. | Visible on range line only. Seasonal. |
| 602<br>*H 0058.4* | **--E.** Range, front. | 58° 29.7′ N<br>68° 10.3′ W | **Iso.W.**<br>period 2s | 65<br>**20** | **16** | Square skeleton tower, orange trapezoidal daymark, black stripe; 26. | Visible on range line only. Seasonal. |
| 602.1<br>*H 0058.41* | ---Rear, 651 meters 189°36′ from front. | 58° 29.4′ N<br>68° 10.4′ W | **Iso.W.**<br>period 2s | 115<br>**35** | **16** | Square tower, orange trapezoidal daymark, black stripe; 66. | Visible on range line only. Seasonal. |
| 603<br>*H 0059* | **-Beacon Point, (Inukshuktuyuk) Range,** front. | 58° 33.1′ N<br>68° 11.5′ W | **F.W.** | 57<br>**17** | **15** | Square tower, orange trapezoidal daymark, black stripe; 26. | Visible on range line only. Seasonal. |
| 603.1<br>*H 0059.1* | --Rear, 1,025 meters 219°49′ from front. | 58° 32.7′ N<br>68° 12.3′ W | **F.W.** | 144<br>**44** | **15** | Square tower, orange trapezoidal daymark, black stripe; 26. | Visible on range line only. Seasonal. |
| 608<br>*H 0053.4* | Cape Poillon Range, front. | 63° 08.0′ N<br>67° 51.8′ W | **Iso.W.**<br>period 2s | 276<br>**84** | 14 | Square skeleton tower, orange trapezoidal daymark, black stripe. | Visible on range line only. Seasonal. |
| 612<br>*H 0053.41* | -Rear, 3427.9 meters 149°28′ from front. | 63° 06.5′ N<br>67° 49.7′ W | **Iso.W.**<br>period 2s | 668<br>**204** | 14 | Square tower, orange trapezoidal daymark. | Visible on range line only. Seasonal. |

| (1) No. | (2) Name and Location | (3) Position | (4) Characteristic | (5) Height | (6) Range | (7) Structure | (8) Remarks |
|---|---|---|---|---|---|---|---|

## CANADA-HUDSON BAY AND STRAIT

| (1) No. | (2) Name and Location | (3) Position | (4) Characteristic | (5) Height | (6) Range | (7) Structure | (8) Remarks |
|---|---|---|---|---|---|---|---|
| 616 *H 0053.5* | Cape Poillon W. | 63° 08.9′ N 67° 54.6′ W | **Fl.Y.** period 6s fl. 1s, ec. 5s | 128 **39** | 8 | Square tower, orange rectangular daymark. | Seasonal. |
| 620 *H 0054* | Basset Point. | 63° 12.8′ N 67° 57.3′ W | **Fl.R.** period 5s fl. 1s, ec. 4s | 60 **18** | 8 | Square tower, orange rectangular daymark. | Seasonal. |
| 624 *H 0054.2* | Pike Island, No. 1 Range, front. | 63° 13.9′ N 67° 59.5′ W | **Iso.W.** period 2s | 92 **28** | 14 | Square tower, orange trapezoidal daymark, black stripe. | Visible on range line only. Seasonal. |
| 628 *H 0054.21* | -Rear, 385.4 meters 329°28′ from front. | 63° 14.1′ N 67° 59.7′ W | **Iso.W.** period 2s | 146 **44** | 8 | Square tower, orange trapezoidal daymark, black stripe. | Visible on range line only. Seasonal. |
| 632 *H 0054.3* | -No. 2 Range, front. | 63° 15.2′ N 68° 01.3′ W | **Iso.W.** period 2s | 69 **21** | 14 | Square tower, orange trapezoidal daymark, black stripe. | Visible on range line only. Seasonal. |
| 636 *H 0054.31* | --Rear, 2463.2 meters 146°04′ from front. | 63° 14.1′ N 67° 59.7′ W | **Iso.W.** period 2s | 171 **52** | 14 | Square tower, orange trapezoidal daymark, black stripe. | Visible on range line only. Seasonal. |
| 640 *H 0054.4* | Quadrifid Island. | 63° 18.3′ N 68° 07.4′ W | **Fl.G.** period 5s fl. 1s, ec. 4s | 110 **34** | 6 | Square tower, orange rectangular daymark. | Seasonal. |
| 644 *H 0054.6* | Lapointe Rock. | 63° 21.7′ N 68° 13.9′ W | **Fl.W.** period 6s fl. 1s, ec. 5s | 46 **14** | 8 | Square tower, orange rectangular daymark. | Seasonal. |
| 648 *H 0056.4* | Monument Island. | 63° 41.9′ N 68° 30.2′ W | **Fl.R.** period 6s fl. 1s, ec. 5s | 135 **41** | 8 | Square tower, orange rectangular daymark; 33. | Seasonal. |
| 650 *H 0055* | Long Island. | 63° 43.5′ N 68° 30.1′ W | **Fl.W.** period 6s fl. 1s, ec. 5s | 46 **14** | 8 | Square tower, orange rectangular daymark; 16. | Seasonal. |
| 652 *H 0056.2* | **Koojesse Inlet Range**, front. | 63° 44.7′ N 68° 31.4′ W | **F.G.** | 42 **13** | **17** | Square tower, orange trapezoidal daymark; 43. | Visible on range line only. Seasonal. |
| 656 *H 0056.21* | -Rear, 419 meters 344°12′ from front. | 63° 45.0′ N 68° 31.5′ W | **F.G.** | 99 **30** | **17** | Square tower, orange trapezoidal daymark; 52. | Visible on range line only. Seasonal. |
| 657 *H 0055.5* | Iqaluit Range, front. | 63° 43.6′ N 68° 31.8′ W | **Iso.R.** period 2s | 57 **18** | 14 | Square tower, orange trapezoidal daymark, black stripe; 56. | Visible on range line only. Seasonal. |
| 658 *H 0055.51* | -Rear, 576 meters 229°57′ from front. | 63° 43.5′ N 68° 32.4′ W | **Iso.R.** period 2s | 183 **56** | 14 | Square tower, orange trapezoidal daymark, black stripe; 26. | Visible on range line only. Seasonal. |
| 659 *H 0056* | Frobisher Landing. | 63° 44.3′ N 68° 31.6′ W | **Fl.Y.** period 6s fl. 1s, ec. 5s | 16 **5** | 7 | Square tower, orange rectangular daymark; 16. | Seasonal. |
| 660 *H 0052* | Cape Hopes Advance. | 61° 04.9′ N 69° 33.4′ W | **Fl.W.** period 6s fl. 1s, ec. 5s | | 8 | Square skeleton tower, orange rectangular daymark. | Seasonal. **Radar reflector.** |
| 668 *H 0048* | Wales Island. | 61° 51.7′ N 71° 58.0′ W | **Fl.W.** period 6s fl. 1s, ec. 5s | 273 **83** | 8 | Square mast, orange rectangular daymark; 22. | Seasonal. **Radar reflector.** |
| | CHARLES ISLAND: | | | | | | |
| 676 *H 0042* | -W. head. | 62° 42.2′ N 74° 38.9′ W | **Fl.W.** period 6s fl. 1s, ec. 5s | 68 **21** | 8 | Square tower, orange rectangular daymark; 53. | Seasonal. **Radar reflector.** |
| | DECEPTION BAY: | | | | | | |
| 680 *H 0041* | -Arctic Island. | 62° 14.3′ N 74° 45.4′ W | **Fl.W.** period 6s fl. 1s, ec. 5s | 97 **30** | 8 | Square tower, orange rectangular daymark; 22. | Seasonal. |
| 700 *H 0040* | Nottingham Island, S. head. | 63° 05.1′ N 77° 56.6′ W | **Fl.W.** period 6s fl. 1s, ec. 5s | 91 **28** | 8 | Square tower, orange rectangular daymark, black stripe; 39. | Seasonal. **Radar reflector.** |
| | RACON | | **N(– •)** | | 10 | | (3 & 10cm). |

| (1) No. | (2) Name and Location | (3) Position | (4) Characteristic | (5) Height | (6) Range | (7) Structure | (8) Remarks |
|---|---|---|---|---|---|---|---|

## CANADA-HUDSON BAY AND STRAIT

| (1) No. | (2) Name and Location | (3) Position | (4) Characteristic | (5) Height | (6) Range | (7) Structure | (8) Remarks |
|---|---|---|---|---|---|---|---|
| 704 *H 0038* | Digges Islet, NW. islet. | 62° 35.0´ N 78° 06.2´ W | **Fl.W.** period 6s fl. 1s, ec. 5s | 91 **28** | 8 | Square tower, orange square daymark; 26. | Seasonal. **Radar reflector.** |
| 708 *H 0036* | Mansel Island. | 62° 24.6´ N 79° 36.0´ W | **Fl.W.** period 5s fl. 1s, ec. 4s | 61 **19** | 8 | Square tower, orange rectangular daymark; 51. | Seasonal. **Radar reflector.** |
| | RACON | | **K(– • –)** | | 10 | (3 & 10cm) | |
| 712 *H 0036.1* | Cape Acadia, S. extremity of island. | 61° 34.5´ N 79° 48.5´ W | **Fl.W.** period 5s fl. 1s, ec. 4s | 77 **24** | 8 | Square tower, orange rectangular daymark; 63. | Seasonal. **Radar reflector.** |
| 714 *H 0036.4* | Ile Broomfield. | 55° 40.4´ N 79° 14.3´ W | **Fl.R.** period 6s fl. 1s, ec. 5s | 144 **44** | 8 | Square skeleton tower, orange rectangular daymark. | Seasonal. **Radar reflector.** |
| | RACON | | **N(– •)** | | 10 | | (3 & 10cm). |
| 716 *H 0032* | Carys Swan Nest. | 62° 02.9´ N 83° 07.9´ W | **Fl.W.** period 6s fl. 1s, ec. 5s | 41 **12** | 8 | Red and white skeleton tower, orange rectangular daymark; 37. | Seasonal. Shoal water surrounds this point and should not be approached nearer than 5 miles. **Radar reflector.** |
| | RACON | | **C(– • – •)** | | 10 | | (3 & 10cm). |
| 720 *H 0033* | -Cape Pembroke. | 62° 46.9´ N 81° 54.1´ W | **Fl.W.** period 5s fl. 1s, ec. 4s | 54 **16** | 8 | Square tower, orange rectangular daymark. | Seasonal. |
| 724 *H 0033.4* | Walrus Island, center. | 63° 11.5´ N 83° 39.8´ W | **Fl.W.** period 6s fl. 1s, ec. 5s | 180 **55** | 8 | Skeleton tower, orange rectangular daymark, black stripe; 32. | Seasonal. **Radar reflector.** |
| 728 *H 0034* | Bear Island, entrance, E. side. | 63° 59.0´ N 83° 13.8´ W | **Fl.W.** period 5s fl. 1s, ec. 4s | 66 **20** | 7 | Square tower, orange rectangular daymark; 39. | Seasonal. **Radar reflector.** |
| 732 *H 0035* | Munn Bay, Southampton Island. | 64° 06.1´ N 83° 14.7´ W | **Fl.W.** period 5s fl. 1s, ec. 4s | 69 **21** | 7 | Square tower, orange rectangular daymark; 38. | Seasonal. **Radar reflector.** |
| 736 *H 0035.4* | Mission Lake, Chesterfield Inlet. | 63° 18.0´ N 90° 42.8´ W | **Fl.W.** period 6s fl. 1s, ec. 5s | 98 **30** | 8 | Square mast, orange rectangular daymark; 32. | Seasonal. |
| 740 *H 0024* | Dunne Foxe Island. | 62° 15.7´ N 91° 59.3´ W | **Fl.W.** period 6s fl. 1s, ec. 5s | 71 **22** | 8 | Square skeleton mast; 33. | Seasonal. |
| 744 *H 0025* | Walrus Island, Mistake Bay. | 61° 58.0´ N 92° 28.7´ W | **Fl.W.** period 6s fl. 1s, ec. 5s | 94 **28** | 8 | Square skeleton mast, orange rectangular daymark; 36. | Seasonal. |
| | RACON | | **Y(– • – –)** | | 10 | | (3 & 10cm) |
| 746 *H 0025.5* | Sentry Island. | 61° 09.6´ N 93° 52.3´ W | **Fl.W.** period 6s fl. 1s, ec. 5s | 116 **35** | 8 | Square skeleton mast; 60. | Seasonal. |
| | RACON | | **C(– • – •)** | | 10 | | (3 & 10cm). |
| | CHURCHILL HARBOR: | | | | | | |
| 749 *H 0028* | **-Fort Prince of Wales Range,** front. | 58° 47.7´ N 94° 12.9´ W | **F.W.** | 26 **8** | **15** | Skeleton tower, orange trapezoidal daymark, black stripe. | Seasonal. |
| 750 *H 0028.1* | --Rear, 385 meters 343°49´ from front. | 58° 47.9´ N 94° 13.0´ W | **F.W.** | 36 **11** | **15** | Tripod skeleton tower, orange trapezoidal daymark, black stripe. | Seasonal. |
| 751 *H 0029* | **-Ship Point Range,** front. | 58° 47.5´ N 94° 13.4´ W | **F.W.** | 30 **9** | **15** | Square skeleton mast, orange trapezoidal daymark, black stripe; 20. | Seasonal. |

| (1) No. | (2) Name and Location | (3) Position | (4) Characteristic | (5) Height | (6) Range | (7) Structure | (8) Remarks |
|---|---|---|---|---|---|---|---|
| | | | **CANADA-HUDSON BAY AND STRAIT** | | | | |
| 751.1 *H 0029.1* | --Rear, 196 meters 317°37′ from front. | 58° 47.5′ N 94° 13.5′ W | **F.W.** | 44 **13** | **15** | Tripod skeleton tower, orange trapezoidal daymark, black stripe. | Seasonal. |
| 752 *H 0027* | **-Churchill Range,** front. | 58° 47.0′ N 94° 14.0′ W | **F.W.** | 75 **23** | **15** | Tripod skeleton tower, orange trapezoidal daymark. | Seasonal. |
| | -RACON | | **G(– – •)** | | 10 | | (3 & 10cm). |
| 756 *H 0027.1* | --Rear, 1633 meters 236°25′ from front. | 58° 46.5′ N 94° 15.4′ W | **F.W.** | 155 **47** | **15** | Tripod skeleton tower, orange trapezoidal daymark, black stripe. | Seasonal. |
| | | | **CANADA-NORTH COAST** | | | | |
| 768 *H 0014.5* | **Resolute Bay Range,** front. | 74° 41.2′ N 94° 48.0′ W | **Iso.W.** period 2s | 154 **47** | **15** | Square skeleton tower; 45. | Visible on range line only. Seasonal. |
| 772 *H 0014.51* | -Rear, 304 meters 023°14′ from front. | 74° 41.3′ N 94° 47.8′ W | **Iso.W.** period 2s | 217 **66** | **15** | Skeleton tower, orange trapezoidal daymark, black stripe; 28. | Visible on range line only. Seasonal. |
| 773 | Taylor Point, RACON. | 69° 37.3′ N 95° 35.5′ W | **Q(– – • –)** | | 6 | Red beacon. | Seasonal. |
| 773.5 | Ristvedt Island, RACON. | 68° 31.2′ N 97° 15.2′ W | **Y(– • – –)** | | 10 | Red beacon. | Seasonal. |
| 774 | Wiik Island, RACON. | 68° 31.4′ N 99° 33.1′ W | **Z(– – • •)** | | 10 | Red beacon. | Seasonal. |
| 774.5 | **M'Clintock Point,** RACON. | 69° 18.7′ N 99° 53.0′ W | **C(– • – •)** | | **20** | Red beacon. | Seasonal. |
| 775 | **Delta Island,** RACON. | 68° 35.4′ N 100° 01.7′ W | **G(– – •)** | | **20** | Red beacon. | Seasonal. |
| 775.5 | Nordenskiold Islands, RACON. | 68° 21.2′ N 100° 47.2′ W | **K(– • –)** | | 10 | Red beacon. | Seasonal. |
| | CAMBRIDGE BAY: | | | | | | |
| 779 *H 0013.8* | -Range No.1, front. | 69° 02.4′ N 104° 55.0′ W | **F.Y.** | 46 **14** | 14 | Tripod skeleton tower, red trapezoidal daymark, white stripe; 30. | Visible on range line only. Seasonal. **Radar reflector.** |
| 780 *H 0013.81* | --Rear, 1,312.5 meters 095° from front. | 69° 02.3′ N 104° 53.0′ W | **F.Y.** | 63 **19** | 14 | Tripod skeleton tower, red trapezoidal daymark, white stripe; 32. | Visible on range line only. Seasonal. **Radar reflector.** |
| 784 *H 0013.84* | -Range No. 2, front. | 69° 05.2′ N 104° 57.1′ W | **F.Y.** | 33 **10** | 14 | Square skeleton tower, red trapezoidal daymark, white stripe; 30. | Visible on range line only. Seasonal. |
| 788 *H 0013.85* | --Rear, 482 meters 015° from front. | 69° 05.5′ N 104° 56.9′ W | **F.Y.** | 42 **13** | 14 | Tripod skeleton tower, red trapezoidal daymark, white stripe; 20. | Visible on range line only. Seasonal. |
| 792 *H 0013.87* | -Range No. 3, front. | 69° 02.9′ N 104° 54.6′ W | **F.Y.** | 16 **5** | 14 | Square skeleton tower, red trapezoidal daymark, white stripe; 14. | Visible on range line only. Seasonal. |
| 796 *H 0013.88* | --Rear, 1,493 meters 137° from front. | 69° 02.3′ N 104° 53.0′ W | **F.Y.** | 59 **18** | 14 | Tripod skeleton tower, red trapezoidal daymark, white stripe; 30. | Visible on range line only. Seasonal. **Radar reflector.** |
| 800 *H 0013.4* | Atkinson Point. | 69° 57.2′ N 131° 26.9′ W | **Fl.W.** period 4s fl. 0.5s, ec. 3.5s | 74 **23** | 7 | Tripod skeleton tower, red rectangular daymark; 60. | Seasonal. **Radar reflector.** |
| | RACON | | **Y(– • – –)** | | 5 | | |
| 804 *H 0013.3* | Tuft Point. | 69° 44.7′ N 132° 29.2′ W | **Fl.W.** period 4s fl. 0.5s, ec. 3.5s | 71 **22** | 7 | Tripod skeleton tower, white daymark, red stripe; 30. | Seasonal. **Radar reflector.** |

| (1) No. | (2) Name and Location | (3) Position | (4) Characteristic | (5) Height | (6) Range | (7) Structure | (8) Remarks |
|---|---|---|---|---|---|---|---|

## CANADA-NORTH COAST

| (1) No. | (2) Name and Location | (3) Position | (4) Characteristic | (5) Height | (6) Range | (7) Structure | (8) Remarks |
|---|---|---|---|---|---|---|---|
| | TUKTOYAKTUK HARBOR: | | | | | | |
| 809<br>*H 0012* | **-Tuktoyaktuk Island Range,** front. | 69° 27.4′ N<br>133° 00.1′ W | **F.G.** | 52<br>**16** | **17** | Square skeleton tower, red trapezoidal daymark, white stripe. | Visible on range line only.<br>Seasonal. |
| 809.5<br>*H 0012.1* | --Rear, 114 meters 144°37′ from front. | 69° 27.4′ N<br>133° 00.0′ W | **F.G.** | 72<br>**22** | **17** | Tripod skeleton tower, red trapezoidal daymark, white stripe; 40. | Visible on range line only.<br>Seasonal.<br>**Radar reflector.** |
| | --RACON | | **C(– • – •)** | | 5 | | |
| 810<br>*H 0012.3* | **-Peninsula Range,** front. | 69° 27.9′ N<br>132° 59.4′ W | **F.W.** | 38<br>**12** | **16** | Tripod skeleton tower, red trapezoidal daymark, white stripe; 30. | Visible on range line only.<br>Seasonal. |
| 810.1<br>*H 0012.4* | --Rear, 274 meters 099° from front. | 69° 27.9′ N<br>132° 58.9′ W | **F.W.** | 55<br>**17** | **16** | Tripod skeleton tower, red trapezoidal daymark, white stripe; 45. | Visible on range line only.<br>Seasonal. |
| 810.5<br>*H 0012.8* | **-Inner harbor Range,** front. | 69° 27.7′ N<br>132° 59.0′ W | **F.W.** | 16<br>**5** | **16** | Tripod skeleton tower, red trapezoidal daymark, white stripe; 20. | Visible on range line only.<br>Seasonal. |
| 810.6<br>*H 0012.81* | --Rear, 122 meters 357° from front. | 69° 27.7′ N<br>132° 59.0′ W | **F.W.** | 42<br>**13** | **16** | Tripod skeleton tower, red trapezoidal daymark, white stripe; 15. | Visible on range line only.<br>Seasonal. |
| 811<br>*H 0012.6* | **-E. entrance Range,** front. | 69° 27.3′ N<br>132° 58.5′ W | **F.W.** | 48<br>**15** | **16** | Square skeleton tower, red trapezoidal daymark, white stripe; 15. | Visible on range line only.<br>Seasonal. |
| 811.5<br>*H 0012.7* | --Rear, 125 meters 134°08′ from front. | 69° 27.2′ N<br>132° 58.4′ W | **F.W.** | 75<br>**23** | **16** | Tripod skeleton tower, red trapezoidal daymark, white stripe; 30. | Visible on range line only.<br>Seasonal. |
| 812<br>*H 0011* | Pullen Island. | 69° 46.6′ N<br>134° 24.4′ W | **Fl.W.**<br>period 6s<br>fl. 0.5s, ec. 5.5s | 135<br>**41** | 7 | Tripod skeleton tower, white daymark, red stripe; 30. | Seasonal.<br>**Radar reflector.** |
| | RACON | | **G(– – •)** | | **20** | | |
| 818 | -Shingle Point beacon, RACON. | 69° 00.0′ N<br>137° 34.5′ W | **Y(– • – –)** | | 10 | Red beacon. | Maintained from Jun. to Nov.<br>**Radar reflector.** |
| 819 | Nipper Island, RACON. | 59° 00.4′ N<br>68° 53.3′ W | **G(– – •)** | | 10 | | |

## CANADA-LABRADOR COAST

| (1) No. | (2) Name and Location | (3) Position | (4) Characteristic | (5) Height | (6) Range | (7) Structure | (8) Remarks |
|---|---|---|---|---|---|---|---|
| 820<br>*H 0060* | Ford Harbor, N. side of entrance. | 56° 28.3′ N<br>61° 10.1′ W | **Fl.W.**<br>period 4s<br>fl. 0.5s, ec. 3.5s | 45<br>**14** | 6 | Square skeleton tower, red and white rectangular daymark; 20. | Seasonal. |
| 820.1<br>*H 0059.7* | Rifle Sight Hill, W. side of Paul Island. | 56° 29.6′ N<br>61° 38.6′ W | **Mo.(A)W.**<br>period 6s | 75<br>**23** | 5 | Square skeleton tower, red and white square daymark; 16. | |
| 821<br>*H 0061* | Big Island. | 56° 13.3′ N<br>61° 19.4′ W | **Fl.W.**<br>period 4s<br>fl. 0.5s, ec. 3.5s | 72<br>**22** | 5 | Square skeleton tower, red and white rectangular daymark; 16. | Seasonal. |
| 821.1<br>*H 0060.5* | Crown Island. | 56° 16.9′ N<br>60° 56.8′ W | **Fl.R.**<br>period 4s | 102<br>**31** | 4 | Square skeleton tower, red and white rectangular daymark; 16. | Seasonal. |
| 822<br>*H 0059.5* | Turnpike Island. | 56° 36.1′ N<br>61° 38.2′ W | **Fl.R.**<br>period 4s | 56<br>**17** | 4 | Square skeleton mast, red and white rectangular daymark; 15. | Seasonal. |
| 823<br>*H 0061.5* | Nameless Island. | 56° 08.2′ N<br>60° 58.0′ W | **Fl.W.**<br>period 4s<br>fl. 0.5s, ec. 3.5s | 75<br>**23** | 5 | Square skeleton tower, red and white rectangular daymark; 16. | Seasonal. |

Many lights on the Labrador coast are maintained seasonally (from June to November).

| (1) No. | (2) Name and Location | (3) Position | (4) Characteristic | (5) Height | (6) Range | (7) Structure | (8) Remarks |
|---|---|---|---|---|---|---|---|

## CANADA-LABRADOR COAST

| (1) No. | (2) Name and Location | (3) Position | (4) Characteristic | (5) Height | (6) Range | (7) Structure | (8) Remarks |
|---|---|---|---|---|---|---|---|
| 824 *H 0062* | Drawbucket Tickle, E. extremity of Cairn Island. | 56° 09.0´ N 60° 52.3´ W | **Fl.W.** period 3s fl. 0.5s, ec. 2.5s | 46 **14** | 6 | Skeleton tower, orange daymark, white band; 20. | Seasonal. |
| 825 *H 0062.1* | -E. | 56° 08.7´ N 60° 50.8´ W | **Q.R.** | 42 **13** | 4 | Square skeleton tower, red and white square daymark; 16. | Seasonal. |
| 825.05 *H 0062.15* | The Horses. | 56° 03.7´ N 60° 44.3´ W | **Fl.W.** period 3s fl. 0.5s, ec. 2.5s | 56 **17** | 5 | Square skeleton tower, red and white rectangular daymark; 16. | Seasonal. |
| 825.1 *H 0062.2* | Ukasiksalik Island. | 55° 56.4´ N 60° 45.0´ W | **Fl.W.** period 6s fl. 1s, ec. 5s | 69 **21** | 6 | Square skeleton tower, red and white rectangular daymark; 16. | |
| 826 *H 0062.5* | Four Meter Islet. | 55° 57.5´ N 60° 24.7´ W | **Fl.W.** period 3s fl. 0.5s, ec. 2.5s | 25 **8** | 7 | Square skeleton tower, red and white rectangular daymark; 12. | Seasonal. |
| 827 *H 0062.6* | Katauyak Island. | 55° 54.0´ N 60° 33.5´ W | **Fl.W.** period 4s | 144 **44** | 5 | Square skeleton tower, red and white rectangular daymark; 16. | Seasonal. |
| 827.1 *H 0062.7* | Entry Island. | 55° 51.4´ N 60° 43.3´ W | **Fl.W.** period 4s | 75 **23** | 5 | Square skeleton tower, red and white rectangular daymark; 16. | Seasonal. |
| 827.2 *H 0063.8* | S. Tikigakjuk Island. | 55° 48.3´ N 60° 29.3´ W | **Fl.G.** period 4s | 122 **37** | 4 | Square skeleton tower, green and white rectangular daymark; 16. | Seasonal. |
| 828 *H 0064* | Cape Harrigan. | 55° 50.6´ N 60° 18.9´ W | **Fl.W.** period 6s fl. 0.5s, ec. 5.5s | 144 **44** | 6 | Cylindrical tower, red and white bands; 13. | Seasonal. |
| | RACON | | **K(– • –)** | | 10 | | (3 & 10cm). |
| 828.1 *H 0064.4* | Farmyard Island. | 55° 49.5´ N 59° 54.1´ W | **Fl.W.** period 3s fl. 0.5s, ec. 2.5s | 177 **54** | 5 | Square skeleton tower, red and white square daymark; 16. | Seasonal. |
| 828.2 *H 0064.3* | Windy Tickle. | 55° 46.6´ N 60° 19.6´ W | **Fl.W.** period 3s fl. 0.5s, ec. 2.5s | 23 **7** | 5 | Square skeleton tower, red and white rectangular daymark; 16. | Seasonal. |
| 829 *H 0065* | Gourley Island. | 55° 43.4´ N 60° 20.5´ W | **Fl.W.** period 4s | 39 **12** | 5 | Square skeleton tower, red and white rectangular daymark; 16. | Seasonal. |
| 830 *H 0066* | Cant Island. | 55° 38.4´ N 60° 23.7´ W | **Fl.W.** period 4s | 72 **22** | 5 | Square skeleton tower, red and white rectangular daymark; 16. | Seasonal. |
| 831 *H 0067* | Cross Island. | 55° 36.1´ N 60° 18.4´ W | **Fl.W.** period 3s fl. 0.5s, ec. 2.5s | 66 **20** | 5 | Square skeleton tower, red and white rectangular daymark; 16. | Seasonal. |
| 832 *H 0068* | Napakataktalik (Manuel Island). | 55° 33.1´ N 60° 14.9´ W | **Fl.W.** period 4s fl. 0.5s, ec. 3.5s | 127 **39** | 5 | Red and white cylindrical tower, red and white rectangular daymark; 16. | Seasonal. |
| 833 *H 0068.4* | Achvitaaksoak Island. | 55° 29.6´ N 60° 13.6´ W | **Fl.R.** period 4s fl. 0.5s, ec. 3.5s | 159 **48** | 4 | Square skeleton tower, red and white rectangular daymark; 16. | Seasonal. |
| 834 *H 0068.42* | Umiaginak Island. | 55° 28.8´ N 60° 12.6´ W | **Q.R.** | 48 **15** | 3 | Square skeleton tower, red and white rectangular daymark; 16. | Seasonal. |
| 836 *H 0068.5* | Hopedale Harbor Range, front. | 55° 27.3´ N 60° 13.5´ W | **F.R.** | 66 **20** | 11 | Skeleton tower, white trapezoidal daymark, red stripe; 19. | Visible on range line only. Seasonal. |
| 840 *H 0068.51* | -Rear, 60 meters 278° from front. | 55° 27.3´ N 60° 13.6´ W | **F.R.** | 85 **26** | 11 | Skeleton tower, white trapezoidal daymark, red stripe; 10. | Visible on range line only. Seasonal. |

Many lights on the Labrador coast are maintained seasonally (from June to November).

| (1) No. | (2) Name and Location | (3) Position | (4) Characteristic | (5) Height | (6) Range | (7) Structure | (8) Remarks |
|---|---|---|---|---|---|---|---|

## CANADA-LABRADOR COAST

| (1) No. | (2) Name and Location | (3) Position | (4) Characteristic | (5) Height | (6) Range | (7) Structure | (8) Remarks |
|---|---|---|---|---|---|---|---|
| 841<br>*H 0068.3* | Satoarsook Island. | 55° 26.2′ N<br>60° 11.4′ W | **L.Fl.W.**<br>period 10s<br>fl. 2s, ec. 8s | 28<br>**9** | 6 | Square skeleton tower, red and white rectangular daymark; 16. | Seasonal. |
| 842<br>*H 0068.6* | Landmark Point. | 55° 24.9′ N<br>60° 01.9′ W | **Fl.G.**<br>period 4s | 111<br>**34** | 4 | Square skeleton tower, green and white rectangular daymark; 16. | Seasonal. |
| 842.1<br>*H 0068.1* | Annaltalik Island. | 55° 27.2′ N<br>59° 46.0′ W | **Fl.W.**<br>period 6s<br>fl. 1s, ec. 5s | 112<br>**34** | 6 | Square skeleton tower, red and white rectangular daymark; 16. | Seasonal. |
| 843<br>*H 0068.8* | Bluff Point. | 55° 15.9′ N<br>60° 02.0′ W | **Fl.W.**<br>period 3s<br>fl. 0.5s, ec. 2.5s | 49<br>**15** | 5 | Square skeleton tower, red and white rectangular daymark; 16. | Seasonal. |
| 844<br>*H 0069* | White Bear Island (NanuakNanuaktok). | 55° 26.0′ N<br>59° 30.7′ W | **Fl.W.**<br>period 6s<br>fl. 0.5s, ec. 5.5s | 77<br>**23** | 5 | Square skeleton tower, red and white rectangular daymark; 24. | Seasonal. |
| | RACON | | **N(– •)** | | 10 | | (3 & 10cm). |
| 848<br>*H 0070* | Winsor Point, Winsor Harbor, NE. point. | 55° 20.9′ N<br>59° 43.9′ W | **Fl.W.**<br>period 3s<br>fl. 0.5s, ec. 2.5s | 105<br>**32** | 5 | Cylindrical tower, red and white rectangular daymark; 16. | Seasonal. |
| 848.5<br>*H 0070.5* | Striped Island. | 55° 19.1′ N<br>59° 38.5′ W | **Fl.W.**<br>period 4s<br>fl. 0.5s, ec. 3.5s | 121<br>**37** | 5 | Square skeleton tower, red and white rectangular daymark; 16. | Seasonal. |
| 849<br>*H 0071* | The Clusters. | 55° 16.8′ N<br>59° 30.2′ W | **Fl.R.**<br>period 4s<br>fl. 0.5s, ec. 3.5s | 17<br>**5** | 7 | Square skeleton tower; 16. | Seasonal. |
| 849.1<br>*H 0071.2* | Drunken Harbor Island. | 55° 13.3′ N<br>59° 30.3′ W | **Fl.R.**<br>period 3s<br>fl. 0.5s, ec. 2.5s | 23<br>**7** | 4 | Square skeleton tower, red and white rectangular daymark; 16. | Seasonal. |
| | KAIPOKOK BAY: | | | | | | |
| 849.2<br>*H 0071.34* | -W. Turnavik Island. | 55° 15.7′ N<br>59° 20.1′ W | **Fl.G.**<br>period 3s<br>fl. 0.5s, ec. 2.5s | 83<br>**25** | | Square skeleton tower, green and white rectangular daymark; 16. | Seasonal. |
| 849.3<br>*H 0071.33* | -Aillik Islands. | 55° 13.5′ N<br>59° 14.3′ W | **Q.R.** | 38<br>**12** | 3 | Square skeleton tower, red and white rectangular daymark; 16. | Seasonal. |
| 849.4<br>*H 0071.3* | -Pigeon Island. | 55° 11.1′ N<br>59° 23.0′ W | **Mo.(A)W.**<br>period 6s<br>fl. 0.3s, ec. 0.6s<br>fl. 1s, ec. 4.1s | 96<br>**29** | 5 | Square skeleton tower, red and white rectangular daymark; 23. | Seasonal. |
| 849.5<br>*H 0071.27* | -Cape Roy. | 55° 09.5′ N<br>59° 24.9′ W | **Fl.R.**<br>period 4s<br>fl. 0.5s, ec. 3.5s | 77<br>**24** | 4 | Square skeleton tower, red and white rectangular daymark; 16. | Seasonal. |
| 849.6<br>*H 0071.26* | -Long Island, N. head. | 55° 08.6′ N<br>59° 22.3′ W | **Fl.G.**<br>period 3s<br>fl. 0.5s, ec. 2.5s | 72<br>**22** | 4 | Square skeleton tower, green and white rectangular daymark; 16. | Seasonal. |
| 849.7<br>*H 0071.25* | -Alkami Island. | 55° 00.1′ N<br>59° 34.3′ W | **Fl.G.**<br>period 4s<br>fl. 0.5s, ec. 3.5s | 115<br>**35** | 4 | Square skeleton tower, green and white rectangular daymark; 20. | Seasonal. |
| 850<br>*H 0071.24* | Postville. | 54° 54.4′ N<br>59° 46.0′ W | **Fl.R.**<br>period 4s<br>fl. 0.5s, ec. 3.5s | 16<br>**5** | 4 | Mast; 7. | Seasonal. |
| | MAKKOVIK BAY: | | | | | | |
| 850.3<br>*H 0071.36* | -Sisters Island. | 55° 13.7′ N<br>59° 07.7′ W | **L.Fl.W.**<br>period 10s<br>fl. 2s, ec. 8s | 58<br>**18** | 6 | Square skeleton tower, red and white rectangular daymark; 20. | Seasonal. |

Many lights on the Labrador coast are maintained seasonally (from June to November).

| (1) No. | (2) Name and Location | (3) Position | (4) Characteristic | (5) Height | (6) Range | (7) Structure | (8) Remarks |
|---|---|---|---|---|---|---|---|
| | | | **CANADA-LABRADOR COAST** | | | | |
| 850.5 *H 0071.45* | -Jackos Island. | 55° 09.8′ N 59° 05.1′ W | **Mo.(A)W.** period 6s fl. 0.3s, ec. 0.6s fl. 1s, ec. 4.1s | 61 **19** | 5 | Square skeleton tower, red and white rectangular daymark; 20. | Seasonal. |
| 850.8 *H 0071.39* | -Ikey's Point. | 55° 09.0′ N 59° 08.6′ W | **Fl.R.** period 4s fl. 0.5s, ec. 3.5s | 39 **12** | 4 | Square skeleton tower, red and white rectangular daymark; 16. | Seasonal. |
| 851 *H 0071.5* | Kidlialuit Island (Ironbound Islands). | 55° 12.0′ N 58° 45.6′ W | **Fl.W.** period 6s fl. 1s, ec. 5s | 470 **143** | 7 | Square skeleton tower, red and white rectangular daymark; 16. | Seasonal. |
| 851.02 *H 0071.48* | Green Island. | 55° 07.8′ N 58° 53.6′ W | **Fl.R.** period 4s fl. 0.5s, ec. 3.5s | 69 **21** | 4 | Square skeleton tower, red and white rectangular daymark; 20. | Seasonal. |
| | ADLAVIK ISLANDS: | | | | | | |
| 851.03 *H 0071.54* | -Double Island. | 55° 04.3′ N 58° 54.7′ W | **Fl.W.** period 4s fl. 0.5s, ec. 3.5s | 233 **71** | 5 | Square skeleteon tower, red and white rectangular daymark; 16. | Seasonal. |
| 851.05 *H 0071.53* | -Blandford Island. | 55° 03.6′ N 58° 44.4′ W | **Q.R.** | 108 **33** | 4 | Square skeleton tower, red and white rectangular daymark; 16. | Seasonal. |
| 851.07 *H 0071.55* | -Conical Island. | 54° 55.7′ N 58° 50.6′ W | **Fl.R.** period 4s fl. 0.5s, ec. 3.5s | 100 **30** | 4 | Square skeleton tower, red and white square daymark; 23. | Seasonal. |
| 851.1 *H 0071.7* | Northern Island. | 54° 58.9′ N 58° 17.7′ W | **Mo.(A)W.** period 6s fl. 0.3s, ec. 0.6s fl. 1s, ec. 4.1s | 190 **58** | 5 | Square skeleton tower, red and white rectangular daymark; 23. | Seasonal. |
| 851.2 *H 0071.9* | Double Point. | 54° 50.4′ N 58° 22.4′ W | **Fl.W.** period 4s fl. 0.5s, ec. 3.5s | 110 **34** | 5 | Square skeleton tower, red and white rectangular daymark; 16. | Seasonal. |
| 852 *H 0072* | Sloop Harbor, N. side of entrance. | 54° 34.1′ N 57° 09.3′ W | **Fl.W.** period 3s fl. 0.5s, ec. 2.5s | 67 **20** | 7 | Square skeleton tower, red and white rectangular daymark; 12. | Seasonal. |
| 854 *H 0071.8* | Cape Harrison. | 54° 55.5′ N 57° 56.5′ W | **Fl.W.** period 4s fl. 0.5s, ec. 3.5s | 610 **186** | 7 | Square skeleton tower, red and white rectangular daymark; 16. | Seasonal. |
| 855 *H 0071.95* | Duck Island. | 54° 43.7′ N 57° 41.4′ W | **Fl.W.** period 4s fl. 0.5s, ec. 3.5s | 66 **20** | 5 | Square skeleton tower, red and white rectangular daymark; 16. | Seasonal. |
| 855.1 *H 0071.97* | Pigeon Island. | 54° 40.4′ N 57° 29.9′ W | **Fl.W.** period 4s fl. 0.5s, ec. 3.5s | 123 **37** | 5 | Square skeleton tower, red and white rectangular daymark; 16. | Seasonal. |
| 855.2 *H 0071.91* | Quaker Hat. | 54° 44.2′ N 57° 20.6′ W | **L.Fl.W.** period 10s fl. 2s, ec. 8s | 118 **36** | 6 | Square skeleton tower, red and white rectangular daymark; 15. | Seasonal. |
| | RACON | | **Q(– – • –)** | | 10 | | (3 & 10cm). |
| 855.3 *H 0071.98* | Holton Island. | 54° 37.6′ N 57° 16.4′ W | **Fl.W.** period 4s | 151 **46** | 5 | Red and white square skeleton tower, red and white rectangular daymark; 16. | Seasonal. |
| 856 *H 0074* | Cut Throat Point. | 54° 29.4′ N 57° 06.4′ W | **Fl.W.** period 4s fl. 0.5s, ec. 3.5s | 92 **28** | 7 | Square skeleton tower, red and white rectangular daymark; 16. | Seasonal. |
| 857 *H 0073* | Run By Guess. | 54° 28.0′ N 57° 19.4′ W | **Fl.W.** period 3s fl. 0.5s, ec. 2.5s | 57 **18** | 4 | Square skeleton tower, red and white rectangular daymark; 16. | Seasonal. |

Many lights on the Labrador coast are maintained seasonally (from June to November).

| (1) No. | (2) Name and Location | (3) Position | (4) Characteristic | (5) Height | (6) Range | (7) Structure | (8) Remarks |
|---|---|---|---|---|---|---|---|

**CANADA-LABRADOR COAST**

| (1) No. | (2) Name and Location | (3) Position | (4) Characteristic | (5) Height | (6) Range | (7) Structure | (8) Remarks |
|---|---|---|---|---|---|---|---|
| 858<br>*H 0074.2* | East Big Island. | 54° 27.2′ N<br>57° 05.6′ W | **Fl.W.**<br>period 3s | 157<br>**48** | 5 | Square skeleton tower, red and white rectangular daymark; 16. | Seasonal. |
| 860<br>*H 0074.5* | Grappling Island. | 54° 27.4′ N<br>56° 52.9′ W | **Fl.W.**<br>period 6s<br>fl. 0.5s, ec. 5.5s | 106<br>**32** | 6 | Square skeleton tower red and white rectangular daymark; 14. | Seasonal. |
| | RACON | | **G(– – •)** | | 10 | | (3 & 10cm). |
| 864<br>*H 0074.7* | Herring Islands, on NE. island. | 54° 20.2′ N<br>57° 05.5′ W | **Fl.W.**<br>period 3s<br>fl. 0.5s, ec. 2.5s | 105<br>**32** | 7 | Square skeleton tower, red and white rectangular daymark; 12. | Seasonal. |
| 868<br>*H 0075* | Little Black Island, N. head. | 54° 18.4′ N<br>57° 50.1′ W | **Fl.W.**<br>period 6s<br>fl. 0.5s, ec. 5.5s | 115<br>**35** | 7 | Square skeleton tower, red and white rectangular daymark; 13. | Seasonal. |
| 872<br>*H 0075.5* | Big Island, SE. side of island. | 54° 17.2′ N<br>58° 02.1′ W | **Fl.W.**<br>period 4s<br>fl. 0.5s, ec. 3.5s | 39<br>**12** | 5 | Skeleton tower, red and white rectangular daymark; 13. | Seasonal. |
| 873<br>*H 0075.55* | Hart Head. | 54° 11.7′ N<br>58° 24.6′ W | **Fl.R.**<br>period 4s | 23<br>**7** | 4 | Square skeleton tower, red and white rectangular daymark; 16. | Seasonal. |
| 874<br>*H 0075.65* | Rigolet Cove. | 54° 10.8′ N<br>58° 25.6′ W | **Fl.R.**<br>period 4s<br>fl. 0.5s, ec. 3.5s | 16<br>**5** | 3 | Mast; 7. | Seasonal. |
| 876<br>*H 0075.6* | Rigolet Point. | 54° 10.7′ N<br>58° 25.6′ W | **Fl.W.**<br>period 6s<br>fl. 1s, ec. 5s | 37<br>**11** | 5 | Square skeleton tower; 30. | Seasonal. |
| 880<br>*H 0075.9* | Eskimo Island. | 54° 03.2′ N<br>58° 33.6′ W | **Fl.W.**<br>period 3s<br>fl. 0.5s, ec. 2.5s | 18<br>**5** | 7 | Square skeleton tower, red and white rectangular daymark; 13. | Seasonal. |
| 884<br>*H 0075.8* | Henrietta Island. | 54° 04.2′ N<br>58° 33.6′ W | **Fl.W.**<br>period 6s<br>fl. 1s, ec. 5s | 18<br>**5** | 6 | Skeleton tower, orange and white rectangular daymark; 16. | Seasonal. |
| 888<br>*H 0075.7* | Snooks Cove. | 54° 04.6′ N<br>58° 34.1′ W | **Fl.W.**<br>period 6s<br>fl. 0.5s, ec. 5.5s | 20<br>**6** | 6 | Skeleton tower, orange and white rectangular daymark; 12. | Seasonal. |
| 892<br>*H 0076* | Green Island. | 53° 55.6′ N<br>58° 59.6′ W | **Fl.W.**<br>period 6s<br>fl. 0.5s, ec. 5.5s | 62<br>**19** | 6 | Square skeleton tower, red and white rectangular daymark; 12. | Seasonal. |
| 894<br>*H 0076.2* | Long Point. | 53° 41.7′ N<br>59° 19.1′ W | **Fl.W.**<br>period 4s | 175<br>**53** | 5 | Square skeleton mast, red and white daymark; 12. | Seasonal. |
| | GOOSE BAY: | | | | | | |
| 896<br>*H 0076.4* | -Brule Point Range, front. | 53° 26.6′ N<br>59° 56.7′ W | **Oc.G.**<br>period 6s<br>lt. 4s, ec. 2s | 26<br>**8** | 13 | Square skeleton tower, white trapezoidal daymark, red stripe; 20. | Seasonal. |
| 900<br>*H 0076.5* | --Rear, 88 meters 163°30′ from front. | 53° 26.5′ N<br>59° 56.7′ W | **Oc.G.**<br>period 6s<br>lt. 4s, ec. 2s | 63<br>**19** | 13 | Square skeleton tower, white trapezoidal daymark, red stripe; 20. | Seasonal. |
| 904<br>*H 0077* | -Kenamu River Range, front, W. side of entrance. | 53° 28.2′ N<br>59° 54.9′ W | **Oc.G.**<br>period 6s<br>lt. 4s, ec. 2s | 22<br>**7** | 13 | Square skeleton tower, white trapezoidal daymark, red stripe; 28. | Visible on range line only. Seasonal. |
| 908<br>*H 0077.1* | --Rear, about 1518 meters 047°30′ from front. | 53° 28.8′ N<br>59° 53.8′ W | **Oc.G.**<br>period 6s<br>lt. 4s, ec. 2s | 62<br>**19** | 13 | Square skeleton tower, white trapezoidal daymark, red stripe; 62. | Visible on range line only. Seasonal. |

Many lights on the Labrador coast are maintained seasonally (from June to November).

| (1) No. | (2) Name and Location | (3) Position | (4) Characteristic | (5) Height | (6) Range | (7) Structure | (8) Remarks |
|---|---|---|---|---|---|---|---|

## CANADA-LABRADOR COAST

| (1) No. | (2) Name and Location | (3) Position | (4) Characteristic | (5) Height | (6) Range | (7) Structure | (8) Remarks |
|---|---|---|---|---|---|---|---|
| 910<br>*H 0076.3* | **Terrington Narrows.** | 53° 20.6′ N<br>60° 24.1′ W | **Dir.W.R.G.** | 34<br>**10** | **19** | Square skeleton tower, red and white rectangular daymark; 33. | F.R. 255°35′-256°55′, Al.R.W.-257°10′, F.W.-257°30′, Al.G.W.-257°45′, F.G.-259°05′.<br>Seasonal. |
| 912<br>*H 0078* | Packs Harbor, N. side of entrance. | 53° 52.0′ N<br>57° 00.0′ W | **Fl.W.**<br>period 3s<br>fl. 0.5s, ec. 2.5s | 106<br>**32** | 6 | Round tower, red daymark, white band; 13. | Seasonal. |
| 913<br>*H 0079.7* | Leading Mark Island. | 53° 45.5′ N<br>57° 04.1′ W | **Fl.G.**<br>period 4s<br>fl. 0.5s, ec. 3.5s | 29<br>**9** | 4 | Square skeleton tower, red and white rectangular daymark; 16. | Seasonal. |
| 914<br>*H 0079* | Cape Horn. | 53° 47.7′ N<br>56° 48.3′ W | **Fl.W.**<br>period 4s<br>fl. 0.5s, ec. 3.5s | 77<br>**23** | 5 | Square skeleton tower, red and white rectangular daymark; 16. | Seasonal. |
| 915.2<br>*H 0079.5* | Cartwright Wharf. | 53° 42.2′ N<br>57° 01.3′ W | **Fl.R.**<br>period 4s<br>fl. 0.5s, ec. 3.5s | 11<br>**3** | 4 | Round mast; 7. | Seasonal. |
| 916<br>*H 0080* | Cape North, NE. extremity. | 53° 47.2′ N<br>56° 28.9′ W | **Fl.W.**<br>period 6s<br>fl. 0.5s, ec. 5.5s | 238<br>**73** | 7 | Square skeleton tower, red and white rectangular daymark; 13. | Seasonal. |
| 920<br>*H 0081* | South Wolf Island, NE. head. | 53° 41.1′ N<br>55° 54.4′ W | **Fl.W.**<br>period 6s<br>fl. 1s, ec. 5s | 289<br>**88** | 6 | Skeleton tower; 45. | Seasonal. |
| 924<br>*H 0082* | White Point. | 53° 34.7′ N<br>56° 01.7′ W | **Fl.W.**<br>period 6s<br>fl. 0.5s, ec. 5.5s | 72<br>**22** | 7 | Square skeleton tower, red and white rectangular daymark; 12. | Seasonal. |
| 928<br>*H 0084* | Domino Point. | 53° 27.6′ N<br>55° 44.8′ W | **Fl.W.**<br>period 6s<br>fl. 0.5s, ec. 5.5s | 127<br>**39** | 7 | Square skeleton tower, red and white rectangular daymark; 13. | Seasonal. |
|  | RACON |  | **Y(– • – –)** |  | 10 |  | (3 & 10cm). |
| 932<br>*H 0085* | Roundhill Island, N. point. | 53° 26.1′ N<br>55° 36.8′ W | **Fl.W.**<br>period 3s<br>fl. 0.5s, ec. 2.5s | 218<br>**66** | 5 | Skeleton tower, red daymark, white band; 23. | Seasonal. |
| 933<br>*H 0085.7* | Fish Island. | 53° 12.8′ N<br>55° 43.5′ W | **Fl.W.**<br>period 6s<br>fl. 0.5s, ec. 5.5s | 58<br>**18** | 6 | Skeleton tower, red daymark, white band; 16. | Seasonal. |
| 934<br>*H 0085.5* | Cod Bag Islets. | 53° 25.9′ N<br>55° 44.9′ W | **Fl.W.**<br>period 4s<br>fl. 0.5s, ec. 3.5s | 108<br>**33** | 6 | Skeleton tower, red daymark, white band; 13. | Seasonal. |
| 936<br>*H 0086* | Red Island, entrance to Hawke Bay. | 53° 00.6′ N<br>55° 45.8′ W | **Fl.W.**<br>period 3s<br>fl. 0.5s, ec. 2.5s | 95<br>**29** | 6 | Square skeleton tower, red and white rectangular daymark; 13. | Seasonal. |
| 938<br>*H 0086.65* | Pigeon Island. | 52° 43.0′ N<br>55° 51.4′ W | **Fl.G.**<br>period 4s | 39<br>**12** | 4 | Square skeleton tower, green and white rectangular daymark; 20. | Seasonal. |
| 940<br>*H 0086.4* | Deepwater Island. | 52° 43.5′ N<br>55° 53.9′ W | **Fl.W.**<br>period 4s<br>fl. 0.5s, ec. 3.5s | 16<br>**5** | 6 | Square skeleton tower, red and white rectangular daymark; 16. | Seasonal. |
| 944<br>*H 0086.6* | Goose Island. | 52° 47.6′ N<br>56° 06.3′ W | **Fl.W.**<br>period 4s<br>fl. 0.5s, ec. 3.5s | 25<br>**8** | 6 | Square skeleton tower, red and white rectangular daymark; 13. | Seasonal. |
| 945<br>*H 0086.7* | Twin Islands. | 52° 40.3′ N<br>55° 45.0′ W | **Fl.W.**<br>period 4s | 102<br>**31** | 5 | Mast, red daymark, white band; 10. | Seasonal. |
| 946<br>*H 0086.8* | Cape St. Francis. | 52° 33.9′ N<br>55° 42.3′ W | **Fl.W.**<br>period 6s<br>fl. 0.5s, ec. 5.5s | 128<br>**39** | 2 | Red mast, white stripe; 10. | Seasonal. |

Many lights on the Labrador coast are maintained seasonally (from June to November).

| (1) No. | (2) Name and Location | (3) Position | (4) Characteristic | (5) Height | (6) Range | (7) Structure | (8) Remarks |
|---|---|---|---|---|---|---|---|
| | | | **CANADA-LABRADOR COAST** | | | | |
| 948 *H 0087* | Bobbs Island, S. side. | 52° 31.0′ N 55° 46.0′ W | **Fl.R.** period 3s fl. 0.5s, ec. 2.5s | 67 **20** | 4 | Square skeleton tower, red and white rectangular daymark; 13. | Seasonal. |
| | ALEXIS RIVER: | | | | | | |
| 952 *H 0089* | -Tickle N.-S. Range, front. | 52° 32.0′ N 56° 10.0′ W | **Iso.R.** period 4s | 26 **8** | 11 | Skeleton tower, white trapezoidal daymark, red stripe; 24. | Seasonal. |
| 956 *H 0089.1* | --Rear, 135 meters 216°13′ from front. | 52° 31.8′ N 56° 10.1′ W | **Iso.R.** period 4s | 46 **14** | 11 | Skeleton tower, white trapezoidal daymark, red stripe; 20. | Seasonal. |
| 960 *H 0088* | -Tickle E.-W. Range, front. | 52° 32.0′ N 56° 10.0′ W | **Iso.R.** period 4s | 28 **9** | 11 | Skeleton tower, white trapezoidal daymark, red stripe; 20. | Visible on range line only. Seasonal. |
| 964 *H 0088.1* | --Rear, 269 meters 106°26′ from front. | 52° 31.9′ N 56° 09.4′ W | **Iso.R.** period 4s | 58 **18** | 11 | Skeleton tower, white trapezoidal daymark, red stripe; 16. | Seasonal. |
| 966 *H 0089.5* | Spear Point. | 52° 26.6′ N 55° 38.0′ W | **Fl.W.** period 3s fl. 0.5s, ec. 2.5s | 128 **39** | 5 | Mast, red and white daymark; 7. | Seasonal. |
| 967 *H 0089.7* | Cape St. Lewis. | 52° 22.0′ N 55° 38.0′ W | **Fl.W.** period 4s fl. 0.5s, ec. 3.5s | 134 **41** | 5 | Square skeleton tower, red and white rectangular daymark, white band; 16. | Seasonal. |
| 967.2 *H 0089.8* | Green Island. | 52° 17.6′ N 55° 41.1′ W | **Fl.W.** period 4s | 46 **14** | 5 | Square skeleton tower, red and white rectangular daymark; 16. | Seasonal. |
| 967.3 *H 0091* | Killik Island. | 52° 16.7′ N 55° 35.6′ W | **Fl.G.** period 4s | 21 **6** | 4 | Square skeleton tower, green and white rectangular daymark; 16. | Seasonal. |
| 968 *H 0092* | Double Island, off Battle Harbor. | 52° 15.3′ N 55° 33.4′ W | **Fl.W.** period 6s fl. 1s, ec. 5s | 126 **38** | 7 | White cilindrical tower, black and white bands; 30. | Seasonal. |
| 972 *H 0090* | Copper Island, SE. head. | 52° 16.0′ N 55° 40.0′ W | **Fl.W.** period 3s fl. 0.5s, ec. 2.5s | 30 **9** | 7 | Red and white cylindrical tower, red daymark, white band; 13. | Seasonal. |
| 974 *H 0093* | Walls Island Point. | 52° 13.2′ N 55° 36.9′ W | **Fl.G.** period 4s | 100 **30** | 4 | Square skeleton tower, green and white rectangular daymark; 16. | Seasonal. |
| 976 *H 0094* | **Camp Island.** | 52° 10.0′ N 55° 38.5′ W | **Fl.W.** period 5s fl. 0.2s, ec. 4.8s | 137 **42** | **15** | White cilindrical tower, red upper portion; 33. | Seasonal. **Horn:** 1 bl. ev. 60s (bl. 4s, si. 56s). Horn points 103°. |
| 980 *H 0108* | **Castle Island.** | 51° 58.3′ N 55° 51.3′ W | **Fl.W.** period 6s fl. 0.5s, ec. 5.5s | 66 **20** | **15** | Square skeleton tower, red and white rectangular daymark; 12. | Seasonal. |
| | BELLE ISLE: | | | | | | |
| 984 *H 0096* | **-Northeast Point.** | 52° 00.8′ N 55° 16.9′ W | **Fl.W.** period 10s fl. 0.2s, ec. 9.8s | 128 **39** | **17** | White cylindrical tower, red upper portion; 57. | Seasonal. **Horn:** 1 bl. ev. 30s (bl. 3s, si. 27s). Horn points 061°. |
| 988 *H 0102* | **-S. head.** (Upper). | 51° 52.8′ N 55° 23.0′ W | **Fl.W.** period 20s fl. 1s, ec. 19s | 450 **137** | **18** | White cylindrical tower, red upper portion; 61. | Visible 240°-110°30′. Seasonal. **Horn:** 2 bl. ev. 60s (bl. 3s, si. 3s, bl. 3s, si. 51s). Horn points 165°. |
| 992 *H 0104* | --(Lower). | 51° 52.6′ N 55° 23.2′ W | **Fl.W.** period 20s fl. 1s, ec. 19s | 163 **50** | **18** | Red cylindrical structure. | Seasonal. |
| 1000 *H 0110* | **Red Bay,** on Saddle Island. | 51° 43.6′ N 56° 26.1′ W | **Fl.W.** period 5s | 118 **36** | **15** | Square skeleton tower; 23. | Seasonal. |

Many lights on the Labrador coast are maintained seasonally (from June to November).

| (1) No. | (2) Name and Location | (3) Position | (4) Characteristic | (5) Height | (6) Range | (7) Structure | (8) Remarks |
|---|---|---|---|---|---|---|---|

## CANADA-LABRADOR COAST

| (1) No. | (2) Name and Location | (3) Position | (4) Characteristic | (5) Height | (6) Range | (7) Structure | (8) Remarks |
|---|---|---|---|---|---|---|---|
| 1009<br>*H 0112.55* | L'Anse au Loup, N. wharf. | 51° 31.3′ N<br>56° 49.7′ W | **Fl.R.**<br>period 4s | | 2 | Mast; 7. | |
| 1010<br>*H 0112.6* | -S. wharf. | 51° 31.0′ N<br>56° 49.7′ W | **Fl.G.**<br>period 4s | 16<br>**5** | 2 | Mast; 10. | |
| | FORTEAU BAY: | | | | | | |
| 1012<br>*H 0114* | **-Amour Pointe.** | 51° 27.7′ N<br>56° 51.5′ W | **Oc.W.**<br>period 20s<br>lt. 16s, ec. 4s | 152<br>**46** | **24** | White round tower, black band; 108. | Seasonal.<br>**Horn:** 1 bl. ev. 30s (bl. 3s, si. 27s). Horn points 156°. |
| 1016<br>*H 0116* | -Forteau. | 51° 28.1′ N<br>56° 57.3′ W | **Fl.R.**<br>period 4s | 16<br>**5** | 4 | Cilindrical mast; 7. | Seasonal. |
| 1020<br>*H 0122* | **Blanc Sablon, near Pointe St. Charles Range,** front. | 51° 25.2′ N<br>57° 07.2′ W | **F.W.** | 116<br>**35** | **19** | Square skeleton tower, orange trapezoidal daymark, black stripe; 50. | Visible on range line only. |
| 1024<br>*H 0122.1* | -Rear, 231 meters 063°16′ from front. | 51° 25.3′ N<br>57° 07.0′ W | **F.W.** | 186<br>**57** | **19** | Square skeleton tower, orange trapezoidal daymark, black stripe; 20. | Visible on range line only. |
| 1028<br>*H 0123* | -Wharf. | 51° 24.9′ N<br>57° 09.2′ W | **Fl.R.**<br>period 6s<br>fl. 1s, ec. 5s | 34<br>**10** | 9 | Mast; 26. | Visible on range line only. |

Many lights on the Labrador coast are maintained seasonally (from June to November).

# Section 2

## Newfoundland

| (1) No. | (2) Name and Location | (3) Position | (4) Characteristic | (5) Height | (6) Range | (7) Structure | (8) Remarks |
|---|---|---|---|---|---|---|---|
| | | | **CANADA-NEWFOUNDLAND** | | | | |
| 1032 *H 0140* | **Cape Norman.** | 51° 37.7′ N 55° 54.4′ W | **Fl.(3)W.** period 30s fl. 0.5s, ec. 5.5s fl. 0.5s, ec. 5.5s fl. 0.5s, ec. 17.5s | 116 **35** | **21** | White octagonal tower; 50. | Year round. **Horn:** 1 bl. ev. 30s. (bl. 3s, si. 27s). Horn points 325°-045°. |
| 1036 *H 0138* | Schooner Island. | 51° 36.4′ N 55° 50.4′ W | **Fl.W.** period 6s fl. 1s, ec. 5s | 34 **10** | 6 | Square skeleton tower, red and white rectangular daymark; 16. | Seasonal. |
| 1038 *H 0137* | Raleigh breakwater. | 51° 34.2′ N 55° 44.3′ W | **Fl.R.** period 3s | | | Cylindrical mast; 7. | Seasonal. |
| 1040 *H 0136* | Quirpon Harbor, NE. point of Jacques Cartier Island. | 51° 36.0′ N 55° 27.5′ W | **Fl.W.** period 6s fl. 0.5s, ec. 5.5s | 72 **22** | 6 | Square skeleton tower, red and white rectangular daymark; 13. | Seasonal. |
| 1044 *H 0135* | **Quirpon Harbor Range,** front, on Merchant Island. | 51° 36.0′ N 55° 27.0′ W | **F.W.** | 32 **10** | **16** | Square skeleton tower, white trapezoidal daymark, orange stripe; 13. | Seasonal. |
| 1048 *H 0135.1* | -Rear, about 343 meters 109° from front. | 51° 35.9′ N 55° 26.8′ W | **F.W.** | 79 **24** | **16** | Square skeleton tower, white trapezoidal daymark, orange stripe; 13. | Seasonal. |
| 1052 *H 0132* | **Cape Bauld.** | 51° 38.4′ N 55° 25.7′ W | **Fl.W.** period 15s fl. 0.5s, ec. 14.5s | 177 **54** | **17** | Red hexagonal tower; 48. | **Horn:** 1 bl. ev. 30s (bl. 3s, si. 27s). Horn points 009°. Emergency light. |
| 1056 | Partridge Point. | 51° 35.0′ N 55° 25.0′ W | **Fl.W.** period 3s | 151 **46** | 7 | Square skeleton tower, red and white rectangular daymark; 13. | Seasonal. |
| 1060 *H 0736* | Griquet Harbor, Cove Point. | 51° 32.7′ N 55° 27.4′ W | **Fl.W.** period 6s fl. 0.5s, ec. 5.5s | 54 **16** | 5 | Square skeleton tower, red rectangular daymark, white band; 13. | Seasonal. |
| 1064 *H 0732* | Moores Point. | 51° 21.6′ N 55° 33.5′ W | **Fl.W.** period 4s | 36 **11** | 5 | Square skeleton tower, red and white rectangular daymark. | Harbor light only. Seasonal. |
| 1068 *H 0730* | **Fishing Point.** | 51° 21.4′ N 55° 33.3′ W | **Fl.W.** period 10s fl. 0.3s, ec. 9.7s | 88 **27** | **17** | White square tower, red bands; 33. | Seasonal. **Horn:** 1 bl. ev. 60s. (bl. 4s, si. 56s). Horn points 115°18′. |
| 1072 *H 0734* | -Harbour Rock. | 51° 21.5′ N 55° 34.2′ W | **Fl.G.** period 4s | 16 **5** | 4 | Square skeleton tower, green and white rectangular daymark; 13. | Harbor light only. Seasonal. |
| 1076 *H 0728* | Goose Cove, Mouse Island. | 51° 18.5′ N 55° 38.5′ W | **Fl.W.** period 4s | 30 **9** | 6 | Round tower, red and white bands; 13. | Seasonal. |
| 1080 *H 0725* | Brent Island. | 51° 15.4′ N 55° 56.0′ W | **Fl.W.** period 6s fl. 0.5s, ec. 5.5s | 28 **9** | 7 | Square skeleton tower, red and white rectangular daymark; 13. | Seasonal. |
| 1084 *H 0724* | Cailloux Islet. | 51° 12.1′ N 55° 59.5′ W | **Fl.R.** period 6s fl. 1s, ec. 5s | 22 **7** | 3 | Square skeleton tower, red and white rectangular daymark; 13. | Seasonal. |
| 1088 *H 0726* | Main Brook wharf, NE. end. | 51° 10.2′ N 55° 59.8′ W | **Fl.R.** period 4s | 16 **5** | 4 | Cylindrical mast; 7. | Seasonal. |
| 1092 *H 0721* | Cape Fox. | 50° 52.0′ N 55° 54.0′ W | **Fl.W.** period 3s | 193 **59** | 6 | Square skeleton tower, red and white rectangular daymark; 13. | Seasonal. |

Many lights of Newfoundland are maintained seasonally (from May to December).

| (1) No. | (2) Name and Location | (3) Position | (4) Characteristic | (5) Height | (6) Range | (7) Structure | (8) Remarks |
|---|---|---|---|---|---|---|---|

**CANADA-NEWFOUNDLAND**

| (1) No. | (2) Name and Location | (3) Position | (4) Characteristic | (5) Height | (6) Range | (7) Structure | (8) Remarks |
|---|---|---|---|---|---|---|---|
| 1096 *H 0722* | Silver Point, S. side of Conche Harbor. | 50° 53.1′ N 55° 54.0′ W | **Fl.R.** period 6s fl. 1s, ec. 5s | 20 **6** | 4 | Square skeleton tower, red and white rectangular daymark; 22. | Seasonal. |
| | CANADA BAY: | | | | | | |
| 1100 *H 0718* | -White Point, Englee Harbor. | 50° 43.3′ N 56° 07.0′ W | **Fl.W.** period 4s | 50 **15** | 7 | Skeleton tower; 12. | Harbor light only. Seasonal. |
| 1104 *H 0718.4* | -Englee wharf, head. | 50° 44.0′ N 56° 06.6′ W | **Fl.R.** period 4s | 13 **4** | 4 | Cylindrical mast; 7. | Seasonal. |
| 1108 *H 0719* | -Bad Rock. | 50° 47.1′ N 56° 09.7′ W | **Fl.G.** period 4s | 14 **4** | 6 | Square skeleton tower, green and white rectangular daymarks; 14. | Seasonal. |
| | -Chimney Bay: | | | | | | |
| 1112 *H 0720* | --Roddickton Point wharf, head. | 50° 51.8′ N 56° 07.9′ W | **Fl.G.** period 4s | 13 **4** | 3 | Mast; 6. | Seasonal. |
| 1116 *H 0716* | Nid Island, W. entrance to Rocky Bay. | 50° 42.2′ N 55° 38.3′ W | **Fl.W.** period 3s | 41 **12** | 7 | Skeleton tower; 14. | Seasonal. |
| 1120 *H 0712* | Duckbill Point. | 50° 35.9′ N 56° 12.4′ W | **Fl.W.** period 3s | 71 **22** | 5 | Square skeleton tower, red and white rectangular daymark; 14. | Seasonal. |
| 1124 *H 0710* | Fourche Harbor, on Granite Point. | 50° 30.5′ N 56° 15.2′ W | **Fl.W.** period 6s fl. 1s, ec. 5s | 81 **25** | 6 | Square skeleton tower, red and white rectangular daymark; 14. | Seasonal. |
| 1128 *H 0708* | Great Harbor Deep, N. side of entrance. | 50° 22.7′ N 56° 24.2′ W | **Fl.W.** period 6s fl. 0.5s, ec. 5.5s | 61 **19** | 6 | Square skeleton tower, red and white rectangular daymark; 14. | Seasonal. |
| 1132 *H 0707* | -Jacksons Arm, N. side of entrance. | 49° 51.7′ N 56° 45.5′ W | **Fl.W.** period 6s fl. 1s, ec. 5s | 66 **20** | 9 | Square skeleton tower, red and white rectangular daymark; 12. | Seasonal. |
| 1136 *H 0705* | -Sops Arm, on White Point. | 49° 45.1′ N 56° 49.3′ W | **Fl.W.** period 4s | 55 **17** | 5 | Square skeleton tower, red and white rectangular daymark; 14. | Seasonal. |
| 1140 *H 0704* | -Westport Cove, on point, N. side of cove. | 49° 47.3′ N 56° 38.4′ W | **Fl.W.** period 4s | 33 **10** | 7 | White octagonal tower; 18. | Seasonal. |
| 1144 *H 0702* | Seal Cove wharf. | 49° 55.9′ N 56° 23.7′ W | **Fl.R.** period 3s fl. 0.5s, ec. 2.5s | 11 **3** | 4 | Mast; 8. | Harbor light. Seasonal. |
| 1148 *H 0698* | Partridge Point. | 50° 09.5′ N 56° 09.1′ W | **Fl.W.** period 3s | 150 **46** | 7 | Square skeleton tower, red and white rectangular daymark; 14. | Seasonal. |
| 1150 *H 0697.7* | Fleur de Lis Harbor. | 50° 06.9′ N 56° 07.2′ W | **Fl.W.** period 6s fl. 0.5s, ec. 5.5s | 10 **3** | 5 | Cylindrical mast; 6. | Seasonal. |
| 1152 *H 0696* | Coachman's Harbor, on French Island. | 50° 03.2′ N 56° 05.7′ W | **Fl.W.** period 3s fl. 0.5s, ec. 2.5s | 37 **11** | 5 | Square skeleton tower, red square daymark, white stripe; 17. | Seasonal. |
| 1154 | Ming's Bight Wharf. | 50° 03.7′ N 56° 04.6′ W | **Fl.G.** period 4s | 11 **3** | 4 | Cylindrical mast; 8. | Seasonal. |
| 1156 *H 0693* | St. Barbe Islands (Horse Islands). | 50° 12.2′ N 55° 44.6′ W | **Fl.W.** period 4s | 70 **21** | 5 | Skeleton tower, white daymark; 14. | Seasonal. |
| 1160 *H 0694* | Pacquet Harbor, S. side of entrance. | 49° 58.6′ N 55° 51.3′ W | **Fl.W.** period 6s fl. 0.5s, ec. 5.5s | 99 **30** | 7 | Square skeleton tower, red and white rectangular daymark; 15. | Seasonal. |

Many lights of Newfoundland are maintained seasonally (from May to December).

| (1) No. | (2) Name and Location | (3) Position | (4) Characteristic | (5) Height | (6) Range | (7) Structure | (8) Remarks |
|---|---|---|---|---|---|---|---|

**CANADA-NEWFOUNDLAND**

| (1) No. | (2) Name and Location | (3) Position | (4) Characteristic | (5) Height | (6) Range | (7) Structure | (8) Remarks |
|---|---|---|---|---|---|---|---|
| 1164 *H 0694.5* | -NW. end of harbor. | 49° 59.4′ N 55° 52.5′ W | **Fl.R.** period 4s | 11 **4** | 2 | Mast; 7. | Seasonal. |
| 1168 *H 0692* | La Scie, Sleepy Point. | 49° 58.7′ N 55° 36.8′ W | **Fl.W.** period 6s fl. 0.5s, ec. 5.5s | 80 **24** | 6 | Square skeleton tower, red and white rectangular daymark; 13. | Seasonal. |
| 1169 *H 0692.4* | -Harbor light. | 49° 57.7′ N 55° 36.2′ W | **Fl.R.** period 4s | 13 **4** | 2 | Cylindrical mast; 7. | Seasonal. |
| | NOTRE DAME BAY: | | | | | | |
| 1172 *H 0686* | **-Gull Island.** | 50° 00.0′ N 55° 22.3′ W | **Fl.W.** period 10s fl. 0.2s, ec. 9.8s | 525 **160** | **17** | Square skeleton tower, red rectangular daymark, white stripe; 17. | Seasonal. **Horn:** 1bl. ev. 30s (bl. 3s, si. 27s). |
| 1176 *H 0681* | -Nippers Islands, Seal Island, off Nippers Harbor. | 49° 47.0′ N 55° 50.8′ W | **Fl.W.** period 3s fl. 0.5s, ec. 2.5s | 111 **34** | 7 | Skeleton tower; 26. | Seasonal. |
| 1178 *H 0682* | -Smiths Harbor, on wharf. | 49° 44.4′ N 55° 59.1′ W | **Fl.R.** period 4s | 10 **3** | 4 | Red cylindrical mast; 7. | Seasonal. |
| 1180 *H 0683* | -Middle Arm Wharf, on outer end of wharf. | 49° 42.5′ N 56° 05.2′ W | **Fl.R.** period 3s | 11 **3** | 4 | Triangular skeleton mast; 8. | Seasonal. |
| 1182 *H 0682.5* | -Jackson's Cove Wharf. | 49° 41.2′ N 56° 00.2′ W | **Fl.R.** period 4s | 13 **4** | 2 | Cylindrical mast; 7. | Seasonal. |
| 1184 *H 0680* | -Springdale Wharf. | 49° 30.0′ N 56° 03.8′ W | **Fl.R.** period 4s | 11 **3** | 4 | Mast; 7. | Seasonal. |
| 1185 *H 0680.7* | -Beachside Wharf. | 49° 38.6′ N 55° 54.2′ W | **Fl.R.** period 4s | 13 **4** | 4 | Cylindrical mast; 7. | Seasonal. |
| 1186 *H 0674.2* | -Pilley's Island Ferry Wharf. | 49° 33.8′ N 55° 44.7′ W | **Fl.R.** period 4s | 13 **4** | 4 | Cylindrical mast, yellow and black daymark; 8. | Private light. |
| 1188 *H 0679* | -Little Bay Island, SE. of Macks Island. | 49° 38.1′ N 55° 46.3′ W | **Fl.W.** period 6s fl. 0.5s, ec. 5.5s | 25 **8** | 5 | Cylindrical tower, red and white bands; 12. | Seasonal. |
| 1192 *H 0679.2* | -Macks Island North, on rock N. of Macks Island. | 49° 38.3′ N 55° 47.0′ W | **Fl.G.** period 4s | 11 **3** | 4 | Square skeleton tower, green and white rectangular daymark; 12. | Seasonal. |
| 1196 *H 0679.3* | -Little Bay Islands Wharf, head. | 49° 38.5′ N 55° 47.3′ W | **Fl.R.** period 4s | 11 **3** | 4 | Cylindrical mast; 8. | |
| 1198 *H 0679.5* | -Suley Ann Cove Ferry. | 49° 38.0′ N 55° 48.4′ W | **Fl.R.** period 4s | 10 **3** | 4 | Mast; 6. | |
| 1200 *H 0677* | -Lushes Bight, Government Wharf, head. | 49° 35.6′ N 55° 43.1′ W | **Fl.R.** period 3s | 10 **3** | 4 | Red skeleton tower; 7. | |
| 1204 *H 0677.6* | --Southern Point. | 49° 35.3′ N 55° 43.3′ W | **Fl.W.** period 6s fl. 0.5s, ec. 5.5s | 21 **6** | 5 | Square skeleton tower, red and white rectangular daymark; 14. | Seasonal. |
| 1206 *H 0680.4* | --Little Bay Arm Ferry Wharf. | 49° 35.4′ N 55° 56.1′ W | **Fl.R.** period 4s | 13 **4** | 2 | Mast. | |
| 1208 *H 0678* | -Gull Rock. | 49° 41.0′ N 55° 42.4′ W | **Fl.W.** period 4s | 62 **19** | 5 | Square skeleton tower; 46. | Seasonal. |
| 1212 *H 0675* | -Long Island, head. | 49° 35.9′ N 55° 35.4′ W | **Fl.W.** period 6s fl. 0.5s, ec. 5.5s | 103 **31** | 7 | Square skeleton tower, red rectangular daymark, white stripe; 31. | Seasonal. |
| 1216 *H 0674* | -Big Triton Island, NE. corner. | 49° 32.8′ N 55° 36.7′ W | **Fl.W.** period 4s | | 5 | Square skeleton tower, red and white rectangular daymark; 14. | Seasonal. |

Many lights of Newfoundland are maintained seasonally (from May to December).

| (1) No. | (2) Name and Location | (3) Position | (4) Characteristic | (5) Height | (6) Range | (7) Structure | (8) Remarks |
|---|---|---|---|---|---|---|---|

## CANADA-NEWFOUNDLAND

| (1) No. | (2) Name and Location | (3) Position | (4) Characteristic | (5) Height | (6) Range | (7) Structure | (8) Remarks |
|---|---|---|---|---|---|---|---|
| 1218 *H 0674.4* | -Roberts Arm. | 49° 29.3′ N 55° 48.3′ W | **Fl.R.** period 4s | 10 **3** | 4 | Red cylindrical mast; 8. | Seasonal. |
| 1220 *H 0672* | -Leading Tickles. | 49° 30.5′ N 55° 24.9′ W | **Fl.W.** period 3s fl. 0.5s, ec. 2.5s | 83 **25** | 6 | Square skeleton tower, red rectangular daymark, white stripe; 14. | Seasonal. |
| 1224 *H 0671.5* | -Leamington Point Wharf, E. head. | 49° 20.4′ N 55° 23.9′ W | **Fl.R.** period 4s | 14 **4** | 4 | Cylindrical mast; 7. | Seasonal. |
| 1228 *H 0670.5* | -Cottrells Cove Point, W. extremity of point. | 49° 28.9′ N 55° 18.3′ W | **Fl.W.** period 4s | 55 **17** | 5 | Square skeleton tower, red rectangular daymark, white stripe; 15. | Seasonal. |
| 1236 *H 0670* | -Fortune Harbor, Bellens Point, W. side of entrance. | 49° 32.1′ N 55° 14.9′ W | **Fl.W.** period 6s fl. 0.5s, ec. 5.5s | 114 **35** | 5 | Square skeleton tower, red and white rectangular daymark; 14. | |
| | -Bay of Exploits: | | | | | | |
| 1240 *H 0656* | **--Surgeon Cove Point.** | 49° 31.2′ N 55° 07.4′ W | **Fl.W.** period 5s fl. 0.1s, ec. 4.9s | 242 **74** | **16** | Cylindrical tower, red and white stripes; 14. | **Horn:** 1 bl. ev. 30s (bl. 3s, si. 27s). Horn points 327°48′. |
| 1244 *H 0658* | --Upper Black Island, islet off NW. point. | 49° 24.8′ N 55° 08.1′ W | **Fl.W.** period 3s fl. 0.5s, ec. 2.5s | 55 **17** | 4 | Square skeleton tower, red rectangular daymark, white stripe; 14. | |
| 1248 *H 0660* | --Grovers Point Island. | 49° 19.7′ N 55° 14.2′ W | **Fl.R.** period 4s | | 4 | Square skeleton tower; 14. | |
| 1252 *H 0664* | --Grassy Island, summit. | 49° 15.6′ N 55° 14.1′ W | **Fl.R.** period 4s | 38 **12** | 4 | Square skeleton tower, white daymark; 12. | |
| 1256 *H 0666* | --Lower Sandy Point. | 49° 12.6′ N 55° 17.8′ W | **Fl.G.** period 3s fl. 0.5s, ec. 2.5s | 17 **5** | 4 | Square skeleton tower, green and white square daymarks; 17. | |
| 1260 *H 0668* | --Mill Point, E. extremity. | 49° 08.9′ N 55° 20.1′ W | **Fl.R.** period 1.5s fl. 0.5s, ec. 1s | 18 **5** | 4 | Cylindrical tower, red and white bands; 14. | |
| 1264 *H 0652* | --Knights Island, near NE. tip, on rock islet. | 49° 25.3′ N 54° 55.0′ W | **Fl.W.** period 4s | 44 **13** | 5 | Square skeleton tower, red and white rectangular daymark; 12. | Seasonal. |
| 1268 *H 0654* | --St. Michaels Island, Burnt Bay. | 49° 17.4′ N 54° 59.9′ W | **Fl.W.** period 3s fl. 0.5s, ec. 2.5s | 186 **57** | 5 | Skeleton tower, red and white rectangular daymark; 25. | Seasonal. |
| 1268.1 *H 0654.5* | --Seal Rock. | 49° 16.4′ N 55° 00.1′ W | **Fl.G.** period 4s | | 4 | Square skeleton tower, green and white square daymark; 12. | Seasonal. |
| 1269 *H 0655.15* | ---Imperial oil pier. | 49° 14.5′ N 55° 03.4′ W | **Fl.R.** period 4s | 10 **3** | | Cylindrical mast. | Private light. |
| 1270 *H 0655.1* | ---C.N.R. pier. | 49° 14.9′ N 55° 03.0′ W | **Fl.R.** period 6s | 12 **4** | | Tower; 7. | Private light. |
| 1271 *H 0654.9* | ---Lewisporte Outer Dolphin, end of breakwater. | 49° 14.5′ N 55° 03.3′ W | **Fl.R.** period 4s | | | Square mast. | Private light. |
| 1272 *H 0640* | **--Long Point.** | 49° 41.3′ N 54° 48.0′ W | **Fl.W.** period 5s | 331 **101** | **16** | Red and white rectangular tower; 47. | **Horn:** 1 bl. ev. 60s. (bl. 4s, si. 56s). Horn points 356°. |
| 1276 *H 0644* | --Twillingate Wharf. | 49° 39.5′ N 54° 46.3′ W | **F.R.** period 4s | 15 **5** | 4 | Cylindrical mast; 7. | Seasonal. |
| 1278 *H 0642* | ---Harbor. | 49° 39.3′ N 54° 46.0′ W | **Fl.G.** period 4s | 20 **6** | 4 | Square skeleton tower, green and white square daymark; 14. | Seasonal. |

Many lights of Newfoundland are maintained seasonally (from May to December).

| (1) No. | (2) Name and Location | (3) Position | (4) Characteristic | (5) Height | (6) Range | (7) Structure | (8) Remarks |
|---|---|---|---|---|---|---|---|

## CANADA-NEWFOUNDLAND

| (1) No. | (2) Name and Location | (3) Position | (4) Characteristic | (5) Height | (6) Range | (7) Structure | (8) Remarks |
|---|---|---|---|---|---|---|---|
| 1280 *H 0645* | --Tickle Point (Shoal Tickle) on S. point of N. island. | 49° 38.7′ N 54° 46.3′ W | **Q.G.** | 45 **14** | 4 | Square skeleton tower, green and white square daymark; 18. | Seasonal. |
| 1284 *H 0648* | --Duck Island. | 49° 35.6′ N 54° 43.6′ W | **Fl.W.** period 6s fl. 1s, ec. 5s | 57 **17** | 6 | Cylindrical tower, red and white bands; 14. | Seasonal. |
| 1288 *H 0650* | --Moretons Harbor. | 49° 35.0′ N 54° 51.8′ W | **Fl.W.** period 6s fl. 0.5s, ec. 5.5s | 59 **18** | 5 | Cylindrical tower, red and white bands; 15. | Seasonal. |
| 1293 *H 0651* | --Moretons Harbor Wharf. | 49° 35.0′ N 54° 52.0′ W | **Fl.R.** period 4s | 13 **4** | 4 | Cylindrical mast; 8. | Seasonal. |
| 1294 *H 0651.2* | --Pond Island Point. | 49° 34.0′ N 54° 53.6′ W | **Fl.R.** period 4s | | 4 | Square skeleton tower, red and white square daymark; 14. | |
| 1296 *H 0651.6* | -Summerford Wharf. | 49° 30.0′ N 54° 47.0′ W | **Fl.R.** period 3s | 12 **4** | 4 | Cylindrical mast; 7. | Seasonal. |
| 1300 *H 0636* | -**Bacalhao Island,** S. side. | 49° 41.2′ N 54° 33.4′ W | **Fl.W.** period 10s fl. 0.2s, ec. 9.8s | 348 **106** | **17** | Cylindrical tower, red and white diagonal stripes; 35. | **Horn:** 1 bl. ev. 30s. (bl. 3s, si. 27s). Horn points 331°48′. |
| 1302 *H 0635* | **Bacalhao Island Sector.** | 49° 41.2′ N 54° 33.3′ W | **Dir.W.R.G.** | 233 **71** | **23** | Square skeleton tower, red rectangular daymark, white stripe; 12. | F.G. 296°- 296°30′, Al.W.G.- 297°30′, F.W.- 299°30′, Al.W.R.- 300°30′, F.R.- 301°. On request by keying VHF 3 times in 5 seconds on channel 65A (156.275 MHz). Extinguishes automatically after 1 hour or by keying VHF 5 times in 5 seconds. |
| 1312 *H 0638* | -Ship Island, E. end. | 49° 39.1′ N 54° 35.9′ W | **Fl.W.** period 3s | 94 **29** | 5 | Skeleton tower, white slatwork daymark; 12. | Seasonal. |
| 1316 *H 0630* | Tickle Point, N. side of entrance to Change Island. | 49° 40.1′ N 54° 24.8′ W | **Fl.G.** period 6s fl. 0.5s, ec. 5.5s | 31 **9** | 4 | Square skeleton tower, green and white rectangular daymark; 12. | Visible 028°-088°. Seasonal. |
| 1320 *H 0632* | Smoker Island. | 49° 36.7′ N 54° 27.1′ W | **Fl.W.** period 6s fl. 0.5s, ec. 5.5s | 35 **11** | 5 | Square skeleton tower, red and white rectangular daymark; 17. | |
| 1324 *H 0634* | Dram Island. | 49° 35.2′ N 54° 31.8′ W | **Fl.W.** period 4s | 33 **10** | 5 | Square skeleton tower, red and white rectangular daymark; 14. | Seasonal. |
| 1326 *H 0625* | Farewell Harbor, ferry wharf. | 49° 33.4′ N 54° 28.5′ W | **Fl.R.** period 4s | 10 **3** | 4 | Cylindrical mast; 9. | |
| 1332 *H 0626* | Change Island, S. head. | 49° 34.2′ N 54° 24.5′ W | **Fl.W.** period 4s | 47 **14** | 5 | Skeleton tower, red rectangular daymark, white stripe; 31. | Seasonal. |
| 1333 *H 0627* | Change Island, SW. Range, front. | 49° 34.6′ N 54° 24.5′ W | **Oc.R.** period 6s lt. 4s, ec. 2s | 39 **12** | 13 | Square skeleton tower, white trapezoidal daymark, red stripe; 17. | Visible on range line only. |
| 1334 *H 0627.1* | -Rear, 91 meters 130°24′ from front. | 49° 34.5′ N 54° 24.5′ W | **Oc.R.** period 6s lt. 4s, ec. 2s | 59 **18** | 13 | Square skeleton tower, white trapezoidal daymark, red stripe; 15. | Visible on range line only. |
| 1335 | Cork Rock. | 49° 33.7′ N 54° 23.1′ W | **Fl.W.** period 6s fl. 0.5s, ec. 5.5s | 19 **6** | 6 | Square skeleton tower, red and white rectangular daymark; 12. | |
| 1336 *H 0624* | Steering Island, entrance to Dog Bay. | 49° 31.0′ N 54° 27.6′ W | **Fl.W.** period 6s fl. 0.5s, ec. 5.5s | 38 **12** | 5 | Square skeleton tower, red rectangular daymark, white stripe; 14. | |
| 1340 *H 0628* | Ruth Island, E. entrance to Change Island. | 49° 40.8′ N 54° 22.8′ W | **Fl.W.** period 3s | 35 **11** | 5 | Square skeleton tower, red and white rectangular daymark; 14. | Seasonal. |

Many lights of Newfoundland are maintained seasonally (from May to December).

| (1) No. | (2) Name and Location | (3) Position | (4) Characteristic | (5) Height | (6) Range | (7) Structure | (8) Remarks |
|---|---|---|---|---|---|---|---|
| | | | **CANADA-NEWFOUNDLAND** | | | | |
| 1344 *H 0629* | Change Island Tickle Range, front. | 49° 40.4′ N 54° 24.3′ W | **F.R.** | 66 **20** | 13 | Square skeleton tower, white trapezoidal daymark, red stripe; 31. | Seasonal. |
| 1348 *H 0629.1* | -Rear, 122 meters 252°45′ from front. | 49° 40.4′ N 54° 24.4′ W | **F.R.** | 80 **24** | 13 | Square skeleton tower, white trapezoidal daymark, red stripe; 19. | Seasonal. |
| 1352 *H 0614* | Tilton Harbor, W. side entrance. | 49° 42.5′ N 54° 04.0′ W | **Fl.R.** period 4s | 91 **28** | | Skeleton tower, white daymark; 21. | Seasonal. |
| 1356 *H 0620* | Seal Cove, wharf, head. | 49° 42.8′ N 54° 17.3′ W | **Fl.R.** period 4s | 14 **4** | 3 | Cylindrical mast; 8. | |
| | FOGO ISLAND: | | | | | | |
| 1360 *H 0618* | -Rags Island, E. approach to Fogo Harbor. | 49° 43.8′ N 54° 15.6′ W | **Fl.W.** period 4s | 82 **25** | 5 | Square skeleton tower, red and white rectangular daymark; 14. | Seasonal. |
| 1372 *H 0619* | -Seal Cove. | 49° 42.9′ N 54° 17.1′ W | **Fl.G.** period 4s | 10 **3** | 3 | Cylindrical mast; 8. | Seasonal. |
| 1376 *H 0617* | -Joe Batts Arm (on Middle Rock). | 49° 43.6′ N 54° 10.1′ W | **Fl.R.** period 4s | 18 **5** | 4 | Square skeleton tower, red and white rectangular daymark; 14. | Seasonal. |
| 1380 *H 0617.4* | --Public Wharf. | 49° 43.5′ N 54° 09.8′ W | **Fl.G.** period 4s | 14 **4** | 4 | Cylindrical mast; 8. | Seasonal. |
| 1384 *H 0617.5* | -Joe Batts Arm Wharf. | 49° 44.2′ N 54° 10.1′ W | **Fl.R.** period 4s | 11 **4** | 3 | Cylindrical mast; 8. | Seasonal. |
| 1386 *H 0617.6* | -Barr'd Island. | 49° 43.5′ N 54° 11.7′ W | **Fl.R.** period 4s | 33 **10** | 4 | Cylindrical mast; 7. | Seasonal. |
| 1388 *H 0616* | -Joe Batts Point. | 49° 45.2′ N 54° 09.2′ W | **Fl.W.** period 6s fl. 0.5s, ec. 5.5s | 95 **29** | 5 | Square skeleton tower, red and white rectangular daymark; 14. | Seasonal. |
| 1390 *H 0623.5* | -Gappy Island. | 49° 46.6′ N 54° 16.7′ W | **Fl.W.** period 3s | 79 **24** | 5 | Square skeleton tower, red and white rectangular daymark; 14. | Seasonal. |
| 1392 *H 0623* | -Storehouse Island. | 49° 49.1′ N 54° 11.1′ W | **Fl.W.** period 6s fl. 1s, ec. 5s | 151 **46** | 6 | Square skeleton tower, red and white rectangular daymark; 14. | Seasonal. |
| 1396 *H 0622* | -Little Fogo Island. | 49° 49.4′ N 54° 05.8′ W | **Fl.W.** period 4s | 158 **48** | 7 | Square skeleton tower, red and white rectangular daymark; 14. | Seasonal. |
| 1400 *H 0612* | **-Burnt Point,** Seldom Cove entrance. | 49° 36.1′ N 54° 09.5′ W | **Fl.W.** period 6s fl. 0.4s, ec. 5.6s | 43 **13** | **16** | Square skeleton tower; 31. | **Horn:** 1 bl. ev. 60s (bl. 4s, si. 56s). Horn points 106°. |
| 1402 *H 0613* | -Seldom Breakwater. | 49° 36.6′ N 54° 10.9′ W | **Fl.G.** period 4s | 11 **3** | | Cylindrical mast; 8. | Seasonal. |
| 1404 *H 0608* | Tinker Rock, E. of Cann Island. | 49° 35.0′ N 54° 10.5′ W | **Fl.W.** period 4s | 34 **10** | 5 | Cylindrical tower, red and white bands; 12. | Seasonal. |
| 1408 *H 0607* | Seldom Harbor, Cann Island. | 49° 35.1′ N 54° 11.2′ W | **Fl.W.** period 6s fl. 0.5s, ec. 5.5s | 71 **22** | 5 | Skeleton tower; 20. | Seasonal. |
| 1410 *H 0606.5* | -Man O'War Cove. | 49° 34.3′ N 54° 18.3′ W | **Fl.G.** period 4s | 22 **7** | 4 | Cylindrical mast; 7. | |
| 1412 *H 0605* | Blundon's Island, E. side | 49° 32.9′ N 54° 13.7′ W | **Fl.W.** period 4s | 12 **4** | 6 | Square skeleton tower, red and white rectangular daymark; 14. | Seasonal. |

Many lights of Newfoundland are maintained seasonally (from May to December).

| (1) No. | (2) Name and Location | (3) Position | (4) Characteristic | (5) Height | (6) Range | (7) Structure | (8) Remarks |
|---|---|---|---|---|---|---|---|

## CANADA-NEWFOUNDLAND

| | | | | | | | |
|---|---|---|---|---|---|---|---|
| 1416<br>*H 0606* | Seal Rock, Stag Harbor Tickle. | 49° 33.3′ N<br>54° 17.8′ W | **Fl.W.**<br>period 3s | 21<br>**6** | 5 | Square skeleton tower, red and white rectangular daymark; 14. | Seasonal. |
| 1420<br>*H 0601* | Grass Islands, on rock. | 49° 27.8′ N<br>54° 19.0′ W | **Fl.W.**<br>period 3s | 22<br>**7** | 7 | Square skeleton tower, red and white rectangular daymark; 14. | Seasonal. |
| 1424<br>*H 0599* | Carmanville Range, front. | 49° 23.5′ N<br>54° 17.1′ W | **F.R.** | 26<br>**8** | 13 | Square skeleton tower, white trapezoidal daymark, red stripe; 12. | Seasonal. |
| 1428<br>*H 0599.1* | -Rear, about 406 meters 203°30′ from front. | 49° 23.3′ N<br>54° 17.3′ W | **F.R.** | 46<br>**14** | 13 | Square skeleton tower, white trapezoidal daymark, red stripe; 24. | Seasonal. |
| 1432<br>*H 0600* | Carmanville Wharf. | 49° 24.2′ N<br>54° 16.8′ W | **Fl.R.**<br>period 3s | 17<br>**5** | 5 | Cylindrical mast; 10. | Seasonal. |
| 1436<br>*H 0597* | Green Island, (Rocky Bay). | 49° 26.9′ N<br>54° 13.7′ W | **Fl.W.**<br>period 6s<br>fl. 0.5s, ec. 5.5s | 30<br>**9** | 5 | Skeleton tower; 12. | Seasonal. |
| | BONAVISTA BAY: | | | | | | |
| 1440<br>*H 0584* | -Offer Wadham Island. | 49° 35.6′ N<br>53° 45.8′ W | **Fl.W.**<br>period 3s | 100<br>**30** | 6 | Square skeleton tower, red and white rectangular daymark; 23. | Seasonal. |
| 1444<br>*H 0586* | **-Peckford Island,** SE. point. | 49° 31.8′ N<br>53° 51.1′ W | **Fl.W.**<br>period 10s<br>fl. 0.2s, ec. 9.8s | 51<br>**16** | **17** | Building, black and white stripes; 7. | **Horn:** 1 bl. ev. 30s. (bl. 3s, si. 27s). Horn points 112°54′. |
| 1448<br>*H 0596* | -Muddy Shag Island. | 49° 29.5′ N<br>53° 56.6′ W | **Fl.W.**<br>period 4s | 33<br>**10** | 5 | Cylindrical tower, red and white bands; 14. | Seasonal. |
| 1452<br>*H 0591* | -Musgrave Harbor, breakwater. | 49° 27.5′ N<br>53° 57.4′ W | **Fl.R.**<br>period 3s<br>fl. 0.5s, ec. 2.5s | 10<br>**3** | 4 | Mast; 7. | Seasonal. |
| 1460<br>*H 0594* | -Muddy Point. | 49° 27.4′ N<br>53° 56.5′ W | **Oc.G.**<br>period 6s<br>lt. 4s, ec. 2s | 26<br>**8** | 4 | Square skeleton tower, green and white rectangular daymark; 14. | Seasonal. |
| 1464<br>*H 0588* | -North Penguin Island, E. head. | 49° 27.0′ N<br>53° 48.7′ W | **Fl.W.**<br>period 6s<br>fl. 0.5s, ec. 5.5s | 47<br>**14** | 5 | Skeleton tower, red and white rectangular daymark; 23. | Seasonal. |
| 1472<br>*H 0582* | -Lumsden Range, front. | 49° 18.2′ N<br>53° 36.4′ W | **F.R.** | 56<br>**17** | 13 | Skeleton tower, white trapezoidal daymark, red stripe; 12. | Seasonal. |
| 1476<br>*H 0582.1* | --Rear, 102 meters 236°11′ from front. | 49° 18.2′ N<br>53° 36.5′ W | **F.R.** | 102<br>**31** | 13 | Skeleton tower, white trapezoidal daymark, red stripe; 12. | Seasonal. |
| 1478<br>*H 0583* | -Lumsden Breakwater, S. outer end. | 49° 18.0′ N<br>53° 35.4′ W | **Fl.G.**<br>period 4s | 26<br>**8** | 4 | Mast; 8. | |
| 1479<br>*H 0583.2* | -South Tickle. | 49° 18.0′ N<br>53° 35.4′ W | **Fl.R.**<br>period 4s | 26<br>**8** | 4 | Mast; 8. | |
| 1484<br>*H 0580* | -Gull Island, off Cape Freels. | 49° 15.4′ N<br>53° 25.8′ W | **Fl.W.**<br>period 3s | 77<br>**23** | 5 | Skeleton tower, red and white rectangular daymark; 14. | Seasonal. |
| 1492<br>*H 0578* | -Kenny's Rocks. | 49° 13.0′ N<br>53° 28.4′ W | **Fl.W.**<br>period 3s | 25<br>**8** | | Square skeleton tower, red and white rectangular daymark; 12. | Seasonal. |
| 1496<br>*H 0576* | **-Cabot Island.** | 49° 10.5′ N<br>53° 22.1′ W | **Fl.W.**<br>period 10s<br>fl. 0.2s, ec. 9.8s | 74<br>**23** | **17** | Octagonal tower, red and white bands; 52. | Seasonal.<br>**Horn (2):** 1 bl. ev. 60s (bl. 4s, si. 56s). Horns point 191° and 341°. |
| 1508<br>*H 0570* | -Pound Cove. | 49° 10.3′ N<br>53° 31.8′ W | **Fl.W.**<br>period 3s | 22<br>**7** | 5 | Square skeleton tower, red and white rectangular daymark; 14. | Seasonal. |

Many lights of Newfoundland are maintained seasonally (from May to December).

| (1) No. | (2) Name and Location | (3) Position | (4) Characteristic | (5) Height | (6) Range | (7) Structure | (8) Remarks |
|---|---|---|---|---|---|---|---|

## CANADA-NEWFOUNDLAND

| (1) No. | (2) Name and Location | (3) Position | (4) Characteristic | (5) Height | (6) Range | (7) Structure | (8) Remarks |
|---|---|---|---|---|---|---|---|
| 1524 *H 0566* | -Wesleyville Harbor. | 49° 08.2′ N 53° 33.8′ W | **Fl.W.** period 3s | 75 **23** | 5 | Square skeleton tower, red and white rectangular daymark; 14. | Seasonal. |
| 1528 *H 0567* | -Wesleyville wharf, head. | 49° 08.6′ N 53° 33.8′ W | **Fl.R.** period 6s fl. 1s, ec. 5s | 12 **4** | 4 | Cylindrical mast; 8. | Seasonal. |
| 1536 *H 0563* | -Valleyfield Range, front. | 49° 06.4′ N 53° 36.5′ W | **F.R.** | 17 **5** | 11 | Square skeleton tower, white trapezoidal daymark, red stripe; 21. | Seasonal. |
| 1540 *H 0563.1* | --Rear, about 457 meters 286°30′ from front. | 49° 06.4′ N 53° 36.9′ W | **F.R.** | 41 **12** | 11 | Square skeleton tower, white trapezoidal daymark, red stripe; 21. | Seasonal. |
| 1544 *H 0563.4* | -Candle Cove Rocks. | 49° 05.8′ N 53° 35.9′ W | **Fl.W.** period 3s | 20 **6** | 5 | Square skeleton tower, red and white rectangular daymark; 12. | Seasonal. |
| 1548 *H 0563.6* | -Valleyfield Wharf. | 49° 07.3′ N 53° 36.5′ W | **Fl.R.** period 4s | 11 **3** | | Cylindrical mast; 7. | Seasonal. |
| 1552 *H 0562* | -South Pound Island, Western Shag. | 49° 05.6′ N 53° 33.4′ W | **Fl.W.** period 4s | 62 **19** | 5 | Square skeleton tower, red and white rectangular daymark; 14. | Seasonal. |
| 1556 *H 0556* | **-Puffin Island.** | 49° 03.7′ N 53° 33.1′ W | **Fl.W.** period 5s fl. 0.2s, ec. 4.8s | 70 **21** | **16** | Red and white hexagonal tower, white daymark, red band; 16. | **Horn:** 1 bl. ev. 30s (bl. 3s, si. 27s). |
| 1560 *H 0558* | -Pound Rocks. | 49° 04.1′ N 53° 33.6′ W | **Q.R.** | 26 **8** | 6 | Square skeleton tower, red and white rectangular daymark; 8. | Seasonal. |
| 1564 *H 0561* | -Greenspond Range, front. | 49° 04.0′ N 53° 34.0′ W | **F.R.** | 19 **6** | 13 | Skeleton tower, white trapezoidal daymark, red stripe; 11. | Visible on range line only. Seasonal. |
| 1568 *H 0561.1* | --Rear, 61 meters 278°50′ from front. | 49° 04.1′ N 53° 34.1′ W | **F.R.** | 26 **8** | 13 | Skeleton tower, white trapezoidal daymark, red stripe; 24. | Visible on range line only. Seasonal. |
| 1572 *H 0560* | -Scammels Lookout. | 49° 04.0′ N 53° 34.2′ W | **Fl.G.** period 6s fl. 0.5s, ec. 5.5s | 20 **6** | 4 | Cylindrical mast; 11. | Seasonal. |
| 1576 *H 0560.2* | -Seine Rock. | 49° 03.9′ N 53° 34.3′ W | **Fl.R.** period 4s | 16 **5** | 4 | Square skeleton tower, red and white rectangualr daymark; 14. | Seasonal. |
| 1580 *H 0555* | -Shoe Cove Point, on S. summit. | 49° 02.2′ N 53° 36.3′ W | **Fl.W.** period 3s | 88 **27** | 5 | Square skeleton tower, red and white rectangular daymark; 12. | Seasonal. |
| 1584 *H 0554.6* | -Fisherman's Wharf. | 49° 01.1′ N 53° 52.7′ W | **Fl.R.** period 3s | 10 **3** | 2 | Cylindrical mast; 7. | Seasonal. |
| 1588 *H 0554* | -Grindstone, head. | 48° 59.0′ N 53° 42.5′ W | **Fl.W.** period 6s fl. 0.5s, ec. 5.5s | 70 **21** | 5 | Square skeleton tower, red and white rectangular daymark; 15. | Seasonal. |
| 1592 *H 0548* | -Gooseberry Harbor on Island, close S. of Inner Gooseberry Islands. | 48° 52.7′ N 53° 37.3′ W | **Fl.W.** period 6s fl. 0.5s, ec. 5.5s | 51 **16** | 5 | Cylindrical tower, red and white bands; 16. | Seasonal. |
| 1594 *H 0543.5* | -Salvage Harbour. | 48° 41.5′ N 53° 38.7′ W | **Fl.G.** period 4s | 12 **4** | 4 | Square skeleton tower, green and white rectangular daymark; 14. | Seasonal. |
| 1595 *H 0546* | Burnside Ferry, wharf. | 48° 42.9′ N 53° 47.2′ W | **Fl.R.** period 4s | 16 **5** | 4 | Cylindrical mast; 7. | |
| 1598 *H 0547.4* | -Penneys Cove Ferry, wharf. | 48° 50.1′ N 53° 41.9′ W | **Fl.R.** period 4s | 16 **5** | 4 | Cylindrical mast; 7. | |
| 1600 *H 0549* | -Hare Cut Point. | 48° 52.5′ N 53° 39.2′ W | **Fl.W.** period 3s | 80 **24** | 5 | Square skeleton tower, red and white rectangular daymark, white band; 15. | Seasonal. |

Many lights of Newfoundland are maintained seasonally (from May to December).

| (1) No. | (2) Name and Location | (3) Position | (4) Characteristic | (5) Height | (6) Range | (7) Structure | (8) Remarks |
|---|---|---|---|---|---|---|---|
| | | | **CANADA-NEWFOUNDLAND** | | | | |
| 1604 *H 0547* | -Puffin Flat Island. | 48° 47.5′ N 53° 36.7′ W | **Fl.W.** period 4s | 120 **37** | 5 | Square skeleton tower, red and white rectangular daymark; 13. | Seasonal. |
| 1608 *H 0543* | -Little Denier Island. | 48° 41.1′ N 53° 35.4′ W | **Fl.W.** period 3s | 298 **91** | 7 | Cylindrical tower, red and white stripes; 25. | Seasonal. |
| 1610 *H 0544* | -Happy Adventure, on western point of entrance. | 48° 37.9′ N 53° 45.3′ W | **Oc.W.** period 6s lt. 4s, ec. 2s | 41 **12** | 7 | Square skeleton tower; 21. | Seasonal. **Whistle:** 1 bl. ev. 60s (bl. 5s, si. 55s). |
| 1612 *H 0545* | -Happy Adventure Wharf. | 48° 37.9′ N 53° 46.1′ W | **Fl.R.** period 4s | 13 **4** | 4 | Mast. | Seasonal. |
| 1620 *H 0540* | -Kings Cove, N. head. | 48° 34.6′ N 53° 19.3′ W | **Fl.W.** period 4s | 176 **54** | 5 | White cylindrical tower; 27. | Seasonal. |
| 1632 *H 0537* | -Squarry Island. | 48° 39.1′ N 53° 07.7′ W | **Fl.W.** period 6s fl. 0.5s, ec. 5.5s | 50 **15** | 5 | Square skeleton tower, red and white rectangular daymark; 12. | Seasonal. |
| 1636 *H 0538* | -Bonavista, breakwater. | 48° 39.0′ N 53° 07.1′ W | **Q.R.** | 18 **6** | 5 | Cylindrical mast; 8. | Seasonal. |
| 1640 *H 0539* | -Long Liner Wharf, seaward end of wharf. | 48° 39.0′ N 53° 06.8′ W | **Fl.G.** period 4s | 9 **3** | | Cylindrical mast; 6. | Seasonal. |
| 1644 *H 0536* | **-Cape Bonavista.** | 48° 42.1′ N 53° 05.1′ W | **Fl.W.** period 10s fl. 1s, ec. 9s | 166 **51** | **16** | Skeleton tower, red and white rectangular daymark; 42. | **Horn:** 1 bl. ev. 30s (bl. 3s, si. 27s). Horn points 354°. |
| | CATALINA HARBOR: | | | | | | |
| 1648 *H 0526* | **-Green Island.** | 48° 30.2′ N 53° 02.6′ W | **Fl.W.** period 4s | 92 **28** | **15** | Red and white octagonal tower; 34. | **Horn:** 1 bl. ev. 60s (bl. 4s, si. 56s). Horn points 115°. |
| 1652 *H 0526.5* | -Burnt Point. | 48° 30.5′ N 53° 03.0′ W | **Fl.W.** period 6s fl. 0.5s, ec. 5.5s | 17 **5** | 6 | Square skeleton tower, red and white rectangular daymark; 15. | Seasonal. |
| 1660 *H 0527* | -Catalina Harbor Outer Range, front. | 48° 30.9′ N 53° 03.7′ W | **F.R.** | 48 **15** | 13 | Skeleton tower, red trapezoidal daymark, black stripe; 14. | Visible on range line only. Seasonal. |
| 1664 *H 0527.1* | --Rear, 66 meters 297°10′ from front. | 48° 30.9′ N 53° 03.8′ W | **F.R.** | 75 **23** | 13 | Skeleton tower, red trapezoidal daymark, black stripe; 16. | Visible on range line only. Seasonal. |
| 1668 *H 0528* | -Manuel Island. | 48° 30.7′ N 53° 04.1′ W | **Fl.R.** period 3s | 22 **7** | 4 | Red and white cylindrical tower; 13. | Seasonal. |
| 1672 *H 0530* | -Catalina Harbor Inner Range, front. | 48° 30.4′ N 53° 04.5′ W | **F.G.** | 33 **10** | 14 | Skeleton tower, black trapezoidal daymark, red stripe; 23. | Visible on range line only. Seasonal. |
| 1676 *H 0530.1* | --Rear, 270 meters 252° from front. | 48° 30.3′ N 53° 04.8′ W | **F.G.** | 56 **17** | 14 | Skeleton tower, black trapezoidal daymark, red stripe; 16. | Visible on range line only. Seasonal. |
| 1680 *H 0531* | -Catalina Wharf. | 48° 30.9′ N 53° 04.5′ W | **Fl.R.** period 3s fl. 0.5s, ec. 2.5s | 12 **4** | 4 | Cylindrical mast; 8. | Seasonal. |
| | TRINITY BAY: | | | | | | |
| 1692 *H 0522* | -Horse Chops, N. side of entrance to Trinity Bay FOG SIGNAL. | 48° 21.0′ N 53° 12.5′ W | | | | Cylindrical tower, red and white diagonal stripe; 35. | **Horn:** 1 bl. ev. 60s. (bl. 4s, si. 56s). Horn points 331°. |
| 1696 *H 0520* | **-Fort Point.** | 48° 21.9′ N 53° 20.7′ W | **Fl.W.** period 5s | 78 **24** | **15** | Square skeleton tower; 41. | **Horn:** 1 bl. ev. 20s. (bl. 2s, si. 18s). Horn points 133°. |
| 1700 *H 0518* | -Ragged Islands. | 48° 14.5′ N 53° 26.5′ W | **Fl.W.** period 4s | 111 **34** | | Red and white cylindrical tower; 14. | Seasonal. |
| 1702 *H 0516.5* | -Lower Lance Cove Wharf, N. side of Random Island. | 48° 08.8′ N 53° 41.8′ W | **Fl.R.** period 4s | 11 **3** | 4 | Cylindrical mast; 7. | Seasonal. |

Many lights of Newfoundland are maintained seasonally (from May to December).

| (1) No. | (2) Name and Location | (3) Position | (4) Characteristic | (5) Height | (6) Range | (7) Structure | (8) Remarks |
|---|---|---|---|---|---|---|---|

## CANADA-NEWFOUNDLAND

| (1) No. | (2) Name and Location | (3) Position | (4) Characteristic | (5) Height | (6) Range | (7) Structure | (8) Remarks |
|---|---|---|---|---|---|---|---|
| 1704 *H 0514* | -Motion Island, E. Random, head. | 48° 05.7′ N 53° 32.7′ W | **Fl.W.** period 3s fl. 0.5s, ec. 2.5s | 126 **38** | 7 | Red and white cylindrical tower; 33. | |
| 1705 *H 0513.7* | -Lower Harbour Point. | 48° 05.6′ N 53° 43.7′ W | **Fl.R.** period 4s | 24 **7** | 4 | Square skeleton tower, red and white rectangular daymark; 15. | Seasonal. |
| 1706 *H 0514.5* | -Southport, wharf. | 48° 02.9′ N 53° 38.6′ W | **Fl.R.** period 4s | 13 **4** | 4 | Cylindrical mast; 7. | Seasonal. |
| 1708 *H 0515* | -Little Hearts Ease. | 48° 00.9′ N 53° 41.4′ W | **Fl.R.** period 4s | 10 **3** | 4 | Cylindrical mast; 7. | Seasonal. |
| 1710 *H 0513* | **-Bull Arm.** | 47° 44.8′ N 53° 50.5′ W | **Dir.W.R.G.** | 49 **15** | **19** | Skeleton tower, red and white rectangular daymark. | F.R. 267°30′-269°, Al.W.R.-269°40′, F.W.-270°20′, Al.W.G.-271°, F.G.-272°30′. On request by keying VHF 3 times at 5 second intervals on channel 65A (156.275 MHz). Extinguishes by keying VHF 7 times at 5 second intervals. |
| 1711 *H 0511.5* | -Dildo, head. | 47° 34.1′ N 53° 34.4′ W | **Fl.G.** period 4s | 80 **24** | 4 | Square skeleton tower, green and white rectangular daymark; 14. | |
| 1712 *H 0512* | -Hopeall, head. | 47° 38.0′ N 53° 33.8′ W | **Fl.W.** period 3s | 204 **62** | 5 | Square skeleton tower, red square daymark, white band; 14. | Seasonal. |
| 1714 *H 0511* | -Whiteway Wharf. | 47° 41.8′ N 53° 28.9′ W | **Fl.G.** period 4s | 14 **4** | 4 | Cylindrical mast; 9. | |
| 1716 *H 0510* | -Heart's Content Harbor, Northern Point. | 47° 52.9′ N 53° 23.1′ W | **Oc.W.** period 6s lt. 4s, ec. 2s | 83 **25** | 8 | Red and white cylindrical tower; 29. | |
| 1717 *H 0510.5* | -Heart's Content Wharf. | 47° 52.8′ N 53° 22.2′ W | **Q.G.** | | | Cylindrical mast; 7. | |
| 1720 *H 0508* | -Bloody Point. | 47° 54.9′ N 53° 21.6′ W | **Fl.R.** period 5s | 37 **11** | 9 | Triangular skeleton tower, red and white rectangular daymark; 14. | **Whistle:** 1 bl. ev. 30s (bl. 3s, si. 27s). |
| 1724 *H 0506* | -Jeans Head. | 47° 55.6′ N 53° 21.8′ W | **Fl.W.** period 4s | 159 **48** | 5 | Square skeleton tower, red and white rectangular daymark; 14. | |
| 1728 *H 0504* | -Hants Harbor, NE. head. | 48° 01.3′ N 53° 15.3′ W | **Iso.W.** period 6s | 65 **20** | 13 | Red and white structure; 26. | |
| 1730 *H 0504.4* | --Breakwater. | 48° 01.2′ N 53° 15.6′ W | **Fl.R.** period 4s | 13 **4** | 4 | Mast; 8. | |
| 1732 *H 0502* | -Old Perlican, on Perlican Island. | 48° 05.4′ N 53° 01.6′ W | **Fl.W.** period 3s fl. 0.5s, ec. 2.5s | 126 **38** | 7 | Red and white cylindrical tower, red daymark, white band; 22. | |
| 1733 *H 0503* | --Outer breakwater. | 48° 05.2′ N 53° 00.6′ W | **Fl.G.** period 3s | 13 **4** | 4 | Cylindrical mast; 6. | |
| 1733.1 *H 0503.2* | --Inner breakwater. | 48° 05.2′ N 53° 00.5′ W | **Fl.R.** period 3s | 16 **5** | 4 | Cylindrical mast; 6. | |
| 1733.2 *H 0503.3* | --Sibleys Cove. | 48° 02.6′ N 53° 06.2′ W | **Fl.R.** period 6s fl. 1s, ec. 5s | 8 **2** | 4 | Cylindrical mast, red and white diagonal stripes; 7. | Seasonal. |
| 1734 *H 0500.5* | --Grates Cove. | 48° 10.2′ N 52° 56.2′ W | **L.Fl.W.** period 10s fl. 2s, ec. 8s | 150 **46** | 7 | Square skeleton tower, red and white rectangular daymark; 15. | Seasonal. |

Many lights of Newfoundland are maintained seasonally (from May to December).

| (1) No. | (2) Name and Location | (3) Position | (4) Characteristic | (5) Height | (6) Range | (7) Structure | (8) Remarks |
|---|---|---|---|---|---|---|---|

## CANADA-NEWFOUNDLAND

| (1) No. | (2) Name and Location | (3) Position | (4) Characteristic | (5) Height | (6) Range | (7) Structure | (8) Remarks |
|---|---|---|---|---|---|---|---|
| 1735 *H 0501* | --Wharf. | 48° 09.9′ N 52° 56.3′ W | **Fl.R.** period 4s | 9 **3** | 4 | Mast; 8. | |
| 1736 *H 0498* | Baccalieu Island, near N. point. | 48° 09.0′ N 52° 47.9′ W | **Fl.W.** period 6s fl. 1s, ec. 5s | 577 **176** | 7 | Square skeleton tower, red and white rectangular daymark; 63. | Often obscured by fog when the lower part of island is clear. |
| 1740 *H 0500* | **-Baccalieu Island,** SW. point. | 48° 06.4′ N 52° 48.5′ W | **Fl.W.** period 10s fl. 1s, ec. 9s | 175 **53** | **16** | White structure; 12. | **Horn:** 1 bl. ev. 60s (bl. 4s, si. 56s). Horn points 202°30′. |
| | CONCEPTION BAY: | | | | | | |
| 1744 *H 0494* | -Western Bay Head, on point. | 47° 53.2′ N 53° 03.4′ W | **Oc.W.** period 10s lt. 7.5s, ec. 2.5s | 94 **29** | 13 | Skeleton tower, red daymark, white band; 22. | |
| 1749 *H 0495* | -Ochre Pit Cove. | 47° 54.7′ N 53° 03.9′ W | **Fl.G.** period 4s | 12 **4** | 4 | Mast; 7. | |
| 1752 *H 0490* | -Carbonear Island, summit. | 47° 44.4′ N 53° 09.9′ W | **Fl.W.** period 6s fl. 0.5s, ec. 5.5s | 178 **54** | 6 | Square skeleton tower, red and white rectangular daymark; 12. | |
| 1756 *H 0492* | -Carbonear Bay, Government Wharf, head. | 47° 44.2′ N 53° 13.4′ W | **Fl.R.** period 6s fl. 1s, ec. 5s | 16 **5** | 4 | Cylindrical mast; 7. | |
| 1760 *H 0484* | -Harbour Grace Islands. | 47° 42.7′ N 53° 08.5′ W | **Fl.W.** period 4s | 136 **41** | 7 | Square skeleton tower, red and white rectangular daymark; 12. | |
| 1768 *H 0487* | -Harbour Grace. | 47° 41.4′ N 53° 12.9′ W | **Dir.W.R.G.** | 21 **6** | 14 | Square skeleton tower; 20. | F.R. 234°30′-235°30′, Al.W.R.-236°, F.W.-238°, Al.W.G.-238°30′, F.G.-239°30′. |
| 1773 *H 0486.2* | -Long Beach, S. breakwater. | 47° 40.4′ N 53° 14.4′ W | **Fl.R.** period 4s | | 2 | Mast; 7. | Seasonal. |
| 1774 *H 0486.3* | --N. breakwater. | 47° 40.4′ N 53° 14.4′ W | **Fl.G.** period 4s | 11 **3** | 2 | Mast; 7. | Seasonal. |
| 1776 *H 0483* | -SE. end Government Wharf, Bay Roberts. | 47° 36.0′ N 53° 16.0′ W | **Fl.R.** period 4s | 15 **5** | 4 | Cylindrical mast; 10. | |
| 1780 *H 0482.5* | -Bait Rocks, off Coley's Point. | 47° 35.4′ N 53° 15.2′ W | **Fl.G.** period 4s | 20 **6** | 5 | Square skeleton tower, green and white rectangular daymark; 14. | |
| 1784 *H 0482* | -Green Point, entrance to Bay Roberts, S. side. | 47° 36.7′ N 53° 10.6′ W | **L.Fl.W.** period 10s fl. 2s, ec. 8s | 56 **17** | 6 | Cylindrical tower, red and white bands; 25. | |
| 1786 *H 0480.2* | -Port de Grave, W. breakwater. | 47° 35.1′ N 53° 12.8′ W | **Fl.G.** period 4s | 13 **4** | 2 | Mast; 9. | |
| 1788 *H 0478* | -North Head, entrance to Brigus Bay. | 47° 32.9′ N 53° 10.9′ W | **Fl.W.** period 3s | 113 **34** | 8 | Cylindrical tower, red and white stripes; 31. | |
| 1792 *H 0479* | -Brigus Wharf. | 47° 32.4′ N 53° 12.3′ W | **Fl.R.** period 4s | 17 **5** | 4 | Triangular skeleton mast; 10. | |
| 1796 *H 0475* | -Salmon Cove Point, E. point of entrance to Gasters Bay. | 47° 27.8′ N 53° 09.0′ W | **Fl.W.** period 5s fl. 1s, ec. 4s | 85 **26** | 7 | Square skeleton tower, red and white rectangular daymark; 21. | |
| 1800 *H 0477* | -Conception Harbor. | 47° 26.4′ N 53° 12.5′ W | **Fl.R.** period 4s | 12 **4** | 3 | Triangular skeleton mast; 11. | |
| 1804 *H 0476* | -Ballyhack. | 47° 26.8′ N 53° 11.5′ W | **Fl.W.** period 6s fl. 0.5s, ec. 5.5s | 37 **11** | 5 | Skeleton mast, red daymark, white band; 16. | |

Many lights of Newfoundland are maintained seasonally (from May to December).

| (1) No. | (2) Name and Location | (3) Position | (4) Characteristic | (5) Height | (6) Range | (7) Structure | (8) Remarks |
|---|---|---|---|---|---|---|---|

## CANADA-NEWFOUNDLAND

| (1) No. | (2) Name and Location | (3) Position | (4) Characteristic | (5) Height | (6) Range | (7) Structure | (8) Remarks |
|---|---|---|---|---|---|---|---|
| 1806 *H 0474.42* | -Holyrood, wharf, N. head. | 47° 26.6′ N 53° 06.5′ W | **F.R.** | 31 **10** | | Mast. Floodlit. | Private light. |
| 1807 *H 0474.4* | --S. head. | 47° 26.6′ N 53° 06.4′ W | **F.R.** | 31 **10** | | Mast. Floodlit. | Private light. |
| 1812 *H 0474.7* | -Holyrood Bay Range, front. | 47° 23.3′ N 53° 07.7′ W | **F.R.** | 27 **8** | 13 | Skeleton tower, red trapezoidal daymark, white stripe; 20. | Visible on range line only. |
| 1816 *H 0474.71* | --Rear, 279.6 meters 183°32′ from front. | 47° 23.2′ N 53° 07.7′ W | **F.R.** | 64 **20** | 13 | Skeleton tower, red trapezoidal daymark, white stripe; 55. | Visible on range line only. |
| 1820 *H 0474* | -Long Pond, Manuels, E. breakwater, head. | 47° 31.1′ N 52° 58.7′ W | **Fl.G.** period 3s | 21 **6** | 5 | Square skeleton tower, green and white rectangular daymark; 14. | |
| 1824 *H 0472* | -Portugal Cove. | 47° 37.6′ N 52° 51.5′ W | **Iso.G.** period 6s | 25 **8** | 5 | Square skeleton tower, green and white rectangular daymark; 12. | **Whistle:** 1 bl. ev. 30s (bl. 3s, si. 27s). |
| 1828 *H 0473* | --Range, front. | 47° 37.5′ N 52° 51.4′ W | **F.G.** | 33 **10** | 14 | Square skeleton tower, white trapezoidal daymark, red stripe; 20. | Visible on range line only. |
| 1832 *H 0473.1* | ---Rear, 62 meters 093°41′ from front. | 47° 37.5′ N 52° 51.3′ W | **F.G.** | 68 **21** | 14 | Square skeleton tower, white trapezoidal daymark, red stripe; 12. | Visible on range line only. |
| 1836 *H 0470* | **-Bell Island.** | 47° 39.3′ N 52° 55.0′ W | **Fl.W.** period 6s fl. 1s, ec. 5s | 173 **53** | **17** | White block; 10. | |
| 1840 *H 0471* | --Ferry wharves. | 47° 37.8′ N 52° 55.4′ W | **Iso.R.** period 6s | 23 **7** | 5 | Square skeleton tower, red and white square daymark; 17. | **Whistle:** 1 bl. ev. 30s. |
| 1844 *H 0468* | **Cape St. Francis.** | 47° 48.5′ N 52° 47.2′ W | **Fl.W.** period 5s | 95 **29** | **15** | Structure; 11. | Visible 084°-316°. **Horn:** 1 bl. ev. 30s. (bl. 3s, si. 27s). Horn points 066°. |
| 1848 *H 0458* | **-Fort Amherst, S. side of entrance.** | 47° 33.8′ N 52° 40.8′ W | **Fl.W.** period 15s fl. 1s, ec. 14s | 132 **40** | **17** | White structure; 25. | **Horn:** 1 bl. ev. 20s. (bl. 2s, si. 18s). Horn points 052°. |
| 1852 *H 0458.4* | -North Head, N. side of entrance. | 47° 34.0′ N 52° 40.7′ W | **Fl.R.** period 4s | 84 **26** | 4 | Cylindrical mast; 9. | |
| 1856 *H 0460* | -Chain Rock. | 47° 34.0′ N 52° 41.3′ W | **Fl.R.** period 3s | 19 **6** | 4 | Red and white octagonal tower; 13. | |
| 1860 *H 0459* | -Range, front, on breastwork between Queen and King wharf. | 47° 34.0′ N 52° 42.2′ W | **F.G.** | 98 **30** | | Red and white skeleton tower, white trapezoidal daymark, red stripe. | Visible on range line only. |
| 1864 *H 0459.1* | --Rear, about 430 meters 276°07′ from front. | 47° 34.1′ N 52° 42.5′ W | **F.G.** | 196 **60** | | White rectangular structure, red diamond in center; 46. | Visible on range line only. |
| 1866.5 *H 0462.2* | --S. jetty. | 47° 33.4′ N 52° 42.5′ W | **F.R.** | 18 **5** | | Mast; 11. | Private light. |
| 1868 *H 0454* | **Cape Spear.** | 47° 31.3′ N 52° 37.3′ W | **Fl.(3)W.** period 15s fl. 0.4s, ec. 2.6s fl. 0.4s, ec. 2.6s fl. 0.4s, ec. 8.6s | 233 **71** | **20** | White hexagonal tower; 45. | **Horn:** 1 bl. ev. 60s. (bl. 4s, si. 56s). Horn points 109°. |
| 1872 *H 0452* | Bay Bulls. | 47° 18.6′ N 52° 44.8′ W | **Fl.W.** period 6s fl. 0.5s, ec. 5.5s | 197 **60** | 7 | White cylindrical tower; 39. | |
| 1874 *H 0451* | Calvert Wharf. | 47° 03.5′ N 52° 54.6′ W | **Fl.R.** period 4s | 11 **3** | 4 | Cylindrical mast; 7. | |
| 1876 *H 0450* | **Ferryland, head.** | 47° 01.0′ N 52° 51.4′ W | **Fl.W.** period 10s fl. 0.2s, ec. 9.8s | 190 **58** | **15** | Red and white cylindrical tower; 34. | |

Many lights of Newfoundland are maintained seasonally (from May to December).

| (1) No. | (2) Name and Location | (3) Position | (4) Characteristic | (5) Height | (6) Range | (7) Structure | (8) Remarks |
|---|---|---|---|---|---|---|---|
| | | | **CANADA-NEWFOUNDLAND** | | | | |
| 1880 *H 0449* | Northern, head. | 46° 57.8´ N 52° 54.1´ W | **Fl.W.** period 3s | 90 **27** | 7 | Cylindrical mast; 8. | |
| 1884 *H 0448* | **Bear Cove Point** (Fermeuse). | 46° 56.4´ N 52° 53.6´ W | **Fl.W.** period 5s fl. 1s, ec. 4s | 108 **33** | **15** | Skeleton tower, red rectangular daymark, white stripe; 10. | **Horn:** 1 bl. ev. 60s (bl. 4s, si. 56s). Horn points 098°. Emergency light. |
| 1904 *H 0444* | **Cape Race.** | 46° 39.5´ N 53° 04.4´ W | **Fl.W.** period 7.5s fl. 0.2s, ec. 7.3s | 170 **52** | **27** | White cylindrical tower, red upper portion; 68. | **Horn:** 2 bl. ev. 60s (bl. 3s, si. 3s, bl. 3s, si. 51s). Horn points 135°. |
| 1908 *H 0442* | **Powles,** head, Trepassey Harbor. | 46° 41.4´ N 53° 24.1´ W | **Fl.W.** period 10s fl. 0.2s, ec. 9.8s | 101 **31** | **22** | Red and white cylindrical tower; 7. | |
| 1912 *H 0443* | -Trepassey Harbor. | 46° 43.5´ N 53° 23.0´ W | **Iso.R.** period 6s | 18 **5** | 4 | Red cylindrical tower, white stripe; 14. | |
| 1916 *H 0443.2* | -Trepassey Wharf. | 46° 44.1´ N 53° 22.2´ W | **Fl.R.** period 4s | 14 **4** | 3 | Cylindrical mast; 7. | |
| 1920 *H 0440* | **Cape Pine.** | 46° 37.0´ N 53° 31.9´ W | **Fl.W.** period 5s fl. 0.5s, ec. 4.5s | 314 **96** | **16** | Cylindrical tower, red and white bands; 60. | **Horn:** 1 bl. ev. 60s (bl. 4s, si. 56s). Horn points 159°. |
| 1924 *H 0438* | St. Shotts at Eastern Head, FOG SIGNAL. | 46° 37.0´ N 53° 36.0´ W | | | | White square building. | Seasonal. **Whistle:** 3 bl. ev. 60s (bl. 2s, si. 8s, bl. 2s, si. 8s, bl. 2s, si. 38s). Standby horn. |
| | ST. MARYS BAY: | | | | | | |
| 1932 *H 0436* | **-La Haye Point,** entrance to St. Mary's Harbor. | 46° 54.3´ N 53° 36.9´ W | **Fl.W.** period 6s fl. 0.4s, ec. 5.6s | 62 **19** | **16** | Square skeleton tower; 37. | **Horn:** 1 bl. ev. 30s (bl. 3s, si. 27s). Horn points 225°. |
| 1934 *H 0435* | -St. Mary's Harbor, Riverhead Wharf. | 46° 57.8´ N 53° 31.3´ W | **Fl.G.** period 4s | 10 **3** | 2 | Mast; 9. | |
| 1936 *H 0434* | -Great Colinet Island, on Dalton Point. | 47° 01.0´ N 53° 41.0´ W | **Fl.W.** period 3s fl. 0.5s, ec. 2.5s | 66 **20** | 5 | Square skeleton tower, red and white square daymark; 14. | |
| 1940 *H 0433* | -Branch, W. breakwater. | 46° 53.0´ N 53° 57.0´ W | **Oc.G.** period 6s lt. 4s, ec. 2s | 7 **2** | 4 | Cylindrical mast; 6. | Seasonal. **Whistle:** 1 bl. ev. 30s (bl. 3s, si. 27s). In operation 0400-2200 (approx.) each day during foggy weather, later if required by fishermen. |
| 1952 *H 0432* | **Cape St. Mary's.** | 46° 49.4´ N 54° 11.8´ W | **Fl.W.** period 5s | 390 **119** | **21** | White octagonal tower; 38. | **Horn:** 1 bl. ev. 30s. (bl. 3s, si. 27s). Horn points 220°. |
| 1954 *H 0429* | St. Brides. | 46° 55.1´ N 54° 10.6´ W | **Fl.R.** period 3s fl. 0.5s, ec. 2.5s | 11 **3** | 3 | Mast; 7. | Seasonal. |
| 1955 *H 0429.5* | -Breakwater. | 46° 55.1´ N 54° 10.7´ W | **Fl.W.** period 3s fl. 0.5s, ec. 2.5s | 26 **8** | 3 | Mast; 7. | Visible 245°-330°. Seasonal. |
| | PLACENTIA BAY: | | | | | | |
| | -Placentia Harbor: | | | | | | |
| 1956 *H 0430* | --St. Brides FOG SIGNAL. | 46° 54.9´ N 54° 10.7´ W | | | | Square skeleton tower. | Seasonal. **Whistle:** 1 bl. ev. 30s. (bl. 3s, si. 27s). In operation 0400-2200 (approx.) each day during foggy weather, later if required by fishermen. |

Many lights of Newfoundland are maintained seasonally (from May to December).

| (1) No. | (2) Name and Location | (3) Position | (4) Characteristic | (5) Height | (6) Range | (7) Structure | (8) Remarks |
|---|---|---|---|---|---|---|---|

## CANADA-NEWFOUNDLAND

| (1) No. | (2) Name and Location | (3) Position | (4) Characteristic | (5) Height | (6) Range | (7) Structure | (8) Remarks |
|---|---|---|---|---|---|---|---|
| 1960 *H 0422* | **--Verde Point.** | 47° 14.3′ N 54° 00.9′ W | **Fl.W.** period 5s | 98 **30** | **16** | Square skeleton tower, red and white square daymark; 37. | **Horn:** 1 bl. ev. 60s. (bl. 4s, si. 56s). Horn points 254°. |
| 1964 *H 0424* | --Range, front. | 47° 14.8′ N 53° 57.9′ W | **F.R.** | 20 **6** | 13 | Square skeleton tower, white trapezoidal daymark, red stripe; 12. | |
| 1968 *H 0424.1* | ---Rear, 59 meters 091°06′ from front. | 47° 14.8′ N 53° 57.8′ W | **F.R.** | 28 **9** | 13 | Square skeleton tower, white trapezoidal daymark, red stripe; 23. | |
| | -Argentia Harbor: | | | | | | |
| 2004 *H 0410* | --Range, front. | 47° 17.2′ N 53° 59.6′ W | **F.G.** | 28 **9** | 14 | Square skeleton tower, red trapezoidal daymark, white stripe; 21. | |
| 2008 *H 0410.1* | ---Rear, 233.8 meters 228° from front. | 47° 17.1′ N 53° 59.7′ W | **F.G.** | 51 **16** | 14 | Square skeleton tower, red trapezoidal daymark, white stripe; 41. | |
| 2012 *H 0400.4* | -Shag Rocks. | 47° 24.6′ N 53° 54.8′ W | **Fl.W.** period 4s | 42 **13** | 5 | Square skeleton tower, red and white rectangular daymark; 14. | |
| 2020 *H 0394* | -Bordeaux Island. | 47° 44.5′ N 54° 01.9′ W | **Fl.W.** period 6s fl. 0.5s, ec. 5.5s | 87 **27** | 5 | Square skeleton tower, red and white rectangular daymark; 12. | |
| 2021 *H 0395.41* | -Whiffin Head. | 47° 46.2′ N 54° 01.2′ W | **F.R.** | | | | Private light. |
| 2021.1 *H 0395.42* | --Center of pier. | 47° 46.4′ N 54° 01.0′ W | **F.Bu.** | | | | **Fog signal.** Private light. |
| 2021.2 *H 0395.4* | --NE. Pier, head. | 47° 46.5′ N 54° 00.9′ W | **4 F.R.** | | | | Private light. |
| 2021.3 *H 0395.5* | --N. pier. | 47° 46.4′ N 54° 00.7′ W | **Q.R.** | | | | Private light. |
| 2021.4 *H 0395.51* | --Harbor entrance, E. end. | 47° 46.4′ N 54° 00.6′ W | **F.G.** | | | | Private light. |
| 2022 *H 0395* | -Long Beach, jetty, SW. head. | 47° 47.8′ N 54° 01.2′ W | **Fl.Y.** | | | | Private light. |
| 2022.1 *H 0395.2* | --Jetty, N. head. | 47° 48.1′ N 54° 01.1′ W | **Fl.Y.** | | | | Private light. |
| 2024 *H 0394.5* | **--Come by Chance Harbor Range,** front. | 47° 48.7′ N 54° 00.5′ W | **F.W.** | 98 **30** | **27** | Skeleton tower, red trapezoidal daymark, white stripe; 65. | |
| 2028 *H 0394.51* | ---Rear, 484.3 meters 039°57′ from front. | 47° 48.9′ N 54° 00.2′ W | **F.W.** | 202 **62** | **27** | Square skeleton tower, red trapezoidal daymark, white stripe; 65. | |
| 2032 *H 0390* | -North Harbor Point, W. side of entrance to North Harbor. | 47° 49.2′ N 54° 05.9′ W | **Fl.W.** period 3s fl. 0.5s, ec. 2.5s | 39 **12** | 5 | Square skeleton tower, red and white square daymark; 12. | |
| 2036 *H 0392* | -Swift Current, wharf. | 47° 52.7′ N 54° 12.1′ W | **Fl.R.** period 4s | 10 **3** | 2 | Cylindrical mast; 7. | |
| 2040 *H 0388* | -Sound Island Point. | 47° 47.4′ N 54° 10.0′ W | **Fl.W.** period 4s | 34 **10** | 5 | Skeleton tower, red and white rectangular daymark; 19. | |
| 2042 *H 0397.5* | -Tobin's Point. | 47° 42.8′ N 54° 12.4′ W | **Fl.W.** period 3s fl. 0.5s, ec. 2.5s | 22 **7** | 5 | Square mast, red and white rectangular daymark; 15. | |
| 2044 *H 0397* | -Long Island Point. | 47° 41.7′ N 54° 04.8′ W | **Fl.W.** period 4s fl. 0.5s, ec. 3.5s | 50 **15** | 5 | Square skeleton tower, red and white rectangular daymark; 15. | |

Many lights of Newfoundland are maintained seasonally (from May to December).

| (1)<br>No. | (2)<br>Name and Location | (3)<br>Position | (4)<br>Characteristic | (5)<br>Height | (6)<br>Range | (7)<br>Structure | (8)<br>Remarks |
|---|---|---|---|---|---|---|---|

## CANADA-NEWFOUNDLAND

| | | | | | | | |
|---|---|---|---|---|---|---|---|
| 2048<br>*H 0398* | -Buffett Island. | 47° 31.6´ N<br>54° 03.0´ W | **Fl.W.**<br>period 3s | 48<br>**15** | 5 | Square skeleton tower, red and white rectangular daymark; 14. | |
| 2052<br>*H 0399* | -Ironskull Rock. | 47° 27.5´ N<br>54° 04.5´ W | **Fl.G.**<br>period 6s<br>fl. 0.5s, ec. 5.5s | 34<br>**10** | 5 | Square skeleton tower; 25. | |
| 2056<br>*H 0400* | -Red Island Harbor, N. side of entrance. | 47° 24.0´ N<br>54° 08.7´ W | **Fl.W.**<br>period 3s | 52<br>**16** | 5 | Square skeleton tower, red and white rectangular daymark; 16. | |
| 2057<br>*H 0387* | -Merasheen Island. | 47° 24.2´ N<br>54° 21.8´ W | **Fl.W.**<br>period 4s | 61<br>**19** | 5 | Cylindrical mast; 7. | |
| 2058<br>*H 0384* | -Little Paradise Point. | 47° 21.1´ N<br>54° 34.8´ W | **Fl.W.**<br>period 6s<br>fl. 0.5s, ec. 5.5s | 29<br>**9** | 5 | Square skeleton tower, red and white rectangular daymark; 14. | |
| 2060<br>*H 0386* | **-Marticot Island,** SE. side. | 47° 19.6´ N<br>54° 34.9´ W | **Fl.W.**<br>period 15s<br>fl. 1s, ec. 14s | 90<br>**27** | **17** | Square skeleton tower; 37. | Visible 227°-075°.<br>**Horn:** 1 bl. ev. 30s. (bl. 3s, si. 27s). Horn points 121°. |
| 2064<br>*H 0382* | -Petit Forte Harbor, on E. side of entrance. | 47° 23.2´ N<br>54° 39.5´ W | **Fl.W.**<br>period 3s<br>fl. 0.5s, ec. 2.5s | 39<br>**12** | 7 | Red and white cylindrical tower, red and white daymark; 15. | |
| 2065<br>*H 0381* | --Wharf. | 47° 23.8´ N<br>54° 40.1´ W | **Fl.R.**<br>period 4s | 9<br>**3** | 4 | Cylindrical mast; 7. | |
| 2066<br>*H 0383* | -Southeast Bight, wharf. | 47° 23.7´ N<br>54° 34.6´ W | **Fl.R.**<br>period 4s<br>fl. 0.5s, ec. 3.5s | 13<br>**4** | 4 | Cylindrical mast; 7. | |
| 2068<br>*H 0380* | -Long Island, S. point. | 47° 17.9´ N<br>54° 42.2´ W | **Fl.W.**<br>period 5s | 237<br>**72** | 5 | Skeleton tower; 28. | |
| 2072<br>*H 0379.7* | -Oderin Harbor Entrance. | 47° 17.7´ N<br>54° 49.3´ W | **Fl.W.**<br>period 6s<br>fl. 0.5s, ec. 5.5s | 30<br>**9** | 5 | Square skeleton tower, red and white rectangular daymark; 16. | |
| 2076<br>*H 0379.4* | -Steering Rock, approach to Baine Harbor. | 47° 21.3´ N<br>54° 53.3´ W | **Fl.G.**<br>period 4s | 18<br>**5** | 4 | Square skeleton tower, green and white rectangular daymark; 12. | |
| 2080<br>*H 0377* | -Collins Island, off the NW. side of Davis Island. | 47° 15.9´ N<br>54° 56.7´ W | **Fl.W.**<br>period 4s | 37<br>**11** | 7 | Square skeleton tower, red and white rectangular daymark; 14. | |
| 2084<br>*H 0375* | -Red Harbor Head. | 47° 16.7´ N<br>54° 58.8´ W | **Fl.R.**<br>period 4s | 60<br>**18** | 4 | Square skeleton tower, red and white rectangular daymark; 14. | |
| 2092<br>*H 0373* | -Go By Point. | 47° 08.4´ N<br>55° 05.3´ W | **Fl.G.**<br>period 4s | 85<br>**26** | 4 | White and green cylindrical tower; 12. | |
| 2096<br>*H 0372.4* | -Duck Rock. | 47° 08.6´ N<br>55° 04.7´ W | **Fl.R.**<br>period 4s | 22<br>**7** | 4 | Square skeleton tower, red and white rectangular daymark; 14. | |
| 2100<br>*H 0372* | **--Tides Cove Point.** | 47° 06.4´ N<br>55° 04.3´ W | **Fl.W.**<br>period 6s<br>fl. 0.4s, ec. 5.6s | 110<br>**34** | **16** | Square skeleton tower; 37. | **Horn:** 1 bl. ev. 60s. (bl. 4s, si. 56s). Horn points 093°. |
| 2104<br>*H 0370* | -Iron Island, off entrance to Burin Inlet. | 47° 02.4´ N<br>55° 07.3´ W | **Fl.R.**<br>period 4s | 118<br>**36** | 4 | Skeleton tower, red and white square daymark; 14. | |
| 2108<br>*H 0368* | -Dodding Head, Burin Island. | 47° 00.2´ N<br>55° 09.1´ W | **Fl.W.**<br>period 6s<br>fl. 1s, ec. 5s | 320<br>**98** | 6 | Square skeleton tower, red and white rectangular daymark; 12. | |
| 2116<br>*H 0367* | -Stag Rock. | 47° 01.6´ N<br>55° 11.1´ W | **Fl.R.**<br>period 4s | 12<br>**4** | 4 | Skeleton tower; 7. | |
| 2120<br>*H 0364* | **-Little Burin Island.** | 46° 58.8´ N<br>55° 11.4´ W | **Fl.W.**<br>period 10s<br>fl. 0.2s, ec. 9.8s | 85<br>**26** | **17** | Skeleton tower, black and white rectangular daymark. | Visible 122°-040°.<br>**Horn:** 1 bl. ev. 30s (bl. 3s, si. 27s). Horn points 096°. |

Many lights of Newfoundland are maintained seasonally (from May to December).

| (1) No. | (2) Name and Location | (3) Position | (4) Characteristic | (5) Height | (6) Range | (7) Structure | (8) Remarks |
|---|---|---|---|---|---|---|---|

## CANADA-NEWFOUNDLAND

| (1) No. | (2) Name and Location | (3) Position | (4) Characteristic | (5) Height | (6) Range | (7) Structure | (8) Remarks |
|---|---|---|---|---|---|---|---|
| 2124 *H 0362* | -Corbin Harbor, Long Point, harbor entrance, N. side. | 46° 57.3´ N 55° 14.0´ W | **Fl.R.** period 6s fl. 1s, ec. 5s | 85 **26** | 5 | Square skeleton tower, red and white rectangular daymark;17. | |
| 2128 *H 0360* | **Middle Head,** on point. | 46° 53.9´ N 55° 20.9´ W | **Fl.W.** period 15s fl. 1s, ec. 14s | 88 **27** | **17** | Square skeleton tower; 31. | **Horn:** 1 bl. ev. 30s. (bl. 3s, si. 27s). Horn points 162°. |
| 2136 *H 0356* | Black Head. | 46° 54.3´ N 55° 33.6´ W | **Fl.W.** period 3s | 190 **58** | 5 | Red and white cylindrical tower, red and white daymark; 15. | |
| | LAMALINE HARBOR: | | | | | | |
| 2140 *H 0350* | **-Alan's Island,** Bluff Head. | 46° 50.8´ N 55° 47.9´ W | **Fl.W.** period 4s | 64 **20** | **16** | Square skeleton tower; 37. | |
| 2144 *H 0352* | -N. side of harbor Range, front. | 46° 52.2´ N 55° 48.0´ W | **F.R.** | 12 **4** | 13 | Skeleton tower, white trapezoidal daymark, red stripe; 12. | Visible on range line only. |
| 2148 *H 0352.1* | --Rear, 146.3 meters 341°30′ from front. | 46° 52.3´ N 55° 48.0´ W | **F.R.** | 30 **9** | 13 | Skeleton tower, white trapezoidal daymark, red stripe; 26. | Visible on range line only. |
| 2156 *H 0348* | **Green Island.** | 46° 52.8´ N 56° 05.1´ W | **Fl.W.** period 10s | 149 **45** | **15** | Square skeleton tower, red and white rectangular daymark; 22. | **Horn:** 1 bl. ev. 60s (bl. 4s, si. 56s). Horn points 089°. |
| | ILE ST. PIERRE (F.): | | | | | | |
| 2160 *H 0332* | **-Tete de Galantry.** | 46° 45.9´ N 56° 09.2´ W | **Fl.(2)W.** period 10s fl. 0.1s, ec. 2.4s fl. 0.1s, ec. 7.4s | 154 **47** | **23** | White tower, red top; 59. | **Horn:** 2 bl. ev. 60s (bl. 2s, si. 3s, bl. 2s, si. 53s). |
| 2172 *H 0338* | -Rocher Petit St. Pierre. | 46° 47.9´ N 56° 08.9´ W | **Fl.W.R.** period 2.5s fl. 0.5s, ec. 2s | 33 **10** | W. 9 R. 6 | White tower, red band; 39. | W. 189°-059°, R.-189°. 2 F.R. on television post 660m W. |
| 2180 *H 0345* | --Harbor entrance, S. end. | 46° 46.7´ N 56° 10.1´ W | **Fl.(3)G.** period 12s | 26 **8** | 6 | White pylon, green top; 21. | |
| 2181 *H 0345.2* | --Harbor, E. end. | 46° 46.6´ N 56° 10.5´ W | **Fl.G.** period 2.5s | 13 **4** | 3 | Post; 10. | |
| 2184 *H 0341* | --N. pier, offshore dike, head. | 46° 47.1´ N 56° 09.7´ W | **Oc.G.** period 4s | 20 **6** | 6 | Green post; 20. | |
| 2188 *H 0341.2* | ---S. pier, head. | 46° 46.9´ N 56° 09.8´ W | **Fl.G.** period 4s fl. 1s, ec. 3s | 20 **6** | 5 | Green post; 20. | Visible 038°30′-190°. |
| 2192 *H 0342* | --Quai Commerce, S. side of breakwater. | 46° 47.2´ N 56° 09.8´ W | **Oc.R.** period 4s lt. 3s, ec. 1s | | 6 | White tower, red lantern; 20. | 2 F.R. on 3 posts 1.35M W. |
| 2193 *H 0343* | --Anse a Rodrigue. | 46° 47.1´ N 56° 10.1´ W | **Fl.(2)R.** period 6s fl. 1s, ec. 1s fl. 1s, ec. 3s | | 1 | Red post; 7. | |
| | ILE MIQUELON (F.): | | | | | | |
| 2208 *H 0330* | -Pointe Plate, SW. point of Ile Langlade (Petite Miquelon). | 46° 49.3´ N 56° 24.1´ W | **Fl.W.R.** period 4s fl. 1s, ec. 3s | 157 **48** | W. 12 R. 9 | White tower, red top; 141. | R. 155°-163°, W.-155°. |
| 2212 *H 0328* | **-Cap Blanc.** | 47° 06.3´ N 56° 23.9´ W | **Fl.(3)W.R.** period 15s fl. 0.6s, ec. 2.4s fl. 0.6s, ec. 2.4s fl. 0.6s, ec. 8.4s | 105 **32** | W. **22** R. **18** | White tower, red top; 62. | R. 036°30′-055°, W.-270°, obsc.-330°, W.-036°30′. Partially obscured by shore 205°-252°. |

Many lights of Newfoundland are maintained seasonally (from May to December).

| (1) No. | (2) Name and Location | (3) Position | (4) Characteristic | (5) Height | (6) Range | (7) Structure | (8) Remarks |
|---|---|---|---|---|---|---|---|
| | | | **CANADA-NEWFOUNDLAND** | | | | |
| 2216 *H 0329* | -Miquelon, on wharf extension. | 47° 06.2´ N 56° 22.6´ W | **Fl.W.R.G.** period 2.5s | 33 **10** | W. 9 R. 6 G. 6 | White tower; 26. | G. 345°-225°, W.-251°, R.-283°, obsc.-345°. |
| | FORTUNE BAY: | | | | | | |
| 2228 *H 0325* | **-Fortune Head.** | 47° 04.5´ N 55° 51.5´ W | **Fl.W.** period 5s fl. 0.5s, ec. 4.5s | 78 **24** | **15** | White skeleton tower, red upper portion; 32. | **Horn:** 1 bl. ev. 30s. (bl. 3s, si. 27s). Horn points 326°18′. |
| 2236 *H 0324* | -Fortune Harbor, E. pier, head. | 47° 04.5´ N 55° 49.7´ W | **Fl.G.** period 4s | 13 **4** | 4 | Cylindrical mast; 11. | |
| 2240 *H 0323..3* | --Western breakwater. | 47° 04.6´ N 55° 49.7´ W | **Fl.R.** period 4s | 16 **5** | 4 | Skeleton tower; 11. | |
| 2241 *H 0323.4* | -Fortune Harbor, Fisherman wharf. | 47° 04.4´ N 55° 49.8´ W | **Fl.G.** period 4s | 11 **4** | | Cylindrical mast; 7. | |
| 2244 *H 0320* | -Grand Bank breakwater, seaward end. | 47° 06.1´ N 55° 44.9´ W | **Fl.R.** period 4s | 19 **6** | 4 | Red cylindrical mast; 10. | |
| 2248 *H 0322* | -Grand Bank, E. pier, head. | 47° 06.1´ N 55° 45.0´ W | **Q.G.** | 27 **8** | 5 | White octagonal tower, red upper portion; 23. | |
| 2260 *H 0321* | --West Pier, head. | 47° 06.0´ N 55° 45.0´ W | **Q.R.** | 20 **6** | 4 | Cylindrical mast; 10. | |
| 2264 *H 0318* | -Garnish, S. side of entrance, breakwater, head. | 47° 14.2´ N 55° 21.5´ W | **Q.R.** | 28 **8** | 6 | Square skeleton tower, red and white rectangular daymark; 14. | |
| 2265 *H 0318.2* | -Garnish inner breakwater. | 47° 14.1´ N 55° 21.5´ W | **Fl.G.** period 4s | 11 **4** | 4 | Cylindrical mast; 7. | |
| 2268 *H 0313* | St. Bernards, breakwater. | 47° 31.7´ N 54° 57.1´ W | **Fl.R.** period 4s | 14 **4** | | Cylindrical mast; 7. | |
| 2272 *H 0314* | -Ragged Point, N. side of entrance to Bay L'Argent. | 47° 33.5´ N 54° 52.6´ W | **Fl.W.** period 3s fl. 0.5s, ec. 2.5s | 204 **62** | 9 | Square skeleton tower, red and white rectangular daymark; 12. | |
| 2280 *H 0312* | -Long Harbour Point. | 47° 34.7´ N 55° 07.1´ W | **Fl.W.** period 6s fl. 0.5s, ec. 5.5s | 165 **50** | 6 | Square skeleton tower, red and white rectangular daymark; 19. | |
| 2284 *H 0310* | -Rencontre East, Mal Bay Island, E. head. | 47° 37.0´ N 55° 12.0´ W | **Fl.W.** period 4s | 52 **16** | 7 | Square skeleton tower, red and white rectangular daymark; 17. | |
| 2286 *H 0309* | -Pool's Cove. | 47° 40.8´ N 55° 25.8´ W | **Fl.R.** period 4s | 11 **3** | 2 | Mast; 7. | |
| 2288 *H 0308* | -Belloram Harbor, on Beach Point. | 47° 31.7´ N 55° 24.5´ W | **Fl.W.** period 3s fl. 0.5s, ec. 2.5s | 34 **10** | 5 | Red and white cylindrical tower, red and white daymark; 23. | |
| 2292 *H 0304* | **-St. Jacques Island,** S. hill. | 47° 28.4´ N 55° 24.4´ W | **Fl.W.** period 6s fl. 1s, ec. 5s | 131 **40** | **16** | White cylindrical tower; 33. | **Horn:** 1 bl. ev. 30s (bl. 3s, si. 27s). Horn points 270°. |
| 2296 *H 0302* | -English Harbor West. | 47° 27.3´ N 55° 29.5´ W | **Fl.R.** period 4s | 45 **14** | 5 | Square mast, red and white square daymark; 14. | |
| 2300 *H 0300* | -Boxey Point. | 47° 24.2´ N 55° 35.1´ W | **Fl.W.** period 3s | 57 **17** | 5 | Square skeleton tower, red and white rectangular daymark; 14. | |
| 2304 *H 0298* | -Bull Point, Coomb's Cove, N. side of entrance. | 47° 27.4´ N 55° 37.9´ W | **Fl.G.** period 4s | 35 **11** | 5 | Square skeleton tower, red and white rectangular daymark; 12. | |
| 2306 *H 0296* | -Wreck Cove. | 47° 29.8´ N 55° 36.5´ W | **Fl.R.** period 4s | 14 **4** | 4 | Cylindrical mast; 7. | |

Many lights of Newfoundland are maintained seasonally (from May to December).

| (1) No. | (2) Name and Location | (3) Position | (4) Characteristic | (5) Height | (6) Range | (7) Structure | (8) Remarks |
|---|---|---|---|---|---|---|---|

## CANADA-NEWFOUNDLAND

| (1) No. | (2) Name and Location | (3) Position | (4) Characteristic | (5) Height | (6) Range | (7) Structure | (8) Remarks |
|---|---|---|---|---|---|---|---|
| 2312<br>*H 0290* | -Brunette Island, Mercer Head, SE. side of island. | 47° 15.4′ N<br>55° 52.0′ W | **Fl.W.**<br>period 4s | 407<br>**124** | 7 | Square skeleton tower, red and white square daymark; 22. | |
| 2316<br>*H 0294* | -Rocky Point, (Harbor Breton). | 47° 28.7′ N<br>55° 47.6′ W | **Fl.W.**<br>period 4s | 53<br>**16** | 9 | Red and white cylindrical tower, red and white daymark; 25. | |
| 2320<br>*H 0286* | Pass Island, summit of island, entrance to Hermitage Bay. | 47° 29.4′ N<br>56° 11.8′ W | **Fl.W.**<br>period 10s<br>fl. 1s, ec. 9s | 281<br>**86** | 12 | White skeleton tower; 31. | |
| | | | **Fl.R.**<br>period 4s | 278<br>**85** | 4 | | Visible 257°-118°. |
| 2324<br>*H 0286.1* | -Pass Island FOG SIGNAL, SW. end of island. | 47° 29.0′ N<br>56° 12.0′ W | | | | Skeleton tower, white rectangular daymark, black band. | **Horn:** 1 bl. ev. 30s. (bl. 3s, si. 27s). Horns point 259°06′. |
| | HERMITAGE BAY: | | | | | | |
| 2328<br>*H 0286.5* | -Grole Point. | 47° 31.5′ N<br>56° 07.5′ W | **Fl.W.**<br>period 4s | 42<br>**13** | 6 | Cylindrical mast; 7. | |
| 2332<br>*H 0288* | -Fox Island. | 47° 33.9′ N<br>55° 58.4′ W | **Fl.W.**<br>period 4s | 74<br>**23** | 5 | Square skeleton tower, red and white rectangular daymark; 14. | |
| 2336<br>*H 0289* | -Gaultois Harbor, on rock W. side of entrance. | 47° 36.3′ N<br>55° 54.1′ W | **Fl.G.**<br>period 3s<br>fl. 0.5s, ec. 2.5s | 18<br>**5** | 5 | Square skeleton tower, green and white rectangular daymark; 15. | |
| 2340<br>*H 0287* | -Tinker Rock. | 47° 36.8′ N<br>56° 03.1′ W | **Fl.W.**<br>period 4s | 48<br>**15** | 5 | Square skeleton tower, red and white rectangular daymark; 15. | |
| 2344<br>*H 0277* | Cape Mark. | 47° 44.5′ N<br>55° 52.1′ W | **Fl.R.**<br>period 4s | 26<br>**8** | 4 | Square skeleton tower, red and white square daymark; 14. | |
| 2347<br>*H 0282* | Day Point. | 47° 41.3′ N<br>55° 55.4′ W | **Fl.W.**<br>period 4s | 33<br>**10** | 5 | Square skeleton tower, red and white square daymark; 22. | |
| 2348<br>*H 0278* | Bay d'Espoir, Roti Point, E. head. | 47° 47.4′ N<br>55° 50.5′ W | **Fl.G.**<br>period 6s<br>fl. 1s, ec. 5s | 26<br>**8** | 4 | Square skeleton tower, green and white rectangular daymark; 12. | |
| 2349<br>*H 0283* | Little Island. | 47° 39.6′ N<br>55° 56.1′ W | **Fl.R.**<br>period 4s | 34<br>**10** | 4 | Square skeleton tower, red and white square daymark; 22. | |
| 2352<br>*H 0276* | **Dawson Point.** | 47° 38.6′ N<br>56° 09.0′ W | **Fl.W.**<br>period 5s | 55<br>**17** | **16** | Square skeleton tower, red and white rectangular daymark. | |
| 2356<br>*H 0275* | Taylor Island, Salmon Point. | 47° 37.0′ N<br>56° 12.0′ W | **Fl.W.**<br>period 4s | 72<br>**22** | 7 | Square skeleton tower, red and white rectangular daymark; 14. | |
| 2358<br>*H 0272* | New Harbour Island. | 47° 35.8′ N<br>56° 39.6′ W | **Fl.G.**<br>period 6s<br>fl. 0.5s, ec. 5.5s | 91<br>**28** | 5 | Square skeleton tower, green and white rectangular daymark; 15. | |
| 2360<br>*H 0270* | Francois Bay. | 47° 33.6′ N<br>56° 44.1′ W | **Fl.G.**<br>period 5s<br>fl. 0.1s, ec. 4.9s | 151<br>**46** | 12 | White square tower, green band on top, attached to building; 15. | Emergency light. |
| 2364<br>*H 0268* | Cape La Hune, SW. point. | 47° 31.8′ N<br>56° 51.6′ W | **Fl.R.**<br>period 6s<br>fl. 1s, ec. 5s | 80<br>**24** | 4 | Square skeleton tower, red and white square daymark; 15. | |
| 2368<br>*H 0266* | **Penguin Islands,** summit of Harbour Island. | 47° 23.0′ N<br>56° 58.7′ W | **Fl.W.**<br>period 10s<br>fl. 0.2s, ec. 9.8s | 72<br>**22** | **17** | Square skeleton tower, red square daymark, white band; 19. | |
| 2376<br>*H 0265* | Grey River Point. | 47° 34.5′ N<br>57° 06.9′ W | **Q.G.** | 89<br>**27** | 4 | Square skeleton tower, green and white rectangular daymark; 14. | |

Many lights of Newfoundland are maintained seasonally (from May to December).

| (1) No. | (2) Name and Location | (3) Position | (4) Characteristic | (5) Height | (6) Range | (7) Structure | (8) Remarks |
|---|---|---|---|---|---|---|---|

## CANADA-NEWFOUNDLAND

| (1) No. | (2) Name and Location | (3) Position | (4) Characteristic | (5) Height | (6) Range | (7) Structure | (8) Remarks |
|---|---|---|---|---|---|---|---|
| 2380<br>*H 0264* | Northwest Head. | 47° 30.7′ N<br>57° 24.5′ W | **Fl.W.**<br>period 3s<br>fl. 0.1s, ec. 2.9s | 125<br>**38** | 13 | White cylindrical tower, red and white diagonal stripes; 21. | Obscured by Eastern Head Ramea Island.<br>**Horn:** 1 bl. ev. 30s (bl. 3s, si. 27s). Horn points 237°06′. |
| 2381<br>*H 0264.4* | -Ramea. | 47° 31.5′ N<br>57° 22.6′ W | **Fl.R.**<br>period 4s | 13<br>**4** | 4 | Cylindrical mast; 7. | |
| 2390<br>*H 0263* | Bay de Loup Point. | 47° 37.3′ N<br>57° 33.6′ W | **Fl.W.**<br>period 4s | 74<br>**23** | 7 | Square skeleton tower, red and white rectangular daymark; 16. | |
| | BURGEO ISLANDS: | | | | | | |
| 2392<br>*H 0260* | -**Boar Island,** summit. | 47° 36.4′ N<br>57° 35.2′ W | **Fl.W.**<br>period 5s<br>fl. 0.2s, ec. 4.8s | 207<br>**63** | **15** | Skeleton tower; 33. | **Horn:** 1 bl. ev. 20s. (bl. 2s, si. 18s). Horn points 140°12′. |
| 2394<br>*H 0262* | -Furber Point, Burgeo Ferry, wharf. | 47° 36.3′ N<br>57° 36.5′ W | **Fl.R.**<br>period 4s | 13<br>**4** | 4 | Cylindrical mast; 7. | |
| 2395<br>*H 0259* | -Rencontre Island. | 47° 35.0′ N<br>57° 36.9′ W | **Fl.W.**<br>period 4s | 188<br>**57** | 7 | Square skeleton tower, red and white rectangular daymark; 15. | |
| 2396<br>*H 0258* | -West Flat Island. | 47° 35.1′ N<br>57° 42.4′ W | **Fl.W.**<br>period 4s | 35<br>**11** | 6 | Square skeleton tower, red and white rectangular daymark; 15. | |
| 2400<br>*H 0254* | Offer Island, approach to Grand Bruit Harbor. | 47° 38.6′ N<br>58° 13.4′ W | **Fl.W.**<br>period 3s | 36<br>**11** | 6 | Square skeleton tower, red and white rectangular daymark; 15. | |
| | LA POILE BAY: | | | | | | |
| 2404<br>*H 0252* | -Ireland Island, E. side of entrance to bay. | 47° 38.1′ N<br>58° 22.3′ W | **Fl.W.**<br>period 6s<br>fl. 1s, ec. 5s | 67<br>**20** | 7 | Square skeleton tower, red and white rectangular daymark; 23. | |
| 2408<br>*H 0250* | -Christmas Head, S. of entrance to Little Bay. | 47° 40.5′ N<br>58° 23.5′ W | **Q.G.** | 39<br>**12** | 4 | Square skeleton tower, green and white rectangular daymark; 15. | |
| | ROSE BLANCHE HARBOR: | | | | | | |
| 2418<br>*H 0242.5* | -Rose Blanche. | 47° 36.1′ N<br>58° 41.7′ W | **Fl.R.**<br>period 10s<br>fl. 0.5s, ec. 9.5s | 95<br>**29** | 13 | Tower. | |
| 2420<br>*H 0244* | -Cains Island. | 47° 36.1′ N<br>58° 41.7′ W | **Fl.R.**<br>period 6s<br>fl. 0.5s, ec. 5.5s | 6<br>**2** | 3 | Mast. | |
| | BURNT ISLANDS: | | | | | | |
| 2428<br>*H 0234* | -Great Burnt Island, front. | 47° 35.8′ N<br>58° 53.5′ W | **F.R.** | 53<br>**16** | 13 | Skeleton tower, white trapezoidal daymark, red stripe; 14. | Visible on range line only. |
| 2432<br>*H 0234.1* | --Rear, 37 meters 034°25′ from front. | 47° 35.9′ N<br>58° 53.5′ W | **F.R.** | 67<br>**20** | 13 | Skeleton tower, white trapezoidal daymark, red stripe; 14. | Visible on range line only. |
| 2436<br>*H 0238* | -**Colombier Islands.** | 47° 35.5′ N<br>58° 53.8′ W | **Fl.W.**<br>period 5s<br>fl. 0.5s, ec. 4.5s | 60<br>**18** | **15** | Square skeleton tower; 37. | **Horn:** 1 bl. ev. 30s. (bl. 3s, si. 27s). Horn points 186°. |
| 2452<br>*H 0232* | Ile aux Morts Harbor, W. end of Pitman's Island. | 47° 34.8′ N<br>58° 58.8′ W | **Fl.W.**<br>period 3s | 30<br>**9** | 6 | Square skeleton tower, red and white rectangular daymark; 18. | |

Many lights of Newfoundland are maintained seasonally (from May to December).

| (1) No. | (2) Name and Location | (3) Position | (4) Characteristic | (5) Height | (6) Range | (7) Structure | (8) Remarks |
|---|---|---|---|---|---|---|---|

## CANADA-NEWFOUNDLAND

| (1) No. | (2) Name and Location | (3) Position | (4) Characteristic | (5) Height | (6) Range | (7) Structure | (8) Remarks |
|---|---|---|---|---|---|---|---|
| 2456 *H 0232.4* | Ile aux Morts, wharf. | 47° 34.9′ N 58° 58.8′ W | **Fl.G.** period 3s | 12 **4** | 4 | Square mast; 8. | |
| 2460 *H 0230* | Margaree Point. | 47° 34.2′ N 59° 04.0′ W | **Fl.W.** period 4s | 21 **6** | 6 | Square skeleton tower, red and white rectangular daymark; 12. | |
| | PORT AUX BASQUES: | | | | | | |
| 2468 *H 0222* | **-Channel Head.** | 47° 34.0′ N 59° 07.4′ W | **Fl.W.** period 10s fl. 1s, ec. 9s | 95 **29** | **17** | White cylindrical tower; 25. | **Horn:** 1 bl. ev. 60s (bl. 4s, si. 56s). Horn points 178°. |
| | -RACON | | **C(– • – •)** | | | | |
| 2469 *H 0222.4* | -Channel Gut Wharf. | 47° 34.0′ N 59° 07.6′ W | **Fl.R.** period 4s | 12 **4** | 2 | Mast; 8. | |
| 2469.5 *H 0222.6* | -Fish Plant Point Wharf (Motherlake Bay). | 47° 34.2′ N 59° 08.5′ W | **Fl.R.** period 4s | | 2 | Mast; 9. | |
| 2472 *H 0224* | -Graveyard Point, breakwater. | 47° 34.4′ N 59° 07.8′ W | **Fl.W.** period 4s | 30 **9** | 5 | Cylindrical mast; 7. | Outer end floodlit. |
| 2476 *H 0226* | -Pikes Island, breakwater. | 47° 34.5′ N 59° 07.9′ W | **Fl.R.** period 4s | 56 **17** | 5 | Triangular mast, red and white rectangular daymark; 33. | |
| 2480 *H 0227* | -Vardys (Rhode) Island, SW. point. | 47° 34.6′ N 59° 08.2′ W | **Fl.R.** period 4s | 19 **6** | 7 | Square skeleton tower, red and white rectangular daymark; 14. | |
| 2484 *H 0223* | -Entrance Range, front. | 47° 34.8′ N 59° 08.5′ W | **F.G.** | 127 **39** | 14 | Square skeleton tower, red trapezoidal daymark, white stripe; 21. | Visible on range line only. |
| 2488 *H 0223.1* | --Rear, about 202 meters 300°43′ from front. | 47° 34.8′ N 59° 08.7′ W | **F.G.** | 220 **67** | 14 | Square skeleton tower, red trapezoidal daymark, white stripe; 22. | Visible on range line only. |
| 2492 *H 0220* | **Cape Ray.** | 47° 37.3′ N 59° 18.2′ W | **Fl.W.** period 15s fl. 1s, ec. 14s | 118 **36** | **17** | White octagonal tower, red daymark, white bands; 58. | **Horn:** 1 bl. ev. 60s (bl. 4s, si. 56s). Horn points 224°. |
| 2496 *H 0219* | Codroy, island, S. head. | 47° 52.2′ N 59° 24.1′ W | **Fl.G.** period 6s fl. 1s, ec. 5s | 23 **7** | | Square skeleton tower, green and white rectangular daymark; 16. | |
| 2504 *H 0218* | **Cape Anquille.** | 47° 54.1′ N 59° 24.7′ W | **Fl.W.** period 5s fl. 0.1s, ec. 4.9s | 81 **25** | **15** | White octagonal tower; 58. | **Horn:** 1 bl. ev. 30s. (bl. 3s, si. 27s). Horn points 289°. |
| | ST. GEORGE'S HARBOR: | | | | | | |
| 2516 *H 0208* | -Sandy Point, N. side of harbor. | 48° 27.4′ N 58° 29.3′ W | **Fl.W.** period 6s fl. 1s, ec. 5s | 35 **11** | 5 | Cylindrical tower, red and white bands; 33. | Seasonal. |
| 2520 *H 0210* | -Flintkote Wharf. | 48° 26.6′ N 58° 28.5′ W | **Fl.G.** period 4s | 21 **6** | 4 | Skeleton tower. | Seasonal. Private light. |
| 2524 *H 0214* | -Public wharf, head. | 48° 25.9′ N 58° 29.2′ W | **Fl.G.** period 6s fl. 1s, ec. 5s | 10 **3** | 2 | Mast; 9. | Seasonal. |
| 2534 *H 0214.2* | St. George's Icebreak. | 48° 26.1′ N 58° 29.6′ W | **F.G.** | 11 **3** | | Square tower, red and yellow bands; 4. | Private light. |
| 2535 *H 0214.3* | -Icebreak, N. | 48° 26.2′ N 58° 30.0′ W | **Fl.R.** period 3s | 17 **5** | | Square tower, yellow and red bands; 4. | Seasonal. Private light. |
| 2536 *H 0205* | Port Harmon. | 48° 30.5′ N 58° 32.5′ W | **Fl.W.** period 3s | 17 **5** | 5 | Cylindrical mast; 8. | |

Many lights of Newfoundland are maintained seasonally (from May to December).

**CANADA-NEWFOUNDLAND**

| (1)<br>No. | (2)<br>Name and Location | (3)<br>Position | (4)<br>Characteristic | (5)<br>Height | (6)<br>Range | (7)<br>Structure | (8)<br>Remarks |
|---|---|---|---|---|---|---|---|
| 2537<br>*H 0205.08* | -SW. breakwater. | 48° 30.5′ N<br>58° 32.3′ W | **Fl.R.**<br>period 4s | 13<br>**4** | 4 | Cylindrical mast; 7. | |
| 2540<br>*H 0206* | -Port Harmon Range, front. | 48° 32.0′ N<br>58° 31.4′ W | **F.G.** | 140<br>**43** | 14 | Square skeleton mast, red trapezoidal daymark, white stripe; 89. | Visible on range line only. |
| 2544<br>*H 0206.1* | --Rear, 244 meters 024° from front. | 48° 32.1′ N<br>58° 31.3′ W | **F.G.** | 183<br>**56** | **15** | Square skeleton mast, red trapezoidal daymark, white stripe; 89. | Visible on range line only. |
| 2548<br>*H 0205.2* | -Port Harmon Channel, W. side. | 48° 30.6′ N<br>58° 32.4′ W | **Fl.G.**<br>period 6s<br>fl. 0.5s, ec. 5.5s | 17<br>**5** | 4 | Cylindrical mast; 8. | |
| 2560<br>*H 0202* | Red Island, NW. side | 48° 33.9′ N<br>59° 13.9′ W | **Fl.W.**<br>period 3s<br>fl. 0.5s, ec. 2.5s | 213<br>**65** | 7 | Skeleton tower, white daymark; 22. | |
| | PORT AU PORT BAY: | | | | | | |
| 2568<br>*H 0196* | -Long Point, near extremity. | 48° 46.7′ N<br>58° 46.3′ W | **Fl.W.**<br>period 6s<br>fl. 0.5s, ec. 5.5s | 48<br>**15** | 5 | Skeleton tower, red slatwork daymark; 36. | |
| 2572<br>*H 0197* | -Beach Point Breakwater. | 48° 46.0′ N<br>58° 46.9′ W | **Fl.R.**<br>period 4s | 14<br>**4** | 4 | Cylindrical mast; 7. | |
| 2576<br>*H 0197.2* | -S. | 48° 45.9′ N<br>58° 47.0′ W | **Fl.G.**<br>period 4s | 14<br>**4** | 4 | Cylindrical mast; 7. | |
| 2580<br>*H 0198* | -Broad Cove Point. | 48° 45.6′ N<br>58° 37.9′ W | **Fl.W.**<br>period 4s<br>fl. 0.5s, ec. 3.5s | 140<br>**43** | 7 | Square skeleton tower, red and white rectangular daymarks; 19. | Seasonal. |
| 2592<br>*H 0201* | -Fox Brook. | 48° 42.3′ N<br>58° 40.1′ W | **Fl.G.**<br>period 3s<br>fl. 0.5s, ec. 2.5s | 10<br>**3** | 3 | Cylindrical mast; 7. | |
| 2596<br>*H 0195* | Shag Island, N. head. | 48° 52.1′ N<br>58° 35.3′ W | **Fl.W.**<br>period 4s<br>fl. 0.5s, ec. 3.5s | 104<br>**32** | 6 | Square skeleton tower, red rectangular daymark, white stripe; 12. | Seasonal. |
| | BAY OF ISLANDS: | | | | | | |
| 2600<br>*H 0194* | -Little Port Head, S. side of entrance. | 49° 06.5′ N<br>58° 25.7′ W | **Fl.W.**<br>period 6s<br>fl. 1s, ec. 5s | 221<br>**67** | 5 | Square skeleton tower, red and white rectangular daymark; 32. | Seasonal. |
| 2604<br>*H 0192* | -South Head. | 49° 08.8′ N<br>58° 22.2′ W | **Fl.W.**<br>period 4s<br>fl. 0.5s, ec. 3.5s | 116<br>**35** | 6 | Red cylindrical tower, white bands; 36. | |
| 2608<br>*H 0190* | -White Point. | 49° 08.5′ N<br>58° 21.1′ W | **Fl.W.**<br>period 6s<br>fl. 1s, ec. 5s | 100<br>**30** | 6 | Skeleton tower, white daymark; 14. | |
| 2616<br>*H 0178* | -Eagle Island, S. head. | 49° 09.7′ N<br>58° 08.8′ W | **Fl.W.**<br>period 6s<br>fl. 1s, ec. 5s | 109<br>**33** | 6 | Square skeleton tower, red rectangular daymark, white stripe; 12. | Seasonal. |
| 2620<br>*H 0179* | -Middle Arm Point. | 49° 07.9′ N<br>58° 08.8′ W | **Fl.W.**<br>period 4s | 72<br>**22** | 6 | Square skeleton tower, red and white rectangular daymark; 12. | Seasonal. |
| 2624<br>*H 0188* | -Woods Island, W. side. | 49° 05.7′ N<br>58° 13.3′ W | **Fl.R.**<br>period 6s<br>fl. 1s, ec. 5s | 36<br>**11** | 3 | Triangular skeleton tower, red and white rectangular daymark; 15. | |
| 2628<br>*H 0186* | -Frenchman's Head, S. of old tower. | 49° 03.4′ N<br>58° 09.5′ W | **Fl.W.**<br>period 6s<br>fl. 0.5s, ec. 5.5s | 271<br>**83** | 7 | Rectangular skeleton tower, red and white rectangular daymark; 32. | |

Many lights of Newfoundland are maintained seasonally (from May to December).

| (1) No. | (2) Name and Location | (3) Position | (4) Characteristic | (5) Height | (6) Range | (7) Structure | (8) Remarks |
|---|---|---|---|---|---|---|---|
| | | | **CANADA-NEWFOUNDLAND** | | | | |
| 2632 *H 0180* | -Meadows Point, on Humber Arm. | 48° 59.5´ N 58° 03.6´ W | **Fl.G.** period 3s fl. 0.5s, ec. 2.5s | 67 **20** | 5 | Square skeleton tower, green and white rectangular daymark; 30. | Seasonal. |
| 2634 *H 0179.5* | -Corner Brook, W. breakwater. | 48° 57.9´ N 58° 01.2´ W | **Fl.R.** period 4s | | 2 | Cylindrical mast. | |
| 2636 *H 0175* | Trout River, W. entrance point. | 49° 28.9´ N 58° 08.2´ W | **Fl.W.** period 6s fl. 1s, ec. 5s | 80 **24** | 5 | Red and white square skeleton tower, red and white rectangular daymark; 12. | Seasonal. |
| 2640 *H 0164* | Lobster Cove Head, N. side of entrance to Bonne Bay. | 49° 36.2´ N 57° 57.4´ W | **Iso.W.** period 4s | 115 **35** | 12 | White round tower; 28. | |
| | BONNE BAY: | | | | | | |
| 2644 *H 0168* | -Woody Point. | 49° 30.3´ N 57° 54.9´ W | **Fl.R.** period 4s | 45 **14** | 4 | White structure; 24. | |
| 2648 *H 0169* | -Norris Point. | 49° 30.9´ N 57° 52.8´ W | **Fl.G.** period 4s | 23 **7** | 5 | Skeleton tower, white rectangular daymark, red stripe; 18. | Seasonal. |
| 2652 *H 0170* | -Gadds Point. | 49° 30.7´ N 57° 52.7´ W | **Fl.W.** period 4s | 46 **14** | 5 | Square skeleton tower, red and white rectangular daymarks; 14. | Seasonal. |
| 2660 *H 0161* | Parson's Pond, S. side of brook. | 50° 01.6´ N 57° 42.9´ W | **Fl.R.** period 6s fl. 0.5s, ec. 5.5s | 33 **10** | 4 | Square skeleton tower, red and white rectangular daymark; 10. | Seasonal. |
| 2668 *H 0156* | **Keppel Island,** NW. point. | 50° 37.9´ N 57° 19.4´ W | **Fl.W.** period 15s fl. 1s, ec. 14s | 120 **36** | **17** | Square skeleton tower, red daymark, white band; 37. | Seasonal. **Horn:** 1 bl. ev. 30s. (bl. 3s, si. 27s). Horn points 143°. |
| 2680 *H 0154* | **Pointe Riche.** | 50° 41.8´ N 57° 24.7´ W | **Fl.W.** period 5s fl. 0.2s, ec. 4.8s | 96 **29** | **15** | White octagonal tower, red upper portion; 65. | Seasonal. |
| 2688 *H 0152* | Port aux Choix, on Querre Island. | 50° 43.2´ N 57° 20.0´ W | **Fl.W.** period 6s fl. 1s, ec. 5s | 28 **8** | 6 | Square skeleton tower, red and white rectangular daymark; 16. | Seasonal. |
| 2692 *H 0152.5* | Port au Choix Range, front. | 50° 42.2´ N 57° 21.5´ W | **F.R.** | 68 **21** | 13 | Skeleton tower, red trapezoidal daymark, white stripe; 29. | Seasonal. |
| 2696 *H 0152.51* | -Rear, 237 meters 224°30′ from front. | 50° 42.2´ N 57° 21.7´ W | **F.R.** | 82 **25** | 13 | Skeleton tower, red trapezoidal daymark, white stripe; 31. | Seasonal. |
| 2700 *H 0150* | White Island, on W. end of islet. | 50° 55.8´ N 57° 01.8´ W | **Fl.W.** period 6s fl. 1s, ec. 5s | 31 **9** | 6 | Square skeleton tower, red rectangular daymark, white stripe; 22. | Seasonal. |
| 2704 *H 0148* | **Ferolle Point.** | 51° 01.3´ N 57° 05.8´ W | **Q.(4)W.** period 7.5s | 91 **28** | **20** | White octagonal tower, red upper portion; 62. | Seasonal. **Horn:** 1 bl. ev. 60s. (bl. 4s, si. 56s). Horn points 314°30′. |
| 2714 *H 0146.5* | Black Duck. | 51° 11.8´ N 56° 47.9´ W | **Fl.R.** period 4s | 13 **4** | 3 | Mast; 10. | Seasonal. |
| 2716 *H 0145* | St. Barbe Point, S. side of St. Barbe Bay. | 51° 12.4´ N 56° 46.6´ W | **Fl.R.** period 4s | 20 **6** | 4 | Skeleton tower, orange daymark; 16. | Seasonal. |
| 2717 *H 0145.7* | St. Barbe Range, front. | 51° 12.5´ N 56° 46.1´ W | **F.G.** | 30 **9** | 11 | Square skeleton tower, white trapezoidal daymark, black stripe; 20. | Seasonal. |
| 2718 *H 0145.71* | -Rear, 140 meters 105° from front. | 51° 12.5´ N 56° 46.0´ W | **F.G.** | 43 **13** | 11 | Square skeleton tower, white trapezoidal daymark, black stripe; 13. | Seasonal. |
| 2720 *H 0144.5* | Anchor Point. | 51° 14.0´ N 56° 48.0´ W | **Fl.G.** period 4s | 23 **7** | 3 | Mast; 8. | Seasonal. |

Many lights of Newfoundland are maintained seasonally (from May to December).

| (1) No. | (2) Name and Location | (3) Position | (4) Characteristic | (5) Height | (6) Range | (7) Structure | (8) Remarks |
|---|---|---|---|---|---|---|---|

## CANADA-NEWFOUNDLAND

| (1) No. | (2) Name and Location | (3) Position | (4) Characteristic | (5) Height | (6) Range | (7) Structure | (8) Remarks |
|---|---|---|---|---|---|---|---|
| 2722 *H 0141.7* | Savage Cove wharf. | 51° 15.5′ N 56° 47.4′ W | **Fl.G.** period 4s | 12 **4** | 4 | Mast; 9. | Seasonal. |
| 2724 *H 0144* | Flowers Cove. | 51° 17.7′ N 56° 44.8′ W | **Fl.G.** period 3s | 18 **5** | 4 | Square skeleton tower, green and white rectangular daymark; 16. | Seasonal. |
| 2728 *H 0143* | -Flowers Cove Range, front. | 51° 17.6′ N 56° 44.6′ W | **F.R.** | 16 **5** | 13 | Skeleton tower, orange trapezoidal daymark, black stripe; 12. | Seasonal. |
| 2732 *H 0143.1* | --Rear, 114 meters 107° from front. | 51° 17.6′ N 56° 44.5′ W | **F.R.** | 26 **8** | 13 | Skeleton tower, orange trapezoidal daymark, black stripe; 18. | Seasonal. |
| 2736 *H 0142* | **Nameless Point.** | 51° 18.7′ N 56° 44.5′ W | **Fl.W.** period 10s fl. 1s, ec. 9s | 52 **16** | **15** | Skeleton tower; 40. | Seasonal. |
| 2736.5 | Sandy Cove. | 51° 20.7′ N 56° 40.6′ W | **Fl.R.** period 4s | 12 **4** | 3 | Mast; 7. | Seasonal. |
| 2737 *H 0141* | Green Island Brook. | 51° 24.0′ N 56° 31.3′ W | **Fl.R.** period 4s | 20 **6** | 3 | Cylindrical mast; 10. | Seasonal. |
| 2739 *H 0141.2* | Green Island Cove. | 51° 23.0′ N 56° 34.7′ W | **Fl.R.** period 6s fl. 1s, ec. 5s | 10 **3** | 4 | Cylindrical tower; 10. | Seasonal. |

Many lights of Newfoundland are maintained seasonally (from May to December).

# Section 3

## North Side of Gulf of St. Lawrence and St. Lawrence River

| (1)<br>No. | (2)<br>Name and Location | (3)<br>Position | (4)<br>Characteristic | (5)<br>Height | (6)<br>Range | (7)<br>Structure | (8)<br>Remarks |
|---|---|---|---|---|---|---|---|
| | | | **CANADA-GULF OF ST. LAWRENCE** | | | | |
| 2740.5<br>*H 0117* | -L'Anse au Clair Wharf. | 51° 25.4′ N<br>57° 04.0′ W | **Fl.G.**<br>period 4s<br>fl. 0.5s, ec. 3.5s | 16<br>**5** | 4 | Mast; 7. | Seasonal. |
| 2752<br>*H 0124* | Bradore Bay Range, front. | 51° 29.5′ N<br>57° 15.0′ W | **Iso.R.**<br>period 2s | 65<br>**20** | 12 | Square skeleton tower, orange trapezoidal daymark, black stripe; 50. | Visible on range line only.<br>Seasonal. |
| 2756<br>*H 0124.1* | -Rear, 96 meters 005°06′ from front. | 51° 29.5′ N<br>57° 15.0′ W | **Iso.R.**<br>period 2s | 103<br>**31** | 12 | Square skeleton tower, orange trapezoidal daymark, black stripe; 15. | Visible on range line only.<br>Seasonal. |
| 2772<br>*H 1890* | Whale Island, summit. | 51° 21.3′ N<br>57° 41.8′ W | **Fl.W.**<br>period 6s<br>fl. 1s, ec. 5s | 92<br>**28** | 7 | Square skeleton tower; 33. | Seasonal. |
| | BONNE ESPERANCE BAY: | | | | | | |
| 2776<br>*H 1887* | -Baie au Saumon Range, front. | 51° 25.8′ N<br>57° 39.2′ W | **Iso.G.**<br>period 2s | 68<br>**21** | 12 | Square skeleton tower, orange trapezoidal daymark, black stripe; 50. | Visible on range line only.<br>Seasonal. |
| 2780<br>*H 1887.1* | --Rear, 249 meters 349°08′ from front. | 51° 25.9′ N<br>57° 39.3′ W | **Iso.G.**<br>period 2s | 98<br>**30** | 12 | Square skeleton tower, orange trapezoidal daymark, black stripe; 20. | Visible on range line only.<br>Seasonal. |
| 2800<br>*H 1889.5* | St. Paul River, (Champlain Passage) E. side of S. entrance. | 51° 25.2′ N<br>57° 42.0′ W | **Fl.R.**<br>period 6s<br>fl. 1s, ec. 5s | 20<br>**6** | 6 | Red and white square skeleton tower; 15. | Seasonal. |
| 2801<br>*H 1889.7* | Chenal du Vieux Fort Range, front. | 51° 23.9′ N<br>57° 48.3′ W | **F.R.** | 67<br>**20** | 14 | Square skeleton tower, orange trapezoidal daymark, black stripe; 30. | Visible on range line only.<br>Seasonal. |
| 2802<br>*H 1889.71* | -Rear, 336 meters 011°02′ from front. | 51° 24.1′ N<br>57° 48.2′ W | **F.R.** | 100<br>**30** | | Square skeleton tower, orange trapezoidal daymark, black stripe; 10. | Seasonal. |
| 2804<br>*H 1889.8* | Old Fort Bay, wharf, head. | 51° 25.3′ N<br>57° 48.9′ W | **Fl.Y.**<br>period 6s<br>fl. 1s, ec. 5s | 28<br>**9** | 7 | Mast; 20. | Seasonal. |
| 2808<br>*H 1890.1* | Mermot Island. | 51° 19.3′ N<br>57° 50.7′ W | **Iso.W.**<br>period 2s | 38<br>**12** | | Square skeleton tower; 23. | |
| | RACON | | **M(– –)** | | 10 | | (3 & 10cm). |
| 2812<br>*H 1890.2* | Mistanoque Island. | 51° 15.3′ N<br>58° 12.7′ W | **Iso.W.**<br>period 2s | 137<br>**42** | 6 | Square skeleton tower; 21. | Seasonal. |
| 2816<br>*H 1890.42* | Northeast Point, outer island. | 51° 10.6′ N<br>58° 25.7′ W | **Fl.W.**<br>period 6s<br>fl. 1s, ec. 5s | 59<br>**18** | 7 | Square skeleton tower, two orange rectangular daymarks; 23. | |
| | RACON | | **N(– •)** | | 10 | | (3 & 10cm). |
| 2820<br>*H 1890.44* | **Northeast Point Range,** front. | 51° 10.5′ N<br>58° 25.4′ W | **F.R.** | 32<br>**10** | **15** | Square skeleton tower, orange trapezoidal daymark, black stripe; 16. | Visible on range line only. |
| 2824<br>*H 1890.45* | -Rear, 274 meters 269°37′ from front. | 51° 10.5′ N<br>58° 25.6′ W | **F.R.** | 63<br>**19** | **15** | Square skeleton tower, orange trapezoidal daymark, black stripe; 16. | Visible on range line only. |
| 2828<br>*H 1890.5* | Ile Paul Nadeau SE. extremity. | 51° 10.7′ N<br>58° 27.8′ W | **Fl.W.**<br>period 6s<br>fl. 1s, ec. 5s | 44<br>**13** | 7 | Red and white square skeleton tower; 16. | |

| (1) No. | (2) Name and Location | (3) Position | (4) Characteristic | (5) Height | (6) Range | (7) Structure | (8) Remarks |
|---|---|---|---|---|---|---|---|

## CANADA-GULF OF ST. LAWRENCE

| (1) No. | (2) Name and Location | (3) Position | (4) Characteristic | (5) Height | (6) Range | (7) Structure | (8) Remarks |
|---|---|---|---|---|---|---|---|
| 2829 *H 1890.63* | St. Augustin Passage. | 51° 10.9′ N 58° 34.1′ W | **Fl.Y.** period 6s fl. 1s, ec. 5s | 30 **9** | 7 | Mast; 26. | |
| 2830 *H 1890.77* | -River mouth. | 51° 13.3′ N 58° 38.7′ W | **Fl.Y.** period 6s fl. 1s, ec. 5s | 75 **23** | 6 | Square skeleton tower; 15. | |
| 2832 *H 1890.6* | Tickle Island Range, front. | 51° 10.4′ N 58° 31.5′ W | **Iso.G.** period 2s | 36 **11** | 5 | Square skeleton tower, orange trapezoidal daymark, black stripe; 10. | |
| 2836 *H 1890.61* | -Rear, 624 meters 271°32′ from front. | 51° 10.4′ N 58° 32.1′ W | **F.G.** | 122 **37** | 14 | Square skeleton tower, orange trapezoidal daymark, black stripe; 20. | Visible on range line only. |
| 2837 *H 1890.7* | Robin Island Range, front. | 51° 08.9′ N 58° 33.4′ W | **Iso.R.** period 2s | 32 **10** | 12 | Square skeleton tower, orange trapezoidal daymark, black stripe; 26. | Visible on range line only. Seasonal. |
| 2838 *H 1890.71* | -Rear, 86 meters 021°11′ from front. | 51° 09.0′ N 58° 33.4′ W | **Iso.R.** period 2s | 59 **18** | 12 | Square skeleton tower, orange trapezoidal daymark, black stripe; 16. | Visible on range line only. Seasonal. |
| 2839 *H 1890.74* | **Inner Island Range,** front. | 51° 08.8′ N 58° 33.7′ W | **F.W.** | 26 **8** | **15** | Square skeleton tower, orange trapezoidal daymark, black stripe; 16. | Visible on range line only. Seasonal. |
| 2839.5 *H 1890.75* | -Rear, 155 meters 242°10′ from front | 51° 08.7′ N 58° 33.8′ W | **F.W.** | 77 **23** | **15** | Square skeleton tower, orange trapezoidal daymark, black stripe; 30. | Visible on range line only. Seasonal. |
| 2840 *H 1894* | Ile Plat. | 50° 45.2′ N 58° 45.3′ W | **Fl.W.** period 15s fl. 1s, ec. 14s | 75 **23** | 13 | Cylindrical mast; 25. | Seasonal. |
| 2844 *H 1890.8* | Ile du Guet. | 50° 55.8′ N 58° 52.7′ W | **Iso.W.** period 2s | 105 **32** | 6 | Square skeleton tower; 16. | |
| 2848 *H 1892* | La Boule. | 50° 50.2′ N 58° 52.5′ W | **Fl.W.** period 6s fl. 1s, ec. 5s | 243 **74** | 8 | Square skeleton tower; 15. | |
| 2852 *H 1891* | Ile Cormandiere, summit. | 50° 51.5′ N 58° 55.9′ W | **Fl.R.** period 6s fl. 1s, ec. 5s | 36 **11** | 6 | Square skeleton tower; 16. | |
| 2856 *H 1891.2* | Baie de Tabatiere Outer Range, front. | 50° 50.6′ N 58° 58.5′ W | **F.G.** | 133 **41** | 14 | Skeleton tower, orange trapezoidal daymark, black stripe; 100. | Visible on range line only. |
| 2860 *H 1891.3* | -Rear, about 157 meters 234°45′ from front. | 50° 50.6′ N 58° 58.6′ W | **F.G.** | 167 **51** | **15** | Square skeleton tower, orange trapezoidal daymark, black stripe; 15. | Visible on range line only. |
| 2864 *H 1891.5* | -Inner Range, front. | 50° 50.2′ N 58° 58.4′ W | **F.R.** | 57 **17** | 14 | Square skeleton tower, orange trapezoidal daymark, black stripe; 51. | Visible on range line only. |
| 2868 *H 1891.6* | --Rear, about 82 meters 193°25′ from front. | 50° 50.1′ N 58° 58.4′ W | **F.R.** | 79 **24** | 14 | Square skeleton tower, orange trapezoidal daymark, black stripe; 16. | Visible on range line only. |
| 2872 *H 1898* | Entrance Island, summit. | 50° 44.1′ N 59° 00.4′ W | **Fl.W.** period 6s fl. 1s, ec. 5s | 60 **18** | 8 | Square skeleton tower; 21. | |
| 2876 *H 1896* | **Mutton Bay Range,** front, W. side of entrance. | 50° 46.2′ N 59° 02.0′ W | **F.G.** | 43 **13** | **16** | Square skeleton tower, orange trapezoidal daymark, black stripe; 43. | Visible on range line only. Seasonal. |
| 2880 *H 1896.1* | -Rear, about 336 meters 322°30′ from front. | 50° 46.3′ N 59° 02.2′ W | **F.G.** | 75 **23** | **16** | Square skeleton tower, orange trapezoidal daymark, black stripe; 20. | Visible on range line only. Seasonal. |
| 2884 *H 1899* | **Whale Head Anchorage Range,** Vatcher Island, NW. side, front. | 50° 39.7′ N 59° 12.0′ W | **F.W.** | 30 **9** | **15** | Square skeleton tower, orange trapezoidal daymark, black stripe; 20. | Visible on range line only. |

| (1) No. | (2) Name and Location | (3) Position | (4) Characteristic | (5) Height | (6) Range | (7) Structure | (8) Remarks |
|---|---|---|---|---|---|---|---|

## CANADA-GULF OF ST. LAWRENCE

| (1) No. | (2) Name and Location | (3) Position | (4) Characteristic | (5) Height | (6) Range | (7) Structure | (8) Remarks |
|---|---|---|---|---|---|---|---|
| 2888 *H 1899.1* | -Rear, 110.4 meters 001°08′ from front. | 50° 39.7′ N 59° 12.0′ W | **F.W.** | 46 **14** | **15** | Square skeleton tower, orange trapezoidal daymark, black stripe; 16. | Visible on range line only. |
| 2892 *H 1899.7* | Whale Head center Range, front. | 50° 39.7′ N 59° 14.1′ W | **F.R.** | 16 **5** | 13 | Square skeleton tower, orange trapezoidal daymark, black stripe; 10. | Visible on range line only. |
| 2896 *H 1899.8* | -Rear, about 422 meters 293°34′ from front. | 50° 39.8′ N 59° 14.4′ W | **F.R.** | 39 **12** | 13 | Square skeleton tower, orange trapezoidal daymark, black stripe; 20. | Visible on range line only. |
| 2900 *H 1899.4* | Ile du Grand Rigolet Range, front. | 50° 40.8′ N 59° 14.5′ W | **F.G.** | 28 **8** | 13 | Square skeleton tower, orange trapezoidal daymark, black stripe; 20. | Visible on range line only. |
| 2904 *H 1899.5* | -Rear, about 96.4 meters 330°04′ from front. | 50° 40.8′ N 59° 14.6′ W | **F.G.** | 66 **20** | 13 | Square skeleton tower, orange trapezoidal daymark, black stripe; 10. | Visible on range line only. |
| 2908 *H 1899.9* | -Wharf, seaward end. | 50° 40.8′ N 59° 14.4′ W | **Fl.Y.** period 3s fl. 1s, ec. 2s | 27 **8** | 6 | Square skeleton tower; 20. | |
| 2912 *H 1901* | Cape Airey, S. end of Cape Island. | 50° 28.2′ N 59° 27.4′ W | **Fl.G.** period 6s fl. 1s, ec. 5s | 59 **18** | 6 | Square skeleton tower; 23. | |
| 2916 *H 1900* | Entry Cliff, S. side of island, N. side of channel to Harrington Harbor. | 50° 29.3′ N 59° 27.7′ W | **Fl.W.** period 6s fl. 1s, ec. 5s | 139 **42** | 8 | Square skeleton tower; 33. | |
| 2920 *H 1900.4* | Entry Island, NW. point of island. | 50° 29.6′ N 59° 28.1′ W | **Fl.G.** period 6s fl. 1s, ec. 5s | 26 **8** | 6 | Square skeleton tower; 23. | |
| 2924 *H 1902* | Harrington Harbor, Entry Passage Range, front. | 50° 29.6′ N 59° 29.0′ W | **F.R.** | 33 **10** | 13 | Square skeleton tower, orange trapezoidal daymark, black stripe; 21. | Visible on range line only. |
| 2928 *H 1902.1* | -Rear, about 189 meters 288°44′ from front. | 50° 29.6′ N 59° 29.2′ W | **F.R.** | 49 **15** | 13 | Square skeleton tower, orange trapezoidal daymark, black stripe; 14. | Visible on range line only. |
| 2932 *H 1904* | St. Mary Islands. | 50° 18.3′ N 59° 39.4′ W | **Fl.W.** period 2.5s fl. 0.1s, ec. 2.4s | 144 **44** | 12 | Square skeleton tower; 52. | Seasonal. |
| 2936 *H 1903* | Netagamu River, outer end of wharf. | 50° 28.4′ N 59° 36.4′ W | **Fl.R.** period 6s fl. 1s, ec. 5s | 29 **9** | 5 | Square mast; 21. | Seasonal. |
| 2940 *H 1906* | **Cape Whittle.** | 50° 09.8′ N 60° 03.6′ W | **Fl.W.** period 15s fl. 1s, ec. 14s | 79 **24** | **15** | Square skeleton tower; 51. | Seasonal. |
| 2948 *H 1907* | Milne Point Range, front. | 50° 13.4′ N 60° 18.9′ W | **F.R.** | 55 **17** | 13 | Square skeleton tower, orange trapezoidal daymark, black stripe; 35. | Visible on range line only. Seasonal. |
| 2952 *H 1907.1* | -Rear, 295 meters 004°40′ from front. | 50° 13.5′ N 60° 18.9′ W | **F.R.** | 101 **31** | 13 | Square skeleton tower, orange trapezoidal daymark, black stripe; 30. | Visible on range line only. Seasonal. |
| | GETHSEMANI (ROMAINE): | | | | | | |
| 2956 *H 1909* | Gethsemani (Romaine) Harbor Channel Range, front. | 50° 12.4′ N 60° 41.2′ W | **F.R.** | 33 **10** | 13 | Square skeleton tower, orange trapezoidal daymark, black stripe; 20. | Visible on range line only. |
| 2960 *H 1909.1* | -Rear, about 80 meters 357°21′ from front. | 50° 12.5′ N 60° 41.2′ W | **F.R.** | 42 **13** | 13 | Square skeleton tower, orange trapezoidal daymark, black stripe; 15. | Visible on range line only. |
| 2968 *H 1909.8* | -Little Lake Point Range, front. | 50° 12.8′ N 60° 41.4′ W | **F.G.** | 39 **12** | 13 | Square skeleton tower, orange trapezoidal daymark, black stripe; 20. | Visible on range line only. |

| (1) No. | (2) Name and Location | (3) Position | (4) Characteristic | (5) Height | (6) Range | (7) Structure | (8) Remarks |
|---|---|---|---|---|---|---|---|
| | | | **CANADA-GULF OF ST. LAWRENCE** | | | | |
| 2972 *H 1909.81* | --Rear, 75 meters 013°11′ from front. | 50° 12.9′ N 60° 41.3′ W | **F.G.** | 46 **14** | 13 | Square skeleton tower, orange trapezoidal daymark, black stripe; 10. | Visible on range line only. |
| 2976 *H 1909.7* | -**Makenzie Point Range,** front. | 50° 12.8′ N 60° 41.8′ W | **F.Y.** | 33 **10** | **15** | Square skeleton tower, orange trapezoidal daymark, black stripe; 10. | Visible on range line only. |
| 2980 *H 1909.71* | --Rear, 106 meters 325°45′ from front. | 50° 12.9′ N 60° 41.9′ W | **F.Y.** | 43 **13** | **15** | Square skeleton tower, orange trapezoidal daymark, black stripe; 20. | Visible on range line only. |
| 2988 *H 1908* | Treble Island, S. side. | 50° 10.1′ N 60° 41.8′ W | **Fl.W.** period 6s fl. 1s, ec. 5s | 62 **19** | 7 | Square skeleton tower; 20. | |
| 2992 *H 1911* | Kegashka Point. | 50° 10.5′ N 61° 16.0′ W | **Fl.W.** period 6s fl. 1s, ec. 5s | 46 **14** | 8 | Square skeleton tower; 20. | |
| 2994 *H 1910.4* | -Kegashka Wharf. | 50° 11.1′ N 61° 15.8′ W | **Fl.R.** period 6s fl. 1s, ec. 5s | 30 **9** | 6 | Square skeleton tower; 20. | |
| 2996 *H 1910* | **Kegashka Bay Range,** front. | 50° 11.8′ N 61° 15.6′ W | **F.W.** | 46 **14** | **16** | Square skeleton tower, orange trapezoidal daymark, black stripe; 20. | Visible on range line only. |
| 3000 *H 1910.1* | -Rear, 91 meters 000°30′ from front. | 50° 11.8′ N 61° 15.6′ W | **F.W.** | 59 **18** | **16** | Square skeleton tower, orange trapezoidal daymark, black stripe; 20. | Visible on range line only. |
| | LITTLE NATASHQUAN HARBOR: | | | | | | |
| 3008 *H 1914* | -W. end of island at entrance to harbor. | 50° 10.9′ N 61° 50.6′ W | **Iso.G.** period 2s | 46 **14** | 6 | Square skeleton tower; 30. | **Radar reflector.** |
| 3012 *H 1918* | -Range, front. | 50° 11.6′ N 61° 50.6′ W | **F.W.** | 33 **10** | 13 | Square skeleton tower, orange trapezoidal daymark, black stripe; 21. | Visible on range line only. |
| 3016 *H 1918.1* | --Rear, 91 meters 009°55′ from front. | 50° 11.6′ N 61° 50.6′ W | **F.W.** | 56 **17** | 13 | Square skeleton tower, orange trapezoidal daymark, black stripe; 30. | Visible on range line only. |
| 3020 *H 1922* | **Aquanish (Goynish),** E. side of river entrance Range, front. | 50° 13.1′ N 62° 05.0′ W | **F.G.** | 36 **11** | **16** | Square skeleton tower, orange trapezoidal daymark, black stripe; 16. | Visible on range line only. Seasonal. |
| 3024 *H 1922.1* | -Rear, 479 meters 330°29′ from front. | 50° 13.3′ N 62° 05.2′ W | **F.G.** | 59 **18** | **16** | Square skeleton tower, orange trapezoidal daymark, black stripe; 25. | Visible on range line only. Seasonal. |
| 3028 *H 1928* | **Johan Beetz Bay Range,** front. | 50° 17.0′ N 62° 47.9′ W | **F.Y.** | 40 **12** | **15** | Square skeleton tower, orange trapezoidal daymark, black stripe; 30. | Visible on range line only. Seasonal. |
| 3032 *H 1928.1* | -Rear, 162.3 meters 043°04′ from front. | 50° 17.1′ N 62° 47.8′ W | **F.Y.** | 69 **21** | **15** | Square skeleton tower, orange trapezoidal daymark, black stripe; 20. | Visible on range line only. Seasonal. |
| 3036 *H 1930* | -Inner Range, front. | 50° 17.0′ N 62° 48.6′ W | **Iso.R.** period 2s | 25 **8** | 4 | Square skeleton tower, orange trapezoidal daymark, black stripe; 15. | Intensified on range line. Seasonal. |
| 3040 *H 1930.1* | --Rear, 126 meters 319°02′ from front. | 50° 17.1′ N 62° 48.7′ W | **Iso.R.** period 2s | 42 **13** | **16** | Square skeleton tower, orange trapezoidal daymark, black stripe; 16. | Visible on range line only. Seasonal. |
| 3046 *H 1933* | La Grande Point. | 50° 12.2′ N 63° 26.9′ W | **Fl.Y.** period 6s fl. 1s, ec. 5s | 36 **11** | 7 | Square skeleton tower; 25. | |
| 3048 *H 1934* | Petite Ile au Marteau. | 50° 12.2′ N 63° 33.5′ W | **Fl.W.** period 2.5s fl. 0.1s, ec. 2.4s | 94 **29** | 12 | Square skeleton tower; 84. | Seasonal. |

| (1) No. | (2) Name and Location | (3) Position | (4) Characteristic | (5) Height | (6) Range | (7) Structure | (8) Remarks |
|---|---|---|---|---|---|---|---|
| | | | **CANADA-GULF OF ST. LAWRENCE** | | | | |
| 3052 *H 1936* | **Havre-St.-Pierre Range,** front. | 50° 14.4′ N 63° 35.7′ W | **F.R.** | 45 **14** | **16** | Square skeleton tower, orange trapezoidal daymark, black stripe; 37. | Visible on range line only. |
| 3056 *H 1936.1* | -Rear, 175 meters 338°30′ from front. | 50° 14.5′ N 63° 35.8′ W | **F.R.** | 80 **24** | **16** | Skeleton tower, orange trapezoidal daymark, black stripe; 61. | Visible on range line only. |
| 3080 *H 1943* | -Ile du Fantome Entrance Range, front. | 50° 15.4′ N 63° 39.3′ W | **F.G.** | 32 **10** | 13 | Skeleton tower, orange trapezoidal daymark, black stripe; 25. | Visible on range line only. |
| 3084 *H 1943.1* | --Rear, 295.7 meters 010°04′ from front. | 50° 15.6′ N 63° 39.3′ W | **F.G.** | 63 **19** | 13 | Skeleton tower, orange trapezoidal daymark, black stripe; 61. | Visible on range line only. |
| 3088 *H 1940* | -**Eskimo Point Range,** front. | 50° 14.3′ N 63° 36.8′ W | **F.R.** | 46 **14** | **16** | Skeleton tower, orange trapezoidal daymark, black stripe; 40. | Visible on range line only. |
| 3092 *H 1940.1* | --Rear, 238 meters 096°31′ from front. | 50° 14.3′ N 63° 36.6′ W | **F.R.** | 76 **23** | **16** | Skeleton tower, orange trapezoidal daymark, black stripe; 59. | Visible on range line only. |
| 3104 *H 1944* | Ile a Firmin, S. end. | 50° 12.2′ N 63° 41.2′ W | **Fl.W.** period 6s fl. 1s, ec. 5s | 36 **11** | 7 | Skeleton tower, orange rectangular daymarks; 26. | |
| | MINGAN HARBOR: | | | | | | |
| 3108 *H 1946* | -Eastern entrance range, front. | 50° 17.4′ N 64° 01.3′ W | **F.G.** | 46 **14** | **16** | Skeleton tower, orange trapezoidal daymark, black stripe; 40. | Visible on range line only. |
| 3112 *H 1946.1* | --Rear, 189 meters 287°50′ from front. | 50° 17.4′ N 64° 01.5′ W | **F.G.** | 73 **22** | **16** | Skeleton tower, orange trapezoidal daymark, black stripe; 65. | Visible on range line only. |
| 3116 *H 1950* | -Western entrance range, front. | 50° 17.4′ N 64° 00.7′ W | **F.G.** | 23 **7** | **16** | Skeleton tower, orange trapezoidal daymark, black stripe; 20. | Visible on range line only. |
| 3120 *H 1950.1* | --Rear, 421 meters 065°47′ from front. | 50° 17.5′ N 64° 00.3′ W | **F.G.** | 69 **21** | **16** | Skeleton tower, two orange trapezoidal daymarks, black stripe; 50. | Visible on range line only. |
| 3124 *H 1958* | Iles aux Perroquets. | 50° 13.2′ N 64° 12.4′ W | **Fl.W.** period 5s fl. 1s, ec. 4s | 79 **24** | 12 | White octagonal tower, red upper portion; 35. | Obscured by Mingan Island between 269° and 292°. Seasonal. |
| | ANTICOSTI ISLAND: | | | | | | |
| 3130 | --AVIATION LIGHT. | 49° 05.1′ N 61° 42.1′ W | **Fl.W.** period 1.5s fl. 0.2s, ec. 1.3s | 420 **128** | **15** | Skeleton tower; 403. | |
| | | | **Fl.W.** period 1.5s | 223 **68** | **15** | | |
| 3132 *H 1864* | -Bagot Bluff, N.W. of South Point. | 49° 04.0′ N 62° 15.6′ W | **Fl.W.** period 6s fl. 1s, ec. 5s | 56 **17** | 7 | Square skeleton tower; 50. | |
| 3136 *H 1866* | -SW. Point, on extremity. | 49° 23.5′ N 63° 35.7′ W | **Fl.W.** period 6s fl. 1s, ec. 5s | 68 **21** | 8 | Square skeleton tower; 50. | |
| 3144 *H 1870* | -**Baie Ellis Main Range,** front, NW. side of bay. | 49° 49.5′ N 64° 22.5′ W | **F.G.** | 40 **12** | **20** | Square skeleton tower, orange trapezoidal daymark, black stripe; 30. | Visible on range line only. Seasonal. |
| 3148 *H 1870.1* | --Rear, 1042 meters 339°25′ from front. | 49° 50.0′ N 64° 22.8′ W | **F.G.** | 88 **27** | **20** | Square skeleton tower, orange trapezoidal daymark, black stripe; 50. | Visible on range line only. Seasonal. |

| (1) No. | (2) Name and Location | (3) Position | (4) Characteristic | (5) Height | (6) Range | (7) Structure | (8) Remarks |
|---|---|---|---|---|---|---|---|

## CANADA-GULF OF ST. LAWRENCE

| (1) No. | (2) Name and Location | (3) Position | (4) Characteristic | (5) Height | (6) Range | (7) Structure | (8) Remarks |
|---|---|---|---|---|---|---|---|
| 3160 *H 1878* | -West Point. | 49° 51.8′ N 64° 31.4′ W | **Fl.W.** period 5s fl. 1s, ec. 4s | 92 **28** | 12 | Skeleton tower; 66. | |
| 3164 *H 1882* | **Cap de Rabast.** | 49° 57.1′ N 64° 08.9′ W | **Fl.(3)W.** period 30s | 78 **24** | **17** | White octagonal tower; 72. | Seasonal. |
| 3168 *H 1884* | -Carleton Point. | 49° 43.9′ N 62° 56.6′ W | **Fl.G.** period 6s fl. 1s, ec. 5s | 126 **38** | 5 | White octagonal tower; 40. | |
| 3172 *H 1886* | -Table Head. | 49° 21.1′ N 61° 53.8′ W | **Fl.R.** period 6s fl. 1s, ec. 5s | 112 **34** | 5 | Red and white octagonal tower; 40. | |

## CANADA-ST. LAWRENCE ESTUARY, NORTH SIDE

| (1) No. | (2) Name and Location | (3) Position | (4) Characteristic | (5) Height | (6) Range | (7) Structure | (8) Remarks |
|---|---|---|---|---|---|---|---|
| 3176 *H 1975* | Riviere-au-Tonnere. | 50° 16.4′ N 64° 47.0′ W | **F.R.** | 33 **10** | 6 | Square skeleton tower, two orange and black rectangular daymarks; 23. | Seasonal. |
| 3184 *H 1974* | **-Riviere-au-Tonnerre Range,** front. | 50° 16.6′ N 64° 46.9′ W | **F.G.** | 62 **19** | **16** | Square skeleton tower, orange trapezoidal daymark, black stripe; 30. | Visible on range line only. Seasonal. |
| 3188 *H 1974.1* | --Rear, 119 meters 359°50′ from front. | 50° 16.6′ N 64° 46.9′ W | **F.G.** | 84 **26** | **16** | Square skeleton tower, orange trapezoidal daymark, black stripe; 35. | Visible on range line only. Seasonal. |
| 3192 *H 1978* | Sheldrake, E. of Sheldrake River. | 50° 15.8′ N 64° 54.5′ W | **Fl.R.** period 6s fl. 2s, ec. 4s | 54 **16** | 4 | Square skeleton tower, orange rectangular daymark; 16. | Seasonal. |
| 3196 *H 1990* | Ile de Corossol. | 50° 05.3′ N 66° 22.6′ W | **Fl.W.** period 2.5s fl. 0.1s, ec. 2.4s | | 12 | Skeleton tower; 60. | |
| | BAY OF SEVEN ISLANDS: | | | | | | |
| 3200 *H 1994* | -Sept-Iles Range, front. | 50° 11.7′ N 66° 22.6′ W | **Iso.G.** period 2s | 56 **17** | | Cylindrical mast, white diamond slatwork daymark; 69. | Visible on range line only. Private light. |
| 3204 *H 1994.1* | --Rear, about 280.2 meters 098°29′ from front. | 50° 11.7′ N 66° 22.4′ W | **Iso.G.** period 2s | 118 **36** | | Cylindrical mast, white diamond slatwork daymark; 79. | Visible on range line only. Private light. |
| 3208 *H 1994.2* | --Wharf, head. | 50° 12.4′ N 66° 23.5′ W | **Iso.G.** period 2s | 44 **13** | 6 | Skeleton tower; 40. | |
| 3209 *H 1994.3* | --Marina breakwater, head. | 50° 12.1′ N 66° 23.2′ W | **Iso.Bu.** period 2s | 16 **5** | | Pyramidal tower; 7. | Private light. |
| 3209.5 *H 1994.34* | ---Elbow. | 50° 12.2′ N 66° 23.3′ W | **F.W.** | 16 **5** | | Pyramidal tower; 7. | Private light. |
| 3211 *H 1994.37* | --Fishing Harbor. | 50° 11.9′ N 66° 23.0′ W | **Iso.G.** period 2s | 12 **4** | 3 | Mast. | |
| 3212 *H 1994.4* | --Imperial Oil Wharf. | 50° 11.8′ N 66° 22.9′ W | **Iso.W.** period 6s | 36 **11** | 9 | Mast, orange rectangular daymark; 26. | Private light. |
| | | | **Iso.R.** period 2s | 28 **9** | | | |
| | | | **Iso.R.** period 2s | 26 **8** | | | |
| 3216 *H 1991* | -West Rocks. | 50° 07.3′ N 66° 26.0′ W | **Fl.R.** period 6s fl. 1s, ec. 5s | 39 **12** | 6 | Square skeleton tower; 20. | |
| 3220 *H 1992* | -Pointe a la Chasse. | 50° 07.6′ N 66° 27.1′ W | **Fl.W.** period 6s fl. 1s, ec. 5s | 39 **12** | 8 | Square skeleton tower; 20. | |

| (1) No. | (2) Name and Location | (3) Position | (4) Characteristic | (5) Height | (6) Range | (7) Structure | (8) Remarks |
|---|---|---|---|---|---|---|---|

## CANADA-ST. LAWRENCE ESTUARY, NORTH SIDE

| (1) No. | (2) Name and Location | (3) Position | (4) Characteristic | (5) Height | (6) Range | (7) Structure | (8) Remarks |
|---|---|---|---|---|---|---|---|
| 3224<br>*H 1992.5* | -Pointe au Corbeau. | 50° 09.0´ N<br>66° 25.5´ W | **Fl.G.**<br>period 6s<br>fl. 1s, ec. 5s | 56<br>**17** | 6 | Square skeleton tower, orange rectangular daymark; 20. | |
| 3228<br>*H 1993* | -Ile Grande-Basque. | 50° 09.2´ N<br>66° 22.6´ W | **Fl.W.**<br>period 6s<br>fl. 1s, ec. 5s | 39<br>**12** | 7 | Square skeleton tower; 20. | |
| 3234<br>*H 1994.6* | --Range, front. | 50° 11.3´ N<br>66° 22.2´ W | **Iso.Y.**<br>period 2s | 36<br>**11** | | Mast; 33. | Visible on range line only.<br>Private light. |
| 3234.1<br>*H 1994.61* | --Rear, 495.8 meters 122°44′ from front. | 50° 11.2´ N<br>66° 21.9´ W | **Iso.Y.**<br>period 2s | 78<br>**24** | | Cylindrical mast between two piles, orange diamond slatwork daymark; 72. | Visible on range line only.<br>Private light. |
| 3244<br>*H 1997.4* | --Range, front (center of wharf). | 50° 09.9´ N<br>66° 28.9´ W | **Iso.Y.**<br>period 2s | 62<br>**19** | | On building; 49. | Visible on range line only.<br>Private light. |
| 3248<br>*H 1997.41* | ---Rear, 173.3 meters 179°59′ from front. | 50° 09.8´ N<br>66° 28.9´ W | **Iso.Y.**<br>period 2s | 87<br>**27** | | Building. | Visible on range line only.<br>Private light. |
| 3249<br>*H 1997.5* | Pointe Noire. | 50° 09.8´ N<br>66° 29.2´ W | **Dir.W.R.G.** | | | Skeleton tower. | F.R. 202°42′-206°57′, Al.W.R.-210°57′, F.W.-216°57′, Al.W.G.-220°57′, F.G.-225°12′.<br>Private light. |
| 3249.5<br>*H 1997.6* | -Ore Wharf terminal. | 50° 09.9´ N<br>66° 29.2´ W | **Fl.R.**<br>period 4s | 17<br>**5** | 6 | Black cylindrical mast; 8. | Private light. |
| 3250<br>*H 1997.8* | --Anse a Brochu Range, front. | 50° 09.4´ N<br>66° 27.7´ W | **Iso.R.**<br>period 2s | | | Cylindrical mast, red daymark, white stripe. | Visible on range line only.<br>Private light. |
| 3251<br>*H 1997.81* | ---Rear, about 270 meters 192°30′ from front. | 50° 09.6´ N<br>66° 27.6´ W | **Iso.R.**<br>period 2s | | | Silo, red daymark, white stripe. | Visible on range line only.<br>Private light. |
| 3256<br>*H 2002* | Port Cartier Range, front. | 50° 02.2´ N<br>66° 46.8´ W | **F.G.** | 166<br>**51** | | Skeleton tower, yellow diamond daymark, black cross. | Visible on range line only.<br>Private light. |
| 3260<br>*H 2002.1* | -Rear, 494.7 meters 016°30′ from front. | 50° 02.4´ N<br>66° 46.7´ W | **F.G.** | 290<br>**88** | | Skeleton tower, orange rectangular daymark, black stripe; 76. | Visible on range line only.<br>Private light. |
| 3264<br>*H 2000* | Port Cartier Entrance, E. | 50° 01.7´ N<br>66° 46.9´ W | **Fl.R.**<br>period 3s<br>fl. 0.5s, ec. 2.5s | 41<br>**12** | 6 | Mast; 16. | **Whistle:** 1 bl. ev. 30s (bl. 3s, si. 27s).<br>Private light.<br>**Radar reflector.** |
| | | | **Fl.R.**<br>period 2s | | | | |
| 3268<br>*H 2001* | -W. | 50° 01.7´ N<br>66° 47.1´ W | **Fl.G.**<br>period 3s<br>fl. 0.5s, ec. 2.5s | 40<br>**12** | 6 | Mast; 16. | Private light.<br>**Radar reflector.** |
| 3272<br>*H 1999* | **Quebec Rayonier Range,** front. | 50° 01.1´ N<br>66° 48.9´ W | **F.W.** | 31<br>**10** | **19** | Triangular skeleton tower, orange slatwork daymark, black stripe; 24. | Visible on range line only.<br>Private light. |
| 3276<br>*H 1999.1* | -Rear, 369 meters 005°25′ from front. | 50° 01.3´ N<br>66° 48.9´ W | **F.W.** | 63<br>**19** | **19** | Triangular skeleton tower, orange slatwork daymark, black stripe; 34. | Visible on range line only.<br>Private light. |
| 3280<br>*H 2010* | Ile du Grand Caouis, near S. point. | 49° 49.6´ N<br>67° 00.4´ W | **Fl.W.**<br>period 6s<br>fl. 1s, ec. 5s | 148<br>**45** | 8 | White octagonal tower, red upper portion; 46. | |
| 3298<br>*H 2027* | Godbout Wharf, on new ferry wharf. | 49° 19.4´ N<br>67° 35.5´ W | **Iso.R.**<br>period 2s | 37<br>**11** | 4 | Square skeleton tower; 23. | Private light. |
| 3304<br>*H 2050* | Pointe St. Pancrace, extremity of point, E. side of entrance to Baie des Anglais. | 49° 15.2´ N<br>68° 04.7´ W | **Fl.W.**<br>period 6s<br>fl. 1s, ec. 5s | 83<br>**25** | 8 | Square skeleton tower, two orange rectangular daymarks; 35. | |
| 3308<br>*H 2050.5* | Baie des Anglais Range, front, on point, N. end of bay. | 49° 16.1´ N<br>68° 07.7´ W | **F.G.** | 89<br>**27** | | Skeleton tower, orange trapezoidal daymark, black stripe; 51. | Visible on range line only.<br>Private light. |
| 3312<br>*H 2050.6* | -Rear, 220 meters 312°19′ from front. | 49° 16.2´ N<br>68° 07.9´ W | **F.G.** | 125<br>**38** | | Skeleton tower, orange square daymark, black stripe; 10. | Visible on range line only.<br>Private light. |

| (1) No. | (2) Name and Location | (3) Position | (4) Characteristic | (5) Height | (6) Range | (7) Structure | (8) Remarks |
|---|---|---|---|---|---|---|---|

## CANADA-ST. LAWRENCE ESTUARY, NORTH SIDE

| (1) No. | (2) Name and Location | (3) Position | (4) Characteristic | (5) Height | (6) Range | (7) Structure | (8) Remarks |
|---|---|---|---|---|---|---|---|
| 3316<br>*H 2051* | Anse du Moulin Range, front. | 49° 15.3′ N<br>68° 08.1′ W | **F.R.** | 119<br>**36** | | Mast, white trapezoidal daymark, red stripe. | Visible on range line only.<br>Private light. |
| 3320<br>*H 2051.1* | -Rear, 229 meters 237°18′ from front. | 49° 15.2′ N<br>68° 08.2′ W | **F.R.** | 221<br>**67** | | Square skeleton tower, white trapezoidal daymark, red stripe; 13. | Visible on range line only.<br>Private light. |
| 3321<br>*H 2052* | Anse du Moulin Entrance Range, front. | 49° 14.9′ N<br>68° 08.3′ W | **Fl.R.**<br>period 4s | 112<br>**34** | | Tank, orange square daymark, white stripe. | Private light. |
| 3322<br>*H 2052.1* | -Rear, 182 meters 239°17′ from front. | 49° 14.8′ N<br>68° 08.4′ W | **Iso.R.**<br>period 6s | 196<br>**60** | | Concrete base, orange square daymark, white stripe. | Visible on range line only.<br>Private light. |
| 3324<br>*H 2054* | **Baie Comeau.** | 49° 14.2′ N<br>68° 07.7′ W | **Fl.R.**<br>period 6s<br>fl. 1s, ec. 5s | 41<br>**12** | **17** | Skeleton tower; 33. | |
| 3325<br>*H 2055* | -Ferry. | 49° 14.1′ N<br>68° 07.9′ W | **F.R.** | 17<br>**5** | 7 | Square tower; 10. | Private light. |
| | OUTARDES BAY: | | | | | | |
| 3336<br>*H 2056* | **-Pointe de Manicouagan.** | 49° 06.1′ N<br>68° 11.6′ W | **Fl.W.**<br>period 6s<br>fl. 1s, ec. 5s | 118<br>**36** | **20** | Skeleton tower; 100. | **Radar reflector.** |
| | -RACON | | **X(– • • –)** | | 10 | | (3 & 10cm). |
| 3348<br>*H 2063* | Cape Colombier. | 48° 49.2′ N<br>68° 52.6′ W | **Fl.W.**<br>period 6s<br>fl. 1s, ec. 5s | 79<br>**24** | 8 | Skeleton tower; 30. | |
| | FORESTVILLE: | | | | | | |
| 3360<br>*H 2064* | --Point Rocheuse, on hill E. of harbor. | 48° 44.4′ N<br>69° 02.9′ W | **Fl.W.**<br>period 6s<br>fl. 1s, ec. 5s | 66<br>**20** | 8 | Square skeleton tower; 52. | |
| 3364<br>*H 2066* | **-Forestville Range,** front. | 48° 44.2′ N<br>69° 03.8′ W | **F.G.** | 58<br>**18** | **16** | Square skeleton tower, orange rectangular daymark, black stripe; 20. | Visible on range line only.<br>Seasonal. |
| 3368<br>*H 2066.1* | --Rear, 241 meters 261°33′ from front. | 48° 44.1′ N<br>69° 03.9′ W | **F.G.** | 105<br>**32** | **16** | Red and white square skeleton tower, orange rectangular daymark, black stripe; 16. | Visible on range line only.<br>Seasonal. |
| | LES ESCOUMINS: | | | | | | |
| 3380<br>*H 2088* | -Wharf, head. | 48° 20.8′ N<br>69° 23.4′ W | **Fl.G.**<br>period 6s<br>fl. 1s, ec. 5s | 40<br>**12** | 6 | On superstructure; 34. | Seasonal.<br>Private light.<br>**Radar reflector.** |
| 3388<br>*H 2090* | **-Anse aux Basques Range,** front. | 48° 19.1′ N<br>69° 24.9′ W | **F.R.** | 22<br>**7** | **16** | Red and white square skeleton tower, orange trapezoidal daymark, black stripe; 15. | Visible on range line only. |
| 3392<br>*H 2090.1* | --Rear, 69 meters 301°48′ from front. | 48° 19.1′ N<br>69° 24.9′ W | **F.R.** | 40<br>**12** | **16** | Red and white square skeleton tower, orange trapezoidal daymark, black stripe; 15. | Visible on range line only. |
| 3396<br>*H 2093* | **Bon Desir.** | 48° 16.3′ N<br>69° 28.1′ W | **Fl.W.**<br>period 6s<br>fl. 1s, ec. 5s | 152<br>**46** | **18** | White octagonal tower, red upper portion; 47. | |
| 3432<br>*H 2104* | **Ile Rouge.** | 48° 04.2′ N<br>69° 33.3′ W | **Fl.W.**<br>period 10s<br>fl. 0.3s, ec. 9.7s | 65<br>**20** | **16** | Cylindrical tower; 66. | |

| (1) No. | (2) Name and Location | (3) Position | (4) Characteristic | (5) Height | (6) Range | (7) Structure | (8) Remarks |
|---|---|---|---|---|---|---|---|

## CANADA-ST. LAWRENCE ESTUARY, NORTH SIDE

| (1) No. | (2) Name and Location | (3) Position | (4) Characteristic | (5) Height | (6) Range | (7) Structure | (8) Remarks |
|---|---|---|---|---|---|---|---|
| 3436<br>*H 2106* | **Haut-fond Prince.** | 48° 06.5′ N<br>69° 36.9′ W | **Fl.W.**<br>period 2.5s<br>fl. 0.1s, ec. 2.4s | 83<br>**25** | **18** | Cylindrical tower; 82. | **Horn (3):** 1 bl. ev. 20s. Horns point 045°, 180° and 288°, sound alternately. Fog signal activated remotely on chan. 69 (156.475MHz). Mariners requiring signal must press button of VHF radio five (5) consecutive times at 1 second interval on chan. 69. Signal in operation for 60 minutes. |
| | SAGUENAY RIVER: | | | | | | |
| 3456<br>*H 2108* | -Baie Ste. Catherine. | 48° 06.9′ N<br>69° 43.2′ W | **Fl.G.**<br>period 6s<br>fl. 1s, ec. 5s | 30<br>**9** | 6 | Red rectangular tower; 3. | |
| 3460<br>*H 2115* | - -Pointe de l'Islet. | 48° 08.1′ N<br>69° 43.0′ W | **Fl.W.**<br>period 6s<br>fl. 1s, ec. 5s | 39<br>**12** | 8 | Skeleton tower; 30. | |
| 3464<br>*H 2112* | **-Pointe Noire Range,** front. | 48° 07.4′ N<br>69° 43.0′ W | **F.W.** | 95<br>**29** | **20** | Square skeleton tower, orange trapezoidal daymark, black stripe; 35. | Visible on range line only.<br>Emergency light. |
| | | | **F.G.** | 95<br>**29** | 6 | | Visible 077°-257°. |
| 3468<br>*H 2112.1* | - -Rear, 427 meters 273°04′ from front. | 48° 07.4′ N<br>69° 43.3′ W | **F.W.** | 144<br>**44** | **20** | Square skeleton tower, orange trapezoidal daymark, black stripe; 25. | Visible on range line only.<br>Emergency light. |
| 3472<br>*H 2113* | -Anse du Portage, on wharf. | 48° 07.6′ N<br>69° 43.8′ W | **F.Y.** | 32<br>**10** | 8 | Skeleton tower; 23. | |
| 3480<br>*H 2118* | - -Anse a l'Eau, wharf, head. | 48° 08.3′ N<br>69° 43.6′ W | **F.G.** | 36<br>**11** | 6 | Skeleton tower; 20. | **Radar reflector.** |
| 3484<br>*H 2122* | -Cap de La Boule, N. side of river. | 48° 08.9′ N<br>69° 48.2′ W | **Fl.W.**<br>period 6s<br>fl. 1s, ec. 5s | 59<br>**18** | 5 | Square skeleton tower; 23. | |
| 3488<br>*H 2124* | -Anse de Sable. | 48° 09.1′ N<br>69° 51.3′ W | **Fl.W.**<br>period 6s<br>fl. 1s, ec. 5s | 22<br>**7** | 5 | Square skeleton tower; 20. | |
| 3492<br>*H 2130* | -Anse a Pierrot, E. side of river, 1.9 kilometers above Grosse Roche. | 48° 14.1′ N<br>69° 53.7′ W | **Fl.W.**<br>period 6s<br>fl. 1s, ec. 5s | 43<br>**13** | 5 | Square skeleton tower; 30. | |
| 3496<br>*H 2128* | -Anse-de-Roche. | 48° 13.1′ N<br>69° 52.5′ W | **Iso.R.**<br>period 2s | 23<br>**7** | 7 | Skeleton tower; 20. | Seasonal.<br>Private light. |
| 3500<br>*H 2126* | -Pointe aux Crepes. | 48° 13.0′ N<br>69° 53.7′ W | **Fl.G.**<br>period 6s<br>fl. 1s, ec. 5s | 42<br>**13** | 5 | Square skeleton tower; 25. | |
| 3504<br>*H 2131* | -Ile St. Louis, N. side of Island. | 48° 15.1′ N<br>70° 01.2′ W | **Fl.W.**<br>period 6s<br>fl. 1s, ec. 5s | 130<br>**40** | 5 | Square skeleton tower; 30. | |
| 3508<br>*H 2133* | -Pointe Claveau. | 48° 15.6′ N<br>70° 06.9′ W | **Fl.W.**<br>period 6s<br>fl. 1s, ec. 5s | 50<br>**15** | 5 | Square skeleton tower; 30. | |
| 3516<br>*H 2136* | -Pointe au Boeuf, near point, S. side of river. | 48° 16.3′ N<br>70° 12.2′ W | **Fl.W.**<br>period 6s<br>fl. 1s, ec. 5s | 49<br>**15** | 5 | Square skeleton tower; 15. | |
| 3520<br>*H 2138* | -Trinity Bay, N. side of river opposite La Niche. | 48° 21.2′ N<br>70° 20.7′ W | **Fl.W.**<br>period 6s<br>fl. 1s, ec. 5s | 52<br>**16** | 8 | Skeleton tower, orange rectangular daymark; 30. | |
| 3524<br>*H 2140* | -Cap Rouge. | 48° 22.5′ N<br>70° 32.2′ W | **Fl.W.**<br>period 6s<br>fl. 1s, ec. 5s | 48<br>**15** | 5 | Square skeleton tower; 26. | |

| (1) No. | (2) Name and Location | (3) Position | (4) Characteristic | (5) Height | (6) Range | (7) Structure | (8) Remarks |
|---|---|---|---|---|---|---|---|

## CANADA-ST. LAWRENCE ESTUARY, NORTH SIDE

| (1) No. | (2) Name and Location | (3) Position | (4) Characteristic | (5) Height | (6) Range | (7) Structure | (8) Remarks |
|---|---|---|---|---|---|---|---|
| 3532 *H 2142* | -Cape East (Cap Est), S. extremity. | 48° 22.6′ N 70° 42.4′ W | **Fl.W.** period 6s fl. 1s, ec. 5s | 56 **17** | 5 | White octagonal tower, red upper portion; 26. | |
| 3536 *H 2142.2* | -Bagotville, wharf, head. | 48° 20.7′ N 70° 52.7′ W | **Iso.R.** period 2s | 36 **11** | 6 | Pipe swing pole; 26. | |
| 3540 *H 2142.3* | Port-Alfred Range, front. | 48° 20.1′ N 70° 52.5′ W | **F.R.** | 50 **15** | | Building, orange trapezoidal daymark, black stripe. | Visible on range line only. Private light. |
| 3544 *H 2142.31* | -Rear, 122.4 meters 261°46′ from front. | 48° 20.1′ N 70° 52.6′ W | **F.R.** | 85 **26** | | Building, orange trapezoidal daymark, black stripe. | Visible on range line only. Private light. |
| | CHICOUTIMI HARBOR: | | | | | | |
| 3564 *H 2142.8* | -Pointe aux Pins. | 48° 25.1′ N 70° 49.9′ W | **Fl.Y.** period 6s fl. 1s, ec. 5s | 36 **11** | 5 | Square skeleton tower, orange rectangular daymark; 20. | |
| 3568 *H 2143* | **Poste St. Martin Range,** front. | 48° 26.6′ N 70° 59.0′ W | **F.W.** | 79 **24** | **15** | Square tower, orange trapezoidal daymark, black stripe. | Visible on range line only. Seasonal. |
| 3572 *H 2143.1* | -Rear, 3,322.3 meters 287°18′ from front. | 48° 26.6′ N 70° 59.0′ W | **F.W.** | 177 **54** | **15** | Square skeleton tower, orange trapezoidal daymark, black stripe; 62. | Visible on range line only. Seasonal. |
| 3584 *H 2143.3* | **Riviere Valin Range,** E. of Riviere Valin mouth. | 48° 27.6′ N 70° 58.9′ W | **F.W.** | 89 **27** | **15** | Skeleton tower, two orange trapezoidal daymarks, black stripe; 86. | Visible on range line only. Seasonal. |
| 3588 *H 2143.31* | -Rear, 1027 meters 314°04′ from front. | 48° 28.0′ N 70° 59.5′ W | **F.W.** | 141 **43** | **15** | Skeleton tower, orange trapezoidal daymark, black stripe; 26. | Visible on range line only. Seasonal. |
| 3592 *H 2143.4* | **Riviere du Caribou Range,** N. side of Saguenay River. | 48° 27.4′ N 71° 00.6′ W | **F.W.** | 43 **13** | **15** | Square skeleton tower, orange trapezoidal daymark, black stripe; 43. | Visible on range line only. Seasonal. |
| 3596 *H 2143.5* | -Rear, on W. bank Riviere du Caribou 229 meters 283°36′ from front. | 48° 27.4′ N 71° 00.8′ W | **F.W.** | 62 **19** | **15** | Square skeleton tower, orange trapezoidal daymark, black stripe; 33. | Visible on range line only. Seasonal. |
| 3608 *H 2143.6* | Simard Range on N. side of Saguenay. | 48° 27.0′ N 71° 01.3′ W | **F.G.** | 29 **9** | 6 | Square skeleton tower, orange trapezoidal daymark, black stripes; 26. | Visible on range line only. Seasonal. |
| 3612 *H 2143.7* | -Rear, 212.9 meters 256°16′ from front. | 48° 27.0′ N 71° 01.5′ W | **F.G.** | 45 **14** | **16** | Square skeleton tower, orange trapezoidal daymark, black stripes; 40. | Visible on range line only. Seasonal. |
| 3616 *H 2143.9* | **Riviere-du-Moulin lower Range,** N. of Riviere-duMoulin. | 48° 26.1′ N 71° 01.5′ W | **F.G.** | 35 **11** | **16** | Square skeleton tower, orange trapezoidal daymark, black stripe; 30. | Visible on range line only. Seasonal. |
| 3620 *H 2143.91* | -Rear, 197 meters 214°47′ from front. | 48° 26.0′ N 71° 01.6′ W | **F.G.** | 58 **18** | **16** | Square skeleton tower, two orange trapezoidal daymarks, black stripe; 26. | Visible on range line only. Seasonal. |
| 3632 *H 2144* | **Riviere-du-Moulin Upper Range,** E. of river mouth. | 48° 26.0′ N 71° 01.7′ W | **F.G.** | 33 **10** | **16** | Skeleton tower, orange trapezoidal daymark, black stripe; 21. | Visible on range line only. Seasonal. |
| 3636 *H 2144.1* | -Rear, 131 meters 081°37′ from front. | 48° 26.0′ N 71° 01.6′ W | **F.G.** | 58 **18** | **16** | Skeleton tower, two orange trapezoidal daymarks, black stripe; 26. | Visible on range line only. Seasonal. |
| 3640 *H 2145* | -Monument Price. | 48° 25.8′ N 71° 02.6′ W | **Dir.W.R.G.** | 43 **13** | 13 | Rectangular skeleton tower. | F.R. 229°30′-231°30′, Al.R.W.-231°50′, F.W.-232°10′, Al.G.W.-232°30′, F.G.-234°30′. |
| 3652 *H 2166* | **Cap de la Tete au Chien.** | 47° 54.7′ N 69° 48.4′ W | **Fl.(2)W.** period 5s fl. 0.2s, ec. 0.8s fl. 0.2s, ec. 3.8s | 207 **63** | **17** | White octagonal tower, red upper portion. | |
| 3656 *H 2168* | St. Simeon, government wharf, head. | 47° 50.4′ N 69° 52.4′ W | **Iso.R.** period 2s | 28 **8** | 7 | Square skeleton tower; 26. | |

| (1) No. | (2) Name and Location | (3) Position | (4) Characteristic | (5) Height | (6) Range | (7) Structure | (8) Remarks |
|---|---|---|---|---|---|---|---|

## CANADA-ST. LAWRENCE ESTUARY, NORTH SIDE

| (1) No. | (2) Name and Location | (3) Position | (4) Characteristic | (5) Height | (6) Range | (7) Structure | (8) Remarks |
|---|---|---|---|---|---|---|---|
| 3660 *H 2182* | **Cap au Saumon.** | 47° 46.2′ N 69° 54.4′ W | **Fl.(3)W.** period 15s | 82 **25** | **20** | White octagonal tower, red upper portion; 46. | |
| 3662 *H 2167* | Hare Island, Ile aux Lievres, SW. head. | 47° 47.9′ N 69° 46.5′ W | **Fl.G.** period 6s fl. 1s, ec. 5s | 30 **9** | 5 | Square skeleton tower, orange and white rectangular daymarks; 23. | Seasonal. **Radar reflector.** |
| 3668 *H 2186* | Cap a l'Aigle. | 47° 39.7′ N 70° 05.8′ W | **Iso.R.** period 2s | 20 **6** | 6 | Square skeleton tower; 16. | |
| 3670 *H 2187* | -Marina breakwater. | 47° 39.8′ N 70° 05.8′ W | **Fl.Y.** period 6s fl. 1s, ec. 5s | 21 **6** | 7 | Square skeleton tower; 15. | Seasonal. Private light. |
| | MURRAY BAY: | | | | | | |
| 3676 *H 2194* | **-Point au Pic.** | 47° 37.4′ N 70° 08.4′ W | **Fl.R.** period 6s fl. 1s, ec. 5s | 64 **20** | **17** | Square skeleton tower; 60. | |
| 3680 *H 2202* | **Goose Cape.** | 47° 29.3′ N 70° 13.9′ W | **Fl.W.** period 6s fl. 1s, ec. 5s | 51 **16** | **20** | Square skeleton tower; 30. | |
| 3684 *H 2204* | -Wharf, head. | 47° 26.9′ N 70° 21.9′ W | **Iso.G.** period 2s | 43 **13** | 7 | Structure; 36. | **Radar reflector.** |
| 3688 *H 2218* | **Cap aux Corbeaux Range,** front. | 47° 26.1′ N 70° 25.7′ W | **F.W.** | 108 **33** | **20** | Skeleton tower, orange trapezoidal daymark, black stripe; 104. | Visible on range line only. Emergency light. |
| | | | **F.W.** | 108 **33** | 8 | | Visible 252°30′-004°30′. |
| 3692 *H 2218.1* | -Rear, 374.6 meters 024°13′ from front. | 47° 26.3′ N 70° 25.6′ W | **F.W.** | 171 **52** | **20** | Square skeleton tower, orange trapezoidal daymark, black stripe; 43. | Visible on range line only. Emergency light. |
| | | | **F.W.** | 171 **52** | 8 | | Visible 256°-004°30′. |
| | ILE AUX COUDRES: | | | | | | |
| 3696 *H 2206* | -Head of wharf. | 47° 25.2′ N 70° 23.6′ W | **F.G.** | 45 **14** | 7 | On landing stage of superstructure. | |
| 3700 *H 2208* | **-Pointe de la Prairie.** | 47° 24.6′ N 70° 25.9′ W | **Fl.W.** period 2.5s fl. 0.5s, ec. 2s | 52 **16** | **16** | Pile. | |
| 3728 *H 2254* | Sault au Cochon. | 47° 11.8′ N 70° 38.3′ W | **Fl.W.** period 6s fl. 1s, ec. 5s | 53 **16** | 4 | Square skeleton tower, orange rectangular daymark; 26. | **Radar reflector.** |
| 3740 *H 2255* | **Cap Gribane Range,** front. | 47° 08.5′ N 70° 41.1′ W | **F.W.** | 43 **13** | **17** | Square skeleton tower, orange rectangular daymark, black stripe; 25. | Visible on range line only. |
| 3744 *H 2255.1* | -Rear, 445.4 meters 023°52′ from front. | 47° 08.7′ N 70° 41.0′ W | **F.W.** | 89 **27** | **17** | Square skeleton tower, orange rectangular daymark, black stripe; 35. | Visible on range line only. |
| 3748 *H 2261* | **Brule Bank,** downstream range, front. | 47° 05.8′ N 70° 42.2′ W | **F.W.** | 30 **9** | **18** | Pile, orange slatwork daymark, black stripe; 23. | Visible on range line only. |
| 3752 *H 2261.1* | -Rear, 1006 meters 213°21′ from front. | 47° 05.4′ N 70° 42.7′ W | **F.W.** | 75 **23** | **18** | White cylindrical tower, orange upper portion, on pile; 59. | Visible on range line only. |
| 3756 *H 2256* | **Cap Rouge Range,** front. | 47° 07.5′ N 70° 42.1′ W | **F.Y.** | 95 **29** | **17** | Square skeleton tower, orange trapezoidal daymark, black stripe; 37. | Visible on range line only. |
| 3760 *H 2256.1* | -Rear, 1025 meters 221°13′ from front. | 47° 07.1′ N 70° 42.6′ W | **F.Y.** | 184 **56** | **17** | Square skeleton tower, orange trapezoidal daymark, black stripe; 27. | Visible on range line only. |

| (1) No. | (2) Name and Location | (3) Position | (4) Characteristic | (5) Height | (6) Range | (7) Structure | (8) Remarks |
|---|---|---|---|---|---|---|---|

## CANADA-ST. LAWRENCE RIVER

| (1) No. | (2) Name and Location | (3) Position | (4) Characteristic | (5) Height | (6) Range | (7) Structure | (8) Remarks |
|---|---|---|---|---|---|---|---|
| 3772 *H 2259* | Cap Brule. | 47° 06.5′ N 70° 43.0′ W | **Iso.W.** period 2s | 134 **41** | 6 | Skeleton tower, orange rectangular daymarks on 3 seaward faces; 16. | |
| 3776 *H 2262* | **Brule Bank,** upstream range, front. | 47° 05.4′ N 70° 42.6′ W | **F.W.** | 29 **9** | **18** | Pile, orange trapezoidal slatwork daymark, black stripe; 23. | Visible on range line only. |
| 3780 *H 2262.1* | -Rear, 1006 meters 033°25′ from front. | 47° 05.8′ N 70° 42.2′ W | **F.W.** | 95 **29** | **18** | White cylindrical tower, orange bands, on pile; 62. | Visible on range line only. |
| 3801 *H 2267* | **Pte. Argentenage Range,** front. | 47° 00.5′ N 70° 48.3′ W | **F.W.** | 82 **25** | **20** | Skeleton tower; 16. | Visible on range line only. Emergency light. |
| 3802 *H 2267.1* | --Rear, 2,769 meters 213°30′ from front. | 46° 59.2′ N 70° 49.5′ W | **F.W.** | 213 **65** | **20** | Skeleton tower; 114. | Visible on range line only. Emergency light. |
| 3812 *H 2278* | **St Francois.** | 46° 59.8′ N 70° 48.5′ W | **Fl.W.** period 5s fl. 1s, ec. 4s | 37 **11** | **20** | Square skeleton tower; 31. | |
| 3836 *H 2274* | **St-Michel-de-Bellechasse Range,** front. | 46° 52.5′ N 70° 55.0′ W | **F.W.** | 97 **30** | **23** | Skeleton tower, orange trapezoidal daymark, black stripe; 79. | Visible on range line only. Emergency light. |
| 3840 *H 2274.1* | -Rear, 1738 meters 213°14′ from front. | 46° 51.7′ N 70° 55.7′ W | **F.W.** | 186 **57** | **20** | Tripod skeleton tower, orange trapezoidal daymark, black stripe; 82. | Visible on range line only. Emergency light. |
| | ORLEANS ISLAND: | | | | | | |
| 3848 *H 2282* | -St. Jean-d'Orleans. | 46° 54.9′ N 70° 53.8′ W | **Fl.R.** period 5s fl. 1s, ec. 4s | 36 **11** | 12 | Square skeleton tower, 3 orange rectangular slatwork daymarks; 30. | |
| | -RACON | | **G(– – •)** | | 10 | | (3 & 10cm). |
| 3852 *H 2284* | -St. Laurent-d'Orleans. | 46° 51.5′ N 71° 00.2′ W | **Fl.G.** period 5s fl. 1s, ec. 4s | 46 **14** | 12 | Pipe swing pole; 43. | |
| 3860 *H 2285* | **-Beaumont Range,** front. | 46° 50.0′ N 71° 01.9′ W | **F.W.** | 175 **53** | **20** | Skeleton tower, orange slatwork daymark, black stripe; 62. | Visible on range line only. Emergency light. |
| 3864 *H 2285.1* | --Rear, 1624 meters 233°40′ from front. | 46° 49.4′ N 71° 02.9′ W | **F.W.** | 291 **89** | **20** | Skeleton tower, orange slatwork daymark, black stripe; 76. | Visible on range line only. Emergency light. |
| 3868 *H 2286* | **-Pointe de la Martiniere Range,** front. | 46° 49.7′ N 71° 07.0′ W | **F.W.** | 486 **148** | **20** | Skeleton tower; 62. | Visible on range line only. Emergency light. |
| 3872 *H 2286.1* | --Rear, 655 meters 252°01′ from front. | 46° 49.6′ N 70° 07.5′ W | **F.W.** | 292 **89** | **20** | Skeleton tower; 112. | Visible on range line only. Emergency light. |
| 3876 *H 2288* | **-Pointe du Bout de l'Ile.** | 46° 50.7′ N 71° 07.9′ W | **Fl.Y.** period 5s fl. 1s, ec. 4s | 49 **15** | **19** | Square skeleton tower; 45. | |
| 3884 *H 2290* | **-Domaine Range,** front. | 47° 01.1′ N 70° 49.7′ W | **F.W.** | 36 **11** | **19** | Red and white square skeleton tower, orange trapezoidal daymark, black stripe; 30. | Visible on range line only. Seasonal. |
| 3888 *H 2290.1* | --Rear, 788 meters 226°14′ from front. | 47° 00.8′ N 70° 50.1′ W | **F.W.** | 122 **37** | **19** | Red and white square skeleton tower, orange trapezoidal daymark, black stripe; 33. | Visible on range line only. Seasonal. |
| | ORLEANS ISLAND CHANNEL: | | | | | | |
| 3900 *H 2293* | **-Ste. Anne de Beaupre.** | 47° 01.2′ N 70° 55.7′ W | **Iso.W.R.G.** period 3s | 36 **11** | **19** | Skeleton tower, orange trapezoidal daymark, black stripe; 30. | R. 251°30′-253°30′, Al.R.W.-253°50′, W.-254°10′, Al.G.W.-254°30′, G.-256°30′. Seasonal. |
| 3924 *H 2300* | **-Pointe St. Pierre,** Orleans Island, S. side of channel, front. | 46° 55.6′ N 71° 02.4′ W | **F.G.** | 21 **6** | **16** | Square skeleton tower, orange trapezoidal daymark, black stripe; 20. | Visible on range line only. Seasonal. |

| (1) No. | (2) Name and Location | (3) Position | (4) Characteristic | (5) Height | (6) Range | (7) Structure | (8) Remarks |
|---|---|---|---|---|---|---|---|

**CANADA-ST. LAWRENCE RIVER**

| (1) No. | (2) Name and Location | (3) Position | (4) Characteristic | (5) Height | (6) Range | (7) Structure | (8) Remarks |
|---|---|---|---|---|---|---|---|
| 3928 *H 2300.1* | --Rear, 167 meters 218°36′ from front. | 46° 55.5′ N 71° 02.5′ W | **F.G.** | 43 **13** | **16** | Square skeleton tower, orange trapezoidal daymark, black stripe; 40. | Visible on range line only. Seasonal. |
| 3932 *H 2294* | **-Ste-Famille Range,** front. | 46° 57.9′ N 70° 58.6′ W | **F.G.** | 61 **19** | **18** | Square skeleton tower, orange trapezoidal daymark, black stripe; 60. | Visible on range line only. Seasonal. |
| 3936 *H 2294.1* | --Rear, 609 meters 052°36′ from front. | 46° 58.1′ N 70° 58.2′ W | **F.G.** | 249 **76** | **18** | Square skeleton tower, orange trapezoidal daymark, black stripe; 50. | Visible on range line only. Seasonal. |
| 3940 *H 2310* | **-L'Ange Gardien Range,** front. | 46° 53.9′ N 71° 07.2′ W | **F.G.** | 46 **14** | **16** | Skeleton tower, orange trapezoidal daymark, black stripe; 40. | Visible on range line only. Seasonal. |
| 3942 *H 2310.1* | --Rear, 415 meters, 023°43′ from front. | 46° 54.1′ N 71° 07.1′ W | **F.G.** | 79 **24** | **16** | Skeleton tower, orange trapezoidal daymark, black stripe; 46. | Visible on range line only. Seasonal. |
| | QUEBEC: | | | | | | |
| 3988 *H 2321* | -Queen's Wharf, on SE. corner of shed. | 46° 48.6′ N 71° 12.2′ W | **Iso.R.** period 2s | 66 **20** | 6 | On building. | Intensified on bearing 280°. |
| 4004 *H 2323* | **-Quebec Yacht Club Range,** front. | 46° 47.0′ N 71° 14.2′ W | **F.R.** | 16 **5** | **16** | Red and white square skeleton tower, orange trapezoidal daymark, black stripe; 10. | Seasonal. Private light. |
| 4008 *H 2323.1* | --Rear, 19.6 meters 298°57′ from front. | 46° 47.0′ N 71° 14.2′ W | **F.R.** | 27 **8** | **16** | Red and white square skeleton tower, orange trapezoidal daymark, black stripe; 20. | Seasonal. Private light. |
| | -Quebec Yacht Club: | | | | | | |
| 4012 *H 2323.3* | --Marina East, E. breakwater, outer end. | 46° 47.0′ N 71° 14.0′ W | **F.Y.** | 16 **5** | 8 | Red and white square skeleton tower; 10. | Seasonal. Private light. |
| 4016 *H 2323.4* | ---West, W. breakwater, outer end. | 46° 47.0′ N 71° 14.1′ W | **Iso.W.** period 2s | 14 **4** | 8 | Red and white square skeleton tower; 11. | Seasonal. Private light. |
| 4020 *H 2324* | **-Pointe a Puiseaux (Sillery).** | 46° 46.3′ N 71° 14.6′ W | **Fl.R.** period 5s fl. 1s, ec. 4s | 27 **8** | **16** | Red and white square skeleton tower; 16. | Emergency light. |
| 4028 *H 2326* | **Le Sault. Quebec Bridge.** | 46° 44.7′ N 71° 17.3′ W | **2 F.W.** | 154 **47** | | On bridge. | Private light. |
| | | | **2 F.R.** | 92 **28** | | On bridge. | Private Light. |
| | | | **Iso.G.** period 2s | 177 **54** | 15 | On bridge. | Visible eastward. |
| | | | **Iso.G.** period 2s | 165 **50** | 7 | On bridge. | Visible westward. |
| 4029 *H 2328* | Pierre Laporte Bridge. | 46° 44.6′ N 71° 17.4′ W | **4 F.W.** | 161 **49** | | On bridge. | Private light. |
| | | | **4 F.R.** | 157 **48** | | | |
| | | | **2 F.G.** | 161 **49** | | | |
| 4032 *H 2330* | **Pointe a Basile Range,** front. | 46° 43.8′ N 71° 19.8′ W | **F.W.** | 197 **60** | **20** | Skeleton tower, orange slatwork daymark, black stripe; 126. | Visible downstream to Quebec Bridge. F.W. visible on range line only. Emergency light. |
| | | | **Iso.R.** period 2s | 194 **59** | **16** | | |
| 4036 *H 2330.1* | -Rear, 1241 meters 077°32′ from front. | 46° 43.9′ N 71° 18.8′ W | **F.W.** | 287 **88** | **20** | Skeleton tower, orange slatwork daymark, black stripe; 116. | Visible on range line only. Emergency light. |

| (1) No. | (2) Name and Location | (3) Position | (4) Characteristic | (5) Height | (6) Range | (7) Structure | (8) Remarks |
|---|---|---|---|---|---|---|---|

**CANADA-ST. LAWRENCE RIVER**

| (1) No. | (2) Name and Location | (3) Position | (4) Characteristic | (5) Height | (6) Range | (7) Structure | (8) Remarks |
|---|---|---|---|---|---|---|---|
| 4048 *H 2332* | Pointe St. Nicholas. | 46° 42.1′ N 71° 26.8′ W | **F.G.** | 266 **81** | 6 | Red and white square skeleton tower, orange rectangular slatwork daymark; 46. | |
| 4082 *H 2333.2* | Vauquelin Range, front, Club Nautique. | 46° 41.8′ N 71° 34.5′ W | **F.G.** | 13 **4** | | Black round mast; 7. | Visible on range line only. Seasonal. Private light. |
| 4086 *H 2333.21* | -Rear, 45.5 meters 321°22′ from front. | 46° 41.9′ N 71° 34.5′ W | **F.G.** | 21 **6** | | Side of boathouse. | Visible on range line only. Seasonal. Private light. |
| 4096 *H 2334* | **Pointe aux Trembles.** | 46° 41.8′ N 71° 34.4′ W | **Fl.W.** period 5s fl. 1s, ec. 4s | 32 **10** | **20** | Skeleton tower; 26. | |
| | RACON | | **G(– – •)** | | 10 | | (3 & 10cm). |
| 4104 *H 2335.9* | **St. Antoine Traverse Range,** front. | 46° 40.0′ N 71° 34.9′ W | **F.G.** | 56 **17** | **15** | White square skeleton tower, orange slatwork daymark, black stripe; 55. | Visible on range line only. Emergency light. |
| 4108 *H 2336* | -Rear, 321 meters 227°37′ from front. | 46° 39.9′ N 71° 35.0′ W | **F.G.** | 188 **57** | **15** | Square skeleton tower, orange slatwork daymark, black stripe; 55. | Visible on range line only. Emergency light. |
| 4112 *H 2336.1* | **St. Antoine Upper Range,** front. | 46° 40.0′ N 71° 35.0′ W | **F.G.** | 33 **10** | **17** | White tower, red upper portion, orange trapezoidal daymark, black stripe; 26. | Visible on range line only. Emergency light. |
| 4116 *H 2335.9* | -Rear, 250 meters 071°56′ from front. | 46° 40.0′ N 71° 34.9′ W | **F.G.** | 55 **17** | **17** | Square skeleton tower, orange trapezoidal daymark, black stripe; 50. | Visible on range line only. Emergency light. |
| 4124 *H 2340* | **Ste. Croix Range,** front. E. of Ste. Croix Wharf. | 46° 37.7′ N 71° 42.0′ W | **F.W.** | 197 **60** | **20** | Square skeleton tower, orange trapezoidal daymark, black stripe; 25. | Visible on range line only. Emergency light. |
| 4128 *H 2340.1* | -Rear, 483.9 meters 117°02′ from front. | 46° 37.6′ N 71° 41.6′ W | **F.W.** | 246 **75** | **20** | Square skeleton tower, orange trapezoidal daymark, black stripe; 51. | Visible on range line only. Emergency light. |
| | | | **F.G.** | 243 **74** | 6 | | Visible E. of 137°. |
| 4130 *H 2338* | Ste. Croix Est. | 46° 38.4′ N 71° 38.2′ W | **F.G.** | | 6 | Skeleton tower, orange rectangular slatwork daymarks on N., E. and W. faces; 30. | |
| 4148 *H 2342* | Ste. Croix. | 46° 37.7′ N 71° 43.9′ W | **Iso.Y.** period 2s | 48 **15** | 7 | Skeleton tower, orange rectangular slatwork daymark; 43. | Visible 189°-262°. Emergency light. |
| 4180 *H 2343* | Pointe au Platon. | 46° 40.2′ N 71° 50.8′ W | **Iso.Y.** period 2s | 33 **10** | 7 | Skeleton tower, orange rectangular slatwork daymarks on N. and W. faces; 30. | Visible 087°45′-272°. Emergency light. **Radar reflector.** |
| 4192 *H 2347* | Portneuf, on outer end of wharf, E. side. | 46° 40.9′ N 71° 52.6′ W | **Iso.R.** period 2s | 28 **9** | 6 | Square skeleton tower; 26. | |
| 4204 *H 2346* | **Portneuf-en-haut Range,** front. | 46° 41.4′ N 71° 52.2′ W | **F.G.** | 66 **20** | **17** | Square skeleton tower, orange trapezoidal daymark, black stripe; 60. | Visible on range line only. Emergency light. |
| 4208 *H 2346.1* | -Rear, 600 meters 028°29′ from front. | 46° 41.7′ N 71° 52.0′ W | **F.G.** | 134 **41** | **17** | Square skeleton tower, orange trapezoidal daymark, black stripe; 50. | Visible on range line only. Emergency light. |
| 4228 *H 2348* | **Lotbiniere Range,** front. | 46° 36.7′ N 71° 57.4′ W | **F.W.** | 51 **16** | **20** | Square skeleton tower, orange trapezoidal daymark, black stripe; 41. | Visible on range line only. Emergency light. |
| 4232 *H 2348.1* | -Rear, 867.8 meters 221°57′ from front. | 46° 36.3′ N 71° 57.8′ W | **F.W.** | 135 **41** | **20** | Skeleton tower, white enclosed upper portion, orange trapezoidal daymark, black stripe; 57. | Visible on range line only. Emergency light. |

| (1) No. | (2) Name and Location | (3) Position | (4) Characteristic | (5) Height | (6) Range | (7) Structure | (8) Remarks |
|---|---|---|---|---|---|---|---|
| | | | **CANADA-ST. LAWRENCE RIVER** | | | | |
| 4236 *H 2350* | **Barre a Boulard Range,** front. | 46° 39.6′ N 71° 52.6′ W | **F.W.** | 169 **52** | **20** | Skeleton tower, orange trapezoidal daymark, black stripe; 62. | Visible on range line only. Emergency light. |
| 4240 *H 2350.1* | -Rear, 1043 meters 054° from front. | 46° 39.9′ N 71° 51.9′ W | **F.W.** | 234 **71** | **20** | Skeleton tower, orange trapezoidal daymark, black stripe; 66. | Visible on range line only. Emergency light. |
| 4244 *H 2349* | **Ile Richelieu.** | 46° 38.6′ N 71° 54.6′ W | **F.Y.** | 19 **6** | **16** | Orange pile; 39. | Visible on bearing 054°. Not to be used as a directional light. |
| | | | **F.G.** | 19 **6** | 6 | | Visible 160°-250°. Intensified on bearing 211°. |
| | RACON | | **M(– –)** | | 10 | | (3 & 10cm). |
| 4284 *H 2354* | Pointe Langlois. | 46° 35.0′ N 71° 59.4′ W | **Iso.G.** period 2s | 71 **22** | 6 | Skeleton tower, orange rectangular daymarks on N., E. and W. faces; 35. | **Radar reflector.** |
| 4308 *H 2356* | **Calvaire (Calvary) Range,** front. | 46° 33.4′ N 72° 05.2′ W | **F.G.** | 131 **40** | **17** | Square skeleton tower, orange slatwork daymark, black stripe; 28. | Visible on range line only. Emergency light. |
| 4312 *H 2356.1* | -Rear, 616 meters 238°29′ from front. | 46° 33.2′ N 72° 05.6′ W | **F.G.** | 177 **54** | **17** | Square skeleton tower, orange slatwork daymark, black stripe; 65. | Visible on range line only. Emergency light. |
| 4316 *H 2358* | **Leclercville (Ste. Emmelie) Range,** front. | 46° 33.7′ N 72° 00.8′ W | **F.G.** | 121 **37** | **17** | Square skeleton tower, orange trapezoidal daymark, black stripe; 33. | Visible on range line only. Emergency light. |
| 4320 *H 2358.1* | -Rear, 1041.8 meters 092°42′ from front. | 46° 33.7′ N 72° 00.0′ W | **F.G.** | 186 **57** | **17** | White skeleton tower, orange trapezoidal daymark, black stripe; 39. | Visible on range line only. Emergency light. |
| | | | **F.G.** | 186 **57** | 6 | | Visible 360°. |
| 4332 *H 2360* | **La Perade Range,** front. | 46° 34.0′ N 72° 10.4′ W | **F.G.** | 49 **15** | **17** | Yellow skeleton tower, orange trapezoidal daymark, black stripe. | Visible on range line only. Emergency light. |
| 4336 *H 2360.1* | -Rear, 1,210.6 meters 272°35′ from front. | 46° 34.1′ N 72° 11.3′ W | **F.G.** | 88 **27** | **17** | Skeleton tower, orange trapezoidal daymark, black stripe. | Visible on range line only. Emergency light. |
| 4340 *H 2362* | **Pointe des Grondines Range,** front. | 46° 34.7′ N 72° 04.2′ W | **F.G.** | 48 **15** | **15** | Square skeleton tower, orange trapezoidal daymark, black stripe; 29. | Visible on range line only. Emergency light. |
| 4344 *H 2362.1* | -Rear, 2441 meters 066°37′ from front. | 46° 35.2′ N 72° 02.4′ W | **F.G.** | 127 **39** | **15** | Skeleton tower, orange trapezoidal slatwork daymark, black stripe; 103. | Visible on range line only. Emergency light. |
| 4348 *H 2364* | **Pointe des Grondines,** upper range, front. | 46° 35.1′ N 72° 05.9′ W | **Iso.W.** period 2s | 30 **9** | **17** | Square skeleton tower, orange trapezoidal daymark, black stripe; 29. | Visible on range line only. Emergency light. |
| 4352 *H 2364.1* | -Rear, 1997.5 meters 047°15′ from front. | 46° 35.8′ N 72° 04.7′ W | **Iso.W.** period 2s | 98 **30** | **17** | Skeleton tower, orange trapezoidal slatwork daymark, black stripe; 47. | Visible on range line only. Emergency light. |
| 4356 *H 2361* | Deschaillons Wharf, NW. corner. | 46° 33.7′ N 72° 06.4′ W | **Fl.G.** period 4s fl. 1s, ec. 3s | 38 **12** | 6 | White cylindrical mast; 32. | **Radar reflector.** |
| 4424 *H 2366* | **Batiscan Range,** front. | 46° 30.6′ N 72° 14.4′ W | **F.G.** | 44 **14** | **17** | Square skeleton tower, orange trapezoidal daymark, black stripe; 26. | Visible on range line only. Emergency light. |
| | | | **F.G.** | 43 **13** | 6 | Square skeleton tower; 59. | Visible on range line only. |

| (1) No. | (2) Name and Location | (3) Position | (4) Characteristic | (5) Height | (6) Range | (7) Structure | (8) Remarks |
|---|---|---|---|---|---|---|---|

## CANADA-ST. LAWRENCE RIVER

| (1) No. | (2) Name and Location | (3) Position | (4) Characteristic | (5) Height | (6) Range | (7) Structure | (8) Remarks |
|---|---|---|---|---|---|---|---|
| 4428 *H 2366.1* | -Rear, 440 meters 240°14′ from front. | 46° 30.4′ N 72° 14.7′ W | **F.G.** | 82 **25** | **17** | Skeleton tower, orange trapezoidal slatwork daymark, black stripe; 69. | Visible on range line only. Emergency light. |
| | | | **F.G.** | 69 **21** | 6 | Skeleton tower; 59. | Visible 360°. |
| 4436 *H 2368* | Les Becquets, root of wharf. | 46° 30.4′ N 72° 12.4′ W | **F.G.** | 28 **9** | 7 | White cylindrical mast; 23. | |
| 4460 *H 2366.4* | Batiscan Wharf. | 46° 30.0′ N 72° 14.8′ W | **Q.R.** | 43 **13** | 5 | White cylindrical mast; 33. | **Radar reflector.** |
| 4472 *H 2370* | Gentilly Range, on flats N. of Gentilly, front. | 46° 25.8′ N 72° 15.8′ W | **F.G.** | 39 **12** | 14 | White tower, orange trapezoidal daymark, black stripe; 13. | Visible on range line only. Emergency light. |
| | RACON | | **K(– • –)** | | 10 | | (3 & 10cm). |
| 4476 *H 2370.1* | -Rear, 2597 meters 197°45′ from front. | 46° 24.5′ N 72° 16.4′ W | **F.G.** | 101 **31** | 14 | Square skeleton tower, orange trapezoidal slatwork daymark, black stripe; 79. | Visible on range line only. Emergency light. |
| 4480 *H 2372* | Pointe a la Citrouille, on beach. | 46° 27.1′ N 72° 16.0′ W | **F.G.** | 59 **18** | 7 | Skeleton tower, orange rectangular daymark; 52. | |
| 4528 *H 2380* | **Champlain,** upper range, front. | 46° 26.1′ N 72° 21.4′ W | **2 F.G.** | 46 **14** | **17** | Mast, orange rectangular daymark, black stripe; 25. | Visible on range line only. Emergency light. |
| 4532 *H 2380.1* | -Rear, 455 meters 264° from front. | 46° 26.1′ N 72° 21.8′ W | **2 F.G.** | 89 **27** | **17** | Square skeleton tower, orange trapezoidal daymark, black stripe; 72. | Visible on range line only. Emergency light. |
| 4544 *H 2382* | **Champlain.** | 46° 26.4′ N 72° 20.7′ W | **F.G.** | 50 **15** | **16** | White skeleton tower, orange trapezoidal daymark; 48. | Visible 210°30′-225°30′. |
| | | | **Fl.R.** period 5s fl. 1s, ec. 4s | 46 **14** | 6 | | Visible 360°. |
| 4560 *H 2387* | Pointe a Bigot. | 46° 24.9′ N 72° 23.0′ W | **Fl.R.** period 6s fl. 1s, ec. 5s | 50 **15** | 4 | White skeleton tower, orange rectangular slatwork daymark; 45. | **Radar reflector.** |
| 4588 *H 2384* | **Becancour Range,** front. | 46° 22.4′ N 72° 27.0′ W | **F.G.** | 14 **4** | **17** | Square tower, orange daymark, black stripe; 6. | Visible on range line only. Emergency light. |
| | | | **F.G.** | 17 **5** | 6 | | Visible 360°. |
| 4592 *H 2384.1* | -Rear, 1798.5 meters 230°10′ from front. | 46° 21.8′ N 72° 28.1′ W | **F.G.** | 74 **22** | **17** | Square skeleton tower, orange slatwork daymark, black stripe; 55. | Visible on range line only. Emergency light. |
| 4608 *H 2386* | **Becancour,** Upper Traverse Range, front. | 46° 23.4′ N 72° 23.7′ W | **F.G.** | 33 **10** | **17** | Square skeleton tower, orange trapezoidal daymark, black stripe; 23. | Emergency light. |
| 4612 *H 2386.1* | -Rear, 669 meters 075°50′ from front. | 46° 23.4′ N 72° 23.2′ W | **F.G.** | 69 **21** | **17** | Square skeleton tower, orange trapezoidal daymark, black stripe; 56. | Emergency light. |
| 4614 *H 2385* | Port of Becancour. | 46° 24.0′ N 72° 22.5′ W | **F.Y.** | 23 **7** | | Yellow structure with black stripes. | Visible on bearing 167°44′. Private light. |
| 4624 *H 2388* | **Cap de la Madeleine Wharf Range,** SW. corner of wharf, front. | 46° 21.9′ N 72° 29.8′ W | **F.G.** | 34 **10** | **17** | Square skeleton tower, orange slatowrk daymark, black stripe; 25. | Visible on range line only. Emergency light. |
| 4628 *H 2388.1* | -Rear, 147 meters 242°32′ from front. | 46° 21.9′ N 72° 30.0′ W | **F.G.** | 66 **20** | **17** | Square skeleton tower, orange slatwork daymark, black stripe; 40. | Visible on range line only. Emergency light. |
| 4636 *H 2390* | **Cap de la Madeleine Lower Range,** front. | 46° 23.6′ N 72° 27.7′ W | **F.G.** | 61 **19** | **17** | Square skeleton tower, orange slatwork daymark, black stripe; 30. | Visible on range line only. Emergency light. |
| 4640 *H 2390.1* | -Rear, 975 meters 037°31′ from front. | 46° 24.0′ N 72° 27.3′ W | **F.G.** | 108 **33** | **17** | Skeleton tower, orange slatwork daymark, black stripe; 77. | Visible on range line and from side. Emergency light. |

| (1) No. | (2) Name and Location | (3) Position | (4) Characteristic | (5) Height | (6) Range | (7) Structure | (8) Remarks |
|---|---|---|---|---|---|---|---|
| | | | **CANADA-ST. LAWRENCE RIVER** | | | | |
| 4656 *H 2389* | Pte. des Chernaux. | 46° 21.4′ N 72° 30.4′ W | **Fl.R.** period 6s fl. 1s, ec. 5s | 46 **14** | 6 | Cylindrical mast; 33. | |
| 4680 *H 2392* | **Ste. Angele Range,** front. | 46° 18.8′ N 72° 34.0′ W | **F.G.** | 25 **8** | **17** | Cylindrical tower, orange rectangular slatwork daymark, black stripe; 26. | Visible on range line only. Emergency light. |
| 4684 *H 2392.1* | -Rear, 223 meters 228°47′ from front. | 46° 18.7′ N 72° 34.1′ W | **F.G.** | 49 **15** | **17** | Cylindrical tower, orange rectangular slatwork daymark, black stripe; 43. | Visible on range line only. Emergency light. |
| 4702 | Trois-Rivieres Bridge, W. RACON. | 46° 18.5′ N 72° 33.8′ W | **T(–)** | | 10 | | (3 & 10cm). |
| 4702.1 | -E. RACON. | 46° 18.4′ N 72° 33.7′ W | **H(• • • •)** | | 10 | | (3 & 10cm). |
| 4728 *H 2398.4* | Port St. Francois wharf. | 46° 16.4′ N 72° 37.2′ W | **Fl.Y.** period 5s fl. 1s, ec. 4s | 33 **10** | 10 | Pipe swing pole; 20. | |
| 4732 *H 2398* | **Port St. Francois Range,** front, on pier. | 46° 16.3′ N 72° 37.2′ W | **F.G.** | 35 **11** | **15** | White square tower, orange trapezoidal daymark, black stripe; 3. | Visible on range line only. Emergency light. **Radar reflector.** |
| 4736 *H 2398.1* | -Rear, 1373 meters 068°25′ from front. | 46° 16.5′ N 72° 36.2′ W | **F.G.** | 62 **19** | **15** | Skeleton tower, orange trapezoidal daymark, black stripe; 47. | Visible on range line only. Emergency light. |
| | LAKE ST. PETER: | | | | | | |
| 4748 *H 2400* | -Nicolet Sector, on pier. | 46° 15.5′ N 72° 39.1′ W | **Iso.W.** period 2s | 29 **9** | 5 | Square tower; 20. | W. 353°-173°, G.-353°. **Radar reflector.** |
| | | | **Iso.G.** period 2s | | 5 | | |
| | -RACON | | **G(– – •)** | | 10 | | (3 & 10cm). |
| 4752 *H 2401* | **-Range,** front. | 46° 15.6′ N 72° 37.8′ W | **F.G.** | 26 **8** | **15** | White cylindrical tower, orange trapezoidal daymark, black stripe; 16. | Visible on range line only. Emergency light. |
| 4756 *H 2401.1* | --Rear, 583 meters 096°45′ from front. | 46° 15.5′ N 72° 37.4′ W | **F.G.** | 94 **29** | **15** | Skeleton tower, orange trapezoidal daymark, black stripe; 71. | |
| 4804 *H 2402* | -Pointe du Lac Range, front. | 46° 16.1′ N 72° 41.7′ W | **F.G.** | 41 **12** | 12 | Square skeleton tower, orange trapezoidal daymark, black stripe; 16. | Visible on range line only. **Radar reflector.** |
| | | | **Iso.Y.** period 2s | | 5 | Square skeleton tower; 16. | |
| 4808 *H 2402.1* | --Rear, 2263 meters 056°08′ from front. | 46° 16.8′ N 72° 40.3′ W | **F.G.** | 161 **49** | 10 | White skeleton tower, orange trapezoidal daymark, black stripe; 112. | Visible on range line only. |
| 4872 *H 2404* | -Yamachiche Bend. | 46° 12.9′ N 72° 49.2′ W | **Iso.R.** period 2s | 33 **10** | 5 | On side of mast; 98. | |
| 4888 *H 2405* | -Curve West Range, front. | 46° 12.3′ N 72° 49.8′ W | **Fl.G.** period 6s fl. 1s, ec. 5s | 39 **12** | 5 | Square skeleton tower; 16. | |
| | -RACON | | **M(– –)** | | 10 | | (3 & 10cm). |
| 4892 *H 2405.1* | --Rear, 763 meters 236°01′ from front. | 46° 12.1′ N 72° 50.3′ W | **F.G.** | 84 **26** | 14 | White tower, orange trapezoidal daymark, black stripe; 56. | Visible on range line only. Emergency light. |
| 4932 *H 2408* | -Lac St. Pierre Upstream Range, front. | 46° 11.2′ N 72° 55.0′ W | **F.G.** | 36 **11** | 14 | Orange and white cylindrical tower, orange rectangular daymark, black stripe; 16. | Visible on range line only. **Radar reflector.** |
| | | | **Iso.G.** period 2s | 36 **11** | 5 | White cylindrical tower, red stripe; 16. | |

| (1) No. | (2) Name and Location | (3) Position | (4) Characteristic | (5) Height | (6) Range | (7) Structure | (8) Remarks |
|---|---|---|---|---|---|---|---|
| | | | **CANADA-ST. LAWRENCE RIVER** | | | | |
| 4936 *H 2408.1* | --Rear, 914 meters 249°57′ from front. | 46° 11.0′ N 72° 55.6′ W | **F.G.** | 75 **23** | 14 | Skeleton tower, orange square daymark, black stripe; 56. | Visible on range line only. **Radar reflector.** |
| | | | **Iso.R.** period 2s | 80 **24** | 5 | Skeleton tower; 59. | |
| | --RACON | | **N(– •)** | | 10 | | (3 & 10cm). |
| 4940 *H 2409* | -Curve No. 2 Downstream Range, front. | 46° 11.7′ N 72° 53.7′ W | **F.G.** | 38 **12** | 12 | Orange rectangular tower, orange rectangular daymark, black stripe; 16. | Visible on range line only. **Radar reflector.** |
| | | | **Iso.W.** period 2s | 39 **12** | 6 | Orange rectangular tower; 16. | Reference light. Visible 360°. |
| 4944 *H 2409.1* | --Rear, 611 meters 044°06′ from front. | 46° 11.9′ N 72° 53.4′ W | **F.G.** | 70 **21** | 12 | White skeleton tower, orange trapezoidal daymark, black stripe; 49. | Visible on range line only. |
| | | | **Iso.G.** period 2s | 72 **22** | 6 | Skeleton tower; 52. | Reference light. Visible 360°. |
| 4956 *H 2410* | -Louiseville. | 46° 13.3′ N 72° 55.5′ W | **F.G.** | 26 **8** | | White cylindrical tower; 20. | Visible on bearing 334.5°. Private light. |
| 4988 *H 2411* | -Maskinonge Curve. | 46° 09.4′ N 72° 56.5′ W | **Iso.Y.** period 2s | 46 **14** | 5 | Orange cylindrical tower, white rectangular daymark, red and white bands; 16. | **Radar reflector.** |
| 5028 *H 2414* | -Ile aux Raisin Range, front. | 46° 06.2′ N 72° 57.9′ W | **F.G.** | 33 **10** | 11 | White cylindrical tower, orange trapezoidal daymark, black stripe; 23. | Visible on range line only. |
| 5032 *H 2414.1* | --Rear, 573.3 meters 193°01′ from front. | 46° 05.9′ N 72° 58.0′ W | **F.G.** | 89 **27** | 11 | Square skeleton tower, orange trapezoidal daymark, black stripe; 75. | |
| | | | **Iso.W.** period 2s | | 6 | Square skeleton tower; 85. | |
| | --RACON | | **K(– • –)** | | 10 | | (3 & 10cm). |
| 5044 *H 2416* | -Isle des Barques Range, front. | 46° 05.3′ N 72° 59.7′ W | **F.G.** | 37 **11** | 13 | Block tower, orange trapezoidal daymark, black stripe; 13. | Visible on range line only. |
| 5046 *H 2416.1* | --Rear, 480 meters 218°26 from front. | 46° 05.1′ N 72° 59.9′ W | **F.G.** | 95 **29** | 13 | Square skeleton tower, orange trapezoidal daymark, black stripe; 66. | Visible on range line only. |
| 5047 *H 2424* | -Ile du Moine Range, front. | 46° 04.0′ N 73° 01.5′ W | **F.G.** | 43 **13** | 14 | White square tower, orange daymark, black stripe; 33. | Visible on range line only. |
| 5048 *H 2424.1* | --Rear 488 meters 082°30′ from front. | 46° 04.0′ N 73° 01.1′ W | **F.G.** | 90 **27** | 14 | Skeleton tower, orange trapezoidal daymark, black stripe; 62. | Visible on range line only. only. |
| 5072 *H 2422* | **Ste. Anne de Sorel Range,** front. | 46° 03.5′ N 73° 03.4′ W | **F.G.** | 43 **13** | **15** | White square tower, orange trapezoidal daymark, black stripe; 26. | Visible on range line only. Emergency light. |
| | | | **F.G.** | 46 **14** | 5 | White square tower; 33. | Visible 360°. |
| 5076 *H 2422.1* | -Rear, 771 meters 231°51′ from front. | 46° 03.3′ N 73° 03.8′ W | **F.G.** | 101 **31** | **15** | Tripod skeleton tower, orange trapezoidal daymark, black stripe; 82. | Visible on range line only. Emergency light. |
| 5104 *H 2426* | **Ile de Grace Range,** front. | 46° 04.1′ N 73° 03.0′ W | **F.G.** | 42 **13** | **15** | White square tower, orange trapezoidal daymark, black stripe; 26. | Visible on range line only. |
| | | | **Iso.G.** period 2s | | 5 | White square tower; 26. | Visible 311°-346°. |

| (1) No. | (2) Name and Location | (3) Position | (4) Characteristic | (5) Height | (6) Range | (7) Structure | (8) Remarks |
|---|---|---|---|---|---|---|---|
| | | | **CANADA-ST. LAWRENCE RIVER** | | | | |
| 5108 *H 2426.1* | -Rear, SE. end of island, 598 meters 073°16′ from front. | 46° 04.2′ N 73° 02.6′ W | **F.G.** | 73 **22** | **15** | Square skeleton tower, enclosed upper portion, orange slatwork daymark, black stripe; 59. | Visible on range line only. |
| | | | **Iso.G.** period 2s | | 5 | Skeleton tower; 59. | Visible 275°-18°. |
| 5136 *H 2450* | Ile Dupas Range, front. | 46° 03.5′ N 73° 09.4′ W | **F.G.** | 46 **14** | 12 | White square tower, orange trapezoidal daymark, black stripe; 13. | Visible on range line only. Emergency light. |
| 5140 *H 2450.1* | -Rear, on S. end of Ile Dupas, 625 meters 015°07′ from front. | 46° 03.8′ N 73° 09.3′ W | **F.G.** | 82 **25** | 12 | Skeleton tower, orange slatwork daymark, black stripe; 65. | Visible on range line only. Emergency light. |
| 5144 *H 2451* | **Ile St. Ours Course,** lower range, front. | 45° 57.9′ N 73° 12.7′ W | **F.G.** | 36 **11** | **17** | Cylindrical tower, orange trapezoidal daymark, black stripe; 20. | Visible on range line only. Emergency light. |
| 5148 *H 2451.1* | -Rear, 713.4 meters 002°22′ from front. | 45° 58.2′ N 73° 12.7′ W | **F.G.** | 112 **34** | **17** | Rectangular tower, orange trapezoidal daymark, black stripe; 72. | Visible on range line only. Emergency light. |
| 5172 *H 2452* | Ile St. Ours Course Range, front. | 45° 53.1′ N 73° 13.0′ W | **F.G.** | 56 **17** | 13 | Skeleton tower, orange slatwork daymark, black stripe; 43. | Visible on range line only. Emergency light. |
| 5176 *H 2452.1* | -Rear, 670 meters 182°20′ from front. | 45° 52.7′ N 73° 13.0′ W | **F.G.** | 109 **33** | 13 | Square skeleton tower, orange slatwork daymark, black stripe; 62. | Visible 066°20′-112°23′ and on range line. Emergency light. |
| 5192 *H 2454* | Petite Traverse Range, front. | 45° 54.7′ N 73° 12.5′ W | **F.G.** | | | Cylindrical tower, orange trapezoidal slatwork daymark, black stripe; 23. | Visible on range line only. Emergency light. |
| 5196 *H 2454.1* | -Rear, 516.5 meters 045°43′ from front. | 45° 54.9′ N 73° 12.2′ W | **F.G.** | 105 **32** | | Square skeleton tower, orange slatwork daymark, black stripe; 65. | Visible on range line only. Emergency light. |
| 5206 *H 2453* | Ile St. Ours, S. end. | 45° 54.3′ N 73° 13.5′ W | **Iso.Y.** period 2s | 49 **15** | 5 | Square skeleton tower; 20. | |
| | RACON | | **M(– –)** | | 10 | | (3 & 10cm). |
| 5208 *H 2456* | **Bellmouth Curve.** | 45° 55.2′ N 73° 12.5′ W | **F.R.** | 73 **22** | **15** | Skeleton tower, orange and white rectangular daymark; 39. | Visible on bearing 024°46′. Emergency light. |
| 5224 *H 2458* | **Contrecoeur Course Range,** front. | 45° 55.3′ N 73° 12.5′ W | **F.Y.** | 85 **26** | **20** | Square skeleton tower, orange trapezoidal daymark, black stripe; 52. | Visible on range line only. Emergency light. |
| 5228 *H 2458.1* | -Rear, 772 meters 033°06′ from front. | 45° 55.7′ N 73° 12.2′ W | **F.Y.** | 139 **42** | **20** | Tripod skeleton tower, orange trapezoidal daymark, black stripe; 82. | Visible on range line only. Emergency light. |
| 5252 *H 2460* | **Lavaltrie Range,** SE. side of Lavaltrie Island, front. | 45° 53.0′ N 73° 15.8′ W | **F.G.** | 26 **8** | **16** | White square tower, orange trapezoidal daymark, black stripe; 13. | Visible on range line only. Emergency light. |
| 5256 *H 2460.1* | -Rear, on pier, 561 meters 208°41′ from front. | 45° 52.7′ N 73° 16.0′ W | **F.G.** | 66 **20** | **16** | Skeleton tower, orange slatowrk daymark, black stripe; 56. | Visible on range line only. Emergency light. |
| | -RACON | | **N(– •)** | | 10 | | (3 & 10cm). |
| 5300 *H 2470* | **Contrecoeur Traverse Range,** front. | 45° 49.9′ N 73° 16.9′ W | **F.G.** | 52 **16** | **15** | White cylindrical tower, orange trapezoidal daymark, black stripe; 36. | Visible on range line only. Emergency light. |
| 5304 *H 2470.1* | -Rear, 401 meters 200°13′ from front. | 45° 49.7′ N 73° 17.0′ W | **F.G.** | 93 **28** | **15** | Square tower, orange trapezoidal daymark, black stripe; 72. | Visible on range line only. Emergency light. |
| 5308 *H 2472* | Contrecoeur to Vercheres Range, front. | 45° 51.9′ N 73° 15.1′ W | **F.G.** | 31 **10** | 14 | Square tower, orange slatwork daymark, black stripe; 13. | Visible on range line only. |

| (1) No. | (2) Name and Location | (3) Position | (4) Characteristic | (5) Height | (6) Range | (7) Structure | (8) Remarks |
|---|---|---|---|---|---|---|---|
| | | | **CANADA-ST. LAWRENCE RIVER** | | | | |
| 5312 *H 2472.1* | -Rear, 1724 meters 040°24′ from front. | 45° 52.6′ N 73° 14.2′ W | **F.G.** | 64 **20** | 14 | Square skeleton tower, orange slatwork daymark, black stripe; 49. | Visible on range line only. |
| | | | **Iso.G.** period 2s | 66 **20** | 6 | Square skeleton tower; 49. | Visible 360°. |
| 5352 *H 2476* | **Vercheres Village Range,** front. | 45° 46.8′ N 73° 21.4′ W | **F.G.** | 33 **10** | **17** | Red and white square tower, orange trapezoidal daymark, black stripe; 22. | Visible on range line only. Emergency light. |
| 5356 *H 2476.1* | -Rear, about 634.5 meters 220°20′ from front. | 45° 46.5′ N 73° 21.7′ W | **F.G.** | 79 **24** | **17** | White square tower, orange trapezoidal daymark, black stripe; 55. | Visible on range line only. Emergency light. |
| 5364 *H 2478* | **Vercheres Traverse Range,** front. | 45° 47.8′ N 73° 19.6′ W | **F.G.** | 52 **16** | **16** | White cylindrical tower, orange rectangular daymark, black stripe. | Visible on range line only. Emergency light. |
| 5368 *H 2478.1* | -Rear, 494 meters 055°56′ from front. | 45° 47.9′ N 73° 19.3′ W | **F.G.** | 85 **26** | **16** | White square tower, orange rectangular daymark, black stripe. | Visible on range line only. Emergency light. |
| 5388 *H 2480* | Ile Bouchard Range, front. | 45° 47.9′ N 73° 20.7′ W | **F.G.** | 43 **13** | 14 | Cylindrical mast, orange rectangular daymark, black stripe; 30. | Visible on range line only. Emergency light. |
| 5392 *H 2480.1* | -Rear, on Ile Bouchard, SE. side, 935 meters 037°36′ from front. | 45° 48.3′ N 73° 20.2′ W | **F.G.** | 73 **22** | 14 | Square tower, orange trapezoidal daymark, black stripe; 61. | Visible on range line only. Emergency light. |
| 5404 *H 2482* | Ile Deslauriers Range, E., front. | 45° 42.7′ N 73° 26.4′ W | **Iso.G.** | 36 **11** | 14 | Square skeleton tower, orange trapezoidal daymark, black stripe; 23. | Visible on range line only. |
| 5408 *H 2482.1* | -Rear, E. side of Ile Ste. Therese, 2653 meters 217°31′ from front. | 45° 41.6′ N 73° 27.6′ W | **Iso.G.** | 105 **32** | 14 | Skeleton tower, orange trapezoidal daymark, black stripe; 89. | Visible on range line only. |
| | | | **Iso.G.** period 2s | 108 **33** | 4 | Skeleton tower; 89. | |
| 5448 *H 2484* | Ile Ste. Therese Lower Range, front. | 45° 41.1′ N 73° 27.5′ W | **F.G.** | 36 **11** | 8 | White cylindrical tower, orange trapezoidal daymark, black stripe; 15. | |
| 5452 *H 2484.1* | -Rear, 152.7 meters 213°07′ from front. | 45° 41.0′ N 73° 27.6′ W | **F.G.** | 52 **16** | 14 | White cylindrical tower, orange trapezoidal daymark, black stripe; 33. | Visible on range line only. |
| 5476 *H 2487* | **Varennes Range,** front. | 45° 41.2′ N 73° 26.5′ W | **F.G.** | 39 **12** | **15** | White cylindrical tower, orange trapezoidal daymark, black stripe; 30. | Visible on range line only. Emergency light. |
| 5480 *H 2487.1* | -Rear, 325.8 meters 032°35′ from front. | 45° 41.4′ N 73° 26.4′ W | **F.G.** | 74 **23** | **15** | Square skeleton tower, orange trapezoidal daymark, black stripe; 62. | Visible on range line only. Emergency light. |
| | | | **F.G.** | 72 **22** | 5 | Square skeleton tower; 59. | Visible 360°. |
| 5496 *H 2486* | Iles de Varennes Range, front. | 45° 40.1′ N 73° 27.4′ W | **F.G.** | 31 **9** | 7 | Cylindrical tower, orange trapezoidal slatwork daymark, black stripe; 20. | Visible on range line only. |
| 5500 *H 2486.1* | -Rear, 122.4 meters 186°11′ from front. | 45° 40.0′ N 73° 27.4′ W | **F.G.** | 51 **16** | 7 | Cylindrical tower, orange trapezoidal slatwork daymark, black stripe; 39. | Visible on range line only. |
| 5512 *H 2490* | Ile Ste. Therese Upper Range, E. side Ile aux Vaches, front. | 45° 39.9′ N 73° 28.0′ W | **F.G.** | 37 **11** | 10 | White cylindrical tower, orange rectangular daymark; 13. | Visible on range line only. Emergency light. |
| | | | **F.G.** | 39 **12** | 5 | | |

| (1) No. | (2) Name and Location | (3) Position | (4) Characteristic | (5) Height | (6) Range | (7) Structure | (8) Remarks |
|---|---|---|---|---|---|---|---|
| | | | **CANADA-ST. LAWRENCE RIVER** | | | | |
| 5516 *H 2490.1* | -Rear, 1262 meters 024°50′ from front. | 45° 40.5′ N 73° 27.6′ W | **F.G.** | 98 **30** | 10 | Square skeleton tower, orange trapezoidal daymark, black stripe; 72. | Visible on range line only. Emergency light. |
| | | | **F.G.** | 98 **30** | 5 | | |
| 5544 *H 2496* | **Tetreaultville Range,** front. | 45° 35.8′ N 73° 30.6′ W | **F.G.** | 48 **15** | **17** | Cylindrical tower, orange trapezoidal daymark, black stripe; 72. | Visible on range line only. Emergency light. |
| 5548 *H 2496.1* | -Rear, 629.8 meters 204°50′ from front. | 45° 35.5′ N 73° 30.8′ W | **F.G.** | 99 **30** | **17** | Cylindrical tower, orange trapezoidal daymark, black stripe; 72. | Visible on range line only. Emergency light. |
| 5564 *H 2497* | **Longue Pointe Traverse Range,** front. | 45° 33.7′ N 73° 29.7′ W | **Iso.G.** period 2s | 46 **14** | **18** | White cylindrical tower, orange trapezoidal daymark, black stripe; 30. | Visible on range line only. |
| 5568 *H 2497.1* | -Rear, 191.5 meters 169°48′ from front. | 45° 33.6′ N 73° 29.7′ W | **Iso.G.** period 2s | 66 **20** | **18** | White cylindrical tower, orange trapezoidal slatwork daymark, black stripe; 43. | Visible on range line only. |
| 5572 *H 2499* | **Grand Battures Trailhandier Range,** front. | 45° 35.7′ N 73° 29.6′ W | **Iso.W.** period 2s | 33 **10** | **15** | Square skeleton tower, orange trapezoidal daymark, black stripe; 23. | Visible on range line only. |
| 5576 *H 2499.1* | -Rear, 478 meters 022°34′ from front. | 45° 35.9′ N 73° 29.4′ W | **Iso.W.** period 2s | 79 **24** | **15** | White cylindrical tower, orange rectangular daymark, black stripe; 62. | Visible on range line only. |

# Section 4

## St. Lawrence Seaway, South Side of St. Lawrence River and New Brunswick

| (1) No. | (2) Name and Location | (3) Position | (4) Characteristic | (5) Height | (6) Range | (7) Structure | (8) Remarks |
|---|---|---|---|---|---|---|---|
| | **CANADA-ST. LAWRENCE SEAWAY** | | | | | | |
| 5632 *H 2506* | Jacques Cartier Bridge. | 45° 31.3′ N 73° 32.6′ W | **2 F.G.** | 178 **54** | | On bridge. | Private light. |
| 5646 *H 2519* | -Range, front. | 45° 25.9′ N 73° 41.7′ W | **F.G.** | 31 **9** | 12 | White cylindrical tower, orange trapezoidal daymark, black stripe. | Visible on range line only. Seasonal. |
| 5647 *H 2519.1* | --Rear, 250.6 meters 067°05′ from front. | 45° 26.0′ N 73° 41.5′ W | **F.G.** | 59 **18** | 12 | White cylindrical tower, orange trapezoidal daymark, black stripe; 49. | Visible on range line only. Seasonal. |
| | LAKE ST LOUIS: | | | | | | |
| 5648 *H 2517.5* | -Kahnawake Dyke. | 45° 24.5′ N 73° 43.2′ W | **F.Y.** | | | | Seasonal. Private light. |
| 5668 *H 2518* | -Pointe Johnson. | 45° 24.0′ N 73° 44.8′ W | **Iso.Y.** period 2s | 26 **8** | 14 | Cylindrical tower; 13. | Visible on bearing 248°30′. Seasonal. |
| 5692 *H 2517.2* | -Kahnawake Range, front. | 45° 24.2′ N 73° 47.8′ W | **F.G.** | 38 **12** | | Orange cylindrical tower, orange rectangular daymark, black stripe; 16. | Seasonal. |
| 5696 *H 2517.21* | --Rear, 513 meters 266°36′ from front. | 45° 24.2′ N 73° 48.2′ W | **F.G.** | 62 **19** | 7 | White cylindrical tower, orange trapezoidal daymark, black stripe; 43. | Visible on range line only. Seasonal. |
| | --RACON | | **G(– – •)** | | 4 | | (3 & 10cm). |
| 5701 *H 2517.04* | -Tekakwitha Island. | 45° 24.6′ N 73° 42.6′ W | **F.Y.** | | | | Private light. |
| 5702 *H 2518.4* | -Dixie Range, front, S. of Ile Dorval. | 45° 25.3′ N 73° 44.7′ W | **Q.G.** | 26 **8** | 4 | Cylindrical tower, orange rectangular daymark, black stripe; 75. | Seasonal. |
| 5703 *H 2518.41* | --Rear, 2038 meters 050°43′ from front. | 45° 26.0′ N 73° 43.5′ W | **Q.G.** | 81 **25** | 12 | Skeleton tower, orange trapezoidal slatwork daymark, black stripe; 75. | Visible on range line only. Seasonal. |
| 5704 *H 2517.1* | -Dorval Range, front. | 45° 25.1′ N 73° 45.6′ W | **F.G.** | 36 **11** | 11 | Orange cylindrical tower, orange rectangular daymark, black stripe; 13. | Visible on range line only. Seasonal. |
| 5708 *H 2517.11* | --Rear, 1069 meters 043°52′ from front. | 45° 25.6′ N 73° 45.0′ W | **F.G.** | 79 **24** | 11 | White cylindrical tower, orange trapezoidal daymark, black stripe; 56. | Visible on range line only. Seasonal. |
| 5748 *H 2522.5* | -Pointe Fortier. | 45° 21.2′ N 73° 53.8′ W | **F.Y.** | 54 **17** | 12 | Square skeleton tower, orange rectangular daymark; 36. | Visible on bearing 024°. Visible at center of E. entrance to Beauharnois Lock. Seasonal. |
| 5788 *H 2522.6* | -**Melocheville Range,** front. | 45° 19.2′ N 73° 56.6′ W | **F.G.** | 35 **11** | **17** | Square skeleton tower, orange trapezoidal daymark, black stripe; 26. | Visible on range line only. Seasonal. |
| 5792 *H 2522.61* | --Rear, 1287 meters 241°29′ from front. | 45° 18.8′ N 73° 57.4′ W | **F.G.** | 98 **30** | **17** | Square skeleton tower, orange trapezoidal daymark, black stripe; 46. | Visible on range line only. Seasonal. |
| 5796 *H 2528.4* | -South Wall Approach. | 45° 17.7′ N 73° 55.9′ W | **F.Y.** | 37 **11** | | Mast. | Private light. |

For other lights along the St. Lawrence Seaway and the Great Lakes see U.S.C.G. Light List Vol. VII, Great Lakes.

| (1) No. | (2) Name and Location | (3) Position | (4) Characteristic | (5) Height | (6) Range | (7) Structure | (8) Remarks |
|---|---|---|---|---|---|---|---|

## CANADA-ST. LAWRENCE SEAWAY

| (1) No. | (2) Name and Location | (3) Position | (4) Characteristic | (5) Height | (6) Range | (7) Structure | (8) Remarks |
|---|---|---|---|---|---|---|---|
| | BEAUHARNOIS CANAL: | | | | | | |
| 5800 *H 2528* | -Upper Beauharnois Lock Range, front. | 45° 18.0′ N 73° 55.7′ W | **F.Y.** | 43 **13** | 14 | White square skeleton tower, orange triangular daymark point up, black stripe; 33. | Seasonal. |
| 5804 *H 2528.1* | --Rear, 329 meters 028°20′ from front. | 45° 18.1′ N 73° 55.6′ W | **F.Y.** | 67 **20** | 14 | White square skeleton tower, orange triangular daymark point down, black stripe;52. | Seasonal. |
| 5816 *H 2530* | **-Powerhouse Range,** front. | 45° 16.7′ N 73° 56.0′ W | **Iso.W.** period 2s | 32 **10** | **15** | White skeleton tower, orange triangular daymark point up, black stripe; 30. | Seasonal. |
| 5820 *H 2530.1* | --Rear, 527 meters 046°17′ from front. | 45° 16.9′ N 73° 55.7′ W | **F.W.** | 74 **23** | **16** | White skeleton tower, orange triangular daymark point down, black stripe; 66. | Seasonal. |
| 5840 *H 2531* | -St. Louis Bridge Range, front. | 45° 15.0′ N 73° 57.6′ W | **Iso.Y.** period 2s | 41 **12** | 14 | White skeleton tower, orange triangular daymark point up, black stripe; 30. | Visible on range line only. Seasonal. |
| 5844 *H 2531.1* | --Rear, 658 meters 060°33′ from front. | 45° 15.1′ N 73° 57.2′ W | **F.Y.** | 61 **19** | **15** | White skeleton tower, orange triangular daymark point down, black stripe; 59. | Visible on range line only. Seasonal. |
| 5872 *H 2532* | -St. Louis Directional, E. side of bridge. | 45° 13.9′ N 74° 00.1′ W | **F.Y.** | 16 **5** | 14 | Bridge, orange triangular daymark point up. | Visible on bearing 226°30′. Seasonal. |
| 5888 *H 2535* | **-Campsite Range,** front. | 43° 13.3′ N 74° 00.8′ W | **Iso.W.** period 2s | 35 **11** | **15** | White square skeleton tower, orange triangular daymark point up, black stripe; 30. | Seasonal. |
| 5892 *H 2535.1* | --Rear, 669 meters 090° from front. | 45° 13.3′ N 74° 00.3′ W | **F.W.** | 51 **16** | **16** | White square skeleton tower, orange triangular daymark point down, black stripe; 36. | Seasonal. |
| 5900 *H 2536* | St. Louis Bridge steering light. | 45° 12.9′ N 74° 02.9′ W | **Dir.Iso.Y.** period 2s | 33 **10** | 14 | White skeleton tower, orange triangular daymark point up; 23. | Visible on bearing 240°30′. |
| 5920 *H 2537* | -Valleyfield Bridge Range, front. | 45° 12.9′ N 74° 03.8′ W | **Iso.Y.** period 2s | 34 **10** | 14 | White square skeleton tower, orange triangular daymark point up, black stripe; 23. | Seasonal. |
| 5924 *H 2537.1* | --Rear, 468 meters 107°26′ from front. | 45° 12.8′ N 74° 03.5′ W | **F.Y.** | 63 **19** | **15** | White square skeleton tower, orange triangular daymark point down, black stripe; 36. | Seasonal. |
| 5928 *H 2533* | **-Duck Range,** front. | 45° 12.8′ N 74° 04.3′ W | **Iso.W.** period 2s | 36 **11** | **15** | White square skeleton tower, orange triangular daymark point up, black stripe; 30. | Seasonal. |
| 5932 *H 2533.1* | --Rear, 552 meters 248°30′ from front. | 45° 12.9′ N 74° 03.9′ W | **F.W.** | 60 **18** | **16** | White skeleton tower, orange triangular daymark point down, black stripe; 30. | Seasonal. |
| 5984 *H 2538* | -W. Entrance Range, front. | 45° 14.1′ N 74° 08.5′ W | **Iso.G.** period 4s | 39 **12** | 8 | White skeleton tower, orange trapezoidal daymark, black stripe; 30. | Visible on range line only. Seasonal. |
| 5988 *H 2538.1* | --Rear, 1501 meters 083°30′ from front. | 45° 14.2′ N 74° 07.3′ W | **F.G.** | 92 **28** | 10 | Skeleton tower, orange trapezoidal daymark, black stripe; 92. | Visible on range line only. Seasonal. |
| 5992 *H 2541* | -Coteau-Landing E. breakwater, SE. head. | 45° 15.2′ N 74° 12.4′ W | **Fl.G.** period 4s | 23 **7** | 3 | White cylindrical tower, green upper portion; 16. | Seasonal. |
| | LAKE ST. FRANCIS: | | | | | | |
| 6064 *H 2543* | -Hay Point (Pte-au-Foin) Range, front. | 45° 13.4′ N 74° 16.5′ W | **F.G.** | 35 **11** | 10 | White skeleton tower, orange triangular daymark point up, black stripe; 33. | Visible on range line only. Seasonal. |

For other lights along the St. Lawrence Seaway and the Great Lakes see U.S.C.G. Light List Vol. VII, Great Lakes.

| (1) No. | (2) Name and Location | (3) Position | (4) Characteristic | (5) Height | (6) Range | (7) Structure | (8) Remarks |
|---|---|---|---|---|---|---|---|

## CANADA-ST. LAWRENCE SEAWAY

| (1) No. | (2) Name and Location | (3) Position | (4) Characteristic | (5) Height | (6) Range | (7) Structure | (8) Remarks |
|---|---|---|---|---|---|---|---|
| 6068 *H 2543.1* | --Rear, 810 meters 263°30′ from front. | 45° 13.4′ N 74° 17.2′ W | **F.G.** | 59 **18** | 10 | White skeleton tower, orange triangular daymark point up, black stripe; 53. | Visible on range line only. Seasonal. |
| 6069 *H 2543.5* | **-Pointe-au-Foin Range,** front. | 45° 13.0′ N 74° 17.4′ W | **Iso.R.** period 4s | 47 **14** | **15** | White cylindrical tower, orange triangular daymark point up, black stripe. | Visible on range line only. Seasonal. |
| 6071 *H 2543.51* | --Rear, 300 meters 029°08′ from front. | 45° 13.2′ N 74° 17.3′ W | **F.R.** | 66 **20** | **15** | White skeleton tower, orange triangular daymark point down, black stripe. | Visible on range line only. Seasonal. |
| 6088 *H 2544* | -Pointe Beaudette Range, front. | 45° 12.1′ N 74° 18.9′ W | **F.G.** | 36 **11** | 14 | White cylindrical tower, orange triangular daymark point up, black stripe; 36. | Visible on range line only. Seasonal. |
| 6092 *H 2544.1* | --Rear, 762 meters 242°30′ from front. | 45° 11.9′ N 74° 19.4′ W | **F.G.** | 59 **18** | 14 | White skeleton tower, orange triangular daymark point down, black stripe; 59. | Visible on range line only. Seasonal. |
| 6096 *H 2550* | -Port Louis Flats Range, front. | 45° 11.2′ N 74° 18.5′ W | **F.W.** | 38 **12** | 13 | White cylindrical tower, orange triangular daymark point up, black stripe; 39. | Visible on range line only. Seasonal. |
| 6100 *H 2550.1* | --Rear, 1219 meters 054°40′ from front. | 45° 11.6′ N 74° 17.7′ W | **F.W.** | 73 **22** | 13 | White cylindrical tower, orange triangular daymark point down, black stripe; 72. | Visible on range line only. Seasonal. |
| 6120 *H 2545* | -Ile Chretien Range, front. | 45° 10.2′ N 74° 19.6′ W | **Iso.R.** period 4s | 36 **11** | 14 | White cylindrical tower, orange triangular daymark point up, black stripe; 36. | Visible on range line only. Seasonal. |
| 6124 *H 2545.1* | --Rear, 642.4 meters 209°11′ from front. | 45° 09.9′ N 74° 19.8′ W | **F.R.** | 56 **17** | 14 | White skeleton tower, orange triangular daymark point down, black stripe; 52. | Visible on range line only. Seasonal. |
| 6132 *H 2546* | -St. Anicet Shoal. | 45° 09.4′ N 74° 22.0′ W | **Iso.W.** period 2s | 33 **10** | 7 | White cylindrical tower, green top, marked D27; 36. | Seasonal. |
| 6146 *H 2547* | Nadeaus Point, (Creg Quay), seaward end of breakwater. | 45° 09.7′ N 74° 25.2′ W | **Fl.G.** period 4s | 25 **8** | 4 | White cylindrical tower, green top; 19. | Seasonal. Private light. |
| 6152 *H 2548* | -Point Dupuis Range, front. | 45° 07.7′ N 74° 24.6′ W | **F.Y.** | 30 **9** | 14 | White square skeleton tower, orange triangular daymark point up, black stripe; 25. | Seasonal. |
| 6156 *H 2548.1* | --Rear, 396 meters 086°20′ from front. | 45° 07.7′ N 74° 24.0′ W | **F.Y.** | 66 **20** | 14 | White skeleton tower, orange triangular daymark point down, black stripe; 62. | Seasonal. |
| 6180 *H 2552* | -Lancaster Bar. | 45° 07.4′ N 74° 26.9′ W | **Fl.W.** period 4s fl. 0.5s, ec. 3.5s | 33 **10** | 9 | White cylindrical tower, green top marked D41; 20. | Seasonal. |
| 6184 *H 2551* | -South Gulby Range, front. | 45° 07.3′ N 74° 26.2′ W | **F.W.** | 33 **10** | 13 | White cylindrical tower, orange triangular daymark point up, black stripe; 33. | Visible on range line only. Seasonal. |
| 6188 *H 2551.1* | --Rear, 2042 meters 234°40′ from front. | 45° 06.7′ N 74° 27.4′ W | **F.W.** | 72 **22** | 13 | White cylindrical tower, orange triangular daymark point down, black stripe; 75. | Visible on range line only. Seasonal. |
| 6228 *H 2556* | --Range, front, D50. | 45° 06.0′ N 74° 29.5′ W | **Iso.W.** period 4s | 39 **12** | 13 | White hexagonal tower, red top, orange triangular daymark point up, black stripe, marked D50; 33. | Visible on range line only. Seasonal. |
| 6232 *H 2556.1* | ---Rear, 785 meters 228°45′ from front. | 45° 05.7′ N 74° 29.9′ W | **F.W.** | 79 **24** | 13 | White cylindrical tower, orange triangular daymark point down, black stripe; 79. | Visible on range line only. Seasonal. |
| 6240 *H 2560* | -Butternut Island Range, front. | 45° 05.6′ N 74° 29.3′ W | **Iso.W.** period 4s | 36 **11** | 13 | White cylindrical tower, orange triangular daymark point up, black stripe; 36. | Visible on range line only. Seasonal. |

For other lights along the St. Lawrence Seaway and the Great Lakes see U.S.C.G. Light List Vol. VII, Great Lakes.

| (1) No. | (2) Name and Location | (3) Position | (4) Characteristic | (5) Height | (6) Range | (7) Structure | (8) Remarks |
|---|---|---|---|---|---|---|---|

**CANADA-ST. LAWRENCE SEAWAY**

| (1) No. | (2) Name and Location | (3) Position | (4) Characteristic | (5) Height | (6) Range | (7) Structure | (8) Remarks |
|---|---|---|---|---|---|---|---|
| 6244 *H 2560.1* | --Rear, 609 meters 045°55′ from front. | 45° 05.8′ N 74° 29.0′ W | **F.W.** | 62 **19** | 13 | White cylindrical tower, orange triangular daymark point down, black stripe; 62. | Visible on range line only. Seasonal. |
| 6256 *H 2558* | -Thompson Island Lower Range, front. | 45° 04.6′ N 74° 30.2′ W | **Iso.W.** period 4s | 31 **9** | 13 | White cylindrical tower, orange triangular daymark point up, black stripe; 30. | Visible on range line only. Seasonal. |
| 6260 *H 2558.1* | --Rear, about 697 meters 207°16′ from front. | 45° 04.2′ N 74° 30.5′ W | **F.W.** | 59 **18** | 13 | White skeleton tower, orange triangular daymark point down, black stripe; 51. | Visible on range line only. Seasonal. |
| 6288 *H 2568* | --Upper Range, front. | 45° 04.0′ N 74° 31.0′ W | **Iso.W.** period 4s | 32 **10** | 13 | White skeleton tower, orange triangular daymark point up, black stripe; 25. | Visible on range line only. Seasonal. |
| 6292 *H 2568.1* | ---Rear, 731 meters 059°15′ from front. | 45° 04.3′ N 74° 30.6′ W | **F.W.** | 58 **18** | 13 | White skeleton tower, orange triangular daymark point down, black stripe; 56. | Visible on range line only. Seasonal. |
| 6316 *H 2571* | Stanley Island East Steering light, E. end of island. | 45° 03.0′ N 74° 33.0′ W | **F.W.** | 30 **9** | 13 | White cylindrical tower, orange triangular daymark point up; 20. | Visible on bearing 226°. Seasonal. |
| 6324 *H 2572* | -Stanley Island. | 45° 03.0′ N 74° 33.3′ W | **Fl.G.** period 4s | 33 **10** | 4 | White cylindrical tower, green top; 26. | Seasonal. |
| 6332 *H 2573* | **-Stanley Crab.** | 45° 02.7′ N 74° 33.6′ W | **Dir.Iso.W.** period 2s | 33 **10** | **15** | White cylindrical tower, orange triangular daymark point up; 26. | Visible on bearing 083°. Seasonal. |
| 6336 *H 2574* | -Clark Island, E. head. | 45° 02.9′ N 74° 34.0′ W | **Fl.R.** period 4s | 30 **9** | 4 | White cylindrical tower, red upper part, marked D70; 26. | Seasonal. |
| 6372 *H 2576* | -McGibbons Point. | 45° 02.4′ N 74° 36.5′ W | **Dir.F.G.** | 33 **10** | 10 | White cylindrical tower, orange triangular daymark point up, marked D80; 30. | Visible on bearing 263°. Seasonal. |
| 6412 *H 2578* | -Cornwall Island Range, front. | 45° 00.9′ N 74° 39.9′ W | **F.W.** | 62 **19** | 14 | White skeleton tower, orange triangular daymark point up, black stripe; 52. | Visible on range line only. Seasonal. |
| 6416 *H 2578.1* | --Rear, 609 meters 241°10′ from front. | 45° 00.7′ N 74° 40.3′ W | **F.W.** | 98 **30** | 14 | White skeleton tower, orange triangular daymark point up, black stripe; 43. | Visible on range line only. Seasonal. |

For other lights along the St. Lawrence Seaway and the Great Lakes see U.S.C.G. Light List Vol. VII, Great Lakes.

**UNITED STATES-ST. LAWRENCE SEAWAY**

| (1) No. | (2) Name and Location | (3) Position | (4) Characteristic | (5) Height | (6) Range | (7) Structure | (8) Remarks |
|---|---|---|---|---|---|---|---|
| 6452 *H 2601* | -Cornwall Island, SE. point (Can.). | 45° 00.2′ N 74° 40.5′ W | **Q.R.** period 1s | 36 **11** | 3 | White cylindrical tower, red upper portion; 20. | Seasonal. |
| 6464 *H 2601.4* | -Cornwall Island (Can.). | 45° 00.0′ N 74° 41.0′ W | **Fl.R.** period 4s | 36 **11** | 4 | White cylindrical tower, red upper portion; 20. | Seasonal. |
| 6492 *H 2604* | -No. 10 (Can.). | 45° 00.1′ N 74° 42.8′ W | **Dir.W.R.G.** | 54 **16** | 8 | White skeleton tower, orange triangular daymark point up; 43. | F.R. 276°-277°45′, F.W.-279°15′, F.G.-281°. Seasonal. |
| | | | **F.R.** | 51 **16** | 13 | | Visible on bearing 048°. Seasonal. |
| | ST. REGIS ISLAND TO CROIL ISLANDS: | | | | | | |
| 6496 *H 2606* | -Raquette Point. | 44° 59.7′ N 74° 43.1′ W | **Fl.G.** period 2.5s | 28 **9** | | Pile, green square daymark. | Seasonal. |
| 6500 *H 2608* | -13. | 44° 59.6′ N 74° 43.4′ W | **Fl.G.** period 4s | 28 **9** | | Pile, green square daymark. | Seasonal. |

For other lights along the St. Lawrence Seaway and the Great Lakes see U.S.C.G. Light List Vol. VII, Great Lakes.

| (1) No. | (2) Name and Location | (3) Position | (4) Characteristic | (5) Height | (6) Range | (7) Structure | (8) Remarks |
|---|---|---|---|---|---|---|---|

## UNITED STATES-ST. LAWRENCE SEAWAY

| (1) No. | (2) Name and Location | (3) Position | (4) Characteristic | (5) Height | (6) Range | (7) Structure | (8) Remarks |
|---|---|---|---|---|---|---|---|
| 6510 *H 2673* | St. Lawrence Seaway No. 73. | 44° 55.6′ N 75° 05.8′ W | **Fl.G.** period 2.5s | 30 **9** | | Tower, green square daymark. | |
| | RACON | | **M(– –)** | | 6 | | |

For other lights along the St. Lawrence Seaway and the Great Lakes see U.S.C.G. Light List Vol. VII, Great Lakes.

## CANADA-ST. LAWRENCE ESTUARY, SOUTH SIDE

| (1) No. | (2) Name and Location | (3) Position | (4) Characteristic | (5) Height | (6) Range | (7) Structure | (8) Remarks |
|---|---|---|---|---|---|---|---|
| 6512 *H 2272* | Ile de Bellechasse. | 46° 55.9′ N 70° 46.0′ W | **Fl.Y.** period 6s fl. 1s, ec. 5s | 43 **13** | 6 | Red and white square skeleton tower; 26. | Seasonal. |
| 6528 *H 2250* | Montmagny Range, front, S. government wharf, head. | 46° 59.2′ N 70° 33.1′ W | **F.R.** | 26 **8** | 12 | Square skeleton tower, orange rectangular daymark, black stripe; 20. | Visible on range line only. Seasonal. |
| 6532 *H 2250.1* | -Rear, 92 meters 169°19′ from front. | 46° 59.1′ N 70° 33.1′ W | **F.R.** | 47 **14** | 12 | Square skeleton tower, orange rectangular daymark, black stripe; 25. | Visible on range line only. Seasonal. |
| 6540 *H 2246* | -Pointe aux Pins. | 47° 02.4′ N 70° 34.5′ W | **Fl.G.** period 6s fl. 1s, ec. 5s | 36 **11** | 6 | Square skeleton tower; 33. | Seasonal. |
| 6546 *H 2238.2* | -Ile aux Grues. | 47° 03.3′ N 70° 31.9′ W | **Fl.G.** period 6s fl. 1s, ec. 5s | 36 **11** | 10 | On wharf structure; 30. | Seasonal. |
| 6552 *H 2244* | **Hospital Rock Range,** front. | 47° 08.0′ N 70° 27.9′ W | **F.W.** | 31 **9** | **16** | Square skeleton tower, orange trapezoidal daymark, black stripe; 20. | Visible on range line only. Seasonal. |
| 6556 *H 2244.1* | -Rear, 1668 meters 025°24′ from front. | 47° 08.8′ N 70° 27.3′ W | **F.W.** | 90 **27** | **16** | Red and white square skeleton tower, orange trapezoidal daymark, black stripe; 60. | Visible on range line only. Seasonal. |
| 6584 *H 2228* | Stone Pillar. | 47° 12.3′ N 70° 21.6′ W | **Fl.W.** period 6s fl. 1s, ec. 5s | 83 **25** | 10 | Cylindrical tower; 43. | Seasonal. |
| 6600 *H 2226* | St. Jean Port Joli. | 47° 13.0′ N 70° 16.5′ W | **Fl.G.** period 6s fl. 1s, ec. 5s | 20 **6** | 5 | Square skeleton tower; 16. | Seasonal. |
| 6652 *H 2174* | Grande Ile. | 47° 37.3′ N 69° 51.7′ W | **Fl.W.** period 6s fl. 1s, ec. 5s | 115 **35** | 8 | Square skeleton tower; 39. | Seasonal. |
| 6664 *H 2172* | Long Pilgrim. | 47° 43.0′ N 69° 44.9′ W | **Fl.W.** period 6s fl. 1s, ec. 5s | 143 **44** | 8 | Square skeleton tower; 45. | Seasonal. |
| 6684 *H 2164* | Brandypot, island, E. head. | 47° 52.3′ N 69° 40.9′ W | **Iso.Y.** period 2s | 119 **36** | 8 | Square skeleton tower; 43. | |
| 6692 *H 2162* | Pointe de la Riviere du Loup. | 47° 50.9′ N 69° 34.2′ W | **Iso.G.** period 2s | 33 **10** | 7 | Pipe swing pole; 26. | |
| 6714 *H 2160.5* | Cacouna Harbor, N. | 47° 55.8′ N 69° 31.2′ W | **Fl.Y.** period 6s fl. 1s, ec. 5s | 27 **8** | 6 | Square skeleton tower; 16. | |
| 6715 *H 2160.6* | -S. | 47° 55.7′ N 69° 31.2′ W | **Iso.W.** period 2s | 26 **8** | 6 | Square skeleton tower; 16. | |
| 6715.1 *H 2160* | **-Harbor Range,** front. | 47° 55.9′ N 69° 29.6′ W | **F.R.** | 97 **30** | **16** | Cylindrical tower, orange trapezoidal daymark, black stripe; 49. | Visible on range line only. |

The lights on the south side of the St. Lawrence estuary are listed in sequence for a vessel proceeding seaward.

| (1) No. | (2) Name and Location | (3) Position | (4) Characteristic | (5) Height | (6) Range | (7) Structure | (8) Remarks |
|---|---|---|---|---|---|---|---|
| | | | | | | | |

## CANADA-ST. LAWRENCE ESTUARY, SOUTH SIDE

| (1) No. | (2) Name and Location | (3) Position | (4) Characteristic | (5) Height | (6) Range | (7) Structure | (8) Remarks |
|---|---|---|---|---|---|---|---|
| 6715.2<br>*H 2160.1* | --Rear, 349 meters 082°09′ from front. | 47° 55.9′ N<br>69° 29.3′ W | **F.R.** | 131<br>**40** | **16** | Square skeleton tower, orange trapezoidal daymark, black stripe; 49. | Visible on range line only. |
| | ILE VERTE: | | | | | | |
| 6724<br>*H 2146* | **-NW. point.** | 48° 03.1′ N<br>69° 25.5′ W | **Fl.W.**<br>period 5s<br>fl. 1s, ec. 4s | 56<br>**17** | **19** | White cylindrical tower; 56. | Mercury vapor light. |
| 6732<br>*H 2148* | -E. wharf, head. | 48° 02.4′ N<br>69° 24.4′ W | **F.G.** | 18<br>**6** | 7 | Square skeleton tower; 15. | Seasonal. |
| 6744<br>*H 2098* | Trois Pistoles Range, front. | 48° 08.1′ N<br>69° 11.2′ W | **F.R.** | 29<br>**9** | 6 | Square skeleton tower, orange trapezoidal daymark, black stripe; 25. | Visible on range line only.<br>Seasonal. |
| 6748<br>*H 2098.1* | -Rear, 241 meters 136°55′ from front. | 48° 08.0′ N<br>69° 11.1′ W | **F.R.** | 56<br>**17** | **16** | Square skeleton tower, orange trapezoidal daymark, black stripe; 50. | Visible on range line only.<br>Seasonal. |
| 6752<br>*H 2096* | Ile aux Basques. | 48° 09.0′ N<br>69° 14.3′ W | **Fl.Y.**<br>period 6s<br>fl. 1s, ec. 5s | 43<br>**13** | 7 | Square skeleton tower; 30. | Seasonal.<br>**Radar reflector.** |
| 6764<br>*H 2086* | Ile du Bic, SW. extremity. | 48° 23.2′ N<br>68° 53.3′ W | **Fl.W.**<br>period 6s<br>fl. 1s, ec. 5s | 36<br>**11** | 8 | Red and white square skeleton tower, orange rectangular daymarks; 31. | Seasonal. |
| 6768<br>*H 2084* | Ile Bicquette. | 48° 24.9′ N<br>68° 53.6′ W | **Fl.W.**<br>period 2s | 112<br>**34** | 12 | White cylindrical tower. | Visible 011°-295°.<br>Seasonal. |
| | | | **Fl.R.**<br>period 6s | | 5 | | Visible 192°-116°.<br>Seasonal. |
| | RIMOUSKI HARBOR: | | | | | | |
| 6776<br>*H 2072* | -Wharf, head. | 48° 28.9′ N<br>68° 31.0′ W | **Iso.G.**<br>period 2s | 47<br>**14** | 6 | Square skeleton tower; 43. | |
| 6780<br>*H 2074* | **-Range,** on government wharf, front. | 48° 28.1′ N<br>68° 31.1′ W | **Iso.R.**<br>period 1s | 37<br>**11** | **16** | Square skeleton tower, orange trapezoidal daymark, black stripe; 35. | Visible on range line only.<br>Emergency light. |
| | -RACON | | **N(– •)** | | 10 | | (3 & 10cm). |
| 6784<br>*H 2074.1* | --Rear, 702 meters 178°23′ from front. | 48° 27.7′ N<br>68° 31.1′ W | **Iso.R.**<br>period 1s | 68<br>**21** | **16** | Square skeleton tower, orange trapezoidal daymark, black stripe; 60. | Visible on range line only.<br>Emergency light. |
| 6800<br>*H 2048* | Pointe Mitis. | 48° 40.8′ N<br>68° 02.0′ W | **Fl.(3)W.**<br>period 7.5s<br>fl. 0.2s, ec. 1s<br>fl. 0.2s, ec. 1s<br>fl. 0.2s, ec. 4.8s | 69<br>**21** | | Hexagonal tower; 82. | Mercury vapor light.<br>Emergency light.<br>Private light. |
| | MATANE: | | | | | | |
| 6812<br>*H 2043* | **-E. breakwater,** head. | 48° 50.8′ N<br>67° 34.6′ W | **Fl.G.**<br>period 6s<br>fl. 1s, ec. 5s | 33<br>**10** | **16** | Square skeleton tower; 23. | |
| 6816<br>*H 2042* | -W. breakwater, head. | 48° 50.9′ N<br>67° 34.7′ W | **Fl.R.**<br>period 6s<br>fl. 1s, ec. 5s | 36<br>**11** | 6 | Square tower; 23. | |
| 6817<br>*H 2041.2* | -E. breakwater, mouth of river. | 48° 51.4′ N<br>67° 32.1′ W | **Fl.G.**<br>period 5s<br>fl. 1s, ec. 4s | 20<br>**6** | | Mast. | Seasonal.<br>Private light. |

The lights on the south side of the St. Lawrence estuary are listed in sequence for a vessel proceeding seaward.

| (1) No. | (2) Name and Location | (3) Position | (4) Characteristic | (5) Height | (6) Range | (7) Structure | (8) Remarks |
|---|---|---|---|---|---|---|---|
| | **CANADA-ST. LAWRENCE ESTUARY, SOUTH SIDE** | | | | | | |
| 6818 *H 2041.3* | -W. breakwater. | 48° 51.4′ N 67° 32.1′ W | **Fl.R.** period 5s fl. 1s, ec. 4s | 20 **6** | | Mast. | Seasonal. Private light. |
| 6820 *H 2044* | -Railway Wharf. | 48° 50.6′ N 67° 34.4′ W | **F.R.** | 24 **7** | 7 | Square skeleton tower; 10. | Private light. |
| 6824 *H 2031* | Les Mechins East. | 49° 00.3′ N 66° 58.4′ W | **Fl.R.** period 6s fl. 1s, ec. 5s | 26 **8** | 6 | Square skeleton tower; 20. | Seasonal. |
| 6828 *H 2032* | Le Gros Mechins Wharf. | 49° 00.4′ N 66° 58.5′ W | **Fl.Y.** period 4s | 26 **8** | 5 | Square skeleton tower; 22. | Seasonal. Private light. |
| 6836 *H 1852* | Ste. Anne des Monts. | 49° 08.1′ N 66° 29.1′ W | **F.R.** | 33 **10** | 7 | Square skeleton tower; 25. | Seasonal. |
| 6837 *H 1854* | -N. breakwater. | 49° 08.1′ N 66° 29.3′ W | **Fl.R.** period 6s | 14 **4** | 3 | Structure on breakwater. | Seasonal. |
| 6838 *H 1853* | -S. breakwater. | 49° 08.0′ N 66° 29.3′ W | **Fl.G.** period 6s | 10 **3** | 3 | Structure on breakwater. | Seasonal. |
| 6840 *H 1846* | **Petite Tourelle,** front. | 49° 10.1′ N 66° 22.3′ W | **F.G.** | 51 **16** | **16** | Square skeleton tower, orange daymark, black stripe; 36. | Visible on range line only. Seasonal. |
| 6844 *H 1846.1* | -Rear, 90.6 meters 204°55′ from front. | 49° 10.1′ N 66° 22.3′ W | **F.G.** | 84 **26** | **16** | Square skeleton tower, orange daymark, black stripe; 30. | Visible on range line only. Seasonal. |
| 6848 *H 1842* | **La-Martre-de-Gaspe.** | 49° 12.5′ N 66° 10.3′ W | **L.Fl.(4)W.** period 30s fl. 2s, ec. 3s fl. 2s, ec. 3s fl. 2s, ec. 3s fl. 2s, ec. 13s | 130 **40** | **17** | Red octagonal tower, white stripe; 62. | Emergency light. Private light. |
| 6856 *H 1830* | **Mont Louis Range,** front. | 49° 13.7′ N 65° 43.9′ W | **Iso.R.** period 2s | 29 **9** | **16** | Square skeleton tower, orange trapezoidal daymark, black stripe; 21. | Visible on range line only. Seasonal. |
| 6860 *H 1830.1* | -Rear, 116.7 meters 176°05′ from front. | 49° 13.7′ N 65° 43.9′ W | **Iso.R.** period 2s | 46 **14** | **16** | Square skeleton tower, orange trapezoidal daymark, black stripe; 30. | Visible on range line only. Seasonal. |
| 6868 *H 1828* | **Cap de la Madeleine.** | 49° 15.0′ N 65° 19.6′ W | **Fl.(3)W.** period 27s fl. 0.2s, ec. 4.3s fl. 0.2s, ec. 4.3s fl. 0.2s, ec. 17.8s | 148 **45** | **20** | White cylindrical tower; 55. | Private light. |
| 6872 *H 1826* | Grande Vallee, on outer end of the wharf. | 49° 13.8′ N 65° 08.0′ W | **Fl.G.** period 6s fl. 1s, ec. 5s | 33 **10** | 6 | Square skeleton tower; 26. | Seasonal. |
| 6884 *H 1808* | **Cloridorme Range,** front. | 49° 10.8′ N 64° 50.9′ W | **F.R.** | 36 **11** | **16** | Square skeleton tower, orange rectangular daymark, black stripe; 16. | Visible on range line only. Seasonal. |
| 6888 *H 1808.1* | -Rear, 74.2 meters 196°25′ from front. | 49° 10.8′ N 64° 50.9′ W | **F.R.** | 72 **22** | **16** | Square skeleton tower, orange rectangular daymark, black stripe; 25. | Visible on range line only. Seasonal. |
| 6892 *H 1811* | -Wharf, head. | 49° 11.2′ N 64° 50.9′ W | **Fl.G.** period 6s fl. 1s, ec. 5s | 29 **9** | 5 | Square skeleton tower; 25. | Seasonal. |
| 6900 *H 1800* | **L'Anse-a-Valleau.** | 49° 05.2′ N 64° 33.5′ W | **Fl.W.** period 10s | 315 **96** | **21** | Skeleton tower. | |
| 6906 *H 1798* | L'Anse-a-Valleau E. | 49° 04.9′ N 64° 32.6′ W | **Iso.R.** period 2s | 56 **17** | 6 | Square skeleton tower; 21. | Seasonal. |
| 6914 *H 1782* | **Riviere-au-Renard Wharf.** | 48° 59.9′ N 64° 23.0′ W | **Fl.G.** period 5s fl. 1s, ec. 4s | 23 **7** | **19** | Square skeleton tower; 16. | Seasonal. |

The lights on the south side of the St. Lawrence estuary are listed in sequence for a vessel proceeding seaward.

| (1) No. | (2) Name and Location | (3) Position | (4) Characteristic | (5) Height | (6) Range | (7) Structure | (8) Remarks |
|---|---|---|---|---|---|---|---|

## CANADA-GULF OF ST. LAWRENCE

| (1) No. | (2) Name and Location | (3) Position | (4) Characteristic | (5) Height | (6) Range | (7) Structure | (8) Remarks |
|---|---|---|---|---|---|---|---|
| 6936 *H 1768* | **Cap des Rosiers.** | 48° 51.4´ N 64° 12.1´ W | **Oc.W.** period 20s lt. 15s, ec. 5s | 138 **42** | **24** | White round tower; 112. | |
| 6940 *H 1770* | -Cap des Rosiers East Wharf, N. jetty, head. | 48° 50.3´ N 64° 12.8´ W | **Iso.R.** period 2s | 25 **8** | 4 | Pipe swing pole; 21. | Seasonal. |
| 6944 *H 1762* | **Cap Gaspe.** | 48° 45.1´ N 64° 09.8´ W | **Fl.W.** period 5s fl. 1s, ec. 4s | 351 **107** | 12 | White octagonal tower; 42. | |
| | GASPE BAY: | | | | | | |
| 6953 *H 1757* | -Grande-Greve. | 48° 47.6´ N 64° 13.6´ W | **Iso.R.** period 2s | 26 **8** | 4 | Pipe swing pole. | Seasonal. |
| 6956 *H 1756* | **-Gros Cap aux Os.** | 48° 49.5´ N 64° 19.0´ W | **Fl.R.** period 5s fl. 1s, ec. 4s | 89 **27** | **18** | Square skeleton tower; 50. | |
| 6960 *H 1754* | **-Penouille Peninsula Range,** front. | 48° 51.1´ N 64° 25.5´ W | **F.W.** | 23 **7** | **19** | Square skeleton tower, fluorescent orange trapezoidal daymark, black stripe; 15. | Visible on range line only. Emergency light. |
| 6964 *H 1754.1* | --Rear, 229.6 meters 307°25′ from front. | 48° 51.2´ N 64° 25.6´ W | **F.W.** | 59 **18** | **19** | Square skeleton tower, orange trapezoidal daymark, black stripe; 52. | Visible on range line only. Emergency light. |
| | --RACON | | **G(– – •)** | | 10 | | (3 & 10cm). |
| 6972 *H 1752.2* | -Marina de Gaspe, breakwater. | 48° 49.7´ N 64° 28.4´ W | **Iso.Y.** period 2s | 23 **7** | 5 | Red and white square skeleton tower; 15. | Seasonal. F.W., F.R., F.G. lights mark bridge 450 meters W. Private light. |
| 6976 *H 1752.4* | -Marina de Gaspe, entrance. | 48° 49.7´ N 64° 28.5´ W | **Fl.G.** period 6s fl. 1s, ec. 5s | 23 **7** | 5 | Red and white square skeleton tower; 15. | Seasonal. Private light. |
| 6978 *H 1740* | **L'Anse-a-Brillant Range,** front. | 48° 43.2´ N 64° 17.5´ W | **F.G.** | 26 **8** | **16** | Square skeleton tower, orange trapezoidal daymark, black stripe; 15. | Visible on range line only. Seasonal. |
| 6979 *H 1740.1* | -Rear, 31 meters 205°10′ from front. | 48° 43.2´ N 64° 17.5´ W | **F.G.** | 32 **10** | **16** | Square skeleton tower, orange trapezoidal daymark, black stripe; 25. | Visible on range line only. Seasonal. |
| 6980 *H 1738* | Ile Plate (Flat Rock), off Pointe St. Pierre, N. entrance to bay. | 48° 37.6´ N 64° 09.4´ W | **Fl.W.** period 6s fl. 1s, ec. 5s | 69 **21** | 9 | Square skeleton tower, orange rectangular daymark; 42. | |
| 6988 *H 1727* | Perce, breakwater, head. | 48° 31.2´ N 64° 12.6´ W | **Fl.R.** period 6s fl. 1s, ec. 5s | 26 **8** | 6 | Black square mast; 20. | Seasonal. |
| 7004 *H 1718* | **Cap d'Espoir.** | 48° 25.2´ N 64° 19.0´ W | **L.Fl.(4)W.** period 30s fl. 2s, ec. 3s fl. 2s, ec. 3s fl. 2s, ec. 3s fl. 2s, ec. 13s | 89 **27** | **17** | White octagonal tower; 37. | |
| 7032 *H 1703* | **Chandler E. Sector.** | 48° 20.5´ N 64° 39.5´ W | **Fl.W.** period 5s fl. 1s, ec. 4s | 46 **14** | **20** | Square skeleton tower; 30. | |
| 7036 *H 1706* | Dupuis Islet (Ile Dupuis). | 48° 20.4´ N 64° 40.2´ W | **Fl.R.** period 6s fl. 1s, ec. 5s | 41 **12** | 6 | Square skeleton tower; 30. | |
| 7038 *H 1708* | Anse a L'Ilot. | 48° 20.6´ N 64° 40.1´ W | **Fl.Y.** period 4s fl. 0.5s, ec. 3.5s | 23 **7** | 4 | Mast; 16. | Private light. |
| 7040 *H 1704* | **Chandler Range,** front. | 48° 20.8´ N 64° 40.4´ W | **Q.W.** | 33 **10** | **19** | Square skeleton tower, orange trapezoidal daymark, black stripe; 25. | Visible on range line only. Emergency light. |

| (1) No. | (2) Name and Location | (3) Position | (4) Characteristic | (5) Height | (6) Range | (7) Structure | (8) Remarks |
|---|---|---|---|---|---|---|---|

## CANADA-GULF OF ST. LAWRENCE

| (1) No. | (2) Name and Location | (3) Position | (4) Characteristic | (5) Height | (6) Range | (7) Structure | (8) Remarks |
|---|---|---|---|---|---|---|---|
| 7044 *H 1704.1* | -Rear, 199 meters 321°08′ from front. | 48° 20.9′ N 64° 40.5′ W | **Q.W.** | 62 **19** | **19** | Square skeleton tower, orange trapezoidal daymark, black stripe; 39. | Visible on range line only. Emergency light. |
| 7052 *H 1701* | **Newport Wharf Range,** front. | 48° 17.1′ N 64° 43.2′ W | **F.R.** | 24 **7** | **16** | White square skeleton tower, red band, orange trapezoidal daymark, black stripe; 20. | Visible on range line only. Seasonal. |
| 7056 *H 1701.1* | -Rear, 235.4 meters 341°50′ from front. | 48° 17.2′ N 64° 43.3′ W | **F.R.** | 56 **17** | **16** | Square skeleton tower, orange trapezoidal daymark, black stripe; 50. | Visible on range line only. Seasonal. |
| 7060 *H 1700* | Newport Point, on island off the point. | 48° 17.0′ N 64° 43.1′ W | **Fl.Y.** period 6s fl. 1s, ec. 5s | 38 **12** | 6 | Square skeleton tower; 30. | Seasonal. |
| | CHALEUR BAY: | | | | | | |
| 7066 *H 1687* | **-Anse aux Gascons Range,** front. | 48° 11.4′ N 64° 51.8′ W | **F.R.** | 31 **9** | **16** | Square skeleton tower, orange trapezoidal daymark, black stripe; 25. | Visible on range line only. Seasonal. |
| 7067 *H 1687.1* | --Rear, 70.3 meters 319°26′ from front. | 48° 11.5′ N 64° 51.9′ W | **F.R.** | 44 **14** | **16** | Square skeleton tower, orange trapezoidal daymark, black stripe; 35. | Visible on range line only. Seasonal. |
| 7068 *H 1686* | -Ruisseau Chapados, outer end of wharf. | 48° 11.4′ N 64° 51.6′ W | **Fl.G.** period 6s fl. 1s, ec. 5s | 16 **5** | 3 | Cylindrical mast; 22. | Seasonal. |
| 7072 *H 1680* | **--West Point.** | 48° 09.1′ N 64° 57.0′ W | **Fl.W.** period 5s fl. 1s, ec. 4s | 75 **23** | **20** | White octagonal tower; 26. | |
| 7080 *H 1674* | -St. Godefroi, head. | 48° 04.3′ N 65° 06.8′ W | **Fl.R.** period 6s fl. 1s, ec. 5s | 26 **8** | 5 | Square skeleton tower; 20. | Seasonal. |
| 7092 *H 1666* | -Paspebiac West. | 48° 01.1′ N 65° 15.5′ W | **Fl.R.** period 6s fl. 1s, ec. 5s | 33 **10** | 6 | Square mast; 26. | Seasonal. |
| 7093 *H 1665* | -Paspebiac Breakwater. | 48° 01.1′ N 65° 15.6′ W | **Fl.G.** period 6s fl. 1s, ec. 5s | 36 **11** | 7 | Square skeleton tower; 23. | Seasonal. |
| 7097 *H 1655* | -Bonaventure Range, front. | 48° 02.2′ N 65° 28.9′ W | **Iso.R.** period 2s | 21 **6** | 13 | Square skeleton tower, orange trapezoidal daymark, black stripe; 15. | Visible on range line only. Seasonal. |
| 7098 *H 1655.1* | --Rear, 142 meters 009°52′ from front. | 48° 02.2′ N 65° 28.9′ W | **Iso.R.** period 2s | 29 **9** | 13 | Square skeleton tower, orange trapezoidal daymark, black stripe; 26. | Visible on range line only. Seasonal. |
| 7108 *H 1638* | **-Pointe Tracadigache.** | 48° 05.2′ N 66° 07.5′ W | **Fl.R.** period 5s fl. 1s, ec. 4s | 30 **9** | **15** | White square skeleton tower, red top; 28. | Seasonal. Private light. |
| 7112 *H 1640* | -Carleton Wharf. | 48° 06.0′ N 66° 07.9′ W | **Iso.Y.** period 2s | 38 **12** | 8 | Square skeleton tower; 30. | Seasonal. |
| | -Restigouche River: | | | | | | |
| 7136 *H 1633* | -Wharf. | 48° 00.8′ N 66° 39.9′ W | **Fl.G.** period 4s fl. 1s, ec. 3s | 16 **5** | 4 | Square skeleton tower; 16. | Seasonal. |

## CANADA-NEW BRUNSWICK-GULF OF ST. LAWRENCE

| (1) No. | (2) Name and Location | (3) Position | (4) Characteristic | (5) Height | (6) Range | (7) Structure | (8) Remarks |
|---|---|---|---|---|---|---|---|
| 7140 *H 1618* | Dalhousie Wharf. | 48° 04.3′ N 66° 21.6′ W | **Fl.G.** period 4s fl. 1s, ec. 3s | 30 **9** | 6 | Square skeleton tower, red and white rectangular daymark; 22. | |

| (1) No. | (2) Name and Location | (3) Position | (4) Characteristic | (5) Height | (6) Range | (7) Structure | (8) Remarks |
|---|---|---|---|---|---|---|---|
| | **CANADA-NEW BRUNSWICK-GULF OF ST. LAWRENCE** | | | | | | |
| 7144 *H 1619* | **Dalhousie Harbor,** E. Range, front. | 48° 04.3′ N 66° 22.0′ W | **Q.G.** | 48 **15** | **16** | Square skeleton tower, white trapezoidal daymark, red stripe; 41. | Visible on range line only. |
| 7148 *H 1619.1* | -Rear, 57 meters 268°10′ from front. | 48° 04.3′ N 66° 22.0′ W | **Iso.G.** period 4s | 59 **18** | **16** | Square skeleton tower, white trapezoidal daymark, red stripe; 51. | Visible on range line only. |
| 7152 *H 1620* | **Dalhousie Island.** | 48° 04.3′ N 66° 21.9′ W | **Fl.W.** period 5s fl. 0.2s, ec. 4.8s | 69 **21** | **15** | Square skeleton tower, red and white rectangular daymark, green square in center; 62. | |
| | CHALEUR BAY: | | | | | | |
| 7156 *H 1620.4* | --Harbor Range, front. | 48° 04.3′ N 66° 22.2′ W | **Q.R.** | 24 **7** | 5 | Square skeleton tower, white trapezoidal daymark, red stripe; 20. | Visible on range line only. |
| 7160 *H 1620.41* | ---Rear, 614.4 meters 264°24′ from front. | 48° 04.3′ N 66° 22.7′ W | **Iso.R.** period 4s | 30 **9** | 13 | Square skeleton tower, white trapezoidal daymark, red stripe; 25. | Visible on range line only. |
| 7164 *H 1616* | -Inch Arran Point Range, front. | 48° 03.7′ N 66° 21.1′ W | **Iso.W.** period 6s | 45 **14** | 11 | White square tower, red upper portion, red stripe; 36. | |
| 7168 *H 1616.1* | --Rear, 365 meters 286°45′ from front. | 48° 03.7′ N 66° 21.3′ W | **F.W.** | 79 **24** | 11 | Square skeleton tower, white trapezoidal daymark, red stripe; 32. | Visible on range line only. |
| 7176 *H 1612* | -New Mills. | 47° 58.5′ N 66° 11.3′ W | **Fl.G.** period 4s fl. 1s, ec. 3s | 20 **6** | | Square skeleton tower; 18. | Seasonal. |
| 7184 *H 1609* | -Belledune Point. | 47° 54.5′ N 65° 49.9′ W | **Oc.G.** period 3s lt. 2s, ec. 1s | 36 **11** | 10 | Square skeleton tower, green and white rectangular daymarks; 32. | |
| 7188 *H 1610* | --Breakwater, head. | 47° 55.0′ N 65° 50.3′ W | **Oc.R.** period 3s lt. 2s, ec. 1s | 33 **10** | 10 | Red square skeleton tower, red and white rectangular daymarks; 33. | |
| 7192 *H 1608.4* | -Green Point, NW. corner of inner wharf. | 47° 51.7′ N 65° 45.6′ W | **F.R.** | 24 **7** | 10 | Square skeleton tower; 23. | |
| 7194 *H 1608* | --Breakwater, head. | 47° 51.7′ N 65° 45.7′ W | **Fl.R.** period 4s fl. 1s, ec. 3s | 23 **7** | 4 | Square skeleton tower; 12. | Seasonal. |
| 7196 *H 1606* | **-Petit Rocher.** | 47° 46.9′ N 65° 42.5′ W | **Fl.Y.** period 5s fl. 0.2s, ec. 4.8s | 25 **8** | **15** | Square skeleton tower; 20. | Seasonal. |
| 7204 *H 1600* | -Bathurst Harbor, front. | 47° 39.1′ N 65° 37.4′ W | **Q.R.** | 25 **8** | 8 | Square skeleton tower, white trapezoidal daymark, red stripe; 22. | Visible on range line only. |
| 7208 *H 1600.1* | --Rear, on shoal, 527.5 meters 208°22′ from front. | 47° 38.9′ N 65° 37.6′ W | **Iso.R.** period 4s | 59 **18** | **16** | Square skeleton tower, white trapezoidal daymark, red stripe; 52. | Visible on range line only. |
| 7240 *H 1596* | -Stonehaven Wharf. | 47° 45.2′ N 65° 21.7′ W | **Fl.W.** period 4s fl. 1s, ec. 3s | | 10 | Pipe swing pole. | Seasonal. |
| 7241 *H 1596.2* | -Stonehaven, breakwater. | 47° 45.3′ N 65° 21.8′ W | **Fl.G.** period 4s | 23 **7** | 5 | Pipe swing pole, green and white square daymarks; 12. | Seasonal. |
| 7252 *H 1591.6* | -Anse-Bleue wharf. | 47° 49.9′ N 65° 04.8′ W | **Fl.G.** period 4s | 21 **6** | 4 | Pipe swing pole; 17. | Seasonal. |
| 7254 *H 1591.8* | -Blue Cove (Anse Bleue) breakwater. | 47° 49.9′ N 65° 04.9′ W | **Fl.R.** period 4s | 26 **8** | 4 | Square skeleton tower; 12. | |
| 7256 *H 1591.4* | -Blue Cove (Anse Bleue) Range, front. | 47° 49.9′ N 65° 04.8′ W | **F.R.** | 21 **6** | 10 | Square skeleton tower, white trapezoidal daymark, red stripe; 17. | Visible on range line only. |

| (1) No. | (2) Name and Location | (3) Position | (4) Characteristic | (5) Height | (6) Range | (7) Structure | (8) Remarks |
|---|---|---|---|---|---|---|---|

**CANADA-NEW BRUNSWICK-GULF OF ST. LAWRENCE**

| (1) No. | (2) Name and Location | (3) Position | (4) Characteristic | (5) Height | (6) Range | (7) Structure | (8) Remarks |
|---|---|---|---|---|---|---|---|
| 7260<br>*H 1591.41* | --Rear, 338.6 meters 195°04′ from front. | 47° 49.7′ N<br>65° 04.9′ W | **F.R.** | 43<br>**13** | 10 | Square skeleton tower, white trapezoidal daymark, red stripe; 32. | Visible on range line only. |
| 7264<br>*H 1590* | **-Maisonnette Point.** | 47° 50.3′ N<br>65° 00.2′ W | **Fl.W.**<br>period 2.4s<br>fl. 0.4s, ec. 2s | 58<br>**18** | **15** | Square skeleton tower; 43. | |
| | -Caraquet Harbor: | | | | | | |
| 7272<br>*H 1588* | --Caraquet Island. | 47° 49.4′ N<br>64° 54.3′ W | **Fl.W.**<br>period 4s<br>fl. 1s, ec. 3s | 73<br>**22** | 9 | Rectangular skeleton tower, white rectangular daymark; 66. | |
| 7273<br>*H 1581.7* | --Stoke Point Range, front. | 47° 48.4′ N<br>64° 51.6′ W | **F.R.** | 27<br>**8** | 14 | Square skeleton tower, red trapezoidal daymark, white stripe; 12. | Visible on range line only.<br>Seasonal. |
| 7274<br>*H 1581.71* | ---Rear, 124 meters 093°46′ from front. | 47° 48.4′ N<br>64° 51.5′ W | **F.R.** | 42<br>**13** | 14 | Square skeleton tower, red trapezoidal daymark, white stripe; 27. | Visible on range line only.<br>Seasonal. |
| 7276<br>*H 1580* | --Range, front, below Stoke Point. | 47° 48.5′ N<br>64° 50.5′ W | **F.Y.** | 27<br>**8** | 13 | White square tower, red stripe; 27. | Seasonal. |
| 7280<br>*H 1580.1* | ---Rear, 1097 meters 226°47′ from front. | 47° 48.1′ N<br>64° 51.1′ W | **F.Y.** | 66<br>**20** | 13 | Square skeleton tower, white trapezoidal daymark, red stripe; 41. | Seasonal. |
| 7284<br>*H 1582* | --Middle Caraquet Wharf. | 47° 48.2′ N<br>64° 52.4′ W | **Fl.W.**<br>period 3s<br>fl. 1s, ec. 2s | 23<br>**7** | 9 | Square skeleton tower; 20. | Seasonal. |
| 7288<br>*H 1582.4* | --Middle Caraquet, E. Wharf. | 47° 48.2′ N<br>64° 52.4′ W | **Fl.G.**<br>period 4s | 14<br>**4** | 4 | Square skeleton tower; 12. | Seasonal. |
| 7291<br>*H 1581.5* | --Caraquet Middle Range, front. | 47° 48.2′ N<br>64° 53.2′ W | **F.R.** | 28<br>**9** | | Square skeleton tower, red trapezoidal daymark, white stripe; 17. | Seasonal. |
| 7291.1<br>*H 1581.51* | ---Rear, 355 meters 244°07′ from front. | 47° 48.0′ N<br>64° 53.4′ W | **F.R.** | 64<br>**20** | | Square skeleton tower, red trapezoidal daymark, white stripe; 46. | Seasonal. |
| 7300<br>*H 1583* | -Young Wharf, SE. corner. | 47° 47.8′ N<br>64° 55.5′ W | **Fl.R.**<br>period 5s<br>fl. 0.2s, ec. 4.8s | 25<br>**8** | 9 | Pipe swing pole; 20. | Seasonal. |
| 7304<br>*H 1584* | -Young Wharf West, NW. corner. | 47° 47.8′ N<br>64° 55.8′ W | **Iso.G.**<br>period 2s | 18<br>**5** | 5 | Square skeleton tower; 16. | Seasonal. |
| 7305<br>*H 1585* | **-Pointe a Brideau Range,** front. | 47° 47.8′ N<br>64° 56.2′ W | **F.W.** | 25<br>**8** | **19** | Square skeleton tower, white trapezoidal daymark, red stripe; 12. | Seasonal. |
| 7306<br>*H 1585.1* | --Rear, 374.8 meters 248°04′ from front. | 47° 47.7′ N<br>64° 56.5′ W | **F.W.** | 44<br>**14** | **19** | White square tower, red stripe; 42. | Seasonal. |
| | -Baie de Shippegan: | | | | | | |
| 7308<br>*H 1566* | --Pokesudie Island, NE. point. | 47° 49.2′ N<br>64° 45.3′ W | **Iso.W.**<br>period 4s | 43<br>**13** | 10 | Square skeleton tower, red and white rectangular daymark; 43. | Seasonal. |
| 7312<br>*H 1567* | --Pointe de Lameque Range, front. | 47° 49.0′ N<br>64° 42.3′ W | **F.W.** | 29<br>**9** | 11 | Square skeleton tower, black trapezoidal daymark, red stripe; 27. | Visible on range line only.<br>Seasonal. |
| 7316<br>*H 1567.1* | ---Rear, 281.3 meters 151°15′ from front. | 47° 48.8′ N<br>64° 42.2′ W | **F.W.** | 56<br>**17** | 11 | Square skeleton tower, black trapezoidal daymark, red stripe; 54. | Visible on range line only.<br>Seasonal. |
| 7320<br>*H 1568* | --Pointe a Marcelle Range, front. | 47° 47.2′ N<br>64° 45.0′ W | **F.W.** | 26<br>**8** | 9 | Square skeleton tower, black trapezoidal daymark, red stripe; 21. | Visible on range line only.<br>Seasonal. |
| 7324<br>*H 1568.1* | ---Rear, 339 meters 194°15′ from front. | 47° 47.0′ N<br>64° 45.0′ W | **F.W.** | 59<br>**18** | 9 | Square skeleton tower, black trapezoidal daymark, red stripe; 56. | Visible on range line only.<br>Seasonal. |

| (1) No. | (2) Name and Location | (3) Position | (4) Characteristic | (5) Height | (6) Range | (7) Structure | (8) Remarks |
|---|---|---|---|---|---|---|---|
| | **CANADA-NEW BRUNSWICK-GULF OF ST. LAWRENCE** | | | | | | |
| 7328<br>*H 1567.3* | --Pointe a Bernache Range, front. | 47° 45.5′ N<br>64° 43.3′ W | **F.R.** | | 13 | Square skeleton tower, black trapezoidal daymark, red stripe; 22. | Seasonal. |
| 7332<br>*H 1567.31* | ---Rear, 170 meters 179°25′ from front. | 47° 45.3′ N<br>64° 43.3′ W | **F.R.** | 52<br>**16** | 13 | Square skeleton tower, black trapezoidal daymark, red stripe; 52. | Seasonal. |
| 7335<br>*H 1535* | --Savoy Landing. | 47° 44.9′ N<br>64° 41.5′ W | **Fl.W.**<br>period 3s<br>fl. 1s, ec. 2s | 20<br>**6** | 6 | Square skeleton tower; 16. | Seasonal. |
| 7354<br>*H 1564.2* | Shippegan Island W. wharf. | 47° 53.0′ N<br>64° 34.5′ W | **Iso.W.**<br>period 2s | 14<br>**4** | 5 | Green pipe swing pole, black and white square daymark; 33. | Seasonal. |
| 7356<br>*H 1562* | -Miscou Wharf. | 47° 53.7′ N<br>64° 34.6′ W | **Iso.R.**<br>period 2s | 16<br>**5** | 3 | Pipe swing pole, red and white triangular daymark, red central triangle; 13. | Seasonal. |
| 7358<br>*H 1559* | -Harper Point. | 47° 53.6′ N<br>64° 34.7′ W | **Fl.G.**<br>period 4s<br>fl. 0.5s, ec. 3.5s | 13<br>**4** | 4 | Green pipe swing pole, green and white square daymark; 13. | Seasonal. |
| 7360<br>*H 1556* | -Black Point. | 47° 53.1′ N<br>64° 37.4′ W | **Oc.(2)Y.**<br>period 10s<br>lt. 4s, ec. 2s<br>lt. 2s, ec. 2s | 58<br>**18** | 12 | Skeleton tower, enclosed center portion, red and white rectangular daymark; 58. | |
| 7368<br>*H 1552* | Miscou Island. | 48° 00.6′ N<br>64° 29.6′ W | **Oc.W.**<br>period 5s<br>lt. 4s, ec. 1s | 79<br>**24** | 12 | White octoganal tower; 83. | |
| | RACON | | **K(– • –)** | | **15** | | (3 & 10cm). |
| 7374<br>*H 1551* | Pigeon Hill Wharf. | 47° 52.7′ N<br>64° 30.4′ W | **Iso.R.**<br>period 2s | 15<br>**4** | 5 | Pipe swing pole, red and white triangular daymark, red triangle in center; 11. | Seasonal. |
| 7376<br>*H 1550* | Fox Dens Gully. | 47° 53.2′ N<br>64° 30.2′ W | **Fl.R.**<br>period 4s | 15<br>**5** | 4 | Square skeleton tower; 10. | Seasonal. |
| 7380<br>*H 1542* | Ste-Marie-sur-Mer Breakwater. | 47° 46.8′ N<br>64° 33.8′ W | **Fl.R.**<br>period 4s<br>fl. 1s, ec. 3s | 23<br>**7** | 4 | Square skeleton tower; 11. | Seasonal. |
| 7382<br>*H 1542.5* | Ste-Marie-sur-Mer. | 47° 46.9′ N<br>64° 34.1′ W | **L.Fl.W.**<br>period 6s<br>fl. 2s, ec. 4s | 51<br>**16** | 13 | Square skeleton tower; 43. | |
| | SHIPPEGAN GULLY: | | | | | | |
| 7392<br>*H 1530* | **-Big Shippegan,** on sand bar, E. side of S. entrance. | 47° 43.3′ N<br>64° 39.6′ W | **Fl.Y.**<br>period 5s<br>fl. 0.2s, ec. 4.8s | 54<br>**16** | **15** | White octagonal tower, red upper portion; 54. | |
| 7396<br>*H 1531* | -W. breakwater, head. | 47° 43.1′ N<br>64° 40.0′ W | **Fl.W.**<br>period 4s<br>fl. 1s, ec. 3s | 15<br>**5** | 6 | Cylindrical mast; 10. | Seasonal. |
| 7400<br>*H 1567.36* | -Government wharf Range, front, head. | 47° 44.8′ N<br>64° 42.1′ W | **F.R.** | 36<br>**11** | 10 | Square skeleton tower, white trapezoidal daymark, red stripe; 31. | Visible on range line only. Seasonal. |
| 7400.1<br>*H 1567.37* | --Rear, 453 meters 154°24′ from front. | 47° 44.6′ N<br>64° 42.0′ W | **F.R.** | 56<br>**17** | 10 | Square skeleton tower, white trapezoidal daymark, red stripe; 54. | Visible on range line only. Seasonal. |
| 7402<br>*H 1564* | Shippegan Wharf. | 47° 44.9′ N<br>64° 42.1′ W | **Q.R.** | 18<br>**6** | 5 | Square skeleton tower; 16. | Seasonal. |
| 7418 | -Pokemouche Gully, wharf, SW. corner. | 47° 40.2′ N<br>64° 48.7′ W | **Fl.R.**<br>period 4s | 19<br>**6** | 4 | Square skeleton tower; 16. | Seasonal. |
| 7424<br>*H 1521* | South Tracadie. | 47° 28.8′ N<br>64° 52.3′ W | **Fl.G.**<br>period 4s<br>fl. 1s, ec. 3s | 20<br>**6** | 5 | Cylindrical mast; 12. | Seasonal. |

| (1) No. | (2) Name and Location | (3) Position | (4) Characteristic | (5) Height | (6) Range | (7) Structure | (8) Remarks |
|---|---|---|---|---|---|---|---|

## CANADA-NEW BRUNSWICK-GULF OF ST. LAWRENCE

| (1) No. | (2) Name and Location | (3) Position | (4) Characteristic | (5) Height | (6) Range | (7) Structure | (8) Remarks |
|---|---|---|---|---|---|---|---|
| 7428 *H 1520.5* | Val Comeau, wharf, head. | 47° 27.9′ N 64° 53.0′ W | **Fl.G.** period 4s fl. 1s, ec. 3s | 20 **6** | 5 | Square skeleton tower; 17. | Seasonal. |
| 7436 *H 1525* | North Tracadie Wharf. | 47° 31.5′ N 64° 54.5′ W | **Fl.G.** period 4s fl. 1s, ec. 3s | 21 **6** | 5 | Square skeleton tower; 17. | Seasonal. |
| 7444 *H 1517* | Lower Neguac Wharf. | 47° 15.4′ N 65° 03.3′ W | **Fl.R.** period 4s fl. 1s, ec. 3s | 20 **6** | 4 | Square skeleton tower, red and white rectangular daymark, red triangle in center; 16. | Seasonal. |
| 7450 *H 1515* | Neguac wharf. | 47° 14.4′ N 65° 04.4′ W | **Fl.R.** period 4s fl. 1s, ec. 3s | 20 **6** | 4 | Cylindrical mast; 10. | Seasonal. |
| 7452 *H 1514* | -Burnt Church, E. side of wharf. | 47° 11.4′ N 65° 08.1′ W | **Fl.R.** period 4s fl. 1s, ec. 3s | 23 **7** | 4 | Square skeleton tower; 22. | Seasonal. |
| 7469 *H 1442* | -Preston Beach West, front. | 47° 04.0′ N 64° 56.5′ W | **Q.Y.** | 35 **11** | 13 | Triangular skeleton tower, red trapezoidal daymark, white stripe; 32. | Visible on range line only. |
| 7470 *H 1442.1* | --Rear, 2067 meters 153°44′ from front | 47° 03.0′ N 64° 55.8′ W | **Iso.Y.** period 4s | 90 **27** | **17** | Triangular skeleton tower, red trapezoidal daymark, white stripe; 41. | Visible on range line only. |
| 7480 *H 1446* | **-Portage Channel Range,** on Fox Island front. | 47° 07.8′ N 65° 02.3′ W | **F.W.** | 38 **12** | **18** | Square skeleton tower, white trapezoidal daymark, red stripe; 30. | Visible on range line only. |
| 7484 *H 1446.1* | --Rear, 373 meters 243°41′ from front. | 47° 07.7′ N 65° 02.5′ W | **F.W.** | 62 **19** | **18** | Skeleton tower, white trapezoidal daymark, red stripe; 66. | Visible on range line only. **Radar reflector.** |
| | --RACON | | **G(– – •)** period 120s | | 10 | | (3cm). |
| 7485 *H 1440* | **-Fox Island,** S. Range, front. | 47° 05.2′ N 64° 58.7′ W | **Q.W.** | 28 **9** | **15** | Square skeleton tower, red trapezoidal daymark, black stripe; 21. | Visible on range line only. |
| 7486 *H 1440.1* | --Rear, 215 meters 248°28′ from front. | 47° 05.2′ N 64° 58.9′ W | **Iso.W.** period 4s | 45 **14** | **15** | Square skeleton tower, red trapezoidal daymark, black stripe; 41. | Visible on range line only. |
| 7496 *H 1464* | -Bay du Vin Island. | 47° 05.4′ N 65° 06.1′ W | **F.W.R.G.** | 31 **10** | 5 | Triangular skeleton tower, red and white rectangular daymark; 22. | R. 284°30′-042°, W.-044°, G.-049°. Seasonal. |
| 7498 *H 1452* | -Grand Dune outer Range, front. | 47° 06.8′ N 65° 02.6′ W | **Q.W.** | 28 **8** | 14 | Pier, red trapezoidal daymark, black stripe; 26. | Visible on range line only. |
| 7499 *H 1452.1* | --Rear, 3499.8 meters 102°11′ from front. | 47° 06.4′ N 64° 59.9′ W | **Iso.W.** period 4s | 107 **32** | **17** | Triangular skeleton tower, red trapezoidal daymark, black stripe; 99. | Visible on range line only. |
| 7500 *H 1472* | -Grand Dune Flats, S. end of Grand Dune Island Range, front. | 47° 08.4′ N 65° 13.6′ W | **F.W.** | 49 **15** | 12 | Triangular skeleton tower, red trapezoidal daymark, black stripe; 46. | Visible on range line only. |
| 7504 *H 1472.1* | --Rear, 1211.3 meters 282°04′ from front. | 47° 08.6′ N 65° 14.6′ W | **F.W.** | 87 **26** | 11 | Triangular skeleton tower, red trapezoidal daymark, black stripe; 69. | Visible on range line only. |
| 7508 *H 1477* | -Moody Point Range, front. | 47° 06.0′ N 65° 19.5′ W | **Q.Y.** | 33 **10** | 14 | Triangular skeleton tower, red trapezoidal daymark, black stripe; 26. | Visible on range line only. |
| 7512 *H 1477.1* | --Rear, about 1810 meters 257°24′ from front. | 47° 05.8′ N 65° 20.9′ W | **Iso.Y.** period 4s | 62 **19** | **17** | Triangular skeleton tower, red trapezoidal daymark, black stripe; 43. | Visible on range line only. |
| 7516 *H 1478* | -Oak Channel Range, front. | 47° 04.3′ N 65° 19.2′ W | **Iso.Y.** period 2s | 29 **9** | 14 | Triangular skeleton tower, red trapezoidal daymark, white stripe; 20. | Visible on range line only. |
| 7520 *H 1478.1* | --Rear, 1200 meters 223°13′ from front. | 47° 03.9′ N 65° 19.8′ W | **Fl.Y.** period 3s fl. 1s, ec. 2s | 69 **21** | **18** | Triangular skeleton tower, red trapezoidal daymark, white stripe; 52. | Visible on range line only. |

| (1) No. | (2) Name and Location | (3) Position | (4) Characteristic | (5) Height | (6) Range | (7) Structure | (8) Remarks |
|---|---|---|---|---|---|---|---|

## CANADA-NEW BRUNSWICK-GULF OF ST. LAWRENCE

| (1) No. | (2) Name and Location | (3) Position | (4) Characteristic | (5) Height | (6) Range | (7) Structure | (8) Remarks |
|---|---|---|---|---|---|---|---|
| 7521 *H 1479* | -Oak Point Range, front. | 47° 06.8′ N 65° 16.5′ W | **Q.W.** | 28 **9** | 14 | Triangular skeleton tower, red trapezoidal daymark, black stripe; 18. | Visible on range line only. |
| 7522 *H 1479.1* | --Rear, 1325 meters, 024°08′ from front. | 47° 07.5′ N 65° 16.1′ W | **Iso.W.** period 4s | 56 **17** | **17** | Triangular skeleton tower, red trapezoidal daymark, black stripe; 23. | Visible on range line only. |
| 7532 *H 1491* | -Grants Beach Range, front. | 47° 05.1′ N 65° 22.5′ W | **Q.R.** | 69 **21** | 12 | Triangular skeleton tower, red trapezoidal daymark, black stripe; 40. | Visible on range line only. |
| 7536 *H 1491.1* | --Rear, 876 meters 278°03′ from front. | 47° 05.1′ N 65° 23.2′ W | **Iso.R.** period 4s | 134 **41** | **16** | Triangular skeleton tower, red trapezoidal daymark, black stripe; 76. | Visible on range line only. |
| 7540 *H 1493* | -St. Andrews Bank Range, front. | 47° 04.2′ N 65° 25.1′ W | **Iso.Y.** period 2s | 30 **9** | 13 | Triangular skeleton tower, red trapezoidal daymark, black stripe; 16. | Visible on range line only. |
| 7544 *H 1493.1* | --Rear, 294 meters 247°53′ from front. | 47° 04.2′ N 65° 25.3′ W | **Fl.Y.** period 3s fl. 1s, ec. 2s | 45 **14** | 13 | Triangular skeleton tower, red trapezoidal daymark, black stripe; 20. | Visible on range line only. |
| 7548 *H 1494* | -Leggett Shoal Range, front. | 47° 04.7′ N 65° 23.9′ W | **Q.R.** | 46 **14** | 12 | Triangular skeleton tower, red trapezoidal daymark, black stripe; 15. | Visible on range line only. |
| 7552 *H 1494.1* | --Rear, 309 meters 043°27′ from front. | 47° 04.8′ N 65° 23.8′ W | **Iso.R.** period 4s | 70 **21** | **16** | Triangular skeleton tower, red trapezoidal daymark, black stripe; 14. | Visible on range line only. |
| 7553 *H 1492* | -Lower Newcastle Range, front. | 47° 04.5′ N 65° 24.6′ W | **Q.W.** | 42 **13** | 14 | Triangular skeleton tower, red trapezoidal daymark, black stripe; 20. | Visible on range line only. |
| 7554 *H 1492.1* | --Rear, 467 meters 256°15′ from front. | 47° 04.5′ N 65° 24.9′ W | **Iso.W.** period 4s | 72 **22** | 14 | Triangular skeleton tower, red trapezoidal daymark, black stripe; 20. | Visible on range line only. |
| 7556 *H 1496* | -Millbank Range, front. | 47° 03.4′ N 65° 27.6′ W | **Q.R.** | 53 **16** | 11 | Triangular skeleton tower, red trapezoidal daymark, black stripe; 20. | Visible on range line only. |
| 7560 *H 1496.1* | --Rear, 306 meters 252°26′ from front. | 47° 03.3′ N 65° 27.8′ W | **Iso.R.** period 4s | 102 **31** | **16** | Triangular skeleton tower, red trapezoidal daymark, black stripe; 39. | Visible on range line only. |
| 7564 *H 1505* | -Chatham Bridge Pier, N. | 47° 01.7′ N 65° 28.8′ W | **Iso.R.** period 2s | 25 **8** | 4 | Square skeleton tower; 17. | |
| 7568 *H 1505.2* | --S. | 47° 01.6′ N 65° 28.7′ W | **Iso.G.** period 2s | 25 **8** | 4 | Square skeleton tower; 17. | |
| 7572 *H 1507* | -Wright Bank Range (Newcastle) N. side of river, front. | 47° 01.0′ N 65° 32.7′ W | **Q.Y.** | 42 **13** | 13 | Triangular skeleton tower, red trapezoidal daymark, black stripe; 13. | Visible on range line only. |
| 7576 *H 1507.1* | --Rear, 49 meters 278°33′ from front. | 47° 01.0′ N 65° 32.8′ W | **Iso.Y.** period 4s | 53 **16** | 13 | Triangular skeleton tower, red trapezoidal daymark, black stripe; 23. | Visible on range line only. |
| 7580 *H 1424* | Point Escuminac. | 47° 04.4′ N 64° 47.9′ W | **Fl.W.** period 3s fl. 1s, ec. 2s | 72 **22** | 13 | White hexagonal tower, red upper portion; 73. | Obscured 110°-120°. **Horn:** 2 bl. ev. 60s (bl. 3s, si. 3s, bl. 3s, si. 51s). |
| 7581 *H 1430* | Escuminac. | 47° 04.9′ N 64° 53.2′ W | **Fl.W.** period 5s fl. 0.2s, ec. 4.8s | 26 **8** | 13 | Square skeleton tower, three red and white rectangular daymarks; 23. | |
| 7592 *H 1418.2* | Point Sapin Sector. | 46° 57.8′ N 64° 49.8′ W | **Dir.W.R.G.** | 22 **7** | | Square skeleton tower. | F.R. 002°07′-003°52′, F.W.-005°52′, F.G.-023°52′. Seasonal. |
| 7597 *H 1419* | Point Sapin. | 46° 57.7′ N 64° 49.8′ W | **Fl.R.** period 4s fl. 1s, ec. 3s | 23 **7** | 5 | Square skeleton tower, red and white rectangular daymark; 21. | Seasonal. |

| (1) No. | (2) Name and Location | (3) Position | (4) Characteristic | (5) Height | (6) Range | (7) Structure | (8) Remarks |
|---|---|---|---|---|---|---|---|
| | | | **CANADA-NEW BRUNSWICK-GULF OF ST. LAWRENCE** | | | | |
| 7598<br>*H 1418.5* | -Point Sapin, outer breakwater. | 46° 57.6′ N<br>64° 49.8′ W | **Fl.W.**<br>period 4s<br>fl. 0.1s, ec. 3.9s | 26<br>**8** | | Square skeleton tower, red and white rectangular daymark. | Seasonal. |
| | RICHIBUCTO HARBOR: | | | | | | |
| 7632<br>*H 1394* | -Pile Sheet Range, front. | 46° 43.0′ N<br>64° 48.0′ W | **Q.W.** | 26<br>**8** | 6 | Square skeleton tower, white trapezoidal daymark, red stripe; 22. | Seasonal. |
| 7636<br>*H 1394.1* | --Rear, 239 meters 045°48′ from front. | 46° 43.0′ N<br>64° 47.9′ W | **Iso.W.**<br>period 4s | 45<br>**14** | 6 | Square skeleton tower, white trapezoidal daymark, red stripe; 32. | Seasonal. |
| 7640<br>*H 1400* | -Fagan Point Range, W. side of South Beach, front. | 46° 42.5′ N<br>64° 48.0′ W | **Q.R.** | 26<br>**8** | 13 | Square skeleton tower, white trapezoidal daymark, red stripe; 16. | Visible on range line only. Seasonal. |
| 7644<br>*H 1400.1* | --Rear, 296 meters 065°44′ from front. | 46° 42.6′ N<br>64° 47.8′ W | **Iso.R.**<br>period 4s | 36<br>**11** | 14 | Square skeleton tower, white trapezoidal daymark, red stripe; 31. | Visible on range line only. Seasonal. |
| 7648<br>*H 1402* | -Town Range, front. | 46° 40.8′ N<br>64° 51.8′ W | **F.Y.** | 50<br>**15** | 13 | Square skeleton tower, white trapezoidal daymark, red stripe; 42. | Visible on range line only. Seasonal. |
| 7652<br>*H 1402.1* | --Rear, 285 meters 227°27′ from front. | 46° 40.7′ N<br>64° 51.9′ W | **F.Y.** | 75<br>**23** | 11 | Square skeleton tower, white trapezoidal daymark, red stripe; 62. | Visible on range line only. Seasonal. |
| 7656<br>*H 1378* | Richibucto Cape, breakwater. | 46° 40.4′ N<br>64° 42.6′ W | **Fl.R.**<br>period 4s<br>fl. 1s, ec. 3s | 14<br>**4** | 5 | Cylindrical mast; 9. | Seasonal. |
| 7660<br>*H 1376* | Richibucto Head. | 46° 40.2′ N<br>64° 42.7′ W | **Fl.W.**<br>period 5s<br>fl. 0.5s, ec. 4.5s | 59<br>**18** | 14 | White square tower, red upper portion; 34. | |
| 7664<br>*H 1374* | Chockpish, on N. breakwater. | 46° 35.0′ N<br>64° 43.2′ W | **Fl.R.**<br>period 4s | 20<br>**6** | 3 | Cylindrical mast; 10. | Seasonal. |
| 7665<br>*H 1375* | Chockpish Range, front. | 46° 34.9′ N<br>64° 43.4′ W | **F.Y.** | 16<br>**5** | 13 | Square skeleton tower; 12. | Seasonal. |
| 7666<br>*H 1375.1* | -Rear, 110 meters 271°02′ from front. | 46° 34.9′ N<br>64° 43.9′ W | **F.Y.** | 23<br>**7** | 13 | Square skeleton tower; 22. | Visible on range line only. Seasonal. |
| 7668<br>*H 1372* | St. Edouard de Kent wharf. | 46° 32.4′ N<br>64° 41.9′ W | **Fl.R.**<br>period 5s<br>fl. 0.2s, ec. 4.8s | 17<br>**5** | 13 | Square skeleton tower, red and white rectangular daymark; 13. | Seasonal. |
| 7680<br>*H 1362* | -Buctouche Bar. | 46° 27.7′ N<br>64° 36.8′ W | **Fl.W.**<br>period 4s<br>fl. 1s, ec. 3s | 36<br>**11** | 7 | White square tower; 37. | Seasonal. |
| 7686<br>*H 1369* | Dixon Point. | 46° 27.4′ N<br>64° 39.0′ W | **Fl.W.**<br>period 5s<br>fl. 1s, ec. 4s | 34<br>**10** | 12 | White square tower, red upper portion; 27. | |
| | BUCTOUCHE RIVER: | | | | | | |
| 7692<br>*H 1368* | -Inner range on Indian (Church) Point, front. | 46° 29.2′ N<br>64° 40.8′ W | **F.W.** | 19<br>**6** | 13 | White square tower, red upper portion, red stripe; 20. | Visible on range line only. Seasonal. |
| 7696<br>*H 1368.1* | --Rear, 382 meters 317°41′ from front. | 46° 29.4′ N<br>64° 41.0′ W | **F.W.** | 58<br>**18** | 13 | White skeleton tower, enclosed upper portion, red stripe; 45. | Visible on range line only. Seasonal. |
| 7700<br>*H 1360* | St. Thomas-de-Kent, NW. corner of wharf. | 46° 26.9′ N<br>64° 38.2′ W | **Fl.G.**<br>period 4s<br>fl. 1s, ec. 3s | 17<br>**5** | 5 | Square skeleton tower; 10. | Seasonal. |
| 7703<br>*H 1359* | Cockagne Bar Wharf. | 46° 24.5′ N<br>64° 36.9′ W | **Fl.R.**<br>period 3s<br>fl. 1s, ec. 2s | 20<br>**6** | 4 | Square skeleton tower; 17. | Seasonal. |
| 7708<br>*H 1354* | Cocagne River Range, front. | 46° 20.1′ N<br>64° 36.9′ W | **F.Y.** | 26<br>**8** | 13 | White square tower, red upper portion, red stripe; 24. | Visible on range line only. Seasonal. |

| (1) No. | (2) Name and Location | (3) Position | (4) Characteristic | (5) Height | (6) Range | (7) Structure | (8) Remarks |
|---|---|---|---|---|---|---|---|
| | **CANADA-NEW BRUNSWICK-GULF OF ST. LAWRENCE** | | | | | | |
| 7712 *H 1354.1* | -Rear, 245 meters 219° 37′ from front. | 46° 20.0′ N 64° 37.0′ W | **F.Y.** | 58 **18** | 13 | Square skeleton tower, white trapezoidal daymark, red stripe; 43. | Visible on range line only. Seasonal. |
| 7720 *H 1352* | Cocagne Cape Wharf, SW. corner. | 46° 21.3′ N 64° 34.5′ W | **Fl.W.** period 3s fl. 1s, ec. 2s | 20 **6** | 6 | Square skeleton tower, red and white rectangular daymark, green square in center; 17. | Seasonal. |
| 7724 *H 1350* | Caissie Point. | 46° 19.2′ N 64° 30.8′ W | **L.Fl.(2)Y.** period 12s fl. 2s, ec. 2s fl. 2s, ec. 6s | 46 **14** | 11 | White square tower, red upper portion; 45. | |
| 7728 *H 1348* | -Breakwater, head. | 46° 18.8′ N 64° 30.6′ W | **Fl.R.** period 4s fl. 1s, ec. 3s | 19 **6** | 4 | Square skeleton tower; 16. | Seasonal. |
| | SHEDIAC HARBOR: | | | | | | |
| 7736 *H 1328* | -North Channel Range, on Pointe du Chene, front. | 46° 14.5′ N 64° 30.7′ W | **F.R.** | 26 **8** | 11 | White square tower, red upper portion, red stripe; 26. | Visible on range line only. Seasonal. |
| 7740 *H 1328.1* | --Rear, 148 meters 189°45′ from front. | 46° 14.4′ N 64° 30.7′ W | **F.R.** | 45 **14** | 11 | White square tower, red upper portion, red stripe; 39. | Seasonal. |
| 7744 *H 1332* | **-Pointe du Chene Range,** front. | 46° 14.5′ N 64° 31.8′ W | **Q.Y.** | 21 **6** | **21** | Square skeleton tower, white trapezoidal daymark, red stripe; 15. | Visible on range line only. Seasonal. |
| 7748 *H 1332.1* | --Rear, 117 meters 194°40′ from front. | 46° 14.4′ N 64° 31.8′ W | **Iso.Y.** period 4s | 39 **12** | **22** | White square tower, red upper portion, red stripe; 46. | Visible on range line only. Seasonal. |
| 7750 *H 1334* | -Yacht Club Breakwater. | 46° 13.7′ N 64° 32.8′ W | **Fl.G.** period 4s | 17 **5** | 4 | Pipe swing pole, green and white square daymarks; 12. | |
| 7756 *H 1325.1* | Cape Bald (L'Aboiteau). | 46° 13.9′ N 64° 17.9′ W | **Fl.G.** period 3s fl. 1s, ec. 2s | 33 **10** | 4 | Square skeleton tower, green and white square daymark, black square in center; 27. | |
| 7764 *H 1324* | Bas-Cap-Pele. | 46° 14.1′ N 64° 15.7′ W | **Fl.W.** period 5s fl. 0.5s, ec. 4.5s | 42 **13** | 11 | Square skeleton tower, red and white rectangular daymark; 22. | Seasonal. |
| 7766 *H 1326* | Robichaud wharf. | 46° 13.5′ N 64° 23.0′ W | **Fl.W.** period 3s fl. 1s, ec. 2s | 20 **6** | 6 | Square skeleton tower; 17. | Seasonal. |
| 7768 *H 1324.4* | Cape Bald wharf, on end of wharf. | 46° 14.2′ N 64° 15.7′ W | **Fl.R.** period 3s fl. 1s, ec. 2s | 20 **6** | 5 | Square skeleton tower; 17. | Seasonal. |
| 7772 *H 1323* | Little Cape Breakwater, SE. corner. | 46° 12.0′ N 64° 09.8′ W | **Fl.R.** period 5s fl. 1s, ec. 4s | 36 **11** | 10 | Square skeleton tower; 33. | Seasonal. |
| 7774 *H 1322* | Little Cape, outer breakwater. | 46° 11.9′ N 64° 09.7′ W | **Fl.R.** period 4s | 23 **7** | 4 | Square skeleton tower; 11. | Seasonal. |
| 7784 *H 1319* | Botsford breakwater, SE. corner. | 46° 10.1′ N 63° 56.0′ W | **Iso.R.** period 2s | 20 **6** | 10 | Square skeleton tower; 17. | |
| 7786 *H 1319.2* | Murray corner. | 46° 10.4′ N 63° 57.3′ W | **Fl.(3)W.** period 12s | 59 **18** | | | Private light. |
| 7812 *H 1313* | Cape Tormentine, Fisherman's wharf. | 46° 08.0′ N 63° 46.7′ W | **Fl.G.** period 4s | 23 **7** | 3 | Pipe swing pole, green and white square daymark; 11. | Seasonal. |
| 7816 *H 1316* | Cape Tormentine Harbor breakwater. | 46° 08.0′ N 63° 46.2′ W | **Fl.G.** period 3s fl. 1s, ec. 2s | 18 **6** | 4 | Square skeleton tower, two green and white square daymarks, black square in center; 11. | Seasonal. |
| 7819 *H 1314* | -Inner wharf. | 46° 08.0′ N 63° 46.5′ W | **Fl.R.** period 3s | 20 **6** | 6 | Round mast; 12. | Seasonal. |
| 7824 *H 1308* | -Outer wharf. | 46° 08.1′ N 63° 46.3′ W | **Iso.R.** period 2s | 39 **12** | 5 | White square tower, white daymark, red stripe; 33. | Seasonal. |

| (1) No. | (2) Name and Location | (3) Position | (4) Characteristic | (5) Height | (6) Range | (7) Structure | (8) Remarks |
|---|---|---|---|---|---|---|---|
| | | | **CANADA-NEW BRUNSWICK-GULF OF ST. LAWRENCE** | | | | |
| 7844 *H 1304* | Fort Monckton Point (Old Fort Point). | 46° 02.6´ N 64° 04.2´ W | **Fl.W.** period 3s fl. 1s, ec. 2s | 31 **10** | 7 | Round tower, red and white bands, red upper portion; 24. | Seasonal. |

# Section 5

## South Side of Gulf of St. Lawrence
## Including Prince Edward Island, Magdalen Islands and Cape Breton Island

| (1) No. | (2) Name and Location | (3) Position | (4) Characteristic | (5) Height | (6) Range | (7) Structure | (8) Remarks |
|---|---|---|---|---|---|---|---|
| | **CANADA-PRINCE EDWARD ISLAND-GULF OF ST. LAWRENCE** | | | | | | |
| 7851 *H 1074.4* | Skinners Pond, N. breakwater. | 46° 58.0′ N 64° 07.5′ W | **Fl.G.** period 4s fl. 0.5s, ec. 3.5s | 14 **4** | 4 | Cylindrical mast; 10. | Seasonal. |
| 7851.5 *H 1074* | -S. breakwater, N. head. | 46° 58.0′ N 64° 07.6′ W | **Fl.R.** period 4s fl. 1s, ec. 3s | 13 **4** | 3 | Cylindrical mast; 10. | Seasonal. |
| 7852 *H 1076* | **North Cape.** | 47° 03.5′ N 63° 59.7′ W | **Fl.Y.** period 5s fl. 1s, ec. 4s | 78 **24** | **18** | White octagonal tower, red upper portion; 62. | R. lights on radio mast close S. |
| 7856 *H 1078* | North Point East, S. breakwater, head. | 47° 01.9′ N 63° 59.3′ W | **Fl.G.** period 3s fl. 1s, ec. 2s | 18 **6** | 4 | Pipe swing pole, green and white square daymark; 15. | Seasonal. |
| 7865 *H 1081.4* | Big Tignish Breakwater. | 46° 57.1′ N 63° 59.7′ W | **Q.R.** | 23 **7** | 5 | Cylindrical mast; 17. | Seasonal. |
| 7892 *H 1094* | **Cascumpeque Island Northport Range,** near outer end of railway wharf, front. | 46° 47.7′ N 64° 03.6′ W | **Q.G.** | 30 **9** | **15** | Square skeleton tower, white rectangular daymark, red stripe; 26. | Visible on range line only. Seasonal. |
| 7896 *H 1094.1* | -Rear, 273 meters 244°54′ from front. | 46° 47.6′ N 64° 03.9′ W | **Iso.G.** period 4s | 43 **13** | **15** | White square tower, red stripe; 37. | Visible on range line only. Seasonal. |
| | MALPEQUE HARBOR: | | | | | | |
| 7912 *H 1116* | **-Darnley Point Range,** front. | 46° 33.8′ N 63° 39.1′ W | **F.R.** | 43 **13** | **16** | White square tower, red upper portion, red stripe; 26. | Visible on range line only. Seasonal. |
| 7916 *H 1116.1* | --Rear, 515 meters 233° from front. | 46° 33.7′ N 63° 39.4′ W | **F.R.** | 69 **21** | **16** | White square tower, red upper portion, red stripe; 26. | Visible on range line only. Seasonal. |
| 7944 *H 1124* | -Port Hill Wharf, SE corner. | 46° 35.6′ N 63° 52.0′ W | **Fl.W.** period 4s fl. 1s, ec. 3s | 16 **5** | 2 | Square skeleton tower; 14. | Seasonal. |
| 7948 *H 1129* | Cape Tryon. | 46° 32.0′ N 63° 30.4′ W | **L.Fl.W.** period 6s fl. 2s, ec. 4s | 110 **33** | 8 | White square tower, red upper portion; 41. | |
| 7956 *H 1130.05* | New London. | 46° 30.7′ N 63° 29.2′ W | **Iso.W.** period 4s | 43 **13** | 7 | White square tower, red upper portion; 43. | Seasonal. |
| | NORTH RUSTICO HARBOR: | | | | | | |
| 7968 *H 1140* | -Northern Breakwater. | 46° 27.4′ N 63° 17.3′ W | **Fl.R.** period 3s fl. 1s, ec. 2s | 9 **3** | 3 | Cylindrical mast; 6. | Seasonal. |
| 7972 *H 1141* | -North Rustico Harbor. | 46° 27.3′ N 63° 17.5′ W | **Iso.Y.** period 10s | 41 **12** | 13 | White square tower, red upper portion; 34. | |
| 7976 *H 1142* | -N. Rustico, inner breakwater. | 46° 27.2′ N 63° 17.5′ W | **Iso.R.** period 4s | 25 **8** | 4 | Pipe swing pole; 22. | Seasonal. |
| 7992 *H 1149* | Covehead Bridge. | 46° 25.8′ N 63° 08.8′ W | **Fl.W.** period 4s | 28 **8** | 5 | Cylindrical mast; 8. | Seasonal. |
| 7996 *H 1150* | Cape Stanhope (Covehead Harbor). | 46° 25.8′ N 63° 08.6′ W | **Fl.W.** period 5s fl. 0.5s, ec. 4.5s | 36 **11** | 11 | White square tower, red upper portion; 27. | Seasonal. **Horn:** 1 bl. ev. 30s (bl. 3s, si. 27s). Horn points 005°. Private light. |

| (1) No. | (2) Name and Location | (3) Position | (4) Characteristic | (5) Height | (6) Range | (7) Structure | (8) Remarks |
|---|---|---|---|---|---|---|---|
| | | | **CANADA-PRINCE EDWARD ISLAND-GULF OF ST. LAWRENCE** | | | | |
| 8000 *H 1156* | Grand Tracadie, wharf. | 46° 24.2′ N 63° 01.7′ W | **Fl.R.** period 4s fl. 1s, ec. 3s | 15 **5** | 2 | Cylindrical mast, red and white triangular daymark, red triangle in center; 12. | Seasonal. |
| 8020 *H 1160* | Savage Harbor. | 46° 26.0′ N 62° 49.9′ W | **Fl.W.** period 4s | 16 **5** | 3 | Pipe swing pole; 11. | Seasonal. |
| 8036 *H 1168* | Shipwreck Point. | 46° 28.1′ N 62° 25.5′ W | **Oc.W.** period 5s lt. 3s, ec. 2s | 84 **26** | 12 | White octagonal tower, red upper portion; 44. | |
| 8048 *H 1170.4* | Naufrage, W. breakwater. | 46° 28.2′ N 62° 25.2′ W | **Fl.R.** period 4s | 15 **5** | 4 | Square skeleton tower; 11. | Seasonal. |
| 8052 *H 1170.3* | -E. breakwater, head. | 46° 28.2′ N 62° 25.2′ W | **Fl.G.** period 4s | 16 **5** | 7 | Square skeleton tower; 10. | Seasonal. |
| 8060 *H 1173* | North Lake Harbor Range, front. | 46° 28.1′ N 62° 04.1′ W | **Q.G.** | 26 **8** | 11 | Square skeleton tower, white trapezoidal daymark, red stripe; 16. | Visible on range line only. Seasonal. |
| 8064 *H 1173.1* | -Rear, 328 meters 204°34′ from front. | 46° 27.9′ N 62° 04.2′ W | **Iso.G.** period 4s | 49 **15** | **15** | Square skeleton tower, white trapezoidal daymark, red stripe; 36. | Visible on range line only. Seasonal. |
| 8065 *H 1174* | -W. breakwater, head. | 46° 28.2′ N 62° 04.2′ W | **Iso.R.** period 2s | 24 **7** | 5 | Pipe swing pole, red and white triangular daymarks, red triangles in center; 16. | Seasonal. |
| 8072 *H 0920* | East Point. | 46° 27.1′ N 61° 58.3′ W | **L.Fl.W.** period 5s fl. 2s, ec. 3s | 89 **27** | 11 | White octagonal tower, red upper portion; 64. | |
| | SOURIS HARBOR: | | | | | | |
| 8084 *H 0922* | -Souris East. | 46° 20.8′ N 62° 14.8′ W | **Iso.W.** period 4s | 89 **27** | 13 | White square tower, red upper portion; 47. | |
| 8088 *H 0924* | -E. breakwater, near extremity. | 46° 20.9′ N 62° 15.3′ W | **Fl.R.** period 4s fl. 1s, ec. 3s | 36 **11** | 8 | Square skeleton tower; 30. | |
| 8092 *H 0928* | **Annandale Range,** front. | 46° 15.5′ N 62° 25.3′ W | **Q.W.** | 31 **10** | **15** | White square tower, red stripe; 17. | Visible on range line only. Seasonal. |
| 8096 *H 0928.1* | -Rear, 1376 meters 303°50′ from front. | 46° 16.0′ N 62° 26.3′ W | **Iso.W.** period 4s | 76 **23** | **18** | White square tower, red stripe; 66. | Visible on range line only. Seasonal. |
| 8100 *H 0925* | Fortune Bay, N. wharf. | 46° 19.7′ N 62° 21.1′ W | **F.W.R.G.** | 23 **7** | 9 | Square skeleton tower, red and white rectangular daymark; 17. | R. 265°-280°, W.-282°, G.-291°. Seasonal. |
| 8104 *H 0930* | Launching Pond, breakwater, head. | 46° 13.2′ N 62° 24.5′ W | **Fl.R.** period 3s fl. 1s, ec. 2s | 16 **5** | 2 | Cylindrical mast; 16. | Seasonal. Private light. |
| 8106 *H 0931* | -S. breakwater. | 46° 13.2′ N 62° 24.6′ W | **Fl.G.** period 3s fl. 1s, ec. 2s | 16 **5** | 2 | Cylindrical mast; 12. | Seasonal. Private light. |
| | CARDIGAN BAY: | | | | | | |
| 8108 *H 0932* | **-Panmure Head.** | 46° 08.7′ N 62° 28.0′ W | **Fl.W.** period 4s | 82 **25** | **19** | White octagonal tower, red upper portion; 61. | |
| 8112 *H 0936* | -St. Andrew Point Range, front. | 46° 09.8′ N 62° 31.7′ W | **F.W.** | 36 **11** | 11 | Cylindrical tower, red and white bands; 25. | Visible on range line only. |
| 8116 *H 0936.1* | --Rear, 618 meters 280°03′ from front. | 46° 09.9′ N 62° 32.2′ W | **F.W.** | 59 **18** | 11 | White square tower, red stripe; 43. | Visible on range line only. |
| 8120 *H 0939* | -Lower Montague Wharf, NE. corner. | 46° 10.2′ N 62° 33.8′ W | **Fl.G.** period 4s fl. 1s, ec. 3s | 20 **6** | 5 | Cylindrical mast; 16. | Seasonal. |
| 8128 *H 0949* | -Graham Pond, on N. breakwater. | 46° 05.8′ N 62° 27.1′ W | **Iso.R.** period 4s | 20 **6** | 6 | Square skeleton tower; 16. | Seasonal. |

| (1) No. | (2) Name and Location | (3) Position | (4) Characteristic | (5) Height | (6) Range | (7) Structure | (8) Remarks |
|---|---|---|---|---|---|---|---|

## CANADA-PRINCE EDWARD ISLAND-GULF OF ST. LAWRENCE

| (1) No. | (2) Name and Location | (3) Position | (4) Characteristic | (5) Height | (6) Range | (7) Structure | (8) Remarks |
|---|---|---|---|---|---|---|---|
| 8132 *H 0949.2* | --S. breakwater. | 46° 05.7′ N 62° 27.1′ W | **Fl.G.** period 6s fl. 1s, ec. 5s | 13 **4** | 4 | Square skeleton tower; 10. | Seasonal. |
| 8140 *H 0954* | Murray Harbor Range, front. | 46° 01.3′ N 62° 28.7′ W | **F.R.** | 21 **6** | 10 | White square tower, red upper portion, red stripe; 23. | Visible on range line only. Seasonal. |
| 8144 *H 0954.1* | -Rear, 1360.9 meters 234°04′ from front. | 46° 00.8′ N 62° 29.6′ W | **F.R.** | 58 **18** | 10 | White square tower, red upper portion, red stripe; 45. | Visible on range line only. Seasonal. |
| 8148 *H 0956* | -Beach Point Breakwater. | 46° 01.0′ N 62° 29.3′ W | **Fl.G.** period 4s | 15 **5** | 4 | Square skeleton tower; 12. | Seasonal. |
| 8156 *H 0950* | Cape Bear, head. | 46° 00.2′ N 62° 27.6′ W | **L.Fl.Y.** period 6s fl. 2s, ec. 4s | 56 **17** | 10 | Square skeleton tower, red and white rectangular daymarks; 27. | |
| 8164 *H 0962* | Wood Island. | 45° 57.0′ N 62° 44.7′ W | **Iso.W.** period 10s | 72 **22** | 12 | White square tower, red upper portion; 50. | |
| 8184 *H 0978* | Pinette River Outer Range, front. | 46° 03.3′ N 62° 57.3′ W | **F.W.** | 33 **10** | 11 | Square skeleton tower, white trapezoidal daymark, red stripe; 17. | Visible on range line only. Seasonal. |
| 8188 *H 0978.1* | -Rear, 302 meters 017°56′ from front. | 46° 03.4′ N 62° 57.2′ W | **F.W.** | 46 **14** | 11 | Square skeleton tower, white trapezoidal daymark, red stripe; 32. | Seasonal. |
| 8192 *H 0982* | **Prim Point.** | 46° 03.0′ N 63° 02.4′ W | **Fl.W.** period 5s fl. 0.2s, ec. 4.8s | 68 **21** | **18** | White cylindrical tower, red upper portion; 60. | |
| 8216 *H 0996* | St. Peters Island, SE. side. | 46° 07.0′ N 63° 10.8′ W | **Fl.W.** period 4s fl. 1s, ec. 3s | 68 **21** | 10 | White square tower, red upper portion; 30. | |
| 8220 *H 0998* | Nine Mile Creek, wharf. | 46° 08.9′ N 63° 13.1′ W | **Fl.W.** period 4s fl. 1s, ec. 3s | 18 **5** | 5 | Square skeleton tower, red and white rectangular daymark, red triangle in center; 16. | Seasonal. |
| | CHARLOTTETOWN HARBOR: | | | | | | |
| 8228 *H 1006* | -Haszard Point Range, front. | 46° 11.7′ N 63° 04.4′ W | **F.Y.** | 59 **18** | 13 | Red square tower, black stripe; 56. | Visible on range line only. |
| 8232 *H 1006.1* | --Rear, 651 meters 019°19′ from front. | 46° 12.0′ N 63° 04.3′ W | **F.Y.** | 152 **46** | 13 | Red square tower, black stripe; 46. | Visible on range line only. |
| 8236 *H 1008* | -Blockhouse Point. | 46° 11.4′ N 63° 07.8′ W | **Oc.W.** period 4s lt. 3s, ec. 1s | 59 **18** | 12 | White square tower, red upper portion; 40. | |
| 8240 *H 1012* | **-Brighton Beach Range,** front. | 46° 13.8′ N 63° 08.9′ W | **F.Y.** | 36 **11** | **19** | White square tower, red upper portion, red stripe; 41. | Visible on range line only. |
| 8244 *H 1012.1* | --Rear, 398 meters 336°56′ from front. | 46° 14.0′ N 63° 09.0′ W | **F.Y.** | 86 **26** | **19** | White hexagonal tower, red stripe; 60. | Visible on range line only. |
| 8248 *H 1016* | -Warren Cove Range, W. side of harbor, front. | 46° 11.9′ N 63° 08.3′ W | **F.Y.** | 56 **17** | 12 | White square tower, red upper portion, red stripe; 36. | |
| 8252 *H 1016.1* | --Rear, 328 meters 197°39′ from front. | 46° 11.8′ N 63° 08.4′ W | **F.Y.** | 69 **21** | 12 | White square tower, red upper portion, red stripe; 25. | |
| 8253 *H 1018* | -Peakes Quay Marina. | 46° 13.9′ N 63° 07.3′ W | **Q.G.** | | 3 | Round mast; 7. | Seasonal. Private light. |
| 8260 *H 1024* | Charlottetown AVIATION LIGHT. | 46° 17.0′ N 63° 08.0′ W | **Fl.W.** period 10s | 250 **76** | | Tower; 75. | |
| | CRAPAUD: | | | | | | |
| 8292 *H 1039* | -Port Borden Pier, head. | 46° 14.7′ N 63° 42.0′ W | **Iso.G.** period 4s | 33 **10** | 7 | White square tower, red upper portion; 28. | Seasonal. |

| (1) No. | (2) Name and Location | (3) Position | (4) Characteristic | (5) Height | (6) Range | (7) Structure | (8) Remarks |
|---|---|---|---|---|---|---|---|

## CANADA-PRINCE EDWARD ISLAND-GULF OF ST. LAWRENCE

| (1) No. | (2) Name and Location | (3) Position | (4) Characteristic | (5) Height | (6) Range | (7) Structure | (8) Remarks |
|---|---|---|---|---|---|---|---|
| 8304 *H 1044* | -Port Borden breakwater. | 46° 14.6′ N 63° 41.8′ W | **Fl.R.** period 4s fl. 1s, ec. 3s | 16 **5** | 3 | Cylindrical mast; 9. | Seasonal. |
| 8306 *H 1039.4* | -Confederation Bridge, on each side of navigation span. | 46° 12.6′ N 63° 45.1′ W | **2 Iso.W.** period 6s | 166 **51** | 13 | On bridge. | Private light. |
| 8306.1 *H 1039.5* | --SE. side. | 46° 12.6′ N 63° 45.1′ W | **Dir.W.R.G.** | 210 **64** | | On bridge. | F.R. 308°39′-310°39′, F.W.-311°39′, F.G.-313°39′. Private light. |
| 8306.2 *H 1039.6* | --NW. side. | 46° 12.6′ N 63° 45.2′ W | **Dir.W.R.G.** | 210 **64** | | On bridge. | F.G. 129°08′-131°08′, F.W.-132°08′, F.R.-134°08′. Private light. |
| 8306.3 *H 1039.7* | --Pier 22. SW. side. | 46° 12.6′ N 63° 45.2′ W | **2 F.G.** | 54 **16** | 11 | On bridge. | On N. and S. sides. Private light. |
| | --RACON | | **B(– • • •)** | | **30** | | (3 & 10cm). |
| 8306.4 *H 1039.8* | --Pier 21. SW. side. | 46° 12.7′ N 63° 45.1′ W | **2 F.R.** | 54 **16** | 11 | On bridge. | On N. and S. sides. Private light. |
| | --RACON | | **T(–)** | | **30** | | (3 & 10cm). |
| 8308 *H 1046* | Seacow Head. | 46° 19.0′ N 63° 48.6′ W | **L.Fl.(2)W.** period 12s fl. 2s, ec. 2s fl. 2s, ec. 6s | 88 **27** | 12 | White pentagonal tower, red upper portion; 60. | |
| 8310 *H 1045* | Richmond Cove. | 46° 19.1′ N 63° 47.2′ W | **Fl.(3)W.** period 12s | 59 **18** | | | Private light. |
| | SUMMERSIDE HARBOR: | | | | | | |
| 8316 *H 1048* | -Indian Head. | 46° 22.8′ N 63° 49.0′ W | **Iso.W.** period 10s | 46 **14** | 10 | White octagonal tower, red upper portion; 42. | |
| 8318 *H 1054* | -Marina. | 46° 23.3′ N 63° 47.2′ W | **Fl.R.** period 4s | 17 **5** | 7 | Square skeleton tower, red and white rectangular daymark, red triangle in center; 11. | Visible 269°-029°. Seasonal. |
| 8320 *H 1050* | **-Range,** on railway wharf, front. | 46° 23.2′ N 63° 47.4′ W | **F.G.** | 35 **11** | **18** | Square skeleton tower, white trapezoidal daymark, red stripe; 30. | Visible on range line only. |
| 8324 *H 1050.1* | --Rear, 1436 meters 072°04′ from front. | 46° 23.5′ N 63° 46.3′ W | **F.G.** | 81 **25** | **18** | White square tower, red upper protion, red stripe; 66. | Visible on range line only. |
| 8328 *H 1056* | Cape Egmont. | 46° 24.1′ N 64° 08.1′ W | **L.Fl.W.** period 5s fl. 2s, ec. 3s | 65 **20** | 12 | White square tower, red upper portion; 41. | |
| | FISHING COVE: | | | | | | |
| 8332 *H 1057* | -Outer End, inner breakwater. | 46° 24.4′ N 64° 08.1′ W | **Fl.R.** period 3s fl. 1s, ec. 2s | 26 **8** | 5 | Pipe swing pole; 23. | Seasonal. |
| 8336 *H 1057.5* | -Fishing Cove, W. breakwater, S. head. | 46° 24.4′ N 64° 08.1′ W | **Fl.G.** period 4s | 10 **3** | 4 | Cylindrical mast; 10. | Seasonal. |
| 8340 *H 1058* | Canoe Gully Outer Range, front. | 46° 26.9′ N 64° 06.4′ W | **F.Y.** | 20 **6** | 13 | Square skeleton tower, white trapezoidal daymark, red stripe; 16. | Visible on range line only. Seasonal. |
| 8344 *H 1058.1* | -Rear, 176 meters 105°49′ from front. | 46° 26.9′ N 64° 06.2′ W | **F.Y.** | 33 **10** | 13 | Square skeleton tower, white trapezoidal daymark, red stripe; 26. | Visible on range line only. Seasonal. |
| 8356 *H 1060* | Egmont Bay Wharf, SW. corner. | 46° 26.4′ N 64° 06.8′ W | **Fl.G.** period 4s | | 2 | Pipe swing pole, green and white square daymark. | Seasonal. |
| 8360 *H 1062* | West Point. | 46° 37.2′ N 64° 23.2′ W | **Iso.W.** period 12s | 66 **20** | 12 | White square tower, black bands, red upper portion; 68. | Private light. |

| (1) No. | (2) Name and Location | (3) Position | (4) Characteristic | (5) Height | (6) Range | (7) Structure | (8) Remarks |
|---|---|---|---|---|---|---|---|

## CANADA-PRINCE EDWARD ISLAND-GULF OF ST. LAWRENCE

| (1) No. | (2) Name and Location | (3) Position | (4) Characteristic | (5) Height | (6) Range | (7) Structure | (8) Remarks |
|---|---|---|---|---|---|---|---|
| 8376<br>*H 1068* | Seal Point wharf, (Howard Cove). | 46° 44.4′ N<br>64° 22.7′ W | **Iso.R.**<br>period 2s | 27<br>**8** | 4 | Square skeleton tower, red and white rectangular daymark, red triangle in center; 21. | |
| 8380<br>*H 1068.1* | Howards Cove, near Seal Point. | 46° 44.4′ N<br>64° 22.6′ W | **L.Fl.W.**<br>period 6s<br>fl. 2s, ec. 4s | 46<br>**14** | 12 | White square tower, red upper portion; 19. | Seasonal. |
| 8384<br>*H 1072* | Miminegash Range, front. | 46° 52.8′ N<br>64° 14.1′ W | **F.R.** | 20<br>**6** | 8 | Square skeleton tower, white trapezoidal daymark, red stripe; 13. | Seasonal. |
| 8388<br>*H 1072.1* | -Rear, 420 meters 173°11′ from front. | 46° 52.6′ N<br>64° 14.1′ W | **F.R.** | 46<br>**14** | 8 | Square skeleton tower, white trapezoidal daymark, red stripe; 43. | Seasonal. |

## CANADA-MAGDALEN ISLANDS-GULF OF ST. LAWRENCE

| (1) No. | (2) Name and Location | (3) Position | (4) Characteristic | (5) Height | (6) Range | (7) Structure | (8) Remarks |
|---|---|---|---|---|---|---|---|
| 8402<br>*H 0907.5* | -Millerand, breakwater. | 47° 12.9′ N<br>61° 59.0′ W | **Iso.R.**<br>period 2s | 36<br>**11** | 4 | Mast; 20. | Seasonal. |
| 8420<br>*H 0913.4* | Etang du Nord, N. breakwater. | 47° 22.2′ N<br>61° 57.7′ W | **Fl.G.**<br>period 3s<br>fl. 1s, ec. 2s | 16<br>**5** | 4 | Mast; 7. | Seasonal. |
| 8422<br>*H 0913.5* | -S. breakwater, head. | 47° 22.2′ N<br>61° 57.7′ W | **Fl.R.**<br>period 3s<br>fl. 1s, ec. 2s | 13<br>**4** | 4 | Mast; 7. | Seasonal. |
| 8423<br>*H 0903* | House Harbor bridge, port. | 47° 24.3′ N<br>61° 50.5′ W | **Iso.G.**<br>period 2s | | 5 | On bridge, black, green and white square daymark. | Seasonal. |
| 8423.5<br>*H 0903.5* | -Starboard. | 47° 24.4′ N<br>61° 50.5′ W | **Iso.R.**<br>period 2s | | 5 | On bridge, red and white triangular daymark. | Seasonal. |
| 8424<br>*H 0886* | Brion Island, near W. extremity. | 47° 46.9′ N<br>61° 30.5′ W | **Fl.W.**<br>period 3s<br>fl. 1s, ec. 2s | 131<br>**40** | 9 | White octagonal tower; 44. | |
| 8432<br>*H 0882* | Bird Rocks. | 47° 50.3′ N<br>61° 08.7′ W | **L.Fl.W.**<br>period 8s<br>fl. 2s, ec. 6s | 161<br>**49** | 9 | Square skeleton tower; 34. | |
| 8444<br>*H 0888* | **Grand Entry Harbor Range,** front. | 47° 33.4′ N<br>61° 33.7′ W | **F.R.** | 21<br>**6** | **15** | Square skeleton tower, orange trapezoidal daymark, black stripe; 16. | Visible on range line only. |
| 8448<br>*H 0888.1* | -Rear, 63 meters 025°57′ from front. | 47° 33.4′ N<br>61° 33.7′ W | **F.R.** | 34<br>**10** | **15** | Square skeleton tower, orange trapezoidal daymark, black stripe; 33. | Visible on range line only. |
| 8464<br>*H 0902* | Pointe Basse. | 47° 23.3′ N<br>61° 47.4′ W | **Iso.R.**<br>period 2s | 26<br>**8** | 5 | Square skeleton tower. | Seasonal. |
| 8469<br>*H 0915.4* | Grindstone (Cap-aux-Meules), W. breakwater. | 47° 22.6′ N<br>61° 51.4′ W | **Iso.R.**<br>period 2s | 16<br>**5** | 4 | Cylindrical mast; 10. | Seasonal. |
| 8470<br>*H 0914* | -Wharf Range, front. | 47° 22.6′ N<br>61° 51.2′ W | **Q.G.** | 22<br>**7** | 13 | Red square skeleton tower, orange trapezoidal daymark, black stripe; 16. | Visible on range line only. |
| 8470.1<br>*H 0914.1* | --Rear, 133 meters 330°13′ from front. | 47° 22.7′ N<br>61° 51.3′ W | **Q.G.** | 39<br>**12** | 13 | Red square skeleton tower, orange trapezoidal daymark, black stripe; 33. | Visible on range line only. |
| 8471<br>*H 0915* | -Breakwater. | 47° 22.5′ N<br>61° 51.1′ W | **Fl.R.**<br>period 6s<br>fl. 1s, ec. 5s | 26<br>**8** | 4 | Cylindrical mast; 7. | |
| 8472<br>*H 0896* | Entry Island, NE. point. | 47° 17.3′ N<br>61° 41.4′ W | **Fl.W.**<br>period 3s<br>fl. 1s, ec. 2s | 236<br>**72** | 8 | Square skeleton tower; 15. | |
| 8484<br>*H 0909* | Amherst Sector. | 47° 13.7′ N<br>61° 50.0′ W | **Dir.Iso.W.R.G.**<br>period 4s | 16<br>**5** | 12 | Gray square skeleton tower, red and white stripes; 15. | R. 211°48′-212°48′, W.-213°48′, G.-214°48′. Seasonal. Private light. |

| (1) No. | (2) Name and Location | (3) Position | (4) Characteristic | (5) Height | (6) Range | (7) Structure | (8) Remarks |
|---|---|---|---|---|---|---|---|

**CANADA-MAGDALEN ISLANDS-GULF OF ST. LAWRENCE**

| (1) No. | (2) Name and Location | (3) Position | (4) Characteristic | (5) Height | (6) Range | (7) Structure | (8) Remarks |
|---|---|---|---|---|---|---|---|
| 8490<br>*H 0910* | Havre-Aubert Sector. | 47° 14.1´ N<br>61° 50.0´ W | **Iso.W.R.G.**<br>period 2s | 14<br>**4** | 5 | White square tower; 10. | R. 305°-322°50′, W.-325°50′, G.-007°.<br>Seasonal.<br>Private light. |
| | PUGWASH HARBOR: | | | | | | |
| 8512<br>*H 1292* | **-Outer Range,** midway between Biglow Point and Fox Point, front. | 45° 51.3´ N<br>63° 40.9´ W | **F.G.** | 50<br>**15** | **16** | Square skeleton tower, white trapezoidal daymark, red stripe; 16. | Visible on range line only.<br>Seasonal. |
| 8516<br>*H 1292.1* | --Rear, 478.5 meters 160°32′ from front. | 45° 51.0´ N<br>63° 40.8´ W | **F.G.** | 92<br>**28** | **16** | Square skeleton tower, white trapezoidal daymark, red stripe; 36. | Visible on range line only.<br>Seasonal. |
| 8520<br>*H 1296* | -Steven Point Range, front. | 45° 51.9´ N<br>63° 40.1´ W | **Iso.R.**<br>period 2s | 32<br>**10** | 5 | Square skeleton tower, white trapezoidal daymark, red stripe; 18. | Visible on range line only.<br>Seasonal. |
| 8524<br>*H 1296.1* | --Rear, 470 meters 086°22′ from front. | 45° 51.9´ N<br>63° 39.7´ W | **Iso.R.**<br>period 4s | 89<br>**27** | 5 | Square skeleton tower, white trapezoidal daymark, red stripe; 21. | Visible on range line only.<br>Seasonal. |
| 8528<br>*H 1300* | -Fishing Point Range, front. | 45° 52.2´ N<br>63° 40.5´ W | **F.G.** | 27<br>**8** | 10 | Square skeleton tower, white trapezoidal daymark, red stripe; 13. | Visible on range line only.<br>Seasonal. |
| 8532<br>*H 1300.1* | --Rear, 258 meters 350°30′ from front. | 45° 52.3´ N<br>63° 40.5´ W | **F.G.** | 40<br>**12** | 10 | Square skeleton tower, white trapezoidal daymark, red stripe; 26. | Visible on range line only.<br>Seasonal. |
| 8536<br>*H 1291* | **-Bergeman Point Range,** front. | 45° 51.7´ N<br>63° 42.5´ W | **Q.Y.** | 39<br>**12** | **16** | Square skeleton tower, white trapezoidal daymark, red stripe; 16. | Visible on range line only.<br>Seasonal. |
| 8540<br>*H 1291.1* | --Rear, 168.6 meters 205°13′ from front. | 45° 51.6´ N<br>63° 42.6´ W | **Iso.Y.**<br>period 4s | 54<br>**17** | **16** | Square skeleton tower, white trapezoidal daymark, red stripe; 31. | Visible on range line only.<br>Seasonal. |
| | WALLACE HARBOR: | | | | | | |
| 8554<br>*H 1283* | **-Wallace Harbor.** | 45° 48.8´ N<br>63° 27.8´ W | **Dir.W.R.G.** | 41<br>**12** | **21** | White square tower, red band; 26. | F.R. 254°-256°, Al.R.W.-257°, F.W.-258°, Al.G.W.-259°, F.G.-261°. |
| 8560<br>*H 1274* | Skinner Cove. | 45° 47.6´ N<br>63° 02.8´ W | **F.W.R.G.** | 21<br>**6** | 5 | Square skeleton tower, red and white rectangular daymark; 17. | R. 109°-182°54′, W.-186°25′, G.-252°.<br>Seasonal. |
| 8564<br>*H 1276* | Amet Island. | 45° 50.1´ N<br>63° 10.7´ W | **Fl.W.**<br>period 4s<br>fl. 1s, ec. 3s | 39<br>**12** | 10 | Square skeleton tower; 22. | Seasonal. |
| 8568<br>*H 1273* | Toney River Wharf. | 45° 46.5´ N<br>62° 53.4´ W | **Fl.R.**<br>period 4s<br>fl. 1s, ec. 3s | 16<br>**5** | 3 | Cylindrical mast; 10. | Seasonal. |
| 8576<br>*H 1272* | Caribou Point. | 45° 45.9´ N<br>62° 40.8´ W | **Fl.(3)W.**<br>period 20s<br>fl. 1s, ec. 1s<br>fl. 1s, ec. 1s<br>fl. 1s, ec. 15s | 44<br>**13** | 9 | White square tower, red upper portion; 41. | Emergency light. |
| 8580 | *Caribou Harbor Buoy SS1.* | 45° 45.1´ N<br>62° 39.9´ W | **Fl.G.**<br>period 4s<br>fl. 0.5s, ec. 3.5s | | | PORT (B)<br>G. | Seasonal.<br>**Bell.** |
| | RACON | | **G(– – •)** | | 10 | | (3 & 10cm). |
| 8584<br>*H 1270* | Caribou Harbor, inner Range, front. | 45° 44.4´ N<br>62° 41.3´ W | **Q.G.** | 23<br>**7** | 4 | Square skeleton tower, white trapezoidal daymark, red stripe; 10. | Visible on range line only.<br>Seasonal. |
| 8588<br>*H 1270.1* | -Rear, 82.7 meters 209°31′ from front. | 45° 44.3´ N<br>62° 41.3´ W | **Iso.G.**<br>period 4s | 33<br>**10** | 4 | Square skeleton tower, white trapezoidal daymark, red stripe; 20. | Visible on range line only.<br>Seasonal. |

| (1) No. | (2) Name and Location | (3) Position | (4) Characteristic | (5) Height | (6) Range | (7) Structure | (8) Remarks |
|---|---|---|---|---|---|---|---|

## CANADA-MAGDALEN ISLANDS-GULF OF ST. LAWRENCE

| (1) No. | (2) Name and Location | (3) Position | (4) Characteristic | (5) Height | (6) Range | (7) Structure | (8) Remarks |
|---|---|---|---|---|---|---|---|
| | PICTOU ISLAND: | | | | | | |
| 8596 *H 1238* | -East End, SE. point. | 45° 49.0′ N 62° 30.9′ W | **Fl.W.** period 4s fl. 1s, ec. 3s | 58 **18** | 9 | Square red skeleton tower, red and white rectangular daymark; 33. | |
| 8600 *H 1238.5* | -Pictou Island (East End), breakwater. | 45° 49.4′ N 62° 30.6′ W | **Fl.R.** period 4s fl. 1s, ec. 3s | 14 **4** | 3 | Cylindrical mast; 11. | Seasonal. |
| 8604 *H 1240* | -Island Breakwater. | 45° 48.2′ N 62° 35.1′ W | **Fl.G.** period 4s | 17 **5** | 4 | Pipe swing pole, green and white square daymark, black square in center; 13. | Seasonal. |
| 8608 *H 1237* | -Island South. | 45° 48.2′ N 62° 35.2′ W | **Iso.W.** period 4s | 35 **11** | 8 | White square tower, red upper portion; 27. | Seasonal. |
| 8612 *H 1244* | -West End. | 45° 48.2′ N 62° 36.1′ W | **Fl.W.** period 4s | 46 **14** | 9 | Square skeleton tower, red and white rectangular daymark; 23. | |
| 8616 *H 1248.05* | -Pictou Bar. | 45° 41.2′ N 62° 39.8′ W | **Fl.W.** period 4s | 29 **9** | 6 | Square skeleton tower, red and white rectangular daymark; 24. | |
| 8617 *H 1248.1* | **-Pictou.** | 45° 40.6′ N 62° 42.1′ W | **Iso.R.** period 4s | 94 **29** | **16** | Square skeleton tower; 42. | |
| 8620 *H 1256* | -Harbor Range, front. | 45° 41.3′ N 62° 40.7′ W | **F.W.** | 23 **7** | 11 | White square tower, red upper portion, red stripe; 23. | Visible on range line only. |
| 8624 *H 1256.1* | --Rear, 142 meters 261°57′ from front. | 45° 41.3′ N 62° 40.8′ W | **F.W.** | 55 **17** | 11 | Square skeleton tower, white trapezoidal daymark, red stripe; 31. | Visible on range line only. |
| 8634 *H 1260.5* | -Pictou Marina. | 45° 40.5′ N 62° 42.7′ W | **Q.G.** | 7 **2** | | Pier; 6. | Seasonal. Private light. |
| 8640 *H 1264* | -East River, Trenton, Stonehouse Point Range, front. | 45° 37.4′ N 62° 38.9′ W | **F.R.** | 26 **8** | 10 | Red and white square tower, white trapezoidal daymark, red stripe; 15. | Visible on range line only. Seasonal. |
| 8644 *H 1264.1* | --Rear, 891 meters 119°43′ from front. | 45° 37.4′ N 62° 38.3′ W | **F.R.** | 66 **20** | 10 | Square skeleton tower, white trapezoidal daymark, red stripe; 33. | Visible on range line only. Seasonal. |
| 8652 *H 1236* | **Baillie Brook.** | 45° 42.4′ N 62° 16.2′ W | **L.Fl.W.** period 6s fl. 2s, ec. 4s | 56 **17** | **15** | Square skeleton tower, red and white rectangular daymark; 25. | Seasonal. |
| 8653 *H 1236.3* | -E. breakwater. | 45° 42.5′ N 62° 16.5′ W | **Fl.G.** period 4s fl. 1s, ec. 3s | 16 **5** | 4 | Cylindrical mast; 9. | Seasonal. |
| 8654 *H 1236.4* | -W. breakwater. | 45° 42.4′ N 62° 16.4′ W | **Fl.R.** period 4s fl. 1s, ec. 3s | 19 **6** | 3 | Cylindrical mast; 10. | Seasonal. |
| 8662 *H 1234.5* | Livingstone Cove. | 45° 52.1′ N 61° 59.0′ W | **Fl.G.** period 4s fl. 1s, ec. 3s | 20 **6** | 4 | Cylindrical mast; 16. | Seasonal. |
| 8664 *H 1234* | **Cape George.** | 45° 52.4′ N 61° 54.0′ W | **Fl.(3)W.** period 12s fl. 1s, ec. 2s fl. 1s, ec. 2s fl. 1s, ec. 5s | 398 **121** | **15** | White octagonal tower, red upper portion; 45. | |
| 8668 *H 1232.5* | -Ballantynes Cove Wharf. | 45° 51.5′ N 61° 55.1′ W | **L.Fl.R.** period 6s fl. 2s, ec. 4s | 26 **8** | 4 | Pipe swing pole; 16. | Seasonal. |
| 8671 *H 1232.35* | Cribbean, head. | 45° 45.4′ N 61° 53.7′ W | **F.W.** | 69 **21** | 13 | Skeleton tower, enclosed lower portion; 12. | |
| 8672 *H 1232.3* | -Wharf, head. | 45° 45.3′ N 61° 53.7′ W | **Fl.R.** period 6s fl. 1s, ec. 5s | 20 **6** | 4 | Skeleton tower, enclosed lower portion; 12. | Seasonal. |

| (1) No. | (2) Name and Location | (3) Position | (4) Characteristic | (5) Height | (6) Range | (7) Structure | (8) Remarks |
|---|---|---|---|---|---|---|---|
| **CANADA-MAGDALEN ISLANDS-GULF OF ST. LAWRENCE** | | | | | | | |
| 8676 *H 1232* | Pomquet Island. | 45° 39.5´ N 61° 44.9´ W | **L.Fl.W.** period 6s fl. 2s, ec. 4s | 46 **14** | 8 | White square tower; 26. | Seasonal. |
| 8684 *H 1231* | Barrios Beach, on shore, approach to breakwater. | 45° 38.7´ N 61° 37.5´ W | **F.W.** | 52 **16** | 13 | Skeleton tower, enclosed lower portion, red and white rectangular slatwork daymark; 22. | Seasonal. |
| 8688 *H 1230* | Havre Boucher Range, front. | 45° 40.9´ N 61° 31.6´ W | **F.G.** | 26 **8** | 8 | Square skeleton tower, white trapezoidal daymark, red stripe; 24. | Visible on range line only. Seasonal. |
| 8692 *H 1230.1* | -Rear, 436 meters 194°31′ from front. | 45° 40.7´ N 61° 31.7´ W | **F.G.** | 105 **32** | 8 | White square tower, red upper portion, red stripe; 31. | Visible on range line only. Seasonal. |
| 8696 *H 3440* | North Canso, W. side of entrance to Strait of Canso. | 45° 41.5´ N 61° 29.3´ W | **Fl.W.** period 3s fl. 1s, ec. 2s | 120 **37** | 11 | White cylindrical tower, two red bands; 35. | Obscured S. of 120°. |
| | STRAIT OF CANSO: | | | | | | |
| 8700 *H 3433* | -Canso Canal, NE. mooring berth. | 45° 39.2´ N 61° 25.2´ W | **Fl.Y.** period 4s | 18 **6** | | Mast. | Private light. |
| 8704 *H 3436* | **-Balache Point Range,** front, N. end of Canso Lock. | 45° 39.0´ N 61° 25.0´ W | **Oc.Y.** period 11s lt. 10s, ec. 1s | 20 **6** | **16** | Square skeleton tower, white trapezoidal daymark, red stripe; 12. | Visible on range line only. Seasonal. |
| 8708 *H 3436.1* | --Rear, 219.4 meters 131°30′ from front. | 45° 38.9´ N 61° 24.9´ W | **Oc.Y.** period 11s lt. 10s, ec. 1s | 43 **13** | **16** | White square tower, red upper portion, red stripe; 25. | Visible on range line only. Seasonal. |
| 8712 *H 3432* | -Canso Canal, SE. mooring dock. | 45° 38.8´ N 61° 24.5´ W | **Fl.Y.** period 4s | 16 **5** | | Mast. | Private light. |
| **CANADA-CAPE BRETON ISLAND-GULF OF ST. LAWRENCE** | | | | | | | |
| 8716 *H 1228* | Judique South, wharf. | 45° 51.5´ N 61° 30.2´ W | **L.Fl.R.** period 6s fl. 2s, ec. 4s | 24 **7** | 4 | Pipe swing pole, red and white triangular daymark, red triangle in center; 20. | Seasonal. |
| 8718 *H 1223.2* | Little Judique Harbor, breakwater. | 45° 57.5´ N 61° 31.7´ W | **F.G.** | 17 **5** | 7 | Round mast; 12. | |
| 8720 *H 1222* | Henry Island. | 45° 58.6´ N 61° 36.0´ W | **Fl.W.** period 4s fl. 1s, ec. 3s | 200 **61** | 9 | Octagonal tower, red upper portion, red and white stripes; 38. | |
| 8724 *H 1224* | Port Hood Island, Smith Point. | 46° 00.9´ N 61° 33.4´ W | **Fl.R.** period 4s | 16 **5** | 5 | Skeleton mast, red and white rectangular daymark; 12. | Seasonal. Private light. |
| 8736 *H 1218* | -Murphy Pond, W. breakwater, head. | 46° 01.6´ N 61° 32.7´ W | **Fl.G.** period 4s | 21 **6** | 2 | Cylindrical tower; 11. | Seasonal. |
| 8740 *H 1223* | -Little Judique Harbor Wharf. | 45° 57.5´ N 61° 31.6´ W | **F.W.R.G.** | 27 **8** | 7 | Skeleton tower, enclosed lower portion, red and white rectangular daymark; 23. | R. 077°-121°, W.-123°, G.-161°. Seasonal. |
| 8748 *H 1216.1* | Mabou Harbor. | 46° 05.2´ N 61° 27.9´ W | **F.G.** | 46 **14** | 6 | White square tower, red upper portion; 44. | Seasonal. |
| 8752 *H 1210* | Inverness Harbor Range, front. | 46° 13.6´ N 61° 19.2´ W | **F.G.** | 20 **6** | 10 | Square skeleton tower, white trapezoidal daymark, red stripe; 11. | Visible on range line only. Seasonal. |
| 8756 *H 1210.1* | --Rear, 24 meters 123° 49′ from front. | 46° 13.6´ N 61° 19.1´ W | **F.G.** | 39 **12** | 10 | Square skeleton tower, white trapezoidal daymark, red stripe; 16. | Visible on range line only. Seasonal. |
| 8757 *H 1210.5* | -Inverness, breakwater. | 46° 13.8´ N 61° 19.5´ W | **Fl.G.** period 4s | 26 **8** | 2 | Cylindrical mast; 10. | Seasonal. |

| (1) No. | (2) Name and Location | (3) Position | (4) Characteristic | (5) Height | (6) Range | (7) Structure | (8) Remarks |
|---|---|---|---|---|---|---|---|

## CANADA-CAPE BRETON ISLAND-GULF OF ST. LAWRENCE

| (1) No. | (2) Name and Location | (3) Position | (4) Characteristic | (5) Height | (6) Range | (7) Structure | (8) Remarks |
|---|---|---|---|---|---|---|---|
| 8760<br>*H 1208* | Margaree, summit of Margaree Island. | 46° 21.5′ N<br>61° 15.8′ W | **Fl.W.**<br>period 4s<br>fl. 1s, ec. 3s | 298<br>**91** | 9 | White hexagonal tower, red upper portion; 27. | |
| 8764<br>*H 1202* | Margaree Harbor Range, front. | 46° 26.4′ N<br>61° 06.8′ W | **F.Y.** | 49<br>**15** | 7 | White square tower, red upper portion, red stripe; 23. | Visible 102°-192°. Seasonal. |
| 8768<br>*H 1202.1* | -Rear, 65 meters 166°45′ from front. | 46° 26.3′ N<br>61° 06.7′ W | **F.Y.** | 68<br>**21** | 8 | White square tower, red upper portion, red stripe; 33. | Visible on range line only. Seasonal. |
| 8776<br>*H 1202.3* | --E. breakwater. | 46° 26.6′ N<br>61° 06.8′ W | **Fl.G.**<br>period 4s | 16<br>**5** | 4 | Cylindrical mast; 6. | Seasonal. |
| 8776.1<br>*H 1202.4* | --W. breakwater. | 46° 26.6′ N<br>61° 06.9′ W | **Fl.R.**<br>period 4s | 19<br>**6** | 2 | Cylindrical mast; 7. | Seasonal. |
| 8778<br>*H 1196.5* | --SW. breakwater. | 46° 33.0′ N<br>61° 02.9′ W | **Q.R.** | 27<br>**8** | 2 | Cylindrical mast; 11. | Seasonal. |
| 8780<br>*H 1196* | **Grande-Etang Range,** front. | 46° 32.9′ N<br>61° 02.5′ W | **Oc.Y.**<br>period 10s<br>lt. 9s, ec. 1s | 32<br>**10** | **16** | Square skeleton tower, white trapezoidal daymark, red stripe; 27. | Visible on range line only. Seasonal. |
| 8784<br>*H 1196.1* | -Rear, 197 meters 130°29′ from front. | 46° 32.8′ N<br>61° 02.4′ W | **Oc.Y.**<br>period 10s<br>lt. 9s, ec. 1s | 59<br>**18** | **16** | Triangular skeleton tower, enclosed lower portion, white trapezoidal daymark, red stripe; 24. | Visible on range line only. Seasonal. |
| | CHETICAMP ISLAND: | | | | | | |
| 8792<br>*H 1197.5* | -Grand Etang, NE. breakwater. | 46° 33.1′ N<br>61° 02.8′ W | **Q.G.** | 30<br>**9** | 4 | Cylindrical mast; 17. | Seasonal. |
| 8796<br>*H 1194* | -La Pointe, wharf, head. | 46° 36.2′ N<br>61° 03.2′ W | **Fl.R.**<br>period 5s<br>fl. 1s, ec. 4s | 14<br>**4** | 2 | Skeleton tower, enclosed lower portion; 10. | Seasonal. |
| 8798<br>*H 1189* | -Cheticamp. | 46° 37.8′ N<br>61° 00.8′ W | **Dir.W.R.G.** | 34<br>**10** | 7 | White cylindrical tower, red band; 25. | F.R.187°57′-189°53′, Al.R.W.-190°03′, F.W.-190°51′, Al.G.W.-191°01′, F.G.-192°57′. |
| 8800<br>*H 1188* | **-Enragee Point Range.** | 46° 39.0′ N<br>61° 01.6′ W | **Fl.(3)W.**<br>period 24s<br>fl. 0.3s, ec. 3.7s<br>fl. 0.3s, ec. 3.7s<br>fl. 0.3s, ec. 15.7s | 74<br>**23** | **18** | White octagonal tower, red upper portion; 42. | |
| 8804<br>*H 1182* | -Caveau Point Range, front. | 46° 38.9′ N<br>61° 00.0′ W | **F.R.** | 56<br>**17** | 14 | Square skeleton tower, white trapezoidal daymark, red stripes; 22. | Visible on range line only. |
| 8808<br>*H 1182.1* | --Rear, 223.1 meters 107°55′ from front. | 46° 38.9′ N<br>60° 59.9′ W | **F.R.** | 95<br>**29** | 14 | White square tower, trapezoidal daymark, red stripe; 28. | Visible on range line only. |
| 8818<br>*H 1176.5* | Pleasant Bay. | 46° 50.0′ N<br>60° 47.9′ W | **Q.R.** | 22<br>**7** | 4 | Cylindrical mast; 12. | Seasonal. |
| 8825<br>*H 1176.4* | -breakwater, NE. | 46° 50.0′ N<br>60° 47.8′ W | **Fl.G.**<br>period 4s | 23<br>**7** | 2 | Cylindrical mast; 13. | Seasonal. |
| 8830<br>*H 1049* | **-Summerside outer Range,** front. | 46° 23.7′ N<br>63° 48.6′ W | **F.R.** | 31<br>**9** | **18** | White square tower, white trapezoidal daymark, red stripe; 30. | Visible on range line only. |
| 8831<br>*H 1049.1* | --Rear, 430.3 meters 028°57′ from front. | 46° 23.9′ N<br>63° 48.5′ W | **F.R.** | 49<br>**15** | **18** | White square tower, white trapezoidal daymark, red stripe; 33. | Visible on range line only. |
| 8832<br>*H 0874* | Cape St. Lawrence. | 47° 02.5′ N<br>60° 35.8′ W | **L.Fl.W.**<br>period 12s<br>fl. 2s, ec. 10s | 88<br>**27** | 8 | Square skeleton tower, red and white rectangular daymark; 22. | Visible 050°- 261°. |
| 8840<br>*H 0873* | St. Lawrence Bay. | 47° 00.2′ N<br>60° 28.0′ W | **Fl.G.**<br>period 3s | 17<br>**5** | 4 | Pipe swing pole; 14. | Seasonal. |
| 8844<br>*H 0873.2* | -Southwest breakwater. | 47° 00.2′ N<br>60° 28.0′ W | **Fl.R.**<br>period 4s | 16<br>**5** | 2 | Pipe swing pole; 10. | Seasonal. |

| (1) No. | (2) Name and Location | (3) Position | (4) Characteristic | (5) Height | (6) Range | (7) Structure | (8) Remarks |
|---|---|---|---|---|---|---|---|
| | | | **CANADA-CAPE BRETON ISLAND-GULF OF ST. LAWRENCE** | | | | |
| 8848 *H 0872* | Cape North. | 47° 01.7′ N 60° 23.5′ W | **L.Fl.W.** period 6s fl. 2s, ec. 4s | 112 **34** | 8 | Square skeleton tower, red and white rectangular daymarks on NW., NE. and SE. faces; 49. | |
| | ST. PAUL ISLAND: | | | | | | |
| 8852 *H 0876* | -S. Point. | 47° 11.0′ N 60° 09.7′ W | **Fl.W.** period 4s | 154 **47** | 7 | White cylindrical tower, red upper portion; 23. | Obscured 132°- 250°. |
| 8856 *H 0878* | -N. Point, on rock off point. | 47° 13.6′ N 60° 08.4′ W | **L.Fl.W.** period 12s fl. 2s, ec. 10s | 131 **40** | 12 | White octagonal tower; 43. | Obscured 351°- 041°. Emergency light. |
| 8864 *H 0870* | Dingwall Harbor. | 46° 54.2′ N 60° 27.3′ W | **Fl.R.** period 4s | 26 **8** | 3 | Square skeleton tower, red and white rectangular daymarks on E. and W. faces;16. | Seasonal. |
| 8868 *H 0870.4* | -S. | 46° 54.2′ N 60° 27.2′ W | **Fl.G.** period 4s | 26 **8** | 4 | Cylindrical mast; 16. | Seasonal. |
| 8880 *H 0866* | Neil Harbor, E. side of entrance. | 46° 48.4′ N 60° 19.2′ W | **L.Fl.W.** period 6s fl. 2s, ec. 4s | 59 **18** | 9 | White square tower, red upper portion; 33. | Seasonal. |
| 8893 *H 0865.1* | The Point Breakwater, outer end of wharf. | 46° 41.2′ N 60° 21.6′ W | **Q.R.** | 13 **4** | 5 | Square skeleton tower, red and white rectangular daymark, red triangle in center; 10. | Seasonal. |
| 8902 *H 0857.5* | Briton Cove Range, front. | 46° 26.7′ N 60° 27.6′ W | **F.Y.** | 23 **7** | 12 | Square skeleton tower, white trapezoidal daymark, red stripe; 16. | Visible on range line only. Seasonal. |
| 8903 *H 0857.51* | -Rear, 80 meters 291°02′ from front. | 46° 26.7′ N 60° 27.7′ W | **F.Y.** | 33 **10** | 12 | Square skeleton tower, white trapezoidal daymark, red stripe; 33. | Visible on range line only. Seasonal. |
| 8904 *H 0856* | Ciboux Island. | 46° 23.1′ N 60° 22.4′ W | **L.Fl.R.** period 12s fl. 2s, ec. 10s | 89 **27** | 7 | White cylindrical tower, two red bands; 33. | |
| | GREAT BRAS D'OR: | | | | | | |
| 8916 *H 0778* | -Black Rock Point. | 46° 18.3′ N 60° 23.5′ W | **L.Fl.W.** period 6s fl. 2s, ec. 4s | 85 **26** | 12 | White square tower; 39. | Visible 047°-227°. **Horn:** 1 bl. ev. 30s (bl. 3s, si. 27s). Horn points 353°. |
| 8920 *H 0779* | **--W.** | 46° 18.3′ N 60° 23.5′ W | **Dir.W.R.G.** | 54 **16** | **19** | Square skeleton tower ; 13. | F.G. 045°15′- 048°15′, Al.G.W.-048°30′, F.W.-049°30′, Al.R.W.-049°45′, F.R.-053°45′. Seasonal. |
| 8932 *H 0782* | -Great Bras d'Or Range, front. | 46° 17.4′ N 60° 24.8′ W | **F.G.** | 52 **16** | 6 | White square tower, red upper portion, red stripe; 33. | Visible on range line only. Seasonal. |
| 8936 *H 0782.1* | --Rear, 515 meters 212°25′ from front. | 46° 17.2′ N 60° 25.0′ W | **F.G.** | 63 **19** | 6 | White square structure, red stripe; 53. | Visible on range line only. Seasonal. |
| 8948 *H 0784* | -Duffus Point. | 46° 16.9′ N 60° 25.5′ W | **Fl.W.** period 4s | 23 **7** | 4 | Pipe swing pole; 23. | Seasonal. |
| 8952 *H 0786* | -Kelly Cove Wharf. | 46° 17.3′ N 60° 26.2′ W | **F.W.** | 16 **5** | 12 | Skeleton tower, enclosed lower portion; 13. | Seasonal. |
| 8981 *H 0792* | -Man of War Point Range, front. | 46° 11.5′ N 60° 32.6′ W | **F.Y.** | 59 **18** | 10 | Triangular skeleton tower, white trapezoidal daymark, red stripe; 33. | Visible on range line only. Seasonal. |
| 8982 *H 0792.1* | --Rear, 769 meters 223°04′ from front. | 46° 11.2′ N 60° 33.1′ W | **F.Y.** | 95 **29** | **16** | Triangular skeleton tower, white trapezoidal daymark, red stripe; 65. | Visible on range line only. Seasonal. |
| 8983 *H 0796* | **-MacFarlane Point Range,** front. | 46° 07.6′ N 60° 36.3′ W | **F.Y.** | 102 **31** | **15** | Triangular skeleton tower, white trapezoidal daymark, red stripe; 33. | Visible on range line only. Seasonal. |

| (1) No. | (2) Name and Location | (3) Position | (4) Characteristic | (5) Height | (6) Range | (7) Structure | (8) Remarks |
|---|---|---|---|---|---|---|---|

## CANADA-CAPE BRETON ISLAND-GULF OF ST. LAWRENCE

| (1) No. | (2) Name and Location | (3) Position | (4) Characteristic | (5) Height | (6) Range | (7) Structure | (8) Remarks |
|---|---|---|---|---|---|---|---|
| 8983.1 *H 0796.1* | --Rear, 277.2 meters 065°15′ from front. | 46° 07.6′ N 60° 36.1′ W | **F.Y.** | 102 **31** | **15** | Triangular skeleton mast, white trapezoidal daymark, red stripe; 32. | Visible on range line only. Seasonal. |
| 8984 *H 0798* | -Mackenzie Point. | 46° 07.0′ N 60° 38.9′ W | **Fl.R.** period 4s | 69 **21** | 2 | Skeleton tower, red and white rectangular daymark; 23. | Seasonal. |
| | ST. PATRICK'S CHANNEL: | | | | | | |
| 8996 *H 0800* | -Kidston Island. | 46° 05.9′ N 60° 44.5′ W | **L.Fl.G.** period 12s fl. 2s, ec. 10s | 44 **13** | 6 | White square tower, red upper portion; 47. | Seasonal. |
| 9000 *H 0801* | --W. head. | 46° 05.6′ N 60° 45.0′ W | **Fl.R.** period 6s | 44 **13** | 4 | White cylindrical tower, two red bands; 36. | Seasonal. |
| 9012 *H 0803* | -Morrison Cove Range, front. | 46° 00.7′ N 60° 56.3′ W | **F.Y.** | 11 **3** | 10 | Square skeleton tower, white trapezoidal daymark, red stripe; 10. | Visible on range line only. Seasonal. |
| 9016 *H 0803.1* | --Rear, 639 meters 195°33′ from front. | 46° 00.3′ N 60° 56.4′ W | **F.Y.** | 20 **6** | 10 | Square skeleton tower, white trapezoidal daymark, red stripe; 20. | Visible on range line only. Seasonal. |
| 9020 *H 0802* | -MacIver Point Range, front. | 46° 02.1′ N 60° 55.5′ W | **Iso.W.** period 2s | 13 **4** | 10 | Triangular skeleton tower, white trapezoidal daymark, red stripe; 10. | Visible on range line only. Seasonal. On request by keying VHF 5 times for 0.5 seconds on channel 65A (156.275 MHz). Remains active for 15 minutes. |
| 9024 *H 0802.1* | --Rear, 33 meters 066° 23′ from front. | 46° 02.1′ N 60° 55.4′ W | **Iso.W.** period 2s | | 10 | Triangular skeleton tower, enclosed lower portion, white trapezoidal daymark, red stripe; 20. | Visible on range line only. Seasonal. On request by keying VHF 5 times for 0.5 seconds on channel 65A (156.275 MHz). Remains active for 15 minutes. |
| 9028 *H 0804.4* | -Little Narrows Range, front. | 45° 59.8′ N 60° 58.1′ W | **F.Y.** | 15 **5** | 10 | Triangular skeleton tower, white trapezoidal daymark, red stripe; 13. | Visible on range line only. Seasonal. |
| 9032 *H 0804.41* | --Rear, 128 meters 206°44′ from front. | 45° 59.8′ N 60° 58.2′ W | **F.Y.** | 33 **10** | 10 | Triangular skeleton tower, white trapezoidal daymark, red stripe; 10. | Visible on range line only. Seasonal. |
| 9040 *H 0806* | Whycocomagh. | 45° 57.7′ N 61° 04.7′ W | **F.W.** | 23 **7** | 11 | Skeleton tower, enclosed lower portion; 23. | Seasonal. |
| | BARRA STRAIT: | | | | | | |
| 9052 *H 0818* | -Grand Narrows Bridge, center of swing. | 45° 57.5′ N 60° 47.8′ W | **F.W.R.G.** | 56 **17** | | Cylindrical mast; 7. | F.R. when closed, F.G. open, F.W. continuous. Private light. |
| 9056 *H 0822* | -Derby Point. | 45° 56.4′ N 60° 48.1′ W | **Fl.R.** period 4s | 52 **16** | 6 | Skeleton tower, enclosed lower portion, red and white rectangular daymark; 23. | Seasonal. |
| 9057 *H 0832* | -Cameron Island. | 45° 48.8′ N 61° 00.4′ W | **Fl.G.** period 4s | 30 **9** | 5 | White square tower; 26. | Seasonal. |
| 9058 *H 0833* | -Clarke Cove Wharf. | 45° 49.2′ N 61° 02.3′ W | **F.R.** | 15 **4** | 9 | Triangular skeleton mast; 13. | Seasonal. |
| | BRAS D'OR LAKE: | | | | | | |
| 9060 *H 0838* | -Cape George, W. side of entrance to St. Peter's Inlet. | 45° 44.1′ N 60° 48.6′ W | **Fl.W.** period 4s | 41 **12** | 6 | White square tower, red upper portion; 26. | Visible 126°-317°. Seasonal. |

| (1) No. | (2) Name and Location | (3) Position | (4) Characteristic | (5) Height | (6) Range | (7) Structure | (8) Remarks |
|---|---|---|---|---|---|---|---|

## CANADA-CAPE BRETON ISLAND-GULF OF ST. LAWRENCE

| (1) No. | (2) Name and Location | (3) Position | (4) Characteristic | (5) Height | (6) Range | (7) Structure | (8) Remarks |
|---|---|---|---|---|---|---|---|
| | ST. PETER'S INLET: | | | | | | |
| 9064<br>*H 0839* | -Gregory Island. | 45° 42.6′ N<br>60° 48.0′ W | **Fl.G.**<br>period 4s | 36<br>**11** | 4 | White cylindrical tower, two red bands; 33. | Seasonal. |
| 9068<br>*H 0842* | -Beaver Island, SE. point. | 45° 40.5′ N<br>60° 50.0′ W | **Fl.W.**<br>period 4s | 33<br>**10** | 6 | White cylindrical tower, red bands; 33. | Seasonal. |
| 9072<br>*H 0843* | -Helen Island, W. of Sandys Point. | 45° 40.0′ N<br>60° 51.3′ W | **Fl.G.**<br>period 4s | 26<br>**8** | 4 | Triangular skeleton tower; 23. | Seasonal. |
| 9080<br>*H 0770* | Point Aconi. | 46° 20.2′ N<br>60° 17.6′ W | **L.Fl.W.**<br>period 6s<br>fl. 2s, ec. 4s | 89<br>**27** | 14 | Square skeleton tower, red and white rectangular daymarks on NW., NE. and SE. faces; 33. | Seasonal. |
| 9092<br>*H 0772* | Little Bras d'Or Range, front. | 46° 18.7′ N<br>60° 17.2′ W | **F.R.** | 30<br>**9** | 6 | Skeleton tower, enclosed lower portion, white trapezoidal daymark, red stripe; 13. | |
| 9096<br>*H 0772.1* | -Rear, 354 meters 211°46′ from front. | 46° 18.6′ N<br>60° 17.4′ W | **F.R.** | 43<br>**13** | **16** | Skeleton tower, enclosed lower portion, white trapezoidal daymark, red stripe; 23. | |
| 9098<br>*H 0774* | **Little Bras d'Or.** | 46° 17.9′ N<br>60° 17.2′ W | **Dir.W.R.G.** | 13<br>**4** | **15** | Skeleton tower, enclosed lower portion; 10. | F.R. 180°15′-182°05′, Al.W.R.-182°30′, F.W.-183°, Al.W.G.-183°25′, F.G.-185°15′. |
| 9100<br>*H 0758* | **Low Point.** | 46° 16.0′ N<br>60° 07.5′ W | **Fl.W.**<br>period 5s<br>fl. 0.5s, ec. 4.5s | 85<br>**26** | **18** | White octagonal tower, red upper portion; 69. | |

## CANADA-CAPE BRETON ISLAND

| (1) No. | (2) Name and Location | (3) Position | (4) Characteristic | (5) Height | (6) Range | (7) Structure | (8) Remarks |
|---|---|---|---|---|---|---|---|
| 9104<br>*H 0761* | -Sydney Range, S. side of W. arm of harbor, 1 mile W. of Edward Point, front. | 46° 10.8′ N<br>60° 15.0′ W | **Iso.Y.**<br>period 4s | 56<br>**17** | 14 | White octagonal tower, red upper portion, red stripe; 49. | Visible on range line only. |
| 9108<br>*H 0761.1* | --Rear, 766 meters 213°34′ from front. | 46° 10.5′ N<br>60° 15.3′ W | **Iso.Y.**<br>period 4s | 121<br>**37** | 14 | Square skeleton tower, red and white trapezoidal daymark; 33. | Visible on range line only. |
| | SYDNEY HARBOR: | | | | | | |
| 9112<br>*H 0760* | -Sydney Bar. | 46° 12.3′ N<br>60° 13.1′ W | **Fl.G.**<br>period 5s<br>fl. 1s, ec. 4s | 30<br>**9** | 4 | On white building; 7. | |
| 9120<br>*H 0762.6* | -Ballast Grounds. | 46° 12.4′ N<br>60° 14.9′ W | **Fl.(2)R.**<br>period 6s<br>fl. 1s, ec. 1s<br>fl. 1s, ec. 3s | 26<br>**8** | 3 | Cylindrical mast; 23. | |
| 9124<br>*H 0764* | -Sydney, South Arm Range, front. | 46° 09.4′ N<br>60° 12.2′ W | **F.G.** | 26<br>**8** | 12 | Triangular skeleton tower, white trapezoidal daymark, red stripe; 23. | Visible on range line only. |
| 9128<br>*H 0764.1* | --Rear, 151 meters 162°32′ from front. | 46° 09.4′ N<br>60° 12.2′ W | **F.G.** | 53<br>**16** | **15** | Triangular skeleton tower, white trapezoidal daymark, red stripe; 43. | Visible on range line only. |
| 9130<br>*H 0767* | Point Edward, main jetty, N. head. | 46° 09.4′ N<br>60° 13.0′ W | **2 F.R.** | 23<br>**7** | 6 | Mast; 16. | |
| 9131<br>*H 0766.2* | --S. head. | 46° 09.2′ N<br>60° 13.0′ W | **2 F.R.** | 26<br>**8** | | Skeleton tower; 13. | |
| 9132<br>*H 0757.5* | Lingan Range, front. | 46° 13.8′ N<br>60° 02.8′ W | **F.G.** | 16<br>**5** | 7 | Skeleton tower, enclosed lower portion, white trapezoidal daymark, red stripe; 13. | Visible on range line only. Seasonal. |

| (1) No. | (2) Name and Location | (3) Position | (4) Characteristic | (5) Height | (6) Range | (7) Structure | (8) Remarks |
|---|---|---|---|---|---|---|---|

## CANADA-CAPE BRETON ISLAND

| (1) No. | (2) Name and Location | (3) Position | (4) Characteristic | (5) Height | (6) Range | (7) Structure | (8) Remarks |
|---|---|---|---|---|---|---|---|
| 9136<br>*H 0757.51* | -Rear, 31 meters 270° from front. | 46° 13.8′ N<br>60° 02.7′ W | **F.G.** | 23<br>**7** | 7 | Triangular skeleton mast, enclosed lower portion, white trapezoidal daymark, red stripe; 23. | Seasonal. |
| 9144<br>*H 0756* | -Glace Bay, breakwater. | 46° 11.9′ N<br>59° 56.9′ W | **Fl.R.**<br>period 3s | 30<br>**9** | 10 | White cylindrical tower, red band; 16. | **Horn:** 1 bl. ev. 20s (bl. 2s, si. 18s). |
| 9148<br>*H 0752* | **-Glace Bay Range,** front. | 46° 11.8′ N<br>59° 56.9′ W | **F.R.** | 26<br>**8** | **16** | Triangular skeleton tower, white trapezoidal daymark, red stripe; 18. | |
| 9152<br>*H 0752.1* | --Rear, 101.7 meters 208°17′ from front. | 46° 11.7′ N<br>59° 57.0′ W | **F.R.** | 43<br>**13** | **16** | Triangular skeleton tower, white trapezoidal daymark, red stripe; 30. | |
| 9156<br>*H 0750* | Flint Island. | 46° 10.9′ N<br>59° 46.2′ W | **Fl.(2)W.**<br>period 25s<br>fl. 1s, ec. 1s<br>fl. 1s, ec. 22s | 75<br>**23** | 9 | White hexagonal tower; 58. | **Horn:** 1 bl. ev. 30s (bl. 3s, si. 27s).<br>Emergency light. |
| 9160<br>*H 0746* | Port Morien. | 46° 07.9′ N<br>59° 52.2′ W | **F.R.** | 16<br>**5** | 10 | Cylindrical mast; 13. | Private light. |
| 9164<br>*H 0742* | **-Scatarie.** | 46° 02.1′ N<br>59° 40.6′ W | **Fl.W.**<br>period 3s<br>fl. 1s, ec. 2s | 66<br>**20** | **15** | White square tower, red upper portion; 46. | **Horn:** 3 bl. ev. 60s. (bl. 2s, si. 3s, bl. 2s, si. 3s, bl. 2s, si. 48s). Horn points 105°.<br>Emergency light. |
| 9168<br>*H 0744* | -Main-a-Dieu. | 46° 00.2′ N<br>59° 47.7′ W | **Fl.W.**<br>period 4s | 82<br>**25** | 7 | White cylindrical tower, two red bands; 33. | |
| 9172<br>*H 0745* | Moque, head. | 46° 00.4′ N<br>59° 49.4′ W | **F.W.** | 40<br>**12** | 12 | Skeleton tower, enclosed lower portion; 23. | **Horn:** 1 bl. ev. 30s (bl. 3s, si. 27s). Horn points 070°. |
| 9180<br>*H 0745.6* | Burke Point, Main-a-Dieu Harbor. | 46° 00.2′ N<br>59° 50.4′ W | **Fl.R.**<br>period 4s | 20<br>**6** | 4 | Skeleton tower, enclosed lower portion; 13. | |
| 9182<br>*H 0745.8* | Mira Gut Swing Bridge, N. side of bridge. | 46° 02.2′ N<br>59° 58.1′ W | **F.R.G.** | 30<br>**9** | | Cylindrical mast; 13. | G. bridge open, R. bridge closed.<br>Privato light. |
| 9184<br>*H 0745.4* | Battery Point (Main-a-Dieu). | 46° 00.3′ N<br>59° 50.4′ W | **L.Fl.G.**<br>period 12s<br>fl. 2s, ec. 10s | 13<br>**4** | 2 | Cylindrical mast; 7. | |
| 9196<br>*H 3342* | Little Lorraine (Lorembec). | 45° 56.9′ N<br>59° 51.5′ W | **F.G.** | 36<br>**11** | 7 | White cylindrical tower, red upper portion; 16. | Seasonal.<br>**Horn:** 1 bl. ev. 20s (bl. 2s, si. 18s). |
| 9204<br>*H 3344* | **Louisbourg.** | 45° 54.4′ N<br>59° 57.5′ W | **Fl.W.**<br>period 10s<br>fl. 1s, ec. 9s | 105<br>**32** | **16** | White octagonal tower, red upper portion; 49. | Visible 250°-100°.<br>**Horn (2):** 1 bl. ev. 20s. (bl. 2s, si. 18s). Horn points 138°.<br>Emergency light. |
| 9208<br>*H 3348* | Louisburg Range, harbor, W. side, front. | 45° 54.1′ N<br>59° 59.4′ W | **F.Y.** | 23<br>**7** | 14 | Square skeleton tower, white trapezoidal daymark, red stripe; 16. | Visible on range line only. |
| 9212<br>*H 3348.1* | -Rear, 166 meters 267°56′ from front. | 45° 54.1′ N<br>59° 59.5′ W | **F.Y.** | 43<br>**13** | | Square skeleton tower, white trapezoidal daymark, red stripe; 20. | |
| 9224<br>*H 3358* | Gabarus Cove. | 45° 50.6′ N<br>60° 08.8′ W | **F.R.** | 56<br>**17** | 8 | White hexagonal tower, red upper portion; 33. | Seasonal. |
| 9226<br>*H 3359* | Rouse Point. | 45° 50.6′ N<br>60° 07.9′ W | **F.Y.** | 30<br>**9** | 9 | White block; 13. | Seasonal. |
| 9232<br>*H 3360* | **Guyon Island.** | 45° 46.0′ N<br>60° 06.8′ W | **Fl.W.**<br>period 20s<br>fl. 1s, ec. 19s | 53<br>**16** | **17** | White octagonal tower, red upper portion; 43. | Seasonal.<br>**Horn:** 1 bl. ev. 60s (bl. 6s, si. 54s). Horn points 147°.<br>Emergency light. |

| (1) No. | (2) Name and Location | (3) Position | (4) Characteristic | (5) Height | (6) Range | (7) Structure | (8) Remarks |
|---|---|---|---|---|---|---|---|

**CANADA-CAPE BRETON ISLAND**

| (1) No. | (2) Name and Location | (3) Position | (4) Characteristic | (5) Height | (6) Range | (7) Structure | (8) Remarks |
|---|---|---|---|---|---|---|---|
| 9236 *H 3362* | Fourchu, head. | 45° 43.0´ N 60° 13.8´ W | **F.W.** | 62 **19** | 13 | White cylindrical tower, two red bands; 36. | Visible 096°-065°. Seasonal. **Horn (2):** 1 bl. ev. 30s (bl. 3s, si. 27s). Horns sound in unison. Horns point 065° and 170°. Seasonal. Emergency light. |
| 9240 *H 3364* | **Fourchu Harbor Range,** front. | 45° 43.1´ N 60° 14.7´ W | **F.Y.** | 10 **3** | **18** | Triangular skeleton mast, white trapezoidal daymark, red stripe; 10. | Visible on range line only. Seasonal. |
| 9244 *H 3364.1* | -Rear, 225.7 meters 255°10′ from front. | 45° 43.1´ N 60° 14.9´ W | **F.Y.** | 26 **8** | **18** | Triangular skeleton mast, white trapezoidal daymark, red stripe; 24. | Visible on range line only. Seasonal. |
| 9252 *H 3368* | St. Esprit Island. | 45° 37.3´ N 60° 29.3´ W | **L.Fl.W.** period 12s fl. 2s, ec. 10s | 79 **24** | 8 | Skeleton tower, enclosed lower portion, red and white rectangular daymark; 33. | |
| 9264 *H 3380* | Jerome Point, St. Peters Bay, near entrance to canal. | 45° 38.9´ N 60° 52.4´ W | **F.R.** | 52 **16** | 10 | White square tower, red upper portion; 36. | Seasonal. |
| 9265 *H 3384* | Ouetique Island. | 45° 36.6´ N 60° 57.5´ W | **Fl.R.** period 4s | 75 **23** | 5 | Triangular skeleton tower, red and white rectangular daymark; 30. | Seasonal. |
| 9266 *H 3388* | Hawk Island. | 45° 35.7´ N 60° 59.7´ W | **Fl.G.** period 4s | 39 **12** | 4 | Skeleton tower, enclosed lower portion, red and white rectangular daymark; 33. | Visible 240°30′-265°30′. Seasonal. |
| 9267 *H 3392* | Grandique Point. | 45° 35.6´ N 61° 01.3´ W | **L.Fl.G.** period 6s fl. 2s, ec. 4s | 30 **9** | 7 | White square tower, red upper portion; 33. | Seasonal. |
| | CHEDABUCTO BAY: | | | | | | |
| 9272 *H 3396* | -Petit-de-Grat Inlet breakwater. | 45° 31.1´ N 60° 57.0´ W | **Fl.G.** period 4s fl. 1s, ec. 3s | | 4 | Square skeleton tower, two green and white rectangular daymarks. | Seasonal. |
| 9280 *H 3372* | Little Harbor Wharf. | 45° 35.0´ N 60° 44.5´ W | **F.R.** | 16 **5** | 8 | Cylindrical mast; 10. | Seasonal. |
| 9312 *H 3376* | -Green Island. | 45° 28.7´ N 60° 54.0´ W | **L.Fl.(2)W.** period 20s fl. 2s, ec. 2s fl. 2s, ec. 14s | 112 **34** | 10 | White cylindrical tower, red upper portion; 39. | Emergency light. |
| 9336 *H 3398* | **-Petit-de-Grat Outer Range,** front. | 45° 29.8´ N 60° 58.4´ W | **F.W.** | 26 **8** | **19** | Skeleton tower, enclosed lower portion, white trapezoidal daymark, red stripe; 11. | Visible on range line only. |
| 9340 *H 3398.1* | --Rear, 60 meters 356°01′ from front. | 45° 29.8´ N 60° 58.4´ W | **F.W.** | 49 **15** | **19** | Skeleton mast, enclosed lower portion, white trapezoidal daymark, red stripe; 33. | Visible on range line only. |
| 9344 *H 3399* | **-Petit-de-Grat Inner Range,** front. | 45° 30.1´ N 60° 57.5´ W | **F.Y.** | 39 **12** | **16** | Triangular skeleton tower, enclosed lower portion, white trapezoidal daymark, red stripe; 13. | Visible on range line only. |
| 9348 *H 3399.1* | --Rear, 64.1 meters 033°56′ from front. | 45° 30.1´ N 60° 57.5´ W | **F.Y.** | 49 **15** | **16** | Triangular skeleton tower, enclosed lower portion, white trapezoidal daymark, red stripe; 11. | Visible on range line only. |
| 9352 *H 3401* | -Cowley Point, breakwater. | 45° 30.1´ N 60° 57.8´ W | **Fl.G.** period 4s fl. 1s, ec. 3s | 16 **5** | 3 | Pipe swing pole, green and white square daymarks on NNE. and SSE. faces; 13. | |
| 9356 *H 3404* | -Marache Point, SE. side of entrance to Arichat Harbor. | 45° 28.8´ N 61° 02.1´ W | **F.W.** | 33 **10** | 13 | White square tower, red upper portion; 26. | Visible 338°-224°. |
| 9364 *H 3406* | -Beach Point, N. extremity of West Jerseyman Island. | 45° 30.2´ N 61° 03.3´ W | **Fl.R.** period 4s | 26 **8** | 5 | White square tower, red upper portion; 26. | Seasonal. |

| (1) No. | (2) Name and Location | (3) Position | (4) Characteristic | (5) Height | (6) Range | (7) Structure | (8) Remarks |
|---|---|---|---|---|---|---|---|

**CANADA-CAPE BRETON ISLAND**

| (1) No. | (2) Name and Location | (3) Position | (4) Characteristic | (5) Height | (6) Range | (7) Structure | (8) Remarks |
|---|---|---|---|---|---|---|---|
| 9380 *H 3416* | -West Arichat Wharf, outer end. | 45° 30.9´ N 61° 05.0´ W | **Fl.W.** period 4s fl. 1s, ec. 3s | 13 **4** | 2 | Pipe swing pole; 13. | Seasonal. |
| 9396 *H 3386* | -River Bourgeois, extremity of point, E. side of entrance. | 45° 37.6´ N 60° 56.8´ W | **F.R.** | 23 **7** | 8 | Square tower, red and white rectangular daymark; 26. | Seasonal. Private light. |

# Section 6

## Nova Scotia
## Including Bay of Fundy

| (1) No. | (2) Name and Location | (3) Position | (4) Characteristic | (5) Height | (6) Range | (7) Structure | (8) Remarks |
|---|---|---|---|---|---|---|---|
| | **CANADA-NOVA SCOTIA** | | | | | | |
| 9400 *H 3423* | **Janvrin Island Range,** front, at Thomas Head. | 45° 32.5′ N 61° 12.0′ W | **F.Y.** | 41 **12** | **15** | Triangular skeleton tower, white trapezoidal daymark, red stripe; 33. | Visible on range line only. |
| | | | **Fl.W.** period 4s | 43 **13** | | | |
| 9404 *H 3423.1* | -Rear, 300 meters 088°10′ from front. | 45° 32.5′ N 61° 11.8′ W | **F.Y.** | 82 **25** | **15** | Triangular skeleton tower, white trapezoidal daymark, red stripe; 49. | Visible on range line only. |
| | | | **Fl.W.** period 4s | 84 **26** | | | |
| | STRAIT OF CANSO: | | | | | | |
| 9416 *H 3421* | **-Eddy Point Range,** front, SE. entrance of strait. | 45° 31.2′ N 61° 15.1′ W | **Oc.Y.** period 11s lt. 10s, ec. 1s | 39 **12** | **15** | Triangular skeleton tower, white trapezoidal daymark, red stripe; 39. | Visible on range line only. |
| | | | **Fl.W.** period 4s | | | | |
| 9420 *H 3421.1* | --Rear, 361 meters 124°51′ from front. | 45° 31.1′ N 61° 14.9′ W | **F.Y.** | 86 **26** | **15** | Triangular skeleton tower, white trapezoidal daymark, red stripe; 62. | Visible on range line only. |
| | | | **Fl.W.** period 4s | 88 **27** | | | |
| 9424 *H 3419* | **-Port Malcolm Range,** front, Seacol Bay entrance. | 45° 34.5′ N 61° 17.3′ W | **Oc.W.** period 11s lt. 10s, ec. 1s | 66 **20** | **25** | Triangular skeleton tower, white trapezoidal daymark, red stripe; 31. | Visible on range line only. |
| 9428 *H 3419.1* | --Rear, 791 meters 319°50′ from front. | 45° 34.9′ N 61° 17.7′ W | **Oc.W.** period 11s lt. 10s, ec. 1s | 154 **47** | **25** | Triangular skeleton tower, white trapezoidal daymark, red stripe; 63. | Visible on range line only. |
| 9432 *H 3422* | -Bear Head, SE. end. | 45° 32.9′ N 61° 17.3′ W | **Fl.W.** period 4s | 49 **15** | 6 | Skeleton tower, enclosed lower portion, red and white rectangular daymark; 23. | Intensified on 297°. |
| 9436 *H 3425* | **-Middle Melford Range,** front. | 45° 32.4′ N 61° 18.9′ W | **F.Y.** | 46 **14** | **15** | Triangular skeleton tower, white trapezoidal daymark, red stripe; 26. | Visible on range line only. |
| | | | **Fl.W.** period 4s | 46 **14** | | | |
| 9440 *H 3425.1* | --Rear, 92 meters 268°05′ from front. | 45° 32.4′ N 61° 19.0′ W | **F.Y.** | 68 **21** | **15** | Triangular skeleton tower, white trapezoidal daymark, red stripe; 45. | Visible on range line only. |
| | | | **Fl.W.** period 4s | 70 **21** | | | |
| 9444 *H 3426* | **-Park Point Range,** front, on point, W. side of strait. | 45° 32.6′ N 61° 19.3′ W | **F.Y.** | 40 **12** | **15** | Triangular skeleton tower, white trapezoidal daymark, red stripe; 36. | Visible on range line only. |
| | | | **Fl.W.** period 4s | 43 **13** | | | |
| 9448 *H 3426.1* | --Rear, 317 meters 146°18′ from front. | 45° 32.5′ N 61° 19.1′ W | **F.Y.** | 82 **25** | **15** | Triangular skeleton tower, white trapezoidal daymark, red stripe; 63. | Visible on range line only. |
| | | | **Fl.W.** period 4s | 84 **26** | | | |

| (1) No. | (2) Name and Location | (3) Position | (4) Characteristic | (5) Height | (6) Range | (7) Structure | (8) Remarks |
|---|---|---|---|---|---|---|---|

## CANADA-NOVA SCOTIA

| (1) No. | (2) Name and Location | (3) Position | (4) Characteristic | (5) Height | (6) Range | (7) Structure | (8) Remarks |
|---|---|---|---|---|---|---|---|
| 9452 *H 3427* | **-Cahil Rock Range,** front, S. of rock. | 45° 34.2′ N 61° 21.3′ W | **F.Y.** | 43 **13** | **18** | Triangular skeleton tower, white trapezoidal daymark, red stripe; 42. | Visible on range line only. |
| | | | **Fl.W.** period 4s | 46 **14** | | | |
| 9456 *H 3427.1* | --Rear, 176 meters 304°46′ from front. | 45° 34.3′ N 61° 21.4′ W | **Oc.Y.** period 11s lt. 10s, ec. 1s | 92 **28** | **18** | Triangular skeleton tower, white trapezoidal daymark, red stripe, 40. | Visible on range line only. |
| | | | **Fl.W.** period 4s | 92 **28** | | | |
| 9472 *H 3430* | -Point Tupper, on gypsum loading pier. | 45° 36.5′ N 61° 22.5′ W | **F.R.** | 98 **30** | | Mast on small shed. | Visible on range line only. Private light. |
| 9476 *H 3434* | **Cape Porcupine Range,** front, S. side of causeway. | 45° 38.7′ N 61° 25.1′ W | **F.G.** | 33 **10** | **18** | Triangular skeleton tower, white trapezoidal daymark, red stripe; 20. | Visible on range line only. Seasonal. |
| 9480 *H 3434.1* | -Rear, 1583 meters 144°06′ from front. | 45° 38.0′ N 61° 24.4′ W | **F.G.** | 72 **22** | **18** | Triangular skeleton tower, white trapezoidal daymark, red stripe; 45. | Visible on range line only. Seasonal. |
| | GUYSBOROUGH HARBOR: | | | | | | |
| 9492 *H 3456* | -Queensport, on Rook Island. | 45° 20.9′ N 61° 16.3′ W | **Fl.W.** period 4s | 52 **16** | 7 | White block, red upper portion; 36. | Visible on range line only. |
| | CANSO HARBOR: | | | | | | |
| 9506 *H 3468* | -Harbor Shoal. | 45° 20.3′ N 60° 59.6′ W | **Fl.G.** period 4s | 20 **6** | 6 | White cylindrical tower, green band, green and white square daymarks on E., W. and N. faces, black square in center; 13. | |
| 9508 *H 3465* | **-Hart Island Range,** front. | 45° 20.6′ N 60° 59.4′ W | **F.R.** | 13 **4** | **17** | Square skeleton tower, white trapezoidal daymark, red stripe; 13. | Increased intensity in line of range. |
| 9512 *H 3465.1* | --Rear, 117 meters 169°49′ from front. | 45° 20.6′ N 60° 59.4′ W | **F.R.** | 34 **10** | **17** | Square skeleton tower, white trapezoidal daymark, red stripe; 26. | **Horn:** 1 bl. ev. 30s. Horn points 348°. |
| 9514 *H 3464.5* | Starling Rock. | 45° 20.4′ N 60° 59.1′ W | **Q.G.** | 21 **6** | 4 | White cylindrical tower, green band, green and white square daymarks on S., W. and N. faces, black square in center; 13. | |
| 9516 *H 3464* | -Piscatiqui Island. | 45° 20.6′ N 60° 59.1′ W | **L.Fl.W.** period 5s fl. 2s, ec. 3s | 16 **5** | 7 | Triangular skeleton tower; 13. | |
| 9520 *H 3462* | -Graves Island breakwater Range, front. | 45° 20.2′ N 60° 59.1′ W | **F.G.** | 17 **5** | 6 | Square skeleton tower, white trapezoidal daymark, red stripe; 10. | |
| 9524 *H 3462.1* | --Rear, 62 meters 164° 31′ from front. | 45° 20.2′ N 60° 59.1′ W | **F.G.** | 23 **7** | 7 | Square skeleton tower, white trapezoidal daymark, red stripe; 16. | |
| 9528 *H 3460* | -Lanigan Beach Range, front. | 45° 19.9′ N 60° 58.8′ W | **F.R.** | 39 **12** | 13 | White square tower, red upper portion, red stripe; 33. | Visible on range line only. |
| 9532 *H 3460.1* | --Canso, rear, 384 meters 266°28′ from front. | 45° 19.9′ N 60° 59.1′ W | **F.R.** | 95 **29** | 13 | White square tower, red upper portion, red stripe; 46. | Visible on range line only. |

| (1) No. | (2) Name and Location | (3) Position | (4) Characteristic | (5) Height | (6) Range | (7) Structure | (8) Remarks |
|---|---|---|---|---|---|---|---|

## CANADA-NOVA SCOTIA

| (1) No. | (2) Name and Location | (3) Position | (4) Characteristic | (5) Height | (6) Range | (7) Structure | (8) Remarks |
|---|---|---|---|---|---|---|---|
| 9540 *H 3458* | **Cranberry Island.** | 45° 19.5′ N 60° 55.6′ W | **Fl.W.** period 15s fl. 1s, ec. 14s | 56 **17** | **23** | White square tower, red upper portion; 49. | **Horn (2):** 2 bl. ev. 60s. (bl. 3s, si. 3s, bl. 3s, si. 51s). Horns sound in unison. Horns point 066° and 141°. Emergency light. |
| | RACON | | **B(– • • •)** | | 10 | | (3cm). |
| 9556 *H 3472* | Little Dover Harbor. | 45° 16.7′ N 61° 01.2′ W | **Fl.W.** period 4s | 26 **8** | 7 | Triangular skeleton tower, red and white rectangular daymark; 23. | Seasonal. |
| 9558 *H 3471* | Rock Island. | 45° 17.0′ N 61° 01.7′ W | **L.Fl.R.** period 6s fl. 2s, ec. 4s | | 5 | Cylindrical mast, two red and white triangular daymarks, red triangle in center. | Seasonal. |
| 9584 *H 3474* | White Head Island, SW. extremity. | 45° 11.8′ N 61° 08.2′ W | **Fl.W.** period 5s fl. 0.5s, ec. 4.5s | 60 **18** | 12 | White block, red upper portion; 36. | **Horn:** 1 bl. ev. 30s (bl. 3s, si. 27s). Horn points 190°. Emergency light. |
| 9588 *H 3476* | Three Top Island. | 45° 12.5′ N 61° 09.5′ W | **L.Fl.W.** period 12s fl. 2s, ec. 10s | 56 **17** | 7 | Square skeleton tower, red and white rectangular daymark; 33. | Visible 150°-033°. |
| 9596 *H 3478* | Port Felix, Hog Island, SE. head. | 45° 13.7′ N 61° 13.2′ W | **Fl.W.** period 4s | 36 **11** | 7 | Square skeleton tower, red and white rectangular daymark; 33. | Visible 196°-062°. Seasonal. **Horn:** 1 bl. ev. 20s. (bl. 2s, si. 18s). |
| 9624 *H 3497* | Larry's River NE. breakwater. | 45° 13.0′ N 61° 22.1′ W | **Iso.R.** period 4s | 13 **4** | 10 | Square skeleton tower, red and white rectangular daymarks on ESE. and WNW. faces, red triangle in center; 10. | |
| 9628 *H 3484* | Torbay, E. point of Berry Head. | 45° 11.5′ N 61° 18.7′ W | **F.W.** | 39 **12** | 12 | White block; 20. | **Horn:** 3 bl. ev. 60s. (bl. 2s, si. 3s, bl. 2s, si. 3s, bl. 2s, si. 48s). Horn points 155°. |
| 9632 *H 3500* | New Harbour Cove, breakwater, head. | 45° 10.2′ N 61° 27.0′ W | **Fl.(2)G.** period 6s fl. 1s, ec. 1s fl. 1s, ec. 3s | 26 **8** | 3 | Skeleton tower, enclosed lower portion; 13. | Seasonal. |
| 9636 *H 3502* | Coddles Harbor. | 45° 09.4′ N 61° 31.0′ W | **Fl.W.** period 4s | 33 **10** | 6 | Triangular skeleton tower, red and white rectangular daymark; 23. | Seasonal. |
| 9648 *H 3504* | Country Island. | 45° 06.0′ N 61° 32.5′ W | **L.Fl.W.** period 20s fl. 2s, ec. 18s | 52 **16** | 14 | White octagonal tower, red upper portion; 45. | Emergency light. |
| 9656 *H 3508* | Drum Head, E. | 45° 08.7′ N 61° 36.2′ W | **Fl.R.** period 4s | 13 **4** | 4 | Cylindrical mast, red and white triangular daymark, red triangle in center; 13. | Seasonal. |
| 9664 *H 3512* | Fishermans Harbor. | 45° 06.7′ N 61° 40.7′ W | **Fl.G.** period 4s | 23 **7** | 7 | Square skeleton tower, white and green daymark; 26. | Seasonal. |
| 9684 *H 3514* | **Port Bickerton,** near W. extremity of Barachois Head. | 45° 05.4′ N 61° 42.0′ W | **Fl.W.** period 3s fl. 1s, ec. 2s | 69 **21** | **17** | White rectangular tower, red upper portion; 30. | Visible 280°-136°. **Horn (2):** 2 bl. ev. 60s. (bl. 3s, si. 3s, bl. 3s, si. 51s). Horns sound in unison. Horns point 156°. Emergency light. |
| 9688 *H 3516.3* | Mouton Harbor. | 45° 05.7′ N 61° 43.5′ W | **Q.R.** period 1s | 13 **4** | 4 | Square skeleton tower, red and white triangular daymark, red triangle in center; 13. | |
| 9692 *H 3516* | -Mouton Harbor Outer Range, front. | 45° 05.5′ N 61° 43.8′ W | **F.W.** | 13 **4** | 14 | Square skeleton tower, white trapezoidal daymark, red stripe; 13. | Visible on range line only. |
| 9696 *H 3516.1* | --Rear, 141 meters 263°42′ from front. | 45° 05.5′ N 61° 43.9′ W | **F.W.** | 26 **8** | 14 | Square skeleton tower, white trapezoidal daymark, red stripe; 20. | Visible on range line only. |
| 9700 *H 3516.4* | -Mouton Harbor Inner. | 45° 05.7′ N 61° 43.6′ W | **Fl.G.** period 4s | 13 **4** | 4 | Cylindrical mast, green and white daymark, green square in center; 12. | |

| (1) No. | (2) Name and Location | (3) Position | (4) Characteristic | (5) Height | (6) Range | (7) Structure | (8) Remarks |
|---|---|---|---|---|---|---|---|
| | | | **CANADA-NOVA SCOTIA** | | | | |
| 9708 *H 3515* | Port Bickerton, E. | 45° 06.3′ N 61° 43.4′ W | **Iso.R.** period 4s | 13 **4** | 4 | Cylindrical mast; 13. | |
| 9736 *H 3526* | Liscomb Island, SW. head. | 44° 59.3′ N 61° 58.0′ W | **Fl.W.** period 10s fl. 1s, ec. 9s | 72 **22** | 14 | White octagonal tower, red upper portion; 45. | **Horn:** 1 bl. ev. 30s (bl. 3s, si. 27s). Horn points 144°. Emergency light. |
| 9748 *H 3530* | Thrumcap Island, E. entrance to Marie Joseph Harbor. | 44° 57.4′ N 62° 02.4′ W | **Fl.R.** period 4s | 40 **12** | 4 | Square skeleton tower, red and white rectangular daymark, red triangle in center; 20. | **Radar reflector.** |
| | BEAVER HARBOR: | | | | | | |
| 9772 *H 3534* | -Beaver Island. | 44° 49.5′ N 62° 20.3′ W | **Fl.W.** period 7s | 65 **20** | 14 | White cylindrical tower; 30. | **Horn:** 1 bl. ev. 60s (bl. 6s, si. 54s). Horn points 144°. Seasonal. Emergency light. |
| 9778 *H 3541* | Sheet Rock, entrance to harbor. | 44° 49.8′ N 62° 29.5′ W | **Fl.W.** period 4s | 85 **26** | 7 | White cylindrical tower, red bands; 30. | |
| 9784 *H 3542* | **Sheet Harbor Passage Range,** E. of Kirby River, front. | 44° 51.5′ N 62° 26.9′ W | **F.W.** | 52 **16** | **18** | White square tower, red upper portion, red stripe; 23. | |
| 9788 *H 3542.1* | -Rear, 278 meters 343°28′ from front. | 44° 51.7′ N 62° 27.0′ W | **F.W.** | 69 **21** | **18** | White square tower, red upper portion, red stripe; 30. | |
| 9814 *H 3557* | Spry Bay. | 44° 49.4′ N 62° 35.9′ W | **F.R.W.G.** | 75 **23** | 10 | White square tower, red upper portion; 23. | F.R. 317°-336°15′, F.W.-338°15′, F.G.-118°15′. Seasonal. |
| 9816 *H 3560* | Popes Harbor. | 44° 47.7′ N 62° 39.0′ W | **L.Fl.R.** period 12s fl. 2s, ec. 10s | 30 **9** | 5 | Skeleton tower, red and white rectangular daymark; 23. | Seasonal. |
| 9820 *H 3564* | Ship Harbor. | 44° 44.9′ N 62° 45.4′ W | **L.Fl.G.** period 6s fl. 2s, ec. 4s | 59 **18** | 4 | Skeleton tower, rectangular daymark, white and red bands; 20. | Seasonal. |
| 9824 *H 3566* | Owls Head, on extremity. | 44° 43.2′ N 62° 48.0′ W | **Fl.W.** period 4s | 85 **26** | 6 | Red skeleton mast, red and white triangular daymarks; 33. | |
| 9836 *H 3568* | Egg Island, center of island. | 44° 39.9′ N 62° 51.8′ W | **L.Fl.W.** period 6s fl. 2s, ec. 4s | 79 **24** | 14 | Square tower; 56. | |
| 9848 *H 3570* | Jeddore Rock. | 44° 39.8′ N 63° 00.7′ W | **L.Fl.W.** period 12s fl. 2s, ec. 10s | 98 **30** | 8 | Skeleton tower; 49. | |
| 9852 *H 3579* | French Point. | 44° 42.3′ N 63° 04.6′ W | **F.R.** | 47 **14** | 9 | White square tower; 31. | Visible 278°-098°. |
| 9872 *H 3578* | Musquodoboit Harbor. | 44° 41.7′ N 63° 04.7′ W | **Q.R.** | 20 **6** | | Red cylindrical mast, red and white triangular daymark; 13. | |
| | HALIFAX APPROACH: | | | | | | |
| 9884 | *-Alpha Buoy HA.* | 44° 21.8′ N 63° 24.2′ W | **Mo.(A)W.** | | | SAFE WATER RW. | **Whistle.** |
| 9892 *H 3596* | -Devils Island, SE. end. | 44° 34.8′ N 63° 27.6′ W | **L.Fl.R.** period 6s fl. 2s, ec. 4s | 20 **6** | 7 | Square framework tower, white and red rectangular daymarks on E., S. and W. faces, red triangle in center; 23. | |
| 9896 *H 3609* | -Eastern Passage, E. | 44° 36.4′ N 63° 29.8′ W | **F.W.R.G.** | 16 **5** | 10 | Triangular skeleton mast; 13. | G. 126°40′-134°, W.-136°, R.-148°40′. |

| (1) No. | (2) Name and Location | (3) Position | (4) Characteristic | (5) Height | (6) Range | (7) Structure | (8) Remarks |
|---|---|---|---|---|---|---|---|

## CANADA-NOVA SCOTIA

| (1) No. | (2) Name and Location | (3) Position | (4) Characteristic | (5) Height | (6) Range | (7) Structure | (8) Remarks |
|---|---|---|---|---|---|---|---|
| | HALIFAX HARBOR: | | | | | | |
| 9904 *H 3600* | -Chebucto Head. | 44° 30.4′ N 63° 31.4′ W | **Fl.W.** period 20s fl. 0.5s, ec. 19.5s | 157 **48** | 10 | White tower, red upper portion; 43. | Visible 155°-360°. **Horn:** 2 bl. ev. 60s. (bl. 3s, si. 3s, bl. 3s, si. 51s). Horn points 113°. Emergency light. |
| | -RACON | | **Z(– – • •)** period 120s | | | | (3cm). |
| 9906 | *-Bear Cove Bell Buoy H6.* | 44° 32.6′ N 63° 31.4′ W | **Q.R.** | | | STARBOARD (B) R. | |
| | -RACON | | **N(– •)** | | 8 | | (3cm). |
| 9908 *H 3604* | -Herring Cove, S. side of entrance. | 44° 34.0′ N 63° 33.3′ W | **F.G.** | 66 **20** | 6 | Triangular skeleton tower, red and white rectangular daymark; 33. | |
| 9912 *H 3605* | -Herring Cove, S.E. corner of breakwater. | 44° 34.2′ N 63° 33.4′ W | **Fl.R.** period 5s fl. 1s, ec. 4s | 13 **4** | | Pipe swing pole, red and white triangular daymark, red triangle in center; 13. | |
| 9916 *H 3602* | -Sandwich Point Range, front. | 44° 34.9′ N 63° 32.9′ W | **F.G.** | 125 **38** | 12 | Triangular skeleton tower, white trapezoidal daymark, red stripe; 20. | |
| 9920 *H 3602.1* | --Rear, 499 meters 336°27′ from front. | 44° 35.2′ N 63° 33.1′ W | **F.G.** | 167 **51** | 12 | Triangular skeleton tower, white trapezoidal daymark, red stripe; 49. | |
| 9924 *H 3606* | -Middle Range, front | 44° 36.8′ N 63° 32.2′ W | **F.R.** | 59 **18** | 12 | Triangular skeleton tower, white trapezoidal daymark, red stripe; 13. | |
| 9928 *H 3606.1* | --Rear, 322 meters 356°13′ from front. | 44° 37.0′ N 63° 32.2′ W | **F.R.** | 95 **29** | 12 | Triangular skeleton tower, white trapezoidal daymark, red stripe; 72. | |
| 9932 *H 3607* | **Maugher Beach.** | 44° 36.1′ N 63° 32.0′ W | **Fl.W.** period 30s fl. 1s, ec. 29s | 57 **17** | **15** | White octagonal tower, red upper portion; 58. | Emergency light. |
| 9944 *H 3618* | **-Inner Range,** front. | 44° 38.4′ N 63° 33.6′ W | **F.W.** | 58 **18** | **15** | White octagonal tower, red stripe, red upper portion; 53. | Visible 290°-181°. Intensified on range line. Emergency light. |
| 9948 *H 3618.1* | --Rear, 3154 meters 339°08′ from front. | 44° 40.0′ N 63° 34.5′ W | **Fl.W.** period 10s fl. 1s, ec. 9s | 124 **38** | 13 | Triangular skeleton tower, white trapezoidal daymark, red stripe; 56. | |
| 9952 *H 3630* | -Bedford Institute of Oceanography Wharf. | 44° 40.8′ N 63° 36.8′ W | **Fl.G.** period 2s | 24 **7** | | Yellow tower. | |
| 9966 *H 3631* | -Dartmouth Yacht Harbor, breakwater. | 44° 42.0′ N 63° 36.8′ W | **Fl.G.** period 4s | 17 **5** | 4 | Square tower; 10. | Private light. |
| 9968 *H 3632* | **Sambro.** | 44° 26.2′ N 63° 33.8′ W | **Fl.W.** period 6s fl. 1s, ec. 5s | 141 **43** | **23** | White octagonal tower, red bands; 68. | |
| 9980 *H 3644* | Sambro Harbor. | 44° 28.5′ N 63° 35.8′ W | **F.G.** | 34 **10** | 7 | White square tower; 26. | |
| 9996 *H 3646* | Pennant Harbor. | 44° 28.3′ N 63° 38.1′ W | **F.G.** | 33 **10** | 7 | White cylindrical tower; 26. | |
| 10004 *H 3650* | Terence Bay. | 44° 27.6′ N 63° 42.4′ W | **F.R.** | 48 **15** | 8 | White square tower; 23. | |
| 10008 *H 3651* | -Government Wharf. | 44° 28.1′ N 63° 42.9′ W | **L.Fl.W.** period 6s fl. 2s, ec. 4s | 16 **5** | 4 | Pipe swing pole; 13. | |
| 10012 *H 3651.4* | -Lower Prospect. | 44° 27.1′ N 63° 43.6′ W | **Fl.W.** period 4s fl. 1s, ec. 3s | 16 **5** | 4 | Pipe swing pole; 13. | |

| (1)<br>No. | (2)<br>Name and Location | (3)<br>Position | (4)<br>Characteristic | (5)<br>Height | (6)<br>Range | (7)<br>Structure | (8)<br>Remarks |
|---|---|---|---|---|---|---|---|
| | | | **CANADA-NOVA SCOTIA** | | | | |
| 10016<br>*H 3652* | **Betty Island.** | 44° 26.3′ N<br>63° 46.1′ W | **L.Fl.W.**<br>period 15s<br>fl. 4s, ec. 11s | 63<br>**19** | 13 | White structure, red upper portion; 30. | Visible from all S. points of approach.<br>**Horn:** 1 bl. ev. 60s (bl. 6s, si. 54s). Horn points S.<br>Emergency light. |
| 10024<br>*H 3655* | -Prospect, public wharf. | 44° 28.2′ N<br>63° 47.1′ W | **Fl.G.**<br>period 4s<br>fl. 1s, ec. 3s | 16<br>**5** | 4 | Pipe swing pole; 13. | |
| 10028<br>*H 3658* | Port Dover, S. end of Callaghan Island. | 44° 29.4′ N<br>63° 51.7′ W | **Fl.G.**<br>period 4s | 50<br>**15** | 5 | Triangular skeleton mast, red and white rectangular daymark; 27. | |
| 10032<br>*H 3659* | Dover West, on wharf. | 44° 29.6′ N<br>63° 52.1′ W | **L.Fl.G.**<br>period 6s<br>fl. 2s, ec. 4s | 16<br>**5** | 4 | Pipe swing pole; 13. | |
| 10036<br>*H 3657* | East Dover wharf. | 44° 29.7′ N<br>63° 50.7′ W | **L.Fl.R.**<br>period 6s<br>fl. 2s, ec. 4s | 16<br>**5** | 4 | Pipe swing pole, red and white triangular daymark, red triangle in center; 13. | |
| 10040<br>*H 3660* | Peggy's Point, E. | 44° 29.5′ N<br>63° 55.1′ W | **Fl.R.**<br>period 5s<br>fl. 1.5s, ec. 3.5s | 72<br>**22** | 10 | White octagonal tower, red upper portion; 43. | Visible 290°-136°. |
| 10044<br>*H 3661* | -Peggy's Cove, Government Wharf, head. | 44° 29.6′ N<br>63° 55.0′ W | **Fl.G.**<br>period 3s<br>fl. 1s, ec. 2s | 16<br>**5** | 4 | Pipe swing pole, white and green square daymark; 13. | |
| | ST. MARGARETS BAY: | | | | | | |
| 10060<br>*H 3663* | -Indian Harbor. | 44° 31.3′ N<br>63° 56.8′ W | **F.W.** | 36<br>**11** | 9 | White square tower, red upper portion; 33. | |
| 10064<br>*H 3664* | -Croucher Island. | 44° 38.4′ N<br>63° 57.5′ W | **L.Fl.W.**<br>period 12s<br>fl. 2s, ec. 10s | 90<br>**27** | 6 | Triangular skeleton mast, red and white rectangular daymark; 36. | |
| 10068<br>*H 3665* | -Hubbards Cove. | 44° 37.3′ N<br>64° 03.2′ W | **Fl.G.**<br>period 6s<br>fl. 1s, ec. 5s | 39<br>**12** | 6 | Square skeleton tower, green and white rectangular daymark; 23. | |
| 10076<br>*H 3667* | -Northwest Cove, on Government wharf. | 44° 32.0′ N<br>64° 01.4′ W | **L.Fl.R.**<br>period 6s<br>fl. 2s, ec. 4s | 16<br>**5** | 4 | Pipe swing pole; 13. | |
| 10088<br>*H 3670* | Pearl Island, off St. Margaret's and Mahone Bays. | 44° 23.0′ N<br>64° 02.9′ W | **Fl.W.**<br>period 10s<br>fl. 0.5s, ec. 9.5s | 62<br>**19** | 8 | White square tower; 39. | |
| 10092<br>*H 3672* | East Ironbound Island, near center. | 44° 26.4′ N<br>64° 06.0′ W | **Iso.W.**<br>period 6s | 146<br>**44** | 13 | White rectangular tower, red upper portion; 46. | Emergency light. |
| | BIG TANCOOK ISLAND: | | | | | | |
| 10100<br>*H 3676* | -Government wharf, N.W. Cove. | 44° 27.9′ N<br>64° 10.3′ W | **Fl.G.**<br>period 6s<br>fl. 1s, ec. 5s | 13<br>**4** | 3 | Cylindrical mast; 7. | |
| 10104<br>*H 3677* | Little Tancook Island, outer end of wharf. | 44° 28.3′ N<br>64° 08.5′ W | **L.Fl.W.**<br>period 6s<br>fl. 2s, ec. 4s | 31<br>**9** | 5 | Square skeleton tower, red and white rectangular daymark; 20. | |
| | MAHONE BAY: | | | | | | |
| 10112<br>*H 3674* | -New Harbor, S. side of entrance. | 44° 28.4′ N<br>64° 05.5′ W | **Fl.R.**<br>period 5s | 20<br>**6** | 4 | Cylindrical mast; 13. | |
| 10120<br>*H 3680* | -Quaker Island, off Chester Harbor. | 44° 30.9′ N<br>64° 14.0′ W | **Fl.R.**<br>period 4s | 101<br>**31** | 3 | White cylindrical tower, red band at top; 20. | |
| 10128<br>*H 3682* | -Kaulbach Island Range, front, N. end of island. | 44° 28.2′ N<br>64° 16.9′ W | **F.W.** | 33<br>**10** | 9 | White square tower, red stripe, red upper portion; 20. | Visible on range line only. |

| (1) No. | (2) Name and Location | (3) Position | (4) Characteristic | (5) Height | (6) Range | (7) Structure | (8) Remarks |
|---|---|---|---|---|---|---|---|
| | | | **CANADA-NOVA SCOTIA** | | | | |
| 10132 *H 3682.1* | --Rear, 113.1 meters 268°03′ from front. | 44° 28.2′ N 64° 17.0′ W | **F.W.** | 66 **20** | 9 | White square tower, red stripe, red upper portion; 20. | Visible on range line only. |
| 10133 *H 3683* | -Western Shore Breakwater, seaward end of breakwater. | 44° 31.4′ N 64° 18.3′ W | **L.Fl.G.** period 6s fl. 2s, ec. 4s | 13 **4** | 3 | Square skeleton tower, green, white and black square daymark; 13. | |
| 10134 *H 3683.2* | --Inner. | 44° 31.4′ N 64° 18.3′ W | **L.Fl.R.** period 6s fl. 2s, ec. 4s | 17 **5** | 3 | Cylindrical mast, enclosed lower portion; 13. | |
| 10136 *H 3688* | -Westhaver Island, Mahone Harbor entrance. | 44° 26.2′ N 64° 20.3′ W | **Fl.W.** period 4s | 31 **10** | 7 | White cylindrical tower, red band at top; 25. | |
| 10148 *H 3694* | -Tanner Island. | 44° 22.0′ N 64° 12.1′ W | **Fl.W.** period 4s | 36 **11** | 6 | White cylindrical tower, red band; 26. | |
| 10152 *H 3699* | East Point Island. | 44° 21.0′ N 64° 12.2′ W | **F.G.** | 33 **10** | 7 | Triangular skeleton mast; 23. | |
| | LUNENBURG BAY: | | | | | | |
| 10160 *H 3698* | -Cross Island. | 44° 18.7′ N 64° 10.1′ W | **Fl.W.** period 10s fl. 1s, ec. 9s | 82 **25** | 10 | White cylindrical tower, red upper portion; 30. | Emergency light. |
| 10168 *H 3700* | Feltzen South. | 44° 19.8′ N 64° 16.8′ W | **Fl.G.** period 6s fl. 1s, ec. 5s | 20 **6** | 4 | Cylindrical mast; 13. | |
| 10172 *H 3702* | Battery Point Breakwater. | 44° 21.6′ N 64° 17.8′ W | **Iso.R.** period 4s | 25 **8** | 9 | White square tower, red upper portion; 26. | **Horn:** 1 bl. ev. 20s. (bl. 2s, si. 18s). Horn points 130°. |
| 10184 *H 3708* | West Ironbound Island. | 44° 13.7′ N 64° 16.5′ W | **Fl.W.** period 12s fl. 2s, ec. 10s | 80 **24** | 8 | Cylindrical tower, red and white bands; 36. | |
| | LAHAVE RIVER: | | | | | | |
| 10192 *H 3710* | -Mosher Island, W. side of entrance to river. | 44° 14.2′ N 64° 19.0′ W | **F.W.** | 76 **23** | 13 | White cylindrical tower; 36. | Visible 106°-351°. **Horn:** 1 bl. ev. 20s. (bl. 2s, si. 18s). Emergency light. |
| 10196 *H 3710.5* | -Kraut Point. | 44° 17.4′ N 64° 20.8′ W | **Fl.R.** period 5s fl. 1s, ec. 4s | 17 **5** | 5 | Square skeleton tower. | |
| 10200 *H 3711* | -Dublin Shore, government wharf. | 44° 16.0′ N 64° 21.8′ W | **Fl.W.** period 4s | 26 **8** | 5 | Cylindrical mast; 23. | |
| 10212 *H 3718* | Cherry Cove. | 44° 09.5′ N 64° 28.8′ W | **Iso.G.** period 4s | 23 **7** | 8 | Cylindrical mast; 13. | Seasonal. **Horn:** 1 bl. ev. 30s. (bl. 3s, si. 27s). Horn points 055°46′. |
| 10224 *H 3722* | Medway Head, W. side of entrance. | 44° 06.2′ N 64° 32.4′ W | **Fl.W.** period 12s fl. 4s, ec. 8s | 79 **24** | 11 | White square tower, red upper portion; 30. | Emergency light. |
| 10226 *H 3721* | Frying Pan Island. | 44° 06.1′ N 64° 31.4′ W | **L.Fl.R.** period 12s fl. 2s, ec. 10s | 36 **11** | 4 | Triangular skeleton tower, red and white rectangular daymark; 16. | |
| 10228 *H 3725* | Voglers Cove. | 44° 09.2′ N 64° 32.7′ W | **Fl.R.** period 3s fl. 1s, ec. 2s | 16 **5** | 4 | Cylindrical mast; 13. | Intensified on a bearing of 350°. |
| | LIVERPOOL BAY: | | | | | | |
| 10235 | -Coffin Island, S point. | 44° 02.0′ N 64° 37.7′ W | **Fl.W.** period 4s | 61 **18** | 7 | White octagonal tower, red upper portion; 52. | |

| (1) No. | (2) Name and Location | (3) Position | (4) Characteristic | (5) Height | (6) Range | (7) Structure | (8) Remarks |
|---|---|---|---|---|---|---|---|
| | | | **CANADA-NOVA SCOTIA** | | | | |
| 10244<br>*H 3740* | **-Western Head.** | 43° 59.4´ N<br>64° 39.8´ W | **Fl.W.**<br>period 15s<br>fl. 0.5s, ec. 14.5s | 56<br>**17** | **15** | White octagonal tower, red upper portion; 46. | Visible 180°-062°.<br>**Horn:** 1 bl. ev. 60s. (bl. 6s, si. 54s). Horn points 104°.<br>Emergency light. |
| 10248<br>*H 3736* | -Moose Point. | 44° 01.2´ N<br>64° 39.8´ W | **Q.G.** | 23<br>**7** | | Cylindrical mast; 13. | **Radar reflector.** |
| 10256<br>*H 3730* | -Brooklyn pier, breakwater, head. | 44° 02.7´ N<br>64° 41.5´ W | **L.Fl.W.**<br>period 12s<br>fl. 2s, ec. 10s | 30<br>**9** | 3 | Cylindrical mast; 16. | |
| 10268<br>*H 3742* | Port Mouton. | 43° 55.1´ N<br>64° 48.2´ W | **L.Fl.W.**<br>period 12s<br>fl. 2s, ec. 10s | 56<br>**17** | 6 | White square tower, red upper portion; 23. | Visible 069°30′-291°30′. |
| 10272<br>*H 3742.04* | -Spectacle Islands West. | 43° 54.5´ N<br>64° 48.7´ W | **Fl.R.**<br>period 4s<br>fl. 1s, ec. 3s | 13<br>**4** | | Red cylindrical mast, red and white rectangular daymark; 10. | |
| 10274<br>*H 3742.5* | -Inner. | 43° 55.2´ N<br>64° 50.8´ W | **L.Fl.R.**<br>period 6s<br>fl. 2s, ec. 4s | 13<br>**4** | 5 | Cylindrical mast, triangular daymark; 11. | |
| 10276<br>*H 3742.6* | -Hunts Landing, on outer end of breakwater. | 43° 57.1´ N<br>64° 46.1´ W | **Iso.R.**<br>period 4s | 26<br>**8** | 4 | Skeleton tower, enclosed lower portion, red and white rectangular daymark, red triangle in center; 10. | |
| 10320<br>*H 3746* | Port Hebert, on Shingle Point, E. side of harbor. | 43° 48.8´ N<br>64° 55.5´ W | **Fl.R.**<br>period 5s<br>fl. 1s, ec. 4s | 28<br>**8** | 4 | Skeleton mast, red and white rectangular daymark, red triangle in center; 23. | |
| 10336<br>*H 3748* | Little Harbor, outer end of public wharf. | 43° 43.0´ N<br>65° 01.8´ W | **Fl.R.**<br>period 4s<br>fl. 1s, ec. 3s | 10<br>**3** | 7 | Pipe swing pole. | |
| | LOCKEPORT HARBOR: | | | | | | |
| 10344<br>*H 3750* | -Gull Rock. | 43° 39.3´ N<br>65° 05.9´ W | **L.Fl.W.**<br>period 15s<br>fl. 4s, ec. 11s | 56<br>**17** | 12 | White rectangular tower, red upper portion; 39. | **Horn:** 1 bl. ev. 30s. (bl. 3s, si. 27s). Horn points 130°30′.<br>Emergency light. |
| 10348<br>*H 3753* | -Carters Island. | 43° 42.3´ N<br>65° 06.1´ W | **Fl.W.**<br>period 6s<br>fl. 1s, ec. 5s | 54<br>**16** | 7 | White cylindrical tower, two red bands; 39. | |
| 10352<br>*H 3754* | --S. breakwater. | 43° 42.1´ N<br>65° 06.4´ W | **Fl.G.**<br>period 5s<br>fl. 1s, ec. 4s | 10<br>**3** | 4 | Cylindrical mast, two green and white square daymarks facing ENE. and WSW.; 10. | |
| 10356<br>*H 3755* | --N. breakwater. | 43° 42.1´ N<br>65° 06.4´ W | **Q.R.** | 10<br>**3** | 3 | Triangular skeleton tower; 12. | |
| 10376<br>*H 3758* | Osborne Harbor, on outer end of wharf. | 43° 42.9´ N<br>65° 06.6´ W | **L.Fl.R.**<br>period 6s | 16<br>**5** | 5 | Cylindrical mast, red and white triangular daymark, red triangle in center; 13. | |
| 10388<br>*H 3759.4* | Lower Jordan Bay Wharf. | 43° 40.9´ N<br>65° 14.4´ W | **Fl.W.**<br>period 4s | 15<br>**4** | 5 | Skeleton tower, enclosed lower portion; 12. | |
| | SHELBURNE HARBOR: | | | | | | |
| 10404<br>*H 3762* | -Cape Roseway. | 43° 37.4´ N<br>65° 15.8´ W | **Fl.W.**<br>period 10s<br>fl. 1s, ec. 9s | 108<br>**33** | 10 | White octagonal tower, red upper portion; 56. | Visible 187°-055°.<br>Emergency light. |
| 10412<br>*H 3763* | -Lower Sandy Point. | 43° 40.8´ N<br>65° 18.2´ W | **Fl.W.**<br>period 4s | 14<br>**4** | 5 | Pipe swing pole; 13. | |
| 10416<br>*H 3765* | -Gunning Cove. | 43° 40.9´ N<br>65° 20.1´ W | **Fl.W.**<br>period 4s | 13<br>**4** | 6 | Triangular skeleton tower; 13. | |

| (1) No. | (2) Name and Location | (3) Position | (4) Characteristic | (5) Height | (6) Range | (7) Structure | (8) Remarks |
|---|---|---|---|---|---|---|---|

## CANADA-NOVA SCOTIA

| (1) No. | (2) Name and Location | (3) Position | (4) Characteristic | (5) Height | (6) Range | (7) Structure | (8) Remarks |
|---|---|---|---|---|---|---|---|
| 10436 *H 3774* | Cape Negro Island. | 43° 30.4′ N 65° 20.7′ W | **Fl.(2)W.** period 15s | 92 **28** | | White octagonal tower, red upper portion; 39. | Visible 187°-106°30′. **Horn:** 1 bl. ev. 60s (bl. 6s, si. 54s). Emergency light. |
| 10440 *H 3776* | Ingomar wharf. | 43° 33.8′ N 65° 21.8′ W | **L.Fl.R.** period 6s fl. 2s, ec. 4s | 16 **5** | 5 | Cylindrical mast, two red and white triangular daymarks, red triangle in center; 13. | |
| 10452 *H 3778* | The Salvages. | 43° 28.1′ N 65° 22.7′ W | **L.Fl.W.** period 12s fl. 2s, ec. 10s | 52 **16** | 10 | White rectangular tower, red upper portion; 39. | **Horn:** 3 bl. ev. 60s (bl. 2s, si. 3s, bl. 2s, si. 3s, bl. 2s, si. 48s). |
| 10460 *H 3779* | Port La Tour Harbour, Whaleback Rock. | 43° 29.6′ N 65° 27.0′ W | **Fl.G.** period 4s | 16 **5** | 2 | Cylindral mast; 13. | |
| 10464 *H 3780* | Port La Tour breakwater. | 43° 30.0′ N 65° 28.3′ W | **L.Fl.G.** period 6s fl. 2s, ec. 4s | 21 **6** | 5 | Cylindrical mast, green and white square daymark; 13. | |
| 10468 *H 3781* | Upper Port La Tour, E. breakwater. | 43° 30.3′ N 65° 28.2′ W | **L.Fl.R.** period 6s | 24 **7** | 5 | Pipe swing pole, red and white triangular daymark, red triangle in center; 23. | |
| 10484 *H 3782* | **Baccaro Point.** | 43° 27.0′ N 65° 28.2′ W | **Mo.(D)W.** period 10s fl. 5s, ec. 1s fl. 1s, ec. 1s fl. 1s, ec. 1s | 49 **15** | **15** | White square tower, red upper portion; 46. | Visible 207°-127°. **Horn:** 1 bl. ev. 20s. (bl. 2s, si. 18s). Horn points 200°. |
| 10492 *H 3787.5* | Cripple Creek Breakwater. | 43° 29.4′ N 65° 33.6′ W | **Iso G** period 4s | | 2 | Mast. | |
| 10494 *H 3787.41* | Stony Island, breakwater, head. | 43° 28.1′ N 65° 34.0′ W | **Fl.G.** period 3s fl. 1s, ec. 2s | 33 **10** | | Square skeleton tower, red and white rectangular daymark, green square in center; 23. | |
| 10496 *H 3784.4* | Daniels Head, on NE. corner of breakwater. | 43° 26.9′ N 65° 35.2′ W | **Fl.G.** period 4s | 30 **9** | 4 | Square skeleton tower; 23. | |
| 10508 *H 3784* | **Cape Sable.** | 43° 23.4′ N 65° 37.3′ W | **Fl.W.** period 5s | 98 **30** | **18** | White octagonal tower, red upper portion; 98. | **Horn:** 1 bl. ev. 60s. (bl. 4s, si. 56s). Horn points 150°. Emergency light. |
| | RACON | | **C(– • – •)** period 120s | | 10 | | (3cm). |
| 10520 *H 3785.6* | Fish Island. | 43° 25.7′ N 65° 39.3′ W | **Fl.R.** period 4s fl. 0.5s, ec. 3.5s | 23 **7** | 4 | Red cylindrical mast; 23. | |
| 10524 *H 3785.4* | Swim Point. | 43° 25.9′ N 65° 37.9′ W | **L.Fl.G.** period 6s fl. 2s, ec. 4s | 26 **8** | 5 | Cylindrical mast, green and white square daymark; 23. | |
| 10528 *H 3785* | Clark's Harbor. | 43° 26.6′ N 65° 38.1′ W | **Fl.G.** period 4s | 24 **7** | 4 | Skeleton tower; 20. | |
| 10532 *H 3786* | West Head, Cape Sable Island. | 43° 27.4′ N 65° 39.3′ W | **F.R.** | 52 **16** | 7 | Red and white cylindrical tower; 20. | **Horn:** 2 bl. ev. 60s. (bl. 3s, si. 3s, bl. 3s, si. 51s). Horn points 254°. |
| 10536 *H 3786.2* | West Head, outer end of breakwater. | 43° 27.6′ N 65° 39.2′ W | **Fl.R.** period 4s fl. 1s, ec. 3s | 33 **10** | 5 | Square skeleton tower, three red and white rectangular daymarks; 20. | |
| 10540 *H 3788* | Bear Point, S. end of wharf. | 43° 29.2′ N 65° 39.3′ W | **Fl.R.** period 4s | 26 **8** | 5 | Cylindrical mast, red and white rectangular daymark, red triangle in center; 13. | |
| 10544 *H 3793.6* | Shag Harbor, outer end of wharf. | 43° 29.5′ N 65° 42.3′ W | **F.R.** period 4s | 23 **7** | 4 | Cylindrical mast; 22. | |
| 10548 *H 3793* | Prospect Point, breakwater, head. | 43° 29.4′ N 65° 43.1′ W | **Fl.Y.** period 4s | 26 **8** | 5 | Cylindrical mast; 23. | |

| (1) No. | (2) Name and Location | (3) Position | (4) Characteristic | (5) Height | (6) Range | (7) Structure | (8) Remarks |
|---|---|---|---|---|---|---|---|

## CANADA-NOVA SCOTIA

| (1) No. | (2) Name and Location | (3) Position | (4) Characteristic | (5) Height | (6) Range | (7) Structure | (8) Remarks |
|---|---|---|---|---|---|---|---|
| 10560<br>*H 3790* | **Outer Island.** | 43° 27.4′ N<br>65° 44.6′ W | **Fl.W.**<br>period 10s<br>fl. 1s, ec. 9s | 46<br>**14** | 10 | White square tower, red upper portion; 39. | **Horn:** 1 bl. ev. 20s (bl. 2s, si. 18s). Horn points 200°. Emergency light. |
| 10572<br>*H 3796.2* | The Falls, NW. end of ledge. | 43° 32.1′ N<br>65° 44.6′ W | **Fl.R.**<br>period 4s | 16<br>**5** | 4 | Red cylindrical mast; 23. | **Radar reflector.** |
| 10576<br>*H 3796* | Falls Point wharf. | 43° 31.8′ N<br>65° 44.4′ W | **Fl.G.**<br>period 5s<br>fl. 1s, ec. 4s | 30<br>**9** | | Cylindrical mast, green and white square daymark; 20. | |
| 10582<br>*H 3797* | Northern End Ledge. | 43° 32.2′ N<br>65° 46.1′ W | **Fl.G.**<br>period 4s | 16<br>**5** | 4 | Square skeleton tower, black and white square daymark. | **Radar reflector.** |
| 10584<br>*H 3795* | Lower Woods Harbor. | 43° 31.4′ N<br>65° 44.3′ W | **Fl.R.**<br>period 6s<br>fl. 1s, ec. 5s | 23<br>**7** | 4 | Skeleton tower; 10. | |
| 10588<br>*H 3794* | Woods Harbor, on Big Ledge. | 43° 31.2′ N<br>65° 44.7′ W | **Fl.W.**<br>period 6s<br>fl. 1s, ec. 5s | 20<br>**6** | 9 | White square tower, red upper portion; 20. | **Horn:** 1 bl. ev. 30s. (bl. 3s, si. 27s). Horn points 201°. |
| 10596<br>*H 3812* | Seal Island, S. end. | 43° 23.7′ N<br>66° 00.9′ W | **Fl.W.**<br>period 10s<br>fl. 1s, ec. 9s | 108<br>**33** | **19** | White octagonal tower, two red bands; 68. | **Horn:** 3 bl. ev. 60s. (bl. 2s, si. 3s, bl. 2s, si. 3s, bl. 2s, si. 48s). Horn points 183°. Emergency light. **Radiobeacon.** |
| 10608<br>*H 3798.4* | Lower East Pubnico, on wharf. | 43° 36.4′ N<br>65° 46.7′ W | **Fl.R.**<br>period 6s<br>fl. 1s, ec. 5s | 26<br>**8** | 4 | Triangular skeleton tower; 23. | |
| 10632<br>*H 3800* | Whitehead Island. | 43° 39.8′ N<br>65° 52.0′ W | **Fl.W.**<br>period 15s | 98<br>**30** | 13 | White square tower on white square building; 39. | **Horn:** 1 bl. ev. 30s (bl. 3s, si. 27s). Horn points 190°. Emergency light. |
| 10633<br>*H 3803.4* | Bar Island. | 43° 42.0′ N<br>65° 54.2′ W | **Fl.G.**<br>period 4s | 13<br>**4** | 4 | Green cylindrical mast; 30. | |
| 10634<br>*H 3805.7* | Snipe Reef. | 43° 40.5′ N<br>65° 59.2′ W | **Fl.R.**<br>period 4s | 14<br>**4** | 4 | Red cylindrical mast; 13. | |
| 10636<br>*H 3804* | **Tusket River.** | 43° 42.2′ N<br>65° 57.1′ W | **Fl.W.**<br>period 10s<br>fl. 1s, ec. 9s | 62<br>**19** | **16** | White square tower, red upper portion; 36. | |
| 10640<br>*H 3805* | Tusket Wedge. | 43° 42.8′ N<br>65° 58.0′ W | **Fl.G.**<br>period 4s | 26<br>**8** | 4 | Pipe swing pole, green and white square daymark, black square in center; 23. | |
| 10640.1<br>*H 3819.5* | Indian Sluice Point Wharf. | 43° 46.3′ N<br>65° 57.0′ W | **Fl.R.**<br>period 4s | | 6 | Cylindrical mast; 10. | |
| 10640.5<br>*H 3805.4* | Goose Bay. | 43° 42.2′ N<br>65° 59.3′ W | **Fl.R.**<br>period 4s | 10<br>**3** | 4 | Skeleton tower on 5-pile dolphin; 7. | **Radar reflector.** |
| 10641<br>*H 3805.5* | Lower Wedgeport. | 43° 42.6′ N<br>65° 59.4′ W | **Fl.R.**<br>period 4s | 10<br>**3** | 4 | Skeleton tower on 5-pile dolphin; 7. | **Radar reflector.** |
| 10644<br>*H 3816* | The Sluice, E. | 43° 40.2′ N<br>66° 00.8′ W | **Fl.W.**<br>period 4s | 14<br>**4** | | Cylindrical mast, three reflective bands; 13. | |
| 10648<br>*H 3815* | -W. | 43° 40.2′ N<br>66° 00.9′ W | **Fl.W.**<br>period 4s | 16<br>**5** | | Cylindrical mast; 13. | |
| 10652<br>*H 3817* | Frenchman Point. | 43° 38.1′ N<br>66° 01.0′ W | **Fl.R.**<br>period 6s<br>fl. 1s, ec. 5s | | 5 | Square skeleton tower, red and white rectangular daymark; 20. | |
| 10668<br>*H 3806* | Pease Island, S. point. | 43° 37.7′ N<br>66° 01.6′ W | **Fl.W.**<br>period 6s<br>fl. 0.5s, ec. 5.5s | 53<br>**16** | 9 | White cylindrical tower, red upper portion; 36. | **Horn:** 2 bl. ev. 60s (bl. 3s, si. 3s, bl. 3s, si. 51s). Horn points 130°. |
| 10670<br>*H 3817.02* | Pearl Rock. | 43° 38.2′ N<br>66° 01.4′ W | **Fl.R.**<br>period 4s | 16<br>**5** | 3 | Red cylindrical mast; 26. | |
| 10672<br>*H 3814* | Candlebox Island. | 43° 39.8′ N<br>66° 02.7′ W | **F.R.** | 46<br>**14** | 10 | White rectangular tower, red upper portion; 39. | **Horn:** 1 bl. ev. 30s (bl. 3s, si. 27s). Horn points 295°. |

| (1) No. | (2) Name and Location | (3) Position | (4) Characteristic | (5) Height | (6) Range | (7) Structure | (8) Remarks |
|---|---|---|---|---|---|---|---|

## CANADA-NOVA SCOTIA

| (1) No. | (2) Name and Location | (3) Position | (4) Characteristic | (5) Height | (6) Range | (7) Structure | (8) Remarks |
|---|---|---|---|---|---|---|---|
| 10684 *H 3817.4* | Little River Harbor. | 43° 42.6′ N 66° 02.0′ W | **Fl.W.** period 4s | 23 **7** | 5 | Square skeleton tower, red and white rectangular daymark, red band; 10. | |
| 10688 *H 3817.5* | -E. breakwater, head. | 43° 42.7′ N 66° 01.9′ W | **Fl.R.** period 4s fl. 1s, ec. 3s | 10 **3** | 4 | Pipe swing pole; 10. | |
| 10692 *H 3819* | Pinkney Point. | 43° 42.2′ N 66° 03.2′ W | **Fl.W.** period 4s | 16 **5** | 6 | Square skeleton tower; 12. | |
| 10700 *H 3818* | **Green Island,** center of island. | 43° 41.4′ N 66° 08.6′ W | **Fl.W.** period 5s fl. 0.5s, ec. 4.5s | 82 **25** | **19** | White square tower, red top, RWR triangular daymark; 30. | **Horn:** 1 bl. ev. 20s. Emergency light. |
| 10728 *H 3820* | -Cape Forchu, E. cape. | 43° 47.6′ N 66° 09.3′ W | **L.Fl.W.** period 12s fl. 2s, ec. 10s | 115 **35** | 12 | Hexagonal tower, red and white stripes; 75. | |
| | -RACON | | **B(– • • •)** | | 10 | | (3cm). |
| | YARMOUTH HARBOR: | | | | | | |
| 10732 *H 3822* | -Ships Stern, N. end. | 43° 48.5′ N 66° 08.8′ W | **Fl.W.** period 4s | 30 **9** | 6 | Triangular skeleton tower; 13. | |
| 10736 *H 3826* | -Bunker Island. | 43° 48.7′ N 66° 08.6′ W | **Iso.R.** period 4s | 33 **10** | 8 | White square tower, red stripe; 30. | Emergency light. |
| 10740 *H 3834* | Yarmouth Bar breakwater. | 43° 48.9′ N 66° 09.1′ W | **F.G.** | 21 **6** | 7 | Cylindrical mast; 10. | |
| 10742 *H 3837* | Chegoggin Point breakwater. | 43° 51.2′ N 66° 09.7′ W | **Fl.G.** period 4s fl. 1s, ec. 3s | | 7 | Square skeleton tower, green and white rectangular daymark; 20. | |
| 10750 | *Lurcher Shoal Buoy NM.* | 43° 49.0′ N 66° 30.0′ W | **Fl.(2+1)R.** period 6s | | | PREFERRED CHANNEL (B) RGR. | |
| | RACON | | **K(– • –)** period 120s | | 8 | | (3cm). |
| 10758 | *Fundy Entrance, S. Buoy M.* | 44° 13.6′ N 66° 50.2′ W | **Mo.(A)W.** | | | SAFE WATER RW. | **Whistle.** **Radar reflector.** |
| | RACON | | **M(– –)** | | 10 | | |
| 10765 *H 3838* | Sanford Sector. | 43° 55.1′ N 66° 09.2′ W | **Iso.W.R.G.** period 2s | 26 **8** | 12 | Square skeleton tower, white rectangular daymark, red band; 23. | R. 090°57′-134°57′, W.-136°57′, G.-180°57′. |
| 10776 *H 3840* | -Port Maitland breakwater. | 43° 59.2′ N 66° 09.5′ W | **L.Fl.G.** period 6s fl. 2s, ec. 4s | 20 **6** | 5 | Square skeleton tower, green and white rectangular daymark facing NNW.; 23. | **Radar reflector.** |
| 10792 *H 3848* | Cape St. Mary, E. side of bay. | 44° 05.2′ N 66° 12.6′ W | **Fl.W.** period 5s fl. 0.5s, ec. 4.5s | 105 **32** | 13 | White rectangular tower, red upper portion; 30. | **Horn:** 1 bl. ev. 60s. (bl. 4s, si. 56s). Horn points 251°30′. |
| 10796 *H 3846* | Cape St. Mary Breakwater. | 44° 05.1′ N 66° 12.3′ W | **Fl.G.** period 4s | 23 **7** | 4 | Cylindrical mast; 23. | |
| 10804 *H 3851* | -Meteghan Breakwater, outer end. | 44° 11.7′ N 66° 10.0′ W | **L.Fl.R.** period 6s fl. 2s, ec. 4s | | 4 | Square skeleton tower, red and white rectangular daymark; 16. | |
| 10808 *H 3852* | -Meteghan River, breakwater, head. | 44° 13.2′ N 66° 08.6′ W | **Fl.W.** period 4s | 26 **8** | 6 | Triangular skeleton tower; 20. | |
| 10810 *H 3855* | -Saulnierville breakwater. | 44° 15.9′ N 66° 08.3′ W | **L.Fl.R.** period 12s fl. 2s, ec. 10s | 28 **9** | 5 | Square skeleton tower, two red and white triangular daymark; 30. | |
| 10816 *H 3858* | -Comeauville wharf. | 44° 17.5′ N 66° 07.9′ W | **Fl.R.** period 4s | 17 **5** | 4 | Triangular skeleton tower; 10. | |

| (1) No. | (2) Name and Location | (3) Position | (4) Characteristic | (5) Height | (6) Range | (7) Structure | (8) Remarks |
|---|---|---|---|---|---|---|---|

## CANADA-NOVA SCOTIA

| (1) No. | (2) Name and Location | (3) Position | (4) Characteristic | (5) Height | (6) Range | (7) Structure | (8) Remarks |
|---|---|---|---|---|---|---|---|
| 10828 *H 3864.5* | -East Sandy Cove. | 44° 29.2′ N 66° 05.1′ W | **Fl.R.** period 4s | 13 **4** | 4 | Pipe swing pole, red and white triangular daymark, red triangle in center. | |
| 10832 *H 3864* | -Little River. | 44° 26.6′ N 66° 07.7′ W | **L.Fl.G.** period 6s fl. 2s, ec. 4s | 23 **7** | 4 | Cylindrical mast, green and white square daymark; 23. | |
| 10834 *H 3865* | -St. Mary's Bay, NE. end of bay. | 44° 34.8′ N 65° 56.2′ W | **Fl.W.** period 4s | 23 **7** | 6 | Square skeleton tower; 16. | **Horn:** 1 bl. ev. 30s (bl. 2s, si. 28s). Horn points 217°. |

## CANADA-NOVA SCOTIA-BAY OF FUNDY

| (1) No. | (2) Name and Location | (3) Position | (4) Characteristic | (5) Height | (6) Range | (7) Structure | (8) Remarks |
|---|---|---|---|---|---|---|---|
| 10844 *H 3872* | **Brier Island.** | 44° 14.9′ N 66° 23.5′ W | **Fl.(3)W.** period 18s fl. 0.2s, ec. 2.8s fl. 0.2s, ec. 2.8s fl. 0.2s, ec. 11.8s | 72 **22** | 14 | White octagonal tower, three red bands; 56. | **Horn (2):** 2 bl. ev. 60s (bl. 3s, si. 3s, bl. 3s, si. 51s). Horns point 270° and 315°, sound in unison. |
| | GRAND PASSAGE: | | | | | | |
| 10852 *H 3874* | **-N. Point, Brier Island.** | 44° 17.2′ N 66° 20.5′ W | **Fl.W.** period 10s fl. 0.3s, ec. 9.7s | 47 **14** | **21** | White triangular tower, red upper portion; 30. | **Horn:** 1 bl. ev. 30s (bl. 3s, si. 27s). |
| 10860 *H 3876* | -Freeport, on wharf. | 44° 16.5′ N 66° 20.1′ W | **F.R.** | 30 **9** | 7 | Pipe swing pole; 23. | |
| 10864 *H 3875* | --Breakwater, S. | 44° 16.0′ N 66° 19.7′ W | **Fl.W.** period 4s | 14 **4** | 6 | Triangular skeleton tower; 13. | |
| 10868 *H 3880* | -Westport. | 44° 15.9′ N 66° 20.8′ W | **Fl.G.** period 4s | 26 **8** | 2 | Cylindrical skeleton mast; 23. | |
| 10872 *H 3878* | -Peter Island, S. entrance to passage. | 44° 15.4′ N 66° 20.3′ W | **Fl.Y.** period 5s fl. 1s, ec. 4s | 59 **18** | 14 | White rectangular tower, red upper portion; 39. | **Horn:** 1 bl. ev. 20s. (bl. 2s, si. 18s). |
| | PETIT PASSAGE: | | | | | | |
| 10880 *H 3884* | **-Boars Head,** W. side of entrance to Petit Passage. | 44° 24.2′ N 66° 12.9′ W | **Fl.W.** period 5s fl. 1s, ec. 4s | 92 **28** | **16** | White square tower, red upper portion; 39. | **Horn:** 3 bl. ev. 60s. (bl. 2s, si. 3s, bl. 2s, si. 3s, bl. 2s, si. 48s). Horn points 315°. |
| 10884 *H 3885* | -Tiverton. | 44° 23.8′ N 66° 12.8′ W | **Fl.Y.** period 4s | 17 **5** | 5 | Triangular skeleton tower; 10. | |
| 10892 *H 3887* | Whale Cove, outer end of wharf. | 44° 26.1′ N 66° 10.5′ W | **Fl.G.** period 4s | 17 **5** | 4 | Green cylindrical mast, black and white square daymark; 16. | |
| 10896 *H 3888* | Centreville, entrance, W. side. | 44° 33.1′ N 66° 02.0′ W | **Fl.G.** period 4s fl. 1s, ec. 3s | 46 **14** | 8 | Square skeleton tower, red and white rectangular daymark, green square in center. | |
| 10904 *H 3889* | Deep Cove Wharf, inner end. | 44° 40.0′ N 65° 49.9′ W | **F.G.** | 16 **5** | 7 | Square skeleton tower; 10. | |
| 10908 *H 3890* | Prim Point, W. side of Digby Gut. | 44° 41.5′ N 65° 47.2′ W | **Iso.W.** period 6s | 82 **25** | 13 | White rectangular tower, red stripes; 46. | **Horn:** 1 bl. ev. 30s. (bl. 3s, si. 27s). Horn points 318°. |
| | ANNAPOLIS BASIN: | | | | | | |
| 10916 *H 3892* | -Digby Gut, E. side of entrance. | 44° 41.3′ N 65° 45.6′ W | **F.W.** | 50 **15** | 10 | Triangular skeleton tower; 23. | **Horn:** 1 bl. ev. 15s. (bl. 1s, si. 14s). Emergency light. |
| 10920 *H 3894* | -Victoria Beach, E. side of Digby Gut. | 44° 40.6′ N 65° 45.2′ W | **Oc.G.** period 10s lt. 6s, ec. 4s | 54 **16** | 7 | White square tower; 26. | |

| (1) No. | (2) Name and Location | (3) Position | (4) Characteristic | (5) Height | (6) Range | (7) Structure | (8) Remarks |
|---|---|---|---|---|---|---|---|
| | **CANADA-NOVA SCOTIA-BAY OF FUNDY** | | | | | | |
| 10936 *H 3896* | -Port Wade. | 44° 40.6′ N 65° 42.7′ W | **F.R.** | 23 **7** | 7 | Triangular skeleton mast; 16. | |
| 10940 *H 3906* | -Schafner Point, N. side of river. | 44° 42.6′ N 65° 37.2′ W | **F.W.** | 43 **13** | 10 | White square tower; red upper portion. | Indicates Goat Island Shoals. |
| | ANNAPOLIS RIVER: | | | | | | |
| 10944 *H 3908* | -Annapolis, NE. of government pier. | 44° 44.7′ N 65° 31.2′ W | **F.R.** | 30 **9** | 8 | White square tower, red upper portion; 26. | Private light. |
| 10946 *H 3914* | Delap Cove Wharf, E. of Digby Gut. | 44° 46.3′ N 65° 38.1′ W | **Fl.W.** period 4s | 20 **6** | 3 | Mast; 23. | Seasonal. |
| 10948 *H 3916* | Parkers Cove, end of E. breakwater. | 44° 48.9′ N 65° 32.4′ W | **L.Fl.G.** period 12s fl. 2s, ec. 10s | 26 **8** | 2 | Cylindrical mast; 26. | |
| 10952 *H 3918* | Hampton, on shore, Chute Cove. | 44° 54.4′ N 65° 21.2′ W | **F.W.** | 69 **21** | 11 | White tower; 33. | |
| 10956 *H 3920* | Port Lorne, S. shore. | 44° 56.9′ N 65° 15.9′ W | **F.W.** | 53 **16** | 13 | Triangular skeleton tower, red square daymark; 26. | |
| 10964 *H 3926* | Margaretsville, extremity of point, S. of breakwater. | 45° 02.9′ N 65° 03.9′ W | **Oc.(2)W.** period 20s lt. 10s, ec. 3s lt. 4s, ec. 3s | 37 **11** | 10 | Square tower, black and white bands; 32. | Visible 095°-236°. |
| 10968 *H 3928* | Ile Haute, summit. | 45° 15.1′ N 65° 00.3′ W | **Fl.W.** period 4s | 367 **112** | 7 | Square skeleton tower; 43. | May be obscured less than 2.5 miles from light. |
| 10972 *H 3930* | Harborville, near outer end of W. pier. | 45° 09.1′ N 64° 48.8′ W | **Fl.R.** period 4s | 32 **10** | 5 | Square skeleton tower, red and white rectangular daymark, red triangle in center; 23. | |
| 10976 *H 3932* | Black Rock, S. shore Minas channel. | 45° 10.2′ N 64° 45.6′ W | **Fl.(2)W.** period 12s fl. 1s, ec. 2s fl. 1s, ec. 8s | 52 **16** | 12 | White cylindrical tower, red bands; 33. | |
| 10980 *H 3938* | Cape D'Or, on extreme point. | 45° 17.5′ N 64° 46.5′ W | **Fl.W.** period 9s fl. 1s, ec. 8s | 67 **20** | 13 | White square tower, red upper portion; 36. | **Horn:** 3 bl. ev. 60s (bl. 2s, si. 3s, bl. 2s, si. 3s, bl. 2s, si. 48s). Horn points 240°. |
| 10984 *H 3934* | Advocate Harbor, on S. side of entrance. | 45° 19.2′ N 64° 47.1′ W | **Fl.W.** period 4s | 24 **7** | 6 | Square skeleton tower, orange trapezoidal daymark; 23. | |
| 10988 *H 3942* | Halls Harbor, on end of wharf. | 45° 12.1′ N 64° 37.2′ W | **Fl.R.** period 4s | 20 **6** | 7 | Cylindrical mast, red and white triangular daymark, red triangle in center; 20. | |
| | MINAS BASIN: | | | | | | |
| 11004 *H 3950* | -Cape Sharp. | 45° 22.0′ N 64° 23.6′ W | **Oc.W.** period 10s lt. 7s, ec. 3s | 56 **17** | 12 | White square tower, red upper portion; 39. | **Horn:** 1 bl. ev. 60s. (bl. 4s, si. 56s). Horn points 250°. |
| 11008 *H 3956* | -Outer SW. corner of wharf. | 45° 12.2′ N 64° 22.9′ W | **F.R.** | 23 **7** | 7 | Triangular skeleton tower; 23. | |
| 11010 *H 3957* | -Upper Pereau. | 45° 12.1′ N 64° 22.8′ W | **Fl.R.** period 4s | 13 **4** | 4 | Triangular skeleton tower; 13. | Seasonal. **Radar reflector.** |
| 11044 *H 3952* | -Parrsboro, at entrance to harbor. | 45° 23.3′ N 64° 19.0′ W | **L.Fl.G.** period 6s fl. 2s, ec. 4s | 26 **8** | 7 | White square tower; 26. | **Horn:** 1 bl. ev. 30s (bl. 3s, si. 27s). Horn points 170°. |
| 11048 *H 3954* | --SE. end of Government wharf. | 45° 23.5′ N 64° 19.2′ W | **Fl.R.** period 4s | 16 **5** | 3 | Pipe swing pole; 13. | |

| (1) No. | (2) Name and Location | (3) Position | (4) Characteristic | (5) Height | (6) Range | (7) Structure | (8) Remarks |
|---|---|---|---|---|---|---|---|

## CANADA-NOVA SCOTIA-BAY OF FUNDY

| (1) No. | (2) Name and Location | (3) Position | (4) Characteristic | (5) Height | (6) Range | (7) Structure | (8) Remarks |
|---|---|---|---|---|---|---|---|
| | CHIGNECTO BAY: | | | | | | |
| 11052 *H 4032* | -Apple River. | 45° 28.4′ N 64° 51.4′ W | **L.Fl.W.** period 12s fl. 2s, ec. 10s | 68 **21** | 9 | White square tower; 36. | |
| 11056 *H 4034* | -Ragged Point, on wharf. | 45° 39.6′ N 64° 29.3′ W | **Fl.G.** period 4s | 23 **7** | 4 | Skeleton tower; 23. | |
| 11064 *H 4060* | -Cape Enrage, slope of cape. | 45° 36.0′ N 64° 56.6′ W | **Fl.G.** period 6s fl. 1s, ec. 5s | 135 **41** | 10 | White square tower, red upper portion; 30. | **Horn:** 3 bl. ev. 60s. (bl. 2s, si. 3s, bl. 2s, si. 3s, bl. 2s, si. 48s). Horn points 220°. |
| 11068 *H 4064* | -Alma, of public wharf, head. | 45° 35.6′ N 64° 46.8′ W | **Iso.R.** period 4s | 26 **8** | 4 | Cylindrical mast. | Seasonal. |
| 11076 *H 4074* | St. Martins, W. breakwater, head. | 45° 21.3′ N 65° 32.0′ W | **L.Fl.R.** period 6s fl. 2s, ec. 4s | 24 **7** | 4 | Triangular skeleton tower; 20. | |
| 11080 *H 4076* | **Quaco Head.** | 45° 19.4′ N 65° 32.2′ W | **Fl.W.** period 10s fl. 0.3s, ec. 9.7s | 85 **26** | **21** | White rectangular tower, red upper portion; 39. | **Horn:** 1 bl. ev. 30s (bl. 3s, si. 27s). Horn points 130°. |
| 11084 *H 4077* | Black River, wharf, head. | 45° 15.4′ N 65° 48.7′ W | **Fl.W.** period 4s | 47 **14** | 6 | Pipe swing pole; 23. | |
| 11088 *H 4078* | Cape Spencer. | 45° 11.7′ N 65° 54.6′ W | **Fl.W.** period 11s fl. 1s, ec. 10s | 203 **62** | 14 | Cylindrical tower, red and white bands; 23. | **Horn:** 3 bl. ev. 60s. (bl. 2s, si. 3s, bl. 2s, si. 3s, bl. 2s, si. 48s). Horn points 165°. |
| | ST. JOHN HARBOR: | | | | | | |
| 11092 | -*Whistle Buoy J.* | 45° 12.9′ N 66° 02.6′ W | **Mo.(A)W.** | | | SAFE WATER RW. | **Whistle. Radar reflector.** |
| | -RACON | | **N(– •)** period 120s | | 8 | | |
| 11096 *H 4080* | -Black Point. | 45° 13.0′ N 66° 00.5′ W | **Fl.R.** period 4s | 37 **11** | 7 | Red and white cylindrical tower; 26. | |
| 11100 *H 4082* | **-Partridge Island.** | 45° 14.4′ N 66° 03.2′ W | **Fl.W.** period 7.5s | 116 **35** | **19** | Hexagonal tower, red and white stripes; 46. | |
| 11104 *H 4089* | **-Saint John Harbor Range,** front. | 45° 16.4′ N 66° 04.1′ W | **F.G.** | 69 **21** | **20** | Triangular skeleton tower, red trapezoidal daymark, black stripe; 59. | |
| 11108 *H 4089.1* | --Rear, 431 meters 333°40′ from front. | 45° 16.6′ N 66° 04.3′ W | **F.G.** | 110 **34** | **20** | Triangular skeleton tower, red trapezoidal daymark, black stripe; 36. | |
| 11112 *H 4083* | -Courtenay Bay. | 45° 15.4′ N 66° 02.7′ W | **Fl.R.** period 4s | 43 **13** | 5 | White hexagonal tower; 33. | |
| 11114 *H 4083.6* | -Single station range. | 45° 16.0′ N 66° 02.8′ W | **F.W.R.G.** | 26 **8** | 12 | Skeleton tower, orange and white rectangular daymark; 23. | F.R. 001°30′-002°30′, Al.W.R.-003°, F.W.-005°, Al.G.W.-005°30′, F.G.-006°30′. |
| 11116 *H 4083.4* | **-Courtenay Bay Inner Range,** front. | 45° 16.4′ N 66° 02.3′ W | **F.G.** | 21 **6** | **15** | Triangular skeleton tower, red trapezoidal daymark, black stripe; 20. | |
| 11120 *H 4083.41* | --Rear, 86 meters 021°10′ from front. | 45° 16.5′ N 66° 02.3′ W | **F.G.** | 33 **10** | **16** | Triangular skeleton tower, red trapezoidal daymark, black stripe; 30. | |
| 11128 *H 4085.5* | -Pier No. 12. | 45° 15.6′ N 66° 03.7′ W | **Iso.G.** period 2s | 8 **2** | 4 | Rectangular skeleton tower; 7. | Private light. |
| 11132 *H 4090* | -Marble Cove, S. side of entrance to cove. | 45° 16.3′ N 66° 05.3′ W | **L.Fl.G.** period 12s fl. 2s, ec. 10s | 92 **28** | 4 | White square tower, red upper portion; 46. | Seasonal. |

| (1) No. | (2) Name and Location | (3) Position | (4) Characteristic | (5) Height | (6) Range | (7) Structure | (8) Remarks |
|---|---|---|---|---|---|---|---|
| | **CANADA-NOVA SCOTIA-BAY OF FUNDY** | | | | | | |
| 11138 | McColgan Point. | 45° 19.9′ N<br>66° 06.6′ W | **L.Fl.W.**<br>period 12s<br>fl. 2s, ec. 10s | 36<br>**11** | 6 | White square tower, red upper portion; 27. | |
| 11140<br>*H 4092* | Lorneville Breakwater. | 45° 11.6′ N<br>66° 08.9′ W | **Fl.W.**<br>period 4s | 23<br>**7** | 6 | Cylindrical tower; 23. | |
| 11148<br>*H 4096* | **Musquash Head.** | 45° 08.6′ N<br>66° 14.2′ W | **Fl.W.**<br>period 3s<br>fl. 1s, ec. 2s | 115<br>**35** | **20** | White hexagonal tower, red band; 46. | **Horn:** 1 bl. ev. 60s. (bl. 4s, si. 56s). Horn points 180°. |
| 11150<br>*H 4098* | Five Fathom Hole, SE. corner of wharf. | 45° 11.2′ N<br>66° 15.4′ W | **Fl.R.**<br>period 3s<br>fl. 1s, ec. 2s | 26<br>**8** | 4 | Cylindrical mast; 23. | |
| 11152<br>*H 4100* | Chance Harbor, Reef Point, W. side of entrance. | 45° 07.1′ N<br>66° 20.9′ W | **L.Fl.W.**<br>period 12s<br>fl. 2s, ec. 10s | 41<br>**12** | 7 | Cylindrical tower, red and white bands; 24. | |
| 11156<br>*H 4104* | Dipper Harbor, breakwater. | 45° 05.7′ N<br>66° 24.9′ W | **Fl.G.**<br>period 4s | 36<br>**11** | 4 | Pipe swing pole, two green, black and white square daymarks on SE. and NW. faces; 20. | |
| 11160<br>*H 4108* | Point Lepreau. | 45° 03.5′ N<br>66° 27.5′ W | **Fl.W.**<br>period 5s<br>fl. 1s, ec. 4s | 84<br>**26** | 14 | Octagonal tower, red and white bands; 59. | **Horn:** 3 bl. ev. 60s. (bl. 2s, si. 3s, bl. 2s, si. 3s, bl. 2s, si. 48s). Horn points 190°. Emergency light. |
| 11172<br>*H 4110* | Southwest Wolf Island. | 44° 56.2′ N<br>66° 44.0′ W | **Fl.W.**<br>period 10s<br>fl. 1s, ec. 9s | 125<br>**38** | 7 | White cylindrical tower; 36. | |
| 11184<br>*H 4112* | Lighthouse Point. | 45° 03.8′ N<br>66° 44.0′ W | **Iso.W.**<br>period 6s | 47<br>**14** | 12 | White cylindrical tower, red upper porton; 30. | **Horn:** 1 bl. ev. 60s (bl. 6s, si. 54s). Horn points 159°. |
| 11188<br>*H 4113* | Beaver Harbor, breakwater, head. | 45° 04.2′ N<br>66° 44.4′ W | **Fl.G.**<br>period 4s | | 4 | Cylindrical mast, green, white and black square daymark; 10. | |
| 11190 | Blacks Harbor, entrance. | 45° 02.8′ N<br>66° 48.5′ W | **F.R.** | 24<br>**7** | 7 | Triangular skeleton tower; 20. | |
| 11191<br>*H 4116.4* | -Wharf. | 45° 03.3′ N<br>66° 47.7′ W | **Fl.R.**<br>period 6s<br>fl. 1s, ec. 5s | 23<br>**7** | 4 | Cylindrical tower; 23. | |
| | LETANG HARBOR: | | | | | | |
| 11192<br>*H 4114* | -Pea Point, on Pea Islet. | 45° 02.3′ N<br>66° 48.5′ W | **F.W.** | 56<br>**17** | 12 | White rectangular tower, red upper portion; 36. | Visible 251°-161°.<br>**Horn:** 2 bl. ev. 60s. (bl. 3s, si. 3s, bl. 3s, si. 51s). Horn points 180°. |
| 11196<br>*H 4115* | Roaring Bull. | 45° 02.4′ N<br>66° 48.8′ W | **Fl.R.**<br>period 4s | 16<br>**5** | 3 | Red cylindrical mast; 20. | |
| 11200<br>*H 4118* | -Bliss Island. | 45° 01.1′ N<br>66° 51.0′ W | **Fl.R.**<br>period 4s | 51<br>**15** | 5 | White rectangular tower, red upper portion; 39. | |
| 11204<br>*H 4119* | -Back Bay. | 45° 03.2′ N<br>66° 51.7′ W | **Fl.G.**<br>period 4s | 13<br>**4** | 4 | Skeleton tower; 13. | |
| | PASSAMAQUODDY BAY: | | | | | | |
| 11208<br>*H 4120* | -Letete Passage Fog Signal. | 45° 02.3′ N<br>66° 53.5′ W | | | | | **Horn:** 1 bl. ev. 30s. (bl. 3s, si. 27s). Horn points 180°. |
| 11212<br>*H 4120.4* | -Morgan Ledge. | 45° 02.2′ N<br>66° 53.6′ W | **Fl.R.**<br>period 6s<br>fl. 1s, ec. 5s | 17<br>**5** | 7 | Red square skeleton tower, red and white rectangular daymark, red triangle in center; 20. | **Radar reflector.** |
| 11220<br>*H 4122* | --Letete Harbor. | 45° 03.1′ N<br>66° 53.8′ W | **Fl.G.**<br>period 4s | 8<br>**2** | 4 | Green cylindrical tower; 23. | **Radar reflector.** |

| (1) No. | (2) Name and Location | (3) Position | (4) Characteristic | (5) Height | (6) Range | (7) Structure | (8) Remarks |
|---|---|---|---|---|---|---|---|
| | | | **CANADA-NOVA SCOTIA-BAY OF FUNDY** | | | | |
| 11225 *H 4123* | --Matthews Ledge. | 45° 03.1´ N 66° 53.8´ W | **L.Fl.R.** period 6s fl. 2s, ec. 4s | 16 **5** | 4 | Skeleton tower, two red and white rectangular daymarks; 30. | |
| 11230 *H 4127* | --St. Andrews, North Point. | 45° 04.0´ N 67° 02.9´ W | **Fl.R.** period 4s | 23 **7** | 4 | Red square skeleton tower; 39. | |
| 11232 *H 4126* | -Tongue Shoal. | 45° 03.8´ N 67° 00.8´ W | **Fl.W.** period 4s | | 7 | Red square skeleton tower, three white and red daymarks. | **Radar reflector.** |
| 11244 *H 4130* | St. Andrews, W. channel. | 45° 04.3´ N 67° 04.1´ W | **Fl.G.** period 4s | 10 **3** | 4 | Green cylindrical mast; 23. | |
| | ST. CROIX RIVER: | | | | | | |
| 11248 *H 4134* | -St. Croix Island (U.S.). | 45° 07.7´ N 67° 08.1´ W | **Fl.W.** period 2.5s fl. 0.5s, ec. 2s | 102 **31** | 7 | White skeleton tower, surmounted by platform. | Higher intensity beam toward Todds Point. |
| 11260 *H 4138* | -Whitlocks Mill, on S. bank (U.S.). | 45° 09.8´ N 67° 13.7´ W | **Iso.G.** period 6s | 32 **10** | 6 | White conical tower. | Seasonal. |
| | DEER ISLAND: | | | | | | |
| 11264 *H 4146* | -Leonardville Harbor. | 44° 58.1´ N 66° 57.3´ W | **F.W.** | 66 **20** | 10 | White square tower, red upper portion; 30. | |
| 11272 *H 4146.4* | -Leonardville wharf. | 44° 58.3´ N 66° 57.2´ W | **F.R.** | 26 **8** | 7 | Cylindrical mast; 23. | |
| 11276 *H 4145* | -Pompey Ledge. | 44° 58.8´ N 66° 56.7´ W | **Fl.W.** period 4s | 11 **3** | 3 | Green cylindrical mast; 23. | **Radar reflector.** |
| 11280 *H 4144* | -Richardson wharf. | 44° 59.7´ N 66° 56.7´ W | **Iso.G.** period 4s | | | Cylindrical mast, green, white and black square daymark; 23. | |
| 11304 *H 4138.6* | -Jameson Island West. | 45° 02.1´ N 66° 55.6´ W | **Fl.G.** period 4s | 13 **4** | 4 | Green square skeleton tower; 20. | **Radar reflector.** |
| 11308 *H 4139* | -Two Hour Rock. | 45° 01.7´ N 66° 56.1´ W | **Fl.R.** period 4s | 8 **2** | 4 | Red square skeleton tower, red and white triangular daymark. | **Radar reflector.** |
| 11310 *H 4140* | -Stuart Town, breakwater. | 45° 01.2´ N 66° 56.1´ W | **Fl.W.** period 4s | 18 **6** | 6 | Triangular skeleton tower; 20. | |
| 11312 *H 4148* | -Fairhaven. | 44° 57.8´ N 67° 00.5´ W | **L.Fl.R.** period 6s fl. 2s, ec. 4s | 13 **4** | 7 | Pipe swing pole; 13. | |
| 11316 *H 4147* | -Deer Point. | 44° 55.5´ N 66° 59.1´ W | **L.Fl.R.** period 12s fl. 2s, ec. 10s | 33 **10** | 7 | White cylindrical tower; 20. | |
| 11324 *H 4150* | Dog Island DI (U.S.). | 44° 55.1´ N 66° 59.3´ W | **Fl.W.R.** period 6s 5 fl. | 36 **11** | W. 10 R. 8 | Skeleton tower, green diamond daymark. | R. 306°-036°. **Horn:** 1 bl. ev. 30s. (bl. 3s, si. 27s). |
| 11328 *H 4152* | **Cherry Island.** | 44° 55.1´ N 66° 58.0´ W | **Fl.W.** period 5s fl. 0.5s, ec. 4.5s | 32 **10** | **17** | Cylindrical tower, red and white bands; 26. | **Horn:** 1 bl. ev. 20s. (bl. 2s, si. 18s). |
| 11332 *H 4154* | Head Harbor, on rock off E. Quoddy Head. | 44° 57.5´ N 66° 54.0´ W | **F.R.** | 58 **18** | 13 | Octagonal tower, red and white bands; 49. | **Horn:** 1 bl. ev. 60s. (bl. 4s, si. 56s). Horn points 116°. |
| 11334 *H 4155* | -Inner. | 44° 56.9´ N 66° 54.8´ W | **L.Fl.W.** period 6s fl. 2s, ec. 4s | 39 **12** | | Pipe swing pole, white bands; 23. | |
| 11336 *H 4156* | Wilsons Beach, wharf. | 44° 55.9´ N 66° 56.4´ W | **L.Fl.G.** period 6s fl. 2s, ec. 4s | | 4 | Cylindrical tower, green, white and black square daymark; 10. | |

| (1)<br>No. | (2)<br>Name and Location | (3)<br>Position | (4)<br>Characteristic | (5)<br>Height | (6)<br>Range | (7)<br>Structure | (8)<br>Remarks |
|---|---|---|---|---|---|---|---|
| | **CANADA-NOVA SCOTIA-BAY OF FUNDY** | | | | | | |
| | CURRY COVE: | | | | | | |
| 11344<br>*H 4157.4* | -Malloch Beach. | 44° 56.0′ N<br>66° 56.5′ W | **L.Fl.R.**<br>period 6s<br>fl. 2s, ec. 4s | 20<br>**6** | 3 | Cylindrical mast, red and white triangular daymark; 20. | |
| 11352 | Roosevelt Memorial Bridge. | 44° 52.0′ N<br>66° 59.0′ W | **F.G.** | | | On center navigable span of bridge. | E. and W. extremities of span marked by F.R. lights. |
| 11356<br>*H 4161* | Lubec Channel (U.S.). | 44° 50.5′ N<br>66° 58.6′ W | **Fl.W.**<br>period 6s | 53<br>**16** | 6 | White conical tower, black cylindrical pier. | **Horn:** 1 bl. ev. 15s. (bl. 2s, si. 13s). |
| | GRAND MANAN: | | | | | | |
| 11360<br>*H 4166* | -Long Eddy Point. | 44° 48.0′ N<br>66° 47.1′ W | **Fl.R.**<br>period 8s | 126<br>**38** | 14 | White rectangular tower, red upper portion; 30. | **Horn:** 1 bl. ev. 60s. (bl. 4s, si. 56s). Horn points 335°. |
| 11364<br>*H 4168* | -Swallow Tail. | 44° 45.9′ N<br>66° 44.0′ W | **Oc.W.**<br>period 6s<br>lt. 4s, ec. 2s | 122<br>**37** | 12 | White octagonal tower, red upper portion; 52. | **Horn:** 1 bl. ev. 20s. (bl. 2s, si. 18s). Horn points 100°. |
| 11372<br>*H 4171* | -Gull Islet. | 44° 41.2′ N<br>66° 43.7′ W | **Fl.G.**<br>period 6s<br>fl. 1s, ec. 5s | 11<br>**3** | 4 | Green square skeleton tower; 33. | |
| 11376<br>*H 4170* | -N. head, on Fisherman's Wharf. | 44° 45.8′ N<br>66° 45.1′ W | **Fl.R.**<br>period 6s<br>fl. 1s, ec. 5s | 14<br>**4** | 4 | Cylindrical mast; 13. | |
| 11380<br>*H 4170.4* | -Farmer Ledge. | 44° 43.4′ N<br>66° 43.6′ W | **Fl.G.**<br>period 4s<br>fl. 1s, ec. 3s | 13<br>**4** | 4 | Square skeleton tower, green and white rectangular daymark; 13. | |
| 11384<br>*H 4174* | **-Great Duck Island.** | 44° 41.1′ N<br>66° 41.6′ W | **Fl.W.**<br>period 10s<br>fl. 1s, ec. 9s | 49<br>**15** | **18** | White rectangular tower, red upper portion; 30. | **Horn:** 1 bl. ev. 60s. (bl. 4s, si. 56s). Horn points 120°.<br>Emergency light. |
| 11388<br>*H 4175* | -Edmunds Rock. | 44° 40.4′ N<br>66° 43.2′ W | **Fl.G.**<br>period 4s | 10<br>**3** | 4 | Green cylindrical mast; 23. | |
| 11392<br>*H 4172* | -Half Tide Rock. | 44° 39.3′ N<br>66° 43.7′ W | **Fl.G.**<br>period 5s<br>fl. 1s, ec. 4s | 13<br>**4** | 4 | Square skeleton tower, two black and white rectangular daymarks on both sides facing traffic; 13. | **Horn:** 1 bl. ev. 15s. (bl. 1s, si. 14s). |
| 11398<br>*H 4178.3* | -White Head Harbor. | 44° 37.8′ N<br>66° 43.7′ W | **Fl.R.**<br>period 4s | 16<br>**5** | 4 | Skeleton tower on 3-pile dolphin; 10. | |
| 11400<br>*H 4178* | -Long Point, S. extremity of White Head Island. | 44° 36.8′ N<br>66° 42.6′ W | **Iso.W.**<br>period 12s | 52<br>**16** | 12 | White rectangular tower, red upper portion; 36. | **Horn:** 1 bl. ev. 20s. (bl. 2s, si. 18s). Horn points 180°. |
| 11416<br>*H 4188* | **Gannet Rock.** | 44° 30.6′ N<br>66° 46.9′ W | **Fl.W.**<br>period 5s | 93<br>**28** | **19** | White octagonal tower, black and white stripes; 75. | **Horn:** 3 bl. ev. 60s (bl. 2s, si. 3s, bl. 2s, si. 3s, bl. 2s, si. 48s). |
| | RACON | | **G(– – •)** | | | | (3 & 10cm). |
| 11420<br>*H 4181.5* | White Horse Islet. | 44° 36.2′ N<br>66° 48.4′ W | **L.Fl.G.**<br>period 12s<br>fl. 2s, ec. 10s | 43<br>**13** | 4 | Square skeleton tower, red and white rectangular daymark, green square in center; 23. | **Radar reflector.** |
| 11424<br>*H 4180* | -Ingalls Head, on breakwater. | 44° 39.7′ N<br>66° 45.3′ W | **Q.G.** | 16<br>**5** | 7 | Cylindrical mast, green and white square daymark; 13. | |
| 11428<br>*H 4184* | -Seal Cove, outer breakwater. | 44° 38.9′ N<br>66° 50.3′ W | **Fl.G.**<br>period 6s<br>fl. 1s, ec. 5s | 16<br>**5** | 4 | Cylindrical mast, black and white square daymark; 13. | |
| 11436<br>*H 4186* | **-Southwest Head,** on Gull Cliff. | 44° 36.0′ N<br>66° 54.3′ W | **Fl.W.**<br>period 10s | 157<br>**48** | **16** | White rectangular tower, red upper portion; 33. | |
| 11444<br>*H 4192* | **Machias Seal Island.** | 44° 30.1′ N<br>67° 06.1′ W | **Fl.W.**<br>period 3s | 82<br>**25** | **17** | White octagonal tower, red upper portion; 59. | |

# Section 7

## Florida, Bermuda, the Bahamas and Turks and Caicos Islands

| (1) No. | (2) Name and Location | (3) Position | (4) Characteristic | (5) Height | (6) Range | (7) Structure | (8) Remarks |
|---|---|---|---|---|---|---|---|
| | | | **UNITED STATES-FLORIDA** | | | | |
| 11608 *J 3060* | **Dry Tortugas.** | 24° 38.0′ N 82° 54.9′ W | **Fl.W.** period 20s | 151 **46** | **20** | Conical tower, white lower, black upper. | Emergency light. |
| | RACON | | **K(– • –)** | | | | (3cm). |
| | For other lights of the U.S., see U.S. Coast Guard Light Lists. | | | | | | |
| | | | **BERMUDA** | | | | |
| 11616 *J 4472* | **St. Davids Island.** | 32° 21.8′ N 64° 39.1′ W | **Fl.(2)W.** period 20s fl. 0.4s, ec. 2.9s fl. 0.4s, ec. 16.3s | 213 **65** | **15** | White octagonal tower, red band; 72. | Partially obscured 044°-135°. |
| | | | **F.R.G.** | 207 **63** | **20** | | R. 135°-221°, G.-276°, R.-044°, R. (partially obscured)-135°. F.R. lights 0.95 mile SSW., 0.63 mile SW., 0.75 mile and 1.12 miles WNW. |
| 11620 *J 4471.3* | NE. breaker. | 32° 28.7′ N 64° 40.9′ W | **Fl.W.** period 2.5s | 45 **14** | 12 | Red fiberglass tower, on concrete tripod, marked "North East"; 46. | **Radar reflector.** |
| | RACON | | **N(– •)** | | 12 | | (3cm). |
| 11624 *J 4471.5* | Kitchen Shoal. | 32° 26.1′ N 64° 37.7′ W | **Fl.(3)W.** period 15s | 45 **14** | 12 | White fiberglass tower, red bands, on concrete tripod, marked "Kitchen" in red, white concrete base; 46. | **Radar reflector.** |
| | ST. GEORGES ISLAND: | | | | | | |
| 11632 *J 4477* | -Town Cut Channel, N. side, outer. | 32° 22.7′ N 64° 39.8′ W | **F.R.** | 46 **14** | 8 | White metal framework tower, red bands at top. | Visible 250°-080°. |
| 11636 *J 4478* | --N. side, inner, Chalk wharf. | 32° 22.7′ N 64° 39.9′ W | **F.R.** | 52 **16** | 8 | White metal framework tower, red bands at top. | Visible 250°-095°. |
| 11640 *J 4476* | -Town Cut Channel, Higgs Island, NE. corner. | 32° 22.7′ N 64° 39.7′ W | **F.G.** | 48 **15** | 8 | White framework tower, green top. | F.R. lights shown from Fort George flagstaff 1 mile W. |
| 11644 *J 4476.5* | -Horseshoe Island. | 32° 22.6′ N 64° 39.8′ W | **F.G.** | | 8 | Framework tower. | |
| 11646 *J 4479* | -Three Sisters. | 32° 22.6′ N 64° 40.0′ W | **V.Q.G.** | | 4 | White beacon, green band. | |
| 11648 *J 4481* | -Hen Island, NW. part. | 32° 22.5′ N 64° 40.5′ W | **Fl.G.** period 1.5s | 16 **5** | 4 | White metal framework tower, green band, red and white checkered diamond daymark. | |
| 11664 *J 4482* | **Kindley Field** AVIATION LIGHT, St. Davids. | 32° 22.0′ N 64° 40.6′ W | **Al.W.G.** period 10s | 141 **43** | **15** | Control tower. | F.R. on tank 0.5 mile WNW. 2 F.R. at Swing Bridge Ferry Reach 0.8 mile WNW. |
| | BERMUDA ISLAND: | | | | | | |
| 11668 *J 4550* | **-Gibbs Hill.** | 32° 15.2′ N 64° 50.1′ W | **Fl.W.** period 10s | 354 **108** | **26** | White round metal tower; 135. | Obscured 223°-228°, 229°-237°. |

| (1) No. | (2) Name and Location | (3) Position | (4) Characteristic | (5) Height | (6) Range | (7) Structure | (8) Remarks |
|---|---|---|---|---|---|---|---|
| | | | **BERMUDA** | | | | |
| 11672 *J 4540* | -Riddells Bay, N. side. | 32° 15.7′ N 64° 49.9′ W | **Fl.G.** period 4s fl. 0.6s, ec. 3.4s | 13 **4** | 4 | | |
| 11676 *J 4539* | -Perots Island, SW head. | 32° 15.6′ N 64° 50.0′ W | **F.W.** | | | | Occasional. |
| 11680 *J 4490* | -Gibbet Island. | 32° 19.4′ N 64° 44.7′ W | **Fl.R.** period 4s | 24 **7** | 2 | Wood column, white base; 10. | |
| 11684 *J 4471* | -North Rock. | 32° 28.5′ N 64° 46.1′ W | **Fl.(4)W.** period 20s | 69 **21** | 12 | Yellow fiberglass tower, black top, marked "North Rock", concrete base; 49. | **Radar reflector.** |
| 11686 *J 4547* | -Eastern Blue Cut, NW. reef. | 32° 24.0′ N 64° 52.7′ W | **Mo.(U)W.** period 10s | 60 **18** | 12 | White fiberglass tower, black bands, black concrete tripod, marked "Eastern Blue Cut" in white; 59. | **Radar reflector.** |
| 11688 *J 4489* | -South Channel, No. 20. | 32° 21.0′ N 64° 44.5′ W | **Fl.G.** period 2.5s | | | PORT (B) G, column. | |
| 11696 *J 4492* | -South Channel, No. 26. | 32° 18.8′ N 64° 47.5′ W | **Fl.G.** period 2.5s | | | PORT (B) G, column. | |
| 11698 *J 4493.5* | -South Channel, No. 29. | 32° 19.3′ N 64° 48.7′ W | **Fl.R.** period 4s | | | STARBOARD (B) R, beacon. | |
| 11700 *J 4493* | -Grassy Bay, No. 30. | 32° 19.1′ N 64° 48.7′ W | **Fl.G.** period 4s | 16 **5** | | PORT (B) G, beacon. | |
| 11704 *J 4494* | -Hogfish. | 32° 18.6′ N 64° 49.4′ W | **Fl.(2)Y.** period 10s | 16 **5** | 5 | White masonry beacon, black band. | F.R. on radio mast 1.07 miles 290°. |
| 11708 *J 4495* | -Stag Rocks, No. 35. | 32° 18.8′ N 64° 49.8′ W | **Fl.R.** period 4s | | | STARBOARD (B) R, beacon, topmark. | |
| 11712 *J 4491* | -Devonshire Dock, W. side of entrance. | 32° 18.5′ N 64° 46.3′ W | **F.G.** | 27 **8** | 2 | White post. | F.R. on radio masts 0.7 mile and 1.2 mile ENE., 0.55 mile and 0.7 mile SE. 2 F.R. mark chimney 460 meters ENE. |
| 11716 *J 4524* | -Ireland Island, Commodore's cottage. | 32° 19.1′ N 64° 50.5′ W | **F.R.** | 11 **3** | 2 | | |
| 11728 *J 4520* | --S. breakwater, head. | 32° 19.3′ N 64° 50.0′ W | **Fl.G.** period 4s | 12 **4** | 3 | Green structure on white bollard; 7. | |
| 11729 *J 4518* | --N. breakwater, head. | 32° 19.3′ N 64° 50.1′ W | **Fl.R.** period 4s | 12 **4** | 2 | Red structure on white bollard. | |
| 11732 *J 4514* | -Pearl Island. | 32° 17.5′ N 64° 50.2′ W | **Fl.Y.** period 4s | 20 **6** | 5 | White concrete beacon; 7. | |
| 11733 *J 4542.5* | -Pompano. | 32° 15.0′ N 64° 52.7′ W | **V.Q.G.** | | | PORT (B) G, beacon, topmark. | |
| 11736 *J 4544* | -Hogfish Cut. | 32° 15.6′ N 64° 53.0′ W | **Fl.R.** period 4s fl. 0.4s, ec. 3.6s | 13 **4** | 5 | Post. | |
| 11740 *J 4543* | -Hogfish Tripod. | 32° 15.4′ N 64° 52.8′ W | **Fl.G.** period 4s fl. 0.4s, ec. 3.6s | | | Tripod. | |
| 11741 *J 4545* | -Wreck Hill. | 32° 16.8′ N 64° 53.3′ W | **V.Q.R.** | | | STARBOARD (B) R, beacon, topmark. | |
| 11742 *J 4546* | -Chub Heads. | 32° 17.3′ N 64° 58.7′ W | **V.Q.(9)W.** period 15s | 60 **18** | 12 | Yellow fiberglass tower, black band, marked "Chub Heads" in white, on tripod. | **Radar reflector.** |
| | -RACON | | **C(– • – •)** | | 12 | | (3 & 10cm). |
| 11743 *J 4531* | -Long Point. | 32° 17.8′ N 64° 51.4′ W | **V.Q.(3)W.** period 5s | 13 **4** | 4 | White fiberglass beacon, black and yellow bands at top. | |

| (1) No. | (2) Name and Location | (3) Position | (4) Characteristic | (5) Height | (6) Range | (7) Structure | (8) Remarks |
|---|---|---|---|---|---|---|---|
| | | | **BERMUDA** | | | | |
| 11744 *J 4532* | -Plaice's Point. | 32° 17.8´ N 64° 51.5´ W | **Fl.R.** period 2.5s | 20 **6** | 4 | White fiberglass beacon, red top. | 2 F.R. shown from center of Watford Bridge 900 meters N. |
| 11748 *J 4508* | -Lane channel, N. side, head. | 32° 17.3´ N 64° 48.9´ W | **Fl.W.** period 4s fl. 0.6s, ec. 3.4s | 15 **5** | 1 | Black round stone tower, white base. | |
| 11750 *J 4537* | -Little Sound, Naval Air Station, Tender Pier. | 32° 16.1´ N 64° 51.2´ W | **Fl.R.** period 4s | | | | |
| | HAMILTON HARBOR: | | | | | | |
| 11752 *J 4506* | -Hinson Island, NW. point, Timlins Narrows. | 32° 17.1´ N 64° 48.4´ W | **Fl.R.** period 2.5s | 12 **4** | 5 | White structure, red band; 13. | |
| 11753 *J 4503* | -Spectacle Island, S. end. | 32° 17.2´ N 64° 48.0´ W | **Fl.G.** period 4s | | | White fiberglass beacon, green top. | |
| 11755 *J 4501* | -Royal Bermuda Yacht Club, SE. corner. | 32° 17.4´ N 64° 47.2´ W | **F.G.** | | | | |
| 11755.2 *J 4501.1* | --SW. corner. | 32° 17.4´ N 64° 47.3´ W | **F.G.** | | | | |
| 11757 | -Ferry Depot, jetty. | 32° 17.5´ N 64° 46.6´ W | **F.G.** | | | | |
| 11760 *J 4498* | -Two Rocks Passage. | 32° 17.5´ N 64° 48.7´ W | **V.Q.G.** | 21 **6** | 5 | White structure, green band at top. | |
| 11761 *J 4499* | --S. side. | 32° 17.5´ N 64° 48.7´ W | **V.Q.R.** | 21 **6** | 5 | White structure, red band at top. | |
| 11764 *J 4542* | -Ricketts Island. | 32° 16.5´ N 64° 49.7´ W | **Fl.R.** period 2.5s | 18 **5** | 4 | White concrete column, red top; 3. | |
| 11768 *J 4509* | -Dagger Rock. | 32° 16.6´ N 64° 48.8´ W | **Fl.R.** period 4s fl. 0.6s, ec. 3.4s | 13 **4** | 4 | White concrete beacon, red band. | |
| | | | **BAHAMA ISLANDS** | | | | |
| 11776 *J 4560* | Little Sale Cay. | 27° 02.7´ N 78° 10.3´ W | **Fl.W.** period 3s | 47 **14** | 12 | Metal tower; 19. | |
| | GREAT ABACO ISLAND: | | | | | | |
| 11780 *J 4562* | -Crab Cay, Angel Fish Point. | 26° 55.6´ N 77° 36.3´ W | **Fl.W.** period 5s | 33 **10** | 11 | Metal tower; 23. | |
| 11784 *J 4565* | -Whale Cay. | 26° 42.9´ N 77° 14.7´ W | **Fl.W.** period 5s | 40 **12** | 8 | Aluminum tower, black bands. | |
| 11788 *J 4566* | -Great Guana Cay. | 26° 39.8´ N 77° 06.9´ W | **Fl.W.** period 3s | 30 **9** | 6 | Metal tower; 20. | |
| 11792 *J 4570* | -Marsh Harbor, N. side, Great Abaco Island. | 26° 33.3´ N 77° 04.1´ W | **Fl.W.** period 3s | 23 **7** | 5 | Metal tower; 13. | |
| 11796 *J 4568* | -Man of War Cay. | 26° 35.4´ N 77° 00.4´ W | **Q.W.** | 30 **9** | 5 | White mast. | |
| 11800 *J 4572* | **-Elbow Cay.** | 26° 32.3´ N 76° 57.9´ W | **Fl.(5)W.** period 15s | 120 **37** | **23** | White round tower, red bands. | |
| 11804 *J 4575* | -Sandy Cay. | 26° 24.1´ N 76° 59.4´ W | **Fl.G.** period 3s | | | Beacon. | |
| 11808 *J 4576* | -Little Harbor. | 26° 19.8´ N 76° 59.7´ W | **Fl.W.** period 4s | 61 **19** | 10 | Metal tower. | F.W. shown when bar is dangerous. |

| (1)<br>No. | (2)<br>Name and Location | (3)<br>Position | (4)<br>Characteristic | (5)<br>Height | (6)<br>Range | (7)<br>Structure | (8)<br>Remarks |
|---|---|---|---|---|---|---|---|
| | | | **BAHAMA ISLANDS** | | | | |
| 11812<br>*J 4578* | -Cherokee Sound, on Duck Cay, Great Abaco Island. | 26° 16.0′ N<br>77° 04.0′ W | **F.R.** | 29<br>**9** | 6 | Metal tower. | Visible 229°-094° except where obscured to the E. by the high land of Cherokee Point. |
| 11816<br>*J 4580* | **-Abaco.** | 25° 51.7′ N<br>77° 11.1′ W | **Fl.W.**<br>period 10s<br>fl. 0.3s, ec. 9.7s | 168<br>**51** | **23** | Red conical stone tower, white base, white lantern; 92. | |
| 11820<br>*J 4581* | -Rocky Point. | 26° 00.0′ N<br>77° 24.3′ W | **Fl.W.**<br>period 6s | 33<br>**10** | 6 | Black metal framework tower, white hut; 26. | |
| 11824<br>*J 4582* | -Sandy Point, near W. extremity of Great Abaco Island. | 26° 01.7′ N<br>77° 24.1′ W | **F.W.** | 25<br>**8** | 5 | Mast; 20. | |
| 11828<br>*J 4583* | -Channel Cay. | 26° 15.3′ N<br>77° 37.8′ W | **Fl.W.**<br>period 2.5s | 38<br>**12** | 7 | Black metal framework tower. | |
| | GRAND BAHAMA ISLAND: | | | | | | |
| 11832<br>*J 4584* | -Sweetings Cay. | 26° 36.7′ N<br>77° 53.6′ W | **Fl.W.**<br>period 6s | 23<br>**7** | 8 | Metal tower. | |
| 11832.1<br>*J 4585* | -Riding Point AVIATION LIGHT. | 26° 42.7′ N<br>78° 09.5′ W | **Oc.R.**<br>period 3s | 269<br>**82** | | Red and white tower. | |
| | | | **3 F.R.** (vert.) | | | | |
| 11833<br>*J 4586* | -South Riding, Point Harbor Range, front. | 26° 37.5′ N<br>78° 13.1′ W | **Oc.G.**<br>period 3s<br>lt. 2.5s, ec. 0.5s | 39<br>**12** | | Framework tower, orange triangular daymark point up. | Visible on range line only. |
| 11833.1<br>*J 4586.1* | --Rear, 60 meters 340° from front. | 26° 37.5′ N<br>78° 13.1′ W | **Oc.G.**<br>period 3s<br>lt. 2.5s, ec. 0.5s | 52<br>**16** | | Framework tower, orange diamond daymark. | Visible on range line only. |
| 11834<br>*J 4587.6* | -Communications Tower. | 26° 37.7′ N<br>78° 14.3′ W | **2 F.R.** (vert.) | 239<br>**73** | | Red and white tower. | |
| 11835<br>*J 4588* | -Platform. | 26° 36.7′ N<br>78° 13.7′ W | **Fl.R.**<br>period 3s | | | Control building. | 2 Q.R. on E. and W. dolphins. |
| 11836<br>*J 4589* | -High Rock, S. side of Grand Bahama Island. | 26° 37.3′ N<br>78° 16.1′ W | **F.W.** | 25<br>**8** | 6 | White mast. | Unreliable. |
| 11837<br>*J 4589.4* | -Ionospheric Tower AVIATION LIGHT. | 26° 37.1′ N<br>78° 18.7′ W | **Oc.R.**<br>period 8s | 210<br>**64** | | Tower. | |
| | | | **F.R.** | | | | |
| 11837.1<br>*J 4589.8* | -Bassett Cove Tower AVIATION LIGHT. | 26° 36.9′ N<br>78° 19.4′ W | **Q.R.** | 407<br>**124** | | Red and white tower. | |
| | | | **2 F.R.** (vert.) | | | | |
| 11837.2<br>*J 4590.4* | -Bore Site Tower AVIATION LIGHT. | 26° 36.6′ N<br>78° 20.8′ W | **Oc.R.**<br>period 4s | 174<br>**53** | | Red and white tower. | |
| | | | **F.W.** | | | | |
| | | | **2 F.R.** (vert.) | | | | |
| 11838<br>*J 4591* | -Grand Lucayan Waterway, W. breakwater head. | 26° 32.4′ N<br>78° 33.4′ W | **Fl.(3)G.**<br>period 10s | 13<br>**4** | 3 | Concrete column; 7. | |
| 11838.1<br>*J 4591.1* | --E. breakwater, head. | 26° 32.4′ N<br>78° 33.3′ W | **Fl.(3)R.**<br>period 10s | 13<br>**4** | 3 | Concrete column; 7. | |
| 11841<br>*J 4593* | -Bahamia Marina, E. breakwater, head. | 26° 29.3′ N<br>78° 42.1′ W | **Q.R.** | | 3 | Concrete pedestal. | |
| 11841.1<br>*J 4593.2* | --W. breakwater, head. | 26° 29.3′ N<br>78° 42.2′ W | **Q.G.** | | 3 | Concrete pedestal. | |
| 11844<br>*J 4593.5* | **-Freeport** International Airport AVIATION LIGHT. | 26° 32.7′ N<br>78° 42.4′ W | **Al.Fl.W.G.**<br>period 10s | 98<br>**30** | **40** | | |

| (1) No. | (2) Name and Location | (3) Position | (4) Characteristic | (5) Height | (6) Range | (7) Structure | (8) Remarks |
|---|---|---|---|---|---|---|---|

## BAHAMA ISLANDS

| (1) No. | (2) Name and Location | (3) Position | (4) Characteristic | (5) Height | (6) Range | (7) Structure | (8) Remarks |
|---|---|---|---|---|---|---|---|
| 11852 *J 4594.4* | -Borco Oil Terminal, No. 1 jetty, SE. head. | 26° 30.0′ N 78° 46.2′ W | **Q.W.** | | | | |
| 11856 *J 4594.44* | --No. 1 jetty, NW. head. | 26° 30.3′ N 78° 46.7′ W | **Fl.(3)W.** period 7s | | 5 | Dolphin. | |
| 11864 *J 4596* | -Freeport, W. breakwater. | 26° 31.1′ N 78° 46.7′ W | **Fl.G.** period 4s | 23 **7** | 6 | Metal structure; 10. | |
| 11868 *J 4596.8* | -Channel entrance, W. side. | 26° 31.2′ N 78° 46.6′ W | **Q.G.** | 12 **4** | 2 | Framework tower. | |
| 11872 *J 4596.6* | --E. side. | 26° 31.2′ N 78° 46.5′ W | **Q.R.** | 12 **4** | 3 | Framework tower. | |
| 11880 *J 4595* | -Pinder Point Range, front. | 26° 31.5′ N 78° 46.4′ W | **F.G.** | 161 **49** | 11 | White framework tower, red bands, two red rectangular daymarks, white stripes. | |
| | | | **Q.W.** | | | | Strobe. |
| 11884 *J 4595.1* | --Rear, 1139 meters 021°47′ from front. | 26° 31.6′ N 78° 46.4′ W | **F.G.** | 266 **81** | 11 | White framework tower, red bands, two red rectangular daymarks, white stripes. | |
| | | | **Q.W.** | | | | Strobe. |
| 11888 *J 4598* | -Settlement Point, W. end of Island. | 26° 41.5′ N 79° 00.0′ W | **Fl.W.** period 4s | 44 **13** | 6 | White metal tower; 33. | |
| 11892 *J 4600* | -Indian Cay. | 26° 42.9′ N 79° 00.2′ W | **Fl.W.** period 6s | 40 **12** | 8 | Aluminum tower; 36. | |
| 11896 *J 4602* | Memory Rock. | 26° 57.0′ N 79° 06.3′ W | **Fl.W.** period 3s | 37 **11** | 11 | Black metal beacon; 23. | |
| | GREAT BAHAMA BANK: | | | | | | |
| 11900 *J 4620* | **-Great Isaac.** | 26° 01.8′ N 79° 05.4′ W | **Fl.W.** period 15s | 152 **46** | **23** | White round tower. | |
| 11904 *J 4616* | -North Rock. | 25° 48.1′ N 79° 15.7′ W | **Fl.W.** period 3s | 40 **12** | 8 | Black metal beacon; 30. | Visible 022°-343°. |
| 11908 *J 4618* | -North Bimini Island, wharf, head. | 25° 43.7′ N 79° 18.1′ W | **F.W.** | 20 **6** | 5 | Gray metal framework beacon. | Two F.R. 2M range lights indicate channel through reef on South Bimini. These lights are unwatched and unreliable. |
| 11912 *J 4613* | --AVIATION LIGHT. | 25° 42.5′ N 79° 16.3′ W | **Mo.(B)R.** period 20s | 282 **86** | **23** | Orange framework tower, white stripe. | |
| | | | **F.R.** | | | | Several lights mark tower. |
| 11916 *J 4610* | **-Gun Cay.** | 25° 34.3′ N 79° 17.8′ W | **Fl.W.** period 10s | 80 **24** | **15** | Red conical stone tower, lower part white. | Obscured by the Bimini Isles, when 8 miles distant, between 176° and 198°. |
| 11920 *J 4608* | -North Cat Cay, breakwater, head. | 25° 33.9′ N 79° 17.3′ W | **Fl.W.** period 2s | 10 **3** | 5 | Beacon; 12. | Not visible W. or SW. of Cat Cay. |
| 11924 *J 4604* | -South Riding Rock. | 25° 14.3′ N 79° 08.6′ W | **Fl.W.** period 5s | 35 **11** | 11 | White metal framework tower. | |
| 11928 *J 4606* | -Sylvia. | 25° 27.4′ N 79° 01.6′ W | **Fl.W.** period 4s | 20 **6** | 8 | Beacon on piles. | |
| 11933 *J 4630* | -Mackie Shoal. | 25° 40.9′ N 78° 39.4′ W | **Fl.W.** period 2s | 20 **6** | | | |
| 11936 *J 4624.5* | -Bullock Harbor. | 25° 45.5′ N 77° 52.5′ W | **Fl.W.** period 6s | 36 **11** | 7 | White metal framework tower, lower half black. | |

| (1) No. | (2) Name and Location | (3) Position | (4) Characteristic | (5) Height | (6) Range | (7) Structure | (8) Remarks |
|---|---|---|---|---|---|---|---|
| | | | **BAHAMA ISLANDS** | | | | |
| 11940 *J 4624* | **-Great Stirrup Cay.** | 25° 49.4′ N 77° 54.0′ W | **Fl.(2)W.** period 20s fl. 0.2s, ec. 1.5s fl. 0.2s, ec. 18.1s | 82 **25** | **22** | White round concrete tower; 56. | |
| 11944 *J 4624.2* | --AVIATION LIGHT, 1189 meters from E. end. | 25° 49.5′ N 77° 54.3′ W | **Fl.R.** period 1.5s **F.R.** | 200 **61** | **18** | Radio mast. | Obstruction light. |
| 11948 *J 4625* | -Little Harbor Cay. | 25° 33.9′ N 77° 42.8′ W | **Fl.W.** period 2s | 94 **29** | 9 | Metal tower; 23. | |
| 11952 *J 4626* | -Whale Point, SW. point of Whale Cay. | 25° 23.7′ N 77° 48.0′ W | **Fl.W.** period 4s | 70 **21** | 7 | Stone tower, white metal structure; 43. | |
| 11954 | Frazers Hog Cay AVIATION LIGHT. | 25° 25.0′ N 77° 53.7′ W | **Fl.W.G.** | | | | **Radiobeacon.** |
| 11956 *J 4627* | -Thompsons Cay (Chub Point). | 25° 24.4′ N 77° 54.6′ W | **Fl.W.R.** period 10s | 44 **13** | 7 | Aluminum framework tower; 33. | W. 320°-054°, R.-320°. Fl.W. and Fl.G. on water tower 0.8 mile NE. |
| 11960 *J 4628* | -Northwest Channel. | 25° 28.1′ N 78° 09.6′ W | **Fl.W.** period 3s | 20 **6** | 8 | White metal tower on piles; 36. | |
| 11960.5 *J 4628,5* | -Northwest Shoal. | 25° 29.9′ N 78° 13.9′ W | **Fl.W.** period 2s | 20 **6** | | | |
| 11964 *J 4629* | -Russell. | 25° 28.5′ N 78° 25.5′ W | **Fl.W.** period 4s | 20 **6** | | | |
| | ANDROS ISLAND: | | | | | | |
| 11968 *J 4635* | -Morgan's Bluff, Range, front. | 25° 10.5′ N 78° 02.1′ W | **Q.W.** | 29 **9** | 6 | | Intensified on range line. |
| 11972 *J 4635.1* | --Rear, 223°44′ from front. | 25° 10.5′ N 78° 02.1′ W | **Oc.W.** period 4s lt. 3s, ec. 1s | 60 **18** | 6 | | Intensified on range line. |
| 11976 *J 4634* | -Morgan's Bluff, dock. | 25° 10.8′ N 78° 01.6′ W | **Fl.W.** period 4s fl. 0.4s, ec. 3.6s | 20 **6** | 4 | | |
| 11980 *J 4636* | -Nicolls Town, Range, front. | 25° 08.1′ N 78° 00.0′ W | **Fl.W.** period 5s | 60 **18** | 8 | Red aluminum structure. | |
| 11984 *J 4636.1* | --Rear, 24 meters 247° from front. | 25° 07.9′ N 78° 00.3′ W | **Fl.W.** period 5s | 65 **20** | 10 | Red aluminum structure. | |
| 11988 *J 4640* | -Staniard Rock. | 24° 51.6′ N 77° 52.7′ W | **Fl.W.** period 4s | 18 **5** | 6 | Gray mast; 16. | |
| 11992 *J 4639* | -Staniard Creek. | 24° 50.5′ N 77° 53.4′ W | **F.R.** | 26 **8** | 6 | Wooden framework tower; 20. | |
| 12000.5 *J 4642* | -Site 1 N. ITT Tower. | 24° 43.9′ N 77° 46.3′ W | **Fl.Y.** period 4s | | 5 | Metal framework tower. | |
| 12001 *J 4641.3* | -OHDF Tower. | 24° 43.7′ N 77° 45.7′ W | **Fl.Y.** period 4s | | 5 | | |
| 12001.5 *J 4642.25* | -Site 1 S. ITT Tower. | 24° 41.5′ N 77° 44.3′ W | **Fl.Y.** period 4s | | 5 | Metal framework tower. | |
| 12002 *J 4641.4* | -AVIATION LIGHT. | 24° 42.3′ N 77° 46.4′ W | **Al.Fl.W.G.Y.** period 2s | 136 **41** | | Tower. | |
| 12004 *J 4642.2* | -Site 1 Range, front. | 24° 42.3′ N 77° 45.9′ W | **Q.G.** | 25 **8** | 10 | White tower, red daymark, white stripe. | |
| 12008 *J 4642.21* | --Rear, 335 meters 223°48′ from front. | 24° 42.2′ N 77° 46.0′ W | **Iso.G.** period 6s | 33 **10** | 10 | White tower, red rectangular daymark, white stripe. | |

| (1) No. | (2) Name and Location | (3) Position | (4) Characteristic | (5) Height | (6) Range | (7) Structure | (8) Remarks |
|---|---|---|---|---|---|---|---|
| | | | **BAHAMA ISLANDS** | | | | |
| 12012 *J 4643.4* | -High Cay. | 24° 38.9′ N 77° 41.7′ W | **Fl.W.** period 4s fl. 0.4s, ec. 3.6s | 70 **21** | 6 | Framework tower, red and white checkered diamond daymark. | |
| 12016 *J 4642.3* | -Site 1, No. 5. | 24° 42.8′ N 77° 45.3′ W | **Fl.G.** period 4s fl. 0.4s, ec. 3.6s | 18 **5** | 6 | Dolphin, black square daymark, green border. | |
| 12020 *J 4642.32* | --No. 6. | 24° 42.9′ N 77° 45.3′ W | **Fl.R.** period 4s fl. 0.4s, ec. 3.6s | 19 **6** | 3 | Dolphin, red triangular daymark point up. | |
| 12024 *J 4642.34* | --No. 7. | 24° 42.6′ N 77° 45.6′ W | **Fl.G.** period 4s fl. 0.4s, ec. 3.6s | 16 **5** | 4 | Dolphin, green square daymark. | |
| 12026 *J 4642.5* | --No. 9. | 24° 42.5′ N 77° 45.7′ W | **Fl.G.** period 6s | 16 **5** | 4 | | |
| 12028 *J 4642.4* | --No. 10. | 24° 42.5′ N 77° 45.8′ W | **Fl.R.** period 4s fl. 0.4s, ec. 3.6s | 16 **5** | 3 | Dolphin, red triangular daymark. | |
| 12030 *J 4642.6* | --No. 15. | 24° 42.3′ N 77° 45.8′ W | **Fl.G.** period 6s | 16 **5** | 4 | | |
| 12032 *J 4646* | -Middle Bight on rock S. side of channel. | 24° 19.0′ N 77° 39.7′ W | **Fl.W.** period 5s | 17 **5** | 7 | White metal framework tower. | |
| 12036 *J 4644* | -Site 2 Range, front. | 24° 29.9′ N 77° 43.1′ W | **Q.G.** | 22 **7** | 10 | White tower, red rectangular daymark, white stripe. | |
| 12040 *J 4644.1* | --Rear, 745 meters 269°54′ from front. | 24° 29.9′ N 77° 43.5′ W | **Iso.G.** period 6s | 42 **13** | 10 | White tower, red rectangular daymark, white stripe. | |
| 12044 *J 4644.3* | -Site 2, No. 3. | 24° 29.9′ N 77° 42.0′ W | **Fl.G.** period 4s fl. 0.4s, ec. 3.6s | 19 **6** | 4 | Dolphin, black square daymark. | Fl.G. and Fl.R. lights mark channel. |
| 12044.4 *J 4644.4* | --No. 4. | 24° 29.9′ N 77° 42.0′ W | **Fl.R.** period 4s | 19 **6** | 3 | Dolphin, red triangular daymark. | |
| 12044.8 *J 4644.5* | --No. 6. | 24° 29.9′ N 77° 42.2′ W | **Fl.R.** period 4s | 19 **6** | 3 | Dolphin, red triangular daymark. | |
| 12045 *J 4644.6* | --No. 9. | 24° 29.9′ N 77° 42.6′ W | **Fl.G.** period 4s | 16 **5** | 4 | Dolphin, black ball daymark. | |
| 12045.2 *J 4644.7* | --No. 10. | 24° 29.9′ N 77° 42.6′ W | **Fl.R.** period 4s | 16 **5** | 3 | Dolphin, red triangular daymark. | |
| 12045.6 *J 4644.8* | --No. 13. | 24° 29.9′ N 77° 43.0′ W | **Fl.G.** period 4s | 17 **5** | 4 | Dolphin, black ball daymark. | |
| 12046 *J 4644.9* | -Site 3 ITT Tower. | 24° 20.9′ N 77° 40.4′ W | **Fl.Y.** period 4s | 33 **10** | 5 | | |
| 12048 *J 4645* | -Site 3 No. 3. | 24° 20.1′ N 77° 40.4′ W | **Fl.G.** period 4s fl. 0.4s, ec. 3.6s | 19 **6** | 4 | Dolphin, green square daymark. | Fl.G. and Fl.R. lights mark channel. |
| 12048.4 *J 4645.1* | --No. 4. | 24° 20.2′ N 77° 40.4′ W | **Fl.R.** period 4s | 20 **6** | 3 | Dolphin, red triangular daymark. | |
| 12048.8 *J 4645.2* | --No. 5. | 24° 20.2′ N 77° 40.6′ W | **Fl.G.** period 4s | 19 **6** | 4 | Dolphin, black square daymark. | |
| 12049 *J 4645.3* | --No. 6. | 24° 20.2′ N 77° 40.9′ W | **Fl.R.** period 4s | 16 **5** | 3 | Dolphin, red triangular daymark. | |
| 12049.4 *J 4645.4* | --No. 9. | 24° 20.2′ N 77° 40.9′ W | **Fl.G.** period 4s | 16 **5** | 4 | Dolphin, black square daymark. | |
| 12052 *J 4647* | -Mangrove Cay, Peats Wharf. | 24° 14.3′ N 77° 38.5′ W | **F.R.** | 20 **6** | 7 | | |
| 12056 *J 4648* | -Sirious Rock. | 24° 13.0′ N 77° 36.0′ W | **Fl.W.** period 3s | 29 **9** | 7 | Black and white mast on white round structure. | |

| (1) No. | (2) Name and Location | (3) Position | (4) Characteristic | (5) Height | (6) Range | (7) Structure | (8) Remarks |
|---|---|---|---|---|---|---|---|

## BAHAMA ISLANDS

| (1) No. | (2) Name and Location | (3) Position | (4) Characteristic | (5) Height | (6) Range | (7) Structure | (8) Remarks |
|---|---|---|---|---|---|---|---|
| 12056.1 *J 4648.2* | -Site 4 ITT Tower. | 24° 13.3´ N 77° 36.0´ W | **Fl.Y.** period 4s | 33 **10** | 5 | | |
| 12056.2 *J 4648.25* | -Site 4 No. 3. | 24° 13.4´ N 77° 36.2´ W | **Fl.G.** period 4s | 23 **7** | 4 | | |
| 12056.4 *J 4648.22* | --No. 2. | 24° 13.4´ N 77° 36.2´ W | **Fl.R.** period 4s | 22 **7** | 3 | | |
| 12056.6 *J 4648.27* | --No. 4. | 24° 13.3´ N 77° 36.2´ W | **Fl.R.** period 4s | 20 **6** | 3 | | |
| 12060 *J 4649* | -Green Cay. | 24° 02.4´ N 77° 10.7´ W | **Fl.W.** period 3s | 33 **10** | 7 | Black metal column, concrete base; 23. | |
| 12060.2 *J 4648.3* | -Site 6 Range, front. | 24° 00.4´ N 77° 31.7´ W | **Q.W.** | 34 **10** | 10 | Framework tower. | |
| 12060.4 *J 4648.31* | --Rear, 760 meters 257° from front. | 24° 00.3´ N 77° 32.1´ W | **Iso.W.** period 6s | 68 **21** | 10 | Framework tower. | |
| 12060.6 *J 4648.32* | -Site 6 No. 4. | 24° 00.6´ N 77° 30.1´ W | **Fl.R.** period 4s | 16 **5** | 3 | | |
| 12060.8 *J 4648.321* | --No. 5. | 24° 00.5´ N 77° 30.1´ W | **Fl.G.** period 4s | 22 **7** | 4 | | |
| 12061 *J 4648.322* | --No. 6. | 24° 00.5´ N 77° 30.2´ W | **Fl.R.** period 4s | 21 **6** | 3 | | |
| 12061.2 *J 4648.323* | --No. 7. | 24° 00.5´ N 77° 30.2´ W | **Fl.G.** period 4s | 21 **6** | 4 | | |
| 12061.4 *J 4648.324* | --No. 8. | 24° 00.6´ N 77° 30.4´ W | **Fl.R.** period 4s | 21 **6** | 3 | | |
| 12061.6 *J 4648.325* | --No. 9. | 24° 00.5´ N 77° 30.4´ W | **Fl.G.** period 4s | 20 **6** | 4 | | |
| 12061.8 *J 4648.326* | --No. 10. | 24° 00.6´ N 77° 30.5´ W | **Fl.R.** period 4s | 20 **6** | 3 | | |
| 12062 *J 4648.327* | --No. 11. | 24° 00.6´ N 77° 30.7´ W | **Fl.G.** period 4s | 18 **5** | 4 | | |
| 12062.2 *J 4648.328* | --No. 12. | 24° 00.6´ N 77° 30.7´ W | **Fl.R.** period 4s | 17 **5** | 3 | | |
| 12062.4 *J 4648.329* | --No. 13. | 24° 00.6´ N 77° 30.9´ W | **Fl.G.** period 4s | 20 **6** | 4 | | |
| 12062.6 *J 4648.33* | --No. 16. | 24° 00.5´ N 77° 31.3´ W | **Fl.R.** period 4s | 16 **5** | 3 | | |
| 12062.8 *J 4648.331* | --No. 17. | 24° 00.4´ N 77° 31.6´ W | **Fl.G.** period 4s | 16 **5** | 4 | | |
| 12064 *J 4648.5* | -Tinker Rocks. | 23° 58.5´ N 77° 29.3´ W | **Fl.W.** period 4.2s | 32 **10** | 8 | Metal tower. | |
| 12068 *J 4648.7* | -High Point Cay. | 23° 55.2´ N 77° 28.5´ W | **Fl.W.** period 5s | | | White building on piles. | |
| 12068.2 *J 4648.75* | -Site 7 No. 4. | 23° 54.0´ N 77° 28.7´ W | **Fl.R.** period 4s | 20 **6** | 3 | | |
| 12068.4 *J 4648.751* | --No. 5. | 23° 53.9´ N 77° 28.7´ W | **Fl.G.** period 4s | 20 **6** | 4 | | |
| 12068.6 *J 4648.752* | --No. 7. | 23° 53.9´ N 77° 28.8´ W | **Fl.G.** period 4s | 17 **5** | 4 | | |
| 12068.8 *J 4648.753* | --No. 10. | 23° 54.0´ N 77° 29.0´ W | **Fl.R.** period 4s | 16 **5** | 3 | | |
| 12069 *J 4648.754* | --No. 11. | 23° 53.9´ N 77° 29.1´ W | **Fl.G.** period 4s | 18 **5** | 4 | | |

| (1) No. | (2) Name and Location | (3) Position | (4) Characteristic | (5) Height | (6) Range | (7) Structure | (8) Remarks |
|---|---|---|---|---|---|---|---|
| | | | **BAHAMA ISLANDS** | | | | |
| 12069.2 *J 4648.755* | --No. 12. | 23° 53.9′ N 77° 29.1′ W | **Fl.R.** period 4s | 19 **6** | 3 | | |
| 12069.4 *J 4648.756* | --No. 14. | 23° 53.9′ N 77° 29.3′ W | **Fl.R.** period 4s | 17 **5** | 3 | | |
| 12072 *J 4632* | -Billy Island, N. end of Williams Island. | 24° 39.6′ N 78° 28.6′ W | **F.W.** | 23 **7** | 5 | Metal tower; 23. | Fishing light. |
| | NEW PROVIDENCE ISLAND: | | | | | | |
| 12076 *J 4650* | -Goulding Cay, off W. point of New Providence Island. | 25° 01.3′ N 77° 34.3′ W | **Fl.W.** period 2s | 36 **11** | 8 | Gray metal structure; 49. | |
| | -Nassau Harbor: | | | | | | |
| 12080 *J 4654* | **--Fort Fincastle** AVIATION LIGHT. | 25° 04.4′ N 77° 20.3′ W | **Fl.W.** period 5s | 219 **67** | **28** | White concrete water tower; 131. | Obscured SW. by island. |
| 12084 *J 4655* | --Paradise (Hog) Island, W. point. | 25° 05.2′ N 77° 21.1′ W | **Fl.W.** period 5s | 68 **21** | 13 | White round tower; 63. | Fl.R. 5s 11M when bar is dangerous. Obscured 334°-025°. |
| 12086 *J 4657.4* | --W. breakwater, head. | 25° 05.1′ N 77° 21.3′ W | **Fl.R.** period 5s | 29 **9** | | Tower. | |
| 12088 *J 4656* | --W. of town, Range, front. | 25° 04.7′ N 77° 21.0′ W | **F.G.** | 37 **11** | 7 | Orange mast; 39. | Difficult to distinguish. |
| 12092 *J 4656.1* | ---Rear, 260 meters 151°36′ from front. | 25° 04.6′ N 77° 20.9′ W | **F.G.** | 61 **19** | 7 | Orange mast; 36. | Difficult to distinguish. |
| 12096 *J 4658* | --Government House. | 25° 04.5′ N 77° 20.7′ W | **Fl.R.** period 3s | 122 **37** | 10 | Building, green cupola; 69. | |
| 12100 *J 4664* | -The Narrows. | 25° 04.7′ N 77° 17.3′ W | **Fl.R.** period 5s | 12 **4** | 2 | White mast; 13. | |
| 12104 *J 4668* | -Porgee Rocks. | 25° 04.0′ N 77° 14.6′ W | **Fl.W.** period 3s fl. 0.3s, ec. 2.7s | 25 **8** | 5 | Metal tower; 23. | |
| 12108 *J 4662* | -Chub Rocks. | 25° 06.5′ N 77° 14.4′ W | **Fl.W.** period 5s | 32 **10** | 4 | White metal framework tower; 26. | |
| 12112 *J 4669* | -On point, S. of East End Point. | 25° 02.0′ N 77° 15.6′ W | **Fl.W.** period 6s | 57 **17** | 8 | White square stone building; 26. | Visible 180°-056°. |
| 12112.5 *J 4669.4* | -Port New Providence Marina, entrance channel. | 25° 00.2′ N 77° 15.7′ W | **Fl.W.** period 4s fl. 0.4s, ec. 3.6s | 7 **2** | 4 | Wooden pile. | |
| 12112.7 *J 4669.6* | --No. 1. | 25° 00.3′ N 77° 15.8′ W | **Fl.W.** period 4s fl. 0.4s, ec. 3.6s | 7 **2** | 4 | Wooden pile. | |
| 12112.9 *J 4669.7* | --No. 2. | 25° 00.4′ N 77° 15.9′ W | **Fl.W.** period 4s fl. 0.4s, ec. 3.6s | 7 **2** | 4 | Wooden pile. | |
| 12114 *J 4670.8* | -Clifton Terminal. | 25° 00.4′ N 77° 32.5′ W | **2 Q.R.** (horiz.) | 121 **37** | 13 | Orange mast, white bands. | |
| | | | **2 F.R.** (horiz.) | 59 **18** | 10 | Same structure. | |
| | GREAT BAHAMA BANK: | | | | | | |
| 12116 *J 4722* | -Beacon Cay (North Rock), Ship Channel. | 24° 52.7′ N 76° 49.9′ W | **Fl.W.R.** period 3s | 58 **18** | 8 | Gray metal framework tower; 30. | R. 292°-303°, W.-292°. Partially obscured by neighboring islands 319°-006°. |
| 12120 *J 4724* | -Elbow Cay. | 24° 30.9′ N 76° 49.0′ W | **Fl.W.** period 2s | 46 **14** | 11 | Gray metal framework tower; 26. | |

## BAHAMA ISLANDS

| (1) No. | (2) Name and Location | (3) Position | (4) Characteristic | (5) Height | (6) Range | (7) Structure | (8) Remarks |
|---|---|---|---|---|---|---|---|
| 12124<br>*J 4728* | -Harvey Cay. | 24° 09.2′ N<br>76° 29.2′ W | **Fl.W.**<br>period 3.3s | 49<br>**15** | 6 | Gray beacon; 13. | |
| 12128<br>*J 4726* | -Bitter Guana Cay, N. end Dotham's Cut. | 24° 07.0′ N<br>76° 23.0′ W | **Fl.W.**<br>period 5s | 33<br>**10** | | | |
| 12132<br>*J 4730* | -Galliot Cut. | 23° 55.1′ N<br>76° 16.7′ W | **Fl.W.**<br>period 4s | 43<br>**13** | 7 | Gray metal framework tower. | |
| | -Eleuthera Island: | | | | | | |
| 12136<br>*J 4694* | --Tarpum Bay, S. end. | 24° 58.2′ N<br>76° 11.2′ W | **F.W.** | 35<br>**11** | 7 | Mast; 20. | |
| 12140<br>*J 4700* | --Powell Point. | 24° 50.3′ N<br>76° 20.7′ W | **Fl.W.**<br>period 3s | 38<br>**12** | 8 | Gray metal framework tower; 30. | |
| 12144<br>*J 4696* | --Poison Point. | 24° 49.3′ N<br>76° 11.7′ W | **Fl.W.**<br>period 15s | 29<br>**9** | 7 | Metal tower; 13. | |
| 12148<br>*J 4698* | ---Rock Sound settlement. | 24° 52.0′ N<br>76° 09.6′ W | **F.R.** | 25<br>**8** | | Mast; 20. | |
| 12152<br>*J 4701* | --Free Town. | 24° 46.1′ N<br>76° 16.8′ W | **F.W.** | 19<br>**6** | 7 | Mast. | |
| 12156<br>*J 4702* | --Wemyss Bight. | 24° 43.6′ N<br>76° 13.2′ W | **F.W.** | 27<br>**8** | 2 | White mast; 16. | |
| 12158<br>*J 4705* | --North Palmetto Point. | 25° 10.8′ N<br>76° 11.4′ W | **Iso.W.**<br>period 4s | 73<br>**22** | 12 | White tower, black top, dwelling. | |
| 12160<br>*J 4692* | --Cupid Cay. | 25° 11.5′ N<br>76° 15.0′ W | **Fl.W.**<br>period 4s | 40<br>**12** | 8 | Gray metal framework. | |
| 12162<br>*J 4691* | --AVIATION LIGHT. | 25° 16.3′ N<br>76° 19.0′ W | **Iso.R.**<br>period 3s | | | Radio mast. | |
| 12164<br>*J 4688* | --Hatchet Bay. | 25° 20.9′ N<br>76° 29.6′ W | **Fl.W.**<br>period 15s | 57<br>**17** | 8 | White metal framework tower; 23. | 2 F.R. range lights in line on 022° are shown from the E. side of the bay. |
| 12168<br>*J 4686* | --Stafford, Gregory Town. | 25° 23.4′ N<br>76° 33.6′ W | **F.W.** | 41<br>**12** | 9 | Mast; 13. | |
| 12172<br>*J 4674* | --Six Shilling Cays. | 25° 16.4′ N<br>76° 54.4′ W | **Fl.W.**<br>period 8s | 32<br>**10** | 10 | Metal framework tower; 33. | |
| 12176<br>*J 4675* | --Six Shilling Channel, 4.3 kilometers 235°30′ from Six Shilling Cays Light. | 25° 15.3′ N<br>76° 56.2′ W | **Fl.R.**<br>period 4s<br>fl. 0.4s, ec. 3.6s | 16<br>**5** | 7 | Metal structure. | |
| 12180<br>*J 4676* | --Current Rock. | 25° 24.0′ N<br>76° 51.1′ W | **Fl.W.**<br>period 8s | 41<br>**12** | 7 | Metal framework tower; 33. | |
| 12184<br>*J 4677* | --Current. | 25° 24.4′ N<br>76° 46.8′ W | **F.W.** | 12<br>**4** | 1 | Mast. | |
| 12188<br>*J 4675.5* | --Current Island. | 25° 22.9′ N<br>76° 48.5′ W | **F.W.** | 20<br>**6** | 1 | Mast. | |
| 12192<br>*J 4680* | --The Bluff. | 25° 29.4′ N<br>76° 44.9′ W | **F.W.** | 20<br>**6** | 1 | Mast. | |
| 12196<br>*J 4681* | --Spanish Wells. | 25° 32.3′ N<br>76° 45.1′ W | **F.W.** | 6<br>**2** | 1 | Concrete column. | |
| 12200<br>*J 4678* | --Egg Island. | 25° 29.8′ N<br>76° 52.9′ W | **Fl.W.**<br>period 3s | 112<br>**34** | 12 | White metal tower; 59. | |
| 12204<br>*J 4682* | --Man Island. | 25° 32.8′ N<br>76° 38.5′ W | **Fl.(3)W.**<br>period 15s<br>fl. 0.5s, ec. 1s<br>fl. 0.5s, ec. 1s<br>fl. 0.5s, ec. 11.5s | 93<br>**28** | 12 | White metal framework tower; 59. | |
| 12208<br>*J 4704* | --Eleuthera Point. | 24° 36.9′ N<br>76° 08.8′ W | **Fl.W.**<br>period 4.6s | 61<br>**19** | 6 | Beacon on white dwelling; 26. | |

| (1) No. | (2) Name and Location | (3) Position | (4) Characteristic | (5) Height | (6) Range | (7) Structure | (8) Remarks |
|---|---|---|---|---|---|---|---|

**BAHAMA ISLANDS**

| (1) No. | (2) Name and Location | (3) Position | (4) Characteristic | (5) Height | (6) Range | (7) Structure | (8) Remarks |
|---|---|---|---|---|---|---|---|
| | EXUMA SOUND: | | | | | | |
| 12212 *J 4708* | -Little San Salvador. | 24° 33.9´ N 75° 56.1´ W | **Fl.W.** period 2.4s | 69 **21** | 13 | Gray metal framework tower; 30. | Visible 240°-110°, obsc.-130°, vis.-140°, obsc.-170°, vis.-190°, obsc.-200°, vis.-220°, obsc.-240°. |
| | -Cat Island: | | | | | | |
| 12220 *J 4712* | --Bennetts Harbor. | 24° 33.6´ N 75° 38.3´ W | **Fl.W.** period 4s | 53 **16** | 12 | Gray metal framework tower; 30. | Visible 350°-130°. |
| 12228 *J 4716* | --Smith Town. | 24° 19.9´ N 75° 28.5´ W | **Fl.W.** period 3.3s | 39 **12** | 7 | Gray metal framework tower. | |
| 12236 *J 4718* | --Devils Point on summit 823 meters NW. of point. | 24° 07.3´ N 75° 27.9´ W | **Fl.W.** period 5s | 143 **44** | 12 | White metal framework tower; 30. | |
| 12240 *J 4748* | -Conception Island. | 23° 49.3´ N 75° 07.0´ W | **Fl.W.** period 2s | 84 **26** | 6 | Gray metal framework tower; 30. | |
| | -Great Exuma Island: | | | | | | |
| 12244 *J 4734* | --Exuma Harbor, Conch Cay. | 23° 33.3´ N 75° 48.0´ W | **Fl.W.** period 5s | 39 **12** | 8 | Gray metal framework tower; 30. | |
| 12248 *J 4732* | --Simon Point. | 23° 32.0´ N 75° 48.0´ W | **F.W.** | 40 **12** | 5 | Mast; 16. | |
| 12252 *J 4737* | --Hawksbill Rocks. | 23° 25.4´ N 76° 05.6´ W | **Fl.W.** period 3.3s | 32 **10** | 6 | White conical metal tower, black bands; 23. | |
| 12256 *J 4736* | --Jewfish Cut. | 23° 27.0´ N 75° 57.6´ W | **Fl.W.** period 2.5s | 38 **12** | 8 | Black conical metal tower, white top; 23. | |
| | -Long Island: | | | | | | |
| 12260 *J 4750* | --Cape St. Maria. | 23° 40.5´ N 75° 20.4´ W | **Fl.W.** period 3.3s | 99 **30** | 14 | Gray metal framework tower; 30. | Obscured 240°-340°. |
| 12264 *J 4752* | --Simms. | 23° 29.4´ N 75° 14.7´ W | **F.W.** | 23 **7** | 4 | Mast. | |
| 12268 *J 4753* | --Great Harbor, Booby Rock. | 23° 06.9´ N 74° 56.9´ W | **Fl.W.** period 2s | 39 **12** | 8 | White tower, red bands; 26. | |
| 12272 *J 4754* | ---Harbor Point. | 23° 06.1´ N 74° 57.5´ W | **F.W.** | 25 **8** | 3 | White mast, hut; 20. | |
| 12276 *J 4760* | --Galloway Landing. | 23° 04.3´ N 74° 59.0´ W | **F.W.** | 14 **4** | 2 | White mast; 23. | |
| 12280 *J 4758* | --South Point, Turbot Hill. | 22° 51.5´ N 74° 51.2´ W | **Fl.W.** period 2.5s | 61 **19** | 12 | Gray metal framework tower; 30. | Partially obscured 140°-245°. |
| 12284 *J 4744* | --Rum Cay, Port Nelson. | 23° 38.7´ N 74° 50.2´ W | **F.W.** | 18 **5** | 5 | Mast; 13. | |
| 12285 *J 4745* | --Cotton Field Point. | 23° 39.2´ N 74° 51.6´ W | **L.Fl.W.Y.R.** period 10s fl. 2s, ec. 8s | 75 **23** | 10 | | R. 083°30′-006°30′, W.-014°30′, Y.-075°30′, W.-083°30′. |
| 12288 *J 4738* | **-San Salvador.** | 24° 06.0´ N 74° 27.1´ W | **Fl.(2)W.** period 10s fl. 0.2s, ec. 1.3s fl. 0.2s, ec. 8.3s | 163 **50** | **23** | White stone tower, dwelling; 72. | Partially obscured 001°-008°, 010°-068°, and 076°-095°. |
| 12292 *J 4740* | -Cockburn Town, near landing. | 24° 03.2´ N 74° 31.8´ W | **F.W.** | 23 **7** | 1 | Mast; 13. | |
| | CROOKED ISLAND AND ACKLINS ISLAND: | | | | | | |
| 12296 *J 4792* | **-Bird Rock.** | 22° 50.7´ N 74° 21.5´ W | **Fl.(2)W.** period 15s | 112 **34** | **22** | White conical stone tower. | |

| (1) No. | (2) Name and Location | (3) Position | (4) Characteristic | (5) Height | (6) Range | (7) Structure | (8) Remarks |
|---|---|---|---|---|---|---|---|
| | | | **BAHAMA ISLANDS** | | | | |
| 12300 *J 4794* | -Majors Cay. | 22° 44.2′ N 74° 09.2′ W | **F.W.** | 30 **9** | 4 | Mast; 20. | Unreliable. |
| 12304 *J 4778* | Acklins Island. | 22° 43.9′ N 73° 50.9′ W | **Fl.W.** period 6s | 56 **17** | 10 | White round metal tower; 33. | |
| 12308 *J 4779* | -Atwood Harbor. | 22° 43.5′ N 73° 53.0′ W | **Fl.W.** period 4.5s | 20 **6** | 5 | Black metal tower. | |
| 12312 *J 4780* | -Spring Point. | 22° 27.9′ N 73° 57.2′ W | **F.W.** | 19 **6** | 7 | White pole; 16. | |
| 12316 *J 4786* | -Long Cay. | 22° 36.1′ N 74° 19.6′ W | **F.W.** | 60 **18** | 4 | White post. | |
| 12320 *J 4788* | -Windsor Point. | 22° 33.1′ N 74° 22.4′ W | **Fl.W.** period 3s | 36 **11** | 8 | Metal tower; 36. | |
| 12324 *J 4782* | **-Castle Island.** | 22° 07.6′ N 74° 19.7′ W | **Fl.(2)W.** period 20s | 131 **40** | **22** | White concrete tower; 112. | |
| | JUMENTOS CAYS: | | | | | | |
| 12328 *J 4764* | -Nuevitas Rocks. | 23° 09.7′ N 75° 22.4′ W | **Fl.W.** period 4s | 38 **12** | 10 | Gray metal tower; 30. | |
| 12332 *J 4766* | -Flamingo Cay. | 22° 52.8′ N 75° 52.0′ W | **Fl.W.** period 6s | 138 **42** | 8 | Gray metal framework tower; 13. | |
| 12336 *J 4768* | -Ragged Island, Duncan Town (Man-O-War Hill). | 22° 11.0′ N 75° 44.0′ W | **Fl.W.** period 3s | 118 **36** | 12 | Black pipe, platform; 23. | F.W. light shown from settlement wharf. |
| 12340 *J 4772* | -Cay Santo Domingo. | 21° 43.2′ N 75° 45.4′ W | **Fl.W.** period 5s | 29 **9** | 7 | Red framework tower, silver bands. | |
| 12344 *J 4774* | **Cay Lobos.** | 22° 22.7′ N 77° 35.3′ W | **Fl.(2)W.** period 20s fl. 0.2s, ec. 1.5s fl. 0.2s, ec. 18.1s | 145 **44** | **22** | White round metal tower; 148. | |
| | MAYAGUANA ISLAND: | | | | | | |
| 12348 *J 4800* | -Guano Point, Abraham Bay. | 22° 21.4′ N 72° 57.9′ W | **Fl.W.** period 3s | 14 **4** | 8 | Gray structure; 7. | |
| 12352 *J 4798* | -Northwest Point. | 22° 27.5′ N 73° 07.9′ W | **Fl.W.** period 5s fl. 1s, ec. 4s | 70 **21** | 12 | White framework tower, red lantern. | |
| 12356 *J 4802* | Hogsty Reef. | 21° 41.7′ N 73° 50.9′ W | **Fl.W.** period 4s | 29 **9** | 8 | Red mast, white bands; 23. | |
| | GREAT INAGUA ISLAND: | | | | | | |
| 12360 *J 4804* | **-Great Inagua.** | 20° 56.1′ N 73° 40.2′ W | **Fl.(2)W.** period 10s fl. 0.4s, ec. 0.9s fl. 0.4s, ec. 8.3s | 120 **37** | **22** | White conical tower; 112. | Partially obscured 165°-183°. |
| | | | **TURKS AND CAICOS ISLANDS** | | | | |
| | CAICOS ISLANDS: | | | | | | |
| 12380 *J 4806.8* | -Providenciales Island, E. head. | 21° 48.5′ N 72° 07.8′ W | **Fl.W.** period 10s | | 12 | | *Temporarily extinguished (2009).* |

Lights in the Caicos and Turks Islands are reported to be unreliable.

| (1) No. | (2) Name and Location | (3) Position | (4) Characteristic | (5) Height | (6) Range | (7) Structure | (8) Remarks |
|---|---|---|---|---|---|---|---|
| | | | **TURKS AND CAICOS ISLANDS** | | | | |
| 12384<br>*J 4806.6* | --NW. point. | 21° 51.8′ N<br>72° 20.0′ W | **Fl.(3)W.**<br>period 15s<br>fl. 0.5s, ec. 2s<br>fl. 0.5s, ec. 2s<br>fl. 0.5s, ec. 9.5s | | 14 | | *Temporarily extinguished (2010).* |
| 12388<br>*J 4807* | -Cape Comete, East Caicos Island. | 21° 43.4′ N<br>71° 28.3′ W | **Fl.(2)W.**<br>period 20s | | 12 | | *Temporarily extinguished (2009).* |
| 12392<br>*J 4808* | -South Caicos Island Cockburn Harbor, on Government Hill. | 21° 29.3′ N<br>71° 31.6′ W | **F.W.** | 50<br>**15** | 9 | White building; 16. | Visible 180°-090°.<br>*Temporarily extinguished (2009).* |
| 12396<br>*J 4809* | -Long Cay, E. end. | 21° 29.0′ N<br>71° 32.1′ W | **Fl.G.**<br>period 2.5s<br>fl. 0.5s, ec. 2s | | 5 | | *Temporarily extinguished (2009).* |
| 12400<br>*J 4809.4* | -Dove Cay, W. end. | 21° 29.1′ N<br>71° 31.8′ W | **Fl.R.**<br>period 2.5s<br>fl. 0.5s, ec. 2s | | 5 | White tower. | *Temporarily extinguished (2009).* |
| 12404<br>*J 4810* | -Bush Cay. | 21° 11.2′ N<br>71° 38.2′ W | **Fl.(2)W.**<br>period 10s<br>fl. 0.5s, ec. 2s<br>fl. 0.5s, ec. 7s | | 14 | | *Temporarily extinguished (2009).* |
| 12405<br>*J 4811* | -French Cay. | 21° 30.5′ N<br>72° 12.7′ W | **Fl.R.** | 10<br>**3** | | Pillar. | *Temporarily extinguished (2009).* |
| 12406<br>*J 4811.5* | -W. Caicos, S. end. | 21° 37.6′ N<br>72° 28.3′ W | **Q.R.** | 52<br>**16** | | Pillar. | *Temporarily extinguished (2009).* |
| | TURKS ISLANDS: | | | | | | |
| 12408<br>*J 4812* | **-Grand Turk.** | 21° 30.7′ N<br>71° 08.0′ W | **Fl.W.**<br>period 7.5s<br>fl. 1s, ec. 6.5s | 108<br>**33** | **18** | White round metal tower; 62. | F.W. on tower 1.1 miles S.<br>F.R. on tower 3 miles S.<br>*Temporarily extinguished (2009).* |
| 12420<br>*J 4814* | -Freighter Dock. | 21° 26.0′ N<br>71° 09.0′ W | **2 F.R.** | | | | *Temporarily extinguished (2009).* |
| 12428<br>*J 4816* | -Salt Cay. | 21° 20.2′ N<br>71° 12.7′ W | **Fl.(4)W.**<br>period 20s | | 8 | | *Temporarily extinguished (2009).* |
| 12432<br>*J 4818* | -Sand Cay. | 21° 11.8′ N<br>71° 14.9′ W | **Fl.W.**<br>period 2s<br>fl. 0.1s, ec. 1.9s | 85<br>**26** | 10 | Red metal framework tower; 49. | *Temporarily extinguished (2009).* |

Lights in the Caicos and Turks Islands are reported to be unreliable.

# Section 8

## Cuba

| (1) No. | (2) Name and Location | (3) Position | (4) Characteristic | (5) Height | (6) Range | (7) Structure | (8) Remarks |
|---|---|---|---|---|---|---|---|
| | | | **CUBA** | | | | |
| 12436<br>*J 4820* | **Cabo San Antonio.** | 21° 52.1´ N<br>84° 57.1´ W | **Fl.(2)W.**<br>period 10s | 102<br>**31** | **18** | Yellow round masonry tower; 75. | Aeromarine light.<br>Reserve light range 7M. |
| 12440<br>*J 4822* | Banco Sancho Pardo. | 22° 09.7´ N<br>84° 44.9´ W | **Fl.W.**<br>period 8s<br>fl. 1s, ec. 7s | 36<br>**11** | 10 | Red framework tower; 26. | |
| 12448<br>*J 4823* | La Tabla. | 22° 18.2´ N<br>84° 39.9´ W | **Fl.W.**<br>period 5s<br>fl. 1s, ec. 4s | 36<br>**11** | 12 | White framework tower, on piles; 26. | |
| 12452<br>*J 4823.5* | Zorrita. | 22° 22.3´ N<br>84° 34.9´ W | **Fl.W.**<br>period 7s<br>fl. 1s, ec. 6s | 36<br>**11** | 10 | Green framework tower, on piles; 26. | |
| 12456<br>*J 4824* | El Pinto. | 22° 24.9´ N<br>84° 31.1´ W | **Fl.W.**<br>period 15s<br>fl. 1s, ec. 14s | 36<br>**11** | 10 | Red framework tower, yellow bands, on piles; 26. | |
| 12460<br>*J 4826* | Cayo Buenavista. | 22° 24.1´ N<br>84° 26.7´ W | **Fl.W.**<br>period 5s<br>fl. 1s, ec. 4s | 108<br>**33** | 6 | Aluminum framework tower; 98. | |
| 12464<br>*J 4824.5* | Quebrado de Buenavista. | 22° 28.1´ N<br>84° 28.1´ W | **Fl.W.**<br>period 7s<br>fl. 1s, ec. 6s | 36<br>**11** | 10 | White framework tower, on piles; 26. | |
| 12468<br>*J 4827.5* | Cabezo Seco. | 22° 32.1´ N<br>84° 20.0´ W | **Fl.W.**<br>period 12s<br>fl. 1s, ec. 11s | 36<br>**11** | 10 | White framework tower, red bands, on piles; 26. | |
| 12472<br>*J 4827* | Puerto de Los Arroys, Baja La Paila. | 22° 21.4´ N<br>84° 22.8´ W | **Fl.G.**<br>period 5s | 16<br>**5** | 3 | PORT (B)<br>G, tower, topmark. | |
| 12476<br>*J 4827.8* | Punta Tabaco. | 22° 34.6´ N<br>84° 15.3´ W | **Fl.W.**<br>period 8s<br>fl. 1s, ec. 7s | 36<br>**11** | 10 | Yellow framework tower, on piles; 26. | |
| 12480<br>*J 4827.9* | Roncadora. | 22° 38.2´ N<br>84° 11.8´ W | **Fl.W.**<br>period 10s | 36<br>**11** | 10 | Red framework tower, on piles; 26. | |
| 12484<br>*J 4828* | **Cayo Jutias.** | 22° 42.9´ N<br>84° 01.4´ W | **L.Fl.W.**<br>period 15s<br>fl. 2s, ec. 13s | 141<br>**43** | **22** | Yellow octagonal metal framework tower, black bands; 135. | |
| | BAHIA DE SANTA LUCIA: | | | | | | |
| 12490<br>*J 4830.2* | -No. 5. | 22° 41.6´ N<br>83° 58.3´ W | **Fl.G.**<br>period 3s | 13<br>**4** | 3 | PORT (B)<br>G, tower, topmark. | |
| 12492<br>*J 4830.4* | -No. 6. | 22° 41.6´ N<br>83° 58.3´ W | **Fl.R.**<br>period 6s | 13<br>**4** | 3 | STARBOARD (B)<br>R, tower, topmark. | |
| 12500<br>*J 4830* | Punta Bano, offshore on W. side of entrance to channel. | 22° 41.2´ N<br>83° 58.2´ W | **Fl.R.**<br>period 4s | 16<br>**5** | 3 | STARBOARD (B)<br>R, tower, topmark. | |
| 12504<br>*J 4832* | Cayo Arenas. | 22° 50.2´ N<br>83° 39.3´ W | **Fl.W.**<br>period 10s<br>fl. 1s, ec. 9s | 46<br>**14** | 10 | Aluminum framework tower; 39. | |
| 12505<br>*J 4833* | No. 13. | 22° 51.4´ N<br>83° 34.8´ W | **Fl.G.**<br>period 5s | 13<br>**4** | 4 | PORT (B)<br>G, tower, topmark. | |
| 12505.2<br>*J 4833.1* | No. 15. | 22° 51.1´ N<br>83° 34.6´ W | **Fl.G.**<br>period 5s | 13<br>**4** | 4 | PORT (B)<br>G, tower, topmark. | |

Many of the lights on the coast of Cuba have been reported to be irregular or extinguished.

| (1) No. | (2) Name and Location | (3) Position | (4) Characteristic | (5) Height | (6) Range | (7) Structure | (8) Remarks |
|---|---|---|---|---|---|---|---|
| | | | **CUBA** | | | | |
| 12512 *J 4836* | **Punta Gobernadora.** | 22° 59.7′ N 83° 13.0′ W | **Fl.W.** period 6s | 108 **33** | **27** | White conical metal tower, red bands; 105. | Aeromarine light. Reserve light range 7M. |
| | BAHIA HONDA: | | | | | | |
| 12516 *J 4838* | -N. of old fort on Punta del Morrillo. | 22° 58.9′ N 83° 09.2′ W | **Fl.(2)W.** period 10s | 89 **27** | 8 | Aluminum framework tower; 26. | |
| | BAHIA CABANAS: | | | | | | |
| 12528 *J 4842* | -Cerro Frias. | 22° 59.8′ N 82° 58.9′ W | **Fl.W.** period 8s | 174 **53** | 10 | White framework tower; 26. | |
| 12536 *J 4843* | -Punta Arenas, edge of shoal S. of Punta Arena (No. 2A). | 22° 59.2′ N 82° 59.0′ W | **Fl.R.** period 6s fl. 0.5s, ec. 5.5s | 16 **5** | 3 | STARBOARD (B) R, tower, topmark. | |
| 12540 *J 4842.5* | -Punta Africana, NE. point of Cayo Juan Tomas (No. 6). | 22° 59.2′ N 82° 58.3′ W | **Fl.R.** period 4s | 16 **5** | 3 | STARBOARD (B) R, tower, topmark. | |
| 12542 *J 4840* | -Peninsula Juan Tomas Entrance Range, front. | 22° 59.2′ N 82° 58.4′ W | **Q.W.** | 39 **12** | 12 | Metal framework tower, red diamond daymark, white border; 33. | |
| 12542.5 *J 4841* | --Rear, 304 meters 170° from front. | 22° 59.0′ N 82° 58.4′ W | **Iso.W.** period 1.5s | 49 **15** | 12 | Metal framework tower, red diamond daymark, white border; 43. | |
| 12544 *J 4843.5* | -Piedra Gloria No. 8. | 22° 59.6′ N 82° 56.7′ W | **Fl.R.** period 6s fl. 0.5s, ec. 5.5s | 16 **5** | 3 | STARBOARD (B) R, tower, topmark. | |
| | BAHIA DEL MARIEL: | | | | | | |
| 12552 *J 4846* | -Puerto del Mariel, W. side of entrance. | 23° 01.3′ N 82° 45.6′ W | **Fl.W.** period 12s | 134 **41** | 11 | White framework tower; 102. | |
| 12556 *J 4847* | -Punta Regula Entrance Range, front. | 23° 00.9′ N 82° 45.5′ W | **Q.W.** | 23 **7** | 7 | Tower, orange rectangular daymark, white border; 16. | |
| 12560 *J 4847.1* | --Rear, 500 meters 187° from front. | 23° 00.7′ N 82° 45.6′ W | **Iso.W.** period 3s | 43 **13** | 9 | Tower, orange rectangular daymark, white border; 30. | |
| 12561 *J 4845* | -Esenada de Laza, front. | 23° 00.8′ N 82° 46.7′ W | **Q.W.** | 33 **10** | 2 | White metal tower, yellow top; 20. | |
| 12561.5 *J 4845.1* | --Rear, 230 meters 270° from front. | 23° 00.8′ N 82° 46.8′ W | **Iso.W.** period 3s | 56 **17** | 2 | White metal tower, yellow top; 16. | |
| 12562 *J 4847.6* | **Rio Santa Ana.** | 23° 03.4′ N 82° 32.5′ W | **Fl.W.** period 10s | 184 **56** | **15** | Blue water tank, blue and white columns. | |
| 12564 *J 4848* | Darsena de Barlovento. | 23° 05.6′ N 82° 29.4′ W | **Fl.W.** period 7s | 118 **36** | 10 | White framework tower on building; 26. | |
| 12565 *J 4849* | -Santa Fe. | 23° 04.9′ N 82° 30.2′ W | **Q.W.R.G.** | 16 **5** | 9 | Framework tower, white square daymark with orange diamond in center; 16. | |
| 12565.6 *J 4849.4* | --E side. No. 3. | 23° 05.1′ N 82° 30.3′ W | **Fl.G.** period 5s | 20 **6** | 3 | Green fiberglass tower, on pile. | |
| | LA HABANA (HAVANA): | | | | | | |
| 12572 *J 4854* | -Bahia Chorrera, entrance (No. 2), W. side. | 23° 08.0′ N 82° 24.7′ W | **Fl.R.** period 6s | 33 **10** | 3 | STARBOARD (B) R, tower, topmark; 26. | |
| 12576 *J 4855* | -No. 3, on mole. | 23° 07.9′ N 82° 24.7′ W | **Fl.G.** period 3s | 10 **3** | 3 | PORT (B) G, column, topmark. | |

Many of the lights on the coast of Cuba have been reported to be irregular or extinguished.

| (1) No. | (2) Name and Location | (3) Position | (4) Characteristic | (5) Height | (6) Range | (7) Structure | (8) Remarks |
|---|---|---|---|---|---|---|---|

## CUBA

| (1) No. | (2) Name and Location | (3) Position | (4) Characteristic | (5) Height | (6) Range | (7) Structure | (8) Remarks |
|---|---|---|---|---|---|---|---|
| 12580 *J 4857* | **-Castillo del Morro.** | 23° 09.0′ N 82° 21.4′ W | **Fl.(2)W.** period 15s | 144 **44** | **26** | Yellow conical tower; 82. Floodlit. | Storm signals. Aeromarine light. Reserve light range 11M. |
| 12585 *J 4858* | -Neptuno. | 23° 08.5′ N 82° 20.9′ W | **Fl.R.** period 4s | 26 **8** | 4 | STARBOARD (B) R, tower, topmark. | |
| 12590 *J 4860* | -Range, front. | 23° 08.1′ N 82° 19.7′ W | **Iso.Y.** | 59 **18** | 9 | Aluminum framework tower, on breakwater; 39. | |
| 12592 *J 4860.1* | --Rear, 480 meters 099°24′ from front. | 23° 08.1′ N 82° 19.5′ W | **Q.Y.** | 59 **18** | 9 | Aluminum framework tower; 105. | |
| 12597 *J 4859* | -Range, front. | 23° 07.9′ N 82° 19.8′ W | **Q.Y.** | 42 **13** | 10 | White framework tower, yellow diamond daymark, black border; 39. | |
| 12598 *J 4859.1* | --Rear, 300 meters 124° from front. | 23° 07.8′ N 82° 19.7′ W | **Iso.Y.** period 6s | 62 **19** | 10 | White framework tower, yellow diamond daymark, black border; 59. | |
| 12600 *J 4862* | Rio Cojimar. | 23° 10.0′ N 82° 17.6′ W | **Fl.G.** period 5s | 30 **9** | 3 | PORT (B) G, column, topmark; 30. | |
| 12612 *J 4867* | -Rio Jaruco, W. side of entrance. | 23° 10.8′ N 82° 00.7′ W | **Fl.W.** period 10s | 56 **17** | 11 | White cylindrical fiberglass tower, red bands; 33. | |
| 12613 *J 4867.5* | **Canasi.** | 23° 08.7′ N 81° 47.6′ W | **Fl.W.** period 7s fl. 1s, ec. 6s | 410 **125** | **15** | White fiberglass tower, red bands; 26. | |
| 12616 *J 4868* | Punta Seboruco. | 23° 09.2′ N 81° 36.4′ W | **Fl.W.** period 15s fl. 1s, ec. 14s | 115 **35** | 10 | White round concrete tower, red bands; 108. | |
| 12620 *J 4872* | **Punta Maya.** | 23° 05.6′ N 81° 28.5′ W | **Fl.W.** period 8s fl. 1s, ec. 7s | 112 **34** | **17** | White round concrete tower; 105. | F.W. on wharf, N. side of port. Reserve light range 7M. |
| | CANALIZO PASO MALO: | | | | | | |
| 12628 *J 4875* | -Kawama W. Jetty. | 23° 08.0′ N 81° 18.8′ W | **Fl.R.** period 4s fl. 0.4s, ec. 3.6s | 23 **7** | 3 | STARBOARD (B) R, column, topmark; 20. | |
| 12632 *J 4875.2* | --E. Jetty. | 23° 08.0′ N 81° 18.7′ W | **Fl.G.** period 3s fl. 0.4s, ec. 2.6s | 23 **7** | 3 | PORT (B) G, column, topmark; 20. | |
| 12636 *J 4875.4* | -Range, front. | 23° 07.8′ N 81° 18.6′ W | **Q.W.** | 9 **3** | 10 | White column, square base; 7. | |
| 12640 *J 4875.41* | --Rear, 108 meters 152°36′ from front. | 23° 07.7′ N 81° 18.6′ W | **Iso.W.** period 6s | 23 **7** | 10 | White column, square base; 20. | |
| 12641 *J 4875.6* | Laguna de Paso Malo, No. 3. | 23° 07.8′ N 81° 18.3′ W | **Fl.G.** period 3s fl. 0.3s, ec. 2.7s | 13 **4** | 3 | PORT (B) G, tower, topmark. | |
| 12642 *J 4875.7* | -No. 6. | 23° 07.8′ N 81° 18.1′ W | **Fl.R.** period 6s fl. 0.5s, ec. 5.5s | 13 **4** | 3 | STARBOARD (B) R, tower, topmark. | |
| 12643 *J 4875.8* | -No. 9. | 23° 07.9′ N 81° 17.7′ W | **Fl.G.** period 5s fl. 0.5s, ec. 4.5s | 13 **4** | 3 | PORT (B) G, tower, topmark. | |
| 12644.5 *J 4875.9* | -No. 11. | 23° 07.9′ N 81° 17.6′ W | **Fl.G.** period 3s fl. 0.3s, ec. 2.7s | 13 **4** | 3 | PORT (B) G, tower, topmark. | |
| 12645 *J 4876.2* | -No. 21. | 23° 07.9′ N 81° 16.7′ W | **Fl.G.** period 3s fl. 0.3s, ec. 2.7s | 13 **4** | 3 | PORT (B) G, tower, topmark. | |

Many of the lights on the coast of Cuba have been reported to be irregular or extinguished.

| (1)<br>No. | (2)<br>Name and Location | (3)<br>Position | (4)<br>Characteristic | (5)<br>Height | (6)<br>Range | (7)<br>Structure | (8)<br>Remarks |
|---|---|---|---|---|---|---|---|
| | | | **CUBA** | | | | |
| 12646<br>*J 4876.3* | -No. 22. | 23° 07.8′ N<br>81° 16.7′ W | **Fl.R.**<br>period 4s<br>fl. 0.3s, ec. 3.7s | 13<br>**4** | 3 | STARBOARD (B)<br>R, tower, topmark. | |
| 12647<br>*J 4877* | Canal Cueva de Muerto, No. 26. | 23° 07.9′ N<br>81° 16.5′ W | **Fl.R.**<br>period 6s | 20<br>**6** | 3 | STARBOARD (B)<br>R, tower, topmark. | |
| 12647.5<br>*J 4877.2* | -No. 27. | 23° 08.2′ N<br>81° 16.1′ W | **Fl.G.**<br>period 5s | 20<br>**6** | 3 | PORT (B)<br>G, tower, topmark. | |
| | BAHIA DE CARDENAS: | | | | | | |
| 12648<br>*J 4879* | -Cayo Piedras, entrance to bay. | 23° 14.6′ N<br>81° 07.2′ W | **Fl.W.**<br>period 10s<br>fl. 1.5s, ec. 8.5s | 79<br>**24** | 10 | White round masonry tower; 62. | Reserve light range 8M. |
| 12656<br>*J 4880* | Cayo Monito. | 23° 13.8′ N<br>81° 08.5′ W | **Fl.(2)W.**<br>period 10s | 20<br>**6** | 5 | ISOLATED DANGER<br>BRB, tower, topmark. | |
| 12660<br>*J 4881* | -Cayo Diana, S. side. | 23° 09.9′ N<br>81° 06.2′ W | **Fl.W.**<br>period 8s | 49<br>**15** | 10 | White framework tower; 39. | |
| 12660.5<br>*J 4881.1* | -Hicacos. | 23° 09.0′ N<br>81° 07.7′ W | **Fl.(2)W.**<br>period 10s | 52<br>**16** | 4 | ISOLATED DANGER<br>BRB, tower, topmark. | |
| 12661<br>*J 4881.3* | -No. 2. | 23° 10.8′ N<br>81° 07.7′ W | **Fl.R.**<br>period 6s | 13<br>**4** | 3 | STARBOARD (B)<br>R, tower, topmark. | |
| 12663 | -No. 6. | 23° 11.4′ N<br>81° 07.8′ W | **Fl.R.**<br>period 4s | 13<br>**4** | 2 | Red concrete tower on square base, triangular daymark; 13. | |
| 12664<br>*J 4882* | -Channel Beacon 4A, Punta Gorda. | 23° 10.0′ N<br>81° 10.3′ W | **Fl.R.**<br>period 4s | 13<br>**4** | 3 | STARBOARD (B)<br>R, tower, topmark. | |
| 12668<br>*J 4883* | --No. 6A. | 23° 09.9′ N<br>81° 11.2′ W | **Fl.R.**<br>period 6s<br>fl. 0.5s, ec. 5.5s | 13<br>**4** | 3 | STARBOARD (B)<br>R, tower, topmark. | |
| 12668.1<br>*J 4883.7* | -Cupey No. 1. | 23° 06.8′ N<br>81° 11.7′ W | **Fl.Y.**<br>period 7s | 10<br>**3** | 3 | SPECIAL<br>Y, tower, "X" topmark. | |
| 12672<br>*J 4886* | Cayo Cruz del Padre. | 23° 16.9′ N<br>80° 53.9′ W | **Fl.W.**<br>period 7s<br>fl. 1s, ec. 6s | 82<br>**25** | 12 | White concrete tower, 3 balconies, square base; 59. | |
| 12676<br>*J 4888* | **Cayo Bahia de Cadiz.** | 23° 12.3′ N<br>80° 28.9′ W | **Fl.(3)W.**<br>period 15s | 177<br>**54** | **21** | White truncated pyramidal tower, black stripes; 161. | Reserve light range 7M. |
| | SAGUA LA GRANDE: | | | | | | |
| 12684<br>*J 4894* | -Cayo Hicacal, on Punta de la Rancheria. | 23° 04.3′ N<br>80° 05.2′ W | **Fl.W.**<br>period 8s | 36<br>**11** | 7 | White framework tower; 26. | |
| 12688<br>*J 4896* | -Cayo del Cristo, on Punta de los Practicos. | 23° 02.1′ N<br>79° 59.4′ W | **Fl.W.**<br>period 10s<br>fl. 1s, ec. 9s | 50<br>**15** | 10 | White framework tower; 39. | |
| 12689<br>*J 4896.6* | -Rio Sagua Entrance, E. side. | 22° 56.8′ N<br>80° 00.0′ W | **Fl.G.**<br>period 3s<br>fl. 0.5s, ec. 2.5s | 13<br>**4** | 3 | PORT (B)<br>G, tower, topmark. | |
| 12696<br>*J 4897.3* | -Boca de Jutias. | 22° 58.0′ N<br>79° 51.9′ W | **Fl.G.**<br>period 5s<br>fl. 0.5s, ec. 4.5s | 13<br>**4** | 3 | PORT (B)<br>G, tower, topmark. | |
| 12700<br>*J 4897.4* | -Canal de Cilindrin. | 22° 56.4′ N<br>79° 49.0′ W | **Fl.G.**<br>period 5s<br>fl. 0.5s, ec. 4.5s | 13<br>**4** | 3 | PORT (B)<br>G, tower, topmark. | |
| 12712<br>*J 4897.6* | -Cayo La Vela. | 22° 56.7′ N<br>79° 45.4′ W | **Fl.W.**<br>period 12s | 39<br>**12** | 10 | White round metal tower; 30. | |

Many of the lights on the coast of Cuba have been reported to be irregular or extinguished.

| (1) No. | (2) Name and Location | (3) Position | (4) Characteristic | (5) Height | (6) Range | (7) Structure | (8) Remarks |
|---|---|---|---|---|---|---|---|

## CUBA

| (1) No. | (2) Name and Location | (3) Position | (4) Characteristic | (5) Height | (6) Range | (7) Structure | (8) Remarks |
|---|---|---|---|---|---|---|---|
| 12716 *J 4900* | -Cayo Fragoso, NW. end. | 22° 48.5′ N 79° 34.7′ W | **Fl.W.** period 15s fl. 1s, ec. 14s | 68 **21** | 10 | White framework tower; 59. | |
| 12720 *J 4899* | -No. 2. | 22° 44.7′ N 79° 36.9′ W | **Fl.R.** period 6s fl. 0.5s, ec. 5.5s | 13 **4** | 3 | STARBOARD (B) R, tower, topmark. | |
| 12728 *J 4899.3* | -No. 5. | 22° 41.0′ N 79° 35.0′ W | **Fl.G.** period 3s fl. 0.3s, ec. 2.7s | 13 **4** | 3 | PORT (B) G, tower, topmark. | |
| 12732 *J 4899.5* | -No. 8. | 22° 40.2′ N 79° 34.2′ W | **Fl.R.** period 4s fl. 0.5s, ec. 3.5s | 13 **4** | 3 | STARBOARD (B) R, tower, topmark. | |
| 12736 *J 4902* | Cayo Frances, W. end, at entrance to Caibarien. | 22° 38.5′ N 79° 13.8′ W | **Fl.W.** period 10s fl. 1s, ec. 9s | 33 **10** | 9 | White concrete tower; 30. | |
| 12746 *J 4904* | -No. 4. | 22° 35.8′ N 79° 17.3′ W | **Fl.R.** period 4s | 16 **5** | 3 | STARBOARD (B) R, tower, topmark. | |
| 12748 *J 4905* | -No. 6. | 22° 34.5′ N 79° 18.4′ W | **Fl.R.** period 6s | 16 **5** | 3 | STARBOARD (B) R, tower, topmark. | |
| 12752 *J 4906* | -No. 8. | 22° 33.5′ N 79° 22.8′ W | **Fl.R.** period 4s | 16 **5** | 3 | STARBOARD (B) R, tower, topmark. | |
| 12756 *J 4908* | -Punta Brava, No. 9. | 22° 32.0′ N 79° 26.8′ W | **Fl.G.** period 5s | 33 **10** | 3 | PORT (B) G, tower, topmark; 26. | |
| 12758.2 *J 4908.08* | -Canal del Refugio, E. No. 1. | 22° 31.9′ N 79° 27.5′ W | **Fl.G.** period 5s | 13 **4** | 3 | PORT (B) G, tower, topmark. | |
| 12759 *J 4909* | Canal de las Piraguas. | 22° 37.0′ N 79° 13.2′ W | **Fl.R.** period 4s | 16 **5** | 3 | STARBOARD (B) R, tower, topmark. | |
| 12772 *J 4913* | Bahia de Buenavista, No. 6. | 22° 27.3′ N 78° 56.7′ W | **Fl.R.** period 4s fl. 0.5s, ec. 3.5s | 16 **5** | 3 | STARBOARD (B) R, tower, topmark. | |
| 12776 *J 4915* | Cayo Borracho, W. end. | 22° 38.9′ N 79° 09.4′ W | **Fl.G.** period 5s | 33 **10** | 3 | PORT (B) G, tower, topmark. | |
| 12780 *J 4916* | **Cayo Caiman Grande de Santa Maria.** | 22° 41.1′ N 78° 53.0′ W | **Fl.W.** period 5s | 158 **48** | **28** | White conical tower, red bands; 105. | Aeromarine light. Reserve light range 7M. |
| 12784 *J 4914* | Paso Manuy, W. beacon. | 22° 24.8′ N 78° 41.4′ W | **Fl.R.** period 6s fl. 0.3s, ec. 5.7s | 13 **4** | 3 | STARBOARD (B) R, tower, topmark. | |
| 12788 *J 4917* | Cayo Jaula. | 22° 34.3′ N 78° 30.9′ W | **Fl.W.** period 10s fl. 1s, ec. 9s | 68 **21** | 10 | White framework tower; 59. | |
| 12792 *J 4920* | Boco De Manati. | 22° 15.2′ N 78° 29.8′ W | **Fl.G.** period 5s | 13 **4** | 3 | PORT (B) G, tower, topmark. | |
| 12800 *J 4918* | **Cayo Paredon Grande.** | 22° 29.0′ N 78° 09.9′ W | **Fl.(3)W.** period 15s | 157 **48** | **27** | Black and yellow checkered truncated pyramidal tower; 135. | Aeromarine light. Reserve light range 7M. |
| 12804 *J 4922* | Cayo Confites. | 22° 11.3′ N 77° 39.7′ W | **Fl.W.** period 7.5s fl. 1s, ec. 6.5s | 75 **23** | 12 | White metal framework tower; 66. | |
| 12806 *J 4923* | -No. 2. | 22° 10.3′ N 77° 39.2′ W | **Fl.R.** period 6s | 13 **4** | 3 | STARBOARD (B) R, tower, topmark. | |
| 12806.5 *J 4923.5* | -No. 3. | 22° 10.2′ N 77° 38.6′ W | **Fl.G.** period 5s | 13 **4** | 3 | PORT (B) G, tower, topmark. | |
| 12807 *J 4924* | -Confites. | 22° 08.8′ N 77° 41.7′ W | **Fl.Y.** period 7s | 13 **4** | 3 | SPECIAL Y, tower, "X" topmark. | |

Many of the lights on the coast of Cuba have been reported to be irregular or extinguished.

| (1) No. | (2) Name and Location | (3) Position | (4) Characteristic | (5) Height | (6) Range | (7) Structure | (8) Remarks |
|---|---|---|---|---|---|---|---|

## CUBA

BAHIA DE NUEVITAS:

| (1) No. | (2) Name and Location | (3) Position | (4) Characteristic | (5) Height | (6) Range | (7) Structure | (8) Remarks |
|---|---|---|---|---|---|---|---|
| 12808 *J 4926* | **-Punta Maternillos.** | 21° 39.7′ N 77° 08.4′ W | **Fl.W.** period 15s | 174 **53** | **23** | White conical masonry tower; 171. | Reserve light range 7M. |
| 12812 *J 4928* | -Punta Practicos, E. side of entrance. | 21° 36.1′ N 77° 05.7′ W | **Fl.W.** period 10s fl. 1s, ec. 9s | 33 **10** | 6 | White concrete tower; 30. | |
| 12816 *J 4930* | -Entrance Range, front. | 21° 35.5′ N 77° 06.3′ W | **Q.W.** | 6 **2** | 8 | Wall, white diamond daymark, black border; 7. | |
| 12820 *J 4930.1* | --Rear, 170 meters 185°36′ from front. | 21° 35.3′ N 77° 06.4′ W | **Iso.W.** period 3s | 23 **7** | 8 | Wall, white diamond daymark, black border; 16. | |
| 12824 *J 4931* | -Punta Salteadores Beacon No. 3. | 21° 35.8′ N 77° 06.2′ W | **Fl.G.** period 3s | 13 **4** | 3 | PORT (B) G, column, topmark. | |
| 12828 *J 4932* | -Pena Redonda Beacon 4. | 21° 35.7′ N 77° 06.4′ W | **Fl.R.** period 4s | 16 **5** | 3 | STARBOARD (B) R, column, topmark. | |
| 12832 *J 4933* | -Playa Chuchu Range, front. | 21° 35.6′ N 77° 06.9′ W | **Q.W.** | 10 **3** | 8 | Wall, white diamond daymark, black border; 20. | |
| 12836 *J 4933.1* | --Rear, 195 meters 000°54′ from front. | 21° 35.7′ N 77° 06.9′ W | **Iso.W.** period 3s | 33 **10** | 8 | Concrete column, white diamond daymark, black border; 33. | |
| 12840 *J 4934* | -Las Calabazas Range, front. | 21° 33.9′ N 77° 06.9′ W | **Q.W.** | 23 **7** | 8 | Wall, white diamond daymark, black border; 20. | |
| 12844 *J 4934.1* | --Rear, 190 meters 180°54′ from front. | 21° 33.9′ N 77° 06.9′ W | **Iso.W.** period 3s | 33 **10** | 8 | Wall, white diamond daymark, black border; 30. | |
| 12848 *J 4936* | -Bajo del Medio Range, front. | 21° 34.2′ N 77° 08.3′ W | **Q.W.** | 20 **6** | 8 | Wall, white diamond daymark, black border; 13. | |
| 12852 *J 4936.1* | --Rear, 265 meters 269°30′ from front. | 21° 34.2′ N 77° 08.5′ W | **Iso.W.** period 3s | 33 **10** | 8 | Square column, white diamond daymark, black border; 30. | |
| 12856 *J 4939* | -Cayo Cayita Range, common front. | 21° 32.8′ N 77° 08.1′ W | **Q.W.** | 16 **5** | 8 | Wall, white diamond daymark, black border; 13. | |
| 12860 *J 4938.9* | --Rear, 290 meters 179°30′ from common front. | 21° 32.7′ N 77° 08.1′ W | **Iso.W.** period 3s | 23 **7** | 8 | Square column on pile, white diamond daymark, black border; 23. | |
| 12864 *J 4939.1* | --Rear, 225 meters 057°48′ from common front. | 21° 32.9′ N 77° 07.9′ W | **Iso.W.** period 3s | 33 **10** | 8 | Square column, white diamond daymark, black border; 30. | |
| 12872 *J 4942* | Bahia de Manati, Punta Roma. | 21° 23.5′ N 76° 48.9′ W | **Fl.W.** period 12s | 43 **13** | 10 | White conical tower; 33. | |
| 12884 *J 4944* | Puerto Padre, Punta Masterlero. | 21° 16.5′ N 76° 32.4′ W | **Fl.W.** period 8s fl. 1s, ec. 7s | 50 **15** | 10 | White conical truncated tower; 33. | |
| 12886 *J 4945* | -No. 20. | 21° 13.0′ N 76° 34.4′ W | **Fl.R.** period 6s | 16 **5** | 3 | STARBOARD (B) R, tower, topmark. | |
| 12892 *J 4946* | Punta Piedra del Mangle. | 21° 15.1′ N 76° 18.8′ W | **Fl.W.** period 10s fl. 1s, ec. 9s | 76 **23** | 10 | White round fiberglass tower, red bands; 59. | |
| 12894 *J 4948* | Punta Rasa. | 21° 09.0′ N 76° 07.8′ W | **Fl.W.** period 15s fl. 1s, ec. 14s | 112 **34** | 12 | White round tower, red bands; 98. | |
| 12896 *J 4950* | Puerto Gibara. | 21° 06.6′ N 76° 06.7′ W | **Fl.G.** period 5s fl. 1s, ec. 4s | 26 **8** | 3 | PORT (B) G, tower, topmark. | |
| 12900 *J 4952* | Puerto de Vita. | 21° 05.8′ N 75° 57.6′ W | **Fl.W.** period 10s fl. 1s, ec. 9s | 115 **35** | 10 | White round concrete tower; 102. | |

Many of the lights on the coast of Cuba have been reported to be irregular or extinguished.

| (1) No. | (2) Name and Location | (3) Position | (4) Characteristic | (5) Height | (6) Range | (7) Structure | (8) Remarks |
|---|---|---|---|---|---|---|---|
| | | | **CUBA** | | | | |
| 12904 *J 4954* | Bahia Naranjo. | 21° 06.8′ N 75° 52.6′ W | **Fl.W.** period 6s | 59 **18** | 6 | White framework tower; 26. | |
| 12908 *J 4956* | Bahia Sama. | 21° 07.6′ N 75° 46.0′ W | **Fl.W.** period 8s | 98 **30** | 7 | White framework tower; 30. | |
| 12912 *J 4958* | **Cabo Lucrecia.** | 21° 04.3′ N 75° 37.3′ W | **Fl.W.** period 5s | 132 **40** | **25** | White round masonry tower, octagonal base; 121. | Aeromarine light. Reserve light range 7M. |
| 12916 *J 4960* | Bahia de Banes, on Caracolillo Beach, S. side of entrance. | 20° 52.6′ N 75° 39.7′ W | **Fl.W.** period 8s fl. 1s, ec. 7s | 43 **13** | 7 | White truncated conical tower; 33. | |
| | BAHIA DE NIPE: | | | | | | |
| 12920 *J 4962* | -Punta Mayari, E. side of entrance. | 20° 47.4′ N 75° 31.5′ W | **Fl.W.** period 6s fl. 1s, ec. 5s | 115 **35** | 10 | White framework tower; 102. | |
| 12924 *J 4964* | -Entrance Range, front. | 20° 46.3′ N 75° 32.8′ W | **Q.W.** | 25 **8** | 5 | Wall, orange diamond daymark; 7. | |
| 12928 *J 4964.1* | --Rear, 230 meters 201°36′ from front. | 20° 46.0′ N 75° 33.0′ W | **Fl.W.** period 4s fl. 1.1s, ec. 2.9s | 90 **27** | 8 | Wall, orange diamond daymark; 7. | |
| 12940 *J 4964.6* | -Bajo La Estrella, No. 9. | 20° 47.5′ N 75° 36.7′ W | **Fl.G.** period 3s | 16 **5** | 3 | PORT (B) G, beacon, topmark. | |
| 12942 *J 4965* | -Bajo Salina Grande S. end, No. 10. | 20° 48.6′ N 75° 41.8′ W | **Fl.R.** period 6s | 13 **4** | 3 | STARBOARD (B) R, beacon, topmark. | |
| | -Antilla Channel: | | | | | | |
| 12944 *J 4966* | --Lengua Tierra No. 11. | 20° 48.7′ N 75° 42.6′ W | **Fl.G.** period 5s | 13 **4** | 3 | PORT (B) G, beacon, topmark. | |
| 12945 *J 4967* | --Bajo Manati, S. end, No. 12. | 20° 49.0′ N 75° 43.2′ W | **Fl.R.** period 6s | 13 **4** | 3 | STARBOARD (B) R, beacon, topmark. | |
| 12945.2 *J 4968* | --Bajo Lengua de Tierra N. end No. 13. | 20° 48.9′ N 75° 43.8′ W | **Fl.G.** period 5s | 13 **4** | 3 | PORT (B) G, beacon, topmark. | |
| 12946 *J 4969* | --Bajo Marabella, S. end, No. 14. | 20° 49.1′ N 75° 43.8′ W | **Fl.R.** period 4s | 13 **4** | 3 | STARBOARD (B) R, beacon, topmark. | |
| 12946.2 *J 4969.4* | --No. 15. | 20° 48.9′ N 75° 44.8′ W | **Fl.G.** period 5s | 13 **4** | 3 | PORT (B) G, beacon, topmark. | |
| 12947 *J 4970* | --No. 17. | 20° 49.1′ N 75° 45.2′ W | **Fl.G.** period 3s | 13 **4** | 3 | PORT (B) G, beacon, topmark. | |
| 12947.2 *J 4971* | -Canal A beacon, No. 1A. | 20° 46.0′ N 75° 34.7′ W | **Fl.G.** period 5s | 13 **4** | 3 | PORT (B) G, beacon, topmark. | |
| 12947.4 *J 4972* | --Bajo Planaca No. 3A. | 20° 44.7′ N 75° 34.6′ W | **Fl.G.** period 5s | 13 **4** | 3 | PORT (B) G, beacon, topmark. | |
| 12948 *J 4975* | Punta Liberal. | 20° 44.7′ N 75° 28.9′ W | **Fl.W.** period 10s | 56 **17** | 7 | White fiberglass tower, red bands; 33. | |
| 12948.52 *J 4980.53* | -No. 19. | 20° 43.4′ N 75° 29.8′ W | **Fl.G.** period 5s | 13 **4** | 3 | PORT (B) G, beacon, topmark. | |
| 12948.54 *J 4980.6* | -No. 22. | 20° 43.6′ N 75° 30.4′ W | **Fl.R.** period 4s | 13 **4** | 3 | STARBOARD (B) R, beacon, topmark. | |
| 12948.56 *J 4980.63* | -No. 23. | 20° 43.4′ N 75° 30.7′ W | **Fl.G.** period 5s | 13 **4** | 3 | PORT (B) G, beacon, topmark. | |
| 12948.62 *J 4981* | -No. 29. | 20° 43.1′ N 75° 32.2′ W | **Fl.G.** period 3s | 13 **4** | 3 | PORT (B) G, beacon, topmark. | |

Many of the lights on the coast of Cuba have been reported to be irregular or extinguished.

| (1) No. | (2) Name and Location | (3) Position | (4) Characteristic | (5) Height | (6) Range | (7) Structure | (8) Remarks |
|---|---|---|---|---|---|---|---|

## CUBA

| (1) No. | (2) Name and Location | (3) Position | (4) Characteristic | (5) Height | (6) Range | (7) Structure | (8) Remarks |
|---|---|---|---|---|---|---|---|
| 12948.64<br>*J 4981.2* | -No. 32. | 20° 43.2´ N<br>75° 32.9´ W | **Fl.R.**<br>period 4s | 13<br>**4** | 3 | STARBOARD (B)<br>R, beacon, topmark. | |
| 12948.7<br>*J 4984* | -Cayo Grande. | 20° 43.1´ N<br>75° 29.4´ W | **Fl.R.**<br>period 4s | 13<br>**4** | 3 | STARBOARD (B)<br>R, beacon, topmark. | |
| | BAHIA DE SAGUA DE TANAMO: | | | | | | |
| 12952<br>*J 4988* | -Punta Barlovento, E. point of entrance. | 20° 43.2´ N<br>75° 19.1´ W | **Fl.W.**<br>period 8s | 43<br>**13** | 10 | White framework tower; 26. | |
| 12956<br>*J 4990* | -Entrance Range, front. | 20° 42.6´ N<br>75° 19.5´ W | **Q.W.** | 22<br>**7** | 5 | Wall, orange diamond daymark; 7. | |
| 12960<br>*J 4990.1* | --Rear, 210 meters 180° from front. | 20° 42.5´ N<br>75° 19.5´ W | **Iso.W.**<br>period 6s | 43<br>**13** | 10 | Wall, orange diamond daymark; 7. | |
| 12964<br>*J 4992* | -No. 3, W. Point. | 20° 42.6´ N<br>75° 19.8´ W | **Fl.G.**<br>period 3s<br>fl. 0.3s, ec. 2.7s | 13<br>**4** | 3 | PORT (B)<br>G, beacon, topmark. | |
| 12968<br>*J 4993* | -No. 5, Cayo Juanillo, W. side. | 20° 42.3´ N<br>75° 20.2´ W | **Fl.G.**<br>period 3s | 13<br>**4** | 3 | PORT (B)<br>G, beacon, topmark. | |
| 12972<br>*J 4994* | -No. 8, Cayo Alto, E. side. | 20° 41.8´ N<br>75° 20.1´ W | **Fl.R.**<br>period 6s<br>fl. 0.4s, ec. 5.6s | 13<br>**4** | 3 | STARBOARD (B)<br>R, beacon, topmark. | |
| 12976<br>*J 4995* | -No. 11, Cayo Medio, W. side. | 20° 41.1´ N<br>75° 19.3´ W | **Fl.G.**<br>period 3s<br>fl. 0.3s, ec. 2.7s | 13<br>**4** | 3 | PORT (B)<br>G, beacon, topmark. | |
| 12978<br>*J 4996* | -No. 12, Punta Gorda. | 20° 41.0´ N<br>75° 19.9´ W | **Fl.R.**<br>period 4s | 13<br>**4** | 3 | STARBOARD (B)<br>R, beacon, topmark. | |
| | PUERTO CAYO MOA: | | | | | | |
| 12980<br>*J 5012* | -Cayo Moa Grande. | 20° 41.7´ N<br>74° 54.4´ W | **Fl.W.**<br>period 10s<br>fl. 1s, ec. 9s | 46<br>**14** | 12 | White framework tower; 39. | |
| 12988<br>*J 5013* | -Punta La Fabrica Range, front. | 20° 40.0´ N<br>74° 53.0´ W | **Q.W.** | 39<br>**12** | 8 | White framework tower on piles, orange diamond daymark; 33. | |
| 12992<br>*J 5013.1* | --Rear, 865 meters 209° from front. | 20° 39.6´ N<br>74° 53.2´ W | **Iso.W.**<br>period 6s | 72<br>**22** | 8 | White concrete post, orange diamond daymark; 69. | |
| 12996<br>*J 5015.5* | Punta Guarico. | 20° 37.1´ N<br>74° 43.9´ W | **Fl.W.**<br>period 6s<br>fl. 1s, ec. 5s | 37<br>**11** | 7 | White truncated conical tower; 33. | |
| 13000<br>*J 5016* | Bahia de Baracoa, Punta Rama, SW. side. | 20° 20.7´ N<br>74° 28.5´ W | **Fl.W.**<br>period 6s | 23<br>**7** | 10 | White fiberglass tower; 10. | |
| 13008<br>*J 5018* | **Punta Maisi.** | 20° 14.5´ N<br>74° 08.8´ W | **Fl.W.**<br>period 5s | 121<br>**37** | **27** | White conical masonry tower, dwelling; 102. | Reserve light range 7M. |
| 13012<br>*J 5020* | Punta Caleta. | 20° 04.0´ N<br>74° 17.8´ W | **Fl.W.**<br>period 10s<br>fl. 1s, ec. 9s | 149<br>**45** | 10 | White framework tower; 98. | |
| 13016<br>*J 5021* | Bahia de Baitiquiri, N. | 20° 01.5´ N<br>74° 51.1´ W | **Fl.W.**<br>period 6s | 30<br>**9** | 8 | White framework tower; 26. | |
| 13017<br>*J 5022.5* | Puerto Escondido. | 19° 54.3´ N<br>75° 03.4´ W | **Fl.W.**<br>period 5s | 66<br>**20** | 6 | White metal post. | |

Many of the lights on the coast of Cuba have been reported to be irregular or extinguished.

| (1) No. | (2) Name and Location | (3) Position | (4) Characteristic | (5) Height | (6) Range | (7) Structure | (8) Remarks |
|---|---|---|---|---|---|---|---|
| | | | **CUBA** | | | | |
| | GUANTANAMO BAY: | | | | | | |
| 13020 *J 5024* | -Windward Point. | 19° 53.7′ N 75° 09.6′ W | **Fl.W.** period 6s | 377 **115** | 9 | Framework tower. | |
| 13028 *J 5026.1* | -Hicacal Beach. | 19° 56.7′ N 75° 09.8′ W | **Fl.W.** period 2.5s | 40 **12** | 7 | Framework tower, black and white checkered diamond daymark. | |
| 13032 *J 5025* | -Leeward Point AVIATION LIGHT. | 19° 54.6′ N 75° 12.5′ W | **Al.Fl.W.G.** | | | | |
| 13033.4 *J 5029* | -No 5. | 19° 54.7′ N 75° 11.7′ W | **Fl.G.** period 2.5s | 16 **5** | 3 | Pile, green square daymark. | |
| 13036 *J 5032* | -Fisherman Point. | 19° 55.2′ N 75° 09.7′ W | **Fl.W.** period 4s | 30 **9** | 5 | Framework tower, pyramidal base, black and white diamond daymark. | Marks Hicacal Range exit point. Various lights mark channel in cove S. of Deer Point. F.R. shown at each end of fuel berth N. of Deer Point. |
| 13040 *J 5032.2* | -Corinaso Point. | 19° 55.1′ N 75° 09.3′ W | **Fl.R.** period 6s | 42 **13** | 5 | Framework tower, black and white checkered diamond daymark. | |
| 13044 *J 5033* | -McCalla Hill. | 19° 55.0′ N 75° 09.6′ W | **F.R.** | 175 **53** | | | Private light. |
| 13048 *J 5034* | -Radio Point, No. 1. | 19° 55.3′ N 75° 09.0′ W | **Fl.G.** period 4s fl. 0.4s, ec. 3.6s | 15 **5** | 5 | Pile, green square daymark. | |
| 13052 *J 5034.1* | --No. 2. | 19° 55.4′ N 75° 08.9′ W | **Q.R.** | 14 **4** | 3 | Pile, red triangular daymark point up. | |
| 13056 *J 5034.3* | --No. 4. | 19° 55.3′ N 75° 08.8′ W | **Fl.R.** period 4s fl. 0.4s, ec. 3.6s | 11 **3** | 3 | Piles, red triangular daymark point up. | |
| 13064 *J 5035* | -Deer Point, No. 1. | 19° 55.5′ N 75° 08.8′ W | **Fl.G.** period 4s fl. 0.4s, ec. 3.6s | 10 **3** | 4 | Piles, green square daymark. | |
| 13068 *J 5035.2* | --No. 3. | 19° 55.4′ N 75° 08.8′ W | **Q.G.** | 12 **4** | 3 | Piles, green square daymark. | |
| 13072 *J 5035.4* | --No. 5. | 19° 55.4′ N 75° 08.7′ W | **Fl.G.** period 4s fl. 0.4s, ec. 3.6s | 14 **4** | 5 | Dolphin, green square daymark. | |
| 13076 *J 5035.6* | -Junction DP. | 19° 55.3′ N 75° 08.7′ W | **Fl.(2+1)R.** period 6s | 13 **4** | 3 | PREFERRED CHANNEL (B) RGR, pile. | |
| 13080 *J 5035.8* | -Evans Point No. 8. | 19° 55.3′ N 75° 08.6′ W | **Fl.R.** period 4s fl. 0.4s, ec. 3.6s | 10 **3** | 3 | Pile, red triangular daymark point up. | |
| 13082 *J 5035.9* | -Mud Island No. 1. | 19° 55.2′ N 75° 08.7′ W | **Fl.G.** period 6s | 7 **2** | 5 | Pile, green square daymark. | |
| 13084 *J 5036* | -Marine Site Two Channel No. 1. | 19° 55.9′ N 75° 08.1′ W | **Fl.G.** period 4s fl. 0.4s, ec. 3.6s | 10 **3** | 5 | Dolphin, green square daymark. | |
| 13088 *J 5036.3* | -Marine Boat Channel No. 2, 457 meters S. of Caravela Point. | 19° 55.9′ N 75° 08.1′ W | **Fl.R.** period 4s fl. 0.4s, ec. 3.6s | 13 **4** | 3 | Pile, red triangular daymark point up. | |
| 13092 *J 5039* | -Granadillo Point W., No. 2. | 19° 56.8′ N 75° 07.5′ W | **Fl.R.** period 4s fl. 0.4s, ec. 3.6s | 13 **4** | 3 | Dolphin, red triangular daymark point up. | |
| 13096 *J 5038* | -Granadillo Bay, Cayo Tomate CT. | 19° 56.9′ N 75° 07.9′ W | **Fl.(2+1)R.** period 6s | 14 **4** | 5 | PREFERRED CHANNEL (B) RGR, dolphin. | |

Many of the lights on the coast of Cuba have been reported to be irregular or extinguished.

| (1)<br>No. | (2)<br>Name and Location | (3)<br>Position | (4)<br>Characteristic | (5)<br>Height | (6)<br>Range | (7)<br>Structure | (8)<br>Remarks |
|---|---|---|---|---|---|---|---|

## CUBA

| (1)<br>No. | (2)<br>Name and Location | (3)<br>Position | (4)<br>Characteristic | (5)<br>Height | (6)<br>Range | (7)<br>Structure | (8)<br>Remarks |
|---|---|---|---|---|---|---|---|
| 13100<br>*J 5036.6* | -Hospital Cay, Watergate channel No. 2. | 19° 56.6′ N<br>75° 08.8′ W | **Q.R.** | 13<br>**4** | 4 | Pile, red triangular daymark point up. | |
| 13104<br>*J 5037* | --No. 4. | 19° 57.1′ N<br>75° 08.7′ W | **Fl.R.**<br>period 4s | 11<br>**3** | 3 | Pile, red triangular daymark point up. | |
| 13108<br>*J 5041* | -Palma Point Shoal, No. 5. | 19° 57.8′ N<br>75° 08.9′ W | **Fl.G.**<br>period 4s | 14<br>**4** | 5 | Dolphin, green square daymark. | |
| 13110<br>*J 5043* | --Cayo Brook. | 19° 59.2′ N<br>75° 07.8′ W | **Fl.(2+1)G.**<br>period 10s | 14<br>**4** | 4 | PREFERRED CHANNEL (B)<br>GRG, beacon, topmark. | |
| 13112<br>*J 5046* | **Morro de Cuba.** | 19° 58.1′ N<br>75° 52.1′ W | **Fl.(2)W.**<br>period 10s | 269<br>**82** | **27** | White round concrete tower; 43. | Aeromarine light.<br>Reserve light range 7M. |
| | BAHIA DE SANTIAGO DE CUBA: | | | | | | |
| 13154<br>*J 5048* | **-Aserradero.** | 19° 59.1′ N<br>76° 10.4′ W | **Fl.W.**<br>period 19s | 197<br>**60** | 10 | White framework tower, daymark; 66. | |
| 13164<br>*J 5052* | Puerto Pilon Range, front. | 19° 54.0′ N<br>77° 17.3′ W | **Q.W.** | 16<br>**5** | 5 | Black framework tower, white diamond daymark, yellow border; 6. | |
| 13168<br>*J 5052.1* | -Rear, on shore 1.5 km. 355°30′ from front. | 19° 54.8′ N<br>77° 17.4′ W | **Fl.W.**<br>period 10s | 26<br>**8** | 10 | White framework tower, white diamond daymark, yellow border; 23. | |
| 13169<br>*J 5052.4* | -Bajo La Javla. | 19° 54.0′ N<br>77° 18.7′ W | **Fl.R.**<br>period 4s | 16<br>**5** | 3 | STARBOARD (B)<br>R, beacon, topmark. | |
| 13170<br>*J 5052.8* | -Beacon No. 11. | 19° 54.0′ N<br>77° 19.0′ W | **Fl.G.**<br>period 5s | 13<br>**4** | 3 | PORT (B)<br>G, topmark. | |
| 13172<br>*J 5054* | **Cabo Cruz.** | 19° 50.5′ N<br>77° 43.8′ W | **Fl.W.**<br>period 5s<br>fl. 0.5s, ec. 4.5s | 112<br>**34** | **22** | Yellow conical masonry tower; 105. | Aeromarine light.<br>Reserve light range 7M. |
| 13176<br>*J 5055* | La Campana. | 19° 50.1′ N<br>77° 44.9′ W | **Fl.R.**<br>period 4s | 16<br>**5** | 3 | STARBOARD (B)<br>R, beacon, topmark. | |
| 13177<br>*J 5055.3* | -No. 2. | 19° 50.3′ N<br>77° 44.7′ W | **Fl.R.**<br>period 6s | 10<br>**3** | 3 | STARBOARD (B)<br>R, beacon, topmark. | |
| 13178<br>*J 5055.35* | -No. 3. | 19° 50.4′ N<br>77° 44.5′ W | **Fl.G.**<br>period 3s | 10<br>**3** | 3 | PORT (B)<br>G, beacon, topmark. | |
| | GOLFO DE GUACANAYABO: | | | | | | |
| | -Banco de Beuna Esperanza: | | | | | | |
| 13178.2<br>*J 5056* | --SW. of Gran Banco. | 20° 12.0′ N<br>77° 47.0′ W | **Fl.R.**<br>period 4s | 16<br>**5** | 4 | STARBOARD (B)<br>R, beacon, topmark. | |
| 13178.4<br>*J 5057* | --W. | 20° 18.3′ N<br>77° 48.3′ W | **Fl.R.**<br>period 6s | 16<br>**5** | 4 | STARBOARD (B)<br>R, beacon, topmark. | |
| | -Banco de Buena: | | | | | | |
| 13179<br>*J 5059* | --Cayo Medano. | 20° 20.4′ N<br>77° 48.7′ W | **Fl.Y.**<br>period 7s | 16<br>**5** | 6 | SPECIAL<br>Y, beacon, X topmark. | |
| | -Canal de Palomino: | | | | | | |
| 13180<br>*J 5060.4* | --No. 9. | 20° 10.1′ N<br>77° 44.9′ W | **Fl.G.**<br>period 5s<br>fl. 0.5s, ec. 4.5s | 13<br>**4** | 3 | PORT (B)<br>G, beacon, topmark. | |
| 13184<br>*J 5061* | --No. 10. | 20° 09.3′ N<br>77° 45.0′ W | **Fl.R.**<br>period 6s<br>fl. 0.5s, ec. 5.5s | 13<br>**4** | 4 | STARBOARD (B)<br>R, beacon, topmark. | |

Many of the lights on the coast of Cuba have been reported to be irregular or extinguished.

| (1) No. | (2) Name and Location | (3) Position | (4) Characteristic | (5) Height | (6) Range | (7) Structure | (8) Remarks |
|---|---|---|---|---|---|---|---|

## CUBA

| (1) No. | (2) Name and Location | (3) Position | (4) Characteristic | (5) Height | (6) Range | (7) Structure | (8) Remarks |
|---|---|---|---|---|---|---|---|
| 13192<br>*J 5062* | --No. 13. | 20° 09.9′ N<br>77° 39.8′ W | **Fl.G.**<br>period 5s<br>fl. 0.5s, ec. 4.5s | 13<br>**4** | 4 | PORT (B)<br>G, beacon, topmark. | |
| 13194<br>*J 5055.5* | -Bajo Orejon Grande. | 20° 06.3′ N<br>77° 40.7′ W | **Fl.Y.**<br>period 7s | 16<br>**5** | 6 | SPECIAL<br>Y, beacon, X topmark. | |
| 13196<br>*J 5062.4* | -Banco Fustete Beacon. | 20° 11.3′ N<br>77° 35.6′ W | **Fl.G.**<br>period 3s | 13<br>**4** | 4 | PORT (B)<br>G, tower, topmark. | |
| | -Cayos Manzanillo: | | | | | | |
| 13204<br>*J 5063* | --Cayo Perla, on S. point, approach to Manzanillo. | 20° 21.4′ N<br>77° 14.6′ W | **Fl.W.**<br>period 9s | 36<br>**11** | 8 | White metal framework tower on piles; 29. | |
| 13208<br>*J 5066.3* | --Punta Socorro. | 20° 20.9′ N<br>77° 12.9′ W | **Fl.G.**<br>period 5s<br>fl. 0.5s, ec. 4.5s | 12<br>**4** | 3 | PORT (B)<br>G, beacon, topmark. | |
| 13212<br>*J 5064* | -Punta Caimanera. | 20° 19.8′ N<br>77° 09.3′ W | **Fl.R.**<br>period 4s<br>fl. 0.5s, ec. 3.5s | 13<br>**4** | 4 | STARBOARD (B)<br>R, beacon, topmark. | |
| 13216<br>*J 5066.6* | --Cayita. | 20° 22.2′ N<br>77° 08.7′ W | **Fl.G.**<br>period 3s<br>fl. 0.3s, ec. 2.7s | 12<br>**4** | 4 | PORT (B)<br>G, beacon, topmark. | |
| 13220<br>*J 5068* | -Bajo Cucharillas. | 20° 31.6′ N<br>77° 17.3′ W | **Fl.R.**<br>period 4s | 13<br>**4** | 3 | STARBOARD (B)<br>R, beacon, topmark. | |
| 13222<br>*J 5068.6* | -Bajo Paticombito. | 20° 34.2′ N<br>77° 28.9′ W | **Fl.G.**<br>period 5s | 13<br>**4** | 3 | PORT (B)<br>G, beacon, topmark. | |
| 13224<br>*J 5068.8* | -Chinchorro Bank. | 20° 32.8′ N<br>77° 22.5′ W | **Fl.R.**<br>period 6s | 13<br>**4** | 4 | STARBOARD (B)<br>R, beacon, topmark. | |
| | -Paso de Chinchorro: | | | | | | |
| 13228<br>*J 5069* | --Bajo de Santa Clara. | 20° 31.7′ N<br>77° 24.0′ W | **Fl.G.**<br>period 3s | 13<br>**4** | 4 | PORT (B)<br>G, beacon, topmark. | |
| 13236<br>*J 5073.4* | --Banco Vibora. | 20° 33.9′ N<br>77° 41.5′ W | **Fl.R.**<br>period 6s | 13<br>**4** | 4 | STARBOARD (B)<br>R, beacon, topmark. | |
| 13236.5<br>*J 5073.5* | -Santa Cruz. | 20° 42.2′ N<br>77° 59.0′ W | **Fl.W.**<br>period 7s | 95<br>**29** | 9 | Red concrete hut, white base; 10. | |
| 13237<br>*J 5073.6* | -No. 2. | 20° 41.7′ N<br>77° 58.1′ W | **Fl.R.**<br>period 4s | 16<br>**5** | 4 | STARBOARD (B)<br>R, beacon, topmark. | |
| 13237.5<br>*J 5073.65* | -Punta Bonita No. 3. | 20° 41.8′ N<br>77° 58.6′ W | **Fl.G.**<br>period 5s | 16<br>**5** | 4 | PORT (B)<br>G, beacon, topmark. | |
| 13238<br>*J 5073.7* | -No. 4. | 20° 41.9′ N<br>77° 58.5′ W | **Fl.R.**<br>period 6s | 16<br>**5** | 4 | STARBOARD (B)<br>R, beacon, topmark. | |
| | -Media Luna Channel: | | | | | | |
| 13240<br>*J 5073.2* | --Cayo Patricio. | 20° 35.8′ N<br>77° 49.6′ W | **Fl.G.**<br>period 5s | 13<br>**4** | 4 | PORT (B)<br>G, beacon, topmark. | |
| 13242<br>*J 5072.2* | --Cayo Blanco. | 20° 27.1′ N<br>77° 58.9′ W | **Fl.R.**<br>period 4s | 16<br>**5** | 4 | STARBOARD (B)<br>R, beacon, topmark. | |
| 13244<br>*J 5070* | --Cayo Culebra. | 20° 33.7′ N<br>77° 50.0′ W | **Fl.R.**<br>period 4s | 16<br>**5** | 3 | STARBOARD (B)<br>R, beacon, topmark. | |
| 13248<br>*J 5071* | --Cayo Medio Luna. | 20° 33.0′ N<br>77° 53.5′ W | **Fl.G.**<br>period 5s<br>fl. 0.5s, ec. 4.5s | 13<br>**4** | 4 | PORT (B)<br>G, beacon, topmark. | |
| 13248.5<br>*J 5071.5* | --Medano de la Ceiba. | 20° 24.1′ N<br>77° 57.6′ W | **Fl.G.**<br>period 3s | 16<br>**5** | 4 | PORT (B)<br>G, beacon, topmark. | |

Many of the lights on the coast of Cuba have been reported to be irregular or extinguished.

| (1) No. | (2) Name and Location | (3) Position | (4) Characteristic | (5) Height | (6) Range | (7) Structure | (8) Remarks |
|---|---|---|---|---|---|---|---|
| | | | **CUBA** | | | | |
| 13249 *J 5069.4* | --Cayo Alacran. | 20° 39.4´ N 77° 43.8´ W | **Q.W.** | 10 **3** | 5 | N. CARDINAL BY, beacon, topmark. | |
| 13250 *J 5069.5* | --Cayo Bajo Bayameses. | 20° 39.8´ N 77° 49.6´ W | **Fl.G.** period 3s | 10 **3** | 3 | PORT (B) G, beacon, topmark. | |
| 13251 *J 5069.6* | --Cayo Navio. | 20° 40.9´ N 77° 51.6´ W | **Fl.G.** period 5s | 10 **3** | 3 | PORT (B) G, beacon, topmark. | |
| 13254 *J 5074.12* | --No. 4. | 20° 36.4´ N 78° 06.2´ W | **Fl.R.** period 4s | 16 **5** | 3 | STARBOARD (B) R, column, topmark. | |
| 13255 *J 5074.22* | --No. 5. | 20° 35.9´ N 78° 06.8´ W | **Fl.G.** period 5s | 13 **4** | 3 | PORT (B) G, tower, topmark. | |
| | -Canal de Cuatro Reales: | | | | | | |
| 13264 *J 5072* | --Cayo Carapacho. | 20° 26.9´ N 78° 02.5´ W | **Fl.W.** period 10s fl. 1s, ec. 9s | 47 **14** | 10 | Aluminum framework tower; 30. | |
| 13265 *J 5072.2* | --Cayo Blanco. | 20° 27.1´ N 77° 58.9´ W | **Fl.R.** period 4s | 16 **5** | 4 | STARBOARD (B) R, beacon, topmark. | |
| 13272 *J 5072.4* | --No. 5. | 20° 28.5´ N 77° 59.7´ W | **Fl.G.** period 5s fl. 0.5s, ec. 4.5s | 13 **4** | 4 | PORT (B) G, beacon, topmark. | |
| 13276 *J 5072.6* | --No. 8. | 20° 28.7´ N 77° 58.9´ W | **Fl.R.** period 4s | 13 **4** | 4 | STARBOARD (B) R, beacon, topmark. | |
| 13280 *J 5072.8* | --No. 9. | 20° 29.2´ N 77° 58.8´ W | **Fl.G.** period 5s fl. 0.5s, ec. 4.5s | 13 **4** | 3 | PORT (B) G, beacon, topmark. | |
| 13284 *J 5076* | -Canal de Cabeza del Este, W. side of entrance, on Cabeza del Este Cay. | 20° 31.0´ N 78° 19.8´ W | **Fl.W.** period 12s fl. 1s, ec. 11s | 47 **14** | 10 | Aluminum framework tower; 39. | |
| | -Canal de Pingue: | | | | | | |
| 13284.5 *J 5078* | --Cayo Orihuela No. 4. | 20° 45.1´ N 78° 18.2´ W | **Fl.R.** period 4s | 13 **4** | 3 | STARBOARD (B) R, tower, topmark. | |
| 13284.6 *J 5078.2* | ---No. 12. | 20° 46.8´ N 78° 18.9´ W | **Fl.R.** period 6s | 13 **4** | 3 | STARBOARD (B) R, tower, topmark. | |
| 13286 *J 5078.7* | Medano de Manuel Gomez. | 21° 01.4´ N 78° 51.6´ W | **Fl.R.** period 6s | 16 **5** | 3 | STARBOARD (B) R, tower, topmark. | |
| 13288 *J 5078.6* | Cayo Manuel Gomez, NW. extremity of reef. | 21° 04.4´ N 78° 50.6´ W | **Fl.R.** period 4s | 16 **5** | 3 | STARBOARD (B) R, tower, topmark. | |
| 13292 *J 5078.8* | Cayo Santa Maria, SW. part of bank. | 21° 11.1´ N 78° 39.2´ W | **Fl.W.** period 5s fl. 1s, ec. 4s | 39 **12** | 7 | White fiberglass tower, red bands; 33. | |
| 13296 *J 5079* | Punta Vertientes. | 21° 24.5´ N 78° 34.5´ W | **Fl.G.** period 3s fl. 0.3s, ec. 2.7s | 13 **4** | 3 | PORT (B) G, tower, topmark. | |
| 13300 *J 5080* | No. 1. | 21° 25.6´ N 78° 44.9´ W | **Fl.G.** period 5s | 13 **4** | 3 | PORT (B) G, tower, topmark. | |
| 13304 *J 5080.2* | No. 3. | 21° 26.5´ N 78° 46.1´ W | **Fl.G.** period 3s fl. 0.3s, ec. 2.7s | 13 **4** | 3 | PORT (B) G, tower, topmark. | |
| | CANAL BALANDRAS: | | | | | | |
| 13306 *J 5082.6* | -Medano de Balandras. | 21° 26.0´ N 78° 49.0´ W | **Fl.G.** period 5s | 13 **4** | 3 | PORT (B) G, tower, topmark. | |

Many of the lights on the coast of Cuba have been reported to be irregular or extinguished.

| (1) No. | (2) Name and Location | (3) Position | (4) Characteristic | (5) Height | (6) Range | (7) Structure | (8) Remarks |
|---|---|---|---|---|---|---|---|
| | | | **CUBA** | | | | |
| 13308<br>*J 5082.7* | -No. 6. | 21° 27.9′ N<br>78° 47.0′ W | **Fl.R.**<br>period 6s | 16<br>**5** | 3 | STARBOARD (B)<br>R, tower, topmark. | |
| 13312<br>*J 5083* | -Cayuelo Sabicu No. 9. | 21° 30.1′ N<br>78° 50.0′ W | **Fl.G.**<br>period 5s | 16<br>**5** | 3 | PORT (B)<br>G, tower, topmark. | |
| 13314<br>*J 5083.2* | Cabezo del Flamenco. | 21° 24.8′ N<br>78° 53.3′ W | **Fl.R.**<br>period 6s | 10<br>**3** | 3 | STARBOARD (B)<br>R, tower, topmark. | |
| 13316<br>*J 5081.8* | Pasa Ana Maria, S. side. | 21° 30.8′ N<br>78° 46.4′ W | **Fl.G.**<br>period 5s | 13<br>**4** | 3 | PORT (B)<br>G, tower, topmark. | |
| | FUERA CHANNEL: | | | | | | |
| 13328<br>*J 5081.6* | -Boca Grande Inlet, E. side of entrance. | 21° 33.2′ N<br>78° 40.4′ W | **Fl.G.**<br>period 5s | 16<br>**5** | 3 | PORT (B)<br>G, tower, topmark. | |
| 13332<br>*J 5082* | Cayo Encantado. | 21° 33.6′ N<br>78° 49.7′ W | **Fl.G.**<br>period 3s<br>fl. 0.5s, ec. 2.5s | 12<br>**4** | 3 | PORT (B)<br>G, tower, topmark. | |
| 13334<br>*J 5083.3* | Cayo Obispito. | 21° 31.7′ N<br>78° 53.0′ W | **Fl.G.**<br>period 5s | 13<br>**4** | 3 | PORT (B)<br>G, tower, topmark. | |
| 13336<br>*J 5082.4* | Jucaro, W. side of channel. | 21° 36.7′ N<br>78° 51.2′ W | **Fl.G.**<br>period 5s | 16<br>**5** | 3 | PORT (B)<br>G, tower, topmark. | |
| 13336.5<br>*J 5082.45* | -Muelle de Mambisas. | 21° 36.9′ N<br>78° 51.2′ W | **Fl.R.**<br>period 4s | 13<br>**4** | 3 | STARBOARD (B)<br>R, tower, topmark. | |
| 13338<br>*J 5083.7* | Tomeguin, N. end of shoal. | 21° 19.1′ N<br>79° 13.0′ W | **Fl.R.**<br>period 6s | 13<br>**4** | 3 | STARBOARD (B)<br>R, tower, topmark. | |
| 13340<br>*J 5077* | Cayo Cachiboca. | 20° 40.9′ N<br>78° 44.9′ W | **Fl.W.**<br>period 15s<br>fl. 1s, ec. 14s | 111<br>**34** | 10 | Aluminum framework tower, on piles; 98. | |
| 13344<br>*J 5084* | Cayo Breton, on W. side. | 21° 07.3′ N<br>79° 26.9′ W | **Fl.W.**<br>period 10s<br>fl. 1s, ec. 9s | 108<br>**33** | 12 | White framework tower; 98. | |
| | CANAL DE BRETON: | | | | | | |
| 13356<br>*J 5084.5* | -La Vela. | 21° 13.4′ N<br>79° 33.4′ W | **Fl.R.**<br>period 4s<br>fl. 0.5s, ec. 3.5s | 16<br>**5** | 3 | STARBOARD (B)<br>R, tower, topmark. | |
| 13358<br>*J 5084.6* | -Beacon No. 6. | 21° 13.8′ N<br>79° 26.1′ W | **Fl.R.**<br>period 4s | 13<br>**4** | 3 | STARBOARD (B)<br>R, tower, topmark. | |
| 13359<br>*J 5084.65* | -Beacon No. 8. | 21° 24.2′ N<br>79° 22.1′ W | **Fl.R.**<br>period 4s | 10<br>**3** | 3 | STARBOARD (B)<br>R, tower, topmark. | |
| 13359.5<br>*J 5084.7* | Bajo Las Charcas. | 21° 27.5′ N<br>79° 04.4′ W | **Fl.G.**<br>period 5s | 10<br>**3** | 3 | PORT (B)<br>G, tower, topmark. | |
| | ENSENADA DE LAS TUNAS: | | | | | | |
| 13364<br>*J 5084.8* | -Cayo Blanco de Zaza. | 21° 35.9′ N<br>79° 35.9′ W | **Fl.W.**<br>period 12s | 48<br>**15** | 8 | White framework tower; 39. | |
| | PUERTO DE CASILDA: | | | | | | |
| 13380<br>*J 5090* | -Cayo Blanco de Casilda. | 21° 38.3′ N<br>79° 53.0′ W | **Fl.W.**<br>period 7s<br>fl. 1s, ec. 6s | 46<br>**14** | 10 | White framework tower; 39. | |
| 13382<br>*J 5090.05* | --NE. | 21° 39.1′ N<br>79° 52.5′ W | **Fl.G.**<br>period 3s | 13<br>**4** | 3 | PORT (B)<br>G, tower, topmark. | |

Many of the lights on the coast of Cuba have been reported to be irregular or extinguished.

| (1) No. | (2) Name and Location | (3) Position | (4) Characteristic | (5) Height | (6) Range | (7) Structure | (8) Remarks |
|---|---|---|---|---|---|---|---|

## CUBA

| (1) No. | (2) Name and Location | (3) Position | (4) Characteristic | (5) Height | (6) Range | (7) Structure | (8) Remarks |
|---|---|---|---|---|---|---|---|
| 13383<br>*J 5090.09* | -Banco Cascajal. | 21° 39.1´ N<br>79° 52.0´ W | **Fl.R.**<br>period 6s | 13<br>**4** | 4 | STARBOARD (B)<br>R, tower, topmark. | |
| 13388<br>*J 5090.2* | -Bajo Los Guairos, No. 3. | 21° 40.3´ N<br>79° 53.3´ W | **Fl.G.**<br>period 5s | 13<br>**4** | 3 | PORT (B)<br>G, pole, topmark. | |
| 13392<br>*J 5090.25* | -Bajo Jobabos, No. 4. | 21° 40.5´ N<br>79° 53.2´ W | **Fl.R.**<br>period 4s | 13<br>**4** | 3 | STARBOARD (B)<br>R, pole, topmark. | |
| 13396<br>*J 5090.3* | -Canal de Los Guairos, No. 5. | 21° 40.7´ N<br>79° 53.8´ W | **Fl.G.**<br>period 3s | 16<br>**5** | 3 | PORT (B)<br>G, tower, topmark. | |
| 13398<br>*J 5090.35* | -No. 7. | 21° 40.8´ N<br>79° 53.9´ W | **Fl.G.**<br>period 5s | 13<br>**4** | 3 | PORT (B)<br>G, tower, topmark. | |
| 13400<br>*J 5090.4* | -No. 9. | 21° 40.7´ N<br>79° 54.0´ W | **Fl.G.**<br>period 3s | 16<br>**5** | 3 | PORT (B)<br>G, tower, topmark. | |
| 13404<br>*J 5090.45* | -No. 11. | 21° 40.6´ N<br>79° 54.1´ W | **Fl.G.**<br>period 5s | 16<br>**5** | 3 | PORT (B)<br>G, pole, topmark. | |
| 13406<br>*J 5090.5* | -No. 12. | 21° 40.7´ N<br>79° 54.2´ W | **Fl.R.**<br>period 6s | 13<br>**4** | 3 | STARBOARD (B)<br>R, tower, topmark. | |
| 13420<br>*J 5090.55* | --Banco Derribada. | 21° 42.1´ N<br>79° 57.9´ W | **Fl.G.**<br>period 5s | 13<br>**4** | 3 | PORT (B)<br>G, tower, topmark. | |
| 13424<br>*J 5090.6* | Bano del Gueyo, No. 14. | 21° 42.3´ N<br>79° 56.6´ W | **Fl.R.**<br>period 6s | 16<br>**5** | 3 | STARBOARD (B)<br>R, tower, topmark. | |
| 13428<br>*J 5091* | Bano del Medio, No. 17. | 21° 43.6´ N<br>79° 57.7´ W | **Fl.G.**<br>period 3s | 13<br>**4** | 3 | PORT (B)<br>G, tower, topmark. | |
| 13432<br>*J 5091.2* | Punta Casilda, No. 21. | 21° 43.8´ N<br>79° 58.2´ W | **Fl.G.**<br>period 3s | 13<br>**4** | 3 | PORT (B)<br>G, tower, topmark. | |
| 13436<br>*J 5091.5* | Punta Lastre, No. 25. | 21° 44.4´ N<br>79° 59.2´ W | **Fl.G.**<br>period 3s | 13<br>**4** | 3 | PORT (B)<br>G, tower, topmark. | |
| 13440<br>*J 5092* | -Cayo Raton, No. 26. | 21° 44.4´ N<br>79° 59.1´ W | **Fl.R.**<br>period 4s | 16<br>**5** | 3 | STARBOARD (B)<br>R, tower, topmark. | |
| 13444<br>*J 5092.2* | -No. 28. | 21° 44.5´ N<br>79° 59.2´ W | **Fl.R.**<br>period 6s | 16<br>**5** | 3 | STARBOARD (B)<br>R, pole, topmark. | |
| 13448<br>*J 5092.3* | -No. 31. | 21° 45.0´ N<br>79° 59.5´ W | **Fl.G.**<br>period 3s | 13<br>**4** | 3 | PORT (B)<br>G, tower, topmark. | |
| 13452<br>*J 5092.4* | -No. 32. | 21° 45.0´ N<br>79° 59.4´ W | **Fl.R.**<br>period 4s | 13<br>**4** | 3 | STARBOARD (B)<br>R, tower, topmark. | |
| 13456<br>*J 5092.6* | -No. 37. | 21° 45.1´ N<br>79° 59.6´ W | **Fl.G.**<br>period 5s | 13<br>**4** | 3 | PORT (B)<br>G, pole, topmark. | |
| 13460<br>*J 5092.8* | Ancon. | 21° 44.6´ N<br>80° 01.3´ W | **Fl.W.**<br>period 5s<br>fl. 1s, ec. 4s | 59<br>**18** | 13 | White pedestal on building; 7. | Reserve light range 7M. |
| 13464<br>*J 5093* | **Rio Yaguanabo.** | 21° 51.5´ N<br>80° 12.5´ W | **Fl.W.**<br>period 10s<br>fl. 1s, ec. 9s | 190<br>**58** | **15** | White round concrete tower; 112. | Reserve light range 7M. |
| | CIENFUEGOS: | | | | | | |
| 13468<br>*J 5094* | **-Punta de los Colorados.** | 22° 02.0´ N<br>80° 26.6´ W | **Fl.W.**<br>period 5s | 82<br>**25** | **23** | White conical masonry tower; 66. | Reserve light range 7M. |
| 13470<br>*J 5097.5* | -Cayo Alcatraz. | 22° 04.3´ N<br>80° 26.6´ W | **Fl.G.**<br>period 5s | 13<br>**4** | 3 | PORT (B)<br>G, pole, topmark. | |
| 13472<br>*J 5097* | -Range No. 1, front. | 22° 03.5´ N<br>80° 27.5´ W | **F.R.** | | 5 | White concrete wall, orange diamond daymark; 16. | |

Many of the lights on the coast of Cuba have been reported to be irregular or extinguished.

| (1) No. | (2) Name and Location | (3) Position | (4) Characteristic | (5) Height | (6) Range | (7) Structure | (8) Remarks |
|---|---|---|---|---|---|---|---|

## CUBA

| (1) No. | (2) Name and Location | (3) Position | (4) Characteristic | (5) Height | (6) Range | (7) Structure | (8) Remarks |
|---|---|---|---|---|---|---|---|
| 13476 *J 5097.1* | --Rear, 220 meters 350°12′ from front. | 22° 03.7′ N 80° 27.5′ W | **F.R.** | | 5 | White concrete wall, orange diamond daymark; 33. | |
| 13480 *J 5097.2* | -Range No. 2, front. | 22° 03.8′ N 80° 27.8′ W | **Fl.W.** period 1.5s | 13 **4** | 7 | White concrete wall, orange diamond daymark; 13. | |
| 13484 *J 5097.21* | --Rear, 60 meters 322°48′ from front. | 22° 03.8′ N 80° 27.9′ W | **Fl.W.** period 1.5s | 13 **4** | 7 | White concrete wall, orange diamond daymark; 13. | |
| 13488 *J 5095* | -Juragua, No. 5. | 22° 03.7′ N 80° 27.8′ W | **Fl.G.** period 3s | 23 **7** | 3 | PORT (B) G, column, topmark. | |
| 13492 *J 5096* | -Pasa Caballos. | 22° 03.7′ N 80° 27.7′ W | **Fl.R.** period 4s | 33 **10** | 4 | STARBOARD (B) R, tower, topmark; 26. | |
| 13496 *J 5097.3* | -Range No. 3, front. | 22° 03.6′ N 80° 27.8′ W | **F.W.** | | 5 | White concrete wall, orange diamond daymark; 10. | |
| 13500 *J 5097.31* | --Rear, 50 meters 204°54′ from front. | 22° 03.6′ N 80° 27.8′ W | **F.W.** | | 5 | White concrete wall, orange diamond daymark; 13. | |
| 13508 *J 5097.4* | -Range No. 4, on Cayo Carenas, front. | 22° 05.1′ N 80° 27.5′ W | **Fl.W.** period 1.5s | 13 **4** | 7 | White concrete wall, orange diamond daymark; 10. | |
| 13512 *J 5097.41* | --Rear, 60 meters 358°30′ from front. | 22° 05.2′ N 80° 27.5′ W | **Fl.W.** period 1.5s | 13 **4** | 7 | White concrete wall, orange diamond daymark; 13. | |
| | -Pasa Bajo de la Cueva: | | | | | | |
| 13512.3 *J 5097.6* | --No. 1. | 22° 05.8′ N 80° 27.3′ W | **Fl.G.** period 3s | 13 **4** | 3 | PORT (B) G, tower, topmark. | |
| 13512.32 *J 5097.65* | --No. 2. | 22° 05.8′ N 80° 27.4′ W | **Fl.R.** period 4s | 13 **4** | 3 | STARBOARD (B) R, tower, topmark. | |
| 13512.34 *J 5097.7* | --No. 3. | 22° 05.8′ N 80° 27.2′ W | **Fl.G.** period 5s | 13 **4** | 3 | PORT (B) G, tower, topmark. | |
| 13512.36 *J 5097.75* | --No. 4. | 22° 05.6′ N 80° 27.2′ W | **Fl.R.** period 6s | 13 **4** | 3 | STARBOARD (B) R, tower, topmark. | |
| 13513 *J 5098* | -Junco Sur. | 22° 06.6′ N 80° 26.3′ W | **Fl.G.** period 5s | 13 **4** | 3 | PORT (B) G, tower, topmark. | |
| 13518 *J 5099* | -Ensenada de Cotica, No. 5B. | 22° 09.4′ N 80° 27.9′ W | **Fl.G.** period 5s | 13 **4** | 3 | PORT (B) G, tower, topmark. | |
| 13518.2 *J 5099.2* | --No. 6B. | 22° 09.3′ N 80° 27.7′ W | **Fl.R.** period 4s | 13 **4** | 3 | STARBOARD (B) R, tower, topmark. | |
| 13518.4 *J 5099.4* | --No. 7B. | 22° 09.3′ N 80° 27.4′ W | **Fl.G.** period 3s | 13 **4** | 3 | PORT (B) G, tower, topmark. | |
| 13518.6 *J 5099.6* | --No. 8B. | 22° 09.2′ N 80° 27.4′ W | **Fl.R.** period 4s | 13 **4** | 3 | STARBOARD (B) R, tower, topmark. | |
| 13524 *J 5104* | Cayo Piedras. | 21° 58.2′ N 81° 07.3′ W | **Fl.W.** period 10s fl. 1s, ec. 9s | 43 **13** | 8 | White round fiberglass tower; 33. | |
| 13532 *J 5104.2* | -Reef, SW. side. | 21° 57.9′ N 81° 08.9′ W | **Fl.R.** period 4s | 13 **4** | 3 | STARBOARD (B) R, tower, topmark. | |
| 13536 *J 5102* | **Cayo Guano del Este.** | 21° 39.8′ N 81° 02.4′ W | **Fl.(2)W.** period 15s | 177 **54** | **19** | White round concrete tower, red bands; 148. | Aeromarine light. Reserve light range 7M. |
| 13538 *J 5103* | Playa Giron. | 22° 04.0′ N 81° 02.3′ W | **Fl.W.** period 15s | 66 **20** | 10 | White pedestal on water tank; 59. | |
| 13540 *J 5105* | No. 1. | 22° 13.5′ N 81° 08.8′ W | **Fl.G.** period 3s | 23 **7** | 3 | PORT (B) G, pillar, topmark. | |
| 13544 *J 5106* | No. 2. | 22° 12.6′ N 81° 08.4′ W | **Fl.R.** period 4s | 26 **8** | 6 | STARBOARD (B) R, tower, topmark; 26. | |

Many of the lights on the coast of Cuba have been reported to be irregular or extinguished.

| (1) No. | (2) Name and Location | (3) Position | (4) Characteristic | (5) Height | (6) Range | (7) Structure | (8) Remarks |
|---|---|---|---|---|---|---|---|

## CUBA

| (1) No. | (2) Name and Location | (3) Position | (4) Characteristic | (5) Height | (6) Range | (7) Structure | (8) Remarks |
|---|---|---|---|---|---|---|---|
| 13544.1 *J 5106.2* | -No. 1. | 22° 12.6′ N 81° 08.4′ W | **Fl.G.** period 3s | 13 **4** | 3 | PORT (B) G, tower, topmark. | |
| 13545 *J 5106.5* | -Cabeta de Buenaventura, No. 2. | 22° 16.7′ N 81° 12.5′ W | **Fl.R.** period 4s | 13 **4** | 3 | STARBOARD (B) R, tower, topmark. | |
| 13546 *J 5106.6* | --No. 5. | 22° 16.9′ N 81° 12.6′ W | **Fl.G.** period 5s | 13 **4** | 3 | PORT (B) G, tower, topmark. | |
| 13547 *J 5106.65* | --No. 6. | 22° 16.9′ N 81° 12.6′ W | **Fl.R.** period 4s | 13 **4** | 3 | STARBOARD (B) R, tower, topmark. | |
| 13548 *J 5107* | Cayo Sigua. | 21° 53.6′ N 81° 24.9′ W | **Fl.W.** period 7s | 30 **9** | 7 | White framework tower; 23. | |
| 13552 *J 5108* | Pasa de Diego Perez, on reef at entrance. | 22° 01.4′ N 81° 30.9′ W | **Fl.W.** period 5s fl. 1s, ec. 4s | 39 **12** | 7 | White framework tower, on piles; 33. | |
| 13556 *J 5114* | Cabezo del Vapor. | 22° 01.5′ N 81° 36.5′ W | **Fl.G.** period 5s fl. 0.4s, ec. 4.6s | 13 **4** | 3 | PORT (B) G, tower, topmark. | |
| 13560 *J 5116* | Cabezo del Carbonero. | 22° 05.9′ N 81° 46.0′ W | **Fl.G.** period 3s | 13 **4** | 3 | PORT (B) G, tower, topmark. | |
| 13566 *J 5120* | Restinga Prieta. | 22° 15.8′ N 81° 58.6′ W | **Fl.G.** period 5s | 13 **4** | 3 | PORT (B) G, tower, topmark. | |
| 13568 *J 5128* | Cayos Ballenatos (Los Ballenatos). | 21° 34.9′ N 81° 38.2′ W | **Fl.W.** period 10s | 30 **9** | 11 | White framework tower; 26. | |
| 13569 *J 5121* | -No. 25. | 22° 03.8′ N 81° 59.6′ W | **Fl.G.** period 5s | 13 **4** | 3 | PORT (B) G, tower, topmark. | |
| 13570 *J 5121.5* | -No. 28. | 22° 08.5′ N 82° 05.4′ W | **Fl.R.** period 6s | 13 **4** | 3 | STARBOARD (B) R, tower, topmark. | |
| 13571 *J 5122* | Bajo Las Gordas, off S.W. side. | 22° 13.1′ N 82° 08.7′ W | **Fl.R.** period 6s | 13 **4** | 3 | STARBOARD (B) R, tower, topmark. | |
| 13571.1 *J 5122.5* | Cayo Amber, off SE. side. | 22° 19.1′ N 82° 09.6′ W | **Fl.G.** period 5s | 13 **4** | 3 | PORT (B) G, tower, topmark. | |
| 13571.2 *J 5123* | Punta Gorda. | 22° 23.8′ N 82° 09.5′ W | **Fl.R.** period 4s | 13 **4** | 3 | STARBOARD (B) R, tower, topmark. | |
| 13572 *J 5130* | Cayo Largo. | 21° 38.6′ N 81° 33.8′ W | **Fl.W.** period 6s fl. 0.5s, ec. 5.5s | 43 **13** | 10 | White octagonal concrete tower; 23. | |
| 13573 *J 5128.1* | -No. 1. | 21° 36.2′ N 81° 34.9′ W | **Fl.G.** period 5s | 10 **3** | 2 | PORT (B) G, tower, topmark. | |
| 13573.1 *J 5128.2* | -No. 2. | 21° 36.2′ N 81° 34.9′ W | **Fl.R.** period 4s | 13 **4** | 3 | STARBOARD (B) R, tower, topmark. | |
| 13573.2 *J 5128.3* | -No. 3. | 21° 36.4′ N 81° 35.1′ W | **Fl.G.** period 7s | 13 **4** | 3 | PORT (B) G, tower, topmark. | |
| 13573.3 *J 5128.4* | -No. 6. | 21° 36.5′ N 81° 35.1′ W | **Fl.R.** period 6s | 13 **4** | 3 | STARBOARD (B) R, tower, topmark. | |
| 13573.4 *J 5128.5* | -No. 7. | 21° 36.7′ N 81° 35.1′ W | **Fl.G.** period 3s | 13 **4** | 3 | PORT (B) G, tower, topmark. | |
| 13573.5 *J 5128.6* | -No. 10. | 21° 36.8′ N 81° 34.9′ W | **Fl.R.** period 4s | 13 **4** | 3 | STARBOARD (B) R, tower, topmark. | |
| 13573.6 *J 5128.7* | -No. 11. | 21° 37.5′ N 81° 33.8′ W | **Fl.G.** period 5s | 13 **4** | 3 | PORT (B) G, tower, topmark. | |
| 13573.7 *J 5128.8* | -No. 14. | 21° 37.1′ N 81° 34.6′ W | **Fl.R.** period 6s | 13 **4** | 3 | STARBOARD (B) R, tower, topmark. | |

Many of the lights on the coast of Cuba have been reported to be irregular or extinguished.

| (1) No. | (2) Name and Location | (3) Position | (4) Characteristic | (5) Height | (6) Range | (7) Structure | (8) Remarks |
|---|---|---|---|---|---|---|---|
| | | | **CUBA** | | | | |
| 13573.8 *J 5128.9* | -No. 15. | 21° 37.2′ N 81° 34.5′ W | **Fl.G.** period 3s | 13 **4** | 3 | PORT (B) G, tower, topmark. | |
| 13574 *J 5130.5* | -No. 6. | 21° 37.2′ N 81° 34.3′ W | **Fl.R.** period 4s | 13 **4** | 3 | STARBOARD (B) R, tower, topmark. | |
| 13575 *J 5130.6* | -No. 11. | 31° 37.5′ N 81° 34.2′ W | **Fl.G.** period 3s | 13 **4** | 3 | PORT (B) G, tower, topmark. | |
| 13575.5 *J 5129* | Playa Sirena. | 21° 36.2′ N 81° 34.1′ W | **Fl.(2)W.** period 10s | 13 **4** | 3 | ISOLATED DANGER BRB, tower, topmark. | |
| 13575.7 *J 5125.05* | No. 20. | 21° 38.8′ N 81° 48.5′ W | **Fl.R.** period 4s | 10 **3** | 2 | STARBOARD (B) R, tower, topmark. | |
| 13576 *J 5136* | Cayo Avalos, S. head. | 21° 32.6′ N 82° 09.9′ W | **Fl.W.** period 8s fl. 1s, ec. 7s | 30 **9** | 7 | White framework tower; 26. | |
| 13580 *J 5138* | **Caleta de Carapachibey.** | 21° 27.0′ N 82° 55.4′ W | **Fl.W.** period 7.5s fl. 1s, ec. 6.5s | 184 **56** | **17** | White round concrete tower, yellow band; 171. | Reserve light range 10M. |
| | GOLFO DE BATABANO: | | | | | | |
| 13592 *J 5156* | --Bajo la Pipa. | 22° 09.6′ N 82° 58.0′ W | **Fl.R.** period 6s fl. 0.5s, ec. 5.5s | 13 **4** | 3 | STARBOARD (B) R, tower, topmark. | |
| 13596 *J 5157* | -Cayo Hambre. | 22° 10.4′ N 82° 51.4′ W | **Fl.G.** period 5s | 13 **4** | 3 | PORT (B) G, tower, topmark. | |
| 13600 *J 5148* | -Punta de los Barcos. | 21° 56.4′ N 82° 59.7′ W | **Fl.R.** period 4s fl. 0.5s, ec. 3.5s | 13 **4** | 3 | STARBOARD (B) R, tower, topmark. | |
| 13604 *J 5146* | -Punta Buenavista. | 21° 47.0′ N 83° 05.8′ W | **Fl.R.** period 6s | 13 **4** | 3 | STARBOARD (B) R, tower, topmark. | |
| 13608 *J 5145* | -Darsena de Siguanea, W. entrance, No. 1. | 21° 37.1′ N 82° 59.1′ W | **Fl.G.** period 5s | 13 **4** | 3 | PORT (B) G, tower, topmark. | |
| 13612 *J 5145.2* | --No. 2. | 21° 37.0′ N 82° 59.1′ W | **Fl.R.** period 6s | 16 **5** | 3 | STARBOARD (B) R, tower, topmark. | |
| 13616 *J 5144* | -Cayos Los Indios. | 21° 43.2′ N 83° 10.0′ W | **Fl.G.** period 5s | 13 **4** | 3 | PORT (B) G, tower, topmark. | |
| 13618 *J 5190* | -Rio Las Casas. E. side. No. 9. | 21° 54.8′ N 82° 48.1′ W | **Fl.G.** period 5s | 10 **3** | 3 | PORT (B) G, tower, topmark. | |
| 13619 *J 5191* | --W. side, No. 10. | 21° 54.8′ N 82° 48.1′ W | **Fl.R.** period 4s | 13 **4** | 3 | STARBOARD (B) R, tower, topmark. | |
| 13622 *J 5143* | -Los Coyuelos. | 21° 38.4′ N 83° 11.2′ W | **Q.W.** | 13 **4** | 3 | N. CARDINAL BY, tower, topmark. | |
| 13623 *J 5192* | -No. 1. | 21° 59.5′ N 82° 43.4′ W | **Fl.G.** period 3s | 13 **4** | 3 | PORT (B) G, tower, topmark. | |
| 13628 *J 5192.6* | -No. 13. | 22° 00.3′ N 82° 42.8′ W | **Fl.G.** period 5s fl. 0.5s, ec. 4.5s | 13 **4** | 3 | PORT (B) G, tower, topmark. | |
| 13630 *J 5193.5* | -Pasa La Manteca. | 22° 00.7′ N 82° 42.8′ W | **Fl.W.** period 8s | 39 **12** | 14 | White metal framework tower; 34. | |
| 13632 *J 5192.8* | -No. 14. | 22° 00.2′ N 82° 42.7′ W | **Fl.R.** period 4s fl. 1s, ec. 3s | 13 **4** | 3 | STARBOARD (B) R, tower, topmark. | |
| 13634 *J 5193* | -No. 21. | 22° 01.4′ N 82° 42.2′ W | **Fl.G.** period 3s | 13 **4** | 3 | PORT (B) G, tower, topmark. | |

Many of the lights on the coast of Cuba have been reported to be irregular or extinguished.

| (1) No. | (2) Name and Location | (3) Position | (4) Characteristic | (5) Height | (6) Range | (7) Structure | (8) Remarks |
|---|---|---|---|---|---|---|---|
| | | | **CUBA** | | | | |
| 13635 *J 5193.2* | -No. 22. | 22° 01.3´ N 82° 42.4´ W | **Fl.R.** period 4s | 13 **4** | 3 | STARBOARD (B) R, tower, topmark. | |
| 13636 *J 5194* | --Beacon No. 2. | 21° 55.8´ N 82° 39.3´ W | **Fl.R.** period 4s | 13 **4** | 3 | STARBOARD (B) R, tower, topmark. | |
| 13638 *J 5197* | --Beacon No. 29. | 21° 56.1´ N 82° 37.5´ W | **Fl.G.** period 3s | 13 **4** | 3 | PORT (B) G, tower, topmark. | |
| 13644 *J 5200* | -Canal del Ingles, NE. of Pasa de Quitasol. | 21° 57.3´ N 82° 36.4´ W | **Fl.G.** period 5s | 13 **4** | 3 | PORT (B) G, tower, topmark. | |
| 13647 *J 5166* | -Surgidero de Batabano. | 22° 41.2´ N 82° 17.9´ W | **Fl.W.** period 10s | 101 **31** | 7 | White pedestal on water tank; 7. | |
| 13647.1 *J 5167* | -Cometa. | 22° 40.5´ N 82° 17.4´ W | **Fl.R.** period 4s | 13 **4** | 3 | STARBOARD (B) R, pedestal, topmark. | |
| | -Isla de Pinos: | | | | | | |
| 13648 *J 5168* | --Refuge Canal, E. breakwater. | 22° 40.6´ N 82° 17.9´ W | **Fl.R.** period 6s fl. 0.5s, ec. 5.5s | 13 **4** | 3 | STARBOARD (B) R, tower, topmark. | |
| 13649 *J 5169* | --W. side. | 22° 40.8´ N 82° 17.9´ W | **Fl.G.** period 5s | 13 **4** | 3 | PORT (B) G, tower, topmark. | |
| 13652 *J 5161* | -Sur Bajo La Gata. | 22° 21.2´ N 82° 25.7´ W | **Fl.G.** period 5s | 13 **4** | 2 | PORT (B) G, tower, topmark. | |
| 13656 *J 5160* | -Cayo Monterrey. | 22° 20.0´ N 82° 20.1´ W | **Fl.W.** period 10s | 36 **11** | 14 | White metal framework tower, on piles; 43. | |
| 13660 *J 5162* | -Cayo Cruz. | 22° 28.2´ N 82° 16.8´ W | **Fl.G.** period 3s fl. 0.3s, ec. 2.7s | 13 **4** | 4 | PORT (B) G, tower, topmark; 26. | |
| 13664 *J 5164* | -Buenavista. | 22° 30.0´ N 82° 21.3´ W | **Fl.R.** period 6s | 13 **4** | 3 | STARBOARD (B) R, tower, topmark. | |
| 13672 *J 5174* | -Cayo Carabela. | 22° 29.2´ N 82° 28.8´ W | **Fl.G.** period 3s | 13 **4** | 3 | PORT (B) G, tower, topmark. | |
| 13676 *J 5176* | -Boqueron del Hacha. | 22° 29.4´ N 82° 27.8´ W | **Fl.R.** period 4s | 13 **4** | 3 | STARBOARD (B) R, tower, topmark. | |
| | ESENADA DE COLOMA: | | | | | | |
| 13678 *J 5202* | -La Coloma. | 22° 14.3´ N 83° 34.4´ W | **Fl.W.** period 15s | 98 **30** | 12 | Green tower on metal tank; 13. | |
| 13680 *J 5203* | -Santo Domingo, approach beacon. | 22° 09.6´ N 83° 36.5´ W | **L.Fl.W.** period 10s | 19 **6** | 4 | SAFE WATER RW, tower, topmark. | |
| 13684 *J 5203.4* | -No. 1, W. side. | 22° 12.1´ N 83° 35.7´ W | **Fl.G.** period 3s fl. 0.5s, ec. 2.5s | 13 **4** | 3 | PORT (B) G, tower, topmark. | |
| 13688 *J 5204* | -No. 4, E. side. | 22° 12.4´ N 83° 35.3´ W | **Fl.R.** period 4s | 13 **4** | 3 | STARBOARD (B) R, tower, topmark. | |
| 13692 *J 5204.4* | -No. 5, W. side. | 22° 13.0´ N 83° 34.9´ W | **Fl.G.** period 5s fl. 0.5s, ec. 4.5s | 13 **4** | 3 | PORT (B) G, tower, topmark. | |
| 13696 *J 5204.6* | -No. 8, E. side. | 22° 13.5´ N 83° 34.6´ W | **Fl.R.** period 4s | 13 **4** | 3 | STARBOARD (B) R, post, topmark. | |
| 13700 *J 5204.8* | -No. 10, E. side. | 22° 14.1´ N 83° 34.2´ W | **Fl.R.** period 6s fl. 0.5s, ec. 5.5s | 13 **4** | 3 | STARBOARD (B) R, tower, topmark. | |

Many of the lights on the coast of Cuba have been reported to be irregular or extinguished.

| (1) No. | (2) Name and Location | (3) Position | (4) Characteristic | (5) Height | (6) Range | (7) Structure | (8) Remarks |
|---|---|---|---|---|---|---|---|

## CUBA

| (1) No. | (2) Name and Location | (3) Position | (4) Characteristic | (5) Height | (6) Range | (7) Structure | (8) Remarks |
|---|---|---|---|---|---|---|---|
| 13708 *J 5210* | Cabo Frances. | 21° 54.5´ N 84° 02.2´ W | **Fl.W.** period 10s fl. 1s, ec. 9s | 30 **9** | 10 | White framework tower; 26. | |
| 13712 *J 4819* | Cabo Corrientes. | 21° 45.7´ N 84° 31.0´ W | **Fl.W.** period 5s fl. 1s, ec. 4s | 88 **27** | 10 | White framework tower; 72. | |

Many of the lights on the coast of Cuba have been reported to be irregular or extinguished.

# Section 9

## Caribbean Islands
## Including Cayman Islands, Jamaica, Hispaniola, Puerto Rico, and Lesser Antilles

| (1)<br>No. | (2)<br>Name and Location | (3)<br>Position | (4)<br>Characteristic | (5)<br>Height | (6)<br>Range | (7)<br>Structure | (8)<br>Remarks |
|---|---|---|---|---|---|---|---|
| | | | **CAYMAN ISLANDS** | | | | |
| 13716<br>*J 5232* | Grand Cayman. | 19° 17.8′ N<br>81° 23.0′ W | **Q.R.** | 43<br>**13** | 6 | Black metal tower, white base. | |
| 13720<br>*J 5222* | **-Boatswain Point.** | 19° 23.1′ N<br>81° 24.5′ W | **Fl.W.**<br>period 15s<br>fl. 1.8s, ec. 13.2s | 90<br>**27** | **15** | White metal tower, black base; 20. | Partially obscured 241°-257°, obscured 257°-316°. |
| 13724<br>*J 5226* | -Gorling Bluff at SE. end of island. | 19° 18.1′ N<br>81° 06.1′ W | **Fl.(2)W.**<br>period 20s<br>2 fl. 1.2s, ec. 18.8s | 72<br>**22** | 12 | White metal tower, black base; 26. | |
| 13728<br>*J 5231* | **-Georgetown** AVIATION LIGHT. | 19° 17.5′ N<br>81° 21.4′ W | **Al.Fl.W.G.** | 39<br>**12** | **20** | | |
| 13733<br>*J 5233* | -Hog Sty Bay Range, front. | 19° 17.7′ N<br>81° 23.1′ W | **F.G.** | 13<br>**4** | | White metal mast; 7. | |
| 13734<br>*J 5233.1* | --Rear, 100 meters 090° from front. | 19° 17.7′ N<br>81° 23.0′ W | **F.G.** | 33<br>**10** | 3 | White metal mast; 30. | |
| 13736<br>*J 5236* | Little Cayman, W. End Point. | 19° 39.5′ N<br>80° 06.5′ W | **Fl.W.**<br>period 5s<br>fl. 0.6s, ec. 4.4s | 30<br>**9** | 10 | White metal tower, black base; 20. | |
| 13740<br>*J 5237* | -E. Point. | 19° 42.4′ N<br>79° 57.7′ W | **Fl.(2)W.**<br>period 15s | 36<br>**11** | 10 | White tower and base. | |
| 13744<br>*J 5238* | **Cayman Brac.** | 19° 41.0′ N<br>79° 53.2′ W | **Fl.(2)W.**<br>period 15s | 41<br>**12** | **15** | White mast. | *Reported extinguished (1993).* |
| 13748<br>*J 5240* | -NE. point. | 19° 45.1′ N<br>79° 43.4′ W | **Fl.W.**<br>period 20s | 150<br>**46** | 12 | White metal tower, black base; 20. | |
| | | | **JAMAICA** | | | | |
| | MONTEGO BAY: | | | | | | |
| 13756<br>*J 5250* | -Lower Range, front. | 18° 28.2′ N<br>77° 55.5′ W | **F.R.** | 22<br>**7** | 5 | Mast, red triangular daymark point up; 16. | Visible 108°-128°. |
| 13760<br>*J 5250.1* | --Rear, 465 meters 118°37′ from front. | 18° 28.1′ N<br>77° 55.3′ W | **F.R.** | 57<br>**17** | 5 | Mast, white triangular daymark point down; 52. | Visible 108°-128°. |
| 13764<br>*J 5250.4* | -Upper Range, front. | 18° 28.7′ N<br>77° 55.6′ W | **F.R.** | 44<br>**13** | 5 | Red round metal tower on white fort, red round daymark; 13. | Visible 026°-046°. Stopping lights. |
| 13768<br>*J 5250.41* | --Rear, 104 meters 035°13′ from front. | 18° 28.7′ N<br>77° 55.5′ W | **F.R.** | 113<br>**34** | 5 | Red round metal tower, red round daymark; 16. | Visible 026°-046°. |
| 13770<br>*J 5251* | -Entrance channel Range, front. | 18° 27.6′ N<br>77° 56.3′ W | **Oc.R.**<br>period 2s<br>lt. 1.5s, ec. 0.5s | 26<br>**8** | | Post, white triangular daymark point up. | |
| 13771<br>*J 5251.1* | --Rear, 300 meters 200°48′ from front. | 18° 27.5′ N<br>77° 56.3′ W | **Oc.R.**<br>period 3s<br>lt. 2s, ec. 1s | 43<br>**13** | | Post, white triangular daymark point down. | |
| 13772<br>*J 5249* | -AVIATION LIGHT. | 18° 29.9′ N<br>77° 55.1′ W | **Fl.W.**<br>period 4s<br>fl. 1s, ec. 3s | 59<br>**18** | 10 | Control tower. | |
| 13775<br>*J 5252.4* | --No. 4. | 18° 27.8′ N<br>77° 56.4′ W | **Fl.R.**<br>period 5s | 16<br>**5** | | Red pile. | |
| 13775.5<br>*J 5252* | --No. 6. | 18° 27.8′ N<br>77° 56.1′ W | **F.G.** | 20<br>**6** | | Green metal column; 20. | |

| (1) No. | (2) Name and Location | (3) Position | (4) Characteristic | (5) Height | (6) Range | (7) Structure | (8) Remarks |
|---|---|---|---|---|---|---|---|
| | | | **JAMAICA** | | | | |
| 13776 *J 5253* | **Rose Hall.** | 18° 31.3′ N 77° 48.7′ W | **Fl.(5)W.** period 30s | 106 **32** | **22** | Metal framework tower. | |
| | FALMOUTH HARBOR | | | | | | |
| 13778 *J 5255* | -Cruise Terminal Range, front. | 18° 29.7′ N 77° 38.8′ W | **Iso.W.** period 6s | 20 **6** | 6 | Beacon, orange rectangular daymark, white stripe. | |
| 13778.1 *J 5255.1* | --Rear, 221°15′ from front. | 18° 29.7′ N 77° 38.9′ W | **Iso.W.** period 6s | 30 **9** | 6 | Beacon, orange rectangular daymark, white stripe. | |
| 13782.2 *J 5254.1* | -Beacon. | 18° 29.9′ N 77° 38.8′ W | **Fl.R.** period 3s | | 4 | STARBOARD (B) R, beacon. | |
| 13782.4 *J 5254.2* | -Beacon. | 18° 29.8′ N 77° 38.8′ W | **Q.R.** | | 3 | STARBOARD (B) R, beacon. | |
| 13782.6 *J 5254.3* | -Beacon. | 18° 29.7′ N 77° 38.7′ W | **Q.G.** | | 3 | PORT (B) G, beacon. | |
| | DISCOVERY BAY: | | | | | | |
| 13784 *J 5256* | -Dry Harbor Range, front. | 18° 27.7′ N 77° 24.6′ W | **F.R.** | 25 **8** | | Mast, white triangular daymark point up. | |
| 13788 *J 5256.1* | --Rear, 220 meters 193°52′ from front. | 18° 27.6′ N 77° 24.6′ W | **F.R.** | 26 **8** | | Framework tower, white triangular daymark point down. | |
| | OCHO RIOS BAY: | | | | | | |
| 13804 *J 5260* | -Range, front. | 18° 24.7′ N 77° 06.9′ W | **Oc.R.** period 5s lt. 4s, ec. 1s | 42 **13** | 10 | Red and white triangular daymark point up. | Shown when vessels are expected. |
| 13808 *J 5260.1* | --Rear, 384 meters 169° from front. | 18° 24.5′ N 77° 06.9′ W | **Oc.R.** period 5s lt. 4s, ec. 1s | 150 **46** | 10 | Metal column, red and white triangular daymark point up. | Synchronized with front. Shown when vessels are expected. |
| 13809 *J 5260.4* | -Beacon. | 18° 24.9′ N 77° 06.7′ W | **Fl.G.** period 5s fl. 0.5s, ec. 4.5s | 16 **5** | | Three pile beacon, square topmark. | |
| 13810 *J 5260.5* | -Beacon. | 18° 24.8′ N 77° 06.6′ W | **Fl.G.** period 1.5s fl. 0.5s, ec. 1s | 16 **5** | | Three pile beacon, square topmark. | |
| 13828 *J 5266* | **Galina Point.** | 18° 24.6′ N 76° 53.7′ W | **Fl.W.** period 12s fl. 1.5s, ec. 10.5s | 62 **19** | **22** | White round concrete tower and hut; 30. | F.R. on radio masts close W. |
| | PORT ANTONIO: | | | | | | |
| 13832 *J 5272* | **-Folly Point.** | 18° 11.1′ N 76° 26.5′ W | **L.Fl.W.** period 10s fl. 2s, ec. 8s | 54 **16** | **23** | White tower, red bands; 49. | |
| 13836 *J 5276* | -Folly Point Range, front. | 18° 11.2′ N 76° 26.6′ W | **F.R.** | | | Beacon. | When required. |
| 13840 *J 5276.1* | --Rear, 146 meters 068°47′ from front. | 18° 11.3′ N 76° 26.5′ W | **F.R.** | | | Beacon. | When required. |
| 13844 *J 5275* | -West Harbor Range, on shore, front. | 18° 10.9′ N 76° 27.6′ W | **F.R.** | 25 **8** | | White beacon; 26. | |
| 13848 *J 5275.1* | --Rear, 1271 meters 248°47′ from front. | 18° 10.7′ N 76° 28.2′ W | **F.R.** | 277 **84** | | White beacon; 20. | |
| 13856 *J 5278* | -Titchfield. | 18° 11.0′ N 76° 27.1′ W | **Q.G.** | | | PORT (B) G, beacon. | |

| (1) No. | (2) Name and Location | (3) Position | (4) Characteristic | (5) Height | (6) Range | (7) Structure | (8) Remarks |
|---|---|---|---|---|---|---|---|
| | | | **JAMAICA** | | | | |
| 13860 *J 5282* | **Morant Point.** | 17° 55.2′ N 76° 11.1′ W | **Fl.(3)W.** period 20s fl. 0.4s, ec. 2.9s fl. 0.4s, ec. 2.9s fl. 0.4s, ec. 13s | 115 **35** | **22** | White metal tower, red bands; 95. | Visible 114° -067°, obsc.-114°. |
| 13864 *J 5356* | Morant Cays, NE. Cay. | 17° 25.0′ N 75° 58.3′ W | **L.Fl.W.** period 10s fl. 4s, ec. 6s | 75 **23** | 12 | Aluminum framework tower, black bands; 69. | **Radar reflector.** |
| | KINGSTON APPROACH: | | | | | | |
| 13908 *J 5294* | **-Plumb Point.** | 17° 55.7′ N 76° 46.7′ W | **Fl.W.R.** period 9s fl. 1.5s, ec. 7.5s | 69 **21** | **19** | White tower; 68. | W. 297°-010°, R.-136°, W.(unintensified)-181°, obscured elsewhere. *Red sector reported difficult to distinguish.* |
| | | | **F.R.** | | | Same structure. | Occasional. |
| 13912 *J 5292* | -Norman Manley AVIATION LIGHT. | 17° 56.3′ N 76° 46.7′ W | **Al.Fl.W.G.** period 5s | 56 **17** | | Tower. | Red lights on radio masts 300 meters E. |
| 13917 | *-Buoy No. 2.* | 17° 54.4′ N 76° 45.8′ W | **Fl.R.** period 10s | | | STARBOARD (B) R, conical. | |
| | -RACON | | **K(– • –)** | | | | |
| | PORT ROYAL: | | | | | | |
| 13924 *J 5297* | -Gun Cay, S. end of shoal. | 17° 55.7′ N 76° 50.2′ W | **Fl.R.** period 5s | 20 **6** | 5 | Beacon. | |
| 13928 *J 5295.95* | -Rackhams Cay Range, front, 2.13 miles 284° to common rear. | 17° 55.9′ N 76° 51.4′ W | **Fl.W.** period 3s | 52 **16** | 8 | Metal framework tower. | Synchronized with common rear. |
| 13932 *J 5296* | --Lazaretto, common rear. | 17° 56.2′ N 76° 52.4′ W | **Fl.W.** period 3s fl. 0.5s, ec. 2.5s | 92 **28** | | White cairn. | 2 F.R. (vert.) on mast 1.6 miles NNW. R. lights 2 miles NNW. |
| 13933 *J 5296.1* | -Boat Channel Range, Bloomfield, middle, 2.37 miles 249°30′ to common rear. | 17° 57.0′ N 76° 50.1′ W | **Q.G.** | | | Beacon, green square daymark. | |
| 13934 *J 5296.4* | -Boat Channel, Angel, front 2.93 miles 249°30′ to common rear. | 17° 57.2′ N 76° 49.6′ W | **Q.W.** | | | Red beacon, white stripes, red ball topmark. | |
| 13940 *J 5300* | -SW. edge of Harbor Shoal. | 17° 56.1′ N 76° 50.9′ W | **Fl.R.** period 5s | 16 **5** | 5 | STARBOARD (B) R, beacon. | |
| 13948 *J 5301.4* | -Chevannes. | 17° 56.4′ N 76° 50.7′ W | **Q.R.** | | | STARBOARD (B) R, beacon. | F.R. lights on 4 masts 600 meters S. |
| 13952 *J 5304* | -Pelican Spit, N. side of Port Royal Harbor. | 17° 56.7′ N 76° 50.7′ W | **Fl.R.** period 5s | 21 **6** | 4 | STARBOARD (B) R, beacon. | |
| 13956 *J 5302* | -Bustamente, SW. of Gallows Point. | 17° 56.7′ N 76° 50.3′ W | **Fl.R.** period 3s | | | Beacon, red square daymark. | |
| | KINGSTON HARBOR: | | | | | | |
| 13960 *J 5306* | -Currey's Gate. | 17° 57.1′ N 76° 50.9′ W | **Fl.R.** period 1.5s | | | STARBOARD (B) R, beacon. | |
| 13962 *J 5307.5* | -Delbert Sicard. | 17° 57.0′ N 76° 51.3′ W | **Fl.G.** period 5s | | | PORT (B) G, beacon. | |
| 13964 *J 5307* | -Morton. | 17° 57.2′ N 76° 51.2′ W | **Fl.G.** period 1.5s | 22 **7** | 6 | PORT (B) G, beacon. | |

| (1) No. | (2) Name and Location | (3) Position | (4) Characteristic | (5) Height | (6) Range | (7) Structure | (8) Remarks |
|---|---|---|---|---|---|---|---|
| | | | **JAMAICA** | | | | |
| 13976 *J 5308* | -Two Sisters, near W. extremity of Middle Ground, E. side of ship channel. | 17° 57.5′ N 76° 50.7′ W | **Q.R.** | 18 **5** | | STARBOARD (B) R, beacon. | |
| 13980 *J 5312* | -Burial Ground. | 17° 57.5′ N 76° 50.9′ W | **Fl.G.** period 3s | 22 **7** | | PORT (B) G, beacon. | |
| 13984 *J 5309* | -Sphinx. | 17° 57.8′ N 76° 50.5′ W | **Fl.R.** period 5s | 18 **5** | | STARBOARD (B) R, beacon. | |
| 13988 *J 5313* | -Augusta. | 17° 57.9′ N 76° 50.7′ W | **Fl.G.** period 5s | | | PORT (B) G, beacon. | |
| 13992 *J 5310* | -Mammee. | 17° 57.9′ N 76° 50.4′ W | **Fl.R.** period 1.5s fl. 0.5s, ec. 1s | 18 **5** | | STARBOARD (B) R, beacon. | |
| 13996 *J 5314* | -St. Albans. | 17° 58.0′ N 76° 50.4′ W | **Fl.G.** period 1.5s | 22 **7** | | PORT (B) G, beacon; 20. | |
| 14000 *J 5317* | -East Horseshoe. | 17° 57.9′ N 76° 49.9′ W | **Fl.R.** period 3s | 26 **8** | | STARBOARD (B) R, beacon. | |
| 14004 *J 5316* | -Hunts Bay. | 17° 57.9′ N 76° 49.9′ W | **Fl.G.** period 3s | | | PORT (B) G, beacon. | |
| 14040 *J 5318* | -Middle Ground. | 17° 57.8′ N 76° 49.5′ W | **Fl.R.** period 5s | 17 **5** | | STARBOARD (B) R, beacon. | |
| 14044 *J 5325* | -Pond Mouth. | 17° 57.8′ N 76° 48.6′ W | **Fl.G.** period 1.5s fl. 0.5s, ec. 1s | 22 **7** | | PORT (B) G, beacon, topmark; 20. | |
| 14048 *J 5325.3* | -Pickering. | 17° 57.2′ N 76° 48.4′ W | **Fl.R.** period 1.5s | | | STARBOARD (B) R, beacon. | |
| 14052 *J 5325.5* | -Tupper. | 17° 57.1′ N 76° 47.8′ W | **Fl.R.** period 3s | | | STARBOARD (B) R, beacon. | |
| 14054 *J 5325.82* | -Royal Jamaican Yacht Club Marina, E side of entrance. | 17° 56.8′ N 76° 46.4′ W | **Fl.G.** period 3s | | | Pile. | |
| 14056 *J 5326* | -Shell pier, on each end of pier. | 17° 58.0′ N 76° 44.7′ W | **2 F.R.** | | | | |
| 14060 *J 5295* | Wreck Reef. | 17° 49.9′ N 76° 55.3′ W | **Fl.R.** period 5s | 16 **5** | 4 | White post, red bands. | |
| | PORTLAND BIGHT: | | | | | | |
| 14072 *J 5328* | -Pigeon Island Range, front. | 17° 47.6′ N 77° 04.4′ W | **Fl.W.** period 3s fl. 1s, ec. 2s | 25 **8** | 9 | White metal column, white triangular daymark point up; 26. | |
| 14080 *J 5327.9* | --Rear, 0.5 mile 343°20′ from front. | 17° 48.1′ N 77° 04.5′ W | **L.Fl.W.** period 6s fl. 2s, ec. 4s | 80 **24** | 10 | White framework tower, white triangular daymark point down; 75. | Visible 339°-347°30′. |
| 14084 *J 5329* | -Rocky Point Pier. | 17° 49.1′ N 77° 08.4′ W | **2 F.R.** | | | | 1 light shows from each end. |
| 14088 *J 5332* | -Range, front. | 17° 53.5′ N 77° 08.4′ W | **Fl.R.** period 3s | 26 **8** | | White conical beacon. | |
| 14092 *J 5332.1* | -Rear, 677 meters 300° from front. | 17° 53.7′ N 77° 08.7′ W | **Q.R.** | 41 **12** | | White conical beacon. | |
| 14112 *J 5327* | **Portland Ridge.** | 17° 44.5′ N 77° 09.5′ W | **Fl.(2)W.** period 15s fl. 1s, ec. 1s fl. 1s, ec. 12s | 650 **198** | **20** | Red metal framework tower, white bands; 115. | |
| 14116 *J 5340* | Kaiser Pier Range, front, outer end. | 17° 51.5′ N 77° 36.2′ W | **F.R.** | 34 **10** | | | |
| 14120 *J 5340.1* | -Rear, 690 meters 347°30′ from front. | 17° 51.9′ N 77° 36.3′ W | **F.R.** | 138 **42** | | Framework tower; 26. | |

| (1) No. | (2) Name and Location | (3) Position | (4) Characteristic | (5) Height | (6) Range | (7) Structure | (8) Remarks |
|---|---|---|---|---|---|---|---|
| | | | **JAMAICA** | | | | |
| 14124 *J 5341* | **Lovers Leap.** | 17° 52.3′ N 77° 39.5′ W | **Fl.W.** period 10s fl. 1s, ec. 9s | 1739 **530** | **40** | White round tower, red bands; 49. | |
| 14144 *J 5244* | **South Negril Point.** | 18° 15.0′ N 78° 21.6′ W | **Fl.W.R.** period 2s fl. 0.8s, ec. 1.2s | 100 **30** | **15** | White tower; 89. | R. 297°-305°, W.-161°, R.-215°. |
| 14148 *J 5352* | Pedro Bank, NE. Cay, NW. extremity of Cay. | 17° 03.1′ N 77° 45.1′ W | **Fl.W.** period 5s | 35 **11** | 11 | Beacon, red square topmark, white bands. | |
| 14149 *J 5347* | South West Rock. | 16° 47.5′ N 78° 11.4′ W | **Fl.(3)R.** period 10s | 16 **5** | 5 | Metal pole. | **Radar reflector.** |
| | | | **HAITI** | | | | |
| 14156 *J 5368* | Cap Jacmel. | 18° 10.6′ N 72° 32.8′ W | **Fl.W.** period 6s fl. 0.6s, ec. 5.4s | 127 **39** | 9 | White metal framework tower, red lantern; 20. | |
| 14158 *J 5370* | Ile Vache. | 18° 03.9′ N 73° 34.5′ W | **Q.(6)+L.Fl.W.** period 15s | | | White square tower. | |
| 14160 *J 5376* | Cap Dame Marie. | 18° 36.3′ N 74° 25.6′ W | **Iso.W.** period 5s | 123 **37** | 9 | Framework structure, white square concrete base; 16. | |
| 14164 *J 5380* | Grande Cayemite, N. point. | 18° 38.6′ N 73° 45.5′ W | **V.Q.W.** | 54 **16** | 12 | White metal framework tower, red lantern; 43. | |
| 14168 *J 5382* | **Pointe Ouest (W. Point).** | 18° 55.7′ N 73° 17.9′ W | **Fl.(4)W.** period 15s | 279 **85** | **20** | White metal framework tower. | |
| 14172 *J 5386* | Banc de Rochelois, in Canal de Sud, on Les Pirogues. | 18° 38.5′ N 73° 12.4′ W | **Mo.(A)W.** period 10s | 30 **9** | 9 | White framework tower with hut, black band, red lantern. | |
| 14182 *J 5388* | Miragoane. | 18° 27.0′ N 73° 06.4′ W | **F.R.** | 20 **6** | | Corner of loading chute. | |
| 14184 *J 5384* | Pointe Fantasque, SE. end of Ile de la Gonave. | 18° 41.6′ N 72° 49.4′ W | **Q.(6)+L.Fl.W.** period 15s | 50 **15** | 9 | White metal framework tower, black bands. | |
| | PORT-AU-PRINCE: | | | | | | |
| 14192 *J 5390* | **-Pointe du Lamentin.** | 18° 33.2′ N 72° 24.6′ W | **Fl.W.** period 3s fl. 0.3s, ec. 2.7s | 106 **32** | **16** | White round metal tower; 95. | Obscured by trees 109°-126°. |
| 14204 *J 5392* | -Range, front. | 18° 32.1′ N 72° 22.8′ W | **F.R.** | | | | |
| 14208 *J 5392.1* | --Rear, inner end of dock, 120 meters 183° from front. | 18° 32.0′ N 72° 22.8′ W | **F.G.** | | | | |
| 14212 *J 5399* | -Lafiteau Range front, pier, head. | 18° 41.7′ N 72° 21.2′ W | **F.R.** | | | Black and white beacon; 66. | |
| 14216 *J 5399.1* | --Rear, 304 meters 044°30′ from front. | 18° 41.8′ N 72° 21.1′ W | **F.R.** | | | Black and white beacon on building. | |
| 14220 *J 5402* | Les Arcadins, NW. point. | 18° 48.2′ N 72° 38.9′ W | **Fl.(2)W.** period 5s | 41 **12** | 9 | White round metal tower; 9. | Obscured by trees 358°-012°. |
| 14224 *J 5404* | Pointe de St. Marc. | 19° 02.5′ N 72° 49.0′ W | **Q.(9)W.** period 15s | 96 **29** | 9 | White framework tower, white round topmark. | |
| 14228 *J 5406* | Point Lapierre, N. side of entrance to Gonaives Bay. | 19° 27.3′ N 72° 46.0′ W | **V.Q.(6)+L.Fl.W.** period 10s | 318 **97** | 11 | White square stone tower. | |
| 14230 *J 5408* | **Cap du Mole St. Nicolas.** | 19° 49.3′ N 73° 24.8′ W | **Oc.W.** period 3s lt. 2s, ec. 1s | | **15** | White tower. | |

Lights along the coast of Haiti have been reported to be unreliable.

| (1) No. | (2) Name and Location | (3) Position | (4) Characteristic | (5) Height | (6) Range | (7) Structure | (8) Remarks |
|---|---|---|---|---|---|---|---|

## HAITI

| (1) No. | (2) Name and Location | (3) Position | (4) Characteristic | (5) Height | (6) Range | (7) Structure | (8) Remarks |
|---|---|---|---|---|---|---|---|
| | PORT-DE-CAP-HAITIEN: | | | | | | |
| 14231.9 *J 5411.4* | -Passenger berth. | 19° 45.6′ N 72° 11.6′ W | **Oc.R.** period 4s lt. 3s, ec. 1s | | | | |
| 14232 *J 5414* | Ile de la Tortue, E. Point. | 19° 59.8′ N 72° 37.3′ W | **Fl.(2)W.** period 6s fl. 0.5s, ec. 1s fl. 0.5s, ec. 4s | 77 **23** | 14 | White metal framework tower, triangular base; 46. | |
| 14234 *J 5412* | -W. Point. | 20° 03.7′ N 72° 58.0′ W | **V.Q.W.** | | | | |

Lights along the coast of Haiti have been reported to be unreliable.

## DOMINICAN REPUBLIC

| (1) No. | (2) Name and Location | (3) Position | (4) Characteristic | (5) Height | (6) Range | (7) Structure | (8) Remarks |
|---|---|---|---|---|---|---|---|
| 14240 *J 5422* | Cayo Arenas, on Bahia de Monte Cristi. | 19° 52.2′ N 71° 51.9′ W | **L.Fl.W.** period 6s fl. 2s, ec. 4s | 65 **20** | 13 | Red tower, black lantern. | |
| 14244 *J 5424* | Puerto Liberatador, steel pier, head. | 19° 42.6′ N 71° 44.6′ W | **Iso.R.** period 20s | 50 **15** | 10 | White tower, red lantern. | |
| 14248 *J 5426* | Cabra Island, NW. side Bahia de Monte Cristi. | 19° 53.4′ N 71° 40.1′ W | **L.Fl.W.** period 12s fl. 3s, ec. 9s | 110 **34** | 13 | White pyramidal metal tower; 49. | |
| 14260 *J 5430* | **Puerto Plata.** | 19° 48.2′ N 70° 41.7′ W | **L.Fl.W.** period 6s fl. 2s, ec. 4s | 137 **42** | **18** | Yellow framework tower, black lantern; 59. | Occasional. |
| 14265 *J 5431.1* | -Harbor light, Dir 218°. | 19° 47.9′ N 70° 42.2′ W | **Dir.F.W.R.G.** | 36 **11** | 9 | | R. 214°45′-217°15′, W.-218°45′, G.-221°15′. |
| 14270 *J 5432* | -AVIATION LIGHT. | 19° 45.8′ N 70° 34.0′ W | **Al.Fl.W.G.** period 10s | | 10 | | |
| 14272 *J 5434* | **Cabo Viejo Frances.** | 19° 40.0′ N 69° 56.2′ W | **L.Fl.W.** period 10s fl. 2s, ec. 8s | 164 **50** | **18** | White pyramidal concrete tower; 85. | Visible 132°-304°. |
| 14280 *J 5438* | Cabo Samana. | 19° 18.0′ N 69° 09.2′ W | **Fl.W.** period 5s fl. 0.5s, ec. 4.5s | 463 **141** | 10 | White pyramidal framework tower; 62. | |
| 14284 *J 5440* | Punta Balandra. | 19° 10.8′ N 69° 13.9′ W | **Fl.W.** period 4s fl. 1s, ec. 3s | 155 **47** | 10 | White framework tower. | |
| 14288 *J 5440.5* | Cayo Vigia. | 19° 11.7′ N 69° 19.6′ W | **Fl.R.** | 23 **7** | 8 | White pyramidal metal tower. | |
| 14292 *J 5442* | Punta Nisibon. | 18° 58.2′ N 68° 46.5′ W | **Fl.(2)W.** period 10s fl. 1s, ec. 2s fl. 1s, ec. 6s | 50 **15** | 12 | White metal tower; 36. | |
| 14296 *J 5444* | Cabo Engano, E. point of island. | 18° 37.0′ N 68° 19.7′ W | **Fl.W.** period 5s fl. 1s, ec. 4s | 141 **43** | 11 | Red and white metal tower; 66. | |
| 14298 *J 5444.5* | Punta Barrachana. | 18° 32.6′ N 68° 21.3′ W | **Iso.R.** period 2s | | | Tower. | |
| 14300 *J 5445* | Boca de Yuma. | 18° 22.7′ N 68° 36.4′ W | **Fl.R.** period 11s | 30 **9** | 10 | Red pyramidal metal tower; 30. | |

## DOMINICAN REPUBLIC

| (1) No. | (2) Name and Location | (3) Position | (4) Characteristic | (5) Height | (6) Range | (7) Structure | (8) Remarks |
|---|---|---|---|---|---|---|---|
| | ISLA SAONA: | | | | | | |
| 14304<br>*J 5446* | **-Isla Saona.** | 18° 06.7′ N<br>68° 34.6′ W | **Fl.W.**<br>period 10s<br>fl. 1s, ec. 9s | 105<br>**32** | **16** | White concrete tower. | |
| 14308<br>*J 5447* | -Punta Laguna. | 18° 08.3′ N<br>68° 45.3′ W | **Fl.W.**<br>period 4s<br>fl. 1s, ec. 3s | 45<br>**14** | 10 | White concrete tower. | |
| 14312<br>*J 5448* | **La Romana.** | 18° 24.9′ N<br>68° 57.5′ W | **Fl.W.**<br>period 6s<br>fl. 1s, ec. 5s | 90<br>**27** | **15** | White framework tower; 69. | |
| | PUERTO DE ANDRES: | | | | | | |
| 14324<br>*J 5454* | -La Caleta AVIATION LIGHT. | 18° 26.0′ N<br>69° 40.1′ W | **Al.Fl.W.G.**<br>period 5s | | 14 | Tower. | On request.<br>**Aero Radiobeacon.** |
| 14333<br>*J 5456.8* | -Cabo Caucedo. | 18° 24.5′ N<br>69° 37.6′ W | **F.R.** | 190<br>**58** | | | Aero light. |
| 14336<br>*J 5457* | Punta Torrecilla. | 18° 27.9′ N<br>69° 52.6′ W | **L.Fl.(2)W.**<br>period 10s<br>fl. 2s, ec. 2s<br>fl. 2s, ec. 4s | 135<br>**41** | 13 | Black tower, yellow diagonal stripes; 125. | |
| | PUERTO DE SANTO DOMINGO: | | | | | | |
| 14344<br>*J 5458* | -Entrance Range, front. | 18° 28.4′ N<br>69° 52.6′ W | **F.G.** | | | White concrete tower. | |
| 14348<br>*J 5458.1* | --Rear, 155 meters 047° from front. | 18° 28.4′ N<br>69° 52.5′ W | **F.G.** | | | White concrete tower. | |
| | PUERTO DE HAINA: | | | | | | |
| 14352<br>*J 5463* | -Entrance. | 18° 25.5′ N<br>70° 01.2′ W | **Dir.F.W.R.G.** | | | Yellow framework tower. | R. 342°18′-347°18′, W.-352°18′, G.-357°18′.<br>Sector bearings not reliable.<br>R. lights mark two chimneys 800 meters SSW. |
| 14353 | -Channel beacon 1. | 18° 24.7′ N<br>70° 01.1′ W | **Iso.G.**<br>period 4s | | | PORT (B)<br>G, beacon. | |
| 14355 | --3. | 18° 24.9′ N<br>70° 01.1′ W | **Fl.G.**<br>period 4s | | | PORT (B)<br>G, beacon. | |
| 14357 | --4. | 18° 24.8′ N<br>70° 01.0′ W | **Fl.R.**<br>period 5s | | | STARBOARD (B)<br>R, beacon. | |
| 14360<br>*J 5466* | Punta Palenque. | 18° 13.8′ N<br>70° 09.4′ W | **Fl.W.**<br>period 7s<br>fl. 1s, ec. 6s | 45<br>**14** | 12 | White concrete tower; 30. | |
| 14364<br>*J 5468* | **Boca Canasta.** | 18° 14.7′ N<br>70° 20.3′ W | **F.R., Fl.R.** (vert.) | | **22** | Mast. | |
| 14368<br>*J 5470* | Punta Salinas, Bahia de las Calderas. | 18° 12.4′ N<br>70° 33.6′ W | **Fl.W.**<br>period 3s<br>fl. 0.3s, ec. 2.7s | 98<br>**30** | 10 | Red pyramidal metal tower; 39. | |
| 14388<br>*J 5482* | Isla Alto Velo. | 17° 28.5′ N<br>71° 38.5′ W | **Fl.(2)W.**<br>period 10s<br>fl. 1s, ec. 2s<br>fl. 1s, ec. 6s | 535<br>**163** | 13 | Yellow concrete tower, black bands, black lantern. | |
| 14392<br>*J 5480* | Punta Beata. | 17° 36.3′ N<br>71° 25.4′ W | **Fl.W.**<br>period 9s<br>fl. 1s, ec. 8s | 80<br>**24** | 14 | Concrete tower. | |
| 14396<br>*J 5482.5* | Los Frailes. | 17° 37.7′ N<br>71° 41.3′ W | **Q.R.** | 32<br>**10** | 5 | | |

| (1) No. | (2) Name and Location | (3) Position | (4) Characteristic | (5) Height | (6) Range | (7) Structure | (8) Remarks |
|---|---|---|---|---|---|---|---|

**DOMINICAN REPUBLIC**

| (1) No. | (2) Name and Location | (3) Position | (4) Characteristic | (5) Height | (6) Range | (7) Structure | (8) Remarks |
|---|---|---|---|---|---|---|---|
| 14404 *J 5484* | Pedernales. | 18° 02.3′ N 71° 44.9′ W | **L.Fl.W.** period 12s fl. 5s, ec. 7s | 40 **12** | 11 | White metal tower, red lantern. | |

**PUERTO RICO**

| (1) No. | (2) Name and Location | (3) Position | (4) Characteristic | (5) Height | (6) Range | (7) Structure | (8) Remarks |
|---|---|---|---|---|---|---|---|
| 14412 *J 5486* | Isla Mona, on Cabo Noroeste. | 18° 06.6′ N 67° 54.5′ W | **Fl.W.** period 5s | 323 **98** | 14 | Metal tower; 39. | Light may be obscured by land masses when viewed from approximate bearings 140° and 270°. |
| 14416 *J 5488* | Punta Higuero. | 18° 21.7′ N 67° 16.2′ W | **Oc.W.** period 4s lt. 3s, ec. 1s | 90 **27** | 9 | Gray round tower; 69. | |
| 14420 *J 5490* | Punta Borinquen. | 18° 29.8′ N 67° 08.9′ W | **Fl.(2)W.** period 15s fl. 0.5s, ec. 4s fl. 0.5s, ec. 10s | 292 **89** | 14 | Gray column. | |
| 14424 *J 5491* | Ramey Air Force Base AVIATION LIGHT. | 18° 29.9′ N 67° 08.3′ W | **Al.Fl.W.G.** period 10s | 297 **91** | | | |
| 14428 *J 5492.6* | Arecibo AVIATION LIGHT. | 18° 26.9′ N 66° 40.4′ W | **Al.Fl.W.G.** | | | | |
| 14432 *J 5492* | Arecibo, on Punta Morillos. | 18° 29.0′ N 66° 41.9′ W | **Fl.W.** period 5s | 120 **37** | 14 | White hexagonal tower with dwelling. | |
| | BAHIA DE SAN JUAN: | | | | | | |
| 14436 *J 5494* | **-Puerto San Juan.** | 18° 28.3′ N 66° 07.4′ W | **Fl.(3)W.** period 40s fl. 1.3s, ec. 8.7s fl. 1.3s, ec. 8.7s fl. 1.3s, ec. 18.7s | 181 **55** | **24** | Beige square tower, octagonal base, on castle; 52. | Visible 061°-281°. |
| 14440 *J 5496* | -Range, W. side of harbor, front. | 18° 27.4′ N 66° 07.7′ W | **Iso.W.** period 2s | 26 **8** | | Framework tower on piles. | Visible 179°30′-182°30′. Shown 24 hours. |
| | -Passing. | | **Fl.W.** period 6s | 27 **8** | 4 | | |
| 14444 *J 5496.1* | --Rear, 220 meters 181° from front. | 18° 27.3′ N 66° 07.7′ W | **Oc.W.** period 4s | 49 **15** | | Framework tower on piles. | Visible 179°30′-182°30′. Shown 24 hours. |
| 14452 *J 5520* | AVIATION LIGHT. | 18° 26.3′ N 66° 00.3′ W | **Al.Fl.W.G.** period 10s | 185 **56** | | | |
| 14456 *J 5518* | Caballo Channel Range, front. | 18° 26.8′ N 65° 59.9′ W | **2 F.R.** (horiz.) | 20 **6** | | Red diamond daymark, orange stripes; 20. | Private light. |
| 14460 *J 5518.1* | -Rear, 27 meters 146°30′ from front. | 18° 26.8′ N 65° 59.9′ W | **2 F.R.** (horiz.) | 25 **8** | | Red circular daymark, orange stripes; 26. | Private light. |
| 14464 *J 5528* | **Cabo San Juan.** | 18° 22.9′ N 65° 37.1′ W | **Fl.W.** period 15s fl. 0.7s, ec. 14.3s | 260 **79** | **26** | Round tower, black band, white dwelling; 46. | Storm signal. |
| 14468 *J 5524* | Las Cucarachas. | 18° 24.0′ N 65° 36.7′ W | **Fl.W.** period 6s fl. 1s, ec. 5s | 38 **12** | 5 | Framework tower, green and white checkered diamond daymark; 16. | |
| 14472 *J 5601* | Cayo Lobito. | 18° 20.0′ N 65° 23.5′ W | **Fl.W.** period 6s fl. 1s, ec. 5s | 110 **34** | 8 | Framework tower, red and white checkered diamond daymark. | |
| 14480 *J 5608* | Isla Culebrita. | 18° 18.8′ N 65° 13.6′ W | **Fl.W.** period 10s | 305 **93** | 14 | Round masonry tower on dwelling; 43. | Obscured 125°-142° by NE. cay. |

Only major coastal and harbor entrance lighted aids are listed for Puerto Rico and the U.S. Virgin Islands. For other lighted aids in this area, see U.S.C.G. Light List Vol. III.

| (1) No. | (2) Name and Location | (3) Position | (4) Characteristic | (5) Height | (6) Range | (7) Structure | (8) Remarks |
|---|---|---|---|---|---|---|---|

## PUERTO RICO

| | | | | | | | |
|---|---|---|---|---|---|---|---|
| | ISLA DE CULEBRA: | | | | | | |
| 14488 *J 5604* | -Punta del Soldado. | 18° 16.7′ N 65° 17.2′ W | **Fl.W.** period 2.5s fl. 0.5s, ec. 2s | 65 **20** | 5 | Tower, red and white checkered diamond daymark. | |
| | ISLA DE VIEQUES: | | | | | | |
| 14496 *J 5594* | -Punta Este. | 18° 08.1′ N 65° 16.1′ W | **Fl.W.** period 6s | 43 **13** | 9 | | |
| 14497 *J 5592* | -Punta Mulas. | 18° 09.3′ N 65° 26.6′ W | **Oc.R.** period 4s | 68 **21** | 7 | White octagonal tower on dwelling. | |
| 14508 *J 5540.8* | Ensenada Honda AVIATION LIGHT. | 18° 14.4′ N 65° 38.2′ W | **Fl.W.** period 60s | 119 **36** | | | **Radiobeacon** about 1 mile eastward. |
| | For other lighted aids in Sonda de Vieques, use U.S.C.G. Light List Vol. III. | | | | | | |
| 14509 *J 5532* | Isla Cabeza de Perro. | 18° 15.0′ N 65° 34.6′ W | **Fl.W.R.** period 6s | 80 **24** | W. 8 R. 6 | Framework tower, red and white checkered diamond daymark. | W. 161°-021°, R.-031°, obsc.-066°, R.-161°. |
| 14510 *J 5533* | Bajo Chinchorro del Sur. | 18° 14.0′ N 65° 31.2′ W | **Fl.W.** period 4s | 25 **8** | 8 | Tower on piles, red and white checkered diamond daymark. | |
| 14512 *J 5545* | **Punta Tuna.** | 17° 59.3′ N 65° 53.1′ W | **Fl.(2)W.** period 30s fl. 0.2s, ec. 19.8s fl. 0.2s, ec. 9.8s | 111 **34** | **16** | White octagonal tower, square flat-roofed dwelling; 111. | |
| 14513 *J 5542* | Puerto Yabucoa Range, front. | 18° 03.3′ N 65° 50.2′ W | **Q.G.** | 75 **23** | | Tower, red rectangular daymark, white stripe. | Visible 295°48′-297°48′. Private light. |
| 14514 *J 5542.01* | -Rear, 832 meters 296°48′ from front. | 18° 03.5′ N 65° 50.6′ W | **Iso.G.** period 6s | 140 **43** | | Tower, red rectangular daymark, white stripe. | Visible 295°48′-297°48′. Private light. |
| 14520 *J 5552* | Bahia de Jobos. | 17° 56.0′ N 66° 17.0′ W | **Fl.W.** period 2.5s | 30 **9** | 5 | Pile, red and white diamond daymark. | |
| 14524 *J 5556* | Isla Caja de Muertos. | 17° 53.7′ N 66° 31.3′ W | **Fl.W.** period 30s | 297 **91** | 10 | Gray cylindrical tower, on center of flat-roofed dwelling; 297. | |
| 14536 *J 5560* | -Cayo Cardona, W. side of entrance. | 17° 57.5′ N 66° 38.1′ W | **Fl.W.** period 4s | 46 **14** | 8 | White cylindrical tower, on center of front of flat-roofed dwelling; 36. | |
| 14540 *J 5564* | -Harbor range, 183 meters S. of Customs Landing, front. | 17° 58.8′ N 66° 37.2′ W | **Fl.G.** period 2.5s | 16 **5** | | On pile. | Visible 013°30′-016°30′. Shown 24 hours. |
| 14544 *J 5564.1* | --Rear, 279 meters 015° from front. | 17° 58.9′ N 66° 37.2′ W | **Iso.G.** period 6s | 49 **15** | | Skeleton tower. | Visible 013°30′-016°30′. Shown 24 hours. |
| | BAHIA DE GUAYANILLA: | | | | | | |
| 14548 *J 5569.8* | -Cayo Maria Langa. | 17° 58.0′ N 66° 45.1′ W | **Fl.W.** period 2.5s | 42 **13** | 7 | Tower, red and white diamond daymark. | |
| | For other lighted aids in Bahia de Guayanilla, use U.S.C.G Light List Vol. III. | | | | | | |
| 14550 *J 5569.9* | -Entrance Range, front. | 17° 58.6′ N 66° 45.8′ W | **Q.R.** | 16 **5** | | Pile, red rectangular daymark, white stripe. | Visible 356°36′-359°36′. |
| 14551 *J 5569.91* | --Rear, 914 meters 358° from front. | 17° 59.1′ N 66° 45.8′ W | **Iso.R.** period 6s | 36 **11** | | Pile, red rectangular daymark, white stripe. | Visible 356°30′-359°30′. |

Only major coastal and harbor entrance lighted aids are listed for Puerto Rico and the U.S. Virgin Islands. For other lighted aids in this area, see U.S.C.G. Light List Vol. III.

| (1) No. | (2) Name and Location | (3) Position | (4) Characteristic | (5) Height | (6) Range | (7) Structure | (8) Remarks |
|---|---|---|---|---|---|---|---|

## PUERTO RICO

| (1) No. | (2) Name and Location | (3) Position | (4) Characteristic | (5) Height | (6) Range | (7) Structure | (8) Remarks |
|---|---|---|---|---|---|---|---|
| | BAHIA DE GUANICA: | | | | | | |
| 14564 *J 5574* | -Range, at Playa de Guanica, front. | 17° 57.9′ N 66° 54.6′ W | **Q.R.** | 36 **11** | | Framework tower, red rectangular daymark, white stripe. | Visible 350°54′-358°54′. |
| 14568 *J 5574.1* | --Rear, 512 meters 354°54′ from front. | 17° 58.2′ N 66° 54.6′ W | **Iso.R.** period 6s | 48 **15** | 5 | Framework tower, red rectangular daymark, white stripe. | Visible 350°54′-358°54′. |
| | For other lighted aids in Bahia de Guanica, use U.S.C.G. Light List Vol. III. | | | | | | |
| 14572 *J 5578* | **Cabo Rojo.** | 17° 56.0′ N 67° 11.5′ W | **Fl.W.** period 20s | 121 **37** | **20** | Gray hexagonal tower, dwelling; 46. | |
| | MAYAGUEZ: | | | | | | |
| 14596 *J 5582* | -Harbor Range, front. | 18° 13.1′ N 67° 09.7′ W | **Q.G.** | 33 **10** | | Square tower, red rectangular daymark, white stripe. | Visible 090°18′-094°18′. |
| 14600 *J 5582.1* | --Rear, 327 meters 092°18′ from front. | 18° 13.1′ N 67° 09.6′ W | **Oc.G.** period 4s | 87 **27** | | Tower on building, red rectangular daymark, white stripe. | Visible 090°18′-094°18′. |

Only major coastal and harbor entrance lighted aids are listed for Puerto Rico and the U.S. Virgin Islands. For other lighted aids in this area, see U.S.C.G. Light List Vol. III.

## LESSER ANTILLES

| (1) No. | (2) Name and Location | (3) Position | (4) Characteristic | (5) Height | (6) Range | (7) Structure | (8) Remarks |
|---|---|---|---|---|---|---|---|
| | VIRGIN ISLANDS (U.S.): | | | | | | |
| | -St. Thomas: | | | | | | |
| 14604 *J 5610* | --Savana Island. | 18° 20.2′ N 65° 04.9′ W | **Fl.W.** period 4s | 300 **91** | 7 | White tower. | |
| | --St. Thomas Harbor: | | | | | | |
| 14624 *J 5618* | ---Berg Hill Range, front. | 18° 20.7′ N 64° 56.0′ W | **Fl.G.** period 2.5s | 210 **64** | | Skeleton tower. | Visible 342°42′-345°42′. Shown 24 hours. |
| 14628 *J 5618.1* | ----Rear, 114 meters 344°12′ from front. | 18° 20.7′ N 64° 56.0′ W | **Iso.G.** period 6s | 299 **91** | | Skeleton tower. | Visible 342°42′-345°42′. Shown 24 hours. |
| 14632 *J 5628* | ---Buck Island, summit, E. side of harbor entrance. | 18° 16.7′ N 64° 53.5′ W | **Fl.W.** period 4s fl. 0.4s, ec. 3.6s | 139 **42** | 8 | Skeleton tower. | |
| 14636 *J 5629* | --Current Rock. | 18° 18.9′ N 64° 50.1′ W | **Fl.W.** period 6s | 20 **6** | 7 | Skeleton tower, red and white diamond daymark. | Intensified toward Buck Island and Two Brothers. |
| | -St. John: | | | | | | |
| 14644 *J 5630* | --Two Brothers. | 18° 20.6′ N 64° 49.0′ W | **Fl.W.** period 6s | 23 **7** | 7 | Skeleton tower, red and white diamond daymark. | |
| 14648 *J 5631* | --Steven Cay. | 18° 19.9′ N 64° 48.5′ W | **Fl.W.** period 4s fl. 0.4s, ec. 3.6s | 14 **4** | 7 | Framework tower, red and white checkered diamond daymark. | |
| 14652 *J 5632* | --Cruz Bay. | 18° 20.0′ N 64° 47.9′ W | **Fl.W.** period 4s | 12 **4** | 5 | Pile, red and white checkered diamond daymark. | |

Only major coastal and harbor entrance lighted aids are listed for Puerto Rico and the U.S. Virgin Islands. For other lighted aids in this area, see U.S.C.G. Light List Vol. III.

| (1) No. | (2) Name and Location | (3) Position | (4) Characteristic | (5) Height | (6) Range | (7) Structure | (8) Remarks |
|---|---|---|---|---|---|---|---|

## LESSER ANTILLES

| (1) No. | (2) Name and Location | (3) Position | (4) Characteristic | (5) Height | (6) Range | (7) Structure | (8) Remarks |
|---|---|---|---|---|---|---|---|
| | -St. Croix: | | | | | | |
| 14656<br>*J 5640* | **--Hams Bluff.** | 17° 46.2′ N<br>64° 53.7′ W | **Fl.(2)W.**<br>period 30s<br>fl. 0.2s, ec. 9.8s<br>fl. 0.2s, ec. 19.8s | 394<br>**120** | **16** | White round tower. | Visible 053°-265°, partially obscured 053°-062°. |
| 14660<br>*J 5639.2* | --Frederiksted Harbor, mooring. | 17° 42.8′ N<br>64° 53.0′ W | **Fl.W.**<br>period 4s | 16<br>**5** | | Dolphin. | Private light. |
| 14664<br>*J 5642* | --Christiansted Harbor Entrance Channel Range, front (Fort Louise Agusta). | 17° 45.3′ N<br>64° 41.7′ W | **Q.G.** | 45<br>**14** | | Framework tower, red rectangular daymark, white stripe. | |
| 14668<br>*J 5642.1* | ---Rear, 672 meters 164° from front. | 17° 45.0′ N<br>64° 41.6′ W | **Iso.G.**<br>period 6s | 93<br>**28** | | Framework tower, red rectangular daymark, white stripe. | |
| 14672<br>*J 5646* | --Buck Island. | 17° 47.2′ N<br>64° 37.1′ W | **Fl.W.**<br>period 4s<br>fl. 0.4s, ec. 3.6s | 339<br>**103** | 6 | Red pyramidal framework tower. | |
| 14673<br>*J 5647.5* | --Krause Lagoon Channel No. 4. | 17° 41.0′ N<br>64° 45.4′ W | **Fl.R.**<br>period 4s | 18<br>**5** | | STARBOARD (B)<br>R, pile, topmark. | Private light. |
| 14674<br>*J 5647.17* | --Lime Tree Bay Channel No. 5. | 17° 40.9′ N<br>64° 44.5′ W | **Fl.G.**<br>period 4s | 14<br>**4** | | PORT (B)<br>G, pile, topmark. | Private light. |
| 14688<br>*J 5638* | --Southwest Cape. | 17° 40.8′ N<br>64° 54.0′ W | **Fl.W.**<br>period 6s<br>fl. 1s, ec. 5s | 45<br>**14** | 7 | Gray framework tower. | |
| 14692<br>*J 5649* | --AVIATION LIGHT. | 17° 42.4′ N<br>64° 47.8′ W | **Al.Fl.W.G.**<br>period 10s | 249<br>**76** | | | |
| | VIRGIN ISLANDS (U.K.): | | | | | | |
| | -Tortola: | | | | | | |
| 14694<br>*J 5634* | --Sopers Hole, passenger terminal, SW. head. | 18° 23.4′ N<br>64° 42.2′ W | **F.R.** | 16<br>**5** | | | |
| 14696<br>*J 5635* | --Roadtown Range, front (Road Harbor). | 18° 25.3′ N<br>64° 37.1′ W | **F.R.** | 37<br>**11** | 3 | Administration building. | F.R. lights on radio mast 1.5 miles WNW.<br>Aero.F.R., F.W. (occas.) 3 miles E. |
| 14696.1<br>*J 5635.1* | ---Rear, about 40 meters 290° from front. | 18° 25.3′ N<br>64° 37.1′ W | **F.R.** | 52<br>**16** | 3 | Administration building. | |
| 14697<br>*J 5635.4* | --Breakwater. | 18° 25.5′ N<br>64° 36.9′ W | **Fl.R.**<br>period 3s | | | | |
| 14697.5<br>*J 5635.3* | --Cruise Ship Dock. | 18° 25.3′ N<br>64° 36.7′ W | **Fl.W.**<br>period 3s | | | Dolphin. | |
| 14698<br>*J 5635.7* | --Fat Hogs Bay. | 18° 26.1′ N<br>64° 33.6′ W | **Fl.(2)W.**<br>period 5s | 25<br>**8** | 5 | | |
| 14699<br>*J 5636.5* | --Bellamy Cay, off Beef Island. | 18° 27.0′ N<br>64° 31.9′ W | **F.W.** | | | White mast. | |
| | -Virgin Gorda: | | | | | | |
| 14700<br>*J 5633* | **--Pajaros Point.** | 18° 30.4′ N<br>64° 18.9′ W | **Fl.(3)W.**<br>period 15s | 200<br>**61** | **16** | | |
| 14702<br>*J 5632.5* | --Anegada, W. head. | 17° 47.6′ N<br>77° 04.4′ W | **Fl.W.**<br>period 10s | 62<br>**19** | 10 | | |
| 14704<br>*J 5637* | -Ginger Island. | 18° 23.5′ N<br>64° 28.1′ W | **Fl.W.**<br>period 5s | 498<br>**152** | 14 | Yellow tower; 13. | |

Only major coastal and harbor entrance lighted aids are listed for Puerto Rico and the U.S. Virgin Islands. For other lighted aids in this area, see U.S.C.G. Light List Vol. III.

| (1) No. | (2) Name and Location | (3) Position | (4) Characteristic | (5) Height | (6) Range | (7) Structure | (8) Remarks |
|---|---|---|---|---|---|---|---|

**LESSER ANTILLES**

| (1) No. | (2) Name and Location | (3) Position | (4) Characteristic | (5) Height | (6) Range | (7) Structure | (8) Remarks |
|---|---|---|---|---|---|---|---|
| 14708<br>*J 5636* | -Salt Island, NW. corner of island. | 18° 22.4´ N<br>64° 31.9´ W | **Fl.W.**<br>period 10s | 175<br>**53** | 14 | | |
| | LEEWARD ISLANDS: | | | | | | |
| | -Anguilla (U.K.): | | | | | | |
| 14712<br>*J 5650* | **--Sombrero.** | 18° 35.1´ N<br>63° 25.5´ W | **Fl.W.**<br>period 10s<br>fl. 0.1s, ec. 9.9s | 92<br>**28** | **17** | White column. | |
| | --RACON | | **T(–)** | | 10 | | (3 & 10cm). |
| 14716<br>*J 5656* | --Anguillita Island. | 18° 09.5´ N<br>63° 10.6´ W | **Fl.(2)W.**<br>period 15s<br>fl. 0.5s, ec. 1.5s<br>fl. 0.5s, ec. 12.5s | 48<br>**15** | 5 | Aluminum framework tower, red lantern; 26. | |
| 14720<br>*J 5656.5* | --Road Point. | 18° 12.2´ N<br>63° 05.7´ W | **Fl.(2)W.R.**<br>period 14s | 59<br>**18** | W. 10<br>R. 6 | White triangular concrete structure; 16. | W. 070°-089°, R.-116°, W.-218°. |
| 14722<br>*J 5656.8* | --Windward Point. | 18° 16.4´ N<br>62° 58.0´ W | **Fl.(3)W.**<br>period 16s<br>fl. 0.5s, ec. 0.5s<br>fl. 0.5s, ec. 0.5s<br>fl. 0.5s, ec. 13.5s | 82<br>**25** | | Framework structure; 33. | 2 R. lights on radio mast 4.4 miles SW. |
| | -Sint Martin (N.): | | | | | | |
| 14727<br>*J 5662.3* | --Philipsburg. | 18° 00.3´ N<br>63° 02.7´ W | **Q.R.** | | | | |
| 14727.5<br>*J 5662.5* | --AC Wathey pier, head. | 18° 00.5´ N<br>63° 02.9´ W | **Fl.(6)+L.Fl.W.**<br>period 10s | | 7 | | |
| 14728<br>*J 5659* | --Simson Baai AVIATION LIGHT. | 18° 02.5´ N<br>63° 06.7´ W | **Al.Fl.W.G.**<br>period 6s | 52<br>**16** | 13 | Control tower. | |
| | -St. Martin (F.): | | | | | | |
| 14730<br>*J 5657.5* | --Breakwater, head, N. end. | 18° 07.0´ N<br>63° 02.4´ W | **Fl.R.**<br>period 2.5s<br>fl. 0.5s, ec. 2s | 10<br>**3** | 5 | White pylon, red top; 7. | |
| 14731<br>*J 5657.6* | ---Spur. | 18° 07.0´ N<br>63° 02.3´ W | **Fl.G.**<br>period 2.5s<br>fl. 0.5s, ec. 2s | 10<br>**3** | 5 | White pylon, green top. | |
| 14731.5<br>*J 5657.7* | --Gailsbay, jetty. | 18° 04.9´ N<br>63° 05.1´ W | **Fl.(3)W.R.G.**<br>period 12s | 33<br>**10** | W. 8<br>R. 6<br>G. 6 | Metal mast. | R. 080°-100°, W. -106°30′, G. -123°. |
| 14732<br>*J 5658* | --Baie du Marigot. | 18° 04.2´ N<br>63° 05.2´ W | **Fl.W.R.G.**<br>period 4s<br>fl. 1s, ec. 3s | 66<br>**20** | W. 11<br>R. 7<br>G. 7 | White tower, red top; 33. | R. 104°-126°, W.-132°, G.-185°. |
| | -St. Barthelemy (F.): | | | | | | |
| 14736<br>*J 5664* | --Fort Gustavia. | 17° 54.1´ N<br>62° 51.1´ W | **Fl.(3)W.R.G.**<br>period 12s<br>fl. 1s, ec. 1.5s<br>fl. 1s, ec. 1.5s<br>fl. 1s, ec. 6s | 210<br>**64** | W. 11<br>R. 8<br>G. 8 | White tower, red top; 33. | R. 340°-103°, W.-111°, G.-160°. |
| 14737.5<br>*J 5666* | --Diamantrots, W. side. | 17° 38.9´ N<br>63° 15.4´ W | **Q.W.** | | | | |
| | -Saba (N.): | | | | | | |
| 14738<br>*J 5667.3* | **--St. Johns.** | 17° 37.2´ N<br>63° 14.6´ W | **Fl.(2)W.**<br>period 10s | | **15** | | |
| 14739.3<br>*J 5667.38* | --Fort Bay, E. side. | 17° 36.9´ N<br>63° 15.1´ W | **F.R.** | | | | |

Only major coastal and harbor entrance lighted aids are listed for Puerto Rico and the U.S. Virgin Islands. For other lighted aids in this area, see U.S.C.G. Light List Vol. III.

| (1) No. | (2) Name and Location | (3) Position | (4) Characteristic | (5) Height | (6) Range | (7) Structure | (8) Remarks |
|---|---|---|---|---|---|---|---|

## LESSER ANTILLES

| (1) No. | (2) Name and Location | (3) Position | (4) Characteristic | (5) Height | (6) Range | (7) Structure | (8) Remarks |
|---|---|---|---|---|---|---|---|
| 14739.6 *J 5667.4* | ---W. side. | 17° 37.0´ N 63° 15.1´ W | **F.G.** | | | | |
| | -St. Eustatius (N.): | | | | | | |
| 14740 *J 5668* | --Tumbledown Dick Bay, oil pier, head. | 17° 29.7´ N 63° 00.4´ W | **Fl.W.** period 5s fl. 0.5s, ec. 4.5s | | 10 | Dolphin. | |
| 14742 *J 5668.5* | **--Oranjestad.** | 17° 28.9´ N 62° 59.2´ W | **Fl.(3)W.** period 15s | 131 **40** | **17** | | |
| | -St. Christopher (St. Kitts and Nevis): | | | | | | |
| 14745 *J 5675* | --Half Moon Point. | 17° 18.8´ N 62° 42.1´ W | **Oc.R.** period 2s lt. 1.5s, ec. 0.5s | | | Tower. | *Reported visible 23M.* |
| | | | **F.R.** | | | | |
| | --Basseterre Bay: | | | | | | |
| 14752 *J 5672* | ---Fort Thomas. | 17° 17.3´ N 62° 44.1´ W | **F.R.** | 67 **20** | | Metal mast; 16. | Aero. Al.Fl.W.G. (occas.) 1.6 miles NE. |
| 14754 *J 5673.21* | ---Market building. | 17° 17.7´ N 62° 43.6´ W | **Q.R.** | 20 **6** | 5 | Green building, cream roof. | |
| 14755.4 *J 5673.13* | ---Cruise ship terminal, N. dolphin. | 17° 17.3´ N 62° 43.4´ W | **Fl.Y.** period 4s | 13 **4** | 3 | Metal mast; 3. | |
| 14755.6 *J 5673.14* | ----S. dolphin. | 17° 17.2´ N 62° 43.4´ W | **Fl.Y.** | | | | |
| 14756 *J 5674* | ---Fort Smith, E. side of harbor. | 17° 17.4´ N 62° 42.5´ W | **F.G.** | 35 **11** | 2 | Concrete block; 20. | Fl.W. 2s 2M on dolphin 370 meters NW. |
| | -St. Christopher (St. Kitts and Nevis): | | | | | | |
| 14760 *J 5678* | --Charlestown, root of pier. | 17° 08.3´ N 62° 37.8´ W | **F.R.** | 15 **5** | | Post. | Iso.R. light on radio mast 0.7 mile SSE. |
| 14761 *J 5678.4* | --Long Point Port. | 17° 06.5´ N 62° 37.5´ W | **Fl.(2)W.R.** period 15s fl. 1s, ec. 2s fl. 1s, ec. 11s | 89 **27** | | | |
| | -Montserrat (U.K.): | | | | | | |
| 14765 *J 5686* | --Plymouth, jetty, root. | 16° 42.3´ N 62° 13.3´ W | **F.R.** | | | Terminal building; 33. | Difficult to distinguish. |
| 14766.5 *J 5687.5* | --Castle Peak AVIATION LIGHT. | 16° 42.5´ N 62° 10.9´ W | **Fl.R.** period 1.5s | 3179 **969** | 6 | Mast; 180. | Obstruction light. |
| 14767 *J 5688* | --Blackburne Airport AVIATION LIGHT. | 16° 45.6´ N 62° 09.5´ W | **Al.Fl.W.G.** period 6s | 33 **10** | | | Obstruction light. *Reported visible 8 miles.* Occasional. |
| 14767.2 *J 5688.2* | ---AVIATION LIGHT. | 16° 46.0´ N 62° 09.9´ W | **Oc.R.** period 1.5s | 197 **60** | | | Obstruction light. *Reported visible 8 miles.* Occasional. |
| | -Antigua: | | | | | | |
| 14768 *J 5690* | --Sandy Island. | 17° 08.1´ N 61° 55.6´ W | **Fl.W.** period 10s fl. 1.5s, ec. 8.5s | 53 **16** | 10 | Aluminum framework tower; 52. | |
| | --St. John's Harbor: | | | | | | |
| 14772 *J 5694* | ---Pillar Rock. | 17° 07.7´ N 61° 52.7´ W | **Fl.G.** period 4s | 106 **32** | 5 | White house. | Visible 067°-093°, obscured-108°, visible thence to shore SE. of light. |

Only major coastal and harbor entrance lighted aids are listed for Puerto Rico and the U.S. Virgin Islands. For other lighted aids in this area, see U.S.C.G. Light List Vol. III.

| (1) No. | (2) Name and Location | (3) Position | (4) Characteristic | (5) Height | (6) Range | (7) Structure | (8) Remarks |
|---|---|---|---|---|---|---|---|

**LESSER ANTILLES**

| (1) No. | (2) Name and Location | (3) Position | (4) Characteristic | (5) Height | (6) Range | (7) Structure | (8) Remarks |
|---|---|---|---|---|---|---|---|
| 14774 *J 5695* | ---Range, front. | 17° 07.1´ N 61° 50.6´ W | **Iso.R.** period 6s | 62 **19** | 6 | Red metal mast, red square daymark; 56. | |
| 14776 *J 5695.1* | ----Rear, 440 meters 113° from front. | 17° 07.0´ N 61° 50.4´ W | **Iso.R.** period 6s | 92 **28** | 6 | Red metal mast, red square daymark; 30. | |
| 14784 *J 5696* | ---Fort James. | 17° 07.8´ N 61° 51.8´ W | **Fl.R.** period 4s | 48 **15** | 5 | White column; 7. | Visible 344°-shore. |
| 14792 *J 5698* | ---Range, front. | 17° 01.4´ N 61° 46.5´ W | **Q.G.** | 75 **23** | | Wooden pile structure, red triangular daymark point up; 33. | |
| 14796 *J 5698.1* | ----Rear, 290 meters 029° from front. | 17° 01.5´ N 61° 46.4´ W | **Iso.G.** period 2s | | | Wooden pile structure, red triangular daymark point up; 33. | |
| 14798 *J 5699.5* | --Prickly Pear Island. | 17° 10.6´ N 61° 47.9´ W | **Q.W.** | 26 **8** | | Black round metal structure. | |
| | --English Harbor: | | | | | | |
| 14800 *J 5698.5* | ---Range, front. | 17° 00.5´ N 61° 45.6´ W | **Fl.R.** period 2s | | | | |
| 14804 *J 5698.51* | ----Rear, about 450 meters 025° from front. | 17° 00.7´ N 61° 45.5´ W | **Fl.R.** period 4s | | | | |
| | -Guadaloupe (F.): | | | | | | |
| 14812 *J 5724* | **--La Desirade.** | 16° 20.0´ N 61° 00.3´ W | **Fl.(2)W.** period 10s fl., ec. 2.5s fl., ec. 7.5s | 164 **50** | **20** | White structure, red top; 66. | |
| 14816 *J 5725* | --Baie Mahault Range, front. | 16° 19.8´ N 61° 00.8´ W | **Fl.R.** period 2s fl. 0.4s, ec. 1.6s | 16 **5** | 4 | White pylon, red top; 16. | |
| 14820 *J 5725.1* | ---Rear, 35 meters 327° from front. | 16° 19.7´ N 61° 01.1´ W | **Fl.R.** period 2s fl. 0.4s, ec. 1.6s | 23 **7** | 4 | White pylon, red top; 16. | Synchronized with front. |
| 14825 *J 5728* | --Port de Beausejour, jetty, head. | 16° 18.2´ N 64° 04.1´ W | **Fl.(2)R.** period 6s | | 2 | White pylon, red top. | |
| 14828 *J 5727* | --Leading light. | 16° 18.2´ N 61° 04.4´ W | **Oc.(2)W.R.G.** period 6s lt. 1s, ec. 1s lt. 3s, ec. 1s | 23 **7** | W. 8 R. 6 G. 6 | White pylon, red top; 23. | R. 250°-335°, W.-339°, G.-056°. |
| 14832 *J 5730* | **--Iles de Petite Terre.** | 16° 10.2´ N 61° 06.5´ W | **Fl.(3)W.** period 12s fl. 1s, ec. 1.5s fl. 1s, ec. 1.5s fl. 1s, ec. 6s | 108 **33** | **15** | Gray tower, green top, on house; 85. | Visible 213°-185°. |
| 14834 *J 5715* | --Vieux-Bourg. | 16° 22.7´ N 61° 29.8´ W | **Fl.W.R.G.** period 4s | 20 **6** | W. 8 R. 5 G. 5 | | R. 016°-081°, W.-091°, G.-119°. |
| 14836 *J 5716* | --Port Louis. | 16° 25.1´ N 61° 32.0´ W | **Q.(9)W.** period 15s | 33 **10** | 11 | W. CARDINAL YBY, tower, topmark. | |
| 14840 *J 5718* | --Anse Bertrand. | 16° 28.4´ N 61° 30.5´ W | **Fl.(2)W.R.G.** period 6s fl. 1s, ec. 1s fl. 1s, ec. 3s | 46 **14** | W. 12 R. 9 G. 9 | White pylon; 26. | R. 120°-163°, W.-170°, G.-200°. |
| 14844 *J 5722* | --Port du Moule. | 16° 19.9´ N 61° 20.6´ W | **Fl.W.R.** period 4s | 39 **12** | W. 9 R. 6 | White pylon, red top, on hut; 36. | R. 110°-202°, W.-312°, R.-340°. |
| 14848 *J 5723* | --E. side of entrance. | 16° 19.9´ N 61° 20.5´ W | **Fl.(2)W.R.G.** period 6s fl. 1s, ec. 1s fl. 1s, ec. 3s | 23 **7** | W. 8 R. 6 G. 6 | White pylon, green top; 23. | R. 353°-133°, W.-138°, G.-165° (white on Hastings Pass). |

Only major coastal and harbor entrance lighted aids are listed for Puerto Rico and the U.S. Virgin Islands. For other lighted aids in this area, see U.S.C.G. Light List Vol. III.

| (1) No. | (2) Name and Location | (3) Position | (4) Characteristic | (5) Height | (6) Range | (7) Structure | (8) Remarks |
|---|---|---|---|---|---|---|---|

## LESSER ANTILLES

| (1) No. | (2) Name and Location | (3) Position | (4) Characteristic | (5) Height | (6) Range | (7) Structure | (8) Remarks |
|---|---|---|---|---|---|---|---|
| 14850<br>*J 5723.5* | ---Jetty, head. | 16° 19.8´ N<br>61° 20.5´ W | **Fl.(3)G.**<br>period 12s | | 2 | White pylon, green top; 10. | |
| 14852<br>*J 5731* | --Port de Saint Francois. | 16° 15.0´ N<br>61° 16.5´ W | **Q.W.R.G.** | 33<br>**10** | W. 9<br>R. 7<br>G. 7 | White tower. | R. 345°-358°, W.-002°, G.-015°. |
| | --Pointe-a-Pitre: | | | | | | |
| 14860<br>*J 5734* | **---Ilet a Gozier.** | 16° 11.9´ N<br>61° 29.4´ W | **Fl.(2)R.**<br>period 10s<br>fl. 0.5s, ec. 2s<br>fl. 0.5s, ec. 7s | 79<br>**24** | **21** | White tower, red top; 69. | Visible 259°-115°, obscured by trees on certain bearings toward Pointe Caraibe. |
| 14862<br>*J 5738.5* | --Port de Lauricisque, jetty, head. | 16° 15.0´ N<br>61° 32.9´ W | **Fl.(4)G.**<br>period 15s | 20<br>**6** | 2 | White pylon, green top, green square daymark. | |
| 14864<br>*J 5736* | ---Entrance Range, front, S. end Monroux peninsula. | 16° 13.2´ N<br>61° 31.9´ W | **Dir.Q.W.** | 49<br>**15** | 13 | White pylon, white rectangular topmark; 46. | Intensified 345°-351°.<br>River marked by lights. |
| 14868<br>*J 5736.1* | ----Rear, Pointe Fouillole, 640 meters 348° from front. | 16° 13.5´ N<br>61° 32.0´ W | **Q.W.** | 69<br>**21** | | White mast, white rectangular daymark; 66. | |
| 14868.5<br>*J 5736.2* | --RoRo Terminal. | 16° 14.0´ N<br>61° 32.5´ W | **Fl.G.**<br>period 2.5s | | 2 | | Marks gangway. |
| 14869<br>*J 5736.3* | --No. 1. | 16° 12.7´ N<br>61° 31.7´ W | **Q.R.** | 10<br>**3** | 5 | STARBOARD (B)<br>R, beacon, topmark. | |
| 14870<br>*J 5736.4* | --No. 2. | 16° 12.8´ N<br>61° 31.8´ W | **Fl.G.**<br>period 4s<br>fl. 1s, ec. 3s | 10<br>**3** | 5 | PORT (B)<br>G, beacon, topmark. | |
| 14871<br>*J 5736.45* | --No. 2a. | 16° 12.8´ N<br>61° 31.9´ W | **Fl.(2)G.**<br>period 6s | | | PORT (B)<br>G, beacon, topmark. | |
| 14872<br>*J 5736.5* | --No. 3. | 16° 12.9´ N<br>61° 31.8´ W | **Fl.(2)R.**<br>period 6s<br>fl. 1s, ec. 1s<br>fl. 1s, ec. 3s | 10<br>**3** | 5 | STARBOARD (B)<br>R, beacon, topmark. | |
| 14873<br>*J 5739* | --Petit Bourg, jetty. | 16° 11.4´ N<br>61° 35.4´ W | **Fl.(2)G.**<br>period 6s | | 4 | White tripod, green top. | |
| 14874<br>*J 5739.5* | --Goyave. | 16° 08.2´ N<br>61° 34.3´ W | **Fl.(3)G.**<br>period 12s<br>fl. 0.5s, ec. 2s<br>fl. 0.5s, ec. 2s<br>fl. 0.5s, ec. 6.5s | 16<br>**5** | 2 | White tripod, green top. | |
| 14878<br>*J 5743* | --Port de Bananier, jetty, head. | 16° 00.2´ N<br>61° 35.9´ W | **Fl.(3)R.**<br>period 6s | 20<br>**6** | 4 | White pylon, red top, red triangular daymark point up. | |
| 14880<br>*J 5702* | --Trois Rivieres. | 15° 58.1´ N<br>61° 38.8´ W | **Iso.W.R.G.**<br>period 4s | 82<br>**25** | W. 10<br>R. 7<br>G. 7 | White tower, green top; 30. | R. 275°-354°, W.-054°, G.-068°. |
| 14882<br>*J 5705* | --Marina, S. breakwater. | 15° 58.9´ N<br>61° 43.0´ W | **Fl.R.**<br>period 2.5s | 30<br>**9** | 5 | White tower; 10. | |
| 14882.5<br>*J 5705.2* | --N. breakwater. | 15° 58.9´ N<br>61° 43.0´ W | **Fl.(2)G.**<br>period 6s | | | Green pylon. | |
| 14884<br>*J 5706* | --Basse Terre, on quay, near customhouse. | 15° 59.8´ N<br>61° 43.9´ W | **Fl.W.G.**<br>period 4s<br>fl. 1s, ec. 3s | 46<br>**14** | W. 9<br>G. 6 | White pylon, green top; 39. | W. 325°-110°, G.-135°. |
| 14888<br>*J 5704* | **--Pointe du Vieux Fort.** | 15° 56.9´ N<br>61° 42.5´ W | **Fl.(2+1)W.**<br>period 15s<br>fl. 0.1s, ec. 2.5s<br>fl. 0.1s, ec. 6.1s<br>fl. 0.1s, ec. 6.1s | 85<br>**26** | **22** | White tower, gray top; 75. | Visible 271°-297° and 331°-176°.<br>Obscured 297°-331° by Les Saintes.<br>Reserve light. |

Only major coastal and harbor entrance lighted aids are listed for Puerto Rico and the U.S. Virgin Islands. For other lighted aids in this area, see U.S.C.G. Light List Vol. III.

| (1) No. | (2) Name and Location | (3) Position | (4) Characteristic | (5) Height | (6) Range | (7) Structure | (8) Remarks |
|---|---|---|---|---|---|---|---|
| | | | **LESSER ANTILLES** | | | | |
| 14892 *J 5712* | --Anse a la Barque. | 16° 05.4′ N 61° 46.0′ W | **Fl.(2)W.R.G.** period 6s fl. 1s, ec. 1s fl. 1s, ec. 3s | 36 **11** | W. 8 R. 5 G. 5 | White tower; 36. | R. 050°-064°, W.-081°, G.-115°. |
| 14896 *J 5710* | --N. side of entrance. | 16° 05.4′ N 61° 46.3′ W | **Q.(9)W.** period 15s | 91 **28** | 9 | W. CARDINAL YBY, tower, topmark; 23. | |
| | --Les Saintes: | | | | | | |
| 14904 *J 5746* | ---Bourg des Saintes, Terre d'en Haut, root of wharf. | 15° 52.1′ N 61° 35.0′ W | **Fl.W.R.G.** period 4s fl. 1s, ec. 3s | 30 **9** | W. 10 R. 7 G. 7 | White square tower; 26. | R. 075°-142°, W.-154°, G.-160°. |
| | --Marie-Galante: | | | | | | |
| 14908 *J 5748* | ---Grand-Bourg, on wharf. | 15° 52.8′ N 61° 35.3′ W | **Fl.(2)G.** period 6s fl. 1s, ec. 1s fl. 1s, ec. 3s | 26 **8** | 7 | White column, green top; 23. | Reserve light range 4M. |
| 14912 *J 5750* | ---St. Louis, W. of church. | 15° 57.4′ N 61° 19.1′ W | **Fl.G.** period 4s fl. 1s, ec. 3s | 36 **11** | 9 | White square tower, green top; 30. | |
| 14916 *J 5752* | ---Capesterre Range, front. | 15° 53.8′ N 61° 13.1′ W | **Q.R.** | 39 **12** | 9 | White tower, red bands, red top; 23. | Visible 246°30′-051°30′. |
| 14920 *J 5752.1* | ----Rear, 100 meters 312°06′ from front. | 15° 53.8′ N 61° 13.1′ W | **Q.R.** | 52 **16** | 9 | White tower, red bands, red top; 20. | Visible 246°30′-051°30′. |
| | DOMINICA: | | | | | | |
| 14926 *J 5760.4* | -Barroui. | 15° 25.9′ N 61° 26.1′ W | **2 F.R.** (vert.) | | | | |
| 14929 *J 5770* | **-Scott Head.** | 15° 12.8′ N 61° 22.3′ W | **Q.W.** | | **17** | | |
| | MARTINIQUE: | | | | | | |
| 14932 *J 5772* | **-La Caravelle.** | 14° 46.4′ N 60° 52.9′ W | **Fl.(3)W.** period 15s fl. 0.2s, ec. 2.8s fl. 0.2s, ec. 2.8s fl. 0.2s, ec. 8.8s | 528 **161** | **22** | Yellow square tower, white lantern; 46. | Visible 113°-345°. |
| 14932.3 *J 5772.23* | -La Trinite, TR10. | 14° 44.4′ N 60° 57.6′ W | **Q.G.** | 10 **3** | 2 | PORT (B) G, beacon, topmark. | |
| 14932.6 *J 5772.25* | --TR11. | 14° 44.4′ N 60° 57.7′ W | **Q.R.** | 10 **3** | 2 | STARBOARD (B) R, beacon, topmark. | |
| 14933 *J 5772.3* | -Baie Trinite Range, front. | 14° 45.3′ N 60° 58.0′ W | **Iso.W.** period 4s | 20 **6** | 12 | White structure; 16. | |
| 14933.1 *J 5772.31* | --Rear, 36 meters 284°12′ from front. | 14° 45.3′ N 60° 58.1′ W | **Iso.W.** period 4s | 23 **7** | 12 | White structure; 20. | |
| 14934 *J 5772.5* | -Baie du Francois. | 14° 38.2′ N 60° 53.5′ W | **Q.W.R.G.** | 92 **28** | W. 8 R. 6 G. 6 | White tower, red top; 30. | R. 200°-245°, W.-248°, G.-280°. |
| 14936 *J 5773* | -Port Vauclin, N. point. | 14° 33.1′ N 60° 50.2′ W | **Q.W.R.G.** | 46 **14** | W. 11 R. 9 G. 9 | White tower, red top; 23. | R. 220°-230°, W.-232°, G.-250°. |
| 14937 *J 5773.5* | --Dique Est, head. | 14° 32.8′ N 60° 50.1′ W | **Fl.(3)G.** period 12s fl. 1s, ec. 1.5s fl. 1s, ec. 1.5s fl. 1s, ec. 6s | 13 **4** | 2 | White tower, green top; 10. | |

Only major coastal and harbor entrance lighted aids are listed for Puerto Rico and the U.S. Virgin Islands. For other lighted aids in this area, see U.S.C.G. Light List Vol. III.

| (1)<br>No. | (2)<br>Name and Location | (3)<br>Position | (4)<br>Characteristic | (5)<br>Height | (6)<br>Range | (7)<br>Structure | (8)<br>Remarks |
|---|---|---|---|---|---|---|---|
| 14937.05<br>*J 5775* | --Baie de Cap Chevalier, Dir Lt 305°. | 14° 26.1′ N<br>60° 49.6′ W | **Q.W.R.G.** | 30<br>**9** | W. 10<br>R. 7<br>G. 7 | White metal post. | R. 291°-304°, W.-306°, G.-319°. |
| 14937.1<br>*J 5774* | --Epi Ouest, head. | 14° 32.8′ N<br>60° 50.1′ W | **Fl.(3)R.**<br>period 12s<br>fl. 1s, ec. 1.5s<br>fl. 1s, ec. 1.5s<br>fl. 1s, ec. 6s | 10<br>**3** | 2 | Pylon; 10. | |
| 14940<br>*J 5776* | **-Ilet Cabrits.** | 14° 23.5′ N<br>60° 52.1′ W | **Fl.(4)W.**<br>period 15s | 115<br>**35** | **15** | White pylon, red top. | Visible 235°-106° and 107°-108°.<br>Reserve light. |
| | -Marin Bay: | | | | | | |
| 14944<br>*J 5777* | --Point du Marin. | 14° 27.0′ N<br>60° 53.0′ W | **Q.W.R.G.** | 23<br>**7** | W. 9<br>R. 6<br>G. 6 | White pylon, red top; 23. | R. 015°-071°, W.-075°, G.-080°. |
| 14948<br>*J 5780* | **-Pointe des Negres.** | 14° 36.0′ N<br>61° 05.4′ W | **Fl.W.**<br>period 5s | 118<br>**36** | **24** | White pylon, gray lantern; 92. | Visible 276°-126°.<br>**Aero Radiobeacon** 0.1 mile NNW. |
| | | | **3 F.R.** (vert.) | | | | |
| 14960<br>*J 5784* | **--Baie du Carenage Range,** front. | 14° 36.2′ N<br>61° 03.7′ W | **Iso.G.**<br>period 4s | 135<br>**41** | **18** | White pylon, black bands, red rectangular daymark; 39. | Intensified 001°-007°. |
| 14964<br>*J 5784.1* | ---Rear, 145 meters 004° from front. | 14° 36.3′ N<br>61° 03.7′ W | **Iso.G.**<br>period 4s | 164<br>**50** | **18** | White pylon, black bands, red rectangular daymark; 46. | Synchronized with front.<br>Intensified 001°-007°. |
| | -Fort-de-France: | | | | | | |
| 14980<br>*J 5785.8* | --Quai des Annexes. | 14° 36.0′ N<br>61° 03.7′ W | **Oc.R.**<br>period 2.5s | 3<br>**1** | 4 | Red structure. | |
| 14981<br>*J 5785.6* | --Quai des Tourelles. | 14° 36.0′ N<br>61° 03.7′ W | **Oc.G.**<br>period 2.5s | 3<br>**1** | 4 | Green structure. | |
| 14983<br>*J 5787* | --No. 7. | 14° 35.6′ N<br>61° 04.0′ W | **Fl.(2)R.**<br>period 6s<br>fl. 1s, ec. 1s<br>fl. 1s, ec. 3s | 23<br>**7** | 4 | STARBOARD (B)<br>R, beacon, topmark. | |
| 14983.5<br>*J 5787.4* | --No. 3. | 14° 35.2′ N<br>61° 03.8′ W | **Fl.R.**<br>period 2.5s<br>fl. 0.5s, ec. 2s | 23<br>**7** | 3 | STARBOARD (B)<br>R, beacon, topmark. | |
| 14984<br>*J 5782* | **--Le Lamentin** AVIATION LIGHT. | 14° 35.7′ N<br>60° 59.7′ W | **Fl.(3+1)W.**<br>period 12s<br>fl. 0.1s, ec. 1.9s<br>fl. 0.1s, ec. 1.9s<br>fl. 0.1s, ec. 3.9s<br>fl. 0.1s, ec. 3.9s | 105<br>**32** | **20** | | |
| 14988<br>*J 5789* | -Pointe du Bout, Marina E. jetty, head. | 14° 33.5′ N<br>61° 03.0′ W | **Fl.(2)G.**<br>period 6s | 13<br>**4** | 2 | Green metal column; 13. | |
| 14992<br>*J 5790* | --Marina W. Jetty, head. | 14° 33.5′ N<br>61° 03.1′ W | **Fl.(2)R.**<br>period 6s | 13<br>**4** | 2 | Red metal column; 13. | |
| 14996<br>*J 5790.5* | **-Precheur Point.** | 14° 48.1′ N<br>61° 13.5′ W | **Fl.R.**<br>period 5s | 72<br>**22** | **15** | White tower; 39. | Visible 338°-162°. |
| | ST. LUCIA: | | | | | | |
| 15000<br>*J 5791* | **-Vigie.** | 14° 01.3′ N<br>61° 00.1′ W | **Fl.(2)W.**<br>period 10s<br>fl. 0.3s, ec. 2s<br>fl. 0.3s, ec. 7.4s | 320<br>**98** | **22** | White round masonry tower, red roof; 36. | Visible 039°-212°, partially obscured by Pigeon Island 206°-209°. |
| 15004<br>*J 5792* | -Tapion Rock. | 14° 01.0′ N<br>61° 00.4′ W | **Q.W.** | 50<br>**15** | 2 | Old battery; 7. | Visible outside harbor from 046°-192°, inside harbor from 192°-287°. |

Only major coastal and harbor entrance lighted aids are listed for Puerto Rico and the U.S. Virgin Islands. For other lighted aids in this area, see U.S.C.G. Light List Vol. III.

| (1) No. | (2) Name and Location | (3) Position | (4) Characteristic | (5) Height | (6) Range | (7) Structure | (8) Remarks |
|---|---|---|---|---|---|---|---|

**LESSER ANTILLES**

| | | | | | | | |
|---|---|---|---|---|---|---|---|
| | -Port of Castries: | | | | | | |
| 15008 *J 5794* | --Airfield extension. | 14° 01.0′ N 61° 00.1′ W | **Q.G.** | 11 **3** | 5 | Mast. | |
| 15016 *J 5793* | --W. wharf Range, front. | 14° 00.7′ N 60° 59.6′ W | **F.R.** | 56 **17** | 5 | Mast, NE. corner of building, white triangular daymark point up, orange stripe. | Emergency light Q.R. |
| 15020 *J 5793.1* | ---Rear, 911 meters 121° from front. | 14° 00.4′ N 60° 59.2′ W | **F.R.** | 110 **34** | 5 | Metal framework tower, white triangular daymark point down, orange stripe; 72. | Emergency light Q.R. |
| 15021 *J 5793.5* | --Pointe Seraphine. | 14° 00.8′ N 60° 59.8′ W | **Fl.Y.** | 13 **4** | 2 | Dolphin. | |
| 15024 *J 5795* | -Cul De Sac Bay Range, front. | 13° 59.3′ N 61° 00.8′ W | **Fl.G.** period 6s fl. 0.6s, ec. 5.4s | 39 **12** | 7 | Tower, green square daymark; 26. | |
| 15024.5 *J 5795.1* | --Rear, 345 meters 105°18′ from front. | 13° 59.3′ N 61° 00.7′ W | **F.G.** | 66 **20** | 7 | Black round tower, yellow bands, green square daymark; 46. | Visible 102°18′-108°18′. |
| 15026 *J 5795.3* | -Range, front. | 13° 58.8′ N 61° 00.5′ W | **F.G.** | 167 **51** | 7 | Black round tower, yellow bands; 89. | Visible 128°06′-134°06′. |
| 15026.1 *J 5795.31* | --Rear, 582 meters 131°06′ from front. | 13° 58.6′ N 61° 00.3′ W | **F.G.** | 203 **62** | 7 | Black round tower, yellow bands, red daymark, white stripe; 26. | Visible 128°06′-134°06′. |
| 15028 *J 5795.5* | -Bananes Point, No. 2. | 13° 59.2′ N 61° 01.6′ W | **Fl.R.** period 4s fl. 0.4s, ec. 3.6s | 85 **26** | 7 | Tower, white triangular daymark point up; 26. | |
| 15036 *J 5799* | -Mathurin Point. | 13° 42.8′ N 60° 57.5′ W | **V.Q.(2)W.** period 5s | 16 **5** | 2 | Red metal framework tower, concrete base; 10. | Visible 003°-shore. |
| 15040 *J 5800* | -Vieux Fort Bay Range, front. | 13° 43.2′ N 60° 57.2′ W | **Q.R.** | 26 **8** | 8 | Mast. | |
| 15044 *J 5800.1* | --Rear, 460 meters 059°53′ from front. | 13° 43.3′ N 60° 57.0′ W | **Iso.R.** period 6s | 65 **20** | 9 | Metal column, red diamond daymark. | |
| 15044.5 *J 5800.2* | -N. entrance channel. | 13° 43.3′ N 60° 57.4′ W | **Q.G.** | 13 **4** | 5 | Green pile. | |
| 15045 *J 5800.4* | -S. entrance channel. | 13° 43.2′ N 60° 57.2′ W | **Q.R.** | 13 **4** | 5 | Red pile. | |
| 15045.5 *J 5800.6* | -Battery Point. | 13° 43.4′ N 60° 57.2′ W | **Fl.Y.** period 2.5s fl. 0.3s, ec. 2.2s | 13 **4** | 5 | Orange pillar. | |
| 15046 *J 5800.7* | --S. | 13° 43.2′ N 60° 57.1′ W | **Fl.Y.** period 2.5s fl. 0.3s, ec. 2.2s | 13 **4** | 5 | Orange pillar. | |
| 15048 *J 5798* | **-Cape Moule a Chique.** | 13° 42.7′ N 60° 56.5′ W | **Fl.W.** period 5s fl. 0.5s, ec. 4.5s | 745 **227** | **22** | Masonry tower; 30. | Visible 197°-123°. |
| 15052 *J 5801* | -Mount Tourney AVIATION LIGHT. | 13° 44.6′ N 60° 57.9′ W | **Iso.R.** | 485 **148** | | Red metal framework tower, white bands; 33. | |
| 15056 *J 5802* | -Mount Bellevue AVIATION LIGHT. | 13° 44.4′ N 60° 56.7′ W | **Al.Fl.W.G.** period 5s | 351 **107** | | Beacon. | |
| 15060 *J 5790.6* | -Cape Marquis. | 14° 03.0′ N 60° 53.0′ W | **Fl.(2)W.** period 20s fl. 0.3s, ec. 6.4s fl. 0.3s, ec. 13s | 197 **60** | | White square support. | |
| 15062 *J 5790.8* | -Fourreur Rock. | 14° 04.3′ N 60° 58.7′ W | **Fl.(2)W.** period 5s | 23 **7** | 2 | | |

Only major coastal and harbor entrance lighted aids are listed for Puerto Rico and the U.S. Virgin Islands. For other lighted aids in this area, see U.S.C.G. Light List Vol. III.

| (1) No. | (2) Name and Location | (3) Position | (4) Characteristic | (5) Height | (6) Range | (7) Structure | (8) Remarks |
|---|---|---|---|---|---|---|---|

## LESSER ANTILLES

| (1) No. | (2) Name and Location | (3) Position | (4) Characteristic | (5) Height | (6) Range | (7) Structure | (8) Remarks |
|---|---|---|---|---|---|---|---|
| 15062.4 *J 5790.9* | -Marina, N. entrance. | 14° 04.7′ N 60° 57.3′ W | **Q.G.** | 10 **3** | 2 | | |
| 15062.6 *J 5790.95* | --S. entrance. | 14° 04.7′ N 60° 57.3′ W | **Q.R.** | 10 **3** | 2 | | |
| 15063 *J 5790.85* | -Marina Range, front. | 14° 04.6′ N 60° 57.0′ W | **Fl.W.** | 15 **5** | 2 | | |
| 15063.1 *J 5790.86* | --Rear, 251 meters 098°36′ from front. | 14° 04.6′ N 60° 56.8′ W | **Fl.W.** | 31 **9** | 2 | | |
| | ST. VINCENT: | | | | | | |
| 15064 *J 5817* | **-Fort Charlotte.** | 13° 09.5′ N 61° 14.5′ W | **Fl.(3)W.** period 20s fl. 1.5s, ec. 3s fl. 1.5s, ec. 3s fl. 1.5s, ec. 9.5s | 640 **195** | **16** | Hexagonal building; 10. | Visible shore-143°. Aero.Oc.R. (occas.) 1.5 miles SE. |
| 15068 *J 5816* | -Duvernette Island. | 13° 07.7′ N 61° 12.2′ W | **V.Q.(2)W.** period 2s | 229 **70** | 6 | White metal framework tower; 30. | Oc.W. (occas.) 250 miles NE. |
| 15068.2 *J 5816.2* | -Calliaqua Bay. | 13° 07.5′ N 61° 11.8′ W | **Fl.R.** period 4s | | | STARBOARD (B) R, pillar, topmark. | |
| 15068.4 *J 5816.4* | --Rookes Point Shoal. | 13° 07.7′ N 61° 11.9′ W | **V.Q.(6)+L.Fl.W.** period 10s | | | S. CARDINAL YB, pillar, topmark. | |
| 15068.6 *J 5816.6* | -Young Island Carenage. | 13° 07.7′ N 61° 12.1′ W | **Fl.G.** period 4s | | | PORT (B) G, pillar, topmark. | |
| 15072 *J 5815.4* | -Brighton. | 13° 07.5′ N 61° 10.1′ W | **Fl.W.** period 4s | 118 **36** | 8 | White metal framework tower; 20. | Visible 217°-077°. |
| 15076 *J 5815* | -Owia (Cow and Calves). | 13° 22.9′ N 61° 08.6′ W | **Fl.W.** period 10s | 118 **36** | 8 | White metal framework tower; 20. | Visible 101°-307°. |
| 15080 *J 5818* | -Dark Head. | 13° 17.2′ N 61° 15.8′ W | **Fl.W.** period 5s | 338 **103** | 12 | Metal framework tower; 10. | Visible 020°-211°. Oc.R. and 2 F.R. (vert.) 2.5 miles NE. |
| 15082 *J 5817.1* | -W. pier head. | 13° 09.2′ N 61° 13.6′ W | **Fl.(2)W.** period 4s | | | | |
| 15084 *J 5817.15* | -E. pier head. | 13° 09.2′ N 61° 13.6′ W | **Q.W.** | | | | |
| 15088 *J 5817.4* | -Kingstown Wharf, NW. head. | 13° 09.1′ N 61° 13.5′ W | **F.R.** | | | Column. | |
| 15092 *J 5817.2* | --SE. head. | 13° 09.0′ N 61° 13.5′ W | **F.R.** | | | Column. | |
| 15093 *J 5817.5* | -Cruise ship jetty, head. | 13° 08.8′ N 61° 13.6′ W | **Fl.G.** period 3s | 33 **10** | | Dolphin. | R. lights shown on S. side and G. lights shown on N. side of channel. |
| | BARBADOS: | | | | | | |
| 15096 *J 5804* | -Ragged Point. | 13° 09.8′ N 59° 26.0′ W | **F.R.** | 213 **65** | 3 | White round stone tower; 98. | Visible 135°-056°. |
| 15100 *J 5806* | **-South Point.** | 13° 02.8′ N 59° 31.8′ W | **Fl.(3)W.** period 30s | 145 **44** | **17** | White tower, red bands; 89. | Storm signal station. |
| 15102 *J 5806.5* | -Oistins Fishing Jetty. | 13° 03.7′ N 59° 32.6′ W | **F.R.** | 20 **6** | 5 | Hut. | |
| 15104 *J 5805* | -Seawell AVIATION LIGHT. | 13° 04.6′ N 59° 29.6′ W | **Al.Fl.W.G.** period 4s | 210 **64** | | | |

Only major coastal and harbor entrance lighted aids are listed for Puerto Rico and the U.S. Virgin Islands. For other lighted aids in this area, see U.S.C.G. Light List Vol. III.

| (1) No. | (2) Name and Location | (3) Position | (4) Characteristic | (5) Height | (6) Range | (7) Structure | (8) Remarks |
|---|---|---|---|---|---|---|---|

## LESSER ANTILLES

| (1) No. | (2) Name and Location | (3) Position | (4) Characteristic | (5) Height | (6) Range | (7) Structure | (8) Remarks |
|---|---|---|---|---|---|---|---|
| 15108 *J 5807* | -Needham Point. | 13° 04.7′ N 59° 36.8′ W | **Fl.R.** period 8s | | 3 | Post; 98. | |
| 15116 *J 5809.2* | -Bridgetown Careenage. | 13° 05.7′ N 59° 37.1′ W | **Fl.(2)R.** period 10s | 26 **8** | 2 | Silver metal framework structure; 16. | |
| 15116.4 *J 5809.4* | --Fishing Harbor Entrance. | 13° 05.7′ N 59° 37.2′ W | **F.G.** | | | | |
| 15116.6 *J 5809.6* | ---N. side. | 13° 05.8′ N 59° 37.2′ W | **F.R.** | | | | |
| 15120 *J 5811* | -Bridgetown breakwater. | 13° 06.4′ N 59° 38.0′ W | **Q.(3)R.** period 10s | 49 **15** | 12 | Red beacon, yellow triangular daymark point up; 30. | |
| 15122 *J 5812.54* | -Entrance Range, front. | 13° 06.5′ N 59° 37.7′ W | **Iso.G.** period 2s | | | Red and yellow stripes. | |
| 15122.1 *J 5812.56* | --Rear, 190 meters 088° from front. | 13° 06.5′ N 59° 37.6′ W | **Oc.G.** period 4.5s | | | Red and yellow stripes. | |
| 15125 *J 5812.5* | -Bulk Facility. | 13° 06.6′ N 59° 37.8′ W | **Fl.G.** period 5s | 29 **9** | | Red metal mast; 13. | |
| 15125.2 *J 5812.6* | -Shallow draft jetty, N. | 13° 06.5′ N 59° 37.6′ W | **F.R.** | 18 **5** | | Red mast. | |
| 15125.4 *J 5812.65* | --S. | 13° 06.4′ N 59° 37.6′ W | **F.R.** | 18 **5** | | Red mast. | |
| 15126 *J 5813.8* | -Maycocks Bay, jetty, N. head. | 13° 17.1′ N 59° 39.1′ W | **Q.R.** | | 3 | | |
| 15127 *J 5813.82* | --S. head. | 13° 17.0′ N 59° 39.1′ W | **Q.G.** | | 3 | | |
| 15128 *J 5814* | -Harrison Point. | 13° 18.5′ N 59° 38.9′ W | **F.R.** | 193 **59** | 3 | White stone tower; 85. | |
| | GRENADA: | | | | | | |
| 15132 *J 5827* | -Carriacou Island, Jack a Dan. | 12° 29.7′ N 61° 28.0′ W | **Fl.G.** period 5s | 14 **4** | 3 | | Visible 243°-182°. Occasional. |
| 15136 *J 5821.8* | -Catholic Island. | 12° 39.7′ N 61° 24.1′ W | **Fl.(2)W.** period 20s | 144 **44** | 8 | White metal framework tower; 10. | |
| 15137 *J 5821.85* | --Jondell. | 12° 39.5′ N 61° 23.7′ W | **V.Q.(3)W.** period 5s | | | E. CARDINAL BYB, beacon, topmark. | |
| 15140 *J 5819.6* | -Petit Cannouan Island. | 12° 47.5′ N 61° 16.8′ W | **Fl.(4)W.** period 40s | 252 **77** | 8 | White metal framework tower; 30. | |
| 15144 *J 5821* | -Canouan, Charlestown Bay Range, front. | 12° 42.8′ N 61° 19.6′ W | **F.W.** | 18 **5** | | White concrete tower. | |
| 15148 *J 5821.1* | --Rear, 450 meters 158°32′ from front. | 12° 41.8′ N 61° 19.7′ W | **F.W.** | 165 **50** | | White concrete tower. | |
| 15148.2 *J 5820.4* | ---Grand Bay. | 12° 42.7′ N 61° 19.9′ W | **Fl.G.** period 4s | | | PORT (B) G, beacon, topmark. | |
| 15148.4 *J 5820.5* | ---S. | 12° 42.4′ N 61° 20.1′ W | **Fl.R.** period 4s | | | STARBOARD (B) R, beacon, topmark. | |
| 15149 *J 5820* | -Range, front. | 12° 42.8′ N 61° 19.6′ W | **Iso.W.** period 4s | 46 **14** | 5 | White framework tower, black and white square daymark; 30. | Visible on range line only. |
| 15150 *J 5820.1* | --Rear, 85 meters 060° from front. | 12° 42.7′ N 61° 19.5′ W | **Fl.W.** period 5s | 91 **28** | 5 | White framework tower, black and white square daymark; 10. | Visible on range line only. |

Only major coastal and harbor entrance lighted aids are listed for Puerto Rico and the U.S. Virgin Islands. For other lighted aids in this area, see U.S.C.G. Light List Vol. III.

| (1) No. | (2) Name and Location | (3) Position | (4) Characteristic | (5) Height | (6) Range | (7) Structure | (8) Remarks |
|---|---|---|---|---|---|---|---|

## LESSER ANTILLES

| (1) No. | (2) Name and Location | (3) Position | (4) Characteristic | (5) Height | (6) Range | (7) Structure | (8) Remarks |
|---|---|---|---|---|---|---|---|
| 15150.1<br>*J 5824* | -Thompson reef, SW. edge. | 12° 35.5′ N<br>61° 24.7′ W | **Fl.R.** | | | STARBOARD (B)<br>R, beacon, topmark. | |
| 15150.2<br>*J 5824.2* | --SE. edge. | 12° 35.6′ N<br>61° 24.7′ W | **Fl.R.** | | | STARBOARD (B)<br>R, beacon, topmark. | |
| 15150.3<br>*J 5825* | -Roundabout Reef, SW. edge. | 12° 35.6′ N<br>61° 24.3′ W | **Fl.R.** | | | STARBOARD (B)<br>R, beacon, topmark. | |
| 15150.4<br>*J 5825.2* | --W. | 12° 35.6′ N<br>61° 25.0′ W | **Fl.G.** | | | PORT (B)<br>G, beacon, topmark. | |
| 15151<br>*J 5821.3* | --Pier, head. | 12° 42.2′ N<br>61° 19.8′ W | **F.W.** | | | | |
| | GRENADINE ISLANDS: | | | | | | |
| 15151.6<br>*J 5822* | -Union Island. Clifton Harbor Range, front. | 12° 36.0′ N<br>61° 25.2′ W | **F.W.** | 13<br>**4** | | White concrete tower. | Lighted beacons mark reef and shoal. |
| 15151.65<br>*J 5822.1* | --Rear, 555 meters 327°30′ from front. | 12° 36.0′ N<br>61° 25.2′ W | **F.W.** | 125<br>**38** | | White concrete tower. | |
| 15151.7<br>*J 5822.4* | -Miss Irene Point. | 12° 35.5′ N<br>61° 27.6′ W | **Fl.(2)W.**<br>period 20s | 410<br>**125** | 8 | Metal framework tower; 20. | |
| 15151.8<br>*J 5823* | -Grand de Coi. | 12° 35.1′ N<br>61° 24.7′ W | **V.Q.(9)W.**<br>period 10s | | | W. CARDINAL<br>YBY, pillar, topmark. | |
| 15152<br>*J 5819.4* | -Battowia Island. | 12° 57.9′ N<br>61° 07.9′ W | **Fl.(2)W.**<br>period 20s | 708<br>**216** | 8 | White metal framework tower; 10. | |
| 15154<br>*J 5819.5* | -Mustique, Montezuma Shoal. | 12° 52.8′ N<br>61° 12.0′ W | **Fl.(2)W.**<br>period 15s | | | ISOLATED DANGER<br>BRB, pillar, topmark. | |
| 15156<br>*J 5819.2* | -Bequia, Admiralty Bay, root of jetty. | 13° 00.7′ N<br>61° 14.2′ W | **Dir.W.R.G.**<br>period 4s | 19<br>**6** | 5 | White metal framework tower; 20. | Fl.R. shore-048°, Fl.W.-058°, Fl.G.-shore. |
| 15158<br>*J 5819.1* | --Devils' Table. | 13° 00.7′ N<br>61° 15.0′ W | **V.Q.(9)W.**<br>period 10s | | | W. CARDINAL<br>YBY, pillar, topmark. | |
| 15160<br>*J 5819* | --West Cay. | 12° 59.5′ N<br>61° 17.5′ W | **Fl.W.**<br>period 10s | 42<br>**13** | 8 | White metal framework tower; 20. | |
| 15161<br>*J 5830.3* | -Prickly Point. | 11° 59.3′ N<br>61° 45.6′ W | **F.R.** | | | Lighthouse. | Occasional.<br>Private light. |
| 15162<br>*J 5830.5* | -Glover Island. | 11° 59.1′ N<br>61° 47.3′ W | **Q.(6)+L.Fl.W.**<br>period 15s | | 7 | Mast; 20. | |
| 15164<br>*J 5830.7* | -Point Salines. | 12° 00.1′ N<br>61° 48.1′ W | **Q.(9)W.**<br>period 15s | | 7 | Hut; 3. | |
| 15174<br>*J 5830.2* | **-Petit Cabrits.** | 12° 01.0′ N<br>61° 46.5′ W | **Fl.(2+1)W.**<br>period 20s<br>fl. 0.4s, ec. 2.9s<br>fl. 0.4s, ec. 7.9s<br>fl. 0.4s, ec. 8s | 354<br>**108** | **18** | Red framework tower. | |
| 15176<br>*J 5834* | **-St. George's Harbor.** | 12° 03.0′ N<br>61° 45.2′ W | **F.R.** | 188<br>**57** | **15** | Brick structure. | Visible 056°30′-151°.<br>R. light on tower 1 mile E. |
| 15177<br>*J 5834.2* | --Range, front. | 12° 02.5′ N<br>61° 45.2′ W | **F.R.** | 46<br>**14** | | Framework tower, orange rectangular daymark, white stripe. | R. lights on radio masts 1.7 miles SW. |
| 15177.1<br>*J 5834.3* | ---Rear, 89 meters 132° from front. | 12° 02.5′ N<br>61° 45.1′ W | **F.R.** | 92<br>**28** | | Framework tower, orange rectangular daymark, white stripe. | |
| 15178<br>*J 5834.4* | --Range, front. | 12° 03.0′ N<br>61° 44.7′ W | **F.R.** | 102<br>**31** | | Framework tower, orange rectangular daymark, white stripe. | |

Only major coastal and harbor entrance lighted aids are listed for Puerto Rico and the U.S. Virgin Islands. For other lighted aids in this area, see U.S.C.G. Light List Vol. III.

| (1)<br>No. | (2)<br>Name and Location | (3)<br>Position | (4)<br>Characteristic | (5)<br>Height | (6)<br>Range | (7)<br>Structure | (8)<br>Remarks |
|---|---|---|---|---|---|---|---|

## LESSER ANTILLES

| (1)<br>No. | (2)<br>Name and Location | (3)<br>Position | (4)<br>Characteristic | (5)<br>Height | (6)<br>Range | (7)<br>Structure | (8)<br>Remarks |
|---|---|---|---|---|---|---|---|
| 15178.1<br>*J 5834.5* | ---Rear, 518 meters 068°30′ from front. | 12° 03.1′ N<br>61° 44.5′ W | **F.R.** | 299<br>**91** | | Framework tower, orange rectangular daymark, white stripe. | |
| | TOBAGO: | | | | | | |
| 15180<br>*J 5837* | **-St. Giles Island.** | 11° 21.4′ N<br>60° 31.0′ W | **Fl.W.**<br>period 7.5s | | **16** | | |
| 15182<br>*J 5837.2* | -Little Tobago. | 11° 17.8′ N<br>60° 29.6′ W | **Fl.(3)W.**<br>period 10s | 59<br>**18** | 5 | | |
| 15183<br>*J 5837.4* | -Smiths Island. | 11° 11.0′ N<br>60° 39.0′ W | **Fl.W.R.**<br>period 5s | 59<br>**18** | W. 7<br>R. 5 | | R. 068°-276°, W.-068°. |
| 15184<br>*J 5838* | **-Scarborough.** | 11° 10.6′ N<br>60° 43.6′ W | **Fl.(2)W.**<br>period 20s<br>fl. 0.7s, ec. 2.6s<br>fl. 0.7s, ec. 16s | 463<br>**141** | **20** | White concrete building, red roof. | Visible 258°-090°. |
| 15196<br>*J 5839* | --Range, front. | 11° 10.9′ N<br>60° 44.4′ W | **Iso.W.R.G.**<br>period 2s | 49<br>**15** | W. 7<br>R. 5<br>G. 5 | White framework tower, red top. | R. 313°30′-323°30′, W.-335°30′, G.-345°30′. |
| 15196.1<br>*J 5839.1* | ---Rear, 244 meters 330°12′ from front. | 11° 11.0′ N<br>60° 44.5′ W | **Oc.W.**<br>period 5s<br>lt. 3s, ec. 2s | 66<br>**20** | 11 | White framework tower, red top. | |
| 15197<br>*J 5839.8* | --Bulldog Shoal. | 11° 08.9′ N<br>60° 44.5′ W | **V.Q.(6)+L.Fl.W.**<br>period 10s | | 5 | S. CARDINAL<br>YB, beacon, topmark. | |
| 15197.2<br>*J 5839.9* | --No. 1. | 11° 09.8′ N<br>60° 44.1′ W | **Fl.G.**<br>period 3s | | 4 | Beacon. | |
| 15197.4<br>*J 5840.1* | --No. 2. | 11° 09.9′ N<br>60° 43.2′ W | **Fl.R.**<br>period 3s | | 5 | Beacon. | |
| 15197.8<br>*J 5840.3* | ---W. | 11° 10.4′ N<br>60° 44.2′ W | **Fl.G.**<br>period 3s | | 5 | Beacon. | |
| 15198<br>*J 5840.4* | --Breakwater, head. | 11° 10.7′ N<br>60° 44.1′ W | **Q.R.** | | 5 | Beacon. | |
| 15200<br>*J 5841.5* | **-Crown Point.** | 11° 08.9′ N<br>60° 50.7′ W | **Fl.(4)W.**<br>period 20s<br>fl. 0.5s, ec. 1.5s<br>fl. 0.5s, ec. 1.5s<br>fl. 0.5s, ec. 1.5s<br>fl. 0.5s, ec. 13.5s | 115<br>**35** | **16** | Aluminum framework tower, topmark; 85. | |
| 15200.05<br>*J 5841.54* | -Milford Bay. | 11° 09.3′ N<br>60° 50.4′ W | **Q.W.R.G.** | 23<br>**7** | W. 5<br>R. 4<br>G. 4 | | R. 073°-083°, W.-128°, G.-138°. |
| 15200.1<br>*J 5841.58* | -Booby Point. | 11° 11.0′ N<br>60° 48.7′ W | **Fl.Y.**<br>period 3s | | 4 | | |
| 15201<br>*J 5841.6* | -Courtland Point. | 11° 13.3′ N<br>60° 46.8′ W | **L.Fl.W.**<br>period 10s<br>fl. 2s, ec. 8s | | 8 | | |
| 15202<br>*J 5841.7* | -The Sisters. | 11° 20.0′ N<br>60° 38.8′ W | **Fl.(2)W.**<br>period 10s | | 8 | | |
| 15202.5<br>*J 5841.8* | -Man of War Bay. | 11° 19.4′ N<br>60° 32.8′ W | **Q.W.R.G.** | 82<br>**25** | W. 5<br>R. 4<br>G. 4 | | R. 098°-108°, W.-131°, G.-141°. |

Only major coastal and harbor entrance lighted aids are listed for Puerto Rico and the U.S. Virgin Islands. For other lighted aids in this area, see U.S.C.G. Light List Vol. III.

# Section 10

## East Coast of Mexico

| (1)<br>No. | (2)<br>Name and Location | (3)<br>Position | (4)<br>Characteristic | (5)<br>Height | (6)<br>Range | (7)<br>Structure | (8)<br>Remarks |
|---|---|---|---|---|---|---|---|
| | | | **MEXICO** | | | | |
| 15203<br>*J 4229.5* | Rio Bravo. | 25° 56.8´ N<br>97° 08.8´ W | **Fl.W.**<br>period 6s<br>fl. 1s, ec. 5s | 59<br>**18** | 10 | White round concrete tower; 52. | |
| 15203.1<br>*J 4230* | **El Mezquital.** | 25° 15.0´ N<br>97° 26.4´ W | **Fl.(3)W.**<br>period 10s | 98<br>**30** | **18** | White truncated pyramidal aluminum tower on four concrete columns; 98. | |
| 15203.15<br>*J 4230.2* | -Breakwater. | 25° 14.5´ N<br>97° 25.6´ W | **Fl.G.**<br>period 5s<br>fl. 0.5s, ec. 4.5s | 39<br>**12** | 7 | White cylindrical concrete tower; 23. | |
| 15203.2<br>*J 4229.55* | -Canal de Chavez. | 25° 52.0´ N<br>97° 10.1´ W | **Fl.W.**<br>period 6s<br>fl. 1s, ec. 5s | 38<br>**12** | 10 | White round concrete tower; 33. | |
| 15206<br>*J 4230.4* | La Carbonera. | 24° 37.7´ N<br>97° 43.1´ W | **Fl.W.**<br>period 6s<br>fl. 1s, ec. 5s | 39<br>**12** | 10 | White round concrete tower, red bands; 33. | |
| 15207<br>*J 4230.5* | **Punta Piedra.** | 24° 29.2´ N<br>97° 44.5´ W | **Fl.(2)W.**<br>period 10s<br>fl. 1s, ec. 2s<br>fl. 1s, ec. 6s | 92<br>**28** | **18** | White pyramidal concrete tower; 82. | |
| 15208<br>*J 4231* | La Pesca. | 23° 46.5´ N<br>97° 44.1´ W | **Fl.(4)W.**<br>period 16s<br>fl. 1s, ec. 2s<br>fl. 1s, ec. 2s<br>fl. 1s, ec. 2s<br>fl. 1s, ec. 6s | 59<br>**18** | 13 | White cylindrical concrete tower; 52. | |
| 15209.1<br>*J 4231.5* | -N. breakwater. | 23° 46.2´ N<br>97° 43.9´ W | **Fl.R.**<br>period 5s<br>fl. 0.5s, ec. 4.5s | 36<br>**11** | 9 | Cylindrical concrete tower; 23. | |
| 15209.2<br>*J 4231.6* | -S. breakwater. | 23° 46.0´ N<br>97° 44.1´ W | **Fl.G.**<br>period 5s<br>fl. 0.5s, ec. 4.5s | 36<br>**11** | 9 | Truncated pyramidal metal tower; 23. | |
| 15211<br>*J 4231.9* | Barra del Tordo. | 23° 03.5´ N<br>97° 46.0´ W | **Fl.W.**<br>period 6s<br>fl. 1s, ec. 5s | 36<br>**11** | 7 | White truncated pyramidal aluminum tower; 23. | |
| 15212<br>*J 4232* | **Punta Jerez.** | 22° 53.6´ N<br>97° 45.8´ W | **Fl.W.**<br>period 6s | 72<br>**22** | **20** | White cylindrical concrete tower; 66. | |
| 15213<br>*J 4232.5* | Barra de Chavarria. | 22° 40.8´ N<br>97° 50.2´ W | **Fl.W.**<br>period 5s<br>fl. 0.5s, ec. 4.5s | 39<br>**12** | 7 | White round concrete tower; 23. | |
| | ALTAMIRA: | | | | | | |
| 15214<br>*J 4233* | -Altamira. | 22° 29.6´ N<br>97° 51.8´ W | **Fl.W.**<br>period 6s | 138<br>**42** | 14 | White octagonal concrete tower; 118. | |
| | -RACON | | **Z(– – • •)** | | **20** | | (3 & 10cm). |
| 15214.2<br>*J 4233.2* | -S. breakwater. | 22° 28.9´ N<br>97° 51.0´ W | **Fl.G.**<br>period 5s<br>fl. 0.5s, ec. 4.5s | 36<br>**11** | 9 | Truncated pyramidal aluminum tower; 23. | |
| 15214.3<br>*J 4233.25* | -N. breakwater. | 22° 29.6´ N<br>97° 50.9´ W | **Fl.R.**<br>period 5s<br>fl. 0.5s, ec. 4.5s | 43<br>**13** | 9 | Truncated pyramidal aluminum tower; 23. | |

The lights of Mexico are characterized by the number of flashes etc., the periods being subject to fluctuations.

| (1) No. | (2) Name and Location | (3) Position | (4) Characteristic | (5) Height | (6) Range | (7) Structure | (8) Remarks |
|---|---|---|---|---|---|---|---|
| | | | **MEXICO** | | | | |
| 15214.4 *J 4233.4* | **-Range,** front. | 22° 29.2´ N 97° 53.4´ W | **Fl.W.** period 3s fl. 1s, ec. 2s | 36 **11** | **15** | Truncated pyramidal aluminum tower; 23. | |
| 15214.45 *J 4233.41* | --Rear, 400 meters 270° from front. | 22° 29.2´ N 97° 53.5´ W | **Iso.W.** period 2s | 56 **17** | **15** | Truncated pyramidal tower; 23. | |
| 15214.5 *J 4233.5* | -S. entrance. | 22° 29.1´ N 97° 51.5´ W | **Fl.G.** period 5s fl. 0.5s, ec. 4.5s | 36 **11** | 9 | Truncated pyramidal aluminum tower; 23. | |
| 15214.6 *J 4233.6* | -N. entrance. | 22° 29.4´ N 97° 51.5´ W | **Fl.R.** period 5s fl. 0.5s, ec. 4.5s | 36 **11** | 9 | Truncated pyramidal aluminum tower; 23. | |
| 15214.7 | Canal de Navigation, No. 3. | 22° 28.9´ N 97° 53.1´ W | **Fl.G.** period 3s fl. 0.5s, ec. 2.5s | 39 **12** | 7 | Truncated pyramidal metal tower; 24. | |
| 15214.8 | -No. 1. | 22° 29.1´ N 97° 52.9´ W | **Fl.G.** period 3s fl. 0.5s, ec. 2.5s | 33 **10** | 7 | Metal tower; 22. | |
| 15215 *J 4233.62* | -No. 4. | 22° 29.4´ N 97° 52.9´ W | **Fl.R.** period 5s fl. 0.5s, ec. 4.5s | 30 **9** | 7 | Truncated pyramidal aluminum tower; 23. | |
| 15215.1 *J 4233.63* | -No. 2. | 22° 29.4´ N 97° 52.1´ W | **Fl.R.** period 3s fl. 0.5s, ec. 2.5s | 33 **10** | 7 | Truncated pyramidal aluminum tower; 23. | |
| 15215.5 *J 4235* | -Arenque to Tierra Range, pipeline, front. | 22° 17.2´ N 97° 48.2´ W | **Fl.W.** period 3s | | | | |
| 15215.51 *J 4235.1* | --Rear, 184 meters from front. | 22° 17.2´ N 97° 48.3´ W | **Fl.W.** period 6s | | | | |
| 15216 *J 4234* | Rihl Field AVIATION LIGHT. | 22° 12.0´ N 97° 49.0´ W | **Al.Fl.W.G.** period 5s | | | Beacon. | |
| | TAMPICO: | | | | | | |
| 15220 *J 4236* | **-Tampico.** | 22° 15.8´ N 97° 47.7´ W | **Fl.(3)W.** period 6s | 141 **43** | **24** | White hexagonal metal tower; 131. | Fl.R. and Fl.G. lights mark bridge at Tamos, above Tampico. **Radar reflector.** |
| 15224 *J 4238* | -Entrance Range, N. bank of river, front. | 22° 15.6´ N 97° 48.0´ W | **Fl.W.** period 3s fl. 1s, ec. 2s | 62 **19** | 14 | Steel post; 62. | |
| 15228 *J 4238.1* | --Rear, 480 yards 256°30′ from front. | 22° 15.5´ N 97° 48.3´ W | **Iso.W.** period 2s | 62 **19** | **15** | Steel post; 131. | |
| 15232 *J 4240* | -N. Breakwater, head. | 22° 16.0´ N 97° 46.4´ W | **Fl.R.** period 5s fl. 0.5s, ec. 4.5s | 33 **10** | 9 | White four-sided concrete tower; 19. | Visible 188°-322°. |
| | -RACON | | **Q(– – • –)** | | **20** | | (3 & 10cm). |
| 15236 *J 4241* | -S. breakwater, head. | 22° 15.8´ N 97° 46.5´ W | **Fl.G.** period 5s fl. 0.5s, ec. 4.5s | 33 **10** | 9 | White cylindrical concrete tower; 20. | Visible 188°-322°. |
| 15240 *J 4241.4* | --Root. | 22° 15.6´ N 97° 47.5´ W | **Dir.Fl.W.** period 3s fl. 1s, ec. 2s | 33 **10** | 5 | Truncated pyramidal aluminum tower; 23. | |
| 15244 *J 4242* | -Canal de Chijol. | 22° 14.7´ N 97° 49.2´ W | **Fl.G.** period 3s fl. 0.5s, ec. 2.5s | 30 **9** | 5 | Cylindrical concrete tower; 20. | |
| 15248 *J 4243* | -Arbol Grande. | 22° 14.0´ N 97° 49.9´ W | **Fl.G.** period 3s fl. 0.5s, ec. 2.5s | 20 **6** | 5 | Four-sided concrete tower; 20. | |

The lights of Mexico are characterized by the number of flashes etc., the periods being subject to fluctuations.

| (1) No. | (2) Name and Location | (3) Position | (4) Characteristic | (5) Height | (6) Range | (7) Structure | (8) Remarks |
|---|---|---|---|---|---|---|---|
| | | | **MEXICO** | | | | |
| 15252 *J 4244* | -Colonia del Golfo. | 22° 13.9′ N 97° 50.0′ W | **Fl.G.** period 3s fl. 0.5s, ec. 2.5s | 33 **10** | 5 | Four-sided concrete tower; 20. | |
| 15256 *J 4244.4* | -Colonia de la Isleta, on E. bank. | 22° 12.9′ N 97° 50.2′ W | **Fl.W.** period 3s fl. 0.5s, ec. 2.5s | 23 **7** | 5 | Truncated pyramidal concrete tower; 20. | |
| 15260 *J 4245* | -Isla Perez. | 22° 12.6′ N 97° 50.2′ W | **Fl.W.** period 3s fl. 0.5s, ec. 2.5s | 30 **9** | 5 | White truncated pyramidal concrete tower; 20. | |
| 15264 *J 4246* | -Canal de Pueblo Viejo Range, front. | 22° 12.3′ N 97° 50.7′ W | **Fl.W.** period 3s fl. 1s, ec. 2s | 23 **7** | 5 | White truncated pyramidal concrete tower; 20. | |
| 15264.1 *J 4246.1* | --Rear, 710 yards 110°30′ from front. | 22° 12.2′ N 97° 50.3′ W | **Iso.W.** period 2s | 36 **11** | 5 | White concrete tower; 30. | |
| 15266 *J 4247* | La Rivera de Tampico Alto. | 22° 06.0′ N 97° 46.9′ W | **Fl.W.** period 3s fl. 1s, ec. 2s | 30 **9** | 5 | Truncated pyramidal metal tower; 16. | |
| 15267.1 *J 4247.6* | Punta Bustos. | 21° 59.3′ N 97° 43.5′ W | **Fl.W.** period 5s fl. 0.5s, ec. 4.5s | 20 **6** | 7 | White truncated pyramidal concrete tower; 18. | |
| 15276 *J 4250* | **Isla de Lobos.** | 21° 28.2′ N 97° 13.6′ W | **Fl.W.** period 3s fl. 0.5s, ec. 2.5s | 105 **32** | **20** | White truncated conical concrete tower; 98. | |
| | RACON | | **O(– – –)** | | **20** | | (3 & 10cm). |
| 15280 *J 4249* | Arrecife La Blanquilla. | 21° 32.6′ N 97° 16.8′ W | **Fl.W.** period 6s fl. 1s, ec. 5s | 33 **10** | 10 | Orange truncated pyramidal concrete tower; 31. | |
| 15284 *J 4249.5* | Arrecife Medio. | 21° 30.9′ N 97° 15.2′ W | **Fl.R.** period 3s fl. 1s, ec. 2s | 33 **10** | 9 | White truncated pyramidal metal tower, orange daymark; 23. | |
| 15288 *J 4253* | Arrecife Tanguijo. | 21° 08.6′ N 97° 16.4′ W | **Fl.(3)W.** period 12s fl. 1s, ec. 2s fl. 1s, ec. 2s fl. 1s, ec. 5s | 36 **11** | 10 | Orange truncated pyramidal concrete tower; 34. | |
| 15290 *J 4253.2* | Arrecife Enmedio. | 21° 05.0′ N 97° 15.5′ W | **Fl.(2)W.** period 10s fl. 1s, ec. 1s fl. 1s, ec. 7s | 40 **12** | 10 | White structure, red bands. | |
| 15292 *J 4254* | Arrecife Tuxpan, Bajo Centro. | 21° 01.5′ N 97° 11.7′ W | **Fl.(2)W.** period 10s fl. 1s, ec. 2s fl. 1s, ec. 6s | 36 **11** | 10 | Orange truncated pyramidal concrete tower; 34. | |
| | RACON | | **X(– • • –)** | | **20** | | (3 & 10cm). |
| | TUXPAN: | | | | | | |
| 15296 *J 4256* | -N. breakwater, head. | 20° 58.4′ N 97° 18.1′ W | **Fl.R.** period 5s fl. 0.5s, ec. 4.5s | 26 **8** | 8 | White round concrete tower, rectangular base; 25. | |
| 15297 *J 4256.4* | --Root. | 20° 58.2′ N 97° 18.6′ W | **Fl.W.** period 5s fl. 0.5s, ec. 4.5s | 23 **7** | 5 | Round fiberglass tower, orange and white bands; 10. | |
| 15300 *J 4257* | -S. breakwater, head. | 20° 58.2′ N 97° 18.1′ W | **Fl.G.** period 5s fl. 0.5s, ec. 4.5s | 26 **8** | 8 | White round concrete tower, rectangular base; 25. | |

The lights of Mexico are characterized by the number of flashes etc., the periods being subject to fluctuations.

| (1) No. | (2) Name and Location | (3) Position | (4) Characteristic | (5) Height | (6) Range | (7) Structure | (8) Remarks |
|---|---|---|---|---|---|---|---|

## MEXICO

| (1) No. | (2) Name and Location | (3) Position | (4) Characteristic | (5) Height | (6) Range | (7) Structure | (8) Remarks |
|---|---|---|---|---|---|---|---|
| 15301 *J 4257.4* | --Root. | 20° 58.0′ N 97° 18.4′ W | **Fl.W.** period 5s fl. 0.5s, ec. 4.5s | 23 **7** | 4 | White round fiberglass tower, orange bands; 11. | |
| 15304 *J 4255* | **-La Barra.** | 20° 58.4′ N 97° 18.5′ W | **Fl.(4)W.** period 7s | 79 **24** | **15** | White truncated conical concrete tower, hut; 72. | Visible 180°-325°. |
| 15305 *J 4258* | -S. side, entrance Range, front. | 20° 57.8′ N 97° 19.1′ W | **Fl.W.** period 3s fl. 1s, ec. 2s | 56 **17** | 9 | White truncated pyramidal metal tower, orange daymark; 56. | |
| 15306 *J 4258.1* | --Rear, 270 meters 238° from front. | 20° 57.7′ N 97° 19.3′ W | **Iso.W.** period 2s | 75 **23** | 10 | White truncated pyramidal metal tower, orange daymark; 75. | |
| 15307 | -La Mata. | 20° 58.2′ N 97° 19.8′ W | **Fl.W.** period 6s fl. 1s, ec. 5s | 20 **6** | 1 | White round fiberglass tower, orange stripes; 18. | |
| 15307.1 | -Potrero. | 20° 58.6′ N 97° 20.5′ W | **Fl.(2)W.** period 10s fl. 1s, ec. 2s fl. 1s, ec. 6s | 20 **6** | 1 | White round fiberglass tower, orange stripes; 20. | |
| 15307.2 | -Pipiloya. | 21° 01.8′ N 97° 21.3′ W | **Fl.G.** period 5s fl. 0.5s, ec. 4.5s | 20 **6** | 3 | White round fiberglass tower, orange stripes; 18. | |
| 15308 *J 4259* | -N. side, Range 1, front. | 20° 57.6′ N 97° 20.2′ W | **Fl.W.** period 3s fl. 1s, ec. 2s | 39 **12** | 8 | White truncated pyramidal metal tower, orange daymark; 36. | |
| 15312 *J 4259.1* | --Rear, 250 meters 255° from front. | 20° 57.6′ N 97° 20.3′ W | **Iso.W.** period 2s | 56 **17** | 8 | White truncated pyramidal metal tower, orange daymark; 52. | |
| 15316 *J 4259.2* | -Range, front. | 20° 57.4′ N 97° 20.6′ W | **Fl.W.** period 3s fl. 1s, ec. 2s | 39 **12** | 8 | White truncated pyramidal metal tower, orange daymark; 36. | |
| 15316.1 *J 4259.21* | --Rear, 95 meters 248° from front. | 20° 57.4′ N 97° 20.6′ W | **Iso.W.** period 2s | 56 **17** | 8 | White truncated pyramidal metal tower, orange daymark; 43. | |
| 15317 *J 4259.3* | Cobos. | 20° 56.4′ N 97° 21.9′ W | **Fl.G.** period 3s fl. 1s, ec. 2s | 36 **11** | 3 | Truncated pyramidal tower; 25. | |
| 15318 *J 4259.32* | Seminario. | 20° 56.3′ N 97° 22.4′ W | **Fl.W.** period 5s fl. 1s, ec. 4s | 49 **15** | 3 | Truncated pyramidal tower; 43. | |
| 15331 *J 4259.4* | Punta Cazones. | 20° 46.0′ N 97° 12.0′ W | **Fl.(2)W.** period 10s fl. 1s, ec. 2s fl. 1s, ec. 6s | 49 **15** | 9 | White truncated pyramidal metal tower; 36. | |
| 15332 *J 4259.5* | **Barra de Cazones.** | 20° 43.3′ N 97° 12.0′ W | **Fl.W.** period 5s fl. 1s, ec. 4s | 85 **26** | **15** | White concrete tower, hut; 52. | |
| 15336 *J 4260* | **Tecolutla.** | 20° 28.5′ N 97° 00.2′ W | **Fl.(2)W.** period 10s fl. 1s, ec. 2s fl. 1s, ec. 6s | 82 **25** | **15** | White truncated conical concrete tower; 74. | Visible 149°-301°. |
| 15340 *J 4261* | -S. breakwater. | 20° 29.0′ N 97° 00.0′ W | **Fl.G.** period 5s fl. 0.5s, ec. 4.5s | 26 **8** | 6 | White truncated pyramidal metal tower, orange daymark; 26. | |
| 15344 *J 4261.2* | -N. breakwater. | 20° 29.0′ N 97° 00.0′ W | **Fl.R.** period 5s fl. 0.5s, ec. 4.5s | 26 **8** | 6 | White truncated pyramidal metal tower, orange daymark; 26. | |
| 15348 *J 4262* | Rio Nautla. | 20° 14.1′ N 96° 47.4′ W | **Fl.W.** period 6s fl. 1s, ec. 5s | 98 **30** | 12 | White cylindrical concrete tower, hut; 72. | Visible 150°-300°. |
| 15352 *J 4266* | **Punta Delgada.** | 19° 51.4′ N 96° 27.7′ W | **Fl.(3)W.** period 25s | 151 **46** | **18** | White cylindrical concrete tower; 72. | |

The lights of Mexico are characterized by the number of flashes etc., the periods being subject to fluctuations.

| (1) No. | (2) Name and Location | (3) Position | (4) Characteristic | (5) Height | (6) Range | (7) Structure | (8) Remarks |
|---|---|---|---|---|---|---|---|

## MEXICO

| (1) No. | (2) Name and Location | (3) Position | (4) Characteristic | (5) Height | (6) Range | (7) Structure | (8) Remarks |
|---|---|---|---|---|---|---|---|
| 15354 *J 4268* | Chachalacas. | 19° 24.7´ N 96° 19.5´ W | **Fl.W.** period 6s fl. 1s, ec. 5s | 30 **9** | 7 | White fiberglass tower; 16. | |
| | VERACRUZ: | | | | | | |
| 15356 *J 4271* | -La Galleguilla. | 19° 13.9´ N 96° 07.3´ W | **Fl.(2)W.** period 10s fl. 1s, ec. 1s fl. 1s, ec. 7s | 36 **11** | 7 | White cylindrical concrete tower; 30. | |
| 15356.1 *J 4271.5* | --N. extremity. | 19° 14.1´ N 96° 07.5´ W | **Fl.(2)W.** period 10s fl. 1s, ec. 1s fl. 1s, ec. 7s | 16 **5** | 5 | Steel pipe. | |
| 15360 *J 4270* | -Arrecife Blanquilla. | 19° 13.7´ N 96° 06.1´ W | **Fl.(4)R.** period 16s fl. 1s, ec. 2s fl. 1s, ec. 2s fl. 1s, ec. 2s fl. 1s, ec. 6s | 49 **15** | 6 | Red truncated conical concrete tower, white bands; 46. | |
| 15364 *J 4270.2* | -Arrecife La Blanquilla, S. side of reef. | 19° 13.4´ N 96° 05.9´ W | **Fl.(2)R.** period 10s fl. 1s, ec. 2s fl. 1s, ec. 6s | 46 **14** | 6 | Red cylindrical concrete tower; 46. | |
| 15368 *J 4272* | -Anegada de Adentro, NW. extremity. | 19° 13.8´ N 96° 03.7´ W | **Fl.(3)G.** period 12s fl. 1s, ec. 2s fl. 1s, ec. 2s fl. 1s, ec. 5s | 36 **11** | 6 | Green cylindrical concrete tower; 30. | |
| 15368.1 *J 4273* | --SE. extremity. | 19° 13.3´ N 96° 03.0´ W | **Fl.Y.** period 2s fl. 0.5s, ec. 1.5s | 16 **5** | 5 | Steel pipe. | |
| 15372 *J 4274* | -Isla Verde. | 19° 11.9´ N 96° 04.1´ W | **Fl.(4)W.** period 16s fl. 1s, ec. 2s fl. 1s, ec. 2s fl. 1s, ec. 2s fl. 1s, ec. 6s | 26 **8** | 6 | Red truncated conical concrete tower; 20. | |
| 15372.2 *J 4273.5* | --NW. reef. | 19° 12.4´ N 96° 04.3´ W | **Fl.(2)W.** period 10s fl. 1s, ec. 1s fl. 1s, ec. 7s | 17 **5** | 6 | Metal post; 17. | |
| 15376 *J 4276* | -Arrecife Pajaros. | 19° 11.7´ N 96° 05.8´ W | **Fl.W.** period 6s fl. 1s, ec. 5s | 20 **6** | 5 | White truncated conical concrete tower; 20. | |
| 15376.1 *J 4275* | --SE. extremity. | 19° 11.1´ N 96° 05.0´ W | **Fl.Y.** period 2s fl. 0.5s, ec. 1.5s | 16 **5** | 5 | Steel pipe. | |
| 15380 *J 4278* | **-Isla de Sacrificios.** | 19° 10.5´ N 96° 05.5´ W | **Fl.W.R.G.** period 15s | 128 **39** | **22** | White cylindrical concrete tower, black bands; 128. | R. 134°-157°, W.-163°, G.-187°, W.-195°, R.-238°. |
| | -RACON | | **Z(– – • •)** | | **25** | | (3 & 10cm). |
| 15380.2 *J 4277* | --N. reef. | 19° 11.0´ N 96° 05.7´ W | **Fl.(2)W.** period 10s fl. 1s, ec. 1s fl. 1s, ec. 7s | 17 **5** | 5 | Steel post. | |
| 15382 *J 4279* | -Bajo de Hornos. | 19° 11.3´ N 96° 07.1´ W | **Fl.R.** period 3s fl. 0.5s, ec. 2.5s | 16 **5** | 4 | Red round concrete tower; 13. | |
| 15382.2 *J 4279.55* | --Hornos 1. | 19° 11.3´ N 96° 07.3´ W | **Fl.W.** period 3s fl. 0.5s, ec. 2.5s | 10 **3** | 3 | White round concrete tower; 8. | |

The lights of Mexico are characterized by the number of flashes etc., the periods being subject to fluctuations.

| (1) No. | (2) Name and Location | (3) Position | (4) Characteristic | (5) Height | (6) Range | (7) Structure | (8) Remarks |
|---|---|---|---|---|---|---|---|

**MEXICO**

| (1) No. | (2) Name and Location | (3) Position | (4) Characteristic | (5) Height | (6) Range | (7) Structure | (8) Remarks |
|---|---|---|---|---|---|---|---|
| 15382.5<br>*J 4279.7* | --Arrecife Hornos. | 19° 11.5′ N<br>96° 07.4′ W | **Iso.W.**<br>period 2s | 13<br>**4** | 3 | Green round concrete tower; 11. | |
| 15384<br>*J 4284* | -NE. breakwater, head. | 19° 12.2′ N<br>96° 07.2′ W | **Fl.R.**<br>period 5s<br>fl. 0.5s, ec. 4.5s | 39<br>**12** | 8 | Red truncated pyramidal concrete tower; 23. | |
| 15388<br>*J 4282* | -SE. breakwater, head. | 19° 12.0′ N<br>96° 07.3′ W | **Fl.G.**<br>period 5s<br>fl. 0.5s, ec. 4.5s | 33<br>**10** | 8 | Green truncated pyramidal concrete tower; 23. | |
| 15392<br>*J 4286* | -Entrance range, front. | 19° 12.1′ N<br>96° 07.6′ W | **Iso.W.**<br>period 2s | 49<br>**15** | 8 | White concrete tower; 39. | |
| 15392.1<br>*J 4286.1* | --Rear, 1050 meters 263°14′ from front. | 19° 12.0′ N<br>96° 08.2′ W | **Iso.W.**<br>period 2s | 102<br>**31** | 10 | Pedestal on building. | |
| 15392.5<br>*J 4286.4* | -Muro de Pescadores. | 19° 12.0′ N<br>96° 07.7′ W | **Fl.W.**<br>period 3s<br>fl. 1s, ec. 2s | 33<br>**10** | 3 | Round metal tower; 26. | |
| 15392.6<br>*J 4286.41* | -Old aquarium. | 19° 11.6′ N<br>96° 07.4′ W | **Iso.W.**<br>period 2s | 39<br>**12** | 5 | Aluminum tower; 39. | |
| 15393<br>*J 4298* | -Pilot pier, N. side. | 19° 12.2′ N<br>96° 07.9′ W | **Iso.G.**<br>period 2s | 16<br>**5** | 3 | White concrete tower; 8. | |
| 15394<br>*J 4298.1* | --S. side. | 19° 12.1′ N<br>96° 07.9′ W | **Iso.G.**<br>period 2s | 16<br>**5** | 3 | White concrete tower; 8. | |
| 15395<br>*J 4286.31* | -Inner harbor. | 19° 12.2′ N<br>96° 08.3′ W | **Iso.W.**<br>period 2s | 121<br>**37** | 7 | Metal tower; 121. | |
| 15395.5<br>*J 4299.6* | -Muelle en Espigon, SE. corner. | 19° 12.7′ N<br>96° 08.2′ W | **Iso.R.**<br>period 2s | 13<br>**4** | 2 | Red concrete tower; 5. | |
| 15395.6<br>*J 4299.5* | --SW. corner. | 19° 12.7′ N<br>96° 08.2′ W | **Iso.G.**<br>period 2s | 13<br>**4** | 2 | Green concrete tower; 5. | |
| 15396<br>*J 4297* | -Muelle de Pemex, E. | 19° 12.3′ N<br>96° 07.4′ W | **Iso.R.**<br>period 2s | 16<br>**5** | 3 | White concrete tower; 8. | |
| 15397<br>*J 4297.2* | --W. | 19° 12.3′ N<br>96° 07.4′ W | **Iso.G.**<br>period 2s | 16<br>**5** | 3 | White concrete tower; 8. | |
| 15406<br>*J 4300* | -Rio Jamapa, N. breakwater. | 19° 06.3′ N<br>96° 05.8′ W | **Fl.R.**<br>period 5s<br>fl. 0.5s, ec. 4.5s | 39<br>**12** | 7 | Red cylindrical concrete tower; 30. | |
| 15407<br>*J 4300.5* | --S. breakwater. | 19° 06.1′ N<br>96° 05.9′ W | **Fl.G.**<br>period 5s<br>fl. 0.5s, ec. 4.5s | 30<br>**9** | 7 | Green triangular concrete tower; 23. | |
| | ANTON LIZARDO ANCHORAGE: | | | | | | |
| 15408<br>*J 4310* | -Blanca Reef. | 19° 05.2′ N<br>96° 00.0′ W | **Fl.(2)W.**<br>period 10s<br>fl. 1s, ec. 2s<br>fl. 1s, ec. 6s | 33<br>**10** | 7 | White truncated pyramidal concrete tower; 30. | |
| 15412<br>*J 4308* | -El Giote Reef. | 19° 04.0′ N<br>95° 59.9′ W | **Fl.R.**<br>period 6s<br>fl. 1s, ec. 5s | 30<br>**9** | 7 | Red four-sided concrete tower; 23. | |
| 15415<br>*J 4311* | -Arrecife Chopas. | 19° 05.8′ N<br>95° 59.5′ W | **Fl.(2)W.**<br>period 10s<br>fl. 1s, ec. 1s<br>fl. 1s, ec. 7s | 17<br>**5** | 6 | Metal post; 17. | |
| 15418<br>*J 4312* | -Polo. | 19° 06.6′ N<br>95° 59.5′ W | **Fl.(2)W.**<br>period 10s<br>fl. 1s, ec. 1s<br>fl. 1s, ec. 7s | 16<br>**5** | 6 | Round white column; 17. | |

The lights of Mexico are characterized by the number of flashes etc., the periods being subject to fluctuations.

| (1)<br>No. | (2)<br>Name and Location | (3)<br>Position | (4)<br>Characteristic | (5)<br>Height | (6)<br>Range | (7)<br>Structure | (8)<br>Remarks |
|---|---|---|---|---|---|---|---|
| | | | **MEXICO** | | | | |
| 15420<br>*J 4314* | -Isla de Enmedio. | 19° 06.1′ N<br>95° 56.3′ W | **Fl.(3)W.R.G.**<br>period 12s<br>fl. 1s, ec. 2s<br>fl. 1s, ec. 2s<br>fl. 1s, ec. 5s | 46<br>**14** | W. 10<br>R. 8<br>G. 7 | Truncated conical concrete tower, dwelling; 46. | W. 147°-220°, R.-260°, W.-268°, G.-299°, W.-327°, R.-032°, W.-057°, R.-147°. |
| 15420.2<br>*J 4313* | --N. reef. | 19° 07.2′ N<br>95° 56.7′ W | **Fl.(2)W.**<br>period 10s<br>fl. 1s, ec. 1s<br>fl. 1s, ec. 7s | 17<br>**5** | 6 | Metal post; 17. | |
| 15424<br>*J 4316* | -Arrecife el Rizo, S. head. | 19° 03.4′ N<br>95° 55.2′ W | **Fl.(3)W.**<br>period 12s<br>fl. 1s, ec. 2s<br>fl. 1s, ec. 2s<br>fl. 1s, ec. 5s | 39<br>**12** | 7 | Red rectangular concrete tower; 33. | |
| 15424.2<br>*J 4315.5* | --NW. head. | 19° 04.4′ N<br>95° 56.0′ W | **Fl.(2)W.**<br>period 10s<br>fl. 1s, ec. 1s<br>fl. 1s, ec. 7s | 17<br>**5** | 6 | Steel post. | |
| 15428<br>*J 4317* | -Arrecife de Cabezo, N. head. | 19° 05.7′ N<br>95° 51.7′ W | **Fl.(2)W.**<br>period 10s<br>fl. 1s, ec. 2s<br>fl. 1s, ec. 6s | 30<br>**9** | 7 | White four-sided concrete tower; 23. | |
| 15432<br>*J 4317.2* | --S. head. | 19° 03.3′ N<br>95° 49.5′ W | **Fl.R.**<br>period 6s<br>fl. 1s, ec. 5s | 26<br>**8** | 7 | Red four-sided concrete tower; 23. | |
| 15436<br>*J 4318* | **Arrecife Santiaguillo.** | 19° 08.6′ N<br>95° 48.5′ W | **Fl.(2)W.R.**<br>period 10s<br>fl. 1s, ec. 2s<br>fl. 1s, ec. 6s | 105<br>**32** | **22** | Red cylindrical concrete tower, white band; 105. | R. 002°-056°, W.-084°, R.-126°, W.-002°. |
| | RACON | | **O(- - -)** | | **25** | | (3 & 10cm). |
| 15437<br>*J 4317.6* | -Anegadilla. | 19° 08.2′ N<br>95° 47.7′ W | **Fl.W.**<br>period 2s<br>fl. 0.5s, ec. 1.5s | 16<br>**5** | 5 | Steel pipe. | |
| 15439<br>*J 4318.5* | -Topatillo. | 19° 08.4′ N<br>95° 50.1′ W | **Fl.Y.**<br>period 2s<br>fl. 0.5s, ec. 1.5s | 16<br>**5** | 5 | Steel post. | |
| 15440<br>*J 4319* | Anegada de Afuera, on NW. point of reef. | 19° 10.3′ N<br>95° 52.2′ W | **Fl.(4)W.**<br>period 16s<br>fl. 1s, ec. 2s<br>fl. 1s, ec. 2s<br>fl. 1s, ec. 2s<br>fl. 1s, ec. 6s | 33<br>**10** | 8 | White cylindrical concrete tower; 39. | |
| 15444<br>*J 4324* | Alvarado. | 18° 47.0′ N<br>95° 44.7′ W | **Fl.(3)G.**<br>period 12s<br>fl. 1s, ec. 2s<br>fl. 1s, ec. 2s<br>fl. 1s, ec. 5s | 125<br>**38** | 12 | White cylindrical concrete tower, red band, dwelling; 26. | Visible 136°-274°. |
| 15445<br>*J 4325* | -E. breakwater. | 18° 47.4′ N<br>95° 44.5′ W | **Fl.G.**<br>period 5s<br>fl. 0.5s, ec. 4.5s | 30<br>**9** | 8 | Green aluminum tower; 23. | |
| 15446<br>*J 4325.5* | -W. breakwater. | 18° 47.7′ N<br>95° 45.0′ W | **Fl.R.**<br>period 5s<br>fl. 0.5s, ec. 4.5s | 30<br>**9** | 8 | Red aluminum framework tower; 23. | |
| 15452<br>*J 4326* | -E. Fortin (Punta Alvarado). | 18° 46.2′ N<br>95° 45.8′ W | **Fl.W.**<br>period 6s<br>fl. 1s, ec. 5s | 30<br>**9** | 8 | Four-sided concrete tower; 23. | |
| 15454 | -Inner breakwater 1. | 18° 46.6′ N<br>95° 44.9′ W | **Fl.R.**<br>period 5s<br>fl. 0.5s, ec. 4.5s | | 8 | Red post; 23. | |
| 15454.5 | --2. | 18° 46.4′ N<br>95° 45.0′ W | **Fl.R.**<br>period 5s<br>fl. 0.5s, ec. 4.5s | | 8 | Red post; 23. | |

The lights of Mexico are characterized by the number of flashes etc., the periods being subject to fluctuations.

| (1) No. | (2) Name and Location | (3) Position | (4) Characteristic | (5) Height | (6) Range | (7) Structure | (8) Remarks |
|---|---|---|---|---|---|---|---|
| | | | **MEXICO** | | | | |
| 15456<br>*J 4330* | Roca Partida. | 18° 42.3′ N<br>95° 11.3′ W | **Fl.(4)W.**<br>period 18s | 328<br>**100** | 13 | White four-sided concrete tower, red bands; 43. | |
| 15460<br>*J 4332* | Punta Zapotitlan. | 18° 31.5′ N<br>94° 48.1′ W | **Fl.W.**<br>period 6s<br>fl. 1s, ec. 5s | 98<br>**30** | 9 | Cylindrical concrete tower; 92. | |
| | COATZACOALCOS: | | | | | | |
| 15464<br>*J 4336* | **-Cerro del Gavilan.** | 18° 09.0′ N<br>94° 24.0′ W | **Fl.(2)W.**<br>period 18s | 197<br>**60** | **18** | White prismatic octagonal masonry tower; 69. | |
| 15468<br>*J 4339* | -Range, front, E. side of river. | 18° 08.1′ N<br>94° 24.2′ W | **Fl.W.**<br>period 3s<br>fl. 1s, ec. 2s | 108<br>**33** | 9 | White truncated pyramidal metal tower, orange bands; 108. | |
| 15472<br>*J 4339.1* | --Rear, 290 meters 162° from front. | 18° 08.0′ N<br>94° 24.2′ W | **Iso.W.**<br>period 2s | 174<br>**53** | 9 | White truncated pyramidal metal tower, orange bands; 167. | |
| 15476<br>*J 4338* | -E. breakwater, head. | 18° 09.9′ N<br>94° 24.7′ W | **Fl.G.**<br>period 5s<br>fl. 0.5s, ec. 4.5s | 79<br>**24** | 9 | White cylindrical concrete tower, red bands; 66. | |
| 15480<br>*J 4337* | -W. breakwater, head. | 18° 09.9′ N<br>94° 24.9′ W | **Fl.R.**<br>period 5s<br>fl. 0.5s, ec. 4.5s | 79<br>**24** | 9 | White cylindrical concrete tower, red bands; 66. | |
| 15484<br>*J 4340* | -Darsena de Pajaritos Range, front. | 18° 07.3′ N<br>94° 24.3′ W | **Iso.W.**<br>period 2s | 33<br>**10** | 8 | Post; 30. | |
| 15488<br>*J 4340.1* | --Rear, 200 meters 180° from front. | 18° 07.1′ N<br>94° 24.3′ W | **Iso.W.**<br>period 2s | 39<br>**12** | 8 | Structure; 33. | |
| 15489.3<br>*J 4341.8* | --Basin, E. | 18° 07.9′ N<br>94° 24.2′ W | **Fl.G.**<br>period 3s<br>fl. 0.5s, ec. 2.5s | 16<br>**5** | 6 | Round metal tower; 3. | |
| 15489.4<br>*J 4341.82* | ---W. | 18° 07.9′ N<br>94° 24.3′ W | **Fl.R.**<br>period 3s<br>fl. 0.5s, ec. 2.5s | 16<br>**5** | 6 | Round metal tower; 3. | |
| 15492<br>*J 4348* | Tonala. | 18° 12.7′ N<br>94° 08.0′ W | **Fl.(3)W.**<br>period 12s<br>fl. 1s, ec. 2s<br>fl. 1s, ec. 2s<br>fl. 1s, ec. 5s | 89<br>**27** | 13 | Red four-sided masonry tower, white bands; 56. | |
| 15496<br>*J 4352* | Tupilco. | 18° 25.0′ N<br>93° 26.3′ W | **Fl.(4)W.**<br>period 16s<br>fl. 1s, ec. 2s<br>fl. 1s, ec. 2s<br>fl. 1s, ec. 2s<br>fl. 1s, ec. 6s | 79<br>**24** | 10 | White cylindrical concrete tower; 75. | |
| 15500<br>*J 4353* | Chiltepec, at river entrance. | 18° 26.4′ N<br>93° 05.8′ W | **Fl.(3)W.**<br>period 12s<br>fl. 1s, ec. 2s<br>fl. 1s, ec. 2s<br>fl. 1s, ec. 5s | 49<br>**15** | 10 | White cylindrical concrete tower; 43. | |
| 15504<br>*J 4354* | **Frontera.** | 18° 36.8′ N<br>92° 41.3′ W | **Fl.W.**<br>period 6s | 98<br>**30** | **15** | White metal tower with 8 columns, red bands; 98. | Visible 045°-245°. |
| 15505<br>*J 4355.5* | -E. breakwater. | 18° 37.1′ N<br>92° 41.2′ W | **Fl.G.**<br>period 5s<br>fl. 0.5s, ec. 4.5s | 23<br>**7** | 5 | White concrete tower; 16. | |
| 15505.5<br>*J 4356.2* | -Isla Azteca. | 18° 36.1′ N<br>92° 41.7′ W | **Fl.R.**<br>period 5s<br>fl. 0.5s, ec. 4.5s | 16<br>**5** | 5 | Red cylindrical metal tower; 16. | |
| 15506<br>*J 4358.6* | Rio San Pedro, W. side of river. | 18° 39.0′ N<br>92° 28.0′ W | **Fl.R.**<br>period 5s<br>fl. 0.5s, ec. 4.5s | 30<br>**9** | 6 | Red round tower; 23. | |

The lights of Mexico are characterized by the number of flashes etc., the periods being subject to fluctuations.

| (1) No. | (2) Name and Location | (3) Position | (4) Characteristic | (5) Height | (6) Range | (7) Structure | (8) Remarks |
|---|---|---|---|---|---|---|---|
| | | | **MEXICO** | | | | |
| 15506.5<br>*J 4358.3* | -E. side of river. | 18° 39.1′ N<br>92° 28.0′ W | **Fl.G.**<br>period 5s<br>fl. 0.5s, ec. 4.5s | 30<br>**9** | 5 | Green cylindrical concrete tower; 30. | |
| 15507<br>*J 4358.7* | -Channel. | 18° 38.7′ N<br>92° 27.9′ W | **Iso.W.**<br>period 2s | 46<br>**14** | 8 | Truncated pyramidal aluminum tower, daymark; 46. | |
| 15508<br>*J 4358.9* | Emiliano Zapata. | 18° 40.3′ N<br>92° 18.7′ W | **Fl.(2)W.**<br>period 10s<br>fl. 1s, ec. 2s<br>fl. 1s, ec. 6s | 36<br>**11** | 10 | Truncated pyramidal aluminum tower; 36. | |
| 15510<br>*J 4358.95* | Campo Pesquero. | 18° 41.0′ N<br>92° 13.2′ W | **Fl.W.**<br>period 6s<br>fl. 1s, ec. 5s | 39<br>**12** | 10 | White cylindrical concrete tower; 36. | |
| 15511 | Darsena de Atasta. | 18° 42.0′ N<br>92° 05.3′ W | **Fl.(2)W.**<br>period 10s<br>fl. 1s, ec. 2s<br>fl. 1s, ec. 6s | 39<br>**12** | 10 | Truncated pyramidal aluminum tower; 36. | |
| 15512<br>*J 4372* | Xicalango Range, front. | 18° 37.8′ N<br>91° 54.0′ W | **Fl.W.**<br>period 3s<br>fl. 1s, ec. 2s | 43<br>**13** | 10 | Truncated pyramidal metal tower; 39. | |
| 15516<br>*J 4372.1* | -Rear, 185 meters 180° from front. | 18° 37.6′ N<br>91° 54.0′ W | **Fl.W.**<br>period 6s | 105<br>**32** | **18** | White truncated conical masonry tower, red bands; 92. | |
| 15517<br>*J 4372.7* | Laguna Azul fishing harbor, W. breakwater. | 18° 37.9′ N<br>91° 49.9′ W | **Fl.G.**<br>period 5s<br>fl. 0.5s, ec. 4.5s | 20<br>**6** | 4 | Green round metal tower; 13. | |
| 15517.5<br>*J 4372.8* | -E. breakwater. | 18° 37.9′ N<br>91° 49.9′ W | **Fl.R.**<br>period 5s<br>fl. 0.5s, ec. 4.5s | 20<br>**6** | 4 | Red round metal tower; 13. | |
| 15518<br>*J 4373* | Government pier, head. | 18° 38.2′ N<br>91° 50.2′ W | **Iso.G.**<br>period 2s | 26<br>**8** | 4 | Red round concrete tower; 16. | |
| 15519<br>*J 4373.05* | -S. side. | 18° 38.2′ N<br>91° 50.2′ W | **Iso.R.**<br>period 2s | 26<br>**8** | 4 | Green round concrete tower; 16. | |
| 15520<br>*J 4374* | Punta Atalaya. | 18° 38.7′ N<br>91° 50.6′ W | **Fl.(3)W.R.**<br>period 12s<br>fl. 1s, ec. 2s<br>fl. 1s, ec. 2s<br>fl. 1s, ec. 5s | 69<br>**21** | 12 | White truncated conical masonry tower, red cupola; 75. | R. 086°-113°, W.-086°. |
| 15528<br>*J 4378* | Laguna de Terminos, Tio Campo, S. head. | 18° 30.7′ N<br>91° 47.2′ W | **Fl.W.**<br>period 6s<br>fl. 1s, ec. 5s | 33<br>**10** | 10 | Truncated conical tower; 30. | |
| 15532<br>*J 4385* | -Boca de los Pargos. | 18° 37.5′ N<br>91° 17.2′ W | **Fl.W.**<br>period 6s<br>fl. 1s, ec. 5s | 46<br>**14** | 10 | White concrete tower; 36. | |
| 15536<br>*J 4384* | Isla Aguada, on Punta del Tigre, entrance Range, front. | 18° 47.3′ N<br>91° 29.7′ W | **Fl.W.**<br>period 3s<br>fl. 1s, ec. 2s | 56<br>**17** | 8 | White cylindrical concrete tower; 26. | |
| 15540<br>*J 4384.1* | -Rear, 400 meters 151° from front. | 18° 47.0′ N<br>91° 29.5′ W | **Fl.(4)W.**<br>period 12s | 75<br>**23** | **18** | White concrete tower; 66. | |
| 15544<br>*J 4386* | Sabancuy. | 19° 00.0′ N<br>91° 11.0′ W | **Fl.(3)W.**<br>period 12s<br>fl. 1s, ec. 2s<br>fl. 1s, ec. 2s<br>fl. 1s, ec. 5s | 69<br>**21** | 10 | Aluminum tower; 66. | |
| 15544.3<br>*J 4386.3* | -SW. jetty. | 18° 59.7′ N<br>91° 11.1′ W | **Fl.G.**<br>period 5s<br>fl. 0.5s, ec. 4.5s | 20<br>**6** | 4 | Green cylindrical steel tower; 23. | |
| 15544.6<br>*J 4386.2* | -NE. jetty. | 18° 59.8′ N<br>91° 11.1′ W | **Fl.R.**<br>period 5s<br>fl. 0.5s, ec. 4.5s | 20<br>**6** | 4 | Red cylindrical steel tower; 23. | |

The lights of Mexico are characterized by the number of flashes etc., the periods being subject to fluctuations.

## MEXICO

| (1)<br>No. | (2)<br>Name and Location | (3)<br>Position | (4)<br>Characteristic | (5)<br>Height | (6)<br>Range | (7)<br>Structure | (8)<br>Remarks |
|---|---|---|---|---|---|---|---|
| 15548<br>*J 4388* | Rio Champoton. | 19° 21.6′ N<br>90° 43.3′ W | **Fl.W.**<br>period 5s | 82<br>**25** | 12 | White four-sided concrete tower; 72. | Visible 045°-180°. |
| 15552<br>*J 4392* | **Punta Morro.** | 19° 40.5′ N<br>90° 42.1′ W | **Fl.(3)W.**<br>period 6s | 177<br>**54** | **18** | White octagonal concrete tower; 52. | Visible 000°-197°. |
| 15553 | Seybaplaya Range, front. | 19° 39.3′ N<br>90° 42.4′ W | **Fl.W.**<br>period 3s<br>fl. 1s, ec. 2s | 26<br>**8** | 5 | Round metal tower; 20. | |
| 15553.5 | -Rear, 26 meters 021°14′ from front. | 19° 39.3′ N<br>90° 42.4′ W | **Iso.W.**<br>period 2s | 39<br>**12** | 6 | Round metal tower; 33. | |
| 15554<br>*J 4390* | -Wharf, No. 1. | 19° 39.1′ N<br>90° 42.4′ W | **Iso.G.**<br>period 2s | 20<br>**6** | 4 | Red cylindrical concrete tower; 13. | |
| 15554.1<br>*J 4390.5* | --No. 2. | 19° 39.1′ N<br>90° 42.5′ W | **Iso.G.**<br>period 2s | 20<br>**6** | 4 | Green cylindrical concrete tower; 13. | |
| 15554.2 | --No. 3. | 19° 39.1′ N<br>90° 42.6′ W | **Iso.W.**<br>period 2s | 20<br>**6** | 4 | White cylindrical concrete tower; 13. | |
| 15556<br>*J 4396* | Lerma Range, front. | 19° 48.4′ N<br>90° 36.0′ W | **Fl.W.**<br>period 3s<br>fl. 1s, ec. 2s | 52<br>**16** | 10 | Truncated pyramidal aluminum tower; 49. | |
| 15560<br>*J 4396.1* | -Rear, 190 meters 139° from front. | 19° 48.3′ N<br>90° 36.0′ W | **Iso.W.**<br>period 2s | 85<br>**26** | 10 | Truncated pyramidal aluminum tower; 13. | |
| 15561.5 | -Kila, No. 2. | 19° 47.9′ N<br>90° 36.8′ W | **Iso.G.**<br>period 2s | 30<br>**9** | 4 | Green round metal tower; 20. | |
| 15562.1<br>*J 4397.2* | -Fishing pier, No. 2. | 19° 48.8′ N<br>90° 35.9′ W | **Iso.G.**<br>period 2s | 20<br>**6** | 4 | Cylindrical concrete tower; 13. | |
| 15562.2<br>*J 4397* | --No. 1. | 19° 48.8′ N<br>90° 35.9′ W | **Iso.R.**<br>period 2s | 20<br>**6** | 4 | Cylindrical concrete tower; 13. | |
| 15562.25<br>*J 4395* | -Breton pier, No. 1. | 19° 49.0′ N<br>90° 35.6′ W | **Iso.W.**<br>period 2s | 30<br>**9** | 6 | White cylindrical concrete tower; 20. | |
| 15562.3<br>*J 4395.3* | --No. 3. | 19° 49.0′ N<br>90° 35.6′ W | **Iso.R.**<br>period 2s | 30<br>**9** | 6 | Red cylindrical concrete tower; 20. | |
| 15562.4<br>*J 4395.2* | --No. 2. | 19° 49.0′ N<br>90° 35.6′ W | **Iso.G.**<br>period 2s | 30<br>**9** | 6 | Green cylindrical concrete tower; 20. | |
| 15564<br>*J 4400* | **San Bartolo Hill.** | 19° 49.0′ N<br>90° 35.0′ W | **Fl.(2)W.**<br>period 12s | 256<br>**78** | **18** | White four-sided concrete tower; 39. | |
| 15565 | San Francisco Pier, No. 1. | 19° 51.8′ N<br>90° 31.9′ W | **Iso.R.**<br>period 2s | 20<br>**6** | 4 | Red round metal tower; 20. | |
| 15565.1 | -No. 2. | 19° 51.8′ N<br>90° 31.9′ W | **Iso.G.**<br>period 2s | 20<br>**6** | 4 | Green round metal tower; 20. | |
| 15565.2 | -No. 3. | 19° 52.0′ N<br>90° 31.7′ W | **Iso.W.**<br>period 2s | 20<br>**6** | 4 | White round metal tower; 20. | |
| 15566 | -Cayo Arcas Oil Terminal. | 20° 11.1′ N<br>91° 59.5′ W | **Fl.Y.**<br>period 2s<br>fl. 0.5s, ec. 1.5s | 125<br>**38** | 12 | | On petroleum transfer structure. |
| 15566.5 | -RACON, Platform Eco-1. | 19° 01.8′ N<br>92° 01.1′ W | **Q(– – • –)** | 262<br>**80** | **18** | Metal structure. | (3 & 10cm). |
| 15567 | -RACON, Platform Akal-C. | 19° 23.9′ N<br>92° 02.3′ W | **Y(– • – –)** | 262<br>**80** | **18** | Complex compound, seven platforms. | (3 & 10cm). |
| 15570.5 | -RACON, Platform Pr-1 Rebombeo. | 18° 56.7′ N<br>92° 37.2′ W | **O(– – –)** | 262<br>**80** | 12 | Complex compound. | |
| 15571<br>*J 4358* | Cayos Arcas, W. side of Cay del Centro Range, front. | 20° 12.9′ N<br>91° 58.1′ W | **Fl.W.**<br>period 3s<br>fl. 1s, ec. 2s | 43<br>**13** | 10 | Truncated pyramidal metal tower. | |

The lights of Mexico are characterized by the number of flashes etc., the periods being subject to fluctuations.

| (1) No. | (2) Name and Location | (3) Position | (4) Characteristic | (5) Height | (6) Range | (7) Structure | (8) Remarks |
|---|---|---|---|---|---|---|---|
| | | | **MEXICO** | | | | |
| 15572 *J 4358.1* | -Rear, 80 meters 107° from front. | 20° 12.3´ N 91° 57.7´ W | **Fl.(2)W.** period 10s fl. 1s, ec. 2s fl. 1s, ec. 6s | 72 **22** | 10 | White cylindrical concrete tower; 66. | |
| 15576 *J 4364* | Isla Triangulos Oeste. | 20° 58.4´ N 92° 18.2´ W | **Fl.(3)W.** period 12s fl. 1s, ec. 2s fl. 1s, ec. 2s fl. 1s, ec. 5s | 79 **24** | 10 | Red rectangular concrete tower; 72. | |
| 15580 *J 4368* | Cayo Arenas. | 22° 07.1´ N 91° 23.8´ W | **Fl.W.** period 6s fl. 1s, ec. 5s | 79 **24** | 10 | White four-sided concrete tower; 66. | |
| | RACON | | **X(– • • –)** | | **20** | | (3 & 10cm). |
| 15584 *J 4403* | Isla Arena. | 20° 37.6´ N 90° 28.0´ W | **Fl.W.** period 6s fl. 1s, ec. 5s | 46 **14** | 10 | White cylindrical concrete tower; 33. | |
| 15585 *J 4403.1* | -Beacon No. 1. | 20° 41.3´ N 90° 27.3´ W | **Iso.G.** period 2s | 16 **5** | 4 | Green round metal tower; 13. | |
| 15585.5 | --No. 2. | 20° 41.3´ N 90° 27.3´ W | **Iso.R.** period 2s | 16 **5** | 4 | Red round metal tower; 13. | |
| 15588 *J 4404* | Celestun. | 20° 51.6´ N 90° 24.0´ W | **Fl.(3)W.** period 12s fl. 1s, ec. 2s fl. 1s, ec. 2s fl. 1s, ec. 5s | 69 **21** | 12 | White cylindrical concrete tower; 39. | Visible 002°-188°. |
| 15588.1 *J 4404.5* | -N. breakwater. | 20° 51.0´ N 90° 53.0´ W | **Fl.G.** period 5s fl. 0.5s, ec. 4.5s | 33 **10** | 7 | White cylindrical concrete tower; 26. | |
| 15588.2 *J 4404.4* | -S. breakwater. | 20° 51.0´ N 90° 53.0´ W | **Fl.R.** period 5s fl. 0.5s, ec. 4.5s | 33 **10** | 7 | White cylindrical concrete tower; 26. | |
| 15588.3 *J 4404.2* | -Celestun Range, front. | 20° 51.0´ N 90° 23.0´ W | **Fl.W.** period 3s fl. 0.5s, ec. 2.5s | 46 **14** | 9 | Truncated pyramidal metal tower; 43. | |
| 15588.4 *J 4404.2* | --Rear. | 20° 51.0´ N 90° 23.0´ W | **Iso.W.** period 2s | 59 **18** | 9 | Truncated pyramidal metal tower; 56. | |
| 15592 *J 4406* | **Punta Palmas.** | 21° 03.7´ N 90° 15.1´ W | **Fl.(2)W.** period 10s | 138 **42** | **20** | White cylindrical concrete tower; 128. | Visible 048°-236°. |
| | RACON | | **Q(– – • –)** | | **25** | | (3 & 10cm). |
| 15596 *J 4414* | **Isla Perez.** | 22° 23.0´ N 89° 41.0´ W | **Fl.(2)W.** period 8s | 69 **21** | **20** | White cylindrical concrete tower, red bands; 59. | |
| | RACON | | **Z(– – • •)** | | **25** | | (3 & 10cm). |
| 15598 | Isla Pajaros. | 22° 22.2´ N 89° 39.5´ W | **Fl.W.** period 6s fl. 1s, ec. 5s | 26 **8** | 5 | Truncated pyramidal aluminum tower; 24. | |
| 15600 *J 4412* | Isla Desterreda. | 22° 31.3´ N 89° 46.4´ W | **Fl.(4)W.** period 16s fl. 1s, ec. 2s fl. 1s, ec. 2s fl. 1s, ec. 2s fl. 1s, ec. 6s | 46 **14** | 10 | Truncated pyramidal aluminum tower; 26. | |
| 15604 *J 4409* | Sisal, on old white fort. | 21° 09.7´ N 90° 02.0´ W | **Fl.(3)W.** period 12s fl. 1s, ec. 2s fl. 1s, ec. 2s fl. 1s, ec. 5s | 43 **13** | 12 | White cylindrical concrete tower, red bands. | |

The lights of Mexico are characterized by the number of flashes etc., the periods being subject to fluctuations.

| (1) No. | (2) Name and Location | (3) Position | (4) Characteristic | (5) Height | (6) Range | (7) Structure | (8) Remarks |
|---|---|---|---|---|---|---|---|

## MEXICO

| (1) No. | (2) Name and Location | (3) Position | (4) Characteristic | (5) Height | (6) Range | (7) Structure | (8) Remarks |
|---|---|---|---|---|---|---|---|
| 15610 *J 4410* | Chuburna, W. breakwater. | 21° 15.3′ N 89° 50.0′ W | **Fl.R.** period 5s fl. 0.5s, ec. 4.5s | 33 **10** | 7 | Cylindrical concrete tower; 23. | |
| 15611 *J 4410.5* | -E. breakwater. | 21° 15.3′ N 89° 50.0′ W | **Fl.G.** period 5s fl. 0.5s, ec. 4.5s | 33 **10** | 7 | Cylindrical concrete tower; 23. | |
| 15617 *J 4411* | Puerto de Yukalpeten Range, front. | 21° 16.2′ N 89° 42.1′ W | **Fl.W.** period 3s fl. 1s, ec. 2s | 46 **14** | 9 | Red truncated pyramidal metal tower; 39. | |
| 15617.1 *J 4411.1* | -Rear, 195 meters 169° from front. | 21° 16.2′ N 89° 42.0′ W | **Iso.W.** period 2s | 59 **18** | 9 | Red truncated pyramidal metal tower; 52. | |
| 15618 *J 4411.3* | -Jetty, E. side. | 21° 17.1′ N 89° 42.2′ W | **Fl.G.** period 5s fl. 0.5s, ec. 4.5s | 39 **12** | 7 | Red truncated pyramidal metal tower; 24. | |
| 15619 *J 4411.5* | --W. side. | 21° 16.9′ N 89° 42.2′ W | **Fl.R.** period 5s fl. 0.5s, ec. 4.5s | 39 **12** | 7 | Red truncated pyramidal metal tower; 24. | |
| | PROGRESO: | | | | | | |
| 15620 *J 4416* | **-Progreso.** | 21° 17.1′ N 89° 39.8′ W | **Fl.W.** period 6s | 108 **33** | **20** | White truncated conical masonry tower; 108. | Visible 066°-250°. |
| 15623.01 *J 4416.5* | -Muelle Fiscal, No. 1. | 21° 18.3′ N 89° 40.0′ W | **Iso.R.** period 2s | 36 **11** | 7 | White cylindrical concrete tower, red bands; 23. | |
| 15623.02 *J 4416.55* | --No. 2. | 21° 18.9′ N 89° 40.1′ W | **Iso.R.** period 2s | 36 **11** | 7 | White cylindrical concrete tower, red bands; 23. | |
| 15623.03 *J 4416.6* | --No. 3. | 21° 19.8′ N 89° 40.1′ W | **Iso.G.** period 2s | 36 **11** | 7 | White cylindrical concrete tower, red bands; 23. | |
| 15623.04 *J 4416.65* | --No. 4. | 21° 20.2′ N 89° 40.2′ W | **Iso.R.** period 2s | 36 **11** | 7 | White cylindrical concrete tower, red bands; 23. | |
| 15623.05 *J 4417.01* | --No. 5. | 21° 20.7′ N 89° 40.3′ W | **Fl.(2)R.** period 10s fl. 1s, ec. 1s fl. 1s, ec. 7s | 36 **11** | 7 | White cylindrical concrete tower, red bands; 26. | |
| 15623.06 *J 4417.02* | --No. 6. | 21° 20.8′ N 89° 40.4′ W | **Fl.G.** period 5s fl. 0.5s, ec. 4.5s | 33 **10** | 7 | White cylindrical concrete tower, red bands; 26. | |
| 15623.07 *J 4417.03* | --No. 7. | 21° 20.9′ N 89° 40.5′ W | **Fl.G.** period 5s fl. 0.5s, ec. 4.5s | 33 **10** | 7 | White cylindrical concrete tower, green bands; 26. | |
| 15623.08 *J 4417.04* | --No. 8. | 21° 20.9′ N 89° 40.9′ W | **Fl.G.** period 5s fl. 0.5s, ec. 4.5s | 33 **10** | 7 | White cylindrical concrete tower, green bands; 26. | |
| 15623.09 *J 4417.05* | --No. 9. | 21° 20.8′ N 89° 41.1′ W | **Fl.G.** period 5s fl. 0.5s, ec. 4.5s | 33 **10** | 7 | White cylindrical concrete tower, green bands; 26. | |
| 15623.1 *J 4417.07* | --No. 10. | 21° 20.7′ N 89° 40.9′ W | **Fl.G.** period 5s fl. 0.5s, ec. 4.5s | 33 **10** | 7 | Green cylindrical concrete tower; 26. | |
| 15625 *J 4417.082* | --Corner between berths 5 and 6. | 21° 20.7′ N 89° 40.6′ W | **F.R.** | 10 **3** | 2 | | |
| 15627 *J 4417.09* | -Cruise wharf, N. side. | 21° 20.5′ N 89° 40.6′ W | **Iso.G.** period 2s | 20 **6** | 5 | Green cylindrical concrete tower; 20. | |
| 15627.1 *J 4417.1* | --S. side. | 21° 20.5′ N 89° 40.5′ W | **Iso.R.** period 2s | 20 **6** | 5 | Green cylindrical concrete tower; 20. | |

The lights of Mexico are characterized by the number of flashes etc., the periods being subject to fluctuations.

| (1) No. | (2) Name and Location | (3) Position | (4) Characteristic | (5) Height | (6) Range | (7) Structure | (8) Remarks |
|---|---|---|---|---|---|---|---|
| | | | **MEXICO** | | | | |
| 15629 *J 4416.15* | -Range, front. | 21° 20.5′ N 89° 41.3′ W | **Fl.W.** period 3s fl. 1s, ec. 2s | 52 **16** | 6 | Truncated pyramidal aluminum tower; 39. | |
| 15629.1 *J 4416.16* | --Rear, 4500 meters 355° from front. | 21° 18.0′ N 89° 41.3′ W | **Iso.W.** period 2s | 92 **28** | 10 | Truncated pyramidal aluminum tower; 79. | |
| 15630 *J 4416.1* | **-Tank.** | 21° 16.8′ N 89° 39.7′ W | **F.R.** | 79 **24** | **15** | On tank. | |
| 15632 *J 4418* | Telchac. | 21° 19.8′ N 89° 15.1′ W | **Fl.(3)W.** period 8s | 39 **12** | 12 | White cylindrical tower; 39. | |
| 15632.1 *J 4418.4* | -Breakwater, W. side. | 21° 20.0′ N 89° 16.0′ W | **Fl.R.** period 5s fl. 0.5s, ec. 4.5s | 30 **9** | 7 | Cylindrical concrete tower; 23. | |
| 15632.2 *J 4418.3* | --E. side. | 21° 20.0′ N 89° 16.0′ W | **Fl.G.** period 5s fl. 0.5s, ec. 4.5s | 30 **9** | 7 | Cylindrical concrete tower; 23. | |
| 15632.3 *J 4418.2* | -Telchac Range, front. | 21° 20.0′ N 89° 16.0′ W | **Fl.W.** period 3s fl. 1s, ec. 2s | 30 **9** | 7 | Rectangular concrete tower; 20. | |
| 15632.4 *J 4418.21* | --Rear. | 21° 19.5′ N 89° 16.0′ W | **Iso.W.** period 2s | 36 **11** | 7 | Rectangular concrete tower; 26. | |
| 15634 *J 4418.7* | Chabihau, E. breakwater. | 21° 21.2′ N 89° 10.0′ W | **Fl.G.** period 5s fl. 0.5s, ec. 4.5s | 33 **10** | 7 | Cylindrical concrete tower; 23. | |
| 15635 *J 4409.6* | Sisal, W. breakwater. | 21° 10.0′ N 89° 04.0′ W | **Fl.R.** period 5s fl. 0.5s, ec. 4.5s | 33 **10** | 8 | Cylindrical concrete tower; 23. | |
| 15635.5 *J 4409.4* | -E. breakwater. | 21° 10.0′ N 89° 04.0′ W | **Fl.G.** period 5s fl. 0.5s, ec. 4.5s | 33 **10** | 8 | Cylindrical concrete tower; 23. | |
| 15636 *J 4419* | Dzilam de Bravo. | 21° 21.9′ N 88° 54.7′ W | **Fl.W.** period 6s fl. 1s, ec. 5s | 59 **18** | 10 | White cylindrical concrete tower; 33. | |
| 15636.1 *J 4419.4* | -Breakwater, W. side. | 21° 22.2′ N 88° 53.6′ W | **Fl.R.** period 5s fl. 0.5s, ec. 4.5s | 39 **12** | 7 | Truncated pyramidal aluminum tower; 23. | |
| 15636.2 *J 4419.3* | --E. side. | 21° 22.2′ N 88° 53.3′ W | **Fl.G.** period 5s fl. 0.5s, ec. 4.5s | 39 **12** | 7 | Truncated pyramidal aluminum tower; 23. | |
| 15636.3 *J 4419.2* | -Dzilam de Bravo Range, front. | 21° 21.9′ N 88° 53.6′ W | **Fl.W.** period 3s fl. 1s, ec. 2s | 46 **14** | 8 | Truncated pyramidal aluminum tower; 39. | |
| 15636.4 *J 4419.21* | --Rear. | 21° 21.9′ N 88° 53.6′ W | **Iso.W.** period 2s | 59 **18** | 9 | Cylindrical concrete tower; 52. | |
| 15640 *J 4420* | Yalkubul. | 21° 31.3′ N 88° 36.6′ W | **Fl.(4)W.** period 16s fl. 1s, ec. 2s fl. 1s, ec. 2s fl. 1s, ec. 2s fl. 1s, ec. 6s | 69 **21** | 10 | White cylindrical concrete tower, red bands; 66. | Visible 057°-251°. |
| 15644 *J 4421* | **Rio Lagartos.** | 21° 36.1′ N 88° 12.4′ W | **Fl.(2)W.** period 10s | 72 **22** | **16** | White four-sided concrete tower; 66. | |
| 15644.1 *J 4421.5* | -Breakwater, W. side. | 21° 40.0′ N 88° 12.0′ W | **Fl.R.** period 5s fl. 0.5s, ec. 4.5s | 39 **12** | 7 | Truncated pyramidal tower; 23. | |
| 15644.2 *J 4421.6* | --E. side. | 21° 40.0′ N 88° 12.0′ W | **Fl.G.** period 5s fl. 0.5s, ec. 4.5s | 39 **12** | 7 | Truncated pyramidal metal tower; 23. | |

The lights of Mexico are characterized by the number of flashes etc., the periods being subject to fluctuations.

| (1) No. | (2) Name and Location | (3) Position | (4) Characteristic | (5) Height | (6) Range | (7) Structure | (8) Remarks |
|---|---|---|---|---|---|---|---|
| | | | **MEXICO** | | | | |
| 15645<br>*J 4421.9* | Coloradas. | 21° 36.6′ N<br>87° 59.5′ W | **Fl.(2)W.**<br>period 10s<br>fl. 1s, ec. 2s<br>fl. 1s, ec. 6s | 43<br>**13** | 10 | Truncated pyramidal aluminum tower; 39. | |
| 15648<br>*J 4422* | Monte de Cuyo, summit. | 21° 31.0′ N<br>87° 41.1′ W | **Fl.(3)W.**<br>period 12s<br>fl. 1s, ec. 2s<br>fl. 1s, ec. 2s<br>fl. 1s, ec. 5s | 82<br>**25** | 14 | Red cylindrical concrete tower; 23. | Visible 100°-273°. |
| 15649<br>*J 4422.8* | -Breakwater, W. side. | 21° 30.0′ N<br>87° 42.0′ W | **Fl.R.**<br>period 5s<br>fl. 0.5s, ec. 4.5s | 26<br>**8** | 6 | Cylindrical concrete tower; 23. | |
| 15649.1<br>*J 4422.7* | --E. side. | 21° 30.0′ N<br>87° 42.0′ W | **Fl.G.**<br>period 5s<br>fl. 0.5s, ec. 4.5s | 26<br>**8** | 6 | Cylindrical concrete tower; 23. | |
| 15650<br>*J 4422.5* | -El Cuyo Range, front. | 21° 30.9′ N<br>87° 41.9′ W | **Fl.W.**<br>period 3s<br>fl. 1s, ec. 2s | 36<br>**11** | 9 | Cylindrical concrete tower; 23. | |
| 15650.1<br>*J 4422.51* | --Rear. | 21° 30.9′ N<br>87° 41.3′ W | **Iso.W.**<br>period 2s | 43<br>**13** | 9 | Cylindrical concrete tower; 46. | |
| 15652<br>*J 4426* | Punta Francisca, (Mosquito). | 21° 32.2′ N<br>87° 18.1′ W | **Fl.(2)W.**<br>period 10s<br>fl. 1s, ec. 2s<br>fl. 1s, ec. 6s | 36<br>**11** | 10 | Truncated pyramidal aluminum tower; 30. | |
| 15656<br>*J 4427* | Isla Holbox, W. head. | 21° 32.1′ N<br>87° 18.1′ W | **Fl.W.**<br>period 6s<br>fl. 1s, ec. 5s | 36<br>**11** | 10 | Truncated pyramidal aluminum tower; 30. | |
| 15657<br>*J 4427.3* | -Holbox Range, front. | 21° 33.0′ N<br>87° 18.0′ W | **Fl.W.**<br>period 3s<br>fl. 1s, ec. 2s | 43<br>**13** | 6 | Truncated pyramidal steel tower; 36. | |
| 15657.1<br>*J 4427.31* | --Rear. | 21° 33.0′ N<br>87° 18.0′ W | **Iso.W.**<br>period 2s | 59<br>**18** | 8 | Truncated pyramidal steel tower; 52. | |
| 15661<br>*J 4424.5* | -Chiquila Range, front. | 21° 26.0′ N<br>87° 17.0′ W | **Fl.W.**<br>period 3s<br>fl. 1s, ec. 2s | 13<br>**4** | 4 | Truncated pyramidal aluminum tower; 10. | |
| 15661.1<br>*J 4424.51* | --Rear. | 21° 25.0′ N<br>87° 17.0′ W | **Iso.W.**<br>period 2s | 46<br>**14** | 4 | Truncated pyramidal aluminum tower; 23. | |
| 15664<br>*J 4428* | **Cabo Catoche.** | 21° 36.3′ N<br>87° 06.1′ W | **Fl.(4)W.**<br>period 20s | 49<br>**15** | **15** | White square masonry tower, red band; 46. | Visible 008°-285°. |
| 15668<br>*J 4430* | **Isla Contoy.** | 21° 31.6′ N<br>86° 48.3′ W | **Fl.W.**<br>period 7s | 105<br>**32** | **21** | White cylindrical masonry tower; 105. | Visible 010°-350°. |
| | RACON | | **T(−)** | | **25** | | (3 & 10cm). |
| 15670<br>*J 4431* | Arrecife El Cabezo. | 21° 19.2′ N<br>86° 46.5′ W | **Fl.R.**<br>period 5s<br>fl. 0.5s, ec. 4.5s | 23<br>**7** | 4 | Truncated pyramidal aluminum tower; 20. | |
| 15672<br>*J 4432* | Isla Mujeres, S. extremity. | 21° 12.2′ N<br>86° 42.8′ W | **Fl.(4)W.**<br>period 16s<br>fl. 1s, ec. 2s<br>fl. 1s, ec. 2s<br>fl. 1s, ec. 2s<br>fl. 1s, ec. 6s | 75<br>**23** | 14 | White octagonal concrete tower; 36. | Visible 150°-131°. |
| 15676<br>*J 4433* | -Roca La Carbonera. | 21° 14.8′ N<br>86° 45.4′ W | **Fl.W.**<br>period 3s<br>fl. 1s, ec. 2s | 20<br>**6** | 6 | White square concrete tower; 16. | |
| 15680<br>*J 4433.1* | -Punta Norte. | 21° 15.8′ N<br>86° 44.9′ W | **Fl.(2)W.**<br>period 10s | 62<br>**19** | 13 | White cylindrical concrete tower; 52 | |

The lights of Mexico are characterized by the number of flashes etc., the periods being subject to fluctuations.

| (1) No. | (2) Name and Location | (3) Position | (4) Characteristic | (5) Height | (6) Range | (7) Structure | (8) Remarks |
|---|---|---|---|---|---|---|---|

## MEXICO

| (1) No. | (2) Name and Location | (3) Position | (4) Characteristic | (5) Height | (6) Range | (7) Structure | (8) Remarks |
|---|---|---|---|---|---|---|---|
| 15684 *J 4431.5* | -Roca El Yunque. | 21° 16.1´ N 86° 45.0´ W | **Fl.G.** period 5s fl. 0.5s, ec. 4.5s | 16 **5** | 4 | Square concrete and aluminum tower; 13. | |
| 15688 *J 4435* | Roca de La Bandera (Becket Rock). | 21° 10.0´ N 86° 43.7´ W | **Fl.(2)W.** period 10s fl. 1s, ec. 1s fl. 1s, ec. 7s | 13 **4** | 5 | Red cylindrical concrete tower, black bands; 20. | Visible 306°-077°. |
| 15692 *J 4436* | El Meco Range, front. | 21° 12.8´ N 86° 48.1´ W | **Fl.W.** period 3s fl. 1s, ec. 2s | 26 **8** | 6 | White truncated pyramidal concrete tower; 17. | |
| 15692.1 *J 4436.1* | -Rear, 140 yards 290° from front. | 21° 12.9´ N 86° 48.1´ W | **Iso.W.** period 2s | 56 **17** | 10 | Truncated pyramidal aluminum tower; 52. | |
| 15693 | Puerto Juarez mole, N. head. | 21° 11.4´ N 86° 48.3´ W | **Iso.W.** period 2s | 13 **4** | | Red wooden framework tower; 13. | |
| 15693.1 | -S. head. | 21° 11.4´ N 86° 48.3´ W | **Iso.W.** period 2s | 13 **4** | | Red wooden framework tower; 13. | |
| 15694 *J 4436.3* | **Gran Puerto de Cancun.** | 21° 11.0´ N 86° 48.4´ W | **Fl.(3)W.** period 20s fl. 1s, ec. 2s fl. 1s, ec. 2s fl. 1s, ec. 13s | 190 **58** | **24** | White truncated pyramidal concrete and metal tower; 190. | |
| 15696 *J 4436.5* | Punta Cancun. | 21° 08.3´ N 86° 44.5´ W | **Fl.(3)W.** period 12s fl. 1s, ec. 2s fl. 1s, ec. 2s fl. 1s, ec. 5s | 49 **15** | 11 | White cylindrical concrete tower, red stripes; 39. | |
| 15700 *J 4437* | Punta Nisuk. | 21° 02.1´ N 86° 46.7´ W | **Fl.(4)W.** period 16s fl. 1s, ec. 2s fl. 1s, ec. 2s fl. 1s, ec. 2s fl. 1s, ec. 6s | 33 **10** | 11 | Truncated pyramidal aluminum tower; 30. | |
| 15704 *J 4438* | **Puerto Morelos.** | 20° 50.2´ N 86° 55.0´ W | **Fl.W.** period 6s fl. 1s, ec. 5s | 52 **16** | **15** | White cylindrical concrete tower; 49. | Visible 205°-035°. |
| 15705 | -E. breakwater. | 20° 49.7´ N 86° 53.4´ W | **Fl.R.** period 5s fl. 0.5s, ec. 4.5s | 23 **7** | 6 | Red concrete structure; 23. | |
| 15705.1 | --Inner point. | 20° 49.8´ N 86° 53.4´ W | **Fl.R.** period 5s fl. 0.5s, ec. 4.5s | 16 **5** | 4 | Red metal structure; 13. | |
| 15706 | -W. breakwater. | 20° 49.7´ N 86° 53.4´ W | **Fl.G.** period 5s fl. 0.5s, ec. 4.5s | 33 **10** | 6 | Red concrete structure; 23. | |
| 15707 | -Diesel pier. | 20° 49.8´ N 86° 53.4´ W | **Fl.Y.** period 2s fl. 0.5s, ec. 1.5s | 16 **5** | 4 | Red metal structure; 13. | |
| 15707.1 | -Pier B. | 20° 49.8´ N 86° 53.4´ W | **Iso.R.** period 2s | 16 **5** | 4 | Red metal structure; 13. | |
| 15708 *J 4440* | Punta Brava. | 20° 48.5´ N 86° 56.5´ W | **Fl.(4)W.** period 16s fl. 1s, ec. 2s fl. 1s, ec. 2s fl. 1s, ec. 2s fl. 1s, ec. 6s | 33 **10** | 11 | Truncated pyramidal aluminum tower; 30. | |
| 15712 *J 4440.5* | Punta Maroma. | 20° 43.8´ N 86° 57.8´ W | **Fl.(2)W.** period 10s fl. 1s, ec. 2s fl. 1s, ec. 6s | 36 **11** | 11 | Truncated pyramidal aluminum tower; 30. | |
| 15716 *J 4441* | Playa del Carmen. | 20° 37.2´ N 87° 04.5´ W | **Fl.(3)W.** period 12s | 56 **17** | 11 | White truncated pyramidal concrete tower; 52. | |

The lights of Mexico are characterized by the number of flashes etc., the periods being subject to fluctuations.

| (1) No. | (2) Name and Location | (3) Position | (4) Characteristic | (5) Height | (6) Range | (7) Structure | (8) Remarks |
|---|---|---|---|---|---|---|---|
| | | | **MEXICO** | | | | |
| 15717 *J 4441.5* | Caleta de Chachalet. | 20° 29.6′ N 87° 13.8′ W | **Fl.(2)W.** period 10s fl. 1s, ec. 2s fl. 1s, ec. 6s | 33 **10** | 10 | Truncated pyramidal aluminum tower; 26. | |
| 15718 *J 4441.55* | Xcaret Range, front. | 20° 35.0′ N 87° 06.0′ W | **Fl.W.** period 3s fl. 1s, ec. 2s | 26 **8** | 5 | | |
| 15718.5 *J 4441.56* | -Rear. | 20° 35.0′ N 87° 06.0′ W | **Iso.W.** period 2s | 26 **8** | 5 | | |
| 15719 *J 4441.6* | -Jetty, N. side. | 20° 35.0′ N 87° 06.0′ W | **Fl.G.** period 5s fl. 0.5s, ec. 4.5s | 26 **8** | 6 | | |
| 15719.5 *J 4441.62* | --S. side. | 20° 35.0′ N 87° 06.0′ W | **Fl.R.** period 5s | 26 **8** | 6 | | |
| 15720 *J 4441.7* | Caleta de Xel-Ha. | 20° 28.4′ N 87° 15.8′ W | **Fl.W.** period 6s fl. 1s, ec. 5s | 39 **12** | 11 | Truncated pyramidal aluminum tower; 26. | |
| | ISLA DE COZUMEL: | | | | | | |
| 15724 *J 4442* | -Punta Molas. | 20° 35.3′ N 86° 43.5′ W | **Fl.(3)W.** period 12s | 105 **32** | 12 | White cylindrical concrete tower, red bands; 105. | |
| | -RACON | | **O(- - -)** | | **20** | | (3 & 10cm). |
| 15728 *J 4445* | -AVIATION LIGHT. | 20° 30.6′ N 86° 55.8′ W | **Al.Fl.W.G.** period 10s | 82 **25** | 14 | Skeleton tower; 72. | |
| 15730 | **-Old Lighthouse.** | 20° 30.4′ N 86° 57.3′ W | **Fl.W.** period 5s | 56 **17** | **15** | White concrete tower; 49. | |
| 15732 *J 4443.1* | **-San Miguel.** | 20° 29.7′ N 86° 57.8′ W | **Fl.(2)W.** period 5s | 121 **37** | **15** | White truncated conical concrete tower; 118. | |
| 15735 *J 4445.2* | -Wharf, W. side. | 20° 29.0′ N 86° 59.0′ W | **Fl.G.** period 3s fl. 0.5s, ec. 2.5s | 10 **3** | 4 | | |
| 15735.5 *J 4445.25* | --E. side. | 20° 29.0′ N 86° 59.0′ W | **Fl.R.** period 3s fl. 0.5s, ec. 2.5s | 10 **3** | 4 | | |
| 15736 *J 4447* | -Banco Playa, entrance, N. side. | 20° 31.7′ N 86° 56.4′ W | **Fl.G.** period 5s fl. 0.5s, ec. 4.5s | 26 **8** | 6 | Green round fiberglass tower; 20. | |
| 15740 *J 4447.2* | --S. side. | 20° 31.6′ N 86° 56.4′ W | **Fl.R.** period 5s fl. 0.5s, ec. 4.5s | 26 **8** | 6 | Red round fiberglass tower; 20. | |
| 15744 *J 4446* | **Punta Celarain.** | 20° 16.4′ N 86° 59.3′ W | **Fl.W.** period 5s | 105 **32** | **15** | White cylindrical masonry tower; 82. | |
| 15748 *J 4448* | Tulum, Salta Iman. | 20° 12.0′ N 87° 26.6′ W | **Fl.W.** period 6s fl. 1s, ec. 5s | 75 **23** | 12 | White truncated pyramidal concrete tower; 36. | |
| 15752 *J 4450* | Punta Allen. | 19° 47.1′ N 87° 27.8′ W | **Fl.(4)W.** period 16s fl. 1s, ec. 2s fl. 1s, ec. 2s fl. 1s, ec. 2s fl. 1s, ec. 6s | 72 **22** | 12 | White cylindrical concrete tower; 66. | |
| 15756 *J 4450.5* | Punta Vigia Chico. | 19° 46.4′ N 87° 35.1′ W | **Fl.(4)W.** period 16s fl. 1s, ec. 2s fl. 1s, ec. 2s fl. 1s, ec. 2s fl. 1s, ec. 6s | 39 **12** | 10 | White cylindrical concrete tower; 33. | |

The lights of Mexico are characterized by the number of flashes etc., the periods being subject to fluctuations.

| (1) No. | (2) Name and Location | (3) Position | (4) Characteristic | (5) Height | (6) Range | (7) Structure | (8) Remarks |
|---|---|---|---|---|---|---|---|

## MEXICO

| (1) No. | (2) Name and Location | (3) Position | (4) Characteristic | (5) Height | (6) Range | (7) Structure | (8) Remarks |
|---|---|---|---|---|---|---|---|
| 15760<br>*J 4450.7* | Cayo Culebras. | 19° 41.8′ N<br>87° 27.8′ W | **Fl.(3)W.**<br>period 12s<br>fl. 1s, ec. 2s<br>fl. 1s, ec. 2s<br>fl. 1s, ec. 5s | 46<br>**14** | 10 | White cylindrical concrete tower; 39. | |
| 15764<br>*J 4450.9* | Punta Nohku. | 19° 38.8′ N<br>87° 27.1′ W | **Fl.(2)W.**<br>period 10s<br>fl. 1s, ec. 2s<br>fl. 1s, ec. 6s | 39<br>**12** | 10 | White truncated pyramidal aluminum tower; 33. | |
| 15768<br>*J 4451* | Punta Pajaros. | 19° 35.8′ N<br>87° 24.6′ W | **Fl.W.**<br>period 6s<br>fl. 1s, ec. 5s | 36<br>**11** | 10 | Truncated pyramidal aluminum tower; 30. | |
| 15772<br>*J 4453* | Punta Owen. | 19° 19.7′ N<br>87° 26.4′ W | **Fl.(3)W.**<br>period 12s<br>fl. 1s, ec. 2s<br>fl. 1s, ec. 2s<br>fl. 1s, ec. 5s | 39<br>**12** | 10 | White truncated pyramidal aluminum tower; 33. | |
| 15776<br>*J 4452* | Punta Herrero. | 19° 18.8′ N<br>87° 26.6′ W | **Fl.(2)W.**<br>period 10s<br>fl. 1s, ec. 2s<br>fl. 1s, ec. 6s | 75<br>**23** | 12 | White truncated pyramidal metal tower; 72. | |
| 15778<br>*J 4454* | El Ubero. | 19° 04.4′ N<br>87° 33.2′ W | **Fl.(3)W.**<br>period 12s<br>fl. 1s, ec. 2s<br>fl. 1s, ec. 2s<br>fl. 1s, ec. 5s | 33<br>**10** | 8 | Truncated pyramidal aluminum tower; 33. | |
| 15780<br>*J 4456* | Banco Chinchorro. | 18° 45.8′ N<br>87° 18.7′ W | **Fl.W.**<br>period 6s<br>fl. 1s, ec. 5s | 52<br>**16** | 8 | White cylindrical concrete tower; 33. | |
| | RACON | | **X(– • • –)** | | | | |
| 15782<br>*J 4455* | **El Majahual.** | 18° 43.9′ N<br>87° 41.7′ W | **Fl.(4)W.**<br>period 16s | 72<br>**22** | **20** | Truncated pyramidal concrete tower; 72. | |
| | RACON | | **M(– –)** | | | | |
| 15784<br>*J 4456.5* | Cayo Centro. | 18° 35.6′ N<br>87° 19.8′ W | **Fl.(2)W.**<br>period 10s<br>fl. 1s, ec. 2s<br>fl. 1s, ec. 6s | 52<br>**16** | 8 | Truncated pyramidal aluminum tower; 49. | |
| 15788<br>*J 4457* | Punta Gavilan. | 18° 25.3′ N<br>87° 46.0′ W | **Fl.W.**<br>period 6s<br>fl. 1s, ec. 5s | 36<br>**11** | 10 | White truncated pyramidal aluminum tower; 39. | |
| 15792<br>*J 4456.7* | -Cayo Lobos. | 18° 23.7′ N<br>87° 23.0′ W | **Fl.(3)W.**<br>period 12s<br>fl. 1s, ec. 2s<br>fl. 1s, ec. 2s<br>fl. 1s, ec. 5s | 46<br>**14** | 8 | Truncated pyramidal metal tower; 43. | |
| | -RACON | | **C(– • – •)** | | **20** | | (3 & 10cm). |
| 15796<br>*J 4462* | Xcalak. | 18° 15.8′ N<br>87° 50.1′ W | **Fl.(3)W.**<br>period 12s<br>fl. 1s, ec. 2s<br>fl. 1s, ec. 2s<br>fl. 1s, ec. 5s | 43<br>**13** | 12 | Cylindrical concrete tower; 39. | Visible 214°-000°. |
| 15797<br>*J 4466* | La Aguada. | 18° 14.1′ N<br>87° 53.8′ W | **Fl.(2)W.**<br>period 10s<br>fl. 1s, ec. 2s<br>fl. 1s, ec. 6s | 39<br>**12** | 10 | Aluminum tower; 33. | |
| | BAHIA DE CHETUMAL: | | | | | | |
| 15800<br>*J 4469* | -Ciudad Chetumal (Payo Obispo). | 18° 31.3′ N<br>88° 16.3′ W | **Fl.W.**<br>period 6s<br>fl. 1s, ec. 5s | 59<br>**18** | 13 | Cylindrical concrete tower; 49. | Visible 115°-064°. |

The lights of Mexico are characterized by the number of flashes etc., the periods being subject to fluctuations.

# Section 11

## Trinidad, East Coast of Central America and Netherland Antilles

| (1) No. | (2) Name and Location | (3) Position | (4) Characteristic | (5) Height | (6) Range | (7) Structure | (8) Remarks |
|---|---|---|---|---|---|---|---|
| | | | **UNITED STATES** | | | | |
| 15816<br>*J 6024* | **Serranilla Bank.** | 15° 47.8′ N<br>79° 50.9′ W | **Fl.(2)W.**<br>period 20s<br>fl. 1s, ec. 3s<br>fl. 1s, ec. 15s | 108<br>**33** | **16** | White tower, red bands, concrete base. | |
| 15818<br>*J 6020* | **Bajo Nuevo.** | 15° 51.2′ N<br>78° 38.0′ W | **Fl.(2)W.**<br>period 15s<br>fl. 1s, ec. 2s<br>fl. 1s, ec. 11s | 72<br>**22** | **15** | White tower, red bands. | |
| | Several other states together with the United States claim sovereignty over Bajo Nuevo and Serranilla Bank. | | | | | | |
| | | | **COLOMBIA** | | | | |
| 15820<br>*J 6028* | **Quita Sueno Bank.** | 14° 29.3′ N<br>81° 08.2′ W | **Fl.(3)W.**<br>period 6.1s<br>fl. 0.4s, ec. 1s<br>fl. 0.4s, ec. 1s<br>fl. 0.4s, ec. 2.9s | 66<br>**20** | **15** | Red tower, white band; 59. | |
| 15821<br>*J 6030* | **-S.** | 14° 09.3′ N<br>81° 09.8′ W | **L.Fl.W.**<br>period 12s<br>fl. 2s, ec. 10s | 66<br>**20** | **15** | Red tower, white band; 59. | |
| 15824<br>*J 6034* | **Serrana Bank.** | 14° 16.4′ N<br>80° 23.5′ W | **Fl.W.**<br>period 10s<br>fl. 1s, ec. 9s | 79<br>**24** | **17** | Red tower, white band; 59. | |
| 15828<br>*J 6038* | **Roncador Bank.** | 13° 35.0′ N<br>80° 05.2′ W | **Fl.W.**<br>period 10s<br>fl. 1s, ec. 9s | 66<br>**20** | **15** | Red tower, white band; 59. | |
| | ISLA DE PROVIDENCIA: | | | | | | |
| 15832<br>*J 6042* | -S. head. | 13° 19.3′ N<br>81° 23.0′ W | **Fl.W.**<br>period 20s<br>fl. 1.6s, ec. 18.4s | 220<br>**67** | **20** | Red tower, white band; 59. | Visible 318°-157°. |
| 15832.3<br>*J 6041.8* | -Catalina Harbor. | 13° 22.3′ N<br>81° 22.2′ W | **Q.G.** | 92<br>**28** | 12 | Red tower, white bands. | |
| 15832.5<br>*J 6041.5* | **-Palma Cay.** | 13° 24.0′ N<br>81° 22.1′ W | **Fl.W.**<br>period 10s<br>fl. 1s, ec. 9s | 66<br>**20** | **15** | Red tower, white bands. | |
| 15832.7<br>*J 6041* | -Low Cay. | 13° 31.8′ N<br>81° 20.6′ W | **Fl.W.**<br>period 10s<br>fl. 1s, ec. 9s | 66<br>**20** | 12 | Red tower, white band; 59. | |
| | ISLA DE SAN ANDRES: | | | | | | |
| 15833<br>*J 6043* | -AVIATION LIGHT. | 12° 34.9′ N<br>81° 42.3′ W | **Al.Fl.W.G.**<br>period 10s | | 14 | Mast. | **Aero Radiobeacon.** |
| 15834<br>*J 6043.5* | Cayo Cordoba. | 12° 33.0′ N<br>81° 41.3′ W | **Fl.W.**<br>period 6.7s<br>fl. 0.5s, ec. 6.2s | 75<br>**23** | 12 | Red tower, white bands. | |
| | RACON | | **S(• • •)** | | **19** | | (3 & 10cm). |
| 15835<br>*J 6043.6* | -Punta Sur. | 12° 28.8′ N<br>81° 43.8′ W | **Fl.W.**<br>period 9s<br>fl. 0.9s, ec. 8.1s | 66<br>**20** | 13 | Red and white metal framework tower. | |

| (1) No. | (2) Name and Location | (3) Position | (4) Characteristic | (5) Height | (6) Range | (7) Structure | (8) Remarks |
|---|---|---|---|---|---|---|---|
| | | | **COLOMBIA** | | | | |
| 15835.5 *J 6043.7* | -Cove. | 12° 31.0′ N 81° 43.8′ W | **Fl.R.** period 5s fl. 1s, ec. 4s | 59 **18** | 12 | Red tower, white bands. | |
| 15835.7 *J 6043.8* | -Punta Evans. | 12° 31.8′ N 81° 44.1′ W | **Fl.G.** period 3s fl. 0.3s, ec. 2.7s | 69 **21** | 12 | Red tower, white bands. | |
| 15840 *J 6044* | **Cayo Bolivar.** | 12° 24.0′ N 81° 28.5′ W | **Fl.W.** period 15s fl. 1.2s, ec. 13.8s | 105 **32** | **15** | Red tower, white bands. | |
| 15844 *J 6045* | **Cayos de Albuquerque.** | 12° 09.9′ N 81° 50.4′ W | **Fl.W.** period 12s fl. 1s, ec. 11s | 105 **32** | **15** | Red tower, white bands. | |
| | | | **ARUBA (N.)-CARIBBEAN SEA** | | | | |
| 15850 *J 6330* | **Noordwestpunt.** | 12° 36.8′ N 70° 03.1′ W | **Fl.(2)W.R.** period 10s fl. 0.8s, ec. 1.7s fl. 0.8s, ec. 6.7s | 180 **55** | **19** | Gray stone tower; 98. | W. 354°-005°, R.-013°, W.-295°. |
| | PAARDEN BAAI: | | | | | | |
| 15852 *J 6343* | -W. entrance, N. side of channel. | 12° 31.6′ N 70° 03.4′ W | **Fl.R.** period 2s | | | | |
| 15853 *J 6343.5* | -W. entrance. | 12° 31.6′ N 70° 03.2′ W | **Fl.(2)R.** period 4s | | | | |
| 15864 *J 6342* | -W. Entrance 7, S. side of entrance. | 12° 31.3′ N 70° 03.0′ W | **Fl.(2)G.** period 4s | | | Concrete column. | |
| 15868 *J 6340* | --Range, front. | 12° 31.3′ N 70° 02.8′ W | **3 F.G.** | | | Beacon, diamond daymark. | |
| 15872 *J 6340.1* | --Rear, 430 meters 110° from front. | 12° 31.2′ N 70° 02.5′ W | **5 F.G.** | | | | F.R. lights are shown from NW. and SW. corners of Oosthaven. |
| 15876 *J 6336.5* | -S. entrance. | 12° 30.3′ N 70° 02.2′ W | **Q.W.** | | | | |
| 15880 *J 6336* | --No. 1. | 12° 30.5′ N 70° 02.2′ W | **Fl.(2)R.** period 4s | | | Concrete column. | |
| 15884 *J 6337* | --No. 4. | 12° 30.6′ N 70° 02.3′ W | **Q.G.** | | | Concrete column. | |
| 15888 *J 6338* | --No. 5. | 12° 30.8′ N 70° 02.3′ W | **Fl.(2)G.** period 4s | 10 **3** | | Concrete column. | |
| 15892 *J 6339* | --No. 2. | 12° 30.8′ N 70° 02.2′ W | **Fl.(3)R.** period 5s | 10 **3** | | Concrete column. | |
| 15896 *J 6339.4* | --No. 6. | 12° 30.8′ N 70° 02.4′ W | **Fl.(3)G.** period 5s | | | Concrete column. | |
| 15900 *J 6346* | Oranjestad, Prinses Beatrix AVIATION LIGHT. | 12° 31.0′ N 69° 59.7′ W | **F.R.** | 604 **184** | | Tower; 62. | Obstruction. |
| 15901 *J 6346.6* | -Haven Barcadera Entrance Range, front. | 12° 28.9′ N 69° 59.9′ W | **F.G.** | 82 **25** | | Mast. | |
| 15902 *J 6346.61* | --Rear, 107 meters 093° from front. | 12° 28.8′ N 69° 59.8′ W | **F.G.** | 105 **32** | | Mast. | |
| 15903 *J 6347.2* | -No. 4, S. side. | 12° 28.8′ N 70° 00.2′ W | **Fl.(2)G.** period 4s | | | | |

| (1) No. | (2) Name and Location | (3) Position | (4) Characteristic | (5) Height | (6) Range | (7) Structure | (8) Remarks |
|---|---|---|---|---|---|---|---|
| | | | **ARUBA (N.)-CARIBBEAN SEA** | | | | |
| | COMMANDEURS BAAI: | | | | | | |
| 15912 *J 6352* | -Range, front. | 12° 26.9´ N 69° 56.9´ W | **2 F.G.** (vert.) | 19 **6** | 1 | Green post, white triangular daymark point up. | |
| 15916 *J 6352.1* | --Rear, 34 meters 057°30′ from front. | 12° 26.9´ N 69° 56.9´ W | **2 F.R.** (vert.) | 23 **7** | 1 | Red post, white triangular daymark point down. | |
| 15918 *J 6352.5* | -Pier, W. end. | 12° 26.5´ N 69° 56.3´ W | **F.R.** | | | | |
| 15919 *J 6352.51* | --E. end. | 12° 26.5´ N 69° 56.3´ W | **F.R.** | | | | |
| 15921 *J 6352.52* | -Reef. | 12° 26.8´ N 69° 56.9´ W | **Q.G.** | | | | |
| 15923 *J 6352.53* | -Narrows. | 12° 26.6´ N 69° 56.6´ W | **Iso.G.** period 2s | | | | |
| 15925 *J 6352.54* | -W. entrance. | 12° 26.8´ N 69° 57.2´ W | **Fl.R.** | | | | |
| 15926 *J 6352.55* | -E. entrance. | 12° 26.8´ N 69° 57.1´ W | **Fl.G.** | | | | |
| | ST. NICHOLAS BAAI: | | | | | | |
| 15932 *J 6356* | -W. entrance Range, front. | 12° 25.9´ N 69° 54.4´ W | **4 F.R.** | 102 **31** | | | Lights arranged in diamond shape. |
| 15936 *J 6356.1* | --Rear, 240 meters 083° from front. | 12° 25.9´ N 69° 54.3´ W | **4 F.R.** | 134 **41** | | | Lights arranged in diamond shape. N. side of channel marked by Fl.R. light on dolphin and two F.R. lights on dock. F.G. and F.R. lights are shown from outer corners of finger piers. |
| 15938 *J 6357* | --Entrance, N. side, No. 2. | 12° 25.9´ N 69° 55.1´ W | **Fl.R.** period 4s | 23 **7** | 7 | Metal column. | |
| 15940 *J 6357.5* | -Mooring post. | 12° 25.8´ N 69° 54.8´ W | **Fl.R.** period 3s | | | | |
| 15941 *J 6358.2* | -South Channel, Janet Range, front. | 12° 25.3´ N 69° 54.1´ W | **Oc.R.** period 3s | | | Beacon. | |
| 15942 *J 6358.21* | --Rear, 180 meters 139° from front. | 12° 25.2´ N 69° 54.1´ W | **Fl.G.** period 4s | | | Beacon. | |
| 15950 *J 6359.2* | -W. side. | 12° 25.4´ N 69° 54.3´ W | **Fl.(2)G.** period 4s | 11 **3** | | Pile. | |
| 15952 *J 6359* | --No. 6. | 12° 25.5´ N 69° 54.2´ W | **Fl.R.** period 4s | 11 **3** | | Pile. | |
| 15954 *J 6358.6* | --No. 8. | 12° 25.3´ N 69° 54.0´ W | **Q.R.** | | | Beacon. | Occasional. |
| 15957 *J 6358.45* | -Range, front. | 12° 25.3´ N 69° 53.7´ W | **F.G.** | | | | |
| 15957.1 *J 6358.451* | --Rear, 075°30′ from front. | 12° 25.4´ N 69° 53.6´ W | **Q.G.** | | | | |
| 15958 *J 6365* | -Indiaanskop. | 12° 24.9´ N 69° 53.8´ W | **Fl.G.** period 2s | 10 **3** | | Metal framework tower. | In line 139° with 15942. |
| 15959 *J 6366* | -Rodgers Lagoon Range, front. | 12° 25.2´ N 69° 53.1´ W | **2 F.G.** | | | Beacon, triangular topmark point up. | |
| 15959.1 *J 6366.1* | --Rear, 120 meters 033° from front. | 12° 25.2´ N 69° 53.1´ W | **2 F.R.** | | | Beacon, triangular topmark point up. | |

| (1) No. | (2) Name and Location | (3) Position | (4) Characteristic | (5) Height | (6) Range | (7) Structure | (8) Remarks |
|---|---|---|---|---|---|---|---|
| | | | **ARUBA (N.)-CARIBBEAN SEA** | | | | |
| 15960 *J 6368* | **-Cerro Colorado.** | 12° 25.1´ N 69° 52.1´ W | **Fl.W.** period 6s | 167 **51** | 21 | | |
| | | | **CURACAO (N.)** | | | | |
| 15964 *J 6372* | Noordpunt. | 12° 23.0´ N 69° 09.2´ W | **Fl.(3)W.** period 15s fl. 0.3s, ec. 2.7s fl. 0.3s, ec. 2.7s fl. 0.3s, ec. 8.7s | 138 **42** | 12 | White round stone tower, gallery and red lantern; 20. | Visible 006°-271°. |
| 15968 *J 6374* | Kaap St. Marie. | 12° 11.2´ N 69° 03.5´ W | **Fl.(2)W.** period 6s | 41 **12** | 9 | Red square metal tower; 20. | |
| 15972 *J 6376* | Bullen Baai. | 12° 10.7´ N 69° 01.0´ W | **Q.W.** | | | | |
| 15976 *J 6375.4* | -First Range, front. | 12° 11.9´ N 69° 02.2´ W | **F.R.** | | | Red daymark. | |
| 15980 *J 6375.41* | --Rear 251 meters 043° from front. | 12° 12.0´ N 69° 02.1´ W | **F.G.** | | | Red daymark. | |
| 15984 *J 6376.6* | -Second Range, front. | 12° 11.5´ N 69° 01.3´ W | **Q.R.** | | | On tank. | |
| 15988 *J 6376.61* | --Rear, 640 meters 095° from front. | 12° 11.5´ N 69° 01.0´ W | **Q.G.** | | | On tank. | |
| 15992 *J 6376.4* | -Third Range, front. | 12° 11.0´ N 69° 01.0´ W | **F.G.** | | | On tank. | |
| 15996 *J 6376.41* | --Rear, 200 meters 123° from front. | 12° 11.0´ N 69° 00.9´ W | **F.R.** | | | On tank. | |
| 16008 *J 6380* | Wilemstad, about 247 meters 263° from Riffort. | 12° 06.2´ N 68° 56.2´ W | **Fl.G.** period 4s | 6 **2** | 1 | Black post; 7. | |
| 16012 *J 6378* | Riffort, Sint Anna (Willemstad), E. side of entrance. | 12° 06.2´ N 68° 56.0´ W | **Oc.W.** period 5s lt. 3s, ec. 2s | 83 **25** | 14 | Gray metal column on fort; 56. | |
| 16013 *J 6381* | -Range, front. | 12° 06.6´ N 68° 55.9´ W | **F.R.** | | | Orange diamond daymark. | |
| 16014 *J 6381.1* | --Rear, 580 meters 043° from front. | 12° 06.9´ N 68° 55.6´ W | **F.R.** | | | Orange diamond daymark. | |
| 16016 *J 6384* | -Entrance, W. side. | 12° 06.3´ N 68° 56.2´ W | **F.R.** | 23 **7** | | Aluminum structure. | |
| 16020 *J 6382* | --E. side. | 12° 06.3´ N 68° 56.1´ W | **F.G.** | 26 **8** | | Aluminum bracket on fort wall. | |
| 16024 *J 6377* | -Range, front. | 12° 06.4´ N 68° 56.1´ W | **3 F.R.** (vert.) | 54 **16** | | Black metal mast, yellow bands, orange square daymark. | |
| 16028 *J 6377.1* | --Rear, 480 meters 023° from front. | 12° 06.7´ N 68° 56.0´ W | **4 F.R.** | 108 **33** | | Metal mast, orange round daymark; 26. | Lights arranged in diamond shape. |
| 16032 *J 6386* | -W. side, near W. wharf, Sint Anna Bay. | 12° 06.7´ N 68° 56.0´ W | **F.R.** | 23 **7** | | | |
| 16036 *J 6389* | -E. side of entrance to Schottegat. | 12° 06.9´ N 68° 55.8´ W | **F.G.** | 67 **20** | | Orange column, black bands; 23. | |
| 16037 *J 6393* | -N. side. | 12° 07.3´ N 68° 55.3´ W | **F.G.** | | | | |
| 16038 *J 6393.5* | -Baai Macola. | 12° 06.9´ N 68° 55.2´ W | **Q.W.** | | | | |
| 16040 *J 6393.7* | Willemstad, pier, head. | 12° 06.7´ N 68° 55.3´ W | **F.R.** | | | | |

| (1) No. | (2) Name and Location | (3) Position | (4) Characteristic | (5) Height | (6) Range | (7) Structure | (8) Remarks |
|---|---|---|---|---|---|---|---|
| | | | **CURACAO (N.)** | | | | |
| 16044 *J 6398* | **Dr. Albert Plesman Field,** AVIATION LIGHT. | 12° 10.9′ N 68° 57.2′ W | **Al.Fl.W.G.** period 10s | 148 **45** | **19** | Concrete pillar with gallery. | |
| 16049 *J 6394.4* | -Range, front. | 12° 04.6′ N 68° 51.9′ W | **F.R.** | | | Gray beacon, red cross topmark. | |
| 16050 *J 6394.41* | --Rear, 90m 043°30′ from front. | 12° 04.7′ N 68° 51.8′ W | **F.R.** | | | Gray beacon, red triangular topmark point up. | |
| 16050.5 *J 6395* | -Fuik Baai Range, front. | 12° 03.0′ N 68° 49.8′ W | **F.G.** | 32 **10** | 2 | Red and white beacon, cross topmark. | |
| 16051 *J 6395.1* | --Rear, 50 meters 027°30′ from front. | 12° 03.1′ N 68° 49.8′ W | **F.R.** | 42 **13** | 4 | Red and white beacon, triangular topmark point up. | |
| 16053 *J 6396* | -Punt Kanon (Oostpunt). | 12° 02.6′ N 68° 44.2′ W | **Fl.W.** period 4s | 39 **12** | 8 | | |
| 16054 *J 6399* | **Klein Curacao** (N.). | 11° 59.4′ N 68° 38.6′ W | **Fl.(2)W.** period 15s | 82 **25** | **15** | Red framework mast, white bands, on white round tower. | |
| | | | **BONAIRE (N.)** | | | | |
| 16056 *J 6416* | **Ceru Bentana.** | 12° 18.3′ N 68° 22.6′ W | **Fl.(4)W.** period 20s | 144 **44** | **15** | Gray square stone tower; 33. | Visible 069°30′-073° and 074°-303°. |
| 16060 *J 6403* | Punt Wekoewa. | 12° 13.6′ N 68° 24.6′ W | **Fl.(3)W.** period 20s | 49 **15** | 12 | White round tower; 36. | Visible 285°-155°. |
| 16064 *J 6414* | **Boca Spelonk.** | 12° 12.7′ N 68° 11.8′ W | **Fl.W.** period 5s fl. 0.3s, ec. 4.7s | 100 **30** | **15** | White round stone tower; 69. | Visible 127°-002°. |
| 16077 *J 6404.31* | Goto oil terminal. | 12° 13.3′ N 68° 22.7′ W | **F.R.** | 82 **25** | 9 | | |
| 16080 *J 6404* | -Range No. 2, front. | 12° 13.2′ N 68° 21.6′ W | **Q.R.** | 26 **8** | 8 | | |
| 16084 *J 6404.1* | --Rear, 126 meters 081°04′ from front. | 12° 13.3′ N 68° 21.5′ W | **Q.G.** | 33 **10** | 6 | | |
| 16088 *J 6406* | Klein Bonaire, SW. point. | 12° 09.4′ N 68° 19.6′ W | **Fl.(2)W.** period 20s | 20 **6** | 9 | | |
| 16093 *J 6408.3* | Kralendijk. | 12° 08.9′ N 68° 16.6′ W | **Fl.W.** period 2s fl. 0.2s, ec. 1.8s | 44 **13** | 5 | White square stone structure; 23. | Visible 027°-150°. |
| 16094 *J 6408.8* | Flamingo Airfield, AVIATION LIGHT. | 12° 08.0′ N 68° 16.6′ W | **Al.Fl.W.R.G.** | | | Tower. | |
| 16096 *J 6409* | Punt Vierkant. | 12° 06.8′ N 68° 17.7′ W | **Fl.(3)W.** period 22s fl. 0.3s, ec. 5.5s fl. 0.3s, ec. 5.5s fl. 0.3s, ec. 10.1s | 30 **9** | 5 | White concrete column, red lantern; 23. | |
| 16100 *J 6411* | Lacre Punt. | 12° 01.7′ N 68° 14.2′ W | **Fl.W.** period 9s fl. 0.1s, ec. 8.9s | 75 **23** | 14 | White round stone tower, red stripes; 69. | Visible 203°-147°. |
| | | | **TRINIDAD** | | | | |
| 16108 *J 5915* | **Brigand Hill.** | 10° 29.8′ N 61° 04.0′ W | **Fl.(2+1)W.** period 30s fl. 0.3s, ec. 2.7s fl. 0.3s, ec. 11.7s fl. 0.3s, ec. 14.7s | 712 **217** | **20** | White metal framework tower; 36. | |
| 16109 *J 5914* | **Galeota Point.** | 10° 08.6′ N 60° 59.6′ W | **Fl.W.** period 5s fl. 0.5s, ec. 4.5s | 285 **87** | **16** | White metal framework tower; 30. | |

| (1) No. | (2) Name and Location | (3) Position | (4) Characteristic | (5) Height | (6) Range | (7) Structure | (8) Remarks |
|---|---|---|---|---|---|---|---|
| | | | **TRINIDAD** | | | | |
| 16110 *J 5913.5* | La Lune Point. | 10° 04.6′ N 61° 18.8′ W | **Fl.(4)W.** period 20s | 148 **45** | 12 | | |
| 16111 *J 5913.4* | Taparo Point. | 10° 03.5′ N 61° 37.6′ W | **Fl.(3)W.** period 15s | 226 **69** | 13 | | |
| 16112 *J 5913* | Chatham Jetty, head. | 10° 05.1′ N 61° 44.0′ W | **F.R.** | | 3 | | Private light. |
| | ICACOS POINT: | | | | | | |
| 16116 *J 5912* | **-Punta del Arenal.** | 10° 02.9′ N 61° 55.6′ W | **Fl.W.** period 7.5s | 72 **22** | **16** | White metal framework tower. | Visible 301°-232°. |
| 16117 *J 5911* | -Wolf Rock. | 10° 03.2′ N 61° 56.2′ W | **Fl.(2)W.** period 8s | 13 **4** | 5 | ISOLATED DANGER BRB, beacon, topmark. | |
| 16118 *J 5909.5* | -Soldado Rock. | 10° 04.6′ N 62° 00.9′ W | **Fl.W.** period 10s | | 8 | | |
| | GULF OF PARIA: | | | | | | |
| | -Point Fortin: | | | | | | |
| 16132 *J 5908* | --Pipeline pier, head. | 10° 12.7′ N 61° 42.1′ W | **Fl.(2)W.** period 10s fl. 0.6s, ec. 1.4s fl. 0.6s, ec. 7.4s | 98 **30** | 14 | Aluminum framework tower; 79. | |
| 16133 *J 5908.5* | --N. breakwater. | 10° 11.3′ N 61° 41.6′ W | **Fl.G.** period 3s | | | | |
| 16133.5 *J 5908.6* | --S. breakwater, head. | 10° 11.2′ N 61° 41.6′ W | **Fl.R.** period 3s | | | | |
| 16134 *J 5908.7* | --Range, front. | 10° 11.2′ N 61° 41.8′ W | **Fl.G.** period 3s fl. 1s, ec. 2s | 105 **32** | 10 | Tower, red rectangular daymark, yellow stripe. | Visible 147°10′-150°10′. |
| 16134.5 *J 5908.71* | ---Rear, 300 meters 148°40′ from front. | 10° 11.0′ N 61° 41.6′ W | **Oc.G.** period 5s lt. 3s, ec. 2s | 138 **42** | 13 | Tower, red rectangular daymark, yellow stripe. | Visible 134°40′-162°40′. |
| 16140 *J 5903* | **-Brighton Range,** front. | 10° 15.1′ N 61° 38.0′ W | **Fl.(3)W.** period 10s fl. 1s, ec. 1s fl. 1s, ec. 1s fl. 1s, ec. 5s | 52 **16** | **15** | White metal tower; 39. | Visible 134°12′-144°12′. Berthing signals. |
| 16144 *J 5903.1* | --Rear, 852 meters 139°15′ from front. | 10° 14.7′ N 61° 37.7′ W | **Fl.W.** period 5s | 100 **30** | 8 | | Visible 134°12′-144°12′. |
| 16148 *J 5900* | --Oropuche Bank Beacon. | 10° 16.9′ N 61° 33.4′ W | **V.Q.W.** | | 4 | Beacon. | |
| | -Pointe-a-Pierre: | | | | | | |
| 16152 *J 5895* | **--La Carriere.** | 10° 19.5′ N 61° 27.6′ W | **Fl.W.** period 2.5s fl. 0.2s, ec. 2.3s | 233 **71** | **17** | Framework tower. | |
| 16156 *J 5896* | --Pipeline viaduct, head. | 10° 19.0′ N 61° 28.8′ W | **Fl.(4)W.** period 10s fl. 0.5s, ec. 1s fl. 0.5s, ec. 1s fl. 0.5s, ec. 1s fl. 0.5s, ec. 5s | 98 **30** | 14 | Metal framework tower. | F.R. at 300 meter intervals along jetty. |
| 16157 *J 5897* | --Turning basin. | 10° 18.9′ N 61° 28.6′ W | **Q.R.** | | | Wooden pile. | |
| 16164 *J 5892* | --Range, front, No. 13. | 10° 22.8′ N 61° 28.9′ W | **Q.W.** | 30 **9** | 8 | | Visible 083°48′-098°48′. |
| | | | **F.R.** | 30 **9** | 4 | | |

| (1) No. | (2) Name and Location | (3) Position | (4) Characteristic | (5) Height | (6) Range | (7) Structure | (8) Remarks |
|---|---|---|---|---|---|---|---|
| | | | **TRINIDAD** | | | | |
| 16168<br>*J 5892.1* | --Rear, No. 14, 530 meters 091°20′ from front. | 10° 22.8′ N<br>61° 28.6′ W | **Oc.W.**<br>period 5s<br>lt. 3.5s, ec. 1.5s | 52<br>**16** | 8 | | Visible 087°18′-095°18′. |
| | | | **F.R.** | 56<br>**17** | 4 | | |
| | -Point Lisas: | | | | | | |
| 16169<br>*J 5894.3* | --Marine Terminal Range, front. | 10° 21.0′ N<br>61° 27.8′ W | **Q.Y.** | 69<br>**21** | 10 | Building. | |
| 16169.5<br>*J 5894.31* | ---Rear, 260 meters 081°25′ from front. | 10° 21.0′ N<br>61° 27.7′ W | **Oc.Y.**<br>period 3s | 82<br>**25** | 10 | Silo. | |
| 16172<br>*J 5892.4* | --Channel entrance, N. side, No. 1. | 10° 22.9′ N<br>61° 30.9′ W | **Fl.(2)G.**<br>period 5s | 26<br>**8** | 8 | White beacon. | |
| 16176<br>*J 5892.5* | ---S. side, No. 2. | 10° 22.8′ N<br>61° 30.9′ W | **Fl.W.**<br>period 3s | 26<br>**8** | 8 | White beacon. | |
| 16180<br>*J 5891* | --Savonneta Range, front. | 10° 24.3′ N<br>61° 29.5′ W | **Fl.W.**<br>period 2s | 98<br>**30** | 8 | Metal framework tower. | Visible 049°18′-055°18′.<br>Identification light Fl.R. 4s. |
| 16184<br>*J 5891.1* | ---Rear, 700 meters 052°12′ from front. | 10° 24.5′ N<br>61° 29.2′ W | **Fl.W.**<br>period 2s | 135<br>**41** | 8 | Metal framework tower. | Synchronized with front.<br>Identification light Fl.R. 4s. |
| | -Port-of-Spain | | | | | | |
| 16190<br>*J 5884.24* | --Grier Channel Range, front. | 10° 39.3′ N<br>61° 31.3′ W | **Oc.W.**<br>period 4s<br>lt. 3s, ec. 1s | 135<br>**41** | 10 | Black and white framework tower, yellow triangular daymark point up. | |
| | | | **F.G.** | | 6 | | |
| 16190.1<br>*J 5884.25* | ---Rear, 3450 meters 061°32′ from front. | 10° 40.2′ N<br>61° 29.6′ W | **Iso.W.**<br>period 2s | 390<br>**119** | 11 | Black and white framework tower, yellow triangular daymark point up. | Visible 058°24′-064°24′. |
| | | | **F.R.** | | 6 | | |
| 16191.7<br>*J 5885* | --No. 20. | 10° 38.9′ N<br>61° 31.9′ W | **Fl.R.**<br>period 3s | 16<br>**5** | 8 | Concrete platform, on tripod. | |
| 16191.8<br>*J 5884.9* | --No. 19. | 10° 39.0′ N<br>61° 31.8′ W | **Fl.G.**<br>period 3s | 16<br>**5** | 8 | Concrete platform, on tripod. | |
| 16191.9<br>*J 5885.3* | --No. 22. | 10° 38.9′ N<br>61° 31.5′ W | **Q.R.** | 13<br>**4** | 3 | Concrete platform, on tripod. | |
| 16191.91<br>*J 5885.2* | --No. 21. | 10° 39.1′ N<br>61° 31.8′ W | **Q.G.** | 13<br>**4** | 3 | Concrete platform, on tripod. | |
| 16191.92<br>*J 5885.4* | --No. 24. | 10° 38.8′ N<br>61° 31.3′ W | **Q.R.** | 13<br>**4** | 3 | Concrete platform, on tripod. | |
| 16191.94<br>*J 5884.43* | --No. 14. | 10° 38.7′ N<br>61° 31.1′ W | **Q.R.** | 13<br>**4** | 3 | Concrete platform, on pilings. | |
| 16192<br>*J 5888* | --Head of St. Vincent Jetty. | 10° 38.8′ N<br>61° 30.8′ W | **F.R.** | 23<br>**7** | 4 | Wooden post. | |
| 16196.1<br>*J 5882.42* | -Sea Lots Channel No. 1, entrance, N. side. | 10° 37.7′ N<br>61° 31.9′ W | **Fl.(2)G.**<br>period 7.5s | | | Pile. | |
| 16196.2<br>*J 5882.4* | --No. 2, entrance, S. side. | 10° 37.7′ N<br>61° 31.9′ W | **V.Q.(9)W.**<br>period 10s | | | Pile. | |
| 16196.3<br>*J 5882.46* | --No. 3. | 10° 37.9′ N<br>61° 31.5′ W | **Q.G.** | | | Pile. | |
| 16196.4<br>*J 5882.44* | --No. 4. | 10° 37.8′ N<br>61° 31.5′ W | **Q.R.** | | | Pile. | |
| 16196.5<br>*J 5882.51* | --No. 5. | 10° 38.0′ N<br>61° 31.0′ W | **V.Q.G.** | | | Pile. | |

| (1) No. | (2) Name and Location | (3) Position | (4) Characteristic | (5) Height | (6) Range | (7) Structure | (8) Remarks |
|---|---|---|---|---|---|---|---|
| | | | **TRINIDAD** | | | | |
| 16196.6 *J 5882.48* | --No. 6. | 10° 38.0′ N 61° 31.0′ W | **V.Q.R.** | | | Pile. | |
| 16196.7 *J 5882.54* | --No. 7. | 10° 38.2′ N 61° 30.5′ W | **Q.G.** | | | Pile. | |
| 16196.8 *J 5882.52* | --No. 8. | 10° 38.2′ N 61° 30.5′ W | **Q.R.** | | | Pile. | |
| 16196.9 *J 5882.58* | --No. 9. | 10° 38.4′ N 61° 30.2′ W | **L.Fl.G.** period 5s | | | Pile. | |
| 16196.91 *J 5882.56* | --No. 10. | 10° 38.3′ N 61° 30.2′ W | **L.Fl.R.** period 5s | | | Pile. | |
| 16196.93 *J 5882.6* | --No. 12. | 10° 38.3′ N 61° 30.0′ W | **Q.R.** | | | Pile. | |
| 16196.94 *J 5882.62* | --No. 14. | 10° 38.2′ N 61° 29.9′ W | **Q.R.** | | | Pile. | |
| 16197 *J 5882* | -Sea Lots Channel Range, front. | 10° 38.5′ N 61° 29.7′ W | **Oc.W.** period 10s lt. 7s, ec. 3s<br>**F.R.** | 85 **26** | 6 | White framework tower, orange rectangular daymark. | |
| 16197.1 *J 5882.1* | --Rear, 640 meters 069°10′ from front. | 10° 38.6′ N 61° 29.4′ W | **Fl.W.** period 2s fl. 0.6s, ec. 1.4s<br>**F.R.** | 128 **39** | 6 | White framework tower, orange rectangular daymark. | |
| 16208 *J 5868* | -Nelson, E. head. | 10° 39.5′ N 61° 35.9′ W | **Fl.W.** period 2s | 62 **19** | 6 | White mast. | |
| 16212 *J 5872* | -Point Sinet Range, front. | 10° 41.0′ N 61° 35.9′ W | **Oc.W.** period 2.5s lt. 1.5s, ec. 1s | 98 **30** | 14 | White square daymark, black stripe. | Visible 038°-046°. |
| 16216 *J 5872.1* | --Rear, 180 meters 042°14′ from front. | 10° 41.1′ N 61° 35.8′ W | **Oc.W.** period 5s lt. 4s, ec. 1s<br>**F.R.** | 102 **31** | 14 | White square daymark, black stripe. | Visible 038°-046°. |
| 16220 *J 5866* | -Cronstadt Island, W. head. | 10° 39.5′ N 61° 37.9′ W | **Q.R.** | | 4 | | |
| 16225 *J 5858* | -Reyna Point. | 10° 40.1′ N 61° 38.7′ W | **Q.G.** | 33 **10** | 4 | | |
| 16228 *J 5861* | -Escondida Cove, off N. point. | 10° 40.4′ N 61° 38.2′ W | **Q.R.** | 17 **5** | | White tripod. | Occasional. |
| 16230 *J 5859.4* | -Furness Smith Floating Dock. | 10° 40.8′ N 61° 38.9′ W | **2 F.R.** | | | | |
| 16236 *J 5856* | -Espolon Point, SW. point of Gaspar Grande Island. | 10° 39.9′ N 61° 40.0′ W | **Fl.W.** period 4s | 42 **13** | 8 | White framework tower. | |
| 16240 *J 5852* | -Gasparillo Island, W. head. | 10° 40.5′ N 61° 39.3′ W | **Q.W.** | 36 **11** | 4 | White mast. | |
| 16244 *J 5851* | -La Retraite Coast Guard Station. | 10° 40.9′ N 61° 39.4′ W | **2 F.R.** | | | | |
| 16248 *J 5850* | -Teteron Rock. | 10° 41.0′ N 61° 40.0′ W | **Fl.G.** period 4s fl. 0.4s, ec. 3.6s | 24 **7** | 4 | White metal structure, concrete base. | |
| 16250 *J 5848.5* | -Le Chapeau Rock. | 10° 42.4′ N 61° 40.5′ W | **Fl.(3)W.** period 10s | | 6 | | |
| 16252 *J 5848* | -Point de Cabras, Huevos, S. head. | 10° 41.2′ N 61° 43.2′ W | **V.Q.(6)+L.Fl.W.** period 10s | 40 **12** | 5 | | |

| (1) No. | (2) Name and Location | (3) Position | (4) Characteristic | (5) Height | (6) Range | (7) Structure | (8) Remarks |
|---|---|---|---|---|---|---|---|

## TRINIDAD

| (1) No. | (2) Name and Location | (3) Position | (4) Characteristic | (5) Height | (6) Range | (7) Structure | (8) Remarks |
|---|---|---|---|---|---|---|---|
| 16256<br>*J 5846* | **Chacachacare.** | 10° 41.9´ N<br>61° 45.1´ W | **Fl.W.**<br>period 10s<br>fl. 0.4s, ec. 9.6s | 825<br>**251** | **26** | White concrete tower; 49. | |
| 16260<br>*J 5846.1* | -Beacon, about 640 meters 216° from main light. | 10° 41.6´ N<br>61° 45.4´ W | **Fl.W.**<br>period 2s<br>fl. 0.1s, ec. 1.9s | 503<br>**153** | 11 | White metal framework tower, white square daymark; 26. | In line 036° with 16256. |
| 16264<br>*J 5844* | North Post, Point a Diable. | 10° 44.9´ N<br>61° 33.7´ W | **Fl.W.**<br>period 5s<br>fl. 1s, ec. 4s | 747<br>**228** | 14 | Beacon. | Visible 087°-252°. |
| 16264.5<br>*J 5843.5* | Saut d'Eau Island. | 10° 46.2´ N<br>61° 30.7´ W | **Q.W.** | | 7 | | |
| 16264.7<br>*J 5843* | **Chupara Point.** | 10° 48.5´ N<br>61° 21.7´ W | **Fl.(2)W.**<br>period 10s | 325<br>**99** | **16** | White metal framework tower and hut. | |
| 16265<br>*J 5842.5* | Petite Matelot Point. | 10° 49.5´ N<br>61° 07.5´ W | **Fl.(3)W.**<br>period 15s | | 7 | | |
| 16266<br>*J 5842* | **Galera Point.** | 10° 50.1´ N<br>60° 54.5´ W | **Oc.W.**<br>period 10s<br>lt. 6s, ec. 4s | 141<br>**43** | **16** | Square brick building, white concrete tower; 75. | |
| | ICACOS POINT: | | | | | | |
| 16267<br>*J 5845* | Hibiscus. | 11° 07.8´ N<br>61° 39.6´ W | **Mo(U).W.** | 72<br>**22** | 10 | Platform. | **Horn.** |
| | RACON | | **B(– • • •)** | | | | (3 & 10cm). |
| 16267.5<br>*J 5844.5* | Poinsettia. | 11° 13.5´ N<br>61° 31.2´ W | **Mo(U).W.**<br>period 15s | 66<br>**20** | 10 | Platform. | **Horn**: Mo.(U) 30s. |
| | RACON | | | | | | |

## BELIZE

| (1) No. | (2) Name and Location | (3) Position | (4) Characteristic | (5) Height | (6) Range | (7) Structure | (8) Remarks |
|---|---|---|---|---|---|---|---|
| | CHETUMAL BAY: | | | | | | |
| 16268<br>*J 5930* | -Bulkhead. | 17° 56.0´ N<br>88° 08.1´ W | **Fl.W.**<br>period 1.5s | 30<br>**9** | 10 | Red metal framework tower, concrete base; 20. | |
| | TURNEFFE CAYS: | | | | | | |
| 16280<br>*J 5940* | -Mauger Cay. | 17° 36.5´ N<br>87° 46.4´ W | **Fl.(2)W.**<br>period 10s | 61<br>**19** | 13 | White metal framework tower; 62. | |
| 16284<br>*J 5942* | -Cay Bokel. | 17° 09.8´ N<br>87° 54.6´ W | **Fl.(3)W.**<br>period 15s<br>fl. 0.5s, ec. 1.5s<br>fl. 0.5s, ec. 1.5s<br>fl. 0.5s, ec. 10.5s | 33<br>**10** | 8 | White metal framework tower; 33. | |
| | LIGHTHOUSE REEF: | | | | | | |
| 16288<br>*J 5934* | **-Sandbore Cay.** | 17° 28.2´ N<br>87° 29.5´ W | **Fl.W.**<br>period 10s | 83<br>**25** | **17** | Red metal framework tower; 82. | |
| 16292<br>*J 5936* | -Half Moon Cay, E. head. | 17° 12.2´ N<br>87° 31.8´ W | **Fl.(4)W.**<br>period 15s | 80<br>**24** | 14 | White metal framework tower; 79. | |
| | GLOVERS REEF: | | | | | | |
| 16296<br>*J 5937* | -NE. side of reef. | 16° 54.6´ N<br>87° 42.3´ W | **Fl.W.**<br>period 5s | | 9 | White metal framework tower; 36. | **Radar reflector.** |

| (1)<br>No. | (2)<br>Name and Location | (3)<br>Position | (4)<br>Characteristic | (5)<br>Height | (6)<br>Range | (7)<br>Structure | (8)<br>Remarks |
|---|---|---|---|---|---|---|---|
| | | | **BELIZE** | | | | |
| 16300<br>*J 5937.5* | -SW. cays. | 16° 06.5′ N<br>88° 16.0′ W | **Fl.(2)W.**<br>period 5s | | 9 | White metal framework tower; 36. | |
| | BELIZE HARBOR: | | | | | | |
| 16304<br>*J 5943* | -Eastern Channel Range, front. | 17° 19.5′ N<br>88° 02.8′ W | **Q.W.** | 23<br>**7** | 9 | Concrete pillar; 23. | |
| 16308<br>*J 5943.1* | --English Cay, rear, 300 meters 300° from front. | 17° 19.6′ N<br>88° 02.9′ W | **Fl.W.**<br>period 2.5s<br>fl. 0.3s, ec. 2.2s | 62<br>**19** | 11 | White metal framework tower; 62. | |
| 16312<br>*J 5943.2* | -Goffs Cay, Sandbore. | 17° 20.3′ N<br>88° 02.1′ W | **Fl.R.**<br>period 5s | 16<br>**5** | 3 | Red concrete pile; 16. | |
| 16316<br>*J 5944* | -Water Cay Spit. | 17° 21.3′ N<br>88° 04.6′ W | **Q.R.** | 16<br>**5** | 5 | Red concrete pile; 16. | |
| 16320<br>*J 5945* | -NE. Spit. | 17° 22.9′ N<br>88° 05.5′ W | **Q.G.** | 16<br>**5** | 5 | Green concrete pile; 16. | |
| 16324<br>*J 5946* | -White Grounds Spit. | 17° 22.8′ N<br>88° 07.0′ W | **Fl.W.**<br>period 2.5s | 16<br>**5** | 5 | Yellow and black concrete pile; 16. | |
| 16328<br>*J 5947* | -Spanish Cay Spit. | 17° 22.6′ N<br>88° 08.4′ W | **Q.G.** | 16<br>**5** | 5 | Green concrete pile; 16. | |
| 16332<br>*J 5948* | -Halfway. | 17° 22.2′ N<br>88° 09.7′ W | **Q.R.** | 16<br>**5** | 5 | Red concrete pile; 16. | |
| 16336<br>*J 5948.4* | -SW. side. | 17° 22.0′ N<br>88° 09.9′ W | **Q.G.** | 16<br>**5** | 5 | Green concrete pile; 16. | |
| 16340<br>*J 5950* | -Robinson Point, W. point of island. | 17° 21.9′ N<br>88° 11.9′ W | **Q.W.** | 38<br>**12** | 8 | White framework tower; 39. | |
| 16344<br>*J 5950.2* | -Triangles. | 17° 21.4′ N<br>88° 12.5′ W | **Fl.G.**<br>period 5s | 16<br>**5** | 5 | Green concrete pile; 16. | |
| 16348<br>*J 5950.4* | -Frank Knoll. | 17° 23.7′ N<br>88° 11.9′ W | **Q.W.** | 16<br>**5** | 5 | Yellow and black concrete pile; 16. | |
| 16352<br>*J 5950.6* | -Sugar Berth B. | 17° 23.5′ N<br>88° 10.7′ W | **Fl.R.**<br>period 2.5s | 16<br>**5** | 5 | Red concrete pile; 16. | |
| 16356<br>*J 5950.7* | -Sugar Berth A. | 17° 25.6′ N<br>88° 08.8′ W | **Fl.G.**<br>period 2.5s | 16<br>**5** | 5 | Green concrete pile; 16. | |
| 16364<br>*J 5952* | -Middle Ground. | 17° 28.2′ N<br>88° 10.6′ W | **Fl.R.**<br>period 5s | 16<br>**5** | 5 | Red concrete pile; 16. | |
| 16368<br>*J 5954* | -Fort George. | 17° 29.5′ N<br>88° 10.9′ W | **Fl.R.**<br>period 5s | 52<br>**16** | 8 | White concrete pillar, red band, on base; 52. | F.R. lights on radio mast 670 meters WNW.<br>F.R. and Fl.R. lights on radio mast 1.3 miles NW. |
| 16369<br>*J 5954.5* | -North Drowned Cay. | 17° 30.0′ N<br>88° 08.8′ W | **Q.W.** | | | Beacon. | |
| 16372<br>*J 5955* | **-Belize City** AVIATION LIGHT. | 17° 32.6′ N<br>88° 18.8′ W | **Q.W.** | | **30** | Mast. | Obstruction. |
| 16374<br>*J 5957* | Manatee River. | 16° 56.2′ N<br>88° 14.2′ W | **F.W.** | 33<br>**10** | 2 | | Occasional. |
| 16376<br>*J 5958* | Colson Point. | 17° 04.3′ N<br>88° 14.4′ W | **Fl.W.**<br>period 10s | 39<br>**12** | 9 | White metal framework tower; 39. | |
| 16380<br>*J 5964* | Sittee Point. | 16° 48.4′ N<br>88° 15.1′ W | **Fl.W.**<br>period 5s | 30<br>**9** | 8 | White metal framework tower; 30. | F.W. shown at all times, in Sapodilla Lagoon 3 miles WSW. and on pier head at Riversdale 7.8 miles SSW. |
| 16384<br>*J 5968* | Bugle Cays (SW. Cay). | 16° 29.3′ N<br>88° 19.3′ W | **Fl.(2)W.**<br>period 10s | 61<br>**19** | 10 | White framework tower; 62. | F.R. 96m 35M obstruction light 6.2 miles NW. |

| (1) No. | (2) Name and Location | (3) Position | (4) Characteristic | (5) Height | (6) Range | (7) Structure | (8) Remarks |
|---|---|---|---|---|---|---|---|
| | | | **BELIZE** | | | | |
| 16388 *J 5970* | Monkey River. | 16° 21.8′ N 88° 29.1′ W | **F.W.** | 52 **16** | 8 | White mast; 52. | |
| 16392 *J 5972* | East Snake Cay. | 16° 12.5′ N 88° 30.5′ W | **Fl.W.** period 3s | 65 **20** | 13 | Concrete framework tower; 66. | |
| 16396 *J 5974* | Hunting Cay, Zapodilla Cays. | 16° 06.5′ N 88° 16.0′ W | **Fl.W.** period 15s | 57 **17** | 13 | White metal framework tower; 56. | |
| 16400 *J 5976* | Punta Gorda. | 16° 06.0′ N 88° 48.2′ W | **F.W.** | 56 **17** | 9 | White mast; 56. | R. lights on radio tower 0.6 mile SW. |
| | | | **GUATEMALA** | | | | |
| 16404 *J 5986* | Bajo Villedo. | 15° 45.4′ N 88° 37.0′ W | **Fl.W.** period 3s fl. 0.4s, ec. 2.6s | 17 **5** | | Aluminum framework tower. | **Radar reflector.** |
| 16410 *J 5990* | -Range, front. | 15° 41.7′ N 88° 37.4′ W | **Fl.Y.** | | | Metal framework structure, white rectangular daymark. | |
| 16411 *J 5990.1* | --Rear, about 290 meters 243° from front. | 15° 41.7′ N 88° 37.5′ W | **Fl.Y.** | | | Metal framework structure, white rectangular daymark. | |
| 16412 *J 5989* | Matias de Galvez Range, front. | 15° 41.6′ N 88° 37.2′ W | **Q.Y.** | 35 **11** | | Metal framework tower, red triangular daymark point up. | Visible on range line only. |
| 16416 *J 5989.1* | -Rear (South), about 347 meters 189°30′ from front. | 15° 41.4′ N 88° 37.3′ W | **Oc.Y.** period 4s lt. 3s, ec. 1s | 80 **24** | | Metal framework tower, red triangular daymark point up. | Visible on range line only. |
| 16418 *J 5985* | **-Puerto Barrios.** | 15° 43.9′ N 88° 35.9′ W | **Fl.W.** period 8s | | **25** | | |
| 16419 *J 5984* | Heredia Shoal. | 15° 50.8′ N 88° 40.4′ W | **Fl.R.** period 3s fl. 0.4s, ec. 2.6s | 20 **6** | | White and orange framework structure. | |
| 16420 *J 5982* | Ox Tongue Shoal. | 15° 53.6′ N 88° 41.1′ W | **Fl.W.** period 3s fl. 0.4s, ec. 2.6s | 13 **4** | 12 | White and orange framework structure. | **Radar reflector.** |
| 16424 *J 5992* | **Cabo Tres Puntas.** | 15° 57.8′ N 88° 35.9′ W | **Fl.W.** period 3s fl. 0.4s, ec. 2.6s | 132 **40** | **17** | White framework tower. | |
| | | | **HONDURAS** | | | | |
| | PUERTO CORTES: | | | | | | |
| 16428 *J 5994* | **-Puerto Cortes.** | 15° 51.3′ N 87° 57.6′ W | **Fl.W.** period 5s | 190 **58** | **20** | Red metal tower, white band; 46. | |
| 16431 *J 5994.1* | -Texaco Pier, W. head. | 15° 50.6′ N 87° 57.7′ W | **Fl.(6)Y.** period 15s | | | | |
| 16431.5 *J 5994.11* | --E. head. | 15° 50.6′ N 87° 57.7′ W | **Fl.(6)Y.** period 15s | | | | |
| 16432 *J 5997* | **Punta Sal.** | 15° 55.5′ N 87° 36.2′ W | **Fl.(4)W.** period 30s | 275 **84** | **15** | White framework tower; 49. | |
| 16440 *J 5999* | **Punta Izopo.** | 15° 50.9′ N 87° 22.5′ W | **Fl.W.** period 5s | 132 **40** | **20** | White framework tower; 49. | |
| 16445 *J 6006* | -E. breakwater, head. | 15° 48.0′ N 86° 45.6′ W | **Fl.G.** period 3s | 30 **9** | 6 | Red and white metal tower. | |
| 16446 *J 6006.1* | -W. breakwater, head. | 15° 47.9′ N 86° 45.7′ W | **Fl.R.** period 3s | 30 **9** | 6 | Red and white metal tower. | |

| (1) No. | (2) Name and Location | (3) Position | (4) Characteristic | (5) Height | (6) Range | (7) Structure | (8) Remarks |
|---|---|---|---|---|---|---|---|
| | | | **HONDURAS** | | | | |
| 16447 *J 6002* | **Pumpkin Hill.** | 16° 07.3´ N 86° 52.8´ W | **Fl.W.** period 9s | 56 **17** | **19** | Red and white round metal tower. | |
| | ISLA DE UTILA: | | | | | | |
| 16448 *J 6003* | -Puerto East, E. Reef. | 16° 05.2´ N 86° 53.9´ W | **F.W.** | | 4 | Wooden building. | |
| 16457 *J 6009.7* | **Punta Caxinas.** | 16° 01.6´ N 86° 00.5´ W | **Fl.W.** period 10s fl. 1s, ec. 9s | 75 **23** | **19** | | |
| 16460 *J 6007* | **Isla de Roatan.** | 16° 18.0´ N 86° 35.3´ W | **Fl.W.** period 9s | 69 **21** | **19** | White concrete tower, red bands. | |
| 16461 *J 6008.2* | **-Punta Oeste.** | 16° 16.1´ N 86° 36.1´ W | **Fl.W.** period 9.5s | 69 **21** | **19** | White round metal tower, red bands. | |
| 16473 *J 6009.6* | **-Cochino Grande.** | 15° 58.6´ N 86° 28.6´ W | **Fl.W.** period 5s | 516 **157** | **18** | Red and white metal structure. | |
| 16476 *J 6010* | Isla de Guanaja, Pond Cay. | 16° 26.2´ N 85° 53.0´ W | **Q.G.** | | 2 | Gray concrete column; 30. | |
| 16477 *J 6010.5* | **Black Rock Point.** | 16° 29.9´ N 85° 49.0´ W | **Fl.W.** period 9s | 72 **22** | **19** | | |
| 16478 *J 6012* | **-Cabo Camaron.** | 15° 59.2´ N 85° 01.7´ W | **Fl.W.** period 5s | 73 **22** | **19** | Red tower, white bands. | |
| 16479 *J 6013* | **-Punta Patuca.** | 15° 48.9´ N 84° 18.2´ W | **Fl.W.** period 10s | 73 **22** | **22** | Red and white metal structure. | |
| 16480 *J 6016* | **Islas de El Cisne** AVIATION LIGHT. | 17° 25.4´ N 83° 56.6´ W | **Fl.W.** period 5s | 70 **21** | **28** | | 3 Fl.R. 1.5s (vert.) on tower 1 mile E. Occasional. |
| 16481 *J 6018* | Cayos Vivorillo. | 15° 50.0´ N 83° 17.7´ W | **Fl.W.** period 10s | | 13 | | |
| 16482 *J 6020* | **-Bajo Nuevo.** | 15° 51.2´ N 78° 38.0´ W | **Fl.(2)W.** period 15s fl. 1s, ec. 2s fl. 1s, ec. 11s | 72 **22** | **15** | White tower, red bands. | |
| 16483 *J 6014* | **-Cabo Falso.** | 15° 15.2´ N 83° 23.7´ W | **Fl.W.** period 5s | 75 **23** | **18** | Red and white metal structure. | |
| | | | **NICARAGUA** | | | | |
| | PUERTO CABEZAS: | | | | | | |
| 16484 *J 6048* | -Puerto Cabezas. | 14° 01.3´ N 83° 23.1´ W | **Fl.W.** period 2.5s | 230 **70** | | | Private light. |
| 16488 *J 6052* | Puerto Isabel Range, front. | 13° 21.7´ N 83° 33.7´ W | **F.R.** | | | Shed. | |
| 16492 *J 6052.1* | -Rear, 90 meters 276° from front. | 13° 21.0´ N 83° 33.0´ W | **F.W.** | | | | |
| 16500 *J 6064* | El Bluff. | 11° 59.6´ N 83° 41.0´ W | **Fl.W.** period 3.8s fl. 0.3s, ec. 3.5s | 163 **50** | 14 | Red metal framework tower; 26. | |
| 16502 *J 6065* | Little Corn Island, summit. | 12° 17.7´ N 82° 58.7´ W | **Fl.W.** | | 8 | | |

| (1) No. | (2) Name and Location | (3) Position | (4) Characteristic | (5) Height | (6) Range | (7) Structure | (8) Remarks |
|---|---|---|---|---|---|---|---|
| | | | **COSTA RICA** | | | | |
| 16504 *J 6068* | Limon, Isla Uvita, summit. | 9° 59.7´ N 83° 00.7´ W | **Fl.W.** period 10s | 134 **41** | 5 | White metal framework tower; 82. | Fl.R. 2s and F.R. on radio tower 0.9 mile WNW. Aero.Al.Fl.W.G. 10s 2 miles SW., R. lights on radio tower 1.5 miles SW. Occasional. |
| 16508 *J 6069* | -Container pier, S. head. | 9° 59.3´ N 83° 01.2´ W | **Fl.R.** period 1.5s | 49 **15** | 10 | | |
| 16516 *J 6067* | Bahia Moin, Isla Pajaros. | 10° 01.1´ N 83° 04.6´ W | **Fl.W.** period 2.5s fl. 0.5s, ec. 2s | | | Tower. | |
| 16520 *J 6067.2* | -Puerto Moin Range, front. | 10° 00.3´ N 83° 04.6´ W | **F.W.** | | | White mast, black bands. | |
| 16524 *J 6067.21* | --Rear, 130 meters 151° from front. | 10° 00.2´ N 83° 04.5´ W | **F.W.** | | | White mast, black bands. | |
| 16527 *J 6072* | Sixaola. | 9° 34.1´ N 82° 33.6´ W | **Fl.W.** period 10s | 46 **14** | 11 | White metal framework tower; 39. | Visible 114°-315°. |
| | RACON | | **K(– • –)** | | **20** | | (3 & 10cm). |
| | | | **PANAMA** | | | | |
| | BAHIA ALMIRANTE: | | | | | | |
| 16528 *J 6081* | -Hospital point. | 9° 20.0´ N 82° 13.2´ W | **Fl.(2)W.** period 10s | 36 **11** | 13 | Metal pedestal; 7. | F.R. lights on radio masts 1.2 miles, 1.9 miles and 2.2 miles WNW. |
| 16530 *J 6081.2* | --Beacon No. 8. | 9° 20.4´ N 82° 13.4´ W | **Q.R.** | 16 **5** | | Red beacon. | |
| 16532 *J 6085* | -Bocas del Toro, pier, NE. corner. | 9° 20.1´ N 82° 14.4´ W | **Fl.G.** | 27 **8** | | White pedestal; 20. | |
| 16544 *J 6085.2* | --Pier, SW. corner. | 9° 20.1´ N 82° 14.4´ W | **Fl.R.** | | | | |
| 16564 *J 6086* | -Juan Point. | 9° 18.1´ N 82° 17.7´ W | **Fl.G.** period 4s fl. 0.5s, ec. 3.5s | 15 **5** | 5 | Green tower. | |
| 16568 *J 6088* | -Pondsock Reef. | 9° 17.3´ N 82° 19.7´ W | **Fl.W.** period 6s fl. 1s, ec. 5s | 15 **5** | 5 | Black tower, red bands. | |
| 16570 *J 6089* | -Almirante, pier. | 9° 17.3´ N 82° 23.4´ W | **Fl.R.** | | | Post. | |
| 16572 *J 6090* | -Isla Pastores, NW. head. | 9° 14.6´ N 82° 21.0´ W | **Fl.W.** period 10s fl. 1.5s, ec. 8.5s | 60 **18** | 9 | Metal windmill tower; 49. | |
| 16576 *J 6090.3* | -Roca Tigre. | 9° 13.1´ N 81° 56.5´ W | **Fl.W.** period 5s fl. 1.5s, ec. 3.5s | 50 **15** | | Metal tower. | |
| | -RACON | | **P(• – – •)** period 70s | | **18** | | (3cm). |
| 16580 *J 6090.5* | -Chiriqui Range, front. | 8° 56.6´ N 82° 06.8´ W | **Q.W.** | | | White round tower, black stripe. | F.R. obstruction lights on tower 1.4 miles W., F.Y. on oil tanks 1.5 miles W. Visible 202°-222°. |
| 16584 *J 6090.51* | --Rear, 60 meters 212° from front. | 8° 56.5´ N 82° 06.8´ W | **Fl.W.** period 4s fl. 0.3s, ec. 3.7s | | | White round tower, black stripe. | Visible 202°-222°. |

| (1) No. | (2) Name and Location | (3) Position | (4) Characteristic | (5) Height | (6) Range | (7) Structure | (8) Remarks |
|---|---|---|---|---|---|---|---|
| | | | **PANAMA** | | | | |
| 16588 *J 6091* | Escudo de Veraguas. | 9° 05.4´ N 81° 32.7´ W | **Fl.W.** period 7s fl. 0.5s, ec. 6.5s | 120 **37** | 6 | White square framework tower; 20. | |
| | LIMON BAY: | | | | | | |
| 16592 *J 6092* | **-Toro Point.** | 9° 22.3´ N 79° 57.0´ W | **L.Fl.W.** period 30s fl. 5s, ec. 25s | 108 **33** | **16** | White metal tower, stone base. | |
| 16600 *J 6102* | **-W. breakwater,** head. | 9° 23.3´ N 79° 55.3´ W | **V.Q.(2)R.** period 2s | 100 **30** | **16** | Tripod on platform, red rectangular daymark. | **Radar reflector.** |
| 16604 *J 6098* | **-E. breakwater,** head. | 9° 23.3´ N 79° 54.9´ W | **Mo.(U)G.** period 20s fl. 0.5s, ec. 3s fl. 0.5s, ec. 3s fl. 5s, ec. 8s | 108 **33** | **16** | Green metal tower, green triangular daymark point up. | F.R. on chimney 5.9 miles E. F.R. on signal station 1.7 miles E., Q.R. and 3 F.R. (vert.) on mast 1.9 miles SSE. 4 F.R. on each of 2 water tanks 3.5 miles SSE. F.R. 2.1 miles SSE. |
| | -RACON | | **U(• • –)** | | 6 | | (3 & 10cm). |
| 16605 *J 6112* | -Explosive Anchorage, near W. limit. | 9° 22.3´ N 79° 56.5´ W | **Fl.Y.** period 2s fl. 0.5s, ec. 1.5s | 15 **5** | | SPECIAL Y, beacon. | |
| 16606 *J 6121* | -Cristobal Harbor, beacon No. 2. | 9° 20.8´ N 79° 54.2´ W | **Q.R.** | | | STARBOARD (B) R, beacon. | |
| 16606.1 *J 6123* | -Beacon No. 3. | 9° 20.8´ N 79° 54.1´ W | **Oc.G** period 5s lt. 4.5s, ec. 0.5s | | | PORT (B) G, beacon. | |
| 16606.2 *J 6124* | --No. 4. | 9° 20.7´ N 79° 54.1´ W | **Oc.R.** period 5s lt. 4.5s, ec. 0.5s | | | STARBOARD (B) R, beacon. | |
| 16606.3 *J 6124.5* | --No. 5. | 9° 20.7´ N 79° 54.0´ W | **Oc.G** period 5s lt. 4.5s, ec. 0.5s | | | PORT (B) G, beacon. | |
| 16606.4 *J 6125* | --No. 6. | 9° 20.7´ N 79° 54.1´ W | **Oc.R.** period 5s lt. 4.5s, ec. 0.5s | | | STARBOARD (B) R, beacon. | |
| 16606.5 *J 6126* | --No. 8. | 9° 20.6´ N 79° 54.1´ W | **Oc.R.** period 5s lt. 4.5s, ec. 0.5s | | | STARBOARD (B) R, beacon. | |
| 16606.6 *J 6127* | --No. 7. | 9° 20.5´ N 79° 54.1´ W | **Oc.G.** period 5s lt. 4.5s, ec. 0.5s | | | PORT (B) G, beacon. | |
| 16606.7 *J 6129* | --No. 9. | 9° 20.5´ N 79° 54.1´ W | **Q.G.** | | | PORT (B) G, beacon. | |
| 16606.8 *J 6130* | --No. 10. | 9° 20.5´ N 79° 54.1´ W | **Oc.R.** period 5s lt. 4.5s, ec. 0.5s | | | STARBOARD (B) R, beacon. | |
| 16612 *J 6132* | -Panama Canal, Atlantic Entrance Range, front. | 9° 17.5´ N 79° 55.2´ W | **F.G.** | | | | R. lights shown on W. side and G. lights shown on E. side of dredged channel and in Limon Bay. The canal is marked by lights, and leading lights mark the center of the channel. |
| 16616 *J 6132.1* | ---Middle, 1037 meters, 180°15′ from front. | 9° 16.9´ N 79° 55.2´ W | **F.G.** | 98 **30** | **15** | Concrete conical tower; 75. | Visible on range line only. |
| 16620 *J 6132.2* | ---Rear, 2278 meters 180°15′ from front. | 9° 16.3´ N 79° 55.2´ W | **Oc.G** | 158 **48** | **15** | Concrete conical tower; 46. | Visible on range line only. F.R. lights shown on each of 2 radio towers 1.1 miles NE. |

| (1) No. | (2) Name and Location | (3) Position | (4) Characteristic | (5) Height | (6) Range | (7) Structure | (8) Remarks |
|---|---|---|---|---|---|---|---|

## PANAMA

| (1) No. | (2) Name and Location | (3) Position | (4) Characteristic | (5) Height | (6) Range | (7) Structure | (8) Remarks |
|---|---|---|---|---|---|---|---|
| | BAHIA LAS MINAS: | | | | | | |
| 16621 *J 6134* | -Range, front. | 9° 23.8′ N 79° 49.3′ W | **F.G.** | | | Framework tower, orange diamond daymark, white stripe. | |
| 16621.1 *J 6134.1* | --Rear, 80 meters 171° from front. | 9° 23.8′ N 79° 49.3′ W | **F.G.** | | | Framework tower, orange diamond daymark, white stripe. | |
| 16622 *J 6134.2* | -Range, front. | 9° 23.3′ N 79° 48.7′ W | **F.G.** | | | Beacon, orange diamond daymark. | |
| 16622.1 *J 6134.21* | --Rear, 160 meters 148°45′ from front. | 9° 23.2′ N 79° 48.6′ W | **F.G.** | | | Beacon, orange diamond daymark. | |
| 16622.5 *J 6134.3* | -Cement Jetty. | 9° 23.3′ N 79° 48.8′ W | **Fl.(2)+L.Fl.Y.** period 15s | | | | *Reported 2006.* |
| 16622.7 *J 6134.36* | -Cargo dock, S. end. | 9° 23.3′ N 79° 48.9′ W | **Fl.R.** | | | | |
| 16622.8 *J 6134.38* | --N. end. | 9° 23.4′ N 79° 48.9′ W | **Fl.(2)+L.Fl.G.** period 15s | | | | |
| 16623 *J 6134.6* | -NW. Pier, N. head. | 9° 23.8′ N 79° 49.1′ W | **F.R.** | | | | |
| 16623.1 *J 6134.8* | -Tanker jetty, N. head. | 9° 23.6′ N 79° 49.1′ W | **F.R.** | | | | |
| 16624 *J 6136* | Farallon Sucio Rock, summit. | 9° 38.6′ N 79° 38.2′ W | **Fl.R.** period 5s fl. 0.5s, ec. 4.5s | 107 **33** | 12 | White concrete pyramidal tower; 23. | |
| 16628 *J 6138* | Isla Grande, off Punta Manzanillo. | 9° 38.2′ N 79° 33.5′ W | **Fl.W.** period 5s fl. 0.3s, ec. 4.7s | 305 **93** | 12 | White metal tower, stone base; 85. | |
| 16630 *J 6143* | Puerto Obaldia. | 8° 40.0′ N 77° 25.0′ W | **L.Fl.W.** period 10s fl. 2s, ec. 8s | 39 **12** | 8 | White framework tower; 38. | |

# Section 12

## North Coast of South America
## Including Colombia, Venezuala, Guyana, Suriname and French Guiana

| (1) No. | (2) Name and Location | (3) Position | (4) Characteristic | (5) Height | (6) Range | (7) Structure | (8) Remarks |
|---|---|---|---|---|---|---|---|
| | | | **COLOMBIA** | | | | |
| 16632 *J 6144* | **Cabo Tiburon.** | 8° 40.6´ N 77° 21.5´ W | **Fl.(3)W.** period 15s fl. 0.5s, ec. 1.5s fl. 0.5s, ec. 1.5s fl. 0.5s, ec. 10.5s | 341 **104** | **15** | Red metal tower, white bands; 59. | |
| 16633 *J 6144.2* | -Sapzurro East. | 8° 39.6´ N 77° 21.5´ W | **Fl.Y.** period 3s fl. 0.3s, ec. 2.7s | 36 **11** | 12 | Red tower, white bands; 16. | |
| 16634 *J 6144.21* | --West. | 8° 39.7´ N 77° 21.7´ W | **Fl.Y.** period 3s fl. 0.3s, ec. 2.7s | 36 **11** | 12 | Red tower, white bands; 16. | |
| 16635 *J 6144.5* | Acandi. | 8° 31.0´ N 77° 16.2´ W | **Fl.(2)W.** period 10s fl. 0.8s, ec. 1.2s fl. 0.8s, ec. 7.2s | 49 **15** | 12 | Red metal framework tower, white bands; 39. | |
| 16636 *J 6147* | Isla de los Muertos. | 8° 07.9´ N 76° 48.8´ W | **Fl.W.** period 6s fl. 0.5s, ec. 5.5s | 66 **20** | 12 | Red metal tower, white bands; 59. | **AIS** (MMSI No 997301001). |
| 16638 *J 6147.5* | Punta Yarumal. | 8° 06.6´ N 76° 44.9´ W | **Fl.W.** period 5s fl. 0.5s, ec. 4.5s | 66 **20** | 10 | Red and white tower; 59. | |
| 16639 *J 6147.8* | Faro de Matuntugo. | 8° 08.2´ N 76° 50.5´ W | **Fl.(3)W.** period 12s fl. 0.8s, ec. 1.2s fl. 0.8s, ec. 1.2s fl. 0.8s, ec. 7.2s | 131 **40** | 12 | Metal framework tower, red and white bands. | |
| 16644 | Turbo Airfield. | 8° 04.4´ N 76° 44.4´ W | **F.R.** | 40 **12** | | Tower. | **Aero Radiobeacon.** |
| 16648 *J 6149* | **Punta de las Vacas.** | 8° 03.8´ N 76° 44.6´ W | **Fl.W.** period 6.6s fl. 0.5s, ec. 6.1s | 66 **20** | **15** | White metal tower, red bands. | |
| | RACON | | **B(– • • •)** | | | | (3 & 10cm). |
| 16649 *J 6149.2* | U6. | 8° 03.9´ N 76° 44.0´ W | **Fl.R.** period 3s fl. 0.3s, ec. 2.7s | 7 **2** | 3 | Red beacon. | . |
| 16650 *J 6148.5* | Bocas del Leoncito. | 8° 01.0´ N 76° 50.2´ W | **Fl.(2)W.** period 8s fl. 0.5s, ec. 1s fl. 0.5s, ec. 6s | 44 **14** | 11 | Red tower, white bands; 39. | |
| 16652 *J 6146.5* | Punta Caiman. | 8° 16.1´ N 76° 46.3´ W | **Fl.W.** period 7.5s fl. 0.8s, ec. 6.7s | 66 **20** | 12 | White metal tower, red bands; 59. | |
| 16656 *J 6146* | Punta Arenas del Norte. | 8° 33.3´ N 76° 56.2´ W | **Fl.W.** period 9s fl. 0.9s, ec. 8.1s | 66 **20** | 10 | White metal tower, red bands; 59. | |
| 16660 *J 6145* | Punta Caribana. | 8° 37.4´ N 76° 53.3´ W | **Q.(4)W.** period 10s | 276 **84** | 10 | White tower, red bands; 7. | |
| 16662 *J 6151* | **Isla Tortuguilla.** | 9° 01.6´ N 76° 20.3´ W | **Fl.W.** period 10s fl. 0.3s, ec. 9.7s | 69 **21** | **15** | Red and white tower; 59. | |
| 16664 *J 6152* | **Isla Fuerte.** | 9° 23.5´ N 76° 10.7´ W | **Fl.W.** period 10s fl. 1s, ec. 9s | 144 **44** | **17** | White metal framework tower, red bands; 108. | |

## COLOMBIA

| (1) No. | (2) Name and Location | (3) Position | (4) Characteristic | (5) Height | (6) Range | (7) Structure | (8) Remarks |
|---|---|---|---|---|---|---|---|
| | GOLFO DE MORROSQUILLO: | | | | | | |
| 16674<br>*J 6153.6* | --*Tanker Loading Unit TLU-3.* | 9° 31.7´ N<br>75° 47.2´ W | **Fl.Y.**<br>period 10s | | | | |
| 16678<br>*J 6154.5* | Roca Morrosquillo. | 9° 35.5´ N<br>75° 59.5´ W | **Fl.W.**<br>period 3s<br>fl. 0.3s, ec. 2.7s | 20<br>**6** | 10 | Red tower, white bands. | |
| 16679<br>*J 6156* | **Isla Ceycen.** | 9° 41.6´ N<br>75° 51.3´ W | **Fl.W.**<br>period 12s<br>fl. 1s, ec. 11s | 66<br>**20** | **17** | Red tower, white bands; 59. | |
| 16680<br>*J 6157* | Isla Mucura. | 9° 47.0´ N<br>75° 52.2´ W | **Fl.W.**<br>period 6.7s<br>fl. 0.5s, ec. 6.2s | 66<br>**20** | 11 | Red tower, white bands; 59. | |
| 16684<br>*J 6159* | Isla Arenas. | 10° 08.7´ N<br>75° 43.6´ W | **Fl.W.**<br>period 12s<br>fl. 1.2s, ec. 10.8s | 66<br>**20** | 13 | White metal tower, red stripes; 59. | |
| 16687.1<br>*J 6159.7* | Isla del Rosario. | 10° 10.1´ N<br>75° 48.0´ W | **Fl.(3)W.**<br>period 10s | 46<br>**14** | 11 | White tower, red bands; 39. | |
| 16688<br>*J 6160* | Isla del Tesoro. | 10° 14.1´ N<br>75° 44.4´ W | **Fl.W.**<br>period 6.6s<br>fl. 0.5s, ec. 6.1s | 66<br>**20** | 12 | White tower, red bands. | |
| | CARTAGENA: | | | | | | |
| 16700<br>*J 6166* | **-Isla Tierra Bomba.** | 10° 20.4´ N<br>75° 34.9´ W | **Fl.W.**<br>period 1.3s<br>fl. 0.3s, ec. 1s | 367<br>**112** | **26** | Red metal framework tower, white bands; 131. | |
| 16701<br>*J 6166.5* | -1, E. entrance. | 10° 18.4´ N<br>75° 31.8´ W | **Fl.G.**<br>period 2s<br>fl. 0.5s, ec. 1.5s | 13<br>**4** | 3 | Green cylindrical post. | |
| 16702<br>*J 6166.7* | -2, W. entrance. | 10° 18.3´ N<br>75° 31.9´ W | **Fl.R.**<br>period 2s<br>fl. 0.5s, ec. 1.5s | 13<br>**4** | 3 | Red cylindrical post. | |
| 16704 | -*Sea buoy.* | 10° 19.0´ N<br>75° 35.9´ W | **Q.W.** | | | SAFE WATER<br>RW, topmark. | |
| | -RACON | | **C(– • – •)** | | | | (3 & 10cm). |
| 16725.5<br>*J 6167.65* | -2 ENAP, Range, front. | 10° 23.3´ N<br>75° 31.8´ W | **Q.Y.** | 59<br>**18** | 10 | White tower, red bands; 30. | |
| 16725.51<br>*J 6167.66* | --1 ENAP, rear, about 110 meters 000° from front. | 10° 23.4´ N<br>75° 31.8´ W | **Q.Y.** | 72<br>**22** | 10 | White tower, red bands; 16. | |
| 16726<br>*J 6167.6* | **Castillo Grande.** | 10° 23.5´ N<br>75° 32.7´ W | **Fl.W.**<br>period 15s<br>fl. 1s, ec. 14s | 79<br>**24** | **17** | Beige concrete tower; 72. | Beacons "E1" Fl G 3s 5M and "E2" Fl R 3s 4M mark small craft passage 1.5 miles W. |
| 16728<br>*J 6164* | Banco Salmedina. | 10° 22.7´ N<br>75° 39.1´ W | **Fl.W.**<br>period 10s<br>fl. 1s, ec. 9s | 13<br>**4** | 8 | Red and white tower. | |
| 16732<br>*J 6172* | **-Crespo** AVIATION LIGHT. | 10° 26.8´ N<br>75° 31.0´ W | **Al.Fl.W.G.**<br>period 10s | | **20** | | |
| 16736<br>*J 6174* | Punta Canoas. | 10° 34.4´ N<br>75° 29.9´ W | **Fl.(2)W.**<br>period 20s<br>fl. 1s, ec. 3s<br>fl. 1s, ec. 15s | 315<br>**96** | 12 | Red and white tower; 39. | |
| 16740<br>*J 6176* | **Punta Galera.** | 10° 47.1´ N<br>75° 16.0´ W | **Fl.W.**<br>period 6s<br>fl. 0.5s, ec. 5.5s | 39<br>**12** | **18** | White tower, red bands; 59. | |
| 16744<br>*J 6180* | **Punta Hermosa.** | 10° 57.8´ N<br>75° 01.1´ W | **Oc.W.**<br>period 4s<br>lt. 2.5s, ec. 1.5s | 440<br>**134** | **28** | White tower, red bands; 39. | |

| (1) No. | (2) Name and Location | (3) Position | (4) Characteristic | (5) Height | (6) Range | (7) Structure | (8) Remarks |
|---|---|---|---|---|---|---|---|

## COLOMBIA

| (1) No. | (2) Name and Location | (3) Position | (4) Characteristic | (5) Height | (6) Range | (7) Structure | (8) Remarks |
|---|---|---|---|---|---|---|---|
| | RIO MAGDALENA: | | | | | | |
| 16747 *J 6190* | **-F-1,** E. breakwater, head. | 11° 06.4′ N 74° 51.0′ W | **L.Fl.G.** period 7s fl. 2s, ec. 5s | 79 **24** | **15** | White tower, red bands. | |
| 16748 *J 6188* | **-F-2,** W. breakwater, head. | 11° 06.4′ N 74° 51.3′ W | **L.Fl.R.** period 7s fl. 2s, ec. 5s | 79 **24** | **15** | White tower, red bands. | |
| | -RACON | | **B(– • • •)** | | | | (3 & 10cm). |
| 16756 *J 6191* | -E-1 Range, front, on E. breakwater, common front. | 11° 06.2′ N 74° 50.9′ W | **Iso.Bu.** period 5s | 33 **10** | 13 | Metal framework tower, white rectangular daymark, red stripe. | Rear 16760. |
| | | | **Iso.W.** period 4s | 33 **10** | 9 | Same structure. | Rear 16761. |
| 16760 *J 6191.1* | --E-3 Rear, 310 meters 139°18′ from front. | 11° 06.1′ N 74° 50.8′ W | **Iso.Bu.** period 5s | 72 **22** | 9 | Orange and white framework tower, white rectangular daymark, red stripe. | |
| 16761 *J 6191.2* | --E-3A Rear, 135°42′ from front. | 11° 06.0′ N 74° 50.7′ W | **Iso.W.** period 3s | 72 **22** | 9 | Orange and white framework tower, white rectangular daymark, red stripe. | |
| 16763 *J 6193.5* | -X-1. | 11° 06.1′ N 74° 51.0′ W | **Iso.Y.** period 4s | 26 **8** | 4 | Orange framework tower, white bands. | |
| 16764 *J 6194* | -X-2, W. side of river. | 11° 06.0′ N 74° 51.2′ W | **Fl.R.** period 1.3s fl. 0.5s, ec. 0.8s | 26 **8** | 6 | Orange framework tower, white bands. | |
| 16768 *J 6196* | -X-4, W. side of river. | 11° 05.6′ N 74° 51.1′ W | **Iso.R.** period 4s | 26 **8** | 4 | Orange framework tower, white bands. | |
| 16772 *J 6198* | -E-4. | 11° 04.2′ N 74° 50.8′ W | **Dir.Iso.W.** period 4s | 36 **11** | 4 | Orange metal tower, white bands. | Visible on bearing 322°12′. |
| | | | **Iso.R.** period 4s | | | | |
| 16776 *J 6200* | -X-5. | 11° 05.4′ N 74° 50.8′ W | **Iso.Y.** period 4s | 26 **8** | 4 | Orange framework tower, white bands. | |
| 16780 *J 6202* | -X-6, W. side of river. | 11° 05.3′ N 74° 51.0′ W | **Q.(6)R.** period 10s | 26 **8** | 4 | Orange framework tower, white bands. | |
| 16784 *J 6191.9* | -E-6 Range, front. | 11° 03.9′ N 74° 50.7′ W | **Iso.Bu.** period 2s | 36 **11** | 11 | Orangee framework tower, white bands, red rectangular daymark, white stripes. | Visible 166°-170°. |
| 16788 *J 6191.91* | --E-8 Rear, 695 meters 167°42′ from front. | 11° 03.5′ N 74° 50.6′ W | **Iso.Bu.** period 4s | 82 **25** | 14 | Red and white framework tower, white rectangular daymark, red stripe. | Visible on range line only. |
| 16790 *J 6193* | -E-16 Range, front. | 11° 03.2′ N 74° 50.2′ W | **Iso.Bu.** period 6s | 39 **12** | 9 | Orange and white framework tower. | |
| 16790.5 *J 6192.1* | --E-14 Rear, 512 meters 302° from front. | 11° 03.4′ N 74° 50.4′ W | **Iso.Bu.** period 6s | 79 **24** | 9 | Tower. | |
| 16792 *J 6204* | -X-8, W. side of river. | 11° 04.9′ N 74° 51.0′ W | **Fl.R.** period 4s fl. 1s, ec. 3s | 26 **8** | 4 | Orange framework tower, white bands. | |
| 16804 *J 6206* | -X-10, W. side of river, below Las Flores. | 11° 04.6′ N 74° 50.9′ W | **Fl.(2)R.** period 8s fl. 1s, ec. 1s fl. 1s, ec. 5s | 26 **8** | 4 | Red framework tower, white bands. | |
| 16806 *J 6216* | **-E-18 Range,** front. | 11° 02.6′ N 74° 49.5′ W | **Iso.Bu.** period 3s | 49 **15** | **15** | White metal framework tower, white rectangular daymark, orange stripe. | |

| (1) No. | (2) Name and Location | (3) Position | (4) Characteristic | (5) Height | (6) Range | (7) Structure | (8) Remarks |
|---|---|---|---|---|---|---|---|

## COLOMBIA

| | | | | | | | |
|---|---|---|---|---|---|---|---|
| 16807 *J 6218* | -E-20 Rear, 522 meters 142° 12′ from front. | 11° 02.4′ N 74° 49.4′ W | **Iso.Bu.** period 4s | 98 **30** | **15** | White and orange metal framework tower, white rectangular daymark, orange stripe. | |
| 16808 *J 6207* | -X-12. | 11° 03.9′ N 74° 50.7′ W | **Iso.R.** period 4s | 26 **8** | 4 | Orange framework tower, white bands. | |
| 16810 *J 6208* | -X-14. | 11° 03.5′ N 74° 50.4′ W | **Q.(2)R.** period 6s | 26 **8** | 4 | Orange framework tower, white bands. | |
| 16811 *J 6222.5* | -X-7. | 11° 02.5′ N 74° 48.9′ W | **Iso.Y.** period 4s | 26 **8** | 4 | Orange framework tower, white bands. | |
| 16812 *J 6214* | -X-16. | 11° 03.0′ N 74° 50.0′ W | **Fl.(3)R.** period 9s fl. 0.8s, ec. 1.2s fl. 0.8s, ec. 1.2s fl. 0.8s, ec. 4.2s | 26 **8** | 4 | Orange framework tower, white bands. | |
| 16813 *J 6222.8* | -X-9. | 11° 02.2′ N 74° 48.3′ W | **Iso.Y.** period 4s | 26 **8** | 4 | Orange framework tower, white bands. | |
| 16813.5 *J 6223* | -X-11. | 11° 01.8′ N 74° 47.7′ W | **Iso.Y.** period 4s | 26 **8** | 4 | Orange framework tower, white bands, red and white rectangular daymark. | |
| 16814 *J 6226* | -X-13. | 11° 01.6′ N 74° 47.4′ W | **Iso.Y.** period 4s | 26 **8** | 4 | Orange framework tower, white bands, red and white rectangular daymark. | |
| 16815 *J 6229* | -X-15. | 11° 01.4′ N 74° 47.1′ W | **Q.(3)Y.** period 5s | 26 **8** | 4 | Orange framework tower, white bands. | |
| 16817 *J 6229.5* | **-E-5 Range,** front. | 11° 00.7′ N 74° 46.2′ W | **Iso.Bu.** period 2s | 39 **12** | **15** | Orange and white framework tower, white rectangular daymark, red stripe. | Visible 118°54′-124°54′. |
| 16818 *J 6229.51* | --E-7 Rear, 262 meters 121°54′ from front. | 11° 00.6′ N 74° 46.0′ W | **Iso.Bu.** period 4s | 75 **23** | **15** | White framework tower, white rectangular daymark, red stripe. | Visible 118°54′-124°54′. |
| 16819 *J 6229.2* | -X-17. | 11° 01.1′ N 74° 46.7′ W | **Q.(3)Y.** period 5s | 26 **8** | 4 | Orange framework tower, white bands. | |
| 16821 *J 6236* | Coal loading jetty, SW corner. | 11° 04.3′ N 74° 14.2′ W | **Fl.R.** | | | | |
| 16822 *J 6236.1* | -NE corner. | 11° 04.3′ N 74° 14.2′ W | **Fl.R.** | | | | |
| 16828 *J 6254* | Simon Bolivar AVIATION LIGHT. | 11° 07.0′ N 74° 14.0′ W | **Al.Fl.W.G.** period 10s | | | Tower. | |
| 16831 *J 6255.3* | *-SBM.* | 11° 09.2′ N 74° 15.2′ W | **Fl.W.** period 8s | | 8 | Yellow CALM superbuoy. | **Radar reflector.** |
| | -RACON | | **C(– • – •)** | | | | (3 & 10cm). |
| | BAHIA DE SANTA MARTA: | | | | | | |
| 16832 *J 6256* | **-Morro Grande.** | 11° 15.0′ N 74° 13.8′ W | **Fl.W.** period 15s fl. 1s, ec. 14s | 279 **85** | **22** | White and gray concrete tower; 76. | Obscured beyond Aguja Island 203°-212°. |
| | -RACON | | **S(• • •)** | | | | (3 & 10cm). |
| 16835 *J 6265* | Puerto Brisa. | 11° 15.6′ N 73° 22.7′ W | **Dir.W.R.G.** period 5s fl. 4s, ec. 1s | 98 **30** | 5 | White tower. | Oc.R. 158°27′-159°27′, Oc.W.-160°09′, Oc.G.-161°09′. |
| 16836 *J 6262* | **Riohacha.** | 11° 32.6′ N 72° 55.8′ W | **Fl.W.** period 10s fl. 1s, ec. 9s | 66 **20** | **15** | White metal framework tower, red bands; 101. | |
| 16840 *J 6260* | **Punta Manaure.** | 11° 47.1′ N 72° 26.3′ W | **Fl.W.** period 12s fl. 1s, ec. 11s | 66 **20** | **15** | Red framework tower, white bands; 59. | |

| (1) No. | (2) Name and Location | (3) Position | (4) Characteristic | (5) Height | (6) Range | (7) Structure | (8) Remarks |
|---|---|---|---|---|---|---|---|
| | | | **COLOMBIA** | | | | |
| 16841<br>*J 6261.2* | Chuchupa A. | 11° 47.2′ N<br>72° 46.3′ W | **Mo.(U)W.**<br>period 15s | | 5 | Platform. | |
| 16842<br>*J 6261.3* | -B. | 11° 49.6′ N<br>72° 49.7′ W | **Mo.(U)W.**<br>period 15s | | 5 | Platform. | |
| 16844<br>*J 6266* | **Cabo de la Vela.** | 12° 13.0′ N<br>72° 10.5′ W | **Fl.W.**<br>period 10s<br>fl. 0.8s, ec. 9.2s | 289<br>**88** | **15** | White metal framework tower, red bands; 26. | |
| 16845 | *Buoy 1.* | 12° 17.5′ N<br>71° 58.9′ W | **Iso.G.**<br>period 4s | | | PORT (B)<br>G, pillar. | |
| | RACON | | **M(– –)** | | **28** | | |
| 16846<br>*J 6266.2* | Puerto Bolivar, coal loading pier, N. | 12° 15.6′ N<br>71° 57.9′ W | **Fl.R.**<br>period 5s<br>fl. 0.5s, ec. 4.5s | | | | |
| 16846.3<br>*J 6266.4* | Punta Latata. | 12° 16.8′ N<br>71° 13.7′ W | **Fl.W.**<br>period 3s<br>fl. 1s, ec. 2s | 13<br>**4** | 6 | Tower. | **Radar reflector.** |
| 16846.6<br>*J 6266.3* | Pier extension, S. | 12° 15.5′ N<br>71° 57.8′ W | **Oc.R.**<br>period 3s<br>lt. 2s, ec. 1s | | | | |
| 16846.8<br>*J 6266.33* | Waieint pier, head. | 12° 15.5′ N<br>71° 57.8′ W | **Oc.R.**<br>period 3s<br>lt. 2s, ec. 1s | | | | |
| 16847<br>*J 6266.5* | Puerto Bolivar Range, front. | 12° 15.3′ N<br>71° 57.5′ W | **Q.W.** | 16<br>**5** | 3 | Pile, red rectangular daymark, white stripe. | **Radar reflector.** |
| 16847.5<br>*J 6266.51* | -Rear, 600 meters 147° from front. | 12° 15.1′ N<br>71° 57.3′ W | **Oc.W.**<br>period 3s<br>lt. 2s, ec. 1s | 33<br>**10** | 3 | Pile, red rectangular daymark, white stripe. | **Radar reflector.** |
| 16848<br>*J 6267* | Punta Gallinas. | 12° 27.5′ N<br>71° 39.8′ W | **Fl.W.**<br>period 10s<br>fl. 1s, ec. 9s | 66<br>**20** | 13 | White tower, red bands; 59. | |
| 16848.2<br>*J 6267.3* | Chimare. | 12° 23.2′ N<br>71° 26.5′ W | **Fl.W.**<br>period 12s<br>fl. 1.2s, ec. 10.8s | 72<br>**22** | 13 | Red tower, white bands; 59. | |
| 16848.3<br>*J 6267.4* | Puerto Estrella. | 12° 21.3′ N<br>71° 18.7′ W | **Fl.W.**<br>period 15s<br>fl. 1s, ec. 14s | 66<br>**20** | 13 | Red framework tower, white bands; 59. | |
| 16848.4<br>*J 6267.6* | **Chichibacoa.** | 12° 18.0′ N<br>71° 13.3′ W | **Fl.W.**<br>period 10s<br>fl. 0.5s, ec. 9.5s | 72<br>**22** | **17** | Red framework tower, white bands; 59. | |
| 16849<br>*J 6267.8* | **Punta Espada.** | 12° 04.8′ N<br>71° 07.8′ W | **Fl.W.**<br>period 20s<br>fl. 1.6s, ec. 18.4s | 164<br>**50** | **18** | White metal framework tower, red bands; 56. | |
| 16850<br>*J 6268* | **Castilletes.** | 11° 51.1′ N<br>71° 19.5′ W | **Fl.W.**<br>period 12s<br>fl. 1s, ec. 11s | 105<br>**32** | **15** | White metal framework tower, red bands; 98. | **AIS** (MMSI No 997301004). |
| | | | **VENEZUELA** | | | | |
| 16851<br>*J 5700* | **Isla Aves.** | 15° 39.9′ N<br>63° 36.8′ W | **Fl.W.**<br>period 5s<br>fl. 1s, ec. 4s | 62<br>**19** | **15** | Black metal framework tower; 7. | |
| | RACON | | **A(• –)** | | **20** | | (3 & 10cm). |
| 16852<br>*J 6270* | **Monjes del Sur.** | 12° 21.3′ N<br>70° 54.1′ W | **Fl.W.**<br>period 10s<br>fl. 0.6s, ec. 9.4s | 253<br>**77** | **25** | White round concrete tower, red bands; 33. | |
| | RACON | | **Y(– • – –)** | | **30** | | (3 & 10cm). |

| (1) No. | (2) Name and Location | (3) Position | (4) Characteristic | (5) Height | (6) Range | (7) Structure | (8) Remarks |
|---|---|---|---|---|---|---|---|
| | | | **VENEZUELA** | | | | |
| 16856 *J 6269* | **Punta Perret.** | 11° 47.7´ N 71° 20.4´ W | **Fl.W.** period 15s fl. 1s, ec. 14s | 95 **29** | **24** | Four-sided concrete tower; 95. | |
| | LAGO DE MARACAIBO ENTRANCE: | | | | | | |
| 16860 *J 6274* | -Malecon Del Este, E. breakwater, head. | 11° 01.2´ N 71° 35.0´ W | **Fl.W.** period 5s | 46 **14** | 10 | | |
| 16860.2 *J 6275* | **-Isla San Carlos.** | 11° 00.0´ N 71° 36.3´ W | **Fl.W.** period 10s fl. 1s, ec. 9s | 75 **23** | **18** | Orange fiberglass tower, white band; 49. | |
| 16872 *J 6279.9* | --Inner channel Range, front, Q. | 10° 47.9´ N 71° 37.6´ W | **Fl.G.** period 1.5s fl. 0.5s, ec. 1s | 89 **27** | 7 | Metal framework tower on concrete piles. | Tide gauge. |
| 16872.1 *J 6280* | ---Rear, P, 1646 meters 188°48′ from front. | 10° 47.0´ N 71° 37.8´ W | **Oc.G.** period 4.5s lt. 4s, ec. 0.5s | 128 **39** | 8 | Metal framework tower on concrete piles. | |
| 16873 *J 6283* | --Maracaibo channel Range, front, R. | 10° 50.5´ N 71° 38.2´ W | **Fl.G.** period 1.5s fl. 0.5s, ec. 1s | 89 **27** | 7 | Metal framework tower on concrete piles. | |
| 16873.1 *J 6283.1* | ---Rear, S, 1829 meters 330°49′ from front. | 10° 51.3´ N 71° 38.6´ W | **Fl.G.** period 4s | 128 **39** | 8 | Truncated metal framework pyramid on concrete piles; 128. | |
| 16873.81 *J 6285.6* | --EP3. | 10° 46.9´ N 71° 37.8´ W | **Fl.G.** period 5s fl. 0.5s, ec. 4.5s | 13 **4** | 5 | Aluminum and green hut on platform, on pile. | |
| | -Inner Channel: | | | | | | |
| 16873.82 *J 6285.4* | --Santa Cruz de Mara jetty. | 10° 38.2´ N 71° 36.2´ W | **Fl.W.** period 5s fl. 0.5s, ec. 4.5s | 20 **6** | 2 | Metal column. | |
| 16873.83 *J 6287* | --Recalada Puerto de Maracaibo. | 10° 38.2´ N 71° 36.2´ W | **Fl.W.** period 4s fl. 1s, ec. 3s | 49 **15** | 11 | Orange hexagonal fiberglass tower, white band; 33. | |
| 16873.84 *J 6288* | --La Arreaga pier. | 10° 36.0´ N 71° 36.5´ W | **Fl.G.** | | | | |
| 16873.85 *J 6288.2* | ---Elbow. | 10° 36.0´ N 71° 36.7´ W | **3 Fl.G.** | | | | |
| 16875 *J 6297* | Punta Borojo. | 11° 12.1´ N 70° 46.7´ W | **Fl.W.** period 12s fl. 1.2s, ec. 10.8s | 62 **19** | 11 | Orange fiberglass tower, white band; 49. | |
| 16875.5 *J 6294* | Moporo. | 9° 34.8´ N 71° 04.0´ W | **Fl.W.** period 10s fl. 1s, ec. 9s | 43 **13** | 11 | Orange fiberglass frame, white band; 39. | |
| | PENINSULA DE PARAGUANA: | | | | | | |
| | -Puerto de Guaranao: | | | | | | |
| 16879.7 *J 6299* | --Guaranao. | 11° 40.0´ N 70° 12.8´ W | **Fl.(2)R.G.** period 12s fl. 1.5s, ec. 2s fl. 1.5s, ec. 7s | 121 **37** | 9 | Orange hexagonal fiberglass tower, white band; 33. | G. 040°-050°, R.-040°. |
| 16879.8 *J 6299.6* | --Muelle Flotante. | 11° 40.3´ N 70° 12.9´ W | **Fl.R.** period 4s fl. 1s, ec. 3s | 20 **6** | 3 | Red hexagonal fiberglass tower, white band; 10. | |
| 16879.9 *J 6299.7* | ---Fijo. | 11° 40.4´ N 70° 12.9´ W | **Fl.G.** period 6s fl. 1s, ec. 5s | 20 **6** | 3 | Green hexagonal fiberglass tower, white band; 10. | |
| 16880 *J 6310* | -Bahia de Amuay, front. | 11° 45.1´ N 70° 12.3´ W | **Fl.G.** period 5s | 122 **37** | 5 | White framework tower, red bands. | Oc.R. 2s and 2 F.R. on each of 2 towers, 0.93 and 1.2 miles ESE. |

## VENEZUELA

| (1)<br>No. | (2)<br>Name and Location | (3)<br>Position | (4)<br>Characteristic | (5)<br>Height | (6)<br>Range | (7)<br>Structure | (8)<br>Remarks |
|---|---|---|---|---|---|---|---|
| 16884<br>*J 6310.1* | --Rear, 365 meters 074°45′ from front. | 11° 45.2′ N<br>70° 12.1′ W | **Fl.G.**<br>period 5s | 156<br>**48** | 5 | White framework tower, red bands. | |
| 16890<br>*J 6300.4* | -Punto Fijo, Recalada BNFA. | 11° 41.9′ N<br>70° 12.7′ W | **L.Fl.G.**<br>period 10s<br>fl. 2s, ec. 8s | 131<br>**40** | 11 | Orange hexagonal fiberglass tower, white band; 33. | |
| 16892<br>*J 6301* | -Las Piedras, Naval Pier, head. | 11° 42.1′ N<br>70° 13.2′ W | **Fl.G.**<br>period 3s<br>fl. 1s, ec. 2s | 30<br>**9** | 7 | Green fiberglass tower, white band; 10. | |
| 16896<br>*J 6312* | **-Macolla.** | 12° 05.8′ N<br>70° 12.5′ W | **Fl.W.**<br>period 10s<br>fl. 1s, ec. 9s | 157<br>**48** | **20** | Gray octagonal metal tower; 135. | |
| 16900<br>*J 6314* | **-Cabo San Roman.** | 12° 11.4′ N<br>69° 59.9′ W | **Fl.W.**<br>period 6s<br>fl. 1s, ec. 5s | 85<br>**26** | **23** | Four-sided masonry tower; 82. | |
| 16904<br>*J 6428* | -Punta Adicora. | 11° 56.7′ N<br>69° 48.1′ W | **Fl.W.**<br>period 16s<br>fl. 1s, ec. 15s | 52<br>**16** | 14 | White round fiberglass tower, orange bands; 49. | |
| 16906<br>*J 6431* | Vela de Coro. | 11° 34.3′ N<br>69° 32.2′ W | **Q.(3)W.**<br>period 10s | 49<br>**15** | 6 | Yellow metal pillar on platform. | |
| 16910<br>*J 6433* | Rompeolas Muaco. | 11° 29.3′ N<br>69° 33.3′ W | **Fl.G.**<br>period 5s<br>fl. 1s, ec. 4s | 16<br>**5** | 9 | Green hexagonal fiberglass tower, white bands. | |
| 16912<br>*J 6434* | Punta Taima-Taima. | 11° 30.2′ N<br>69° 30.9′ W | **Fl.W.**<br>period 7s<br>fl. 1s, ec. 6s | 167<br>**51** | 14 | Orange fiberglass framework tower, white bands; 39. | |
| 16920<br>*J 6438* | Punta Tomoro. | 11° 31.9′ N<br>69° 16.2′ W | **Fl.W.**<br>period 6s<br>fl. 0.5s, ec. 5.5s | 148<br>**45** | 11 | Orange hexagonal fiberglass tower, white band; 39. | |
| 16924<br>*J 6440* | Punta Zamuro. | 11° 26.4′ N<br>68° 49.9′ W | **Fl.W.**<br>period 10s<br>fl. 1s, ec. 9s | 52<br>**16** | 13 | Orange fiberglass tower, white bands; 39. | |
| 16928<br>*J 6441* | Punta Aguide. | 11° 20.8′ N<br>68° 40.6′ W | **Fl.W.R.**<br>period 3s<br>fl. 1s, ec. 2s | 23<br>**7** | 9 | White metal framework tower, orange bands; 39. | |
| 16932<br>*J 6442* | Cayo Noroeste, W. side. | 11° 13.1′ N<br>68° 26.8′ W | **Fl.W.**<br>period 6s | 49<br>**15** | 12 | Orange fiberglass tower, white band; 39. | |
| 16936<br>*J 6444* | Cayo Borracho. | 10° 58.4′ N<br>68° 14.8′ W | **Fl.W.**<br>period 8s<br>fl. 1s, ec. 7s | 52<br>**16** | 12 | White truncated conical fiberglass tower, orange bands; 46. | |
| | PUERTO CABELLO: | | | | | | |
| 16950<br>*J 6446.5* | -Silos Caribe, pier. | 10° 29.4′ N<br>68° 05.7′ W | **Fl.G.**<br>period 3s | 79<br>**24** | 10 | Black framework tower; 13. | |
| 16952<br>*J 6446* | -Puerto Cabello AVIATION LIGHT. | 10° 28.6′ N<br>68° 04.4′ W | **Al.Fl.W.G.**<br>period 4s | 73<br>**22** | 14 | Tower. | |
| 16956<br>*J 6448.4* | -Isla Guaiguaza. | 10° 29.6′ N<br>68° 02.5′ W | **Fl.W.**<br>period 8s<br>fl. 1s, ec. 7s | 43<br>**13** | 14 | Red hexagonal fiberglass tower, white band; 39. | |
| 16959<br>*J 6448.7* | -La Planchita. | 10° 29.0′ N<br>68° 00.5′ W | **Fl.G.**<br>period 4s<br>fl. 1s, ec. 3s | 49<br>**15** | 9 | Green hexagonal fiberglass tower, white band; 43. | |
| 16960<br>*J 6452* | -Isla Alcatraz. | 10° 30.5′ N<br>67° 58.5′ W | **Fl.W.**<br>period 10s<br>fl. 1s, ec. 9s | 62<br>**19** | 11 | Orange fiberglass tower, white band; 49. | |
| | -RACON | | **M(– –)** | | | | |
| 16961<br>*J 6449* | -Naval quay, SW. head. | 10° 29.1′ N<br>68° 00.1′ W | **Fl.G.**<br>period 3s<br>fl. 1s, ec. 2s | 16<br>**5** | 3 | Green hexagonal fiberglass tower, white band; 10. | |

| (1) No. | (2) Name and Location | (3) Position | (4) Characteristic | (5) Height | (6) Range | (7) Structure | (8) Remarks |
|---|---|---|---|---|---|---|---|

## VENEZUELA

| (1) No. | (2) Name and Location | (3) Position | (4) Characteristic | (5) Height | (6) Range | (7) Structure | (8) Remarks |
|---|---|---|---|---|---|---|---|
| 16961.3 *J 6449.5* | -Naval Base M-7. | 10° 28.8′ N 68° 00.0′ W | **Fl.R.** period 5s fl. 1.5s, ec. 3.5s | 20 **6** | 4 | Red hexagonal fiberglass structure, white band; 46. | |
| 16961.7 *J 6449.7* | --M-32. | 10° 28.4′ N 67° 59.6′ W | **Fl.R.** period 5s fl. 0.9s, ec. 4.1s | 20 **6** | 4 | Red hexagonal fiberglass structure, white band; 39. | |
| 16962 *J 6448.9* | -Inner harbor. | 10° 29.1′ N 68° 00.2′ W | **Fl.(2+1)G.** period 15s fl. 1s, ec. 2s fl. 1s, ec. 5s fl. 1s, ec. 5s | 16 **5** | 4 | PREFERRED CHANNEL (B) GRG, tower; 10. | |
| 16964 *J 6448* | **-Punta Brava.** | 10° 29.4′ N 68° 00.5′ W | **Fl.W.** period 6s fl. 1s, ec. 5s | 121 **37** | **20** | White concrete tower, orange bands; 121. | F.R. lights on radio mast 0.6 mile S. |
| 16965 | Range, front. | 10° 29.1′ N 67° 59.0′ W | **Q.W.** | 36 **11** | | White fiberglass tower, black stripes. | |
| 16966 | -Rear, 222 meters 140° from front. | 10° 29.0′ N 67° 58.9′ W | **Q.W.** | 43 **13** | | White fiberglass tower, black stripes. | |
| 16973.5 *J 6448.7* | -Muelle La Planchita. | 10° 29.0′ N 68° 00.5′ W | **Fl.G.** period 4s fl. 1s, ec. 3s | 49 **15** | 9 | Green hexagonal fiberglass tower, white band; 43. | |
| 16976 *J 6447* | **-Fortin Solano.** | 10° 27.9′ N 68° 01.2′ W | **Fl.(3)W.** period 15.5s fl. 1s, ec. 2s fl. 1s, ec. 2s fl. 1s, ec. 8.5s | 551 **168** | **25** | Orange and white metal framework tower; 20. | |
| 16988 *J 6452.6* | Isla Turiamo. | 10° 29.0′ N 67° 50.3′ W | **Fl.W.** period 9s fl. 0.7s, ec. 8.3s | 23 **7** | 10 | Metal framework tower, orange and white bands; 10. | |
| 16992 *J 6453* | Bahia de Turiamo, pier, head. | 10° 27.2′ N 67° 50.7′ W | **L.Fl.G.** period 7s fl. 3s, ec. 4s | 49 **15** | 6 | Green hexagonal metal framework tower, white band; 43. | |
| 16993 *J 6453.2* | -S. head. | 10° 27.1′ N 67° 50.6′ W | **Fl.Y.** period 1.5s | 13 **4** | 4 | Yellow framework tower; 10. | |
| 16996 *J 6453.4* | **Morro Choroni.** | 10° 30.6′ N 67° 36.2′ W | **Fl.W.** period 5s fl. 0.9s, ec. 4.1s | 348 **106** | **18** | White metal structure; 20. | |
| 17000 *J 6420* | -Aves de Barlovento. | 11° 56.5′ N 67° 26.6′ W | **Fl.W.** period 10s fl. 1.5s, ec. 8.5s | 46 **14** | 12 | Orange fiberglass tower, white band; 39. | |
| 17004 *J 6419* | -Aves de Sotavento. | 12° 03.5′ N 67° 41.0′ W | **Fl.W.** period 7s fl. 0.5s, ec. 6.5s | 52 **16** | 12 | Orange fiberglass tower, white band; 39. | |
| | -RACON | | **S(• • •)** | 52 **16** | **30** | | |
| 17008 *J 6424* | **El Gran Roque.** | 11° 57.5′ N 66° 41.1′ W | **Fl.W.** period 10s fl. 1s, ec. 9s | 374 **114** | **18** | White hexagonal fiberglass tower, orange bands; 20. | |
| | RACON | | **R(• – •)** | | **20** | | (3 & 10cm). |
| 17012 *J 6425* | -Cayo de Agua. | 11° 50.2′ N 66° 57.3′ W | **Fl.W.** period 15s fl. 1s, ec. 14s | 52 **16** | 12 | Orange truncated conical fiberglass tower, white band; 46. | |
| 17014 *J 6476* | **Isla La Blanquilla.** | 11° 49.2′ N 64° 36.2′ W | **Fl.W.** period 6s fl. 1s, ec. 5s | 89 **27** | **20** | White fiberglass framework tower, orange bands; 39. | |
| | RACON | | **Q(– – • –)** | 89 **27** | **25** | | |
| 17016 *J 6425.4* | -Cayo Grande, Sebastopol. | 11° 46.7′ N 66° 35.0′ W | **Fl.W.** period 6s fl. 1s, ec. 5s | 52 **16** | 12 | Orange truncated conical fiberglass tower, white band; 46. | |

| (1) No. | (2) Name and Location | (3) Position | (4) Characteristic | (5) Height | (6) Range | (7) Structure | (8) Remarks |
|---|---|---|---|---|---|---|---|

## VENEZUELA

| (1) No. | (2) Name and Location | (3) Position | (4) Characteristic | (5) Height | (6) Range | (7) Structure | (8) Remarks |
|---|---|---|---|---|---|---|---|
| 17020 *J 6427* | La Orchila, jetty. | 11° 48.4´ N 66° 11.6´ W | **Fl.W.** period 4s fl. 0.3s, ec. 3.7s | 16 **5** | 10 | Orange metal pole, white band; 7. | |
| 17024 *J 6426* | **-Cerro Walker.** | 11° 49.0´ N 66° 11.0´ W | **Fl.W.** period 10s fl. 1s, ec. 9s | 449 **137** | **20** | Orange iron tower, white band; 20. | |
| | -RACON | | **O(– – –)** | 449 **137** | 20 | | |
| 17025 *J 6427.5* | -Range, front. | 11° 47.0´ N 66° 09.4´ W | **Q.Y.** | 43 **13** | 10 | Red fiberglass framework tower, white band; 39. | |
| 17025.5 *J 6427.51* | --Rear, 539 meters 054° from front. | 11° 47.2´ N 66° 09.1´ W | **Q.Y.** | 52 **16** | 10 | Red fiberglass framework tower, white band; 49. | |
| 17026 | -SE. Point. | 11° 46.4´ N 66° 07.1´ W | **Fl.W.** period 6s fl. 1.2s, ec. 4.8s | 10 **3** | 5 | Red iron skeleton tower, white stripes; 10. | **Radar Reflector.** |
| | ISLA LA TORTUGA: | | | | | | |
| 17028 *J 6472* | -Cayo Herradura. | 10° 59.8´ N 65° 23.1´ W | **Fl.W.** period 15s fl. 1s, ec. 14s | 46 **14** | 13 | Orange truncated conical fiberglass tower, white band; 49. | |
| | -RACON | | **T(–)** | 49 **15** | 20 | | |
| 17032 *J 6474* | -Punta Oriental. | 10° 54.0´ N 65° 12.3´ W | **Fl.W.** period 7.5s fl. 0.5s, ec. 7s | 56 **17** | 11 | Orange round fiberglass tower, white band; 39. | F.R. on radio towers 3.7 miles W., 8 miles WNW. and 4.1 miles NW. |
| 17036 *J 6462* | **Isla Farallin.** | 10° 48.9´ N 66° 05.5´ W | **Fl.W.** period 12s fl. 1s, ec. 11s | 125 **38** | **25** | Orange fiberglass framework tower, white band; 20. | |
| | RACON | | **C(– • – •)** | | 20 | | |
| 17037 *J 6453.5* | **Puerto Cruz.** | 10° 32.2´ N 67° 20.9´ W | **Fl.W.** period 10s fl. 1s, ec. 9s | 1053 **321** | **15** | Orange fiberglass tower, white band; 39. | |
| 17039 *J 6453.8* | Venezuelan Naval Squadron. | 10° 35.6´ N 67° 03.1´ W | **Fl.W.** period 10s fl. 1s, ec. 9s | 325 **99** | 11 | Red hexagonal structure, white band; 33. | |
| 17049 *J 6455* | -Range, front. | 10° 35.8´ N 67° 02.2´ W | **Fl.W.** period 10s | | | | |
| 17049.5 *J 6455.1* | --Rear, 124° from front. | 10° 35.8´ N 67° 02.2´ W | **Fl.W.** period 10s | | | | |
| | LA GUAIRA: | | | | | | |
| 17052 *J 6457* | **-AVIATION LIGHT.** | 10° 36.5´ N 67° 00.3´ W | **Fl.W.G.** period 10s | 465 **142** | **15** | Metal framework tower. | |
| 17058 *J 6458.5* | **-La Guaira.** | 10° 34.9´ N 66° 56.8´ W | **L.Fl.W.** period 15.5s fl. 2s, ec. 13.5s | 1394 **425** | **25** | Orange concrete tower, white band; 82. | |
| 17064 *J 6459.5* | -N. breakwater. | 10° 36.4´ N 66° 57.1´ W | **Fl.G.** period 3s fl. 0.8s, ec. 2.2s | 46 **14** | 13 | Green fiberglass tower, white band; 33. | |
| 17068 *J 6459* | -S. breakwater. | 10° 36.1´ N 66° 57.2´ W | **Fl.R.** period 3s fl. 0.2s, ec. 2.8s | 49 **15** | 8 | Red hexagonal fiberglass tower, white band; 43. | |
| 17069 *J 6460.3* | -Breakwater, head. | 10° 36.1´ N 66° 56.7´ W | **Fl.R.** period 2.5s fl. 0.5s, ec. 2s | 43 **13** | 8 | Red hexagonal fiberglass tower, white band; 33. | |

| (1) No. | (2) Name and Location | (3) Position | (4) Characteristic | (5) Height | (6) Range | (7) Structure | (8) Remarks |
|---|---|---|---|---|---|---|---|
| | | | **VENEZUELA** | | | | |
| 17073 *J 6461.5* | --Carballeda, W. side of entrance. | 10° 37.4′ N 66° 50.8′ W | **Fl.G.** period 8s fl. 0.5s, ec. 7.5s | 23 **7** | 4 | Green hexagonal fiberglass tower, white band; 20. | |
| 17074 *J 6461.52* | ---E. side of entrance. | 10° 37.3′ N 66° 50.7′ W | **Fl.R.** period 8s fl. 0.5s, ec. 7.5s | 23 **7** | 4 | Red hexagonal fiberglass tower, white band; 20. | |
| 17076 *J 6461.6* | Naiguata. | 10° 36.9′ N 66° 44.9′ W | **Fl.W.** period 2s | 52 **16** | 8 | White concrete tower, black bands. | |
| 17077 *J 6461.85* | **-Club Puerto Azul.** | 10° 37.4′ N 66° 44.6′ W | **Fl.W.** period 11s fl. 1s, ec. 10s | 180 **55** | **20** | Black metal post; 180. | |
| 17082 *J 6461.95* | La Sabana. | 10° 37.2′ N 66° 23.0′ W | **Fl.W.** period 7.5s fl. 0.8s, ec. 6.7s | 197 **60** | 11 | Orange hexagonal fiberglass tower, white band; 33. | |
| 17084 *J 6469* | Cabo Codera. | 10° 34.2′ N 66° 03.2′ W | **Fl.W.** period 2.5s fl. 0.5s, ec. 2s | 551 **168** | 13 | Red fiberglass tower, white band; 33. | |
| 17085 *J 6470* | Puerto Carenero, Bahia de los Piratas. | 10° 31.7′ N 66° 07.0′ W | **Fl.W.** period 10s fl. 1s, ec. 9s | 138 **42** | 12 | Gray iron framework tower; 3. | |
| 17087 *J 6477.5* | **Unare.** | 10° 05.5′ N 65° 10.7′ W | **Fl.W.** period 12s fl. 1s, ec. 11s | 49 **15** | **18** | Orange fiberglass tower, white band; 39. | |
| 17088 *J 6478* | Islas Piritu. | 10° 09.6′ N 64° 58.4′ W | **Fl.W.** period 10s fl. 1s, ec. 9s | 66 **20** | 11 | Orange round fiberglass tower, white band; 39. | |
| 17088.5 *J 6478.2* | -E. island, E. head. | 10° 08.6′ N 64° 54.8′ W | **Fl.W.** period 7s fl. 0.5s, ec. 6.5s | 52 **16** | 11 | Orange round fiberglass tower, white band; 39. | |
| 17089 *J 6479* | Isla Borrachitos del Este. | 10° 15.1′ N 64° 45.7′ W | **Fl.W.** period 15s fl. 1s, ec. 14s | 82 **25** | 6 | Orange hexagonal fiberglass tower, white band; 20. | |
| 17090 *J 6479.5* | **Cayo Borracha.** | 10° 18.2′ N 64° 44.1′ W | **Fl.W.** period 6s fl. 1s, ec. 5s | 1250 **381** | **19** | Orange fiberglass framework tower, white band; 33. | |
| | RACON | | **B(– • • •)** | 1250 **381** | **20** | | (3 & 10cm). |
| 17100 *J 6477* | Barcelona. | 10° 07.2′ N 64° 41.0′ W | **Al.Fl.W.G.** period 20s | | | | Fl.R. on radio tower 4 miles N., 5 F.R. on radio tower 1 mile NW., F.R. on 2 radio towers 5 miles NE., F.W. and F.R. on radio towers 9 miles NE. |
| 17106 *J 6480.36* | -Cargo dock, W. | 10° 14.5′ N 64° 38.2′ W | **Fl.G.** period 3s | | | Green structure, green cone topmark. | |
| 17107 *J 6480.37* | -Cargo dock, E. | 10° 14.4′ N 64° 38.0′ W | **Fl.G.** period 3s | | | Green structure, green cone topmark. | |
| | BAHIA BERGANTIN: | | | | | | |
| 17108 *J 6480.4* | -3. | 10° 14.7′ N 64° 38.1′ W | **Fl.G.** period 3s fl. 0.7s, ec. 2.3s | 13 **4** | 3 | PORT (B) G, beacon. | |
| 17112 *J 6480.42* | -4. | 10° 14.6′ N 64° 37.9′ W | **Fl.G.** period 3s fl. 1s, ec. 2s | 13 **4** | 3 | PORT (B) G, beacon. | |
| 17116 *J 6480.44* | -5. | 10° 14.8′ N 64° 37.8′ W | **Fl.R.** period 3s fl. 1s, ec. 2s | 13 **4** | 3 | STARBOARD (B) R, beacon. | |

| (1)<br>No. | (2)<br>Name and Location | (3)<br>Position | (4)<br>Characteristic | (5)<br>Height | (6)<br>Range | (7)<br>Structure | (8)<br>Remarks |
|---|---|---|---|---|---|---|---|
| | | | **VENEZUELA** | | | | |
| | BAHIA GUANTA: | | | | | | |
| 17128<br>*J 6483* | -Isla Pitahaya. | 10° 15.4′ N<br>64° 35.7′ W | **Fl.R.**<br>period 3s<br>fl. 0.3s, ec. 2.7s | 43<br>**13** | 6 | White hexagonal concrete tower, red bands; 10. | |
| 17132<br>*J 6483.2* | -Isla Redonda. | 10° 15.4′ N<br>64° 35.6′ W | **Fl.G.**<br>period 6s<br>fl. 1s, ec. 5s | 20<br>**6** | 9 | Green fiberglass tower, white band; 10. | |
| 17136<br>*J 6483.4* | -Punta Queque. | 10° 15.1′ N<br>64° 35.5′ W | **Fl.G.**<br>period 4s<br>fl. 1s, ec. 3s | 23<br>**7** | 5 | Green fiberglass tower, white band; 10. | |
| 17138<br>*J 6484* | Isla de Plata. | 10° 15.0′ N<br>64° 34.0′ W | **Fl.R.**<br>period 4s<br>fl. 1s, ec. 3s | 26<br>**8** | 9 | Red hexagonal fiberglass tower, white band; 10. | |
| 17139<br>*J 6485* | Isla Picuda Chica. | 10° 18.5′ N<br>64° 33.7′ W | **Fl.W.**<br>period 7s<br>fl. 1s, ec. 6s | 131<br>**40** | 11 | Orange hexagonal fiberglass tower, white band; 20. | |
| 17140<br>*J 6481* | Isla Chimana Segunda, W. end. | 10° 17.5′ N<br>64° 36.4′ W | **Fl.W.**<br>period 10s<br>fl. 1s, ec. 9s | 164<br>**50** | 11 | Orange truncated conical fiberglass tower, white band; 39. | |
| 17141<br>*J 6488* | **Cumana Landfall.** | 10° 27.9′ N<br>64° 10.0′ W | **Fl.W.**<br>period 12s<br>fl. 1.5s, ec. 10.5s | 200<br>**61** | **25** | Orange fiberglass framework tower, white band; 39. | |
| 17142<br>*J 6487* | Cumana, Puerto Sucre, pier, head. | 10° 27.6′ N<br>64° 11.7′ W | **Fl.W.**<br>period 5s<br>fl. 1s, ec. 4s | 20<br>**6** | 11 | Orange hexagonal fiberglass tower, white band; 10. | |
| 17144<br>*J 6489* | -Punta Arena. | 10° 30.9′ N<br>64° 14.6′ W | **Fl.W.**<br>period 12s | 135<br>**41** | 11 | Orange hexagonal fiberglass tower, white band; 39. | |
| 17148<br>*J 6490* | Morro de Chacopata. | 10° 42.5′ N<br>63° 48.7′ W | **Fl.W.**<br>period 15s<br>fl. 1s, ec. 14s | 187<br>**57** | 11 | Orange hexagonal fiberglass structure, white band; 33. | |
| | ISLA DE MARGARITA: | | | | | | |
| 17152<br>*J 6508* | -Punta Mosquito. | 10° 53.2′ N<br>63° 53.7′ W | **Fl.W.**<br>period 6s<br>fl. 0.5s, ec. 5.5s | 98<br>**30** | 14 | Orange fiberglass tower, white band; 39. | R. lights mark mast 7 miles NNW. |
| | -RACON | | **M(– –)** | 98<br>**30** | **19** | | |
| 17153<br>*J 6508.5* | Isla Los Frailes. | 11° 11.8′ N<br>63° 44.0′ W | **Fl.W.**<br>period 15s<br>fl. 1s, ec. 14s | 525<br>**160** | 13 | Orange fiberglass tower, white band; 39. | |
| | RACON | | **K(– • –)** | 525<br>**160** | 13 | | |
| 17153.6<br>*J 6508.8* | -Isla Sola. | 11° 18.8′ N<br>63° 34.3′ W | **Fl.W.**<br>period 8s<br>fl. 0.5s, ec. 7.5s | 33<br>**10** | 5 | Orange pole, white band; 10. | |
| 17154<br>*J 6503* | -La Puntilla. | 10° 57.0′ N<br>63° 50.9′ W | **Fl.W.**<br>period 10s<br>fl. 1.5s, ec. 8.5s | 66<br>**20** | 11 | Red masonry tower, white band; 49. | |
| 17155<br>*J 6502.5* | -Isla Blanca. | 10° 57.9′ N<br>63° 47.5′ W | **Fl.W.**<br>period 4s<br>fl. 0.8s, ec. 3.2s | 72<br>**22** | 6 | Orange round fiberglass tower, white band; 10. | |
| 17155.5<br>*J 6502.25* | **-Punta Ballena.** | 10° 59.8′ N<br>63° 46.6′ W | **Fl.W.**<br>period 10s<br>fl. 1s, ec. 9s | 249<br>**76** | **30** | Orange hexagonal stone tower, white band; 33. | |
| 17156<br>*J 6504* | -AVIATION LIGHT. | 10° 54.5′ N<br>63° 57.8′ W | **Al.Fl.W.G.**<br>period 10s | | | Tower. | |

| (1) No. | (2) Name and Location | (3) Position | (4) Characteristic | (5) Height | (6) Range | (7) Structure | (8) Remarks |
|---|---|---|---|---|---|---|---|
| | | | **VENEZUELA** | | | | |
| 17160 *J 6502* | **-Cabo de la Isla.** | 11° 10.5′ N 63° 53.0′ W | **Fl.W.** period 5s fl. 1s, ec. 4s | 230 **70** | **19** | Orange hexagonal fiberglass tower, white band; 39. | |
| 17161 *J 6502.1* | -El Tirano. | 11° 07.0′ N 63° 50.6′ W | **Fl.W.** period 6s fl. 1s, ec. 5s | 49 **15** | 11 | Orange fiberglass tower, white band; 39. | |
| 17162 *J 6501* | **-Punta Faragoza.** | 11° 07.6′ N 63° 56.0′ W | **Fl.W.** period 8s fl. 1s, ec. 7s | 279 **85** | **20** | Orange concrete tower, white band; 75. | |
| 17162.1 *J 6500.8* | -Ensenada La Guardia. | 11° 03.0′ N 64° 00.9′ W | **Fl.W.** period 8s | 39 **12** | 14 | | |
| 17162.3 *J 6499* | -Punta Tigre. | 11° 04.9′ N 64° 13.0′ W | **Fl.W.** period 12s fl. 1.2s, ec. 10.8s | 39 **12** | 11 | Orange round fiberglass tower, white band; 39. | |
| 17162.5 *J 6500.6* | -Punta Manglillo. | 10° 57.7′ N 64° 21.1′ W | **Fl.W.** period 10s fl. 0.8s, ec. 9.2s | 39 **12** | 11 | Orange round fiberglass tower, white band; 39. | |
| 17163 *J 6500.1* | Robledal, Muelle Pesquero. | 11° 01.5′ N 64° 22.5′ W | **Fl.W.** period 5s fl. 1s, ec. 4s | 20 **6** | 5 | Orange hexagonal fiberglass tower, white band; 10. | |
| 17164 *J 6500* | **-Morro de Robledal.** | 11° 02.6′ N 64° 23.0′ W | **Fl.W.** period 8s fl. 1s, ec. 7s | 262 **80** | **19** | Orange hexagonal fiberglass tower, white band; 10. | |
| 17167 | -Punta Mangle. | 10° 51.8′ N 64° 04.1′ W | **Fl.R.** period 3s fl. 0.7s, ec. 2.3s | 13 **4** | 3 | STARBOARD (B) R, metal tower. | |
| | ISLA CUBAGUA: | | | | | | |
| 17168 *J 6492* | -Punta Palanquete. | 10° 49.9′ N 64° 12.6′ W | **Fl.W.** period 8s fl. 1s, ec. 7s | 43 **13** | 11 | Orange round fiberglass tower, white band; 39. | |
| | -RACON | | **G(– – •)** | 46 **14** | 11 | | |
| 17172 *J 6494* | -Punta Charagato, NE. extremity. | 10° 50.4′ N 64° 09.4′ W | **Fl.W.** period 12s fl. 1s, ec. 11s | 49 **15** | 11 | Orange fiberglass tower, white band; 39. | |
| 17184 *J 6510* | **Carupano.** | 10° 40.3′ N 63° 14.9′ W | **Fl.W.** period 9s fl. 1.5s, ec. 7.5s | 673 **205** | **25** | Gray metal framework tower; 3. | |
| 17188 *J 6512* | Hernan Vasquez breakwater, head. | 10° 40.7′ N 63° 14.7′ W | **Fl.W.** period 4s fl. 1s, ec. 3s | 26 **8** | 9 | Green fiberglass tower, white band; 20. | |
| 17190 *J 6509.8* | **Puerto Santo.** | 10° 43.6′ N 63° 10.0′ W | **Fl.W.** period 12s fl. 1s, ec. 11s | 131 **40** | **15** | Orange fiberglass framework tower, white band; 39. | |
| 17192 *J 6509* | **Isla Testigo Grande.** | 11° 22.9′ N 63° 07.2′ W | **Fl.W.** period 10s fl. 1s, ec. 9s | 1460 **445** | **23** | White fiberglass framework tower, orange band; 10. | |
| | RACON | | **Z(– – • •)** | 1450 **442** | **20** | | |
| 17192.5 *J 6509.1* | -Los Testigos. | 11° 22.4′ N 63° 07.8′ W | **Fl.G.** period 4s fl. 1s, ec. 3s | 26 **8** | 4 | Green fiberglass tower, white band; 10. | |
| 17193 *J 6509.2* | Isla Iguana. | 11° 21.8′ N 63° 07.9′ W | **Fl.R.** period 4s fl. 1s, ec. 3s | 30 **9** | 4 | Red fiberglass tower, white band. | |
| 17194 *J 6514* | **Cabo Tres Puntas.** | 10° 45.8′ N 62° 42.9′ W | **Fl.W.** period 5s fl. 1s, ec. 4s | 656 **200** | **19** | Orange fiberglass tower, white band; 30. | |

| (1)<br>No. | (2)<br>Name and Location | (3)<br>Position | (4)<br>Characteristic | (5)<br>Height | (6)<br>Range | (7)<br>Structure | (8)<br>Remarks |
|---|---|---|---|---|---|---|---|
| | | | **VENEZUELA** | | | | |
| 17195<br>*J 6515* | Punta Mejillones. | 10° 42.2′ N<br>62° 08.4′ W | **Fl.W.**<br>period 12s<br>fl. 1.2s, ec. 10.8s | 141<br>**43** | 12 | Orange fiberglass tower, white band; 39. | |
| 17195.5<br>*J 6516* | -Promontorio de Paria. | 10° 44.1′ N<br>61° 51.0′ W | **Fl.W.**<br>period 15s | 246<br>**75** | 11 | Orange fiberglass tower, white band; 39. | |
| | GULF OF PARIA: | | | | | | |
| 17196<br>*J 6518* | -Macuro. | 10° 39.3′ N<br>61° 56.6′ W | **Fl.W.**<br>period 4s<br>fl. 1s, ec. 3s | 249<br>**76** | 11 | Orange fiberglass tower, white band; 20. | |
| 17200<br>*J 6517* | **-Isla de Patos.** | 10° 38.3′ N<br>61° 52.0′ W | **Fl.W.**<br>period 5s<br>fl. 1s, ec. 4s | 374<br>**114** | **20** | Orange metal framework tower, white band; 39. | Q.R. marks platform 15 miles S. |
| | -RACON | | **P(• – – •)** | 374<br>**114** | **20** | | |
| 17204<br>*J 6521* | Puerto de Hierro. | 10° 38.0′ N<br>62° 05.8′ W | **Fl.W.**<br>period 6s<br>fl. 1s, ec. 5s | 213<br>**65** | 11 | Orange fiberglass tower, white band; 39. | |
| 17210<br>*J 6524* | **-Recalada Guiria.** | 10° 34.8′ N<br>62° 17.5′ W | **Fl.W.**<br>period 10s<br>fl. 1s, ec. 9s | 207<br>**63** | **23** | Orange masonry tower, white band; 108. | |
| 17212<br>*J 6525* | -Guiria E. breakwater, S. extremity. | 10° 33.9′ N<br>62° 17.3′ W | **Fl.R.**<br>period 9s<br>fl. 1s, ec. 8s | 33<br>**10** | 8 | Red round concrete tower, white band; 26. | F.R. lights on radio tower 0.9 mile N. |
| 17216<br>*J 6526* | --S. breakwater, E. extremity. | 10° 34.0′ N<br>62° 17.4′ W | **Fl.G.**<br>period 9s<br>fl. 1s, ec. 8s | 16<br>**5** | 4 | Green round concrete tower, white band; 13. | |
| | -Rio San Juan: | | | | | | |
| 17224<br>*J 6530.3* | --No. 1. | 10° 18.5′ N<br>62° 29.2′ W | **Fl.G.**<br>period 4s | | | | |
| 17227<br>*J 6615* | Isla Cotorra. | 10° 03.2′ N<br>62° 14.5′ W | **Fl.W.**<br>period 15s<br>fl. 1s, ec. 14s | 46<br>**14** | 11 | Orange fiberglass framework tower, white band; 39. | |
| 17230<br>*J 5912.5* | ***Serpents Mouth,*** *storage vessel.* | 9° 56.5′ N<br>61° 34.8′ W | **Fl.W.**<br>period 10s<br>fl. 1s, ec. 9s | 174<br>**53** | **20** | Yellow fiberglass tower; 10. | |
| | RACON | | **F(• • – •)** | 174<br>**53** | **25** | | (3 & 10cm). |
| 17240 | *Rio Orinoco Approach Lighted Buoy O.1.* | 8° 56.1′ N<br>60° 11.0′ W | **Fl.W.**<br>period 10s<br>fl. 1s, ec. 9s | | 4 | SAFE WATER<br>RW, pillar. | **Radar reflector.** |
| | RACON | | **O(– – –)** | | 14 | | |
| 17242<br>*J 6800* | **Punta Barima.** | 8° 35.1′ N<br>60° 25.0′ W | **Fl.W.**<br>period 10s<br>fl. 1s, ec. 9s | 79<br>**24** | **15** | Orange fiberglass tower, white band; 49. | |
| | RACON | | **A(• –)** | 79<br>**24** | **20** | | (3 & 10cm). |
| | | | **GUYANA** | | | | |
| 17244<br>*J 6810* | Waini Point. | 8° 27.5′ N<br>59° 47.5′ W | **Fl.W.**<br>period 12s | | 11 | Metal tower on platform. | Passage upstream marked by lights. |

| (1) No. | (2) Name and Location | (3) Position | (4) Characteristic | (5) Height | (6) Range | (7) Structure | (8) Remarks |
|---|---|---|---|---|---|---|---|

## GUYANA

| (1) No. | (2) Name and Location | (3) Position | (4) Characteristic | (5) Height | (6) Range | (7) Structure | (8) Remarks |
|---|---|---|---|---|---|---|---|
| | ESSEQUIBO RIVER: | | | | | | |
| 17278 *J 6836* | -Middle Ground. | 6° 54.6´ N 58° 22.2´ W | **Fl.W.** period 10s | 30 **9** | 10 | White framework tower on platform. | |
| | DEMERARA RIVER: | | | | | | |
| 17292 *J 6841* | **-Georgetown.** | 6° 49.4´ N 58° 09.9´ W | **Fl.W.R.** period 60s | 103 **31** | **16** | White hexadecagonal tower, red stripes; 98. | R. 275°-040°, W.-275°. |
| 17296 *J 6843* | -Range, front. | 6° 49.7´ N 58° 10.5´ W | **Q.W.** | 46 **14** | **20** | Metal tower on platform. | |
| 17300 *J 6843.1* | --Rear, 1630 meters 225° from front. | 6° 49.1´ N 58° 11.1´ W | **Fl.(2)W.** period 4s | 66 **20** | **20** | Metal tower on platform, diamond daymark. | |
| 17309 *J 6847* | -Range, front. | 6° 46.2´ N 58° 10.7´ W | **Q.W.** | 19 **6** | | | |
| 17310 *J 6847.1* | --Rear, 610 yards 189° from front. | 6° 46.0´ N 58° 10.7´ W | **Oc.W.** period 6s | 49 **15** | | | |
| | BERBICE RIVER: | | | | | | |
| 17324 *J 6858* | -River entrance Range, front. | 6° 20.8´ N 57° 31.4´ W | **Q.W.** | 43 **13** | 6 | Metal tower on platform. | |
| 17328 *J 6858.1* | --Rear, 1.4 km. 216° from front. | 6° 20.2´ N 57° 31.9´ W | **Fl.(2)W.** period 4s | 59 **18** | 6 | Metal tower on platform, diamond daymark. | |
| 17329 *J 6858.5* | -Crab Island Range, front. | 6° 21.7´ N 57° 31.3´ W | **Q.W.** | 30 **9** | 9 | | |
| 17330 *J 6858.51* | --Rear, 1.6 km. 003° from front. | 6° 22.6´ N 57° 31.3´ W | **Q.W.** | 36 **11** | 9 | Pile. | |
| 17332 *J 6862* | Corentyn River, Springlands, wharf, head. | 5° 53.8´ N 57° 08.9´ W | **Fl.W.** period 10s | 45 **14** | 12 | Metal framework tower. | 2 F.R. on radio mast 0.7 mile SSW. |

## SURINAME

| (1) No. | (2) Name and Location | (3) Position | (4) Characteristic | (5) Height | (6) Range | (7) Structure | (8) Remarks |
|---|---|---|---|---|---|---|---|
| 17352 *J 6864.4* | **-Nickerie River** AVIATION LIGHT. | 5° 56.9´ N 56° 59.5´ W | **F.R.** | 295 **90** | **23** | Mast. | Obstruction. **Aero Radiobeacon.** |
| 17353 *J 6866* | --N1. | 5° 58.2´ N 57° 01.0´ W | **Fl.R.** period 3s | | | Red beacon. | |
| 17354 | --N4. | 5° 59.7´ N 57° 00.7´ W | **Iso.G.** period 4s | | | | |
| 17355 *J 6866.5* | --N6. | 5° 59.0´ N 57° 00.8´ W | **Iso.G.** period 8s | | | Pole. | |
| 17358 *J 6867.2* | **Totness** AVIATION LIGHT. | 5° 53.2´ N 56° 20.1´ W | **Oc.R.** | 299 **91** | **23** | Mast. | Obstruction. |
| 17360 *J 6868* | **Coppename River** AVIATION LIGHT. | 5° 47.3´ N 55° 53.6´ W | **F.R.** | 299 **91** | **24** | Mast. | Obstruction. |
| 17364 *J 6870* | **Entrance.** | 5° 53.5´ N 55° 12.9´ W | **Oc.W.** period 10s | 161 **49** | **15** | Mast. | |
| | SURINAME RIVER: | | | | | | |
| 17368 *J 6870.6* | -Approach. | 5° 57.4´ N 55° 13.0´ W | **Fl.(2)W.** period 15s | 23 **7** | 10 | White beacon. | River marked by buoys and lights. **Radiobeacon** 7.5 miles SSE. |

| (1) No. | (2) Name and Location | (3) Position | (4) Characteristic | (5) Height | (6) Range | (7) Structure | (8) Remarks |
|---|---|---|---|---|---|---|---|
| | | | **SURINAME** | | | | |
| 17370 *J 6870.7* | -R6. | 5° 55.2′ N 55° 08.4′ W | **Iso.G.** period 8s | | | | |
| 17376 *J 6878.9* | **-Paramaribo** AVIATION LIGHT. | 5° 49.8′ N 55° 09.2′ W | **Oc.R.** | 253 **77** | **23** | Mast. | Obstruction. |
| 17388 *J 6873* | -Range, front. | 5° 54.4′ N 55° 06.6′ W | **Fl.R.** period 2s | 16 **5** | 6 | Red hut on piles, red diamond daymark, white bands. | |
| 17392 *J 6873.1* | --Rear, 227 meters 332°30′ from front. | 5° 54.6′ N 55° 06.7′ W | **Fl.W.** period 5s | 29 **9** | 6 | Pyramidal tower on piles, red diamond daymark, white bands. | |
| 17399.4 *J 6879.9* | -D8. | 5° 45.0′ N 55° 07.4′ W | **Iso.G.** period 4s | | | | |
| 17399.6 *J 6879.4* | -D1. | 5° 44.1′ N 55° 06.8′ W | **Iso.R.** period 8s | | | Red beacon. | |
| 17399.8 *J 6880* | -D10. | 5° 44.2′ N 55° 06.7′ W | **Iso.G.** period 8s | | | | |
| | | | **FRENCH GUIANA** | | | | |
| | ILES DU SALUT: | | | | | | |
| 17416 *J 6894* | **-Ile Royale.** | 5° 17.2′ N 52° 35.5′ W | **Fl.(2)W.** period 10s fl. 0.4s, ec. 2.1s fl. 0.4s, ec. 7.1s | 213 **65** | **25** | Red tower; 95. | |
| 17420 *J 6895* | --E. jetty, head, front. | 5° 17.1′ N 52° 35.2′ W | **F.G.** | 26 **8** | 11 | White tower, green bands; 23. | Visible 053°30′-071°30′. |
| 17424 *J 6895.1* | --SE. point, rear, about 150 meters 062°30′ from front. | 5° 17.1′ N 52° 35.1′ W | **F.G.** | 33 **10** | 11 | White tower, green band; 13. | Visible 053°30′-071°30′. |
| 17428 *J 6901* | L'Enfant Perdu, on rock, 11.1 kilometers 355° from Cayenne. | 5° 02.5′ N 52° 21.3′ W | **Fl.W.** period 4s fl. 1s, ec. 3s | 56 **17** | 11 | White truncated conical tower, red top; 49. | Reserve light F.W. |
| 17432 | *Riviere de Cayenne Entrance Buoy CA.* | 4° 56.8′ N 52° 20.2′ W | **Iso.W.** period 4s | | | SAFE WATER RW, pillar, topmark. | **Radar reflector.** |
| | CAYENNE: | | | | | | |
| 17436 *J 6902* | **-Fort Ceperou.** | 4° 56.3′ N 52° 20.2′ W | **Fl.(2+1)W.R.** period 15s fl. 1s, ec. 1.5s fl. 1s, ec. 5.2s fl. 1s, ec. 5.2s | 131 **40** | W. **16** R. 13 | White column, red top; 30. | W. 318°-166°, R.-175°, W.-228°. Reserve light range R. 7M 166°-175°, W. 10M -166°. F.R. on radio masts close NE. and S., on radio tower 2.1 miles E., and on water towers 3.6 miles ESE. and 2.4 miles SE. |
| 17440 *J 6904* | -Cheval Blanc. | 4° 55.6′ N 52° 20.7′ W | **Q.R.** | 39 **12** | 5 | White pylon, red top. | |
| | RIVIERE DE MAHURY: | | | | | | |
| 17448 | *-Entrance Buoy DC.* | 4° 57.0′ N 52° 10.0′ W | **L.Fl.W.** period 10s | | | SAFE WATER RW, pillar, topmark. | **Whistle.** |

| (1) No. | (2) Name and Location | (3) Position | (4) Characteristic | (5) Height | (6) Range | (7) Structure | (8) Remarks |
|---|---|---|---|---|---|---|---|
| | | | **FRENCH GUIANA** | | | | |
| 17455.5<br>*J 6907.3* | --D20. | 4° 51.0´ N<br>52° 14.8´ W | **V.Q.W.** | 13<br>**4** | 2 | N. CARDINAL BY, topmark. | |
| | | | **Dir.W.R.G.** | 13<br>**4** | W. **18**<br>R. **15**<br>G. 14 | | F.R. 218°46.2′-219°28.2′, Al.W.R.-220°22.2′, F.W.-220°40.2′, Al.W.G.-221°34.2′, F.G.-222°16.2′. |
| 17456.5<br>*J 7000* | -Naval Base, E. head. | 4° 51.1´ N<br>52° 16.0´ W | **Oc.(2)W.**<br>period 6s<br>lt. 3s, ec. 1s<br>lt. 1s, ec. 1s | 36<br>**11** | 7 | Mast. | |
| 17456.6<br>*J 7000.1* | --W. head. | 4° 51.1´ N<br>52° 16.0´ W | **Oc.(2)W.**<br>period 6s<br>lt. 3s, ec. 1s<br>lt. 1s, ec. 1s | 36<br>**11** | 7 | Mast. | |
| 17456.7<br>*J 7000.8* | --E. dolphin. | 4° 51.1´ N<br>52° 16.0´ W | **Fl.(3)W.**<br>period 12s<br>fl. 0.5s, ec. 2s<br>fl. 0.5s, ec. 2s<br>fl. 0.5s, ec. 6.5s | 13<br>**4** | | | |
| 17456.8<br>*J 7000.9* | --W. dolphin. | 4° 51.1´ N<br>52° 16.0´ W | **Fl.(3)W.**<br>period 12s<br>fl. 0.5s, ec. 2s<br>fl. 0.5s, ec. 2s<br>fl. 0.5s, ec. 6.5s | 13<br>**4** | | | |

| (1) No. | (2) Name and Location | (3) Position | (4) Characteristic | (5) Height | (6) Range | (7) Structure | (8) Remarks |
|---|---|---|---|---|---|---|---|
| | | | **BRAZIL** | | | | |
| 17458 *G 0000.5* | **Cabo Orange.** | 4° 26.0´ N 51° 32.2´ W | **Fl.(2)W.** period 15s fl. 1s, ec. 3s fl. 1s, ec. 10s | 164 **50** | **18** | White four-sided metal framework tower; 154. Helicopter platform. | Visible 035°-255°. |
| 17460 *G 0001* | Rio Calcoene, S. side of entrance. | 2° 30.4´ N 50° 48.4´ W | **Fl.W.** period 3s fl. 0.5s, ec. 2.5s | 79 **24** | 13 | White four-sided metal framework structure; 66. | |
| 17464 *G 0002* | Amapa AVIATION LIGHT. | 2° 04.6´ N 50° 51.6´ W | **Al.Fl.W.G.** | 98 **30** | | White metal framework structure, red and white bands. | |
| | RIO AMAZONAS: | | | | | | |
| 17470 *G 0004* | **-Guara.** | 1° 11.3´ N 49° 54.0´ W | **Fl.W.** period 6s fl. 1s, ec. 5s | 144 **44** | **16** | White four-sided truncated pyramidal metal framework structure; 138. | |
| | -RACON | | **Q(– – • –)** | | **25** | | (3 & 10cm). |
| 17472 *G 0005* | -Bailique. | 0° 59.4´ N 49° 56.8´ W | **Fl.W.** period 10s fl. 1s, ec. 9s | 135 **41** | 14 | White four-sided truncated pyramidal metal framework structure, daymarks; 128. | |
| | -RACON | | **M(– –)** | | **25** | | (3 & 10cm). |
| 17474 *G 0005.5* | **-Ilha do Para.** | 0° 52.8´ N 49° 59.2´ W | **Fl.(3)W.** period 10s fl. 1s, ec. 1s fl. 1s, ec. 1s fl. 1s, ec. 5s | 108 **33** | **16** | White four-sided metal framework tower, daymarks; 98. | |
| | -RACON | | **B(– • • •)** | | **20** | | (3 & 10cm). |
| 17480 *G 0006.5* | -Ponta do Ceu. | 0° 45.6´ N 50° 07.0´ W | **Fl.W.** period 6s fl. 0.5s, ec. 5.5s | 36 **11** | 9 | White four-sided truncated pyramidal metal framework structure; 30. | |
| 17484 *G 0006.8* | -Ponta do Santarem. | 0° 38.8´ N 50° 05.7´ W | **Fl.(2)W.** period 15s fl. 1s, ec. 3s fl. 1s, ec. 10s | 43 **13** | 12 | White four-sided truncated pyramidal metal framework structure; 36. | |
| | -RACON | | **Y(– • – –)** | | **20** | | (3 & 10cm). |
| 17488 *G 0006.9* | Taia. | 0° 39.2´ N 50° 17.6´ W | **Fl.(3)W.** period 12s fl. 0.5s, ec. 1.5s fl. 0.5s, ec. 1.5s fl. 0.5s, ec. 7.5s | 43 **13** | 10 | White four-sided truncated pyramidal metal framework structure; 36. | |
| 17496 *G 0007.4* | **-Espirito Santo.** | 0° 15.6´ N 50° 31.4´ W | **L.Fl.W.** period 15s fl. 2s, ec. 13s | 79 **24** | **16** | White four-sided truncated pyramidal metal framework structure; 72. | **Radar reflector.** |
| 17500 *G 0007.5* | -Pau Cavado. | 0° 11.5´ N 50° 47.2´ W | **Fl.W.** period 6s fl. 0.5s, ec. 5.5s | 154 **47** | 11 | White four-sided truncated pyramidal metal framework structure; 148. | |
| | -RACON | | **X(– • • –)** | | **25** | | (3 & 10cm). |
| 17504 *G 0007.7* | -Fugitivo, on N. bank. | 0° 10.2´ N 50° 55.1´ W | **Fl.(2)W.** period 12s fl. 1s, ec. 2s fl. 1s, ec. 8s | 43 **13** | 12 | White four-sided metal structure; 36. | |
| 17510 *G 0008.4* | -Water tower. | 0° 02.2´ N 51° 03.3´ W | **F.W.R.** | | | | Private light. |

| (1) No. | (2) Name and Location | (3) Position | (4) Characteristic | (5) Height | (6) Range | (7) Structure | (8) Remarks |
|---|---|---|---|---|---|---|---|
| | | | **BRAZIL** | | | | |
| 17511 *G 0008.5* | -Macapa, SW. Water tower. | 0° 01.4´ N 51° 03.6´ W | **F.R.** | | | | Private light. |
| 17512 *G 0009* | -Cascalheira. | 0° 01.4´ S 51° 03.7´ W | **Fl.(2)W.** period 10s fl. 0.5s, ec. 1.5s fl. 0.5s, ec. 7.5s | 43 **13** | 10 | White four-sided truncated pyramidal metal framework tower; 36. | |
| 17528 *G 0010.6* | --E. bank. | 0° 04.1´ S 51° 07.9´ W | **Fl.(3)W.** period 10s fl. 0.5s, ec. 1s fl. 0.5s, ec. 1s fl. 0.5s, ec. 6.5s | 33 **10** | 6 | White four-sided metal framework tower on metal structure; 26. | |
| 17530 *G 0010.7* | -Porto de Santana. | 0° 03.5´ S 51° 10.6´ W | **F.Y.** | | 2 | Hulk. | |
| 17534 *G 0011.5* | **Camaleao.** | 0° 09.2´ S 48° 54.6´ W | **L.Fl.W.** period 15s fl. 2s, ec. 13s | 121 **37** | **16** | White four-sided truncated pyramidal metal framework tower; 115. | |
| 17536 *G 0012* | Ilha do Machadinho. | 0° 10.8´ S 48° 45.9´ W | **Fl.W.** period 10s fl. 1s, ec. 9s | 75 **23** | 11 | White four-sided truncated pyramidal metal framework structure; 66. | Visible 256°-143°. |
| | RIO DO PARA: | | | | | | |
| 17540 *G 0014* | **-Simao Grande.** | 0° 15.4´ S 48° 24.1´ W | **Fl.W.** period 5s fl. 0.5s, ec. 4.5s | 138 **42** | **16** | White four-sided truncated pyramidal metal framework tower, diamond daymark; 131. | Visible 138°-320°. |
| | -RACON | | **O(– – –)** | | **25** | | (3 & 10cm). |
| 17548 *G 0018* | **-Ponta Tijoca.** | 0° 33.4´ S 47° 53.9´ W | **Fl.(2)W.** period 10s fl. 0.5s, ec. 1s fl. 0.5s, ec. 8s | 115 **35** | **18** | Four-sided metal framework tower, red and white bands; 16. | Visible 085°-265°. |
| | -RACON | | **B(– • • •)** | | 14 | | (3 & 10cm). |
| 17550 *G 0019* | -Coroa das Gaivotas. | 0° 34.7´ S 48° 01.9´ W | **Fl.G.** period 10s fl. 1s, ec. 9s | 26 **8** | 8 | Metal pipe, green and white bands; 26. | |
| 17552 *G 0020* | **-Taipu.** | 0° 39.7´ S 48° 02.6´ W | **Fl.(3)W.** period 15s fl. 0.5s, ec. 1s fl. 0.5s, ec. 1s fl. 0.5s, ec. 11.5s | 128 **39** | **16** | White four-sided truncated pyramidal metal framework tower, white diamond daymark; 98. | |
| 17556 *G 0021* | **-Ponta Maria Teresa.** | 0° 46.6´ S 48° 09.1´ W | **Fl.W.** period 6s fl. 1s, ec. 5s | 138 **42** | **15** | White four-sided metal lattice tower, daymark; 131. | Visible 057°-221°. |
| 17560 *G 0021.5* | **-Soure.** | 0° 44.5´ S 48° 30.4´ W | **Fl.(2)W.** period 10s fl. 1s, ec. 1s fl. 1s, ec. 7s | 114 **35** | **16** | Four-sided concrete tower, red and white bands; 98. | |
| 17562 *G 0022* | -Ilha dos Amores, Salvaterra. | 0° 45.2´ S 48° 30.5´ W | **Fl.W.** period 3s fl. 0.5s, ec. 2.5s | 46 **14** | 5 | White four-sided truncated pyramidal metal framework structure, daymark; 26. | |
| 17564 *G 0024* | -Joanes, on Ponta da Guarita. | 0° 52.9´ S 48° 30.5´ W | **Fl.W.** period 10s fl. 1s, ec. 9s | 75 **23** | 14 | White four-sided truncated pyramidal metal framework tower, daymark; 56. | |
| 17568 *G 0028* | -Colares. | 0° 55.1´ S 48° 17.5´ W | **Fl.(2)W.** period 6s fl. 0.5s, ec. 1s fl. 0.5s, ec. 4s | 46 **14** | 10 | White metal pipe, concrete base, white diamond daymark; 33. | |
| 17572 *G 0029* | -Banco Coroa Grande. | 1° 01.7´ S 48° 35.8´ W | **Fl.(3)W.** period 12s fl. 0.5s, ec. 1.5s fl. 0.5s, ec. 1.5s fl. 0.5s, ec. 7.5s | 59 **18** | 10 | White round metal structure; 36. | Visible 255°-031°. |

| (1) No. | (2) Name and Location | (3) Position | (4) Characteristic | (5) Height | (6) Range | (7) Structure | (8) Remarks |
|---|---|---|---|---|---|---|---|

**BRAZIL**

| | | | | | | | |
|---|---|---|---|---|---|---|---|
| 17576 *G 0030* | -Ponta do Chapeu Virado, SW. extremity. | 1° 08.1′ S 48° 28.2′ W | **Iso.G.** period 2s | 36 **11** | 13 | White metal pipe, concrete base, white diamond daymark, red bands; 33. | |
| 17584 *G 0034* | -Ilha Tatuoca. | 1° 12.0′ S 48° 30.4′ W | **Q.(2)W.** period 6s | 39 **12** | 9 | White four-sided truncated pyramidal metal framework structure, daymark; 36. | Visible 081°-301°. |
| 17588 *G 0036* | -Ilha Cotejuba, SW. side of island. | 1° 16.0′ S 48° 33.8′ W | **Fl.W.** period 6s fl. 0.5s, ec. 5.5s | 33 **10** | 9 | White metal pipe, concrete base, white diamond daymarks; 26. | Visible 334°-147°. |
| 17589 *G 0035.2* | -Ilha das Barreiras, W. mole, head. | 1° 16.5′ S 48° 29.3′ W | **F.G.** | | | | Private light. |
| 17590 *G 0035.3* | --E. mole, head. | 1° 16.3′ S 48° 29.1′ W | **Q.G.** | | | | Private light. |
| 17592 *G 0038* | -Forte de Barra. | 1° 22.7′ S 48° 29.6′ W | **Q.W.** | 43 **13** | 9 | White four-sided truncated pyramidal concrete tower, daymark; 39. | Forms range 028°30′ with chimney 1.6 miles NNE. |
| 17596 *G 0039* | -Val de Caes AVIATION LIGHT. | 1° 23.3′ S 48° 28.8′ W | **Al.Fl.W.G.** | | | Metal framework structure, red and white bands; 56. | |
| 17597 *G 0040* | -Cais de Oleo. | 1° 24.2′ S 48° 29.7′ W | **F.Y.** | | | Yellow metal post. | Private light. |
| 17598 *G 0041* | -Trapiche. | 1° 24.6′ S 48° 29.7′ W | **F.Y.** | | | | Private light. |
| 17598.5 *G 0041.8* | --Pontoon. | 1° 27.2′ S 48° 30.3′ W | **F.Y.** | | | | |
| 17599 *G 0042.3* | **-Belem.** | 1° 27.9′ S 48° 30.3′ W | **Fl.W.** period 20s fl. 0.5s, ec. 19.5s | 148 **45** | **15** | Four-sided metal tower; 138. | |
| 17599.3 *G 0042.05* | -Belem Pontoon. | 1° 28.6′ S 48° 29.8′ W | **F.Y.** | | | | |
| 17599.6 *G 0042.08* | --Pontoon. | 1° 28.6′ S 48° 29.5′ W | **F.Y.** | | | | |
| 17600 *G 0052* | -Itaguary. | 1° 25.5′ S 48° 49.0′ W | **Fl.W.** period 5s fl. 0.5s, ec. 4.5s | 39 **12** | 9 | White four-sided concrete tower; 39. | |
| 17604 *G 0044* | -Rio Arari, Ilha das Pombas. | 1° 11.5′ S 48° 44.6′ W | **Fl.W.** period 6s fl. 0.5s, ec. 5.5s | 39 **12** | 10 | White metal pipe, concrete base, white diamond daymark; 33. | Visible 230°-350°. |
| 17608 *G 0045* | -Carnapijo. | 1° 21.8′ S 48° 38.9′ W | **Fl.(2)W.** period 10s fl. 1s, ec. 1.5s fl. 1s, ec. 6.5s | 26 **8** | 8 | White metal pipe, concrete base, white diamond daymark; 26. | |
| 17610 *G 0045.4* | Machadinho. | 1° 22.6′ S 48° 38.6′ W | **Fl.(3)W.** period 10s fl. 1s, ec. 1s fl. 1s, ec. 1s fl. 1s, ec. 5s | 26 **8** | 7 | White metal pipe, red bands, concrete base; 16. | |
| 17612 *G 0046* | -Rio Arrozal, E. side of river. | 1° 27.5′ S 48° 42.2′ W | **Q.(2)W.** period 6s | 33 **10** | 10 | White metal pipe, white diamond daymark; 23. | Visible 345°-174°. |
| 17614 *G 0047* | -Boco do Furo. Arrozal. | 1° 27.9′ S 48° 42.6′ W | **Fl.(2)W.** period 5s fl. 0.3s, ec. 0.8s fl. 0.3s, ec. 3.6s | 36 **11** | 9 | ISOLATED DANGER BRB, tower; 26. | |
| 17616 *G 0048* | -Pedra da Manteiga. | 1° 28.5′ S 48° 42.6′ W | **Fl.G.** period 3s fl. 0.3s, ec. 2.7s | 16 **5** | 5 | White four-sided truncated pyramidal concrete tower, diamond daymark; 16. | |
| 17620 *G 0050* | -Ilha do Capim. | 1° 33.3′ S 48° 51.9′ W | **Fl.W.** period 3s fl. 0.3s, ec. 2.7s | 26 **8** | 10 | White metal pipe, diamond daymark; 23. | Visible 066°-246°. |

| (1) No. | (2) Name and Location | (3) Position | (4) Characteristic | (5) Height | (6) Range | (7) Structure | (8) Remarks |
|---|---|---|---|---|---|---|---|
| | | | **BRAZIL** | | | | |
| 17624 *G 0054* | -Ilha Mandi. | 1° 36.7´ S 49° 08.6´ W | **Fl.W.** period 6s fl. 0.5s, ec. 5.5s | 49 **15** | 12 | White four-sided truncated pyramidal metal framework tower, white diamond daymarks; 36. | Visible 228°-039°. |
| 17634 *G 0053.7* | -Ponta do Frechal. | 1° 43.4´ S 49° 16.7´ W | **Fl.G.** period 10s fl. 1s, ec. 9s | 75 **23** | 9 | White four-sided truncated pyramidal metal framework tower, daymark; 66. | |
| 17636 *G 0056* | -Ilha Cameleao, N. side of island. | 1° 49.2´ S 49° 56.8´ W | **Fl.W.** period 3s fl. 0.3s, ec. 2.7s | 43 **13** | 10 | White four-sided truncated pyramidal metal framework tower, white diamond daymarks; 36. | Visible 089°-287°. |
| 17640 *G 0056.5* | -Ilha das Araras. | 1° 48.7´ S 50° 09.2´ W | **Fl.W.** period 6s fl. 0.5s, ec. 5.5s | 43 **13** | 8 | White four-sided metal tower, daymark; 36. | Visible 269°-099°. |
| 17648 *G 0058* | -Boiucu, E. side of island. | 1° 48.5´ S 50° 18.4´ W | **Fl.W.** period 3s fl. 0.3s, ec. 2.7s | 43 **13** | 4 | White metal pipe, white diamond daymark; 33. | Visible 277°-086°. |
| 17652 *G 0062* | **Curuca.** | 0° 33.9´ S 47° 46.0´ W | **Fl.(3)W.** period 15s fl. 1s, ec. 2s fl. 1s, ec. 2s fl. 1s, ec. 8s | 144 **44** | **18** | Four-sided truncated pyramidal metal framework tower, white daymark, red bands; 138. | Visible 105°-238°. |
| 17656 *G 0063* | **Ponta Marapanim.** | 0° 34.8´ S 47° 35.1´ W | **Fl.(2)W.** period 10s fl. 0.5s, ec. 1.5s fl. 0.5s, ec. 7.5s | 112 **34** | **16** | Four-sided truncated pyramidal metal framework tower, white diamond daymark, red bands; 105. | Visible 108°-276°. |
| 17660 *G 0064* | **Salinopolis.** | 0° 36.9´ S 47° 21.4´ W | **Fl.W.** period 6s fl. 1s, ec. 5s | 200 **61** | **46** | Red conical metal framework structure, center column; 128. | **Radiobeacon.** |
| | RACON | | **K(– • –)** | | **25** | | (3 & 10cm). |
| 17662 *G 0065* | **Quatipuru.** | 0° 42.8´ S 46° 57.6´ W | **Fl.(3)W.** period 15s fl. 1s, ec. 2s fl. 1s, ec. 2s fl. 1s, ec. 8s | 89 **27** | **15** | White four-sided truncated pyramidal metal framework tower, red bands, white diamond daymark, red bands; 82. | |
| 17664 *G 0066* | **Caete.** | 0° 49.0´ S 46° 36.9´ W | **Q.(2)W.** period 6s | 66 **20** | **15** | White rectangular metal tower, white diamond daymarks; 52. | |
| 17668 *G 0070* | **Ilha do Apeu.** | 0° 54.7´ S 46° 11.3´ W | **Fl.(2)W.** period 15s fl. 1s, ec. 2s fl. 1s, ec. 11s | 135 **41** | **15** | White four-sided truncated pyramidal metal framework structure, red bands, white diamond daymark, red bands; 125. | |
| 17670 *G 0070.5* | **Ponta da Praia Grande.** | 1° 10.0´ S 45° 38.1´ W | **Fl.(5)W.** period 60s fl. 1s, ec. 9s fl. 1s, ec. 9s fl. 1s, ec. 9s fl. 1s, ec. 9s fl. 1s, ec. 19s | 157 **48** | **24** | White four-sided metal framework tower, daymarks; 148. | |
| 17672 *G 0072* | **Ilha Maiau.** | 1° 16.9´ S 44° 54.2´ W | **L.Fl.W.** period 10s fl. 2s, ec. 8s | 125 **38** | **20** | White cylindrical concrete tower, black bands; 98. | Obscured 311°-shore. |
| | RACON | | **O(– – –)** | | **25** | | (3 & 10cm). |
| 17674 *G 0073* | Ilha Lencois, Ponta do Gino. | 1° 20.8´ S 44° 53.4´ W | **Fl.W.** period 6s fl. 1s, ec. 5s | 23 **7** | 8 | White metal post; 16. | Visible 245°-120°. |
| 17676 *G 0074* | **Ilha do Mangunca.** | 1° 36.9´ S 44° 39.3´ W | **Fl.W.** period 10s fl. 0.2s, ec. 9.8s | 151 **46** | **28** | White four-sided truncated pyramidal metal framework tower; 131. | |

| (1) No. | (2) Name and Location | (3) Position | (4) Characteristic | (5) Height | (6) Range | (7) Structure | (8) Remarks |
|---|---|---|---|---|---|---|---|

**BRAZIL**

| (1) No. | (2) Name and Location | (3) Position | (4) Characteristic | (5) Height | (6) Range | (7) Structure | (8) Remarks |
|---|---|---|---|---|---|---|---|
| 17677<br>*G 0071* | ***Recife Manoel Luis Lightfloat (BF-1).*** | 0° 49.0′ S<br>44° 16.0′ W | **Fl.(3)W.**<br>period 10s<br>fl. 1s, ec. 1s<br>fl. 1s, ec. 1s<br>fl. 1s, ec. 5s | 46<br>**14** | **16** | Red four-sided truncated pyramidal metal framework tower on red hull. | |
| | RACON | | **T(–)** | | 14 | | (3 & 10cm). |
| | BAIA DE SAO MARCOS: | | | | | | |
| 17680<br>*G 0078* | **-Pirajuba.** | 2° 12.7′ S<br>44° 24.2′ W | **Fl.(3)W.**<br>period 15s<br>fl. 1s, ec. 2s<br>fl. 1s, ec. 2s<br>fl. 1s, ec. 8s | 210<br>**64** | **21** | White four-sided truncated pyramidal metal framework tower; 72. | |
| | -RACON | | **Z(– – • •)** | | **25** | | (3 & 10cm). |
| 17684<br>*G 0080* | -Alcantara. | 2° 24.6′ S<br>44° 25.1′ W | **Q.(2)W.**<br>period 6s | 125<br>**38** | 10 | White metal pipe. | |
| 17688<br>*G 0084* | **-Ponta de Sao Marcos.** | 2° 29.3′ S<br>44° 18.1′ W | **Fl.W.**<br>period 10s<br>fl. 1.1s, ec. 8.9s | 118<br>**36** | **23** | White cylindrical masonry tower, white four-sided masonry base; 26. | **Radiobeacon.**<br>**DGPS Station.** |
| 17695<br>*G 0079* | **-Pirarema.** | 2° 20.3′ S<br>44° 21.7′ W | **Fl.W.**<br>period 6s<br>fl. 1s, ec. 5s | 180<br>**55** | **20** | White octagonal masonry tower; 39. | |
| 17696<br>*G 0087* | **-Ilha do Medo.** | 2° 31.3′ S<br>44° 21.9′ W | **Fl.(3)W.**<br>period 15s<br>fl. 0.3s, ec. 2.2s<br>fl. 0.3s, ec. 2.2s<br>fl. 0.3s, ec. 9.7s | 197<br>**60** | **25** | White four-sided metal framework structure, four-sided masonry tower; 102. | |
| 17700<br>*G 0087.2* | -Itauna. | 2° 32.0′ S<br>44° 30.6′ W | **Fl.W.**<br>period 5s<br>fl. 0.5s, ec. 4.5s | 82<br>**25** | 11 | White truncated conical masonry tower. | |
| 17701<br>*G 0087.5* | --N. breakwater, head. | 2° 33.5′ S<br>44° 22.7′ W | **F.Y.** | | | | |
| 17702<br>*G 0087.6* | --S. breakwater, head. | 2° 34.2′ S<br>44° 22.7′ W | **F.Y.** | | | | Private light. |
| 17703.1<br>*G 0087.7* | --Wharf, N. head. | 2° 34.6′ S<br>44° 22.2′ W | **F.Y.** | | | | Private light. |
| 17704<br>*G 0087.4* | -Ilha de Guarapira. | 2° 34.7′ S<br>44° 22.4′ W | **Fl.W.**<br>period 3s<br>fl. 0.3s, ec. 2.7s | 56<br>**17** | 9 | White metal pipe; 20. | Visible 312°-245°. |
| 17708<br>*G 0088* | **-Sao Luis** AVIATION LIGHT, SE. of city. | 2° 35.0′ S<br>44° 14.2′ W | **Al.Fl.W.G.** | 200<br>**61** | **20** | Truncated pyramidal metal framework tower, red and white bands; 46. | Occasional.<br>**Aero Radiobeacon.** |
| 17712<br>*G 0090* | **Ponta do Aracagi.** | 2° 27.0′ S<br>44° 08.9′ W | **Fl.(4)W.**<br>period 10s<br>fl. 0.3s, ec. 1.8s<br>fl. 0.3s, ec. 1.8s<br>fl. 0.3s, ec. 1.8s<br>fl. 0.3s, ec. 3.4s | 299<br>**91** | **33** | Black and white diamond checkered four-sided truncated pyramidal masonry tower; 131. | |
| | RACON | | **Q(– – • –)** | | **25** | | (3 & 10cm). |
| 17713<br>*G 0091* | Papagaio. | 2° 33.7′ S<br>43° 55.7′ W | **Fl.W.**<br>period 6s<br>fl. 0.5s, ec. 5.5s | 98<br>**30** | 9 | White metal post; 16. | |
| 17716<br>*G 0092* | **Ilha de Santana.** | 2° 16.2′ S<br>43° 37.4′ W | **Al.L.Fl.W.W.R.**<br>period 51s<br>W. fl. 6s, ec. 11s<br>W. fl. 6s, ec. 11s<br>R. fl. 6s, ec. 11s | 187<br>**57** | W. **31**<br>R. **25** | White truncated conical masonry tower; 161. | |
| | RACON | | **B(– • • •)** | | **25** | | (3 & 10cm). |

| (1) No. | (2) Name and Location | (3) Position | (4) Characteristic | (5) Height | (6) Range | (7) Structure | (8) Remarks |
|---|---|---|---|---|---|---|---|
| | | | **BRAZIL** | | | | |
| 17718 *G 0093* | **Lencois Grandes.** | 2° 22.8´ S 43° 16.2´ W | **L.Fl.W.** period 15s fl. 2s, ec. 13s | 236 **72** | **17** | Red four-sided truncated pyramidal metal framework structure; 138. | |
| 17720 *G 0094* | **Barra das Prequicas.** | 2° 35.6´ S 42° 42.5´ W | **Fl.W.** period 3s fl. 1s, ec. 2s | 151 **46** | **43** | White truncated conical concrete tower, black bands; 115. | |
| 17724 *G 0097* | Tutoia. | 2° 43.6´ S 42° 22.4´ W | **Fl.W.** period 10s fl. 1s, ec. 9s | 59 **18** | 12 | White four-sided truncated pyramidal metal framework structure, white diamond daymark; 39. | |
| 17728 *G 0098* | Andreza. | 2° 45.8´ S 42° 15.7´ W | **Fl.R.** period 6s fl. 1s, ec. 5s | 79 **24** | 6 | Red triangular pyramidal metal framework tower; 36. | |
| 17736 *G 0102* | Pedra do Sal, on point. | 2° 48.3´ S 41° 43.8´ W | **Fl.W.** period 6s fl. 0.5s, ec. 5.5s | 49 **15** | 10 | White octagonal concrete tower; 46. | **Radiobeacon** about 5 miles S. |
| 17740 *G 0104* | **Luis Correia.** | 2° 54.1´ S 41° 33.4´ W | **Fl.W.** period 5s fl. 1s, ec. 4s | 95 **29** | **15** | White cylindrical fiberglass tower, red band, concrete base; 33. | |
| 17742 *G 0103* | -Molhe de Acesso. | 2° 50.9´ S 41° 38.9´ W | **Fl.G.** period 3s fl. 0.5s, ec. 2.5s | 33 **10** | 5 | White four-sided masonry tower; 10. | |
| 17744 *G 0105* | **Ponta das Almas.** | 2° 53.5´ S 41° 16.3´ W | **Fl.W.** period 10s fl. 1s, ec. 9s | 92 **28** | **16** | White cylindrical fiberglass tower; 30. | |
| 17748 *G 0108* | **Camocim.** | 2° 51.8´ S 40° 51.6´ W | **Fl.(3)W.** period 10s fl. 1s, ec. 1s fl. 1s, ec. 1s fl. 1s, ec. 5s | 66 **20** | **15** | White four-sided masonry tower; 49. | |
| 17756 *G 0110* | **Jericoacoara.** | 2° 47.3´ S 40° 30.0´ W | **L.Fl.W.** period 10s fl. 2s, ec. 8s | 331 **101** | **19** | White four-sided concrete tower, black bands; 20. | |
| 17760 *G 0114* | **Ponta de Itapage.** | 2° 52.3´ S 39° 56.7´ W | **Fl.(2)W.** period 15s fl. 1s, ec. 3s fl. 1s, ec. 10s | 151 **46** | **20** | White four-sided truncated pyramidal metal framework tower, black bands, white daymark, black bands; 141. | |
| | RACON | | **N(– •)** | | **25** | | (3 & 10cm). |
| 17764 *G 0116* | Mundau. | 3° 10.6´ S 39° 21.7´ W | **Fl.W.** period 3s fl. 0.5s, ec. 2.5s | 108 **33** | 14 | White four-sided concrete tower, red bands; 23. | |
| 17766 *G 0117* | **Ponta Paracuru.** | 3° 24.0´ S 39° 00.7´ W | **Fl.W.** period 10s fl. 1s, ec. 9s | 262 **80** | **27** | White four-sided truncated pyramidal metal framework tower, orange bands; 246. | |
| 17766.5 *G 0119* | **Ponta Pecem.** | 3° 33.0´ S 38° 49.1´ W | **Al.Fl.W.W.R.** period 30s W. fl. 1s, ec. 9s W. fl. 1s, ec. 9s R. fl. 1s, ec. 9s | 246 **75** | W. **26** R. **21** | White four-sided truncated pyramidal metal framework tower, red bands; 98. | |
| 17766.7 *G 0119.3* | -Pier, No. 1. | 3° 32.0´ S 38° 48.0´ W | **Fl.R.** period 5s fl. 0.5s, ec. 4.5s | | 6 | Red structure. | |
| 17766.71 *G 0119.4* | --No. 2. | 3° 31.8´ S 38° 47.9´ W | **F.Y.** | | 5 | Metal post; 3. | |
| 17766.73 *G 0119.5* | -Quebra-Mar, SE. | 3° 32.2´ S 38° 47.9´ W | **Fl.Y.** period 6s fl. 0.5s, ec. 5.5s | | 8 | White pyramidal fiberglass tower; 7. | |
| 17766.75 *G 0119.6* | --Center. | 3° 31.9´ S 38° 47.5´ W | **Fl.Y.** period 6s fl. 0.5s, ec. 5.5s | 16 **5** | 8 | White truncated pyramidal fiberglass lattice tower; 7. | |

| (1) No. | (2) Name and Location | (3) Position | (4) Characteristic | (5) Height | (6) Range | (7) Structure | (8) Remarks |
|---|---|---|---|---|---|---|---|

## BRAZIL

| (1) No. | (2) Name and Location | (3) Position | (4) Characteristic | (5) Height | (6) Range | (7) Structure | (8) Remarks |
|---|---|---|---|---|---|---|---|
| 17766.77<br>*G 0119.7* | --NW. | 3° 31.6′ S<br>38° 47.8′ W | **Fl.G.**<br>period 6s<br>fl. 0.5s, ec. 5.5s | 16<br>**5** | 6 | White truncated pyramidal fiberglass lattice tower; 7. | |
| 17767<br>*G 0121.4* | Marina, N. breakwater. | 3° 43.0′ S<br>38° 31.6′ W | **F.G.** | | | | |
| 17767.3<br>*G 0121.45* | -Elbow. | 3° 42.9′ S<br>38° 31.6′ W | **F.G.** | | | | |
| 17767.5<br>*G 0121.5* | -S. breakwater. | 3° 43.1′ S<br>38° 31.7′ W | **F.R.** | | | | |
| 17768<br>*G 0122* | **Ponta de Mucuripe.** | 3° 43.6′ S<br>38° 28.3′ W | **Fl.(2)W.**<br>period 10s<br>fl. 0.6s, ec. 2s<br>fl. 0.6s, ec. 6.8s | 279<br>**85** | **43** | Black cylindrical masonry tower, white bands; 72. | Q.W. 80m 23M on mast 2 miles W.<br>Q.W. 112m 23M on mast 2.5 miles W.<br>**Radiobeacon** 40 meters W. |
| 17772<br>*G 0124* | -Titan breakwater, head. | 3° 41.9′ S<br>38° 28.9′ W | **Fl.G.**<br>period 3s<br>fl. 0.5s, ec. 2.5s | 49<br>**15** | 10 | White truncated pyramidal fiberglass framework structure, daymark; 39. | |
| 17778<br>*G 0125* | -Pier. | 3° 42.5′ S<br>38° 29.0′ W | **F.R.** | | | | Private light. |
| 17780<br>*G 0123* | -Praia do Futuro. | 3° 42.3′ S<br>38° 27.6′ W | **Fl.W.**<br>period 10s<br>fl. 1s, ec. 9s | 36<br>**11** | 5 | White four-sided masonry tower, black bands; 16. | |
| 17784<br>*G 0120* | **Fortaleza** AVIATION LIGHT. | 3° 46.4′ S<br>38° 32.2′ W | **Al.Fl.W.G.**<br>period 12s<br>W. fl. 1s, ec. 5s<br>G. fl. 1s, ec. 5s | 121<br>**37** | **20** | White metal framework structure, red bands. | |
| 17786<br>*G 0130* | **Penedos de Sao Pedro e Sao Paulo.** | 0° 55.2′ N<br>29° 20.6′ W | **Fl.W.**<br>period 10s<br>fl. 1s, ec. 9s | 95<br>**29** | **15** | White cylindrical fiberglass tower, red bands; 20. | |
| | ARQUIPELAGO DE FERNANDO DE NORONHA: | | | | | | |
| 17788<br>*G 0132* | **-Ilha Rata.** | 3° 48.8′ S<br>32° 23.2′ W | **Fl.W.**<br>period 15s<br>fl. 1.5s, ec. 13.5s | 207<br>**63** | **16** | White four-sided masonry tower; 69. | Visible 054°-009°. |
| 17792<br>*G 0144* | **-Alto da Bandeira.** | 3° 52.5′ S<br>32° 27.7′ W | **Al.Fl.W.W.R.**<br>period 30s<br>W. fl. 1s, ec. 9s<br>W. fl. 1s, ec. 9s<br>R. fl. 1s, ec. 9s | 666<br>**203** | W. **28**<br>R. **24** | White octagonal masonry tower; 33. | |
| 17796<br>*G 0138* | -Morro do Pico AVIATION LIGHT. | 3° 50.7′ S<br>32° 25.3′ W | **Al.Fl.W.G.**<br>period 10s | 1079<br>**329** | | Metal framework structure; 20. | **Radiobeacon** about 0.7 mile S. |
| 17800<br>*G 0146* | -Atol das Rocas. | 3° 51.4′ S<br>33° 48.9′ W | **Q.(2)W.**<br>period 6s | 59<br>**18** | 13 | White four-sided truncated pyramidal metal framework structure; 46. | **Radar reflector.** |
| 17802<br>*G 0125.5* | **Morro Branco.** | 4° 09.5′ S<br>38° 06.5′ W | **Fl.(5)W.**<br>period 60s<br>fl. 1s, ec. 9s<br>fl. 1s, ec. 9s<br>fl. 1s, ec. 9s<br>fl. 1s, ec. 9s<br>fl. 1s, ec. 19s | 351<br>**107** | **24** | White four-sided masonry tower; 82. | |
| 17804<br>*G 0126* | Aracati, W. side of Rio Jaquaribe entrance. | 4° 24.5′ S<br>37° 46.2′ W | **Fl.W.**<br>period 6s<br>fl. 0.5s, ec. 5.5s | 112<br>**34** | 14 | Red cylindrical masonry tower and dwelling; 39. | |
| 17808<br>*G 0148* | **Ponta Cajuais.** | 4° 42.6′ S<br>37° 21.6′ W | **Fl.(3)W.**<br>period 15s<br>fl. 1s, ec. 2s<br>fl. 1s, ec. 2s<br>fl. 1s, ec. 8s | 210<br>**64** | **19** | White cylindrical fiberglass tower, red bands; 46. | |
| 17810<br>*G 0152.5* | Pontal. | 4° 56.4′ S<br>37° 08.7′ W | **Fl.W.**<br>period 6s<br>fl. 0.5s, ec. 5.5s | 69<br>**21** | 10 | Black cylindrical fiberglass tower, white band; 26. | |

| (1)<br>No. | (2)<br>Name and Location | (3)<br>Position | (4)<br>Characteristic | (5)<br>Height | (6)<br>Range | (7)<br>Structure | (8)<br>Remarks |
|---|---|---|---|---|---|---|---|
| | | | **BRAZIL** | | | | |
| 17812<br>*G 0152* | Areia Branca, on Ponta Upanema. | 4° 55.6′ S<br>37° 06.9′ W | **Fl.(3)R.**<br>period 15s<br>fl. 1s, ec. 2s<br>fl. 1s, ec. 2s<br>fl. 1s, ec. 8s | 46<br>**14** | 13 | White metal pipe with balcony, green masonry base; 36. | |
| 17816<br>*G 0154* | **Ponte do Mel.** | 4° 57.7′ S<br>36° 52.6′ W | **L.Fl.W.**<br>period 30s<br>fl. 3.5s, ec. 26.5s | 348<br>**106** | **41** | White cylindrical metal framework tower, column in center, black bands; 46. | |
| 17824<br>*G 0156* | -Macau, at lagoon. | 5° 05.7′ S<br>36° 39.3′ W | **Fl.W.**<br>period 6s<br>fl. 0.5s, ec. 5.5s | 59<br>**18** | 13 | White four-sided truncated pyramid concrete structure; 56. | |
| 17826<br>*G 0157* | Ponta do Tubarao. | 5° 04.0′ S<br>36° 29.7′ W | **Fl.W.**<br>period 3s<br>fl. 0.3s, ec. 2.7s | 23<br>**7** | 8 | White four-sided metal framework structure; 16. | |
| 17828<br>*G 0158* | Galinhos. | 5° 05.3′ S<br>36° 17.4′ W | **Fl.W.**<br>period 10s<br>fl. 1s, ec. 9s | 46<br>**14** | 12 | White cylindrical concrete tower, red bands; 43. | |
| 17830 | Caicaras. | 5° 03.4′ S<br>36° 03.3′ W | **Fl.(2)W.**<br>period 10s | | 2 | ISOLATED DANGER<br>Beacon, topmark. | Private light. |
| 17832<br>*G 0162* | **Santo Alberto.** | 5° 03.2′ S<br>36° 02.3′ W | **Fl.(2)W.**<br>period 15s<br>fl. 1s, ec. 2s<br>fl. 1s, ec. 11s | 138<br>**42** | **20** | Black and white checkered hexagonal concrete tower, black four-sided truncated pyramidal base; 125. | |
| 17836<br>*G 0164* | **Ponta de Calcanhar.** | 5° 09.7′ S<br>35° 29.2′ W | **Fl.W.**<br>period 10s<br>fl. 0.3s, ec. 9.7s | 243<br>**74** | **38** | White truncated conical concrete tower, black bands; 203. | Aeromarine light.<br>**Radiobeacon.**<br>**DGPS Station.** |
| | RACON | | **Y(– • – –)** | | **25** | | (3 & 10cm). |
| | CANAL DE SAO ROQUE: | | | | | | |
| 17840<br>*G 0166* | -Ponta da Gameleira. | 5° 13.2′ S<br>35° 25.3′ W | **Fl.W.R.**<br>period 6s<br>fl. 0.5s, ec. 5.5s | 89<br>**27** | W. 13<br>R. 9 | Black four-sided concrete post, white band; 20. | R. 121°-203°, W.-233°, R.-309°. |
| 17844<br>*G 0168* | -Baixio do Rio do Fogo, SW. side. | 5° 13.8′ S<br>35° 20.8′ W | **Fl.R.**<br>period 6s<br>fl. 0.5s, ec. 5.5s | 39<br>**12** | 10 | Four-sided concrete tower, red and white bands; 39. | |
| 17848<br>*G 0170* | -Baixo da Teresa Panca. | 5° 24.1′ S<br>35° 17.8′ W | **Fl.W.**<br>period 6s<br>fl. 0.5s, ec. 5.5s | 33<br>**10** | 11 | Cylindrical concrete tower, black and white bands; 33. | |
| 17852<br>*G 0172* | **Cabo de Sao Roque.** | 5° 29.4′ S<br>35° 15.7′ W | **Fl.(3)W.**<br>period 10s<br>fl. 1s, ec. 1s<br>fl. 1s, ec. 1s<br>fl. 1s, ec. 5s | 164<br>**50** | **21** | Four-sided masonry tower structure, red and white bands; 105. | |
| | PORTO DE NATAL: | | | | | | |
| 17856<br>*G 0177* | **-Natal.** | 5° 47.7′ S<br>35° 11.1′ W | **Fl.(5)W.**<br>period 25s<br>fl. 1s, ec. 2s<br>fl. 1s, ec. 2s<br>fl. 1s, ec. 2s<br>fl. 1s, ec. 2s<br>fl. 1s, ec. 12s | 285<br>**87** | **39** | White truncated conical masonry tower; 121. | Visible 168°-342°.<br>F.R. 147m on TV tower 1.5 miles SSW. |
| 17860<br>*G 0178* | **-Recife de Natal.** | 5° 45.1′ S<br>35° 11.7′ W | **Fl.G.**<br>period 5s<br>fl. 0.5s, ec. 4.5s | 43<br>**13** | **17** | Green four-sided masonry tower; 33. | |
| 17864<br>*G 0180* | -Pedra Baixinha, W. side of entrance. | 5° 45.0′ S<br>35° 11.8′ W | **Fl.R.**<br>period 6s<br>fl. 1s, ec. 5s | 26<br>**8** | 7 | Red truncated conical concrete tower with balcony, white latticework on top; 20. | |
| 17872<br>*G 0180.6* | -Potengi. | 5° 46.9′ S<br>35° 12.6′ W | **Fl.G.**<br>period 3s<br>fl. 0.5s, ec. 2.5s | 23<br>**7** | 5 | Green four-sided masonry tower, two white bands; 16. | |

| (1) No. | (2) Name and Location | (3) Position | (4) Characteristic | (5) Height | (6) Range | (7) Structure | (8) Remarks |
|---|---|---|---|---|---|---|---|
| | | | **BRAZIL** | | | | |
| 17876 *G 0180.8* | -Naval pier. | 5° 47.3´ S 35° 13.3´ W | **F.Y.** | | | Yellow four-sided masonry tower; 10. | Private light. |
| 17880 *G 0182* | -Parnamirim airport AVIATION LIGHT. | 5° 54.2´ S 35° 14.8´ W | **Al.Fl.W.G.** | 210 **64** | | Metal framework structure, red and white bands; 49. | |
| 17882 *G 0183* | **Ponta da Tabatinga.** | 6° 02.7´ S 35° 06.8´ W | **Fl.(5)W.** period 60s fl. 1s, ec. 9s fl. 1s, ec. 9s fl. 1s, ec. 9s fl. 1s, ec. 9s fl. 1s, ec. 19s | 315 **96** | **24** | Gray cylindrical concrete tower; 266. | |
| 17884 *G 0184* | **Cabo de Bacopari.** | 6° 22.5´ S 34° 59.6´ W | **Fl.(2)W.** period 10s fl. 0.5s, ec. 1.5s fl. 0.5s, ec. 7.5s | 98 **30** | **15** | White and black checkered octagonal masonry tower; 56. | |
| 17888 *G 0186* | Baia da Traicao. | 6° 40.5´ S 34° 56.0´ W | **Fl.W.** period 6s fl. 0.5s, ec. 5.5s | 39 **12** | 12 | White four-sided truncated pyramidal masonry, concrete base; 33. | |
| | PORTO DE CABEDELO: | | | | | | |
| 17892 *G 0188* | **-Pedra Seca.** | 6° 57.4´ S 34° 49.4´ W | **Fl.(3)W.** period 10s fl. 1s, ec. 1s fl. 1s, ec. 1s fl. 1s, ec. 5s | 52 **16** | **16** | White octagonal truncated pyramidal metal tower, four-sided masonry base; 49. | |
| 17900 *G 0189* | -Cabedelo breakwater, head. | 6° 57.7´ S 34° 50.6´ W | **Fl.G.** period 6s fl. 1s, ec. 5s | 26 **8** | 7 | Green four-sided truncated pyramidal masonry tower; 20. | |
| 17904 *G 0190* | **Cabo Branco.** | 7° 08.9´ S 34° 47.9´ W | **Fl.W.** period 10s fl. 1.2s, ec. 8.8s | 151 **46** | **27** | White truncated pyramidal triangular masonry tower, black band, concrete base with three points; 59. | |
| 17907.5 *G 0191.5* | Pitimbu. | 7° 27.7´ S 34° 47.7´ W | **Fl.W.** period 3s fl. 0.5s, ec. 2.5s | 16 **5** | 5 | White metal pipe; 20. | |
| 17908 *G 0192* | **Ponta de Pedras.** | 7° 37.7´ S 34° 48.7´ W | **Fl.(3)W.** period 15s fl. 1s, ec. 2s fl. 1s, ec. 2s fl. 1s, ec. 8s | 184 **56** | **18** | White four-sided truncated pyramidal metal frame structure, circular balcony; 23. | |
| | RECIFE: | | | | | | |
| 17912 *G 0202* | **-Olinda.** | 8° 00.7´ S 34° 50.8´ W | **Fl.(2)W.** period 35s fl. 1s, ec. 7.5s fl. 1s, ec. 25.5s | 295 **90** | **46** | Truncated conical concrete tower, black and white bands; 138. | F.R. 130m on TV tower 1.2 miles NW. |
| 17920 *G 0204* | **-Recife.** | 8° 03.3´ S 34° 51.9´ W | **Al.Fl.W.R.** period 12s fl. 0.4s, ec. 3.6s fl. 0.4s, ec. 7.6s | 66 **20** | W. **17** R. 13 | White octagonal masonry tower, red band, four-sided concrete base; 59. | Q.R. and Q.W. on radio towers 0.8 mile WNW. |
| 17932 *G 0205* | -Banco Ingles Breakwater, N. | 8° 02.7´ S 34° 51.0´ W | **Fl.G.** period 6s fl. 1s, ec. 5s | 39 **12** | 11 | Green four-sided concrete tower; 23. | |
| 17936 *G 0205.4* | -S. breakwater. | 8° 03.3´ S 34° 51.2´ W | **Fl.R.** period 6s fl. 1s, ec. 5s | 39 **12** | 11 | Four-sided concrete tower, red and white bands; 23. | |
| 17944 *G 0208* | -N. breakwater, head. | 8° 02.6´ S 34° 51.6´ W | **L.Fl.R.** period 8s fl. 2s, ec. 6s | 39 **12** | 7 | Red cylindrical concrete tower; 30. | |
| 17948 *G 0206* | -S. breakwater, head. | 8° 02.8´ S 34° 51.5´ W | **L.Fl.G.** period 8s fl. 2s, ec. 6s | 39 **12** | 5 | Green cylindrical concrete tower; 36. | |

| (1) No. | (2) Name and Location | (3) Position | (4) Characteristic | (5) Height | (6) Range | (7) Structure | (8) Remarks |
|---|---|---|---|---|---|---|---|
| | | | **BRAZIL** | | | | |
| 17960<br>*G 0212* | **Cabo de Santo Agostinho.** | 8° 21.1′ S<br>34° 56.8′ W | **Fl.W.**<br>period 10s<br>fl. 1s, ec. 9s | 299<br>**91** | **22** | White cylindrical concrete tower; 49. | |
| 17961<br>*G 0212.4* | Porto de Suape, breakwater. | 8° 23.6′ S<br>34° 56.8′ W | **Iso.G.**<br>period 2s | 52<br>**16** | 8 | Four-sided concrete post, black and white bands; 26. | |
| 17962<br>*G 0212.6* | -Pier de Graneis Liquidos de Gasosos. No.1. | 8° 23.9′ S<br>34° 57.4′ W | **F.Y.** | 16<br>**5** | 2 | White metal structure, red bands; 10. | Private light. |
| 17962.3<br>*G 0212.65* | --No. 2. | 8° 23.8′ S<br>34° 57.2′ W | **F.Y.** | | 2 | | |
| 17962.5<br>*G 0212.5* | -Pier de Cargas Multiplas. | 8° 23.8′ S<br>34° 57.5′ W | **F.Y.** | 26<br>**8** | 2 | Four-sided concrete tower, red and white bands; 13. | Private light. |
| 17964<br>*G 0214* | **Tamandare.** | 8° 45.4′ S<br>35° 06.2′ W | **Fl.(3)W.**<br>period 10s<br>fl. 1s, ec. 1s<br>fl. 1s, ec. 1s<br>fl. 1s, ec. 5s | 89<br>**27** | **18** | White cylindrical concrete tower; 72. | N. limit of visibility 236°. |
| 17966 | Maragogi. | 9° 00.8′ S<br>35° 13.4′ W | **F.R.** | 440<br>**134** | | Tower. | Private light. |
| 17968<br>*G 0218* | **Porto de Pedras.** | 9° 09.4′ S<br>35° 17.9′ W | **Fl.(2)W.**<br>period 15s<br>fl. 1s, ec. 3s<br>fl. 1s, ec. 10s | 295<br>**90** | **24** | Truncated conical concrete tower, black and white bands; 118. | |
| 17970 | Barra Santo Antonio. | 9° 24.5′ S<br>35° 30.5′ W | **F.R.** | 289<br>**88** | | Tower. | Private light. |
| 17971 | Floriano. | 9° 30.9′ S<br>35° 35.8′ W | **F.R.** | 318<br>**97** | | Tower. | Private light. |
| 17972<br>*G 0220* | Ponta Verde. | 9° 40.0′ S<br>35° 41.5′ W | **L.Fl.W.**<br>period 10s<br>fl. 2s, ec. 8s | 43<br>**13** | 13 | Cylindrical masonry tower, red and white bands, truncated pyramidal concrete pillars; 36. | |
| | PORTO DE MACEIO: | | | | | | |
| 17976<br>*G 0222* | **-Maceio.** | 9° 39.4′ S<br>35° 43.5′ W | **Al.Fl.W.R.**<br>period 20s<br>W. fl. 1s, ec. 9s<br>R. fl. 1s, ec. 9s | 223<br>**68** | W. **43**<br>R. **36** | White truncated conical masonry tower, black diamonds, black base; 85. | Visible 012°-010°.<br>Iso.R. on tower 0.6 mile W.<br>F.R. on silos 0.4 mile and 0.6 mile SSE. |
| 17977 | -Jatiuca. | 9° 39.0′ S<br>35° 42.6′ W | **F.R.** | 308<br>**94** | | Tower. | Private light. |
| 17980<br>*G 0219* | --AVIATION LIGHT. | 9° 30.7′ S<br>35° 48.1′ W | **Al.Fl.W.G.** | 371<br>**113** | | Metal framework stucture, red and white bands; 59. | Occasional. |
| 17984<br>*G 0223* | -Ponta do Molhe. | 9° 40.9′ S<br>35° 43.8′ W | **Fl.R.**<br>period 5s<br>fl. 0.5s, ec. 4.5s | 33<br>**10** | 5 | White cylindrical masonry tower; 33. | |
| 17989<br>*G 0223.4* | -Salgema. | 9° 41.7′ S<br>35° 45.6′ W | **Q.R.** | 30<br>**9** | 9 | Four-sided concrete tower, red and white bands; 7. | Private light. |
| 17991 | Barra Sao Miguel. | 9° 50.3′ S<br>35° 53.3′ W | **F.R.** | 243<br>**74** | | Tower. | Private light. |
| 17992<br>*G 0224* | Rio de Sao Miguel. | 9° 52.0′ S<br>35° 54.4′ W | **Fl.W.**<br>period 3s<br>fl. 0.3s, ec. 2.7s | 49<br>**15** | 13 | White truncated pyramidal concrete tower, white lattice at top, red four-sided concrete base; 43. | |
| 17996<br>*G 0226* | Ponta Coruripe. | 10° 09.6′ S<br>36° 08.2′ W | **Fl.(2)W.**<br>period 15s<br>fl. 1s, ec. 3s<br>fl. 1s, ec. 10s | 66<br>**20** | 14 | White cylindrical masonry tower, black bands, black truncated pyramidal concrete base; 33. | |
| 18000<br>*G 0227* | **Peba.** | 10° 29.5′ S<br>36° 23.2′ W | **L.Fl.W.**<br>period 15s<br>fl. 2s, ec. 13s | 141<br>**43** | **17** | White four-sided truncated pyramidal metal framework tower, red band; 131. | |

| (1)<br>No. | (2)<br>Name and Location | (3)<br>Position | (4)<br>Characteristic | (5)<br>Height | (6)<br>Range | (7)<br>Structure | (8)<br>Remarks |
|---|---|---|---|---|---|---|---|
| | | | **BRAZIL** | | | | |
| 18002 | **Platform PRB-1.** | 10° 39.2´ S<br>36° 38.3´ W | **Fl.W.**<br>period 10s<br>fl. 1s, ec. 9s | 82<br>**25** | **26** | Orange platform; 82. | Visible 225°-070°.<br>Additional lights on platform Fl.W. 10M and F.R. |
| 18004<br>*G 0229.5* | **Santa Isabel.** | 10° 49.5´ S<br>36° 56.1´ W | **Al.Fl.W.W.R.**<br>period 30s<br>W. fl. 1s, ec. 9s<br>W. fl. 1s, ec. 9s<br>R. fl. 1s, ec. 9s | 223<br>**68** | W. **26**<br>R. **21** | Cylindrical concrete tower, white band; 207. | |
| | PORTO DE ARACAJU: | | | | | | |
| 18010<br>*G 0230* | **-Sergipe.** | 10° 58.2´ S<br>37° 02.2´ W | **Oc.(6)W.**<br>period 60s<br>lt. 30s, ec. 2s<br>lt. 2.4s, ec. 3.5s<br>lt. 2.4s, ec. 3.5s<br>lt. 2.4s, ec. 3.5s<br>lt. 2.4s, ec. 3.5s<br>lt. 2.4s, ec. 2s | 135<br>**41** | **39** | Four-sided concrete tower, white and black bands; 131. | F.R. on 3 towers 2.7 miles SW.<br>**Radiobeacon.**<br>**DGPS Station.** |
| 18011<br>*G 0233* | **Sao Cristovao.** | 11° 07.8´ S<br>37° 08.7´ W | **L.Fl.W.**<br>period 20s<br>fl. 2s, ec. 18s | 138<br>**42** | **23** | White four-sided concrete tower, two red bands; 131. | |
| 18012 | **Mangue Seco.** | 11° 27.9´ S<br>37° 22.0´ W | **Fl.W.**<br>period 6s<br>fl. 1s, ec. 5s | 180<br>**55** | **15** | White four-sided metal framework tower; 82. | |
| 18013<br>*G 0234.5* | **Itariri.** | 11° 57.3´ S<br>37° 37.3´ W | **Fl.(5)W.**<br>period 60s<br>fl. 1s, ec. 9s<br>fl. 1s, ec. 9s<br>fl. 1s, ec. 9s<br>fl. 1s, ec. 9s<br>fl. 1s, ec. 19s | 246<br>**75** | **26** | Four-sided concrete tower, white and black bands; 98. | |
| 18014<br>*G 0235* | **Subauma**. | 12° 14.4´ S<br>37° 46.4´ W | **Fl.W.**<br>period 10s<br>fl. 1s, ec. 9s | 157<br>**48** | **23** | Four-sided concrete tower, red and white bands; 135. | |
| 18016<br>*G 0236* | **Garcia d'Avila.** | 12° 34.7´ S<br>38° 00.2´ W | **Fl.(2)W.**<br>period 12s<br>fl. 1s, ec. 2s<br>fl. 1s, ec. 8s | 92<br>**28** | **21** | White cylindrical masonry tower; 82. | |
| 18018<br>*G 0236.2* | **Camacari.** | 12° 44.5´ S<br>38° 08.9´ W | **Fl.W.**<br>period 10s<br>fl. 1s, ec. 9s | 66<br>**20** | **16** | White cylindrical concrete tower; 66. | |
| 18020<br>*G 0237* | Salvador AVIATION LIGHT. | 12° 54.8´ S<br>38° 19.7´ W | **Al.Fl.W.G.** | 75<br>**23** | | White metal framework structure, red bands; 56. | Occasional.<br>**Aero Radiobeacon.** |
| 18024<br>*G 0238* | **Ponta Itapua.** | 12° 57.4´ S<br>38° 21.2´ W | **Fl.W.**<br>period 6s<br>fl. 0.5s, ec. 5.5s | 79<br>**24** | **15** | Truncated conical metal tower, red and white bands, white masonry base; 69. | F.R. on building 0.5 mile N. |
| | BAIA DE TODOS OS SANTOS: | | | | | | |
| 18028<br>*G 0242* | **--Ponta de Santo Antonio.** | 13° 00.6´ S<br>38° 32.0´ W | **Al.Iso.W.W.R.**<br>period 30s<br>W. lt. 5s, ec. 5s<br>W. lt. 5s, ec. 5s<br>R. lt. 5s, ec. 5s | 128<br>**39** | W. **38**<br>R. **34** | Cylindrical masonry tower, black and white bands; 72. | |
| | -Porto do Salvador: | | | | | | |
| 18032<br>*G 0244* | --Mar Grande. | 12° 57.7´ S<br>38° 36.0´ W | **Fl.W.**<br>period 3s<br>fl. 0.3s, ec. 2.7s | 26<br>**8** | 9 | White four-sided masonry tower; 26. | |
| 18033 | --Barra da Penha. | 12° 58.9´ S<br>38° 36.4´ W | **Q.W.** | 30<br>**9** | 3 | White metal pipe, concrete base; 30. | |
| 18034<br>*G 0244.5* | --Barra do Pote. | 13° 01.2´ S<br>38° 38.7´ W | **Q.(2)W.**<br>period 6s | 20<br>**6** | 6 | White metal pipe, concrete base; 16. | |

| (1) No. | (2) Name and Location | (3) Position | (4) Characteristic | (5) Height | (6) Range | (7) Structure | (8) Remarks |
|---|---|---|---|---|---|---|---|
| | | | **BRAZIL** | | | | |
| 18035 *G 0244.3* | --Barra do Gil. | 12° 59.7′ S 38° 37.4′ W | **Fl.W.** period 6s fl. 0.5s, ec. 5.5s | 23 **7** | 6 | White metal pipe, concrete base; 20. | |
| 18035.5 *G 0244.6* | --Barra Grande. | 13° 02.6′ S 38° 40.4′ W | **Fl.W.** period 3s fl. 0.5s, ec. 2.5s | 23 **7** | 6 | White metal pipe, concrete base; 20. | |
| 18036 *G 0246* | --S. breakwater, N. head. | 12° 58.1′ S 38° 31.2′ W | **Fl.R.** period 3s fl. 0.3s, ec. 2.7s | 33 **10** | 5 | Red four-sided truncated pyramid masonry tower, concrete base; 20. | |
| 18040 *G 0247* | --Detached breakwater, S. head. | 12° 58.0′ S 38° 31.0′ W | **Fl.G.** period 3s fl. 0.3s, ec. 2.7s | 20 **6** | 5 | Green four-sided truncated pyramidal masonry, concrete base; 20. | |
| 18044 *G 0247.2* | ---N. head. | 12° 57.3′ S 38° 30.7′ W | **F.Y.** | 20 **6** | 5 | Yellow four-sided truncated pyramidal masonry tower, concrete base; 20. | |
| 18048 *G 0249* | --Ponta de Monte Serrat. | 12° 55.7′ S 38° 31.2′ W | **Fl.R.** period 10s fl. 1s, ec. 9s | 33 **10** | 11 | Truncated conical masonry tower, red and white bands; 33. | |
| 18060 *G 0254* | -Caboto. | 12° 45.3′ S 38° 30.2′ W | **Fl.W.** period 6s fl. 1s, ec. 5s | 112 **34** | 14 | White four-sided masonry tower; 26. | |
| 18061 *G 0252.2* | -Solids pier. | 12° 46.8′ S 38° 30.1′ W | **F.R.** | | 3 | Red metal pipe. | Private light. |
| 18062 *G 0252* | -Liquids pier. | 12° 47.0′ S 38° 30.0′ W | **F.R.** | | 3 | Red metal pipe. | Private light. |
| 18063 *G 0251.3* | -Naval pier. | 12° 47.5′ S 38° 29.6′ W | **F.R.** | | 3 | Red metal pipe; 16. | Private light. |
| 18064 *G 0251* | -Cotegipe. | 12° 47.4′ S 38° 29.9′ W | **Fl.R.** period 5s fl. 0.5s, ec. 4.5s | 49 **15** | 5 | Red truncated conical masonry tower; 20. | |
| 18064.5 *G 0251.6* | -Aratu. | 12° 47.6′ S 38° 29.4′ W | **Mo.(N)Y.** period 5s fl. 1.5s, ec. 0.5s fl. 0.5s, ec. 2.5s | 16 **5** | 6 | Yellow metal pole; 7. | |
| 18065 *G 0251.7* | -Ponta do Forte. | 12° 47.4′ S 38° 29.1′ W | **Fl.W.** period 5s fl. 0.5s, ec. 4.5s | 23 **7** | 8 | White metal pole, concrete base; 20. | |
| 18066 *G 0256* | **-Itamoabo.** | 12° 47.7′ S 38° 32.0′ W | **Q.(2)W.** period 3s | 164 **50** | **15** | White cylindrical masonry tower; 16. | |
| 18067 | -Terminal da Usiba. | 12° 49.5′ S 38° 29.9′ W | **Iso.W.R.** period 2s | 115 **35** | W. 8 R. 6 | Gray metallic framework structure on fixed crane. | W. 038°-136°, R.-038°. |
| 18067.2 | --N. dolphin. | 12° 49.4′ S 38° 29.9′ W | **F.Y.** | 10 **3** | 5 | Yellow iron column. | |
| 18067.4 | --S. dolphin. | 12° 49.5′ S 38° 29.9′ W | **F.Y.** | 10 **3** | 5 | Yellow iron column. | |
| 18126 *G 0262.3* | -Baixio do Capeta. | 12° 45.0′ S 38° 38.1′ W | **Fl.(2)W.** period 5s fl. 0.5s, ec. 1s fl. 0.5s, ec. 3s | | 5 | Metal tube, triangular concrete base, black and red bands. | |
| 18127 *G 0262* | -Baixio de Madre de Deus. | 12° 44.9′ S 38° 37.6′ W | **Fl.(2+1)G.** period 12s fl. 1s, ec. 1s fl. 1s, ec. 3s fl. 1s, ec. 5s | | 5 | Metal pipe, triangular concrete base, red and black bands. | |
| 18128 *G 0267* | -Oureis, on Bancode Oureis. | 12° 43.2′ S 38° 39.3′ W | **Fl.(2)W.** period 10s fl. 0.5s, ec. 1.5s fl. 0.5s, ec. 7.5s | 26 **8** | 8 | Four-sided masonry tower, red and black bands; 26. | |
| 18132 *G 0266* | -Ilha do Frade, Ponta de Nossa Senhora de Guadalupe. | 12° 48.9′ S 38° 38.5′ W | **Q.(2)W.** period 6s | 115 **35** | 10 | White four-sided concrete tower; 16. | Visible 253°-145°. |

| (1) No. | (2) Name and Location | (3) Position | (4) Characteristic | (5) Height | (6) Range | (7) Structure | (8) Remarks |
|---|---|---|---|---|---|---|---|

## BRAZIL

| (1) No. | (2) Name and Location | (3) Position | (4) Characteristic | (5) Height | (6) Range | (7) Structure | (8) Remarks |
|---|---|---|---|---|---|---|---|
| 18136 *G 0268* | -Saubara. | 12° 44.4´ S 38° 43.1´ W | **Fl.W.** period 5s fl. 0.5s, ec. 4.5s | 26 **8** | 11 | White four-sided masonry tower; 26. | |
| | -Rio Paraguacu: | | | | | | |
| 18140 *G 0269* | --Ponta Alambique. | 12° 50.4´ S 38° 47.6´ W | **Fl.W.** period 6s fl. 0.5s, ec. 5.5s | 36 **11** | 14 | White four-sided truncated pyramidal metal framework structure, four-sided masonry base; 23. | |
| 18144 *G 0270* | --Cabeca de Negro. | 12° 49.5´ S 38° 51.5´ W | **Fl.R.** period 3s fl. 0.3s, ec. 2.7s | 23 **7** | 5 | Red metal pipe, red four-sided masonry base; 20. | |
| 18145 *G 0270.2* | --Salamina. | 12° 47.9´ S 38° 51.3´ W | **Fl.R.** period 5s fl. 0.5s, ec. 4.5s | 46 **14** | 6 | White metal pipe, red bands; 16. | |
| 18148 *G 0274* | **Morro de Sao Paulo.** | 13° 22.6´ S 38° 54.9´ W | **Fl.(2)W.** period 15s fl. 1s, ec. 3s fl. 1s, ec. 10s | 292 **89** | **23** | White truncated conical masonry tower; 85. | Southern limit of visibility 355°. |
| 18154 *G 0279* | Ponta Muta. | 13° 52.7´ S 38° 56.9´ W | **Fl.G.** period 3s fl. 0.5s, ec. 2.5s | 36 **11** | 11 | White four-sided masonry tower; 33. | |
| 18155 | **Morro Taipus.** | 13° 57.2´ S 38° 56.5´ W | **Fl.(3)W.** period 15s fl. 1s, ec. 2s fl. 1s, ec. 2s fl. 1s, ec. 8s | 249 **76** | **23** | Four-sided concrete tower, red and white bands; 82. | |
| 18156 *G 0282* | **Ilhota de Contas.** | 14° 16.5´ S 38° 59.1´ W | **Fl.W.** period 10s fl. 1s, ec. 9s | 69 **21** | **15** | White four-sided masonry tower; 66. | Obscured 320°-shore. |
| 18160 *G 0288* | **Ilheus.** | 14° 48.3´ S 39° 01.5´ W | **Fl.W.** period 10s fl. 1.3s, ec. 8.7s | 115 **35** | **23** | White cylindrical masonry tower; 33. | Southern limit of visibility 340°30´. **Aero Radiobeacon** 0.74 mile WSW. |
| 18164 *G 0286* | Ilheu Grande. | 14° 46.2´ S 39° 01.1´ W | **Fl.(3)W.** period 10s fl. 1s, ec. 1s fl. 1s, ec. 1s fl. 1s, ec. 5s | 66 **20** | 8 | White four-sided masonry tower; 13. | |
| 18168 *G 0287* | Porto do Malhado, breakwater, head. | 14° 46.1´ S 39° 01.6´ W | **Fl.G.** period 3s fl. 0.5s, ec. 2.5s | 46 **14** | 5 | Green four-sided truncated pyramidal metal framework structure, green four-sided masonry base; 26. | F.R. on 2 radio towers 1.3 miles SW. |
| 18170 *G 0290.5* | **Comandatuba.** | 15° 21.1´ S 38° 58.7´ W | **Fl.(3)W.** period 15s fl. 1s, ec. 2s fl. 1s, ec. 2s fl. 1s, ec. 8s | 148 **45** | **23** | White four-sided concrete tower; 131. | |
| 18172 *G 0292* | **Belmonte.** | 15° 51.8´ S 38° 52.5´ W | **Fl.W.** period 6s fl. 1s, ec. 5s | 118 **36** | **21** | White conical metal framework structure, central column, red bands, on red dwelling; 112. | |
| 18173 *G 0292.9* | Terminal Belmonte, N. end. | 16° 01.7´ S 38° 55.1´ W | **Fl.G.** period 5s fl. 0.5s, ec. 4.5s | 39 **12** | 5 | Green four-sided concrete tower; 16. | Private light. |
| 18173.5 *G 0293.1* | -S. end. | 16° 01.9´ S 38° 55.2´ W | **Fl.R.** period 5s fl. 0.5s, ec. 4.5s | 39 **12** | 5 | Red four-sided concrete tower; 16. | Private light. |
| 18174 *G 0294* | **Araripe.** | 16° 08.1´ S 38° 57.9´ W | **L.Fl.W.** period 10s fl. 2s, ec. 8s | 230 **70** | **17** | White four-sided concrete tower, two black bands; 131. | |

| (1)<br>No. | (2)<br>Name and Location | (3)<br>Position | (4)<br>Characteristic | (5)<br>Height | (6)<br>Range | (7)<br>Structure | (8)<br>Remarks |
|---|---|---|---|---|---|---|---|
| | | | **BRAZIL** | | | | |
| 18176<br>*G 0296* | **Porto Seguro.** | 16° 26.1′ S<br>39° 03.8′ W | **Al.Fl.W.W.R.**<br>period 30s<br>W. fl. 1s, ec. 9s<br>W. fl. 1s, ec. 9s<br>R. fl. 1s, ec. 9s | 187<br>**57** | W. **26**<br>R. **21** | White four-sided masonry tower; 39. | Visible 190°-347°. |
| 18180<br>*G 0298* | Ponta Corumbau. | 16° 53.7′ S<br>39° 06.9′ W | **Fl.W.**<br>period 10s<br>fl. 1s, ec. 9s | 49<br>**15** | 12 | White four-sided truncated pyramidal concrete tower; 39. | |
| 18182<br>*G 0298.5* | -Cumuruxatiba. | 17° 06.0′ S<br>39° 10.0′ W | **Fl.(3)W.**<br>period 10s<br>fl. 1s, ec. 1s<br>fl. 1s, ec. 1s<br>fl. 1s, ec. 5s | 20<br>**6** | 7 | White metal pipe, masonry base; 13. | |
| 18184<br>*G 0299* | **Barreiras do Prado.** | 17° 17.2′ S<br>39° 13.2′ W | **Fl.(2)W.**<br>period 12s<br>fl. 1s, ec. 2s<br>fl. 1s, ec. 8s | 138<br>**42** | **16** | White four-sided truncated pyramidal metal framework tower; 72. | |
| 18188<br>*G 0300* | **Alcobaca.** | 17° 31.0′ S<br>39° 11.4′ W | **Fl.W.**<br>period 15s<br>fl. 1s, ec. 14s | 92<br>**28** | **15** | White four-sided masonry tower, red band; 79. | |
| 18192<br>*G 0301* | Caravelas AVIATION LIGHT. | 17° 39.3′ S<br>39° 15.0′ W | **Al.Fl.W.G.** | 89<br>**27** | | Metal framework; 75. | Occasional.<br>**Aero Radiobeacon.** |
| 18196<br>*G 0302* | Ponta da Baleia. | 17° 41.3′ S<br>39° 08.1′ W | **Fl.W.**<br>period 5s<br>fl. 0.5s, ec. 4.5s | 62<br>**19** | 14 | White four-sided truncated pyramidal metal framework structure; 49. | |
| 18200<br>*G 0306* | **Canal dos Abrolhos.** | 17° 57.9′ S<br>38° 41.5′ W | **Fl.W.**<br>period 6s<br>fl. 0.5s, ec. 5.5s | 197<br>**60** | **51** | Truncated conical metal tower, black and white bands; 72. | **Radiobeacon.**<br>**DGPS Station.** |
| | RACON | | **Q(– – • –)** | | **25** | | (3 & 10cm). |
| 18204<br>*G 0304* | Ponta Catoeiro. | 17° 52.0′ S<br>39° 16.2′ W | **Fl.W.**<br>period 10s<br>fl. 1s, ec. 9s | 66<br>**20** | 14 | White four-sided metal framework tower; 52. | |
| 18206<br>*G 0305* | **Nova Vicosa.** | 17° 53.9′ S<br>39° 22.4′ W | **L.Fl.W.**<br>period 15s<br>fl. 2s, ec. 13s | 210<br>**64** | **23** | Four-sided truncated pyramidal metal framework structure, orange and white bands; 180. | |
| 18208<br>*G 0308* | Coroa Vermelha. | 17° 58.1′ S<br>39° 12.4′ W | **Fl.(3)W.**<br>period 15s<br>fl. 1s, ec. 2s<br>fl. 1s, ec. 2s<br>fl. 1s, ec. 8s | 53<br>**16** | 13 | Red octagonal masonry tower; 46. | |
| 18210<br>*G 0310* | **Mucuri.** | 18° 03.7′ S<br>39° 32.0′ W | **Fl.W.**<br>period 6s<br>fl. 1s, ec. 5s | 79<br>**24** | **16** | White cylindrical concrete tower; 66. | |
| 18213<br>*G 0312* | **Sao Mateus.** | 18° 36.9′ S<br>39° 43.9′ W | **Fl.(2)W.**<br>period 15s<br>fl. 1s, ec. 3s<br>fl. 1s, ec. 10s | 46<br>**14** | **15** | White cylindrical fiberglass tower, red bands; 23. | |
| 18214<br>*G 0313.5* | **Sucuraca.** | 19° 05.8′ S<br>39° 43.4′ W | **Fl.(2)W.**<br>period 30s<br>fl. 1s, ec. 9s<br>fl. 1s, ec. 19s | 210<br>**64** | **24** | White four-sided concrete tower, black bands; 131. | |
| 18216<br>*G 0316* | **Rio Doce.** | 19° 39.3′ S<br>39° 49.5′ W | **Fl.W.**<br>period 6s<br>fl. 1s, ec. 5s | 151<br>**46** | **18** | White four-sided concrete tower, red bands; 138. | |
| 18220<br>*G 0317* | Barra do Riacho, N. mole, head. | 19° 50.6′ S<br>40° 03.3′ W | **Fl.R.**<br>period 5s<br>fl. 0.5s, ec. 4.5s | 33<br>**10** | 9 | Red metal pipe; 13. | |
| 18224<br>*G 0317.2* | -S. mole, head. | 19° 50.7′ S<br>40° 03.2′ W | **Fl.G.**<br>period 5s<br>fl. 0.5s, ec. 4.5s | 33<br>**10** | 8 | Green metal frame; 13. | |

| (1) No. | (2) Name and Location | (3) Position | (4) Characteristic | (5) Height | (6) Range | (7) Structure | (8) Remarks |
|---|---|---|---|---|---|---|---|
| | | | **BRAZIL** | | | | |
| 18228 *G 0316.5* | Barra do Riacho. | 19° 50.0′ S 40° 03.8′ W | **Fl.(2)W.** period 10s fl. 0.5s, ec. 1.5s fl. 0.5s, ec. 7.5s | 112 **34** | 14 | White cylindrical concrete tower; 72. | |
| | ILHA DA TRINIDADE: | | | | | | |
| 18232 *G 0314* | -Ponta do Valado. | 20° 30.0′ S 29° 19.3′ W | **Fl.W.** period 3s fl. 0.3s, ec. 2.7s | 46 **14** | 8 | White four-sided truncated pyramidal masonry tower, red bands; 10. | Occasional. |
| 18234 *G 0315* | -Enseada dos Portugueses Range, front. | 20° 30.5′ S 29° 18.9′ W | **Q.R.** | 148 **45** | 4 | White four-sided metal framework structure, yellow diamond daymark; 36. | Occasional. |
| 18236 *G 0315.1* | --Rear, 65 meters 194° from front. | 20° 30.5′ S 29° 18.9′ W | **Iso.R.** period 2s | 151 **46** | 4 | Red four-sided metal framework structure, daymark; 10. | Visible 147°-286°. Occasional. |
| 18237 *G 0315.3* | -Calheta Range, front. | 20° 30.5′ S 29° 18.6′ W | **Q.W.** | 16 **5** | 5 | White four-sided truncated pyramidal masonry tower, red stripe; 16. | Occasional. |
| 18238 *G 0315.4* | --Rear, 55 meters 137° from front. | 20° 30.5′ S 29° 18.6′ W | **Iso.W.** period 2s | 16 **5** | 6 | White four-sided truncated pyramidal masonry tower, red stripe; 16. | Occasional. |
| | BAHIA DO ESPIRITO SANTO: | | | | | | |
| 18240 *G 0320* | **-Ponta de Santa Luzia.** | 20° 19.5′ S 40° 16.1′ W | **Fl.(4)W.** period 12s fl. 0.5s, ec. 1.5s fl. 0.5s, ec. 1.5s fl. 0.5s, ec. 1.5s fl. 0.5s, ec. 5.5s | 95 **29** | **34** | White octagonal metal tower; 46. | |
| | -RACON | | **M(– –)** | | **25** | | (3 & 10cm). |
| 18240.5 *G 0320.19* | -Port Tubarao Range, front. | 20° 16.5′ S 40° 15.4′ W | **Fl.W.** period 3s fl. 0.3s, ec. 2.7s | 49 **15** | 5 | Cylindrical fiberglass tower, orange and white bands; 26. | |
| 18241 *G 0320.2* | --Rear, 0.65 mile 344°30′ from front. | 20° 15.9′ S 40° 15.6′ W | **Q.W.** | 85 **26** | 5 | Cylindrical fiberglass tower, orange and white bands; 33. | |
| 18243 *G 0320.3* | -Mole, head. | 20° 18.1′ S 40° 14.4′ W | **Q.R.** | 46 **14** | 6 | Cylindrical fiberglass tower, red and white bands; 20. | |
| 18244 *G 0320.31* | -Mole, elbow. | 20° 17.7′ S 40° 13.8′ W | **Q.R.** | 46 **14** | 5 | Metal pipe, red and white bands; 20. | |
| 18245 *G 0320.7* | -Praia Mole (pier). | 20° 17.9′ S 40° 14.2′ W | **Q.R.** | 30 **9** | 3 | Red cylindrical metal tower; 16. | Private light. |
| 18246 *G 0320.8* | -Cais Siderurgico. | 20° 17.7′ S 40° 14.2′ W | **Q.G.** | 33 **10** | 3 | Green cylindrical metal tower; 16. | Private light. |
| 18247 *G 0320.4* | -S. breakwater, head. | 20° 17.6′ S 40° 14.8′ W | **Q.R.** | 46 **14** | 5 | Cylindrical fiberglass tower, orange and white bands; 33. | |
| 18248 *G 0320.6* | -N. breakwater, head. | 20° 17.5′ S 40° 14.8′ W | **F.Y.** | | 3 | | Private light. |
| 18249 *G 0320.65* | -Pier II, head. | 20° 17.3′ S 40° 15.0′ W | **F.Y.** | 30 **9** | 7 | Yellow cylindrical fiberglass tower; 26. | |
| 18252 *G 0321* | -Baleia, Pedra de Baleia, N. side. | 20° 19.1′ S 40° 16.3′ W | **Fl.(2)W.** period 6s fl. 1s, ec. 2s fl. 1s, ec. 2s | 16 **5** | 9 | White cylindrical masonry tower; 13. | |
| 18256 *G 0318* | -Vitoria AVIATION LIGHT. | 20° 15.4′ S 40° 17.4′ W | **Al.Fl.W.G.** | 59 **18** | | Metal framework structure, red and white bands; 49. | Occasional. **Radiobeacon** 4.52 miles NE. |
| 18259 *G 0318.5* | -Carapebus. | 20° 15.6′ S 40° 13.2′ W | **Fl.W.** period 5s fl. 1s, ec. 4s | 39 **12** | 9 | White cylindrical metal structure; 13. | |

| (1) No. | (2) Name and Location | (3) Position | (4) Characteristic | (5) Height | (6) Range | (7) Structure | (8) Remarks |
|---|---|---|---|---|---|---|---|
| | | | **BRAZIL** | | | | |
| 18264<br>*G 0322* | -Ilha do Boi, A Range, front. | 20° 18.6′ S<br>40° 16.9′ W | **Dir.W.R.G.** | 233<br>**71** | W. 13<br>R. 9<br>G. 9 | White truncated conical concrete tower, horizontal disk. | F.R. 282°-284°, Al.W.R.-286°, F.W.-288°, Al.W.G.-290°, F.G.-292°.<br>F.W., F.R. and F.G. on bridge 1000 meters SW., center span marked by Q.W.<br>Range 4/3M by day. |
| 18268<br>*G 0322.1* | **-Morro Grande**, rear, 1.67 mile 287° from front. | 20° 18.2′ S<br>40° 18.6′ W | **Iso.W.**<br>period 2s | 682<br>**208** | **20** | White four-sided truncated pyramidal metal framework structure, red bands. | |
| 18272<br>*G 0323* | **-Ponta Uchuria, B 3** Range, front. | 20° 19.4′ S<br>40° 17.2′ W | **Q.R.** | 23<br>**7** | **16** | White four-sided concrete tower, red triangular daymark point up; 16. | |
| 18276<br>*G 0323.1* | --Rear, 4, 120 meters 245°30′ from front. | 20° 19.4′ S<br>40° 17.3′ W | **Iso.R.**<br>period 2s | 112<br>**34** | **16** | White four-sided concrete tower, red triangular daymark point down; 13. | |
| 18280<br>*G 0324* | **-Ponta do Tagano, C 5** Range, front. | 20° 19.3′ S<br>40° 16.5′ W | **Q.R.** | 69<br>**21** | **15** | White four-sided concrete tower, red triangular daymark point up; 13. | |
| 18284<br>*G 0324.1* | --Rear, 6, 130 meters 087° from front. | 20° 19.3′ S<br>40° 16.5′ W | **Iso.R.**<br>period 2s | 85<br>**26** | **15** | White four-sided concrete tower, red triangular daymark point down; 13. | |
| 18288<br>*G 0325* | -Ponta do Soares. | 20° 19.4′ S<br>40° 18.0′ W | **Fl.(3)W.**<br>period 15s<br>fl. 1s, ec. 2s<br>fl. 1s, ec. 2s<br>fl. 1s, ec. 8s | 20<br>**6** | 5 | White metal framework structure; 10. | |
| 18292<br>*G 0327* | -Ilha das Pombas. | 20° 19.3′ S<br>40° 19.0′ W | **Fl.G.**<br>period 3s<br>fl. 0.3s, ec. 2.7s | 23<br>**7** | 5 | Green metal framework structure; 10. | |
| 18296<br>*G 0326* | -Ilha da Fumaca, pier. | 20° 19.2′ S<br>40° 18.8′ W | **Fl.W.**<br>period 6s<br>fl. 0.5s, ec. 5.5s | 46<br>**14** | 5 | White metal framework structure; 10. | |
| 18300<br>*G 0327.3* | -Ilha do Urubu. | 20° 19.2′ S<br>40° 19.1′ W | **Fl.R.**<br>period 3s<br>fl. 0.3s, ec. 2.7s | 33<br>**10** | 7 | Red hexagonal masonry tower; 10. | |
| 18304<br>*G 0327.6* | -Recife de Sao Joao. | 20° 19.3′ S<br>40° 19.6′ W | **Fl.(2)W.**<br>period 10s<br>fl. 1s, ec. 1s<br>fl. 1s, ec. 7s | 23<br>**7** | 8 | White metal framework structure, cylindrical concrete base; 16. | |
| 18308<br>*G 0327.8* | -Argolas. | 20° 19.4′ S<br>40° 20.5′ W | **Fl.(3)W.**<br>period 6s<br>fl. 0.5s, ec. 1s<br>fl. 0.5s, ec. 1s<br>fl. 0.5s, ec. 2.5s | 23<br>**7** | 5 | White metal post, white concrete base. | |
| 18310<br>*G 0327.9* | -Pedra das Argolas. | 20° 19.5′ S<br>40° 20.6′ W | **Fl.(3)W.**<br>period 8s<br>fl. 0.5s, ec. 1s<br>fl. 0.5s, ec. 1s<br>fl. 0.5s, ec. 4.5s | 23<br>**7** | 6 | White cylindrical concrete tower; 23. | |
| 18312<br>*G 0328* | Ilha do Pacotes, N. side of rock. | 20° 21.1′ S<br>40° 15.0′ W | **Fl.W.**<br>period 6s<br>fl. 1s, ec. 5s | 23<br>**7** | 8 | White cylindrical masonry tower; 13. | |
| | RACON | | **N(– •)** | | **15** | | (3 & 10cm). |
| 18316<br>*G 0330* | **Ilha Escalvada.** | 20° 42.2′ S<br>40° 24.4′ W | **Q.(2)W.**<br>period 6s | 89<br>**27** | **15** | Red cylindrical metal tower; 39. | |
| 18320<br>*G 0331* | Point Ubu. | 20° 46.9′ S<br>40° 34.7′ W | **Fl.W.**<br>period 5s<br>fl. 0.5s, ec. 4.5s | 89<br>**27** | 14 | White truncated pyramidal masonry tower; 16. | |
| 18321<br>*G 0331.2* | -Range, front. | 20° 46.9′ S<br>40° 34.7′ W | **F.W.** | 92<br>**28** | 10 | White rectangular concrete post, daymark; 20. | Occasional. |
| 18322<br>*G 0331.21* | --Rear, about 120 meters 270° from front. | 20° 46.9′ S<br>40° 34.8′ W | **F.W.** | 105<br>**32** | 10 | White rectangular concrete post, daymark; 33. | Occasional. |

| (1) No. | (2) Name and Location | (3) Position | (4) Characteristic | (5) Height | (6) Range | (7) Structure | (8) Remarks |
|---|---|---|---|---|---|---|---|

## BRAZIL

| (1) No. | (2) Name and Location | (3) Position | (4) Characteristic | (5) Height | (6) Range | (7) Structure | (8) Remarks |
|---|---|---|---|---|---|---|---|
| 18324 *G 0332* | **Ilha do Frances.** | 20° 55.6´ S 40° 45.3´ W | **L.Fl.W.** period 15s fl. 2s, ec. 13s | 157 **48** | **18** | Brown four-sided masonry tower, white top and edges; 39. | |
| 18328 *G 0334* | **Itapemirim.** | 21° 00.1´ S 40° 47.1´ W | **Fl.W.** period 10s fl. 1s, ec. 9s | 16 **5** | **15** | White four-sided masonry tower; 10. | |
| 18330 *G 0335* | Barra de Itabapoana. | 21° 18.8´ S 40° 57.9´ W | **Fl.G.** period 6s fl. 0.5s, ec. 5.5s | 115 **35** | 11 | White four-sided metal framework tower, white daymarks; 49. | |
| 18330.5 *G 0335.5* | **Ponta do Retiro.** | 21° 21.5´ S 40° 57.8´ W | **Fl.(3)W.** period 15s fl. 1s, ec. 2s fl. 1s, ec. 2s fl. 1s, ec. 8s | 131 **40** | **23** | White cylindrical concrete tower, red band, four-sided masonry base; 98. | |
| 18331 *G 0336* | **Guaxindiba.** | 21° 27.9´ S 41° 02.6´ W | **Fl.(2)W.** period 10s fl. 0.5s, ec. 1.5s fl. 0.5s, ec. 7.5s | 75 **23** | **15** | White four-sided metal framework tower, daymark; 66. | |
| 18332 *G 0338* | **Atafona.** | 21° 37.5´ S 41° 00.9´ W | **Fl.(2)W.** period 15s fl. 1s, ec. 2s fl. 1s, ec. 11s | 98 **30** | **16** | Four-sided pyramidal framework structure, black and white bands; 82. | |
| 18336 *G 0340* | Barra do Acu. | 22° 00.0´ S 40° 59.2´ W | **Fl.W.** period 3s fl. 0.3s, ec. 2.7s | 43 **13** | 12 | Cylindrical fiberglass tower, black and white bands; 33. | |
| 18340 *G 0342* | **Cabo Sao Tome.** | 22° 02.5´ S 41° 03.2´ W | **L.Fl.(2)W.** period 67.5s fl. 3s, ec. 10.5s fl. 3s, ec. 51s | 161 **49** | **40** | Red metal framework structure with central column; 148. | **DGPS Station.** **Radiobeacon** tower marked by 3 F.R. lights. |
| | RACON | | **O(- - -)** | | **25** | | (3 & 10cm). |
| 18342 *G 0343* | **Quissama.** | 22° 09.7´ S 41° 17.9´ W | **L.Fl.W.** period 10s fl. 2s, ec. 8s | 131 **40** | **17** | White cylindrical concrete tower, two red bands, four-sided masonry base; 131. | |
| 18344 *G 0346* | **Macae.** | 22° 24.9´ S 41° 42.4´ W | **Al.L.Fl.W.R.** period 20s fl. 2.3s, ec. 7.7s fl. 2.3s, ec. 7.7s | 512 **156** | W. **28** R. **22** | White four-sided masonry tower; 52. | |
| 18348 *G 0348* | Ilha dos Papagaios. | 22° 23.0´ S 41° 45.6´ W | **Q.(2)W.R.** period 6s | 89 **27** | W. 9 R. 6 | Red four-sided metal framework structure; 16. | R. 270°-315°. |
| 18352 *G 0349* | Ilha Branca. | 22° 43.8´ S 41° 52.5´ W | **Fl.W.** period 5s fl. 0.5s, ec. 4.5s | 125 **38** | 8 | White metal pipe, white four-sided masonry base; 16. | F.R. light on mast 2 miles S. |
| 18356 *G 0350* | Lajinha (Laginha), E. of new bar. | 22° 53.3´ S 42° 00.2´ W | **Fl.R.** period 3s fl. 0.3s, ec. 2.7s | 161 **49** | 9 | White four-sided truncated pyramidal concrete tower, lower half masonry; 23. | |
| 18360 *G 0352* | **Cabo Frio.** | 23° 00.8´ S 42° 00.1´ W | **Fl.W.** period 10s fl. 1.2s, ec. 8.8s | 459 **140** | **49** | White truncated conical metal tower; 52. | Visible 231°-118°. |
| 18362 *G 0352.5* | Ilha dos Franceses. | 22° 59.0´ S 42° 02.3´ W | **Iso.R.** period 2s | 43 **13** | 4 | Red concrete tower; 20. | |
| 18364 *G 0356* | **Ponta Negra.** | 22° 57.7´ S 42° 41.6´ W | **Fl.(2)W.** period 10s fl. 1s, ec. 1s fl. 1s, ec. 7s | 233 **71** | **21** | White cylindrical concrete tower; 36. | |
| 18368 *G 0358* | **Ilhas Maricas.** | 23° 00.9´ S 42° 55.2´ W | **L.Fl.W.** period 15s fl. 2s, ec. 13s | 262 **80** | **16** | Truncated conical masonry tower, black and white bands; 33. | |

| (1) No. | (2) Name and Location | (3) Position | (4) Characteristic | (5) Height | (6) Range | (7) Structure | (8) Remarks |
|---|---|---|---|---|---|---|---|

**BRAZIL**

| | | | | | | | |
|---|---|---|---|---|---|---|---|
| | BAIA DE GUANABARA: | | | | | | |
| | -Rio de Janeiro: | | | | | | |
| 18372 *G 0360* | **--Ilha Rasa.** | 23° 03.8´ S 43° 08.7´ W | **Al.Fl.W.W.R.** period 15s fl. 0.5s, ec. 4.5s fl. 0.5s, ec. 4.5s fl. 0.5s, ec. 4.5s | 331 **101** | W. **51** R. **45** | White four-sided masonry tower, cylindrical top, brown edges. | Visible 085°-077°. 3 F.R. lights shown from tower at light. **Radiobeacon.** **DGPS Station.** |
| 18374 *G 0367.4* | **--Morro do Pico.** | 22° 56.2´ S 43° 07.4´ W | **Q.W.** | 823 **251** | **30** | | Private light. |
| 18376 *G 0362* | --Ilha de Palmas, W. end of island. | 23° 01.6´ S 43° 12.3´ W | **Fl.W.R.** period 6s fl. 1s, ec. 5s | 105 **32** | W. 10 R. 7 | White truncated conical concrete tower, four-sided base; 10. | W. 008°-076°, R.-081°, W.-252°. |
| 18380 *G 0367* | --Fort Santa Cruz. | 22° 56.3´ S 43° 08.1´ W | **Iso.R.** period 2s | 85 **26** | 14 | White masonry column, hexagonal lantern; 20. | |
| 18384 *G 0368* | --Ilha da Laje. | 22° 56.1´ S 43° 08.8´ W | **Iso.G.** period 2s | 55 **17** | 11 | Green four-sided truncated pyramidal concrete tower; 33. | |
| 18388 *G 0372* | --Ilha de Villegagnon. | 22° 54.8´ S 43° 09.5´ W | **Fl.W.** period 6s fl. 0.5s, ec. 5.5s | 23 **7** | 5 | Two white four-sided concrete towers, green band; 23. | |
| 18389 *G 0374* | --Isla Fiscal. | 22° 54.0´ S 43° 10.1´ W | **Fl.R.** period 6s fl. 0.5s, ec. 5.5s | 26 **8** | 8 | Gray truncated pyramidal concrete tower; 20. | |
| 18392 *G 0365* | --TV tower. | 22° 57.0´ S 43° 13.8´ W | **Q.W.** | 2844 **867** | **24** | Four-sided metal framework structure, white and red bands; 341. | Private light. |
| 18396 *G 0364* | --TV tower. | 22° 57.1´ S 43° 14.2´ W | **Q.W.** | 2792 **851** | **40** | | Private light. |
| 18400 *G 0366* | **--Santos Dumont** AVIATION LIGHT. | 22° 54.6´ S 43° 10.0´ W | **Al.Fl.W.G.** | 246 **75** | **22** | Four-sided metal framework structure, red and white bands; 10. | |
| 18401 *G 0369.5* | --Pescadores, mole, head. | 22° 55.0´ S 43° 10.0´ W | **Fl.R.** period 6s fl. 0.5s, ec. 5.5s | 30 **9** | 5 | Red concrete pipe, red balcony; 16. | |
| 18404 *G 0376* | --Feiticeiras, on shoal. | 22° 52.9´ S 43° 10.1´ W | **Fl.(2)W.** period 10s fl. 1s, ec. 1.5s fl. 1s, ec. 6.5s | 29 **9** | 7 | ISOLATED DANGER BRB, tower, topmark. | |
| 18408 | -President Costa and Silva Bridge RACON. | 22° 52.3´ S 43° 09.3´ W | **G(– – •)** | | **25** | | |
| 18409 *G 0380.3* | --W. pillar. | 22° 52.3´ S 43° 09.4´ W | **F.G.** | 26 **8** | 5 | Green metal framework structure; 16. | |
| 18410 *G 0380.32* | --E. pillar. | 22° 52.3´ S 43° 09.2´ W | **F.R.** | 26 **8** | 5 | Red metal framework structure; 16. | |
| 18412 *G 0381.8* | -Mocangue, W. pier, head. | 22° 51.9´ S 43° 08.3´ W | **Fl.R.** period 3s fl. 0.5s, ec. 2.5s | 23 **7** | 5 | White metal post; 20. | F.Y. mark pier heads on N. and E. sides of Ilha do Mocangue. |
| 18413 *G 0382.25* | **-Ponta da Armacao.** | 22° 53.1´ S 43° 08.0´ W | **Fl.W.** period 10s fl. 1s, ec. 9s | 69 **21** | **19** | Four-sided truncated pyramidal masonry tower, black and white bands; 62. | F.Y. on pier 200 meters NW. |
| 18414 *G 0382.4* | -BACS(E). | 22° 52.5´ S 43° 08.1´ W | **F.Y.** | | | | |
| 18416 *G 0382.5* | -BACS(W). | 22° 52.4´ S 43° 07.9´ W | **F.Y.** | | | | |
| 18420 *G 0385* | -Galeao AVIATION LIGHT. | 22° 48.4´ S 43° 14.2´ W | **Al.Fl.W.G.** | 164 **50** | | Four-sided truncated pyramidal metal framework structure, white and red bands; 33. | Occasional. |

| (1) No. | (2) Name and Location | (3) Position | (4) Characteristic | (5) Height | (6) Range | (7) Structure | (8) Remarks |
|---|---|---|---|---|---|---|---|

## BRAZIL

| (1) No. | (2) Name and Location | (3) Position | (4) Characteristic | (5) Height | (6) Range | (7) Structure | (8) Remarks |
|---|---|---|---|---|---|---|---|
| 18424 *G 0385.4* | -Ponta da Ribeira, mole. | 22° 49.4′ S 43° 09.8′ W | **3 F.Y.** | | 3 | Two black posts. | Lights arranged in triangular shape. Private light. |
| 18425 *G 0385.41* | --Tower. | 22° 49.4′ S 43° 10.1′ W | **3 F.W.** | | 3 | Black post on building. | Lights arranged in triangular shape. Private light. |
| 18432 *G 0386* | -Terminal Alte. Tamandare, S. beacon. | 22° 49.3′ S 43° 09.2′ W | **Q.Y.** | 43 **13** | 3 | White metal post; 33. | Private light. |
| 18433 *G 0386.4* | --N. beacon. | 22° 49.1′ S 43° 09.2′ W | **Q.Y.** | 43 **13** | 3 | White metal post; 33. | Private light. |
| 18434 *G 0389* | --Secondary pier, N. beacon. | 22° 48.2′ S 43° 09.1′ W | **Q.Y.** | 46 **14** | 3 | White metal post; 33. | Private light. |
| 18434.5 *G 0389.1* | ---S. beacon. | 22° 48.3′ S 43° 09.0′ W | **Q.Y.** | 43 **13** | 3 | White metal post; 33. | Private light. |
| 18435 *G 0391* | -Ilha Rasa de Dentro. | 22° 48.0′ S 43° 09.5′ W | **Fl.(2)W.** period 5s fl. 0.5s, ec. 1s fl. 0.5s, ec. 3s | 30 **9** | 4 | ISOLATED DANGER BRB, column, topmark; 10. | |
| 18436 *G 0387* | -Manue is de Dentro. | 22° 48.5′ S 43° 09.2′ W | **Fl.G.** period 3s fl. 0.3s, ec. 2.7s | 36 **11** | 5 | Green cylindrical masonry tower; 26. | |
| 18438 *G 0390* | -Pedra da Sardinha. | 22° 48.1′ S 43° 07.6′ W | **Fl.(2)W.** period 10s fl. 0.5s, ec. 1s fl. 0.5s, ec. 8s | 23 **7** | 5 | ISOLATED DANGER BRB, post, topmark; 10. | |
| 18439 *G 0388.8* | --Ilha Comprida. | 22° 48.3′ S 43° 07.4′ W | **Iso.W.** period 2s | 36 **11** | 4 | White metal tube; 23. | |
| 18439.2 *G 0388.7* | --Ponte. | 22° 48.2′ S 43° 07.3′ W | **Iso.W.** period 2s | 49 **15** | 4 | White metal tube; 10. | |
| 18439.4 *G 0388.63* | --Ilha Redonda. | 22° 48.2′ S 43° 07.2′ W | **Iso.W.** period 2s | 49 **15** | 4 | White metal tube; 10. | |
| 18440 *G 0388* | -Cocois. | 22° 48.5′ S 43° 07.7′ W | **Fl.R.** period 3s fl. 0.3s, ec. 2.7s | 20 **6** | 5 | Red metal tower, four-sided concrete base; 10. | Q.Y. 8m 5M on dolphin 0.5 mile NE. |
| 18441 *G 0388.4* | -Alinhamento Range, front. | 22° 48.1′ S 43° 07.2′ W | **Q.R.** | 43 **13** | 5 | White metal pipe, red triangular daymark point up; 33. | Private light. |
| 18441.1 *G 0388.41* | --Rear, about 230 meters 073°42′ from front. | 22° 48.1′ S 43° 07.1′ W | **Iso.R.** period 2s | 49 **15** | 6 | White framework tower, red triangular daymark point down; 33. | Private light. |
| 18444 *G 0392* | -Pedra do Xareu. | 22° 47.8′ S 43° 08.5′ W | **Fl.(2)W.** period 5s fl. 0.5s, ec. 1s fl. 0.5s, ec. 3s | 36 **11** | 7 | ISOLATED DANGER BRB, pipe, topmark; 30. | |
| 18448 *G 0394* | -Gravatais. | 22° 47.6′ S 43° 07.0′ W | **Fl.(2)W.** period 10s fl. 0.5s, ec. 1.5s fl. 0.5s, ec. 7.5s | 20 **6** | 8 | ISOLATED DANGER BRB, tower, topmark; 13. | |
| 18452 *G 0396* | -Ilha de Itapacis. | 22° 46.6′ S 43° 06.4′ W | **Fl.R.** period 3s fl. 0.3s, ec. 2.7s | 32 **10** | 5 | Red cylindrical concrete tower; 23. | |
| 18452.3 *G 0398.5* | -Ilha de Lobos. | 22° 45.8′ S 43° 06.1′ W | **Fl.(2)G.** period 6s fl. 0.5s, ec. 0.5s fl. 0.5s, ec. 4.5s | 16 **5** | 5 | Green metal pipe; 16. | |
| 18452.5 *G 0398* | -Ponta da Ribeira. | 22° 45.9′ S 43° 06.2′ W | **Fl.G.** period 6s fl. 1s, ec. 5s | 46 **14** | 8 | White four-sided masonry tower; 36. | |
| 18453 *G 0397* | -Laje Tijolo do Boqueirao. | 22° 46.4′ S 43° 09.9′ W | **Fl.Y.** period 3s fl. 0.5s, ec. 2.5s | 13 **4** | 5 | Yellow metal pipe, concrete base; 10. | |

| (1) No. | (2) Name and Location | (3) Position | (4) Characteristic | (5) Height | (6) Range | (7) Structure | (8) Remarks |
|---|---|---|---|---|---|---|---|

**BRAZIL**

| (1) No. | (2) Name and Location | (3) Position | (4) Characteristic | (5) Height | (6) Range | (7) Structure | (8) Remarks |
|---|---|---|---|---|---|---|---|
| 18455 *G 0384* | -Pedras da Passagem. | 22° 50.5′ S 43° 10.0′ W | **Q.W.** | 30 **9** | 10 | Cylindrical concrete tower, black and white bands; 26. | |
| 18456 *G 0402* | -Ilha Pontuda. | 23° 02.3′ S 43° 18.2′ W | **Fl.W.R.** period 10s fl. 0.5s, ec. 9.5s | 285 **87** | W. 11 R. 7 | White cylindrical metal tower, concrete base; 10. | W. 213°-027°, R.-055°, W.-085°, R.-096°, W.-205°, R.-213°. |
| 18460 *G 0404* | **Ponta de Guaratiba.** | 23° 04.9′ S 43° 33.8′ W | **Fl.W.** period 6s fl. 1s, ec. 5s | 138 **42** | **18** | White four-sided concrete tower; 26. | |
| 18464 *G 0418* | **Santa Cruz** AVIATION LIGHT. | 22° 55.7′ S 43° 42.8′ W | **Al.Fl.W.G.** | 246 **75** | **22** | Metal framework structure, red and white bands; 16. | Occasional. **Aero Radiobeacon** 1.6 miles SW. |
| 18468 *G 0406* | **Laje Marambaia.** | 23° 07.0′ S 43° 50.2′ W | **Fl.(2)W.** period 10s fl. 1s, ec. 1s fl. 1s, ec. 7s | 79 **24** | **18** | Black truncated pyramidal masonry tower, red bands; 23. | |
| 18472 *G 0408* | **Ponta de Castelhanos.** | 23° 10.1′ S 44° 05.6′ W | **Oc.(3)W.** period 10s lt. 6s, ec. 0.8s lt. 0.5s, ec. 1.4s lt. 0.5s, ec. 0.8s | 397 **121** | **27** | White four-sided masonry tower, white dwelling; 52. | Visible 149°-027°. |
| | BAIA DA ILHA GRANDE: | | | | | | |
| 18476 *G 0409* | -Ilha Pau a Pino. | 23° 06.0′ S 44° 07.1′ W | **Q.(3)W.** period 10s | 82 **25** | 10 | White cylindrical masonry tower; 6. | |
| 18478 *G 0409.5* | -Ilha do Abraao. | 23° 06.9′ S 44° 09.9′ W | **Fl.W.** period 6s fl. 0.5s, ec. 5.5s | 29 **9** | 6 | White metal pipe, diamond daymark; 16. | Visible 093°-066°. |
| 18480 *G 0411* | -Channel A and B Range, common front. | 23° 02.5′ S 44° 06.3′ W | **Fl.(2)R.** period 10s fl. 0.5s, ec. 1s fl. 0.5s, ec. 8s | 23 **7** | 3 | White triangular metal framework structure, four-sided concrete base, white diamond daymark. | **Radar reflector.** |
| | | | **Dir.Q.Y.** | | 8 | | |
| | | | **Dir.Q.Y.** | | 5 | | |
| | -RACON | | **M(– –)** | | **19** | | (3 & 10cm). |
| 18484 *G 0410.9* | --A, rear, 2300 meters. 328°30′ from front. | 23° 01.4′ S 44° 07.0′ W | **Dir.Iso.Y.** period 2s | | 9 | White triangular metal framework structure, four-sided concrete base, white diamond daymark. | |
| 18492 *G 0411.1* | --B, rear, 940 meters 249° from front. | 23° 02.7′ S 44° 06.8′ W | **Iso.R.** period 2s | 56 **17** | 7 | White triangular metal framework structure, four-sided concrete base, white diamond daymark. | **Radar reflector.** |
| | | | **Dir.Iso.Y.** period 2s | | 6 | | |
| 18496 *G 0412* | -Laje de Mangaratiba. | 23° 00.7′ S 44° 04.6′ W | **Fl.(2)W.** period 10s fl. 0.5s, ec. 1.5s fl. 0.5s, ec. 7.5s | 20 **6** | 7 | ISOLATED DANGER BRB, tower, topmark; 16. | |
| 18497 *G 0414* | -Terminal da Ilha Guaiba, W. head. | 23° 00.8′ S 44° 02.1′ W | **F.Y.** | | 3 | Yellow metal framework structure. | Private light. |
| 18498 *G 0414.2* | --E. end. | 23° 00.7′ S 44° 01.9′ W | **Q.G.** | | 3 | Green metal framework structure. | |
| 18500 *G 0415* | -Laje Alagada. | 23° 02.0′ S 43° 58.4′ W | **Q.R.** | 13 **4** | 5 | Red four-sided masonry tower; 10. | |

| (1) No. | (2) Name and Location | (3) Position | (4) Characteristic | (5) Height | (6) Range | (7) Structure | (8) Remarks |
|---|---|---|---|---|---|---|---|

## BRAZIL

| (1) No. | (2) Name and Location | (3) Position | (4) Characteristic | (5) Height | (6) Range | (7) Structure | (8) Remarks |
|---|---|---|---|---|---|---|---|
| | BAIA DE SEPETIBA: | | | | | | |
| 18501 *G 0416.3* | -Laje de Pedra Branca. | 22° 57.9´ S 43° 53.3´ W | **Fl.(2)W.** period 10s fl. 1s, ec. 1.5s fl. 1s, ec. 6.5s | 23 **7** | 5 | Black four-sided masonry tower; red bands. | |
| 18502 *G 0416.5* | -Laje Preta. | 22° 57.6´ S 43° 52.6´ W | **Q.(9)W.** period 15s | 13 **4** | 5 | W. CARDINAL YBY, tower, topmark. | |
| 18503 *G 0416.8* | -Ilha do Martins. | 22° 57.3´ S 43° 51.5´ W | **Fl.W.** period 6s fl. 1s, ec. 5s | 13 **4** | 8 | White four-sided masonry tower; 10. | |
| 18503.5 *G 0417* | -Sepetiba. | 22° 56.2´ S 43° 50.4´ W | **F.Y.** | | 3 | White metal structure, yellow lantern. | Private light. |
| | BAIA DA ILHA GRANDE: | | | | | | |
| 18504 *G 0416* | -Ilha Jurubaiba. | 22° 57.6´ S 43° 57.0´ W | **Fl.W.** period 3s fl. 0.3s, ec. 2.7s | 75 **23** | 7 | White four-sided truncated pyramidal concrete tower; 16. | Visible 290°-258°. |
| 18506 *G 0415.5* | -Jaguanum. | 22° 59.9´ S 43° 56.2´ W | **Fl.W.** period 6s fl. 0.5s, ec. 5.5s | 13 **4** | 7 | White metal pipe; 13. | |
| 18508 *G 0414.6* | -Laje do Cabrito. | 22° 57.9´ S 44° 00.4´ W | **Q.(9)W.** period 15s | 16 **5** | 7 | W. CARDINAL YBY, tower, topmark; 10. | |
| 18512 *G 0414.8* | Laje Preta de Fora. | 22° 58.6´ S 44° 01.3´ W | **Q.(3)W.** period 10s | 16 **5** | 5 | E. CARDINAL BYB, tower, topmark; 10. | |
| 18516 *G 0420* | -Ilha da Itacuatiba. | 23° 04.2´ S 44° 15.1´ W | **Fl.W.** period 6s fl. 0.3s, ec. 5.7s | 148 **45** | 7 | White four-sided masonry tower; 16. | |
| 18517 *G 0419* | -Ponte Leme, E. pier head. | 23° 03.7´ S 44° 13.6´ W | **F.Y.** | | 3 | | Private light. |
| 18518 *G 0419.2* | --Pier elbow. | 23° 03.6´ S 44° 13.9´ W | **F.Y.** | | 3 | | Private light. |
| 18520 *G 0424* | -Ilha Saracura. | 23° 03.3´ S 44° 16.1´ W | **Fl.R.** period 5s fl. 0.5s, ec. 4.5s | 56 **17** | 5 | Red four-sided truncated pyramidal masonry tower; 13. | |
| 18522 *G 0417.5* | -Ponta do Funil, E. range marker. | 23° 05.2´ S 44° 12.7´ W | **Fl.W.** period 10s fl. 1s, ec. 9s | 20 **6** | 7 | White four-sided concrete post; 13. | |
| 18524 *G 0426* | -Laje Grande. | 23° 00.9´ S 44° 15.2´ W | **Fl.G.** period 3s fl. 0.5s, ec. 2.5s | 23 **7** | 6 | Green cylindrical metal tower; 13. | |
| 18525 *G 0427* | -Lajes Pretas. | 23° 01.4´ S 44° 16.1´ W | **Fl.(2)W.** period 5s fl. 0.5s, ec. 1s fl. 0.5s, ec. 3s | | 5 | Black cylindrical concrete tower, red band; 10. | |
| 18526 *G 0427.5* | -Ilha do Peregrino. | 23° 01.5´ S 44° 17.4´ W | **Fl.G.** period 3s fl. 0.3s, ec. 2.7s | 13 **4** | 8 | Green cylindrical concrete tower; 13. | |
| 18528 *G 0432* | -Laje Preta. | 23° 03.0´ S 44° 18.5´ W | **Fl.G.** period 3s fl. 0.5s, ec. 2.5s | 39 **12** | 6 | Green cylindrical concrete tower; 20. | |
| 18532 *G 0428* | -Laje dos Homens, S. extremity. | 23° 02.3´ S 44° 17.9´ W | **Iso.R.** period 2s | 26 **8** | 4 | Red cylindrical concrete tower; 16. | |
| 18534 *G 0429* | -Laje Alagada. | 23° 02.1´ S 44° 18.0´ W | **Fl.R.** period 3s fl. 0.3s, ec. 2.7s | | 5 | Red cylindrical concrete tower. | |

| (1) No. | (2) Name and Location | (3) Position | (4) Characteristic | (5) Height | (6) Range | (7) Structure | (8) Remarks |
|---|---|---|---|---|---|---|---|
| | | | **BRAZIL** | | | | |
| 18536 *G 0430* | Calombo, W. head. | 23° 01.6′ S 44° 18.8′ W | **Fl.R.** period 3s fl. 0.3s, ec. 2.7s | 10 **3** | 5 | Red four-sided concrete post; 10. | |
| 18537 *G 0431.5* | -Ilha dos Coqueiros. | 23° 00.6′ S 44° 18.5′ W | **Fl.G.** period 3s fl. 0.3s, ec. 2.7s | 13 **4** | 5 | Green concrete tower; 13. | |
| 18538 *G 0431* | -Naval College, pier. | 23° 00.9′ S 44° 19.7′ W | **F.Y.** | | | White masonry tower, square base; 7. | |
| 18539 *G 0435* | -Laje Branca. | 23° 00.0′ S 44° 22.0′ W | **Fl.(2)W.** period 5s fl. 0.5s, ec. 1s fl. 0.5s, ec. 3s | | 5 | Black cylindrical concrete tower, red band; 10. | |
| 18540 *G 0434* | -Laje da Figueira. | 23° 01.3′ S 44° 22.2′ W | **Fl.(2)W.** period 5s fl. 0.5s, ec. 1s fl. 0.5s, ec. 3s | 13 **4** | 5 | ISOLATED DANGER BRB, tower, topmark. | |
| 18541 *G 0440* | -Laje do Sitio. | 22° 59.1′ S 44° 23.5′ W | **Q.(2)W.** period 4s | 13 **4** | 8 | White cylindrical metal tower, red band; 10. | |
| 18542 *G 0433.5* | -Ilha de Piedade. | 23° 02.3′ S 44° 20.8′ W | **Fl.Y.** period 3s fl. 0.5s, ec. 2.5s | | 5 | Yellow metal pipe. | Private light. |
| 18543 *G 0439.2* | -Bracui Marina, E. | 22° 57.3′ S 44° 23.7′ W | **F.R.** | | 5 | Red metal pipe. | Private light. |
| 18543.5 *G 0439* | --W. | 22° 57.3′ S 44° 23.8′ W | **F.G.** | | 5 | Green metal pipe. | Private light. |
| 18544 *G 0450* | -Laje do Coronel. | 23° 06.0′ S 44° 24.0′ W | **Fl.(2)W.** period 10s fl. 1s, ec. 1s fl. 1s, ec. 7s | 26 **8** | 10 | ISOLATED DANGER BRB, tower, topmark; 13. | |
| | -RACON | | **T(−)** | | **25** | | (3 & 10cm). |
| 18548 *G 0448* | -Laje Branca. | 23° 08.3′ S 44° 20.8′ W | **Fl.(2)W.** period 5s fl. 0.5s, ec. 1s fl. 0.5s, ec. 3s | 20 **6** | 5 | ISOLATED DANGER BRB, tower, topmark; 13. | |
| 18552 *G 0454* | -Ilha Rapada, S. head. | 23° 09.6′ S 44° 39.8′ W | **Fl.R.** period 3s fl. 0.3s, ec. 2.7s | 180 **55** | 5 | Red four-sided truncated pyramidal metal framework tower, topmark; 23. | |
| 18556 *G 0458* | **-Juatinga.** | 23° 17.6′ S 44° 30.3′ W | **Fl.W.** period 10s fl. 1s, ec. 9s | 574 **175** | **17** | White four-sided truncated pyramidal concrete tower; 26. | Visible 137°-045°. |
| 18558 *G 0459* | **-Ponta dos Meros.** | 23° 13.5′ S 44° 20.8′ W | **Fl.(2)W.** period 15s fl. 1s, ec. 2s fl. 1s, ec. 11s | 148 **45** | **15** | Metal pipe, red and white bands, diamond daymark; 13. | |
| 18560 *G 0462* | **-Ubatuba.** | 23° 27.6′ S 45° 01.2′ W | **Fl.(3)W.** period 10s fl. 1s, ec. 1s fl. 1s, ec. 1s fl. 1s, ec. 5s | 213 **65** | **16** | Metal pipe, white four-sided concrete base; 10. | Visible 128°-047°. |
| 18568 *G 0466* | **Ilha da Vitoria.** | 23° 45.0′ S 45° 00.5′ W | **Fl.W.** period 6s fl. 1s, ec. 5s | 331 **101** | **16** | White four-sided masonry tower; 13. | Visible 137°-353°. |
| 18570 *G 0464* | Massaguacu. | 23° 37.7′ S 45° 22.2′ W | **Fl.(2)W.** period 12s fl. 1s, ec. 2s fl. 1s, ec. 8s | 246 **75** | 12 | White four-sided masonry tower; 16. | |
| 18571 *G 0468* | **Ponta Grossa.** | 23° 46.6′ S 45° 13.8′ W | **L.Fl.W.** period 15s fl. 2s, ec. 13s | 197 **60** | **16** | White four-sided metal framework tower, daymarks; 33. | |

## BRAZIL

| (1) No. | (2) Name and Location | (3) Position | (4) Characteristic | (5) Height | (6) Range | (7) Structure | (8) Remarks |
|---|---|---|---|---|---|---|---|
| | CANAL DE SAO SEBASTIAO: | | | | | | |
| 18572<br>*G 0470* | -Ponta das Canas. | 23° 43.7′ S<br>45° 20.5′ W | **Fl.W.**<br>period 6s<br>fl. 0.5s, ec. 5.5s | 43<br>**13** | 9 | Cylindrical concrete tower, red and white bands; 36. | Visible 029°-240°. |
| 18576<br>*G 0472* | -Sao Sebastiao. | 23° 43.5′ S<br>45° 21.9′ W | **Fl.R.**<br>period 5s<br>fl. 0.5s, ec. 4.5s | 20<br>**6** | 4 | Red four-sided masonry tower, red concrete base; 20. | |
| 18580<br>*G 0474* | -Ponta do Viana. | 23° 45.5′ S<br>45° 21.1′ W | **Fl.W.**<br>period 3s<br>fl. 0.3s, ec. 2.7s | 19<br>**6** | 7 | White metal tower, white four-sided concrete base; 10. | |
| 18584<br>*G 0475* | -Ilhabela. | 23° 46.2′ S<br>45° 22.5′ W | **Fl.R.**<br>period 3s<br>fl. 0.3s, ec. 2.7s | 20<br>**6** | 5 | Red four-sided masonry tower, red concrete platform, red metal framework base; 20. | |
| 18585<br>*G 0476* | -Terminal Maritimo de Sao Sebastiao, N. pier, No. 1. | 23° 48.0′ S<br>45° 23.0′ W | **F.Y.** | | 5 | | Private light. |
| 18585.1<br>*G 0476.2* | --N. pier, No. 2. | 23° 48.2′ S<br>45° 23.1′ W | **F.Y.** | | 5 | | Private light. |
| 18585.2<br>*G 0476.4* | --S. pier, No. 1. | 23° 48.4′ S<br>45° 23.2′ W | **F.Y.** | | 5 | | Private light. |
| 18585.3<br>*G 0476.6* | ---No. 2. | 23° 48.6′ S<br>45° 23.3′ W | **F.Y.** | | 5 | | Private light. |
| 18585.4<br>*G 0476.8* | --Mole. | 23° 48.5′ S<br>45° 23.8′ W | **F.R.** | | 5 | | Private light. |
| 18588<br>*G 0477* | -Pontinha, E. side of Channel. | 23° 49.2′ S<br>45° 22.6′ W | **Fl.R.**<br>period 5s<br>fl. 0.5s, ec. 4.5s | 82<br>**25** | 6 | Red four-sided metal framework structure; 33. | |
| 18592<br>*G 0478* | -Laje dos Moleques, W. side of channel. | 23° 49.7′ S<br>45° 24.8′ W | **Fl.G.**<br>period 10s<br>fl. 1s, ec. 9s | 33<br>**10** | 9 | Green four-sided concrete tower; 13. | |
| 18610<br>*G 0479* | Ilha do Toque-Toque. | 23° 51.3′ S<br>45° 31.5′ W | **Fl.W.**<br>period 6s<br>fl. 1s, ec. 5s | 115<br>**35** | 12 | White four-sided metal framework tower; 33. | Visible 236°-149°. |
| 18612<br>*G 0480* | -Ponta da Sela. | 23° 53.3′ S<br>45° 27.7′ W | **Fl.(3)W.**<br>period 15s<br>fl. 1s, ec. 1s<br>fl. 1s, ec. 1s<br>fl. 1s, ec. 10s | 56<br>**17** | 9 | Cylindrical concrete tower, red and white bands; 36. | Visible 000°-226°. |
| 18616<br>*G 0484* | **Ponta do Boi.** | 23° 58.0′ S<br>45° 15.1′ W | **L.Fl.W.**<br>period 10s<br>fl. 2.5s, ec. 7.5s | 230<br>**70** | **22** | White four-sided masonry tower; 56. | Visible 247°-092°. |
| | RACON | | **B(– • • •)** | | **25** | | (3 & 10cm). |
| 18620<br>*G 0486* | Ponta de Pirabura. | 23° 56.6′ S<br>45° 13.6′ W | **Fl.R.**<br>period 3s<br>fl. 0.3s, ec. 2.7s | 49<br>**15** | 10 | Red four-sided concrete tower; 10. | Visible 185°-020°. |
| 18624<br>*G 0490* | **Arquipelago de Alcatrazes.** | 24° 05.7′ S<br>45° 42.2′ W | **Fl.W.**<br>period 6s<br>fl. 0.5s, ec. 5.5s | 79<br>**24** | **15** | White four-sided truncated pyramidal concrete tower; 23. | Visible 014°-244°. |
| 18628<br>*G 0492* | Pedra do Corvo, S. side of entrance to Enseada de Bertioga. | 23° 51.4′ S<br>46° 07.5′ W | **Fl.W.**<br>period 6s<br>fl. 0.3s, ec. 5.7s | 95<br>**29** | 7 | Red four-sided concrete tower; 13. | Visible 113°-358°. |
| 18632<br>*G 0495* | Laje de Santos. | 24° 19.2′ S<br>46° 10.9′ W | **Fl.W.**<br>period 3s<br>fl. 0.3s, ec. 2.7s | 125<br>**38** | 14 | Cylindrical masonry tower, black and white bands; 16. | |
| 18636<br>*G 0496* | **Ilha da Moela.** | 24° 03.0′ S<br>46° 15.8′ W | **Al.Oc.W.R.**<br>period 60s<br>W. lt. 15s, ec. 4s<br>W. lt. 1.5s, ec. 4s<br>W. lt. 15s, ec. 9.5s<br>R. lt. 1.5s, ec. 9.5s | 361<br>**110** | W. **40**<br>R. **39** | White cylindrical masonry tower; 33. | **Radiobeacon.**<br>**DGPS Station.** |

| (1) No. | (2) Name and Location | (3) Position | (4) Characteristic | (5) Height | (6) Range | (7) Structure | (8) Remarks |
|---|---|---|---|---|---|---|---|

## BRAZIL

| (1) No. | (2) Name and Location | (3) Position | (4) Characteristic | (5) Height | (6) Range | (7) Structure | (8) Remarks |
|---|---|---|---|---|---|---|---|
| | BAIA DE SANTOS: | | | | | | |
| 18640<br>*G 0497* | -Palmas, W. extremity of Ilha das Palmas. | 24° 00.5′ S<br>46° 19.5′ W | **Fl.R.**<br>period 3s<br>fl. 0.3s, ec. 2.7s | 59<br>**18** | 5 | Red cylindrical concrete tower; 13. | |
| 18644<br>*G 0498* | -Range A, front, Praia do Boqueirao No. 1. | 23° 59.1′ S<br>46° 19.7′ W | **Q.W.** | 26<br>**8** | 10 | White cylindrical concrete tower, red band; 23. | |
| 18648<br>*G 0498.1* | --Rear, Praia do Boqueirao No. 2, 1372 meters 021°30′ from front. | 23° 58.4′ S<br>46° 19.4′ W | **Iso.W.**<br>period 2s | 56<br>**17** | 11 | Four-sided concrete tower, red and white bands; 56. | |
| | --RACON | | **N(– •)** | | **19** | | (3 & 10cm). |
| 18656<br>*G 0499.1* | -Ponta da Praia No. 4. | 23° 59.1′ S<br>46° 18.6′ W | **Dir.W.R.G.** | 43<br>**13** | W. 9<br>R. 5<br>G. 5 | Four-sided concrete tower, black and white bands; 39. | F.R. 053°-057°, F.W.-058°, F.G.-062°.<br>Range 5/2M by day. |
| 18660<br>*G 0501* | -Range C, front Rio do Meio No. 5. | 23° 59.6′ S<br>46° 17.6′ W | **Q.W.** | 26<br>**8** | 10 | White four-sided concrete tower, red band; 23. | |
| 18664<br>*G 0501.1* | --Rear, Rio No. 6, 250 meters 094° from front. | 23° 59.6′ S<br>46° 17.5′ W | **Iso.W.**<br>period 2s | 43<br>**13** | 11 | Four-sided concrete tower, red and white bands; 43. | |
| 18668<br>*G 0500* | -Fortaleza. | 23° 59.7′ S<br>46° 18.4′ W | **Fl.R.**<br>period 3s<br>fl. 0.3s, ec. 2.7s | 13<br>**4** | 6 | Red metal framework structure; 10. | |
| 18673<br>*G 0502.5* | -Cable tower, W. side. | 23° 57.2′ S<br>46° 18.6′ W | **F.R.** | | | Tower. | Private light. |
| 18674<br>*G 0502.55* | --E. side. | 23° 57.1′ S<br>46° 18.3′ W | **F.R.** | | | Tower. | Private light. |
| 18676<br>*G 0502.4* | -Itapema Norte. | 23° 56.2′ S<br>46° 18.5′ W | **Fl.R.**<br>period 3s<br>fl. 0.3s, ec. 2.7s | 36<br>**11** | 5 | White four-sided metal framework tower; 46. | |
| 18680<br>*G 0502* | -Naval Aviation Base. No. 4. | 23° 55.5′ S<br>46° 18.5′ W | **Fl.Y.**<br>period 3s<br>fl. 0.5s, ec. 2.5s | | 5 | SPECIAL<br>Y, beacon, topmark. | Private light. |
| 18684<br>*G 0502.2* | --Rio Diana, W. side No. 3. | 23° 55.2′ S<br>46° 18.6′ W | **Fl.Y.**<br>period 3s<br>fl. 0.5s, ec. 2.5s | | 5 | SPECIAL<br>Y, beacon, topmark. | Private light. |
| 18688<br>*G 0502.6* | -Barnabe. | 23° 55.5′ S<br>46° 19.7′ W | **Q.R.** | 26<br>**8** | 5 | White four-sided metal framework structure. | |
| 18689<br>*G 0503* | -Valongo. No. 1. | 23° 55.4′ S<br>46° 20.6′ W | **Fl.Y.**<br>period 3s<br>fl. 0.5s, ec. 2.5s | | 5 | SPECIAL<br>Y, beacon, topmark. | Private light. |
| 18689.2<br>*G 0503.2* | --No. 2. | 23° 55.1′ S<br>46° 20.1′ W | **Fl.Y.**<br>period 3s<br>fl. 0.5s, ec. 2.5s | | 5 | SPECIAL<br>Y, beacon, topmark. | Private light. |
| 18690<br>*G 0504* | -Pier No. 4, E. head. | 23° 55.2′ S<br>46° 21.6′ W | **F.Y.** | 13<br>**4** | 5 | Gray four-sided metal post; 3. | |
| 18692<br>*G 0506* | **Laje da Conceicao.** | 24° 14.2′ S<br>46° 41.5′ W | **Fl.(2)W.R.**<br>period 12s<br>fl. 1s, ec. 2s<br>fl. 1s, ec. 8s | 112<br>**34** | W. **16**<br>R. **17** | Red four-sided concrete tower; 20. | R. 276°-286°, W.-276°. |
| 18696<br>*G 0509* | Guarau Island. | 24° 22.9′ S<br>46° 59.2′ W | **Fl.W.R.**<br>period 3s<br>fl. 0.5s, ec. 2.5s | 220<br>**67** | W. 14<br>R. 11 | White cylindrical fiberglass tower; 23. | W. 206°-000°, R.-206°. |
| 18700<br>*G 0512* | **Ilha Queimada Grande.** | 24° 28.7′ S<br>46° 40.6′ W | **Fl.W.**<br>period 10s<br>fl. 1s, ec. 9s | 272<br>**83** | **23** | White four-sided concrete tower; 33. | Visible 014°-337°. |
| 18702<br>*G 0513.5* | **Icapara.** | 24° 41.0′ S<br>47° 27.2′ W | **L.Fl.W.**<br>period 15s<br>fl. 2s, ec. 13s | 240<br>**73** | **19** | White four-sided metal framework tower, daymark; 33. | |

| (1) No. | (2) Name and Location | (3) Position | (4) Characteristic | (5) Height | (6) Range | (7) Structure | (8) Remarks |
|---|---|---|---|---|---|---|---|
| | | | **BRAZIL** | | | | |
| 18704 *G 0516* | **Ilha do Bom Abrigo.** | 25° 07.4´ S 47° 51.8´ W | **Al.Fl.W.W.R.** period 30s W. fl. 1s, ec. 9s W. fl. 1s, ec. 9s R. fl. 1s, ec. 9s | 479 **146** | W. **28** R. **23** | White octagonal masonry tower; 52. | |
| | PORTO DE PARANAGUA: | | | | | | |
| | -Ilha do Mel: | | | | | | |
| 18724 *G 0520* | **--Ponta das Conchas.** | 25° 32.3´ S 48° 17.4´ W | **Fl.W.** period 10s fl. 1s, ec. 9s | 220 **67** | **25** | White truncated conical metal tower; 59. | Visible 146°-004°30′. |
| 18726 *G 0524* | --Caraguata. | 25° 34.4´ S 48° 19.2´ W | **Fl.W.** period 6s fl. 1s, ec. 5s | 141 **43** | 8 | White four-sided masonry tower, red band; 33. | |
| | --RACON | | **C(– • – •)** | | **25** | | (3 & 10cm). |
| 18748 *G 0528* | -Ilha das Cobras. | 25° 29.3´ S 48° 25.9´ W | **Fl.W.** period 5s fl. 0.5s, ec. 4.5s | 36 **11** | 7 | White four-sided truncated pyramidal concrete tower; 20. | |
| 18752 *G 0530* | -Ponta da Cruz. | 25° 30.0´ S 48° 29.3´ W | **Fl.W.** period 6s fl. 1s, ec. 5s | 20 **6** | 8 | White metal post on concrete pillar, daymark; 7. | Q.W. 64m on antenna 1.5 miles SW. |
| 18753 *G 0532* | -Petroleum Terminal jetty. | 25° 30.1´ S 48° 32.0´ W | **F.Y.** | | | | |
| 18756 *G 0538* | **Ilha Caioba.** | 25° 51.2´ S 48° 32.1´ W | **Fl.W.** period 5s fl. 0.5s, ec. 4.5s | 88 **27** | **15** | White four-sided truncated pyramidal metal framework structure; 30. | Visible 225°-000°. Q.W. on antennas 0.5 mile NW. and 2.8 miles SW. |
| 18760 *G 0540* | **Ilha da Paz.** | 26° 10.6´ S 48° 29.1´ W | **L.Fl.W.** period 20s fl. 3.5s, ec. 16.5s | 276 **84** | **26** | White four-sided masonry tower, dwelling; 52. | |
| 18761 *G 0541* | -Ponto Zero. | 26° 13.9´ S 48° 30.1´ W | **Fl.Y.** period 3s fl. 0.3s, ec. 2.7s | 30 **9** | 5 | Yellow structure; 16. | Private light. |
| 18762 *G 0542* | -Cabo Joao Diaz. | 26° 10.1´ S 48° 31.5´ W | **Fl.W.** period 6s fl. 0.5s, ec. 5.5s | 26 **8** | 7 | White four-sided masonry tower; 13. | |
| 18763 *G 0544* | -Sumidouro. | 26° 10.2´ S 48° 33.3´ W | **Fl.W.** period 10s fl. 1s, ec. 9s | 49 **15** | 8 | White four-sided fiberglass framework skeleton tower, two white diamond daymarks. | |
| 18764 *G 0545* | -Trincheira, 3.2 km. 260° from Ponta do Sumidouro. | 26° 10.5´ S 48° 35.2´ W | **Fl.R.** period 6s fl. 0.5s, ec. 5.5s | 30 **9** | 10 | White octagonal masonry tower, red bands; 26. | Fl.Y. 3s 0.2 km. NE. and F.Y. 2.0 km. SE. mark pipeline area. |
| 18768 *G 0545.4* | -Laje Grande de Baixo. | 26° 13.1´ S 48° 38.4´ W | **Q.(2)R.** period 6s | | 5 | Red structure. | |
| 18769 *G 0545.6* | -Sai Pier, E. side of pier head. | 26° 13.3´ S 48° 39.9´ W | **Q.R.** | 16 **5** | 5 | White cylindrical metal tower; 10. | |
| 18770 *G 0545.7* | --W. side of pier, head. | 26° 13.3´ S 48° 39.9´ W | **Q.R.** | 16 **5** | 5 | White cylindrical metal tower; 10. | |
| 18772 *G 0546* | -Abreu de Fora. | 26° 14.6´ S 48° 38.8´ W | **Fl.G.** period 3s fl. 0.3s, ec. 2.7s | 23 **7** | 8 | Green truncated pyramidal concrete tower, triangular base; 20. | |
| 18776 *G 0548* | -Laje do Fundao. | 26° 15.9´ S 48° 40.6´ W | **Fl.R.** period 7s fl. 0.5s, ec. 6.5s | 26 **8** | 5 | Red triangular concrete tower; 20. | |
| 18778 *G 0548.5* | -Pernambuco. | 26° 15.9´ S 48° 41.0´ W | **Fl.R.** period 3s fl. 0.5s, ec. 2.5s | 13 **4** | 6 | Red concrete column; 7. | |

| (1) No. | (2) Name and Location | (3) Position | (4) Characteristic | (5) Height | (6) Range | (7) Structure | (8) Remarks |
|---|---|---|---|---|---|---|---|

## BRAZIL

| (1) No. | (2) Name and Location | (3) Position | (4) Characteristic | (5) Height | (6) Range | (7) Structure | (8) Remarks |
|---|---|---|---|---|---|---|---|
| 18781 *G 0550* | Araquari. | 26° 27.1′ S 48° 35.7′ W | **F.Y.** | 20 **6** | 7 | White cylindrical masonry tower; 13. | |
| 18784 *G 0551* | **Ponta do Varrido.** | 26° 47.1′ S 48° 35.2′ W | **Fl.W.** period 6s fl. 1s, ec. 5s | 164 **50** | **18** | White four-sided truncated pyramidal metal framework tower, black band, daymark; 33. | |
| 18786 | *Lightfloat.* | 26° 46.7′ S 46° 48.2′ W | **Fl.Y.** period 3s | | 5 | | |
| 18788 *G 0552* | **Ponta das Cabecudas.** | 26° 55.6′ S 48° 37.4′ W | **Al.Fl.W.W.R.** period 30s W. fl. 1s, ec. 9s W. fl. 1s, ec. 9s R. fl. 1s, ec. 9s | 190 **58** | W. **28** R. **23** | White metal column, four-sided masonry base. | |
| 18794 *G 0552.4* | **Cabecudas.** | 26° 55.2′ S 48° 38.6′ W | **F.R.** | 548 **167** | **15** | Antenna. | Private light. |
| | RIO ITAJAI: | | | | | | |
| 18796 *G 0555* | -S. jetty head, No. 8. | 26° 54.9′ S 48° 38.0′ W | **Fl.G.** period 3s fl. 0.5s, ec. 2.5s | 52 **16** | 10 | White cylindrical fiberglass tower, concrete base, green bands; 46. | |
| 18800 *G 0554* | -N. jetty head, No. 7. | 26° 54.8′ S 48° 38.2′ W | **Fl.(3)R.** period 10s fl. 1s, ec. 1s fl. 1s, ec. 1s fl. 1s, ec. 5s | 49 **15** | 10 | White cylindrical fiberglass tower, concrete base, red bands; 46. | |
| 18804 *G 0555.5* | -No. 10. | 26° 54.9′ S 48° 38.5′ W | **Q.(2)G.** period 3s | 20 **6** | 5 | Green cylindrical fiberglass tower, concrete base, white bands; 13. | |
| 18808 *G 0555.8* | -No. 12. | 26° 54.8′ S 48° 38.8′ W | **Fl.G.** period 3s fl. 0.3s, ec. 2.7s | 16 **5** | 5 | Green cylindrical fiberglass tower, concrete base, white band; 13. | |
| 18810 *G 0555.48* | -No. 9. | 26° 54.7′ S 48° 38.5′ W | **Fl.R.** period 6s fl. 0.5s, ec. 5.5s | 20 **6** | 6 | Red cylindrical fiberglass tower, concrete base, white band; 13. | |
| 18812 *G 0555.4* | -No. 11. | 26° 54.6′ S 48° 38.8′ W | **Fl.R.** period 3s fl. 0.3s, ec. 2.7s | 16 **5** | 5 | Red cylindrical fiberglass tower, concrete base, white band; 13. | |
| 18820 *G 0555.7* | -No. 14. | 26° 54.7′ S 48° 39.0′ W | **Fl.(3)G.** period 12s fl. 0.5s, ec. 1.5s fl. 0.5s, ec. 1.5s fl. 0.5s, ec. 7.5s | 16 **5** | 5 | Green cylindrical fiberglass tower, concrete base, white band; 13. | |
| 18828 *G 0555.45* | -No. 13. | 26° 54.3′ S 48° 39.1′ W | **Q.(2)R.** period 3s | 20 **6** | 5 | Red cylindrical fiberglass tower, concrete base, white band. | |
| 18830 *G 0555.6* | -No. 15. | 26° 54.1′ S 48° 39.2′ W | **Fl.(3)R.** period 10s fl. 1s, ec. 1s fl. 1s, ec. 1s fl. 1s, ec. 5s | 20 **6** | 5 | Red cylindrical fiberglass tower, concrete base, white band; 13. | |
| 18848 *G 0558* | Pedrada Gale. | 27° 10.9′ S 48° 24.5′ W | **Fl.W.** period 10s fl. 1s, ec. 9s | 256 **78** | 8 | White four-sided masonry tower, black bands; 33. | |
| 18852 *G 0560* | Calhau de Sao Pedro. | 27° 15.1′ S 48° 25.3′ W | **Fl.W.** period 3s fl. 0.3s, ec. 2.7s | 62 **19** | 8 | White four-sided truncated pyramidal tower; masonry base; 16. | |
| 18856 *G 0562* | **Ilha do Arvoredo.** | 27° 17.8′ S 48° 21.4′ W | **Oc.(2+2)W.** period 60s lt. 20s, ec. 6.6s lt. 1.8s, ec. 6.6s lt. 20s, ec. 1.6s lt. 1.8s, ec. 1.6s | 295 **90** | **24** | Red truncated conical metal tower, white bands; 52. | Visible 168°-099°. |

| (1) No. | (2) Name and Location | (3) Position | (4) Characteristic | (5) Height | (6) Range | (7) Structure | (8) Remarks |
|---|---|---|---|---|---|---|---|

**BRAZIL**

| (1) No. | (2) Name and Location | (3) Position | (4) Characteristic | (5) Height | (6) Range | (7) Structure | (8) Remarks |
|---|---|---|---|---|---|---|---|
| 18857 *G 0562.5* | **Ponta da Galheta.** | 27° 34.5´ S 48° 25.0´ W | **Fl.W.** period 10s fl. 1s, ec. 9s | 492 **150** | **16** | White cylindrical concrete tower; 33. | |
| 18858 *G 0563* | -Barra de Lagoa, W. side. | 27° 34.4´ S 48° 25.4´ W | **Fl.R.** period 6s fl. 0.5s, ec. 5.5s | 20 **6** | 5 | White conical concrete tower, red bands; 13. | |
| 18859 *G 0564* | --E. side. | 27° 34.4´ S 48° 25.3´ W | **Fl.G.** period 6s fl. 0.5s, ec. 5.5s | 33 **10** | 5 | White conical concrete tower, green bands, hexagonal base; 20. | |
| | CANAL DE SANTA CATARINA: | | | | | | |
| 18860 *G 0566* | -Ilha Anhatomirin. | 27° 25.7´ S 48° 33.9´ W | **Fl.R.** period 6s fl. 1s, ec. 5s | 128 **39** | 9 | White metal framework structure; 26. | |
| 18864 *G 0570* | -Ratones. | 27° 29.6´ S 48° 34.0´ W | **Fl.G.** period 3s fl. 0.3s, ec. 2.7s | 20 **6** | 8 | White cylindrical tower, four-sided concrete base; 16. | |
| 18872 *G 0572* | -Guarazes, E. side of dredged channel. | 27° 32.9´ S 48° 34.0´ W | **Fl.(3)G.** period 12s fl. 0.5s, ec. 1.5s fl. 0.5s, ec. 1.5s fl. 0.5s, ec. 7.5s | | 3 | Green structure; 23. | |
| 18878 *G 0578* | **Ilha de Santa Catarina** AVIATION LIGHT. | 27° 40.1´ S 48° 32.5´ W | **Al.Fl.W.G.** period 5s | 79 **24** | **20** | White and orange checkered four-sided tower; 72. | Occasional. **Aero Radiobeacon** 2.75 miles SE. |
| 18880 *G 0580* | -Ponta da Enseada. | 27° 46.2´ S 48° 36.9´ W | **Fl.G.** period 10s fl. 1s, ec. 9s | 26 **8** | 8 | White truncated conical masonry tower; 20. | |
| 18884 *G 0582* | -Ilha dos Cardos. | 27° 48.9´ S 48° 34.9´ W | **Fl.R.** period 3s fl. 0.3s, ec. 2.7s | 20 **6** | 5 | Red four-sided concrete tower, masonry base; 13. | Visible 284°-232°. |
| 18888 *G 0584* | **-Ponta dos Naufragados.** | 27° 50.1´ S 48° 34.2´ W | **Fl.(2)W.** period 15s fl. 1s, ec. 3s fl. 1s, ec. 10s | 140 **43** | **18** | White truncated conical masonry tower; 33. | Visible 285°-177°. |
| 18892 *G 0588* | Ilha de Coral. | 27° 56.0´ S 48° 32.6´ W | **Fl.W.** period 3s fl. 0.3s, ec. 2.7s | 266 **81** | 14 | White four-sided truncated pyramidal concrete tower; 39. | |
| 18896 *G 0591* | Ponta do Catalao. | 28° 12.6´ S 48° 39.8´ W | **Fl.R.** period 3s fl. 0.3s, ec. 2.7s | 207 **63** | 10 | White truncated pyramidal masonry tower, red four-sided concrete base; 13. | |
| 18900 *G 0592* | **Morro de Imbituba.** | 28° 14.1´ S 48° 38.7´ W | **Fl.(3)W.** period 15s fl. 1s, ec. 2s fl. 1s, ec. 2s fl. 1s, ec. 8s | 226 **69** | **21** | White four-sided truncated pyramidal masonry tower; 23. | F.R. on building 1 mile WSW. |
| 18904 *G 0594* | Ilhas das Araras. | 28° 19.3´ S 48° 38.9´ W | **Q.(2)W.** period 6s | 177 **54** | 11 | Red cylindrical concrete tower, white bands; 36. | |
| 18908 *G 0596* | Ilha dos Lobos. | 28° 26.8´ S 48° 42.5´ W | **Fl.W.** period 5s fl. 0.3s, ec. 4.7s | 164 **50** | 11 | White truncated conical masonry tower; 20. | |
| | LAGUNA: | | | | | | |
| 18912 *G 0598* | -N. mole, head. | 28° 29.7´ S 48° 44.9´ W | **Fl.R.** period 3s fl. 0.3s, ec. 2.7s | 43 **13** | 5 | Red truncated conical masonry tower; 20. | |
| 18916 *G 0599* | -S. mole, head. | 28° 29.8´ S 48° 44.7´ W | **Fl.G.** period 3s fl. 0.5s, ec. 2.5s | 39 **12** | 7 | White four-sided concrete tower, green bands; 16. | |

| (1) No. | (2) Name and Location | (3) Position | (4) Characteristic | (5) Height | (6) Range | (7) Structure | (8) Remarks |
|---|---|---|---|---|---|---|---|

## BRAZIL

| (1) No. | (2) Name and Location | (3) Position | (4) Characteristic | (5) Height | (6) Range | (7) Structure | (8) Remarks |
|---|---|---|---|---|---|---|---|
| 18920 *G 0600* | **Cabo Santa Marta.** | 28° 36.3′ S 48° 48.8′ W | **Oc.(3)W.R.** period 30s lt. 15s, ec. 5.5s lt. 0.3s, ec. 3.4s lt. 0.3s, ec. 5.5s | 243 **74** | W. **46** R. **39** | White four-sided masonry tower with dwelling; 95. | W. 056°-045°, R.-056°. **Radiobeacon.** **DGPS Station.** |
| | RACON | | **Z(– – • •)** | | **25** | | (3 & 10cm). |
| 18924 *G 0602* | **Ararangua.** | 28° 56.3′ S 49° 21.6′ W | **Fl.(3)W.** period 20s fl. 0.4s, ec. 2.9s fl. 0.4s, ec. 2.9s fl. 0.4s, ec. 13s | 269 **82** | **25** | White truncated conical masonry tower, black band; 26. | |
| | RACON | | **Y(– • – –)** | | **25** | | (3 & 10cm). |
| 18928 *G 0604* | **Torres.** | 29° 20.7′ S 49° 43.8′ W | **L.Fl.W.** period 10s fl. 2s, ec. 8s | 278 **85** | **23** | White cylindrical concrete tower, black stripes; 151. | |
| 18930 *G 0605* | **Itapeva.** | 29° 33.4′ S 49° 53.4′ W | **Fl.(5)W.** period 30s fl. 0.5s, ec. 4.5s fl. 0.5s, ec. 4.5s fl. 0.5s, ec. 4.5s fl. 0.5s, ec. 4.5s fl. 0.5s, ec. 9.5s | 138 **42** | **24** | White four-sided masonry tower, red bands; 131. | |
| 18932 *G 0606* | **Capao da Canoa.** | 29° 44.7′ S 50° 00.3′ W | **Fl.(2)W.** period 10s fl. 0.4s, ec. 2s fl. 0.4s, ec. 7.2s | 89 **27** | **15** | White four-sided concrete tower, black bands; 85. | |
| 18936 *G 0607.4* | **Tramandai.** | 30° 00.5′ S 50° 08.2′ W | **L.Fl.W.** period 15s fl. 2s, ec. 13s | 82 **25** | **23** | Black and white diamond checkered truncated conical masonry tower; 75. | **Radar reflector.** **Radiobeacon.** |
| | RACON | | **Z(– – • •)** | | **25** | | (3 & 10cm). |
| 18944 *G 0608* | **Cidreira.** | 30° 09.5′ S 50° 11.9′ W | **Fl.W.** period 6s fl. 0.5s, ec. 5.5s | 108 **33** | **20** | Red cylindrical concrete tower, white diagonal stripes; 98. | |
| 18945 *G 0610* | **Berta.** | 30° 23.9′ S 50° 17.4′ W | **Fl.W.** period 10s fl. 1s, ec. 9s | 138 **42** | **23** | White four-sided masonry tower, black band; 131. | |
| | RACON | | **Q(– – • –)** | | **25** | | (3 & 10cm). |
| 18946 *G 0633* | Itapua da Lagoa. | 30° 23.1′ S 51° 03.6′ W | **Fl.W.** period 6s fl. 1s, ec. 5s | 56 **17** | 12 | White octagonal masonry tower; 43. | |
| | CANAL DO JUNCO: | | | | | | |
| 18946.1 | -No. 97. | 30° 20.8′ S 51° 03.6′ W | **Fl.R.** period 6s fl. 1s, ec. 5s | 20 **6** | 7 | Red metal framework structure, on piles. | |
| 18946.12 | -No.99. | 30° 20.6′ S 51° 03.9′ W | **Fl.R.** period 5s fl. 0.5s, ec. 4.5s | | 7 | Red metal framework structure. | |
| 18946.13 | -No. 102. | 30° 20.7′ S 51° 03.9′ W | **Fl.G.** period 5s fl. 0.5s, ec. 4.5s | | 5 | Green metal framework structure, on piles. | |
| 18946.16 | -No. 103. | 30° 19.9′ S 51° 05.5′ W | **Fl.R.** period 5s | | 2 | Red metal framework structure, on piles. | |
| 18946.2 | -No. 106. | 30° 19.9′ S 51° 05.5′ W | **Fl.G.** period 5s fl. 0.5s, ec. 4.5s | 16 **5** | 9 | Green metal framework structure. | |

| (1) No. | (2) Name and Location | (3) Position | (4) Characteristic | (5) Height | (6) Range | (7) Structure | (8) Remarks |
|---|---|---|---|---|---|---|---|

## BRAZIL

| | | | | | | | |
|---|---|---|---|---|---|---|---|
| | CANAL DO CRISTAL: | | | | | | |
| 18946.21<br>*G 0634.5* | -Veleiros do Sul. | 30° 05.7′ S<br>51° 15.4′ W | **Iso.R.**<br>period 4s | 23<br>**7** | 3 | White truncated conical masonry tower, blue bands; 20. | Private light. |
| 18946.22 | -No. 1. | 30° 04.3′ S<br>51° 14.8′ W | **Fl.R.**<br>period 6s<br>fl. 1s, ec. 5s | 23<br>**7** | 7 | Red metal framework tower. | |
| 18946.23 | -Cristal, No. 5. | 30° 03.5′ S<br>51° 14.9′ W | **Fl.R.**<br>period 6s<br>fl. 1s, ec. 5s | 23<br>**7** | 7 | Red metal framework tower. | |
| 18946.24 | -Pedras Brancas No. 5. | 30° 05.9′ S<br>51° 16.3′ W | **Fl.R.**<br>period 5s<br>fl. 0.5s, ec. 4.5s | 16<br>**5** | 7 | Red metal framework structure; 13. | |
| 18946.3 | -No. 14. | 30° 19.1′ S<br>51° 07.2′ W | **Fl.G.**<br>period 5s<br>fl. 0.5s, ec. 4.5s | 16<br>**5** | 9 | Green metal framework structure. | |
| 18946.5<br>*G 0632.2* | Barba Negra. | 30° 32.0′ S<br>51° 08.5′ W | **Fl.G.**<br>period 5s<br>fl. 0.5s, ec. 4.5s | 26<br>**8** | 9 | Green metal framework structure. | |
| 18946.6<br>*G 0632.4* | Desertas. | 30° 32.7′ S<br>50° 50.6′ W | **Fl.G.**<br>period 5s<br>fl. 0.5s, ec. 4.5s | 20<br>**6** | 9 | Green metal framework structure. | |
| 18946.7<br>*G 0631.6* | Arambare. | 30° 56.2′ S<br>51° 27.8′ W | **Fl.G.**<br>period 5s<br>fl. 0.5s, ec. 4.5s | 26<br>**8** | 5 | Green metal framework structure. | |
| 18946.8<br>*G 0631.8* | Desertores. | 30° 57.5′ S<br>51° 15.3′ W | **Fl.G.**<br>period 5s<br>fl. 0.5s, ec. 4.5s | 26<br>**8** | 9 | Green metal framework structure, on piles. | |
| 18946.9<br>*G 0631.4* | Cristovao Pereira. | 31° 03.8′ S<br>51° 10.0′ W | **Fl.W.**<br>period 10s<br>fl. 1s, ec. 9s | 98<br>**30** | 13 | White four-sided masonry tower; 92. | |
| 18947<br>*G 0632.15* | Alvaro Alberto. | 30° 47.5′ S<br>51° 10.8′ W | **Fl.(2)W.**<br>period 10s<br>fl. 1s, ec. 1s<br>fl. 1s, ec. 7s | 43<br>**13** | 9 | Black metal structure, red band, on wreck. | |
| 18948<br>*G 0612* | **Solidao.** | 30° 42.0′ S<br>50° 28.8′ W | **Fl.(2)W.**<br>period 12s<br>fl. 1s, ec. 2s<br>fl. 1s, ec. 8s | 78<br>**24** | **15** | Red truncated conical concrete tower; 69. | |
| | RACON | | **K(– • –)** | | **19** | | (3 & 10cm). |
| 18956<br>*G 0614* | **Mostardas.** | 31° 14.8′ S<br>50° 54.4′ W | **Al.Oc.W.W.R.R.**<br>period 40s<br>W. lt. 10s, ec. 4.5s<br>W. lt. 1s, ec. 4.5s<br>R. lt. 10s, ec. 4.5s<br>R. lt. 1s, ec. 4.5s | 128<br>**39** | W. **40**<br>R. **34** | White truncated conical concrete tower, black bands; 125. | |
| | RACON | | **C(– • – •)** | | **25** | | (3 & 10cm). |
| 18957<br>*G 0631.2* | Capao da Marca. | 31° 19.0′ S<br>51° 10.0′ W | **L.Fl.R.**<br>period 10s<br>fl. 2s, ec. 8s | 62<br>**19** | 13 | White truncated conical metal tower; 46. | |
| 18958<br>*G 0630.2* | Sao Lourenco (Curva). | 31° 22.9′ S<br>51° 58.2′ W | **Fl.R.**<br>period 5s<br>fl. 0.5s, ec. 4.5s | 26<br>**8** | 7 | Red metal framework structure, on piles. | |
| 18958.5<br>*G 0630.4* | Sao Lourenco. | 31° 23.4′ S<br>51° 57.6′ W | **Fl.G.**<br>period 5s<br>fl. 0.5s, ec. 4.5s | 20<br>**6** | 8 | Green metal framework structure, on piles. | |
| 18959<br>*G 0630.8* | Quilombo. | 31° 26.5′ S<br>51° 45.6′ W | **Fl.G.**<br>period 5s<br>fl. 0.5s, ec. 4.5s | 23<br>**7** | 7 | Green metal framework structure, on piles. | |

| (1) No. | (2) Name and Location | (3) Position | (4) Characteristic | (5) Height | (6) Range | (7) Structure | (8) Remarks |
|---|---|---|---|---|---|---|---|
| | | | **BRAZIL** | | | | |
| 18959.5 *G 0631* | Bojuru. | 31° 28.3´ S 51° 24.9´ W | **Fl.R.** period 8s fl. 1s, ec. 7s | 26 **8** | 6 | Red metal framework structure, on piles. | |
| 18959.7 *G 0615* | **Capao da Marca de Fora.** | 31° 30.0´ S 51° 11.1´ W | **Fl.(3)W.** period 10s fl. 1s, ec. 1s fl. 1s, ec. 1s fl. 1s, ec. 5s | 138 **42** | **17** | White round concrete tower, red band; 131. | |
| 18960 *G 0616* | **Conceicao.** | 31° 43.7´ S 51° 28.8´ W | **Fl.(2)W.** period 10s fl. 1s, ec. 1s fl. 1s, ec. 7s | 108 **33** | **16** | White four-sided metal framework tower, red bands; 98. | |
| | RACON | | **B(– • • •)** | | **25** | | (3 & 10cm). |
| 18962 *G 0618* | **Estreito.** | 31° 52.8´ S 51° 46.3´ W | **L.Fl.W.** period 15s fl. 2s, ec. 13s | 138 **42** | **17** | White four-sided metal tower; 131. | |
| | RIO GRANDE: | | | | | | |
| 18964 *G 0620* | **-Barra.** | 32° 07.1´ S 52° 04.6´ W | **Oc.(6)W.** period 21s lt. 10s, ec. 1s lt. 0.6s, ec. 1.5s lt. 0.6s, ec. 1.5s lt. 0.6s, ec. 1.5s lt. 0.6s, ec. 1.5s lt. 0.6s, ec. 1.5s | 105 **32** | **30** | White truncated conical metal tower, black bands; 102. | **Radiobeacon** and **DGPS Station** 2.3 miles SW. |
| | -RACON | | **K(– • –)** | | **25** | | (3 & 10cm). |
| 18968 *G 0624* | -E. mole, head. | 32° 11.2´ S 52° 04.5´ W | **L.Fl.R.** period 10s fl. 2s, ec. 8s | 43 **13** | 8 | White round concrete tower; 33. | |
| 18972 *G 0622* | -W. mole, head. | 32° 11.3´ S 52° 04.8´ W | **L.Fl.G.** period 10s fl. 2s, ec. 8s | 39 **12** | 11 | White round concrete tower; 39. | |
| 18974 *G 0625.2* | -ENRG Pier, N. head. | 32° 08.3´ S 52° 06.1´ W | **F.Y.** | 30 **9** | 5 | Building, yellow lantern; 20. | |
| 18975 *G 0625* | --S. head. | 32° 08.4´ S 52° 06.1´ W | **Mo.(N)Y.** period 5s fl. 1.5s, ec. 0.5s fl. 0.5s, ec. 2.5s | 30 **9** | 5 | Yellow metal post; 16. | |
| 18975.5 *G 0625.4* | -Honorio Bicalho. | 32° 02.0´ S 52° 04.6´ W | **Fl.G.** period 6s fl. 1s, ec. 5s | 13 **4** | 5 | Green metal framework tower, round topmark; 10. | |
| 18976 *G 0626.2* | -No. 2. | 32° 01.7´ S 52° 04.7´ W | **Fl.G.** period 5s fl. 1s, ec. 4s | 20 **6** | 2 | Green four-sided metal framework structure, conical base; 20. | |
| 18980 *G 0626* | -Ligacao Channel, No. 1, NE. side. | 32° 01.6´ S 52° 04.7´ W | **Fl.R.** period 5s fl. 0.5s, ec. 4.5s | 16 **5** | 2 | Red four-sided concrete tower, on concrete piles; 16. | |
| 18984 *G 0626.4* | --No. 3, N. side. | 32° 01.6´ S 52° 04.9´ W | **Fl.R.** period 5s fl. 0.5s, ec. 4.5s | 16 **5** | 2 | Red square concrete structure, on concrete piles; 16. | |
| 18988 *G 0626.6* | --No. 5. | 32° 01.7´ S 52° 05.1´ W | **Fl.R.** period 5s fl. 0.5s, ec. 4.5s | 16 **5** | 2 | Red square concrete structure, on concrete piles; 16. | |
| 18996 *G 0627.4* | --Balizao No. 18. | 32° 00.8´ S 52° 03.8´ W | **Fl.(2)G.** period 6s fl. 0.5s, ec. 1s fl. 0.5s, ec. 4s | 16 **5** | 5 | Green four-sided concrete tower, on concrete piles; 16. | |

| (1) No. | (2) Name and Location | (3) Position | (4) Characteristic | (5) Height | (6) Range | (7) Structure | (8) Remarks |
|---|---|---|---|---|---|---|---|
| | | | **BRAZIL** | | | | |
| 18998 *G 0627.5* | --Sao Jose No. 20. | 31° 59.4´ S 52° 04.4´ W | **Q.(3)G.** period 10s fl. 0.3s, ec. 0.7s fl. 0.3s, ec. 0.7s fl. 0.3s, ec. 7.7s | 16 **5** | 5 | Green concrete tower, four-sided concrete base, on piles; 16. | |
| 18999 *G 0627.2* | -Sao Jose do Norte. | 32° 00.7´ S 52° 02.7´ W | **Fl.R.** period 5s fl. 0.5s, ec. 4.5s | 16 **5** | 5 | Red metal post, concrete base; 10. | |
| 18999.06 *G 0627.6* | -Diamante No. 22. | 31° 57.2´ S 52° 04.8´ W | **Fl.G.** period 5s fl. 0.5s, ec. 4.5s | 20 **6** | 9 | Green metal framework structure, on piles. | |
| 18999.11 *G 0627.8* | -Baleias No. 25. | 31° 55.1´ S 52° 07.1´ W | **Fl.R.** period 5s fl. 0.5s, ec. 4.5s | 26 **8** | 7 | Red metal framework structure, on piles. | |
| 18999.18 *G 0628* | -Canal da Setia No. 28. | 31° 53.1´ S 52° 09.1´ W | **Fl.G.** period 5s fl. 0.5s, ec. 4.5s | 23 **7** | 9 | Green metal framework structure, on piles. | |
| 18999.23 *G 0628.1* | --No. 37. | 31° 52.1´ S 52° 09.5´ W | **Fl.R.** period 5s fl. 0.5s, ec. 4.5s | 20 **6** | 7 | Red metal framework structure, on piles. | |
| 18999.25 *G 0628.15* | --No. 32. | 31° 52.2´ S 52° 09.7´ W | **Fl.G.** period 5s fl. 0.5s, ec. 4.5s | | 2 | Green metal framework tower, on piles; 26. | |
| 18999.29 *G 0628.2* | -Sao Goncalo No. 3. | 31° 47.8´ S 52° 11.7´ W | **Fl.R.** period 5s fl. 0.5s, ec. 4.5s | 20 **6** | 7 | Red metal framework structure, on piles. | |
| 18999.35 *G 0628.4* | --No. 11. | 31° 47.3´ S 52° 13.0´ W | **Fl.R.** period 5s fl. 0.5s, ec. 4.5s | 20 **6** | 7 | Red metal framework structure, on piles. | |
| 18999.42 *G 0628.6* | -Laranjal No. 50. | 31° 46.4´ S 52° 10.8´ W | **Fl.G.** period 5s fl. 0.5s, ec. 4.5s | 23 **7** | 9 | Green metal framework structure, on piles. | |
| 18999.48 *G 0628.8* | -Coroa do Meio No. 56. | 31° 44.3´ S 52° 09.3´ W | **Fl.G.** period 5s fl. 0.5s, ec. 4.5s | 23 **7** | 9 | Green metal framework structure, on piles. | |
| 18999.53 *G 0629* | -Gambeta No. 55. | 31° 43.9´ S 52° 08.2´ W | **Fl.R.** period 5s fl. 0.5s, ec. 4.5s | 23 **7** | 7 | Red metal framework structure, on piles. | |
| 18999.6 *G 0629.1* | -Coroa dos Patos, No. 60. | 31° 43.0´ S 52° 04.4´ W | **Fl.G.** period 5s fl. 0.5s, ec. 4.5s | 23 **7** | 9 | Green metal framework structure, on piles. | |
| 18999.65 *G 0629.2* | -Canal da Feitoria No. 67. | 31° 43.5´ S 52° 00.2´ W | **Fl.R.** period 5s fl. 0.5s, ec. 4.5s | 20 **6** | 7 | Red metal framework structure, on piles. | |
| 18999.72 *G 0629.3* | --No. 66. | 31° 43.3´ S 52° 00.1´ W | **Fl.G.** period 5s fl. 0.5s, ec. 4.5s | 20 **6** | 9 | Green metal framework structure, on piles. | |
| 18999.78 *G 0629.5* | --No. 68. | 31° 43.0´ S 51° 59.3´ W | **Fl.G.** period 5s fl. 0.5s, ec. 4.5s | 20 **6** | 9 | Green metal framework structure, on piles. | |
| 18999.83 *G 0629.4* | --No. 71. | 31° 43.0´ S 51° 59.2´ W | **Fl.R.** period 5s fl. 0.5s, ec. 4.5s | 20 **6** | 7 | Red metal framework structure, on piles. | |
| 18999.89 *G 0629.6* | --No. 73. | 31° 42.6´ S 51° 58.1´ W | **Fl.R.** period 5s fl. 0.5s, ec. 4.5s | 20 **6** | 7 | Red metal framework structure, on piles. | |
| 18999.91 *G 0629.8* | --No. 83. | 31° 41.7´ S 51° 55.8´ W | **Fl.R.** period 5s fl. 0.5s, ec. 4.5s | | 2 | Red metal framework tower, on piles. | |
| 18999.95 *G 0629.7* | --No. 79. | 31° 41.9´ S 51° 56.5´ W | **Fl.R.** period 5s fl. 0.5s, ec. 4.5s | 23 **7** | 7 | Red metal framework structure, on piles. | |

| (1) No. | (2) Name and Location | (3) Position | (4) Characteristic | (5) Height | (6) Range | (7) Structure | (8) Remarks |
|---|---|---|---|---|---|---|---|

## BRAZIL

| (1) No. | (2) Name and Location | (3) Position | (4) Characteristic | (5) Height | (6) Range | (7) Structure | (8) Remarks |
|---|---|---|---|---|---|---|---|
| 19000 *G 0636* | **Sarita.** | 32° 37.8´ S 52° 25.9´ W | **Fl.(3)W.** period 15s fl. 1s, ec. 2s fl. 1s, ec. 2s fl. 1s, ec. 8s | 131 **40** | **18** | Red square masonry tower, white bands; 121. | |
| 19004 *G 0639* | Verga. | 32° 58.7´ S 52° 33.6´ W | **Fl.W.** period 5s fl. 0.5s, ec. 4.5s | 49 **15** | 11 | Red four-sided metal framework structure, white masonry base; 36. | **Radar reflector.** |
| 19008 *G 0640* | **Albardao.** | 33° 12.2´ S 52° 42.5´ W | **Fl.(4)W.** period 25s fl. 1s, ec. 3s fl. 1s, ec. 3s fl. 1s, ec. 3s fl. 1s, ec. 12s | 164 **50** | **42** | Black and white checkered round concrete tower; 144. | |
| | RACON | | **X(– • • –)** | | **25** | | (3 & 10cm). |
| 19012 *G 0644* | **Chui.** | 33° 44.6´ S 53° 22.5´ W | **Fl.(2)W.** period 35s fl. 1s, ec. 8s fl. 1s, ec. 25s | 141 **43** | **46** | Red truncated conical concrete tower, white bands; 98. | **Radiobeacon.** |
| | RACON | | **O(– – –)** | | **25** | | (3 & 10cm). |

# Section 14

## East Coast of South America
## Including Uruguay, Argentina, Falkland Islands and Straits of Magellan

| (1)<br>No. | (2)<br>Name and Location | (3)<br>Position | (4)<br>Characteristic | (5)<br>Height | (6)<br>Range | (7)<br>Structure | (8)<br>Remarks |
|---|---|---|---|---|---|---|---|
| | | | **URUGUAY** | | | | |
| 19016<br>*G 0658* | Sandra (Punta del Diablo). | 34° 02.6´ S<br>53° 32.0´ W | **Fl.W.**<br>period 5s<br>fl. 0.5s, ec. 4.5s | 49<br>**15** | 8 | White masonry structure. | |
| 19020<br>*G 0660* | Punta Palmar. | 34° 04.0´ S<br>53° 33.1´ W | **Fl.W.**<br>period 6s<br>fl. 0.3s, ec. 5.7s | 69<br>**21** | 10 | White fiberglass tower, red bands; 39. | |
| 19024<br>*G 0662* | **Cabo Polonio.** | 34° 24.3´ S<br>53° 46.7´ W | **Fl.W.**<br>period 12s<br>fl. 0.2s, ec. 11.8s | 131<br>**40** | **22** | White round stone tower with dwelling, white cupola, red bands; 85. | |
| 19028<br>*G 0664* | Maria Victoria. | 34° 38.7´ S<br>54° 09.2´ W | **Fl.W.R.**<br>period 4s<br>fl. 0.6s, ec. 3.4s | 23<br>**7** | W. 8<br>R. 6 | White tower, red bands. | R. 232°-270°, W.-284°. |
| 19030<br>*G 0667* | Maria Magdalena. | 34° 38.9´ S<br>54° 08.7´ W | **Fl.G.**<br>period 5s<br>fl. 0.5s, ec. 4.5s | 46<br>**14** | 5 | Green tower; 25. | |
| 19032<br>*G 0668* | **Cabo Santa Maria.** | 34° 40.0´ S<br>54° 09.2´ W | **Fl.W.**<br>period 60s<br>fl. 0.3s, ec. 59.7s | 138<br>**42** | **20** | White round stone tower with dwelling, white cupola, red stripes; 98. | |
| 19036<br>*G 0672* | **Punta Jose Ignacio.** | 34° 50.6´ S<br>54° 38.0´ W | **Fl.W.**<br>period 2s<br>fl. 0.3s, ec. 1.7s | 105<br>**32** | **15** | White round stone tower with dwelling, white cupola, red stripes; 82. | |
| 19040<br>*G 0676* | **Isla de Lobos.** | 35° 01.5´ S<br>54° 53.0´ W | **Fl.W.**<br>period 5s<br>fl. 0.5s, ec. 4.5s | 217<br>**66** | **23** | White round concrete tower with dwelling, white cupola, red stripes; 194. | |
| | | | **F.R.** | 174<br>**53** | 4 | | Red sector 250°-290° (over shoals E. of the Island). |
| | BAHIA DE MALDONADO: | | | | | | |
| 19044<br>*G 0682* | **-Punta del Este.** | 34° 58.1´ S<br>54° 57.1´ W | **Fl.W.**<br>period 8s<br>fl. 0.5s, ec. 7.5s | 144<br>**44** | **21** | White round masonry tower with dwelling, white cupola, red stripes; 82. | Signal station. |
| 19048<br>*G 0684* | --W. breakwater, head. | 34° 57.6´ S<br>54° 57.1´ W | **Fl.R.**<br>period 5s<br>fl. 0.5s, ec. 4.5s | 23<br>**7** | 8 | Red tower. | |
| 19056<br>*G 0683* | -Isla Gorriti. | 34° 57.6´ S<br>54° 58.2´ W | **Fl.G.**<br>period 5s<br>fl. 0.5s, ec. 4.5s | 30<br>**9** | 5 | Concrete tower, green and white bands; 16. | Visible 357°-097°. |
| 19068<br>*G 0688* | Punta Negra. | 34° 54.2´ S<br>55° 15.6´ W | **Fl.W.**<br>period 5s<br>fl. 0.5s, ec. 4.5s | 56<br>**17** | 7 | Tower, black and white bands; 13. | |
| 19076<br>*G 0689.1* | Piriapolis breakwater, head. | 34° 52.4´ S<br>55° 16.9´ W | **Fl.R.**<br>period 5s<br>fl. 0.5s, ec. 4.5s | | 8 | Red aluminium tower. | |
| 19076.5<br>*G 0689.2* | Piriapolis breakwater. | 34° 52.5´ S<br>55° 16.9´ W | **Fl.G.**<br>period 5s<br>fl. 0.5s, ec. 4.5s | | 8 | Green aluminum tower. | |
| 19080<br>*G 0690* | **Isla de Flores.** | 34° 56.8´ S<br>55° 56.0´ W | **Fl.(2)W.**<br>period 16s<br>fl. 0.3s, ec. 3.7s<br>fl. 0.3s, ec. 11.7s | 121<br>**37** | **19** | White round masonry tower with dwelling, white cupola, red stripes; 62. | |
| 19084<br>*G 0692* | **Carrasco Airport** AVIATION LIGHT. | 34° 49.5´ S<br>56° 01.0´ W | **Al.W.G.**<br>period 2s | 190<br>**58** | **17** | Control tower; 69. | **Aero Radiobeacon.** |

| (1) No. | (2) Name and Location | (3) Position | (4) Characteristic | (5) Height | (6) Range | (7) Structure | (8) Remarks |
|---|---|---|---|---|---|---|---|
| | | | **URUGUAY** | | | | |
| | PUERTO DEL BUCEO: | | | | | | |
| 19104 *G 0696* | -W. breakwater, head. | 34° 54.5´ S 56° 07.7´ W | **Fl.G.** period 5s fl. 0.5s, ec. 4.5s | 43 **13** | 10 | Green tower; 26. | |
| 19108 *G 0698* | -E. breakwater, head. | 34° 54.6´ S 56° 07.6´ W | **Fl.R.** period 5s fl. 0.5s, ec. 4.5s | 23 **7** | 10 | Red tower; 26. | |
| 19112 *G 0699* | -Yacht Club. | 34° 54.6´ S 56° 07.9´ W | **Fl.W.** period 4s fl. 1s, ec. 3s | 131 **40** | 8 | Club tower. | |
| 19124 *G 0700* | **Punta Brava.** | 34° 56.1´ S 56° 09.6´ W | **Al.Fl.W.R.** period 10s fl. 0.2s, ec. 4.8s fl. 0.2s, ec. 4.8s | 69 **21** | **15** | White round stone tower, red stripes; 62. | |
| 19126 *G 0717* | **Montecarlo TV tower** AVIATION LIGHT. | 34° 53.9´ S 56° 10.0´ W | **Fl.W.** period 1.5s | 682 **208** | **35** | Mast. | |
| | PUERTO DE MONTEVIDEO: | | | | | | |
| 19136 *G 0704* | -Sarandi, E. breakwater, head. | 34° 54.8´ S 56° 13.4´ W | **Fl.R.** period 3s fl. 0.3s, ec. 2.7s | 72 **22** | 10 | Red round metal tower, white bands, concrete base; 40. | |
| 19140 *G 0706* | -Detached W. breakwater, SE. head. | 34° 54.8´ S 56° 13.6´ W | **Fl.G.** period 3s fl. 0.3s, ec. 2.7s | 72 **22** | 10 | Green round metal tower, white bands, concrete base; 49. | |
| 19144 *G 0707* | --NW. head. | 34° 54.2´ S 56° 14.0´ W | **Fl.R.** period 5s fl. 0.5s, ec. 4.5s | 30 **9** | 5 | Red framework tower. | |
| 19148 *G 0710* | -Muelle de Escala, outer harbor, NE. corner of pier. | 34° 54.2´ S 56° 13.0´ W | **Fl.R.** period 5s fl. 0.5s, ec. 4.5s | 33 **10** | 5 | Red metal framework tower; 7. | |
| 19152 *G 0709* | --SW. end. | 34° 54.4´ S 56° 13.4´ W | **Fl.R.** period 5s fl. 0.5s, ec. 4.5s | 37 **11** | 5 | Red tower. | |
| 19156 *G 0712* | -S. side of W. entrance to inner harbor, Mole A, head. | 34° 54.1´ S 56° 12.9´ W | **Fl.R.** period 5s fl. 0.5s, ec. 4.5s | 26 **8** | 5 | Red framework tower. | Traffic signals. |
| 19160 *G 0714* | -Head of Espigon A, N. side of W. entrance to inner harbor (W. arm of Dique de Cintura). | 34° 54.0´ S 56° 12.9´ W | **Fl.G.** period 5s fl. 0.5s, ec. 4.5s | 26 **8** | 5 | Green framework tower. | |
| 19164 *G 0715* | --B (E. arm of Dique de Cintura). | 34° 53.9´ S 56° 12.5´ W | **Fl.G.** period 5s fl. 0.5s, ec. 4.5s | 26 **8** | 5 | Green tower. | |
| 19168 *G 0718* | -Espigon F, E. side of N. entrance. | 34° 53.6´ S 56° 12.1´ W | **Fl.R.** period 5s fl. 0.5s, ec. 4.5s | 26 **8** | 5 | Red tower. | |
| 19169 *G 0721* | -Darsena La Teja Range beacon, front. | 34° 54.5´ S 56° 12.7´ W | **Fl.W.** period 3.5s fl. 1.5s, ec. 2s | | | On building. | |
| 19169.1 *G 0721.1* | --Rear, 133 meters 157°37′ from front. | 34° 54.6´ S 56° 12.7´ W | **Fl.W.** period 3.5s fl. 1.5s, ec. 2s | | | On building. | |
| 19172 *G 0722* | -Darsena A.N.C.A.P., S. Quay, outer end. | 34° 52.9´ S 56° 13.9´ W | **Fl.G.** period 6s | 30 **9** | 5 | Black tower. | |
| 19173 *G 0724* | -Punta Lobos. Navy Dry Dock Range, front. | 34° 54.4´ S 56° 15.4´ W | **F.Y.** | 20 **6** | 6 | Red tower, white bands, triangular daymark point up. | For vessels approaching the dock. Occasional. |

| (1) No. | (2) Name and Location | (3) Position | (4) Characteristic | (5) Height | (6) Range | (7) Structure | (8) Remarks |
|---|---|---|---|---|---|---|---|
| | | | **URUGUAY** | | | | |
| 19174 *G 0724.1* | --Rear, 254° from front. | 34° 54.4´ S 56° 15.4´ W | **F.R.** | 23 **7** | 4 | Red structure, white bands, square daymark. | |
| 19184 *G 0702* | **-Cerro de Montevideo.** | 34° 53.3´ S 56° 15.6´ W | **Fl.(3)W.** period 10s fl. 0.4s, ec. 1.6s fl. 0.4s, ec. 1.6s fl. 0.4s, ec. 5.6s | 486 **148** | **19** | White round masonry tower on roof of fort; 26. | |
| 19190 *G 0726* | Radio tower. | 34° 51.9´ S 56° 20.7´ W | **F.R.** | 679 **207** | 14 | Metal tower; 597. | |
| 19196 *G 0736* | La Panela. | 34° 54.9´ S 56° 26.9´ W | **Fl.(4)W.** period 10s fl. 0.5s, ec. 1s fl. 0.5s, ec. 1s fl. 0.5s, ec. 1s fl. 0.5s, ec. 5s | 57 **17** | 8 | White fiberglass tower, red bands, concrete base. | |
| 19200 *G 0740* | El Arriero. | 34° 47.8´ S 56° 24.9´ W | **Fl.R.** period 5s fl. 0.5s, ec. 4.5s | 30 **9** | 5 | Red tower. | |
| 19228 *G 0743* | -Rio Rosario Range, front, S. side. | 34° 26.1´ S 57° 21.3´ W | **Fl.R.** period 5s fl. 0.5s, ec. 4.5s | 33 **10** | 5 | Red tower. | Safe water buoy showing L.Fl.W. 10s marks outer end of channel. |
| 19232 *G 0744* | --Rear, 641 meters 037°31´ from front, N. side of entrance. | 34° 25.9´ S 57° 21.1´ W | **Fl.G.** period 5s fl. 0.5s, ec. 4.5s | 23 **7** | 5 | Green tower; 23. | |
| 19240 *G 0748* | -Puerto Sauce breakwater, head. | 34° 26.4´ S 57° 27.2´ W | **Fl.R.** period 5s fl. 0.5s, ec. 4.5s | 20 **6** | 5 | Red tower. | |
| 19253 *G 0754.6* | Arroyo Riachuelo, E. mole. | 34° 27.5´ S 57° 43.9´ W | **Fl.R.** period 5s fl. 0.5s, ec. 4.5s | 23 **7** | 5 | Red tower. | |
| 19254 *G 0754.4* | -W. mole. | 34° 27.5´ S 57° 44.0´ W | **Fl.G.** period 5s fl. 0.5s, ec. 4.5s | 23 **7** | 5 | Green tower. | |
| 19257 *G 0754* | -N. end of channel. | 34° 27.2´ S 57° 43.9´ W | **Fl.W.** period 5s fl. 0.5s, ec. 4.5s | 26 **8** | 8 | White tower; 7. | |
| 19258 *G 0755* | **-Real San Carlos Radio Antenna.** | 34° 26.4´ S 57° 51.6´ W | **Fl.W.R.** | 384 **117** | W. **25** R. **15** | | |
| | -Puerto de Colonia: | | | | | | |
| 19260 *G 0756* | --SW. angle of plaza. | 34° 28.4´ S 57° 51.1´ W | **Fl.R.** period 9s fl. 0.9s, ec. 8.1s | 112 **34** | 11 | White round masonry tower, white cupola, red stripes; 89. | |
| 19264 *G 0760* | --Santa Rita mole, head. | 34° 28.1´ S 57° 51.2´ W | **Fl.R.** period 4.5s fl. 0.5s, ec. 4s | 16 **5** | 5 | Red tower. | |
| | RIO DE LA PLATA: | | | | | | |
| 19268 *G 0759* | --Breakwater, head. | 34° 28.6´ S 57° 50.7´ W | **Fl.G.** period 5s fl. 0.5s, ec. 4.5s | 33 **10** | 8 | Green tower; 16. | |
| 19272 *G 0757* | --Detached breakwater, NE. head. | 34° 28.7´ S 57° 50.3´ W | **Fl.G.** period 5s fl. 0.5s, ec. 4.5s | 26 **8** | 8 | Green tower. | |
| 19276 *G 0758* | --W. extremity of detached breakwater. | 34° 28.7´ S 57° 50.9´ W | **Fl.R.** period 5s fl. 0.5s, ec. 4.5s | 26 **8** | 8 | Red tower; 16. | Numerous lighted buoys shown above Colonia. |
| 19280 *G 0762* | -Isla Farallon. | 34° 29.1´ S 57° 55.1´ W | **Fl.(2)W.** period 10s fl. 0.3s, ec. 2.2s fl. 0.3s, ec. 7.2s | 85 **26** | 10 | White round masonry tower, white cupola, red stripes; 79. | |

| (1) No. | (2) Name and Location | (3) Position | (4) Characteristic | (5) Height | (6) Range | (7) Structure | (8) Remarks |
|---|---|---|---|---|---|---|---|

**URUGUAY**

| (1) No. | (2) Name and Location | (3) Position | (4) Characteristic | (5) Height | (6) Range | (7) Structure | (8) Remarks |
|---|---|---|---|---|---|---|---|
| 19281 *G 0763* | -Beacon ODAS. | 34° 37.7´ S 57° 55.2´ W | **Fl.Y.** period 4s fl. 0.2s, ec. 3.8s | 26 **8** | | SPECIAL Y, beacon, X topmark. | |
| 19284 *G 0789* | -Piedra Diamante Barra San Pedro. | 34° 25.4´ S 57° 57.7´ W | **Fl.(2)W.** period 6s fl. 0.8s, ec. 1.2s fl. 0.8s, ec. 3.2s | 60 **18** | 10 | Conical concrete beacon, metal base. | |
| 19287 *G 0764* | -Rio San Juan. | 34° 16.4´ S 57° 59.0´ W | **Fl.G.** period 5s fl. 0.5s, ec. 4.5s | 16 **5** | 5 | White tower. | F.W. (occas.) light on tower 0.3 mile SSW. |
| 19290 *G 0765* | -Punta Conchillas. | 34° 12.4´ S 58° 04.6´ W | **Fl.R.** period 5s fl. 1s, ec. 4s | 13 **4** | 5 | Red tower. | |
| 19292 *G 0791* | -Isla Martin Garcia. | 34° 11.4´ S 58° 15.4´ W | **Fl.(2)Y.** period 10s fl. 0.5s, ec. 1s fl. 0.5s, ec. 8s | 33 **10** | 6 | Square tower; 33. | |
| 19296 *G 0766* | --Puerto de Carmelo, S. dyke, head. | 34° 00.5´ S 58° 18.1´ W | **Fl.R.** period 5s fl. 0.5s, ec. 4.5s | 20 **6** | 5 | Red tower. | |
| 19300 *G 0767* | ---N. breakwater, head. | 34° 00.5´ S 58° 18.2´ W | **Fl.G.** period 5s fl. 0.5s, ec. 4.5s | 20 **6** | 5 | Green tower. | |
| 19302 *G 0768.5* | --Water intake. | 34° 00.4´ S 58° 18.5´ W | **Fl.Y.** period 3s fl. 0.3s, ec. 2.7s | 7 **2** | - | SPECIAL Y, beacon, X topmark. | |
| 19304 *G 0768* | --N. side of river mouth near root of N. breakwater. | 34° 00.4´ S 58° 17.8´ W | **Fl.G.** period 5s fl. 0.5s, ec. 4.5s | 20 **6** | 6 | White tower. | |
| | PUERTO DE NUEVA PALMIRA: | | | | | | |
| 19305 *G 0771* | -S. pier, S. end. | 33° 53.0´ S 58° 25.5´ W | **Fl.W.R.** period 5s fl. 0.5s, ec. 4.5s | 32 **10** | W. 11 R. 8 | White tower, red bands. | R. 342°-021°, W.-180°. |
| 19306 *G 0772* | -N. pier, N. end. | 33° 52.6´ S 58° 25.4´ W | **Fl.G.** period 5s fl. 0.5s, ec. 4.5s | 26 **8** | 5 | Green tower; 19. | |
| 19307 *G 0773* | -Dolphin, 100 meters N. of N. pier. | 33° 52.5´ S 58° 25.4´ W | **Fl.Y.** period 4s fl. 0.3s, ec. 3.7s | | 5 | | |
| 19307.1 *G 0773.2* | -Muelle Ontur, S. end. | 33° 52.4´ S 58° 25.4´ W | **Fl.R.** period 5s | | | | |
| 19307.2 *G 0773.3* | --N. end. | 33° 52.3´ S 58° 25.4´ W | **Fl.G.** period 5s | | | | |
| 19307.3 *G 0773.4* | -N. of muelle. | 33° 52.3´ S 58° 25.4´ W | **Fl.Y.** period 4s | | | Dolphin. | |
| 19307.5 *G 0774* | -Darsena Higueritas, S. breakwater, head. | 33° 52.2´ S 58° 25.2´ W | **Fl.R.** period 5s fl. 0.5s, ec. 4.5s | 13 **4** | 5 | Red tower. | |
| 19307.6 *G 0775* | -N. breakwater, head. | 33° 52.2´ S 58° 25.2´ W | **Fl.G.** period 5s fl. 0.5s, ec. 4.5s | 13 **4** | 6 | Green tower. | |

| (1) No. | (2) Name and Location | (3) Position | (4) Characteristic | (5) Height | (6) Range | (7) Structure | (8) Remarks |
|---|---|---|---|---|---|---|---|

## ARGENTINA

| (1) No. | (2) Name and Location | (3) Position | (4) Characteristic | (5) Height | (6) Range | (7) Structure | (8) Remarks |
|---|---|---|---|---|---|---|---|
| | RIO DE LA PLATA: | | | | | | |
| 19308 *G 0812* | -*PRACTICOS RECALADA LIGHTSHIP.* | 35° 06.5´ S 55° 57.9´ W | **Fl.(2)W.** period 12s fl. 1s, ec. 3s fl. 1s, ec. 7s | 75 **23** | 13 | Orange funnel on white superstructure, orange hull, two masts, marked DE-15 RECALADA. | **Siren:** 30s (bl. 5s, si. 25s). Pilot station. |
| | -Aero | | **2 F.R.** | | | | |
| 19316 *G 0896* | **-Punta Atalaya.** | 35° 01.4´ S 57° 32.0´ W | **Fl.W.** period 6s fl. 0.5s, ec. 5.5s | 82 **25** | 10 | Coast Guard red and white framework radio mast. | |
| | | | **2 Fl.R.** (vert.) period 2.5s fl. 0.5s, ec. 2s | 344 **105** | **30** **15** | | |
| 19320 *G 0872* | -La Plata breakwater, E. beacon., Km. 7,700. | 34° 48.0´ S 57° 51.6´ W | **Iso.G.** period 2s | 26 **8** | 5 | PORT (B) G, beacon, topmark. | **Radar reflector.** |
| 19324 *G 0874* | --Breakwater, W. beacon, Km. 7,700. | 34° 47.9´ S 57° 51.8´ W | **Iso.R.** period 2s | 26 **8** | 5 | STARBOARD (B) R, beacon, topmark. | **Radar reflector.** |
| 19328 *G 0877* | --Km. 6,600, W. | 34° 48.5´ S 57° 52.0´ W | **Fl.(2)R.** period 8s | 20 **6** | 3 | STARBOARD (B) R, tower, topmark. | **Radar reflector.** |
| 19332 *G 0876* | --Km. 6,600, E. | 34° 48.5´ S 57° 51.9´ W | **Fl.(2)G.** period 8s fl. 0.5s, ec. 1s fl. 0.5s, ec. 6s | 20 **6** | 3 | PORT (B) G, tower, topmark. | **Radar reflector.** |
| | -Puerto la Plata: | | | | | | |
| 19336 *G 0878* | ---Km. 5,360, E. | 34° 49.1´ S 57° 52.2´ W | **Fl.(2)G.** period 8s fl. 0.5s, ec. 1s fl. 0.5s, ec. 6s | 20 **6** | 3 | PORT (B) G, tower, topmark. | **Radar reflector.** |
| 19340 *G 0879* | ---Km. 5,360, W. | 34° 49.1´ S 57° 52.3´ W | **Fl.(2)R.** period 8s fl. 0.5s, ec. 1s fl. 0.5s, ec. 6s | 20 **6** | 3 | STARBOARD (B) R, tower, topmark. | **Radar reflector.** |
| 19344 *G 0880* | ---Km. 4,540, E. | 34° 49.5´ S 57° 52.4´ W | **Fl.(2)G.** period 8s fl. 0.5s, ec. 1s fl. 0.5s, ec. 6s | 20 **6** | 3 | PORT (B) G, tower, topmark. | **Radar reflector.** |
| 19348 *G 0881* | ---Km. 4,540, W. | 34° 49.5´ S 57° 52.5´ W | **Fl.(2)R.** period 8s fl. 0.5s, ec. 1s fl. 0.5s, ec. 6s | 20 **6** | 3 | STARBOARD (B) R, tower, topmark. | **Radar reflector.** |
| 19350 *G 0882* | ---Km. 2,505, W. side of channel. | 34° 50.8´ S 57° 53.2´ W | **Fl.(3)R.** period 9s fl. 0.8s, ec. 1.2s fl. 0.8s, ec. 1.2s fl. 0.8s, ec. 4.2s | 30 **9** | 3 | STARBOARD (B) R, tower, topmark. | |
| 19351 *G 0882.5* | --Guard post No. 4. | 34° 50.8´ S 57° 53.7´ W | **Fl.W.** period 1.5s fl. 0.5s, ec. 1s | 10 **3** | 4 | Concrete lookout station. | |
| 19360 *G 0883.2* | --Beacon, Km. 1,300, W. side of Gran Dock entrance. | 34° 51.1´ S 57° 53.3´ W | **Fl.(3)R.** period 9s fl. 0.8s, ec. 1.2s fl. 0.8s, ec. 1.2s fl. 0.8s, ec. 4.2s | 30 **9** | 3 | STARBOARD (B) R, tower, topmark. | |
| 19361 *G 0883* | ---Km. 1,300, E. side of Gran Dock entrance. | 34° 51.1´ S 57° 53.3´ W | **Fl.(2)G.** period 8s fl. 0.5s, ec. 1s fl. 0.5s, ec. 6s | 30 **9** | 2 | PORT (B) G, tower, topmark. | |
| 19368 *G 0871* | --La Toma. | 34° 49.1´ S 57° 53.8´ W | **Iso.W.** period 2s | | 6 | Water tower. | |

| (1) No. | (2) Name and Location | (3) Position | (4) Characteristic | (5) Height | (6) Range | (7) Structure | (8) Remarks |
|---|---|---|---|---|---|---|---|

## ARGENTINA

| (1) No. | (2) Name and Location | (3) Position | (4) Characteristic | (5) Height | (6) Range | (7) Structure | (8) Remarks |
|---|---|---|---|---|---|---|---|
| 19372<br>*G 0865* | -Tower Difusora, No. 1. | 34° 43.5´ S<br>58° 10.0´ W | **L.Fl.W.**<br>period 6s<br>fl. 2s, ec. 4s | | | Concrete tower. | |
| 19373<br>*G 0864* | -Toma Ducilo. | 34° 43.0´ S<br>58° 11.2´ W | **Fl.W.**<br>period 4.3s<br>fl. 0.3s, ec. 4s | | | Water tower. | |
| 19374<br>*G 0861.6* | -Toma Bernal. | 34° 40.9´ S<br>58° 13.8´ W | **Fl.(2)W.**<br>period 10s<br>fl. 0.5s, ec. 1s<br>fl. 0.5s, ec. 8s | | 1 | ISOLATED DANGER<br>BRB, tower, topmark; 26. | Water intake tower. |
| 19375<br>*G 0861.8* | -Tower, 0.33 mile NE. of Quilmes Marina breakwater. | 34° 41.9´ S<br>58° 14.5´ W | **L.Fl.Y.**<br>period 6s<br>fl. 2s, ec. 4s | | | Concrete tower. | |
| 19376<br>*G 0862* | -Quilmes Marina, N. breakwater. | 34° 41.9´ S<br>58° 13.7´ W | **Fl.R.**<br>period 3s<br>fl. 0.3s, ec. 2.7s | | 5 | | |
| 19377<br>*G 0862.2* | --S. breakwater. | 34° 42.0´ S<br>58° 13.6´ W | **Fl.G.**<br>period 3s<br>fl. 0.3s, ec. 2.7s | | 5 | | |
| | -Buenos Aires:--Puerto Nuevo: | | | | | | |
| 19380<br>*G 0834* | ---Darsena Norte, N. side. | 34° 35.7´ S<br>58° 21.9´ W | **Fl.(4)R.** | 26<br>**8** | | Red square metal framework tower; 10. | |
| 19382<br>*G 0836* | ---Darsena Norte, S. side. | 34° 35.7´ S<br>58° 21.8´ W | **Fl.(4)G.** | 26<br>**8** | | Green square tower; 10. | |
| 19383<br>*G 0843* | ---AVIATION LIGHT. | 34° 36.7´ S<br>58° 21.6´ W | **Fl.R.**<br>period 3s | 574<br>**175** | **27** | Red and white tower on building. | |
| 19384<br>*G 0828* | ---Km. 0.8, S. end, outer detached breakwater. | 34° 35.5´ S<br>58° 21.3´ W | **Fl.(2)R.**<br>period 8s<br>fl. 0.5s, ec. 1s<br>fl. 0.5s, ec. 6s | 46<br>**14** | 7 | Red square tower. | |
| 19384.5<br>*G 0826* | ---Km. 1.35, S. pier, head. | 34° 35.7´ S<br>58° 21.0´ W | **Fl.(2)G.**<br>period 8s | | | PORT (B)<br>G, tower, topmark. | |
| 19388<br>*G 0840* | ---Outer detached breakwater, N. end, Km. 3.2 of new port. | 34° 34.4´ S<br>58° 22.2´ W | **Fl.R.**<br>period 4s<br>fl. 0.5s, ec. 3.5s | 39<br>**12** | | Red square metal framework tower. | |
| 19401<br>*G 0845* | ---Sports Complex. | 34° 37.2´ S<br>58° 20.7´ W | **Fl.W.**<br>period 4s<br>fl. 0.5s, ec. 3.5s | | 6 | Black beacon. | |
| 19401.5<br>*G 0851* | -Cabecera Muella, head. | 34° 37.9´ S<br>58° 19.9´ W | **Q.W.** | 7<br>**2** | 4 | N. CARDINAL<br>BY, beacon, topmark. | 2 pairs Fl.W. range lights for approach on either side of pier. |
| | | | **Dir.Iso.W.R.G.**<br>period 2s | | | | |
| 19401.7<br>*G 0851.3* | -E. breakwater, head. | 34° 37.9´ S<br>58° 19.8´ W | **Fl.Y.**<br>period 2s | | | | |
| 19401.8<br>*G 0851.5* | -W. breakwater, head. | 34° 37.9´ S<br>58° 20.1´ W | **Fl.Y.**<br>period 2s | | | | |
| | | | **Dir.Iso.W.R.G.**<br>period 2s | | | | |
| 19402<br>*G 0848.5* | -Darsena de Inflamables. | 34° 38.0´ S<br>58° 20.4´ W | **Fl.R.**<br>period 7s<br>fl. 1s, ec. 6s | 20<br>**6** | | | E. cardinal beacon V.Q.(3)W. 5s on pier head 150 meters N.<br>Q.(3)G. 10s 13m 8M 380 meters ENE. |
| 19402.2 | -Darsena de Inflamables. E. side of entrance. | 34° 38.0´ S<br>58° 20.3´ W | **Fl.G.**<br>period 7s<br>fl. 1s, ec. 6s | 24<br>**7** | | | |

| (1) No. | (2) Name and Location | (3) Position | (4) Characteristic | (5) Height | (6) Range | (7) Structure | (8) Remarks |
|---|---|---|---|---|---|---|---|

## ARGENTINA

| (1) No. | (2) Name and Location | (3) Position | (4) Characteristic | (5) Height | (6) Range | (7) Structure | (8) Remarks |
|---|---|---|---|---|---|---|---|
| 19402.3<br>*G 0793* | --No. 7. | 34° 31.2´ S<br>58° 19.7´ W | **Fl.(5)Y.**<br>period 13s<br>fl. 0.5s, ec. 1.5s<br>fl. 0.5s, ec. 1.5s<br>fl. 0.5s, ec. 1.5s<br>fl. 0.5s, ec. 1.5s<br>fl. 0.5s, ec. 4.5s | 26<br>**8** | | SPECIAL<br>Y, beacon, X topmark. | |
| 19402.6<br>*G 0854* | -Water intake No.3. | 34° 32.6´ S<br>58° 25.1´ W | **Fl.(2)W.**<br>period 6s<br>fl. 0.5s, ec. 1s<br>fl. 0.5s, ec. 4s | 28<br>**8** | 2 | Black round tower, black circular daymark. | **Radar reflector.** |
| 19402.65<br>*G 0853* | -Fisherman's club. | 34° 33.7´ S<br>58° 24.0´ W | **Q.(3)W.**<br>period 10s | | | Beacon. | Tide gauge. |
| 19402.7<br>*G 0860* | -San Isidro, pier, head. | 34° 27.0´ S<br>58° 30.3´ W | **Fl.G.**<br>period 5s<br>fl. 1s, ec. 4s | 39<br>**12** | 2 | 3 green wooden piles. | |
| 19402.8<br>*G 0860.2* | --Rio Lujan, entrance. | 34° 27.0´ S<br>58° 30.4´ W | **Fl.R.**<br>period 5s<br>fl. 1s, ec. 4s | 46<br>**14** | 8 | Red truncated metal tower, concrete base; 30. | |
| 19403<br>*G 0900* | **Punta Piedras.** | 35° 26.8´ S<br>57° 08.6´ W | **Fl.W.**<br>period 9s<br>fl. 0.5s, ec. 8.5s | 148<br>**45** | **15** | White truncated pyramidal tower, orange bands; 102. | |
| 19404<br>*G 0901* | Rio Salado, N. side of entrance. | 35° 44.6´ S<br>57° 22.3´ W | **Fl.W.**<br>period 8s<br>fl. 0.5s, ec. 7.5s | 34<br>**10** | 7 | Orange metal column; 20. | |
| 19406<br>*G 0903* | -San Clemente del Tuyu. | 36° 18.9´ S<br>56° 46.7´ W | **Fl.R.**<br>period 5s<br>fl. 0.5s, ec. 4.5s | 26<br>**8** | 6 | Black framework column; 26. | |
| 19408<br>*G 0902* | Rio Ajo. | 36° 19.8´ S<br>56° 54.5´ W | **Fl.(2)W.**<br>period 8.4s<br>fl. 0.2s, ec. 0.1s<br>fl. 0.1s, ec. 8s | 16<br>**5** | 4 | Metal column; 16. | |
| 19412<br>*G 0905* | Toledo. | 36° 17.6´ S<br>56° 46.9´ W | **Fl.G.**<br>period 5.5s<br>fl. 0.5s, ec. 5s | 16<br>**5** | 5 | Triangular tower on tripod; 16. | |
| 19420<br>*G 0904* | **Cabo San Antonio.** | 36° 18.4´ S<br>56° 46.3´ W | **Fl.W.**<br>period 17s<br>fl. 1.4s, ec. 15.6s | 207<br>**63** | **20** | White truncated pyramidal tower with glass cabin, black bands; 190. | Visible 160°-300°.<br>Reserve light Fl.(3)W. 30s fl. .75s, ec. 3.5s, fl. .75s, ec. 3.5s, fl. .75s, ec. 20.75s 9M. |
| 19421<br>*G 0905.5* | San Clemente Anchorage, leading light. | 36° 18.1´ S<br>56° 46.2´ W | **Fl.W.**<br>period 3.5s<br>fl. 0.5s, ec. 3s | 55<br>**17** | 6 | White triangular framework tower; 43. | 614 meters, 021° from light 19420. |
| 19422<br>*G 0904.3* | -Dos Bocas. | 36° 19.7´ S<br>56° 46.3´ W | **Fl.W.**<br>period 5s<br>fl. 0.5s, ec. 4.5s | 98<br>**30** | 4 | Wooden mast; 16. | |
| 19424<br>*G 0908* | **Punta Medanos.** | 36° 53.0´ S<br>56° 40.5´ W | **Fl.(5)W.**<br>period 40s<br>fl. 1.5s, ec. 4.5s<br>fl. 1.5s, ec. 4.5s<br>fl. 1.5s, ec. 4.5s<br>fl. 1.5s, ec. 4.5s<br>fl. 1.5s, ec. 14.5s | 223<br>**68** | **18** | Red metal framework tower, white bands, on building; 194. | Reserve light Fl.(5)W. 40s. |
| 19428<br>*G 0910* | **Querandi.** | 37° 27.8´ S<br>57° 06.6´ W | **Fl.(5)W.**<br>period 26s<br>fl. 1s, ec. 3s<br>fl. 1s, ec. 3s<br>fl. 1s, ec. 3s<br>fl. 1s, ec. 3s<br>fl. 1s, ec. 9s | 213<br>**65** | **18** | Black truncated pyramidal concrete tower, white bands; 177. | Reserve light Fl.(4)W. 60s. |
| 19430<br>*G 0912* | Mar Chiquita. | 37° 46.3´ S<br>57° 26.8´ W | **Fl.(2)W.**<br>period 15s | 69<br>**21** | 12 | | |

| (1) No. | (2) Name and Location | (3) Position | (4) Characteristic | (5) Height | (6) Range | (7) Structure | (8) Remarks |
|---|---|---|---|---|---|---|---|

## ARGENTINA

MAR DEL PLATA:

| (1) No. | (2) Name and Location | (3) Position | (4) Characteristic | (5) Height | (6) Range | (7) Structure | (8) Remarks |
|---|---|---|---|---|---|---|---|
| 19436 *G 0915* | -Cabo Corrientes. | 38° 01.1′ S 57° 31.5′ W | **Fl.W.** period 10s fl. 0.2s, ec. 9.8s | 246 **75** | 10 | Lookout tower terrace; 190. | |
| 19436.5 *G 0916* | -N. breakwater, head. | 38° 02.2′ S 57° 31.4′ W | **Fl.R.** period 3s fl. 0.3s, ec. 2.7s | 49 **15** | 9 | Red round column; 33. | |
| 19437 *G 0917* | -S. breakwater, head. | 38° 02.3′ S 57° 31.1′ W | **Fl.G.** period 3s fl. 0.3s, ec. 2.7s | 59 **18** | 9 | Green round column; 33. | |
| 19464 *G 0920* | -Inner breakwater. | 38° 02.5′ S 57° 32.0′ W | **Iso.G.** period 3s | 56 **17** | 5 | Triangular tower, red rectangular daymark, white stripe; 7. | |
| 19465 *G 0919* | -Submarine Dock Range, front. | 38° 02.2′ S 57° 32.0′ W | **Q.R.** | 16 **5** | 7 | Red triangular daymark point up, white rectangular daymark. | |
| 19466 *G 0919.1* | --Rear, 50 meters 314°30′ from front. | 38° 02.2′ S 57° 32.0′ W | **Q.R.** | 39 **12** | 7 | Building, red triangular daymark point down and white rectangular daymark. | |
| 19468 *G 0917.7* | -Abrigo breakwater. | 38° 02.3′ S 57° 31.7′ W | **Fl.R.** period 4s fl. 1s, ec. 3s | 26 **8** | 5 | Red and white checkered tower; 10. | |
| 19469 *G 0917.4* | -S. breakwater, range, front. | 38° 02.5′ S 57° 31.5′ W | **L.Fl.G.** period 5s fl. 2s, ec. 3s | 33 **10** | 5 | Triangular tower, black rectangular daymark, white stripe, orange rectangular daymark; 26. | Shown 24 hours. |
| 19470 *G 0917.5* | --Rear, about 711 meters 216°39′ from front. | 38° 02.9′ S 57° 31.8′ W | **Oc.G.** period 5s lt. 3s, ec. 2s | 56 **17** | 5 | Rectangular tubular tower, orange square daymark, black rectangular daymark, white stripe; 33. | Shown 24 hours. |
| 19470.5 *G 917.62* | -Inflammables berth. | 38° 02.7′ S 57° 31.8′ W | **Mo.(U)Y.** period 5s fl. 0.5s, ec. 0.5s fl. 0.5s, ec. 0.5s fl. 1.5s, ec. 1.5s | 30 **9** | 6 | Yellow iron column; 16. | |
| 19470.7 *G 917.64* | -Espigon 7. | 38° 02.7′ S 57° 31.9′ W | **Fl.(2)G.** period 6s fl. 1s, ec. 1s fl. 1s, ec. 3s | 30 **9** | 6 | Green iron column, white bands; 16. | |
| 19471 *G 920.2* | -Espigon 3. | 38° 02.7′ S 57° 32.2′ W | **Iso.R.** period 2s | 30 **9** | 6 | Red iron column, white bands; 16. | |
| 19471.2 *G 920.4* | -Espigon 2. | 38° 02.8′ S 57° 32.1′ W | **Iso.G.** period 2s | 30 **9** | 6 | Green iron column, white bands; 16. | |
| 19471.4 *G 920.6* | -Espigon 1. | 38° 02.9′ S 57° 32.2′ W | **Iso.G.** period 4s | 30 **9** | 6 | Green iron column, white bands; 16. | |
| 19472 *G 0913* | **Punta Mogotes.** | 38° 05.5′ S 57° 32.7′ W | **Fl.W.** period 19s fl. 1.5s, ec. 17.5s | 180 **55** | **25** | White conical tower, red band and dwellings; 115. | Visible 216°-026°. Reserve light range 12M. |
| 19475 *G 0922* | Miramar. | 38° 16.6′ S 57° 50.0′ W | **Fl.W.** period 5s fl. 0.5s, ec. 4.5s | 256 **78** | 12 | White concrete pedestal. | |
| 19480 *G 0926* | **Quequen.** | 38° 34.0′ S 58° 41.4′ W | **Fl.(2)W.** period 15s fl. 0.5s, ec. 3.3s fl. 0.5s, ec. 10.7s | 207 **63** | **26** | Black truncated conical concrete tower, white band; 112. | Reserve light range 19M. |
| 19484 *G 0930* | -N. breakwater, head. | 38° 34.9′ S 58° 41.8′ W | **Fl.R.** period 3s | 26 **8** | 6 | Red truncated pyramidal tower, square base; 7. | Reserve light. |
| 19488 *G 0928* | -S. breakwater, head. | 38° 35.3′ S 58° 41.4′ W | **Oc.G.** period 6s | 69 **21** | 9 | Round column, black and yellow bands; 33. | |
| 19496 *G 0928.19* | -Pescador Range, front. | 38° 35.1′ S 58° 41.8′ W | **Iso.G.** period 2s | 23 **7** | 4 | Yellow square masonry tower; 7. | Visible 134°-222°. Reserve light. |

| (1) No. | (2) Name and Location | (3) Position | (4) Characteristic | (5) Height | (6) Range | (7) Structure | (8) Remarks |
|---|---|---|---|---|---|---|---|
| | | | **ARGENTINA** | | | | |
| 19497 G 0928.2 | --Rear, about 33 meters 134°42′ from front. | 38° 35.1′ S 58° 41.7′ W | **Iso.G.** period 2s | 26 **8** | 3 | Orange truncated conical tower; 10. | Reserve light. |
| 19501 G 0932.6 | -Segunda, on S. breakwater. | 38° 35.0′ S 58° 42.0′ W | **Q.G.** | 39 **12** | 7 | Black masonry tower; 13. | Visible 157° - 242°. Reserve light. |
| 19504 G 0932 | -Entrance Range, front, on S. breakwater. | 38° 34.9′ S 58° 42.1′ W | **Iso.R.** period 2s | 33 **10** | 10 | White round tower, red band; 20. | |
| 19508 G 0932.1 | --Rear, 919 meters 293° from front. | 38° 34.7′ S 58° 42.6′ W | **2 Iso.W.** period 2s | 141 **43** 75 **23** | 9 | On factory chimney, red triangular daymark point down. | |
| 19516 G 0934 | -Breakwater Range (Enfilacion Escollera), front. | 38° 35.1′ S 58° 41.7′ W | **Q.R.** period 1s fl. 0.5s, ec. 0.5s | 30 **9** | 4 | Tower, yellow triangular daymark point up, black base; 13. | Visible 131°-139°. Reserve light. |
| 19520 G 0934.1 | --Rear, about 26 meters 134°42′ from front. | 38° 35.1′ S 58° 41.6′ W | **Iso.W.** period 2s | 43 **13** | 6 | Black tower, yellow triangular daymark point down, red band; 20. | Visible 131°-139°. Reserve light. |
| 19524 G 0935 | -Inner Range (Enfilacion del Fondo), front. | 38° 34.5′ S 58° 42.5′ W | **Fl.R.** period 3s fl. 0.5s, ec. 2.5s | 98 **30** | 9 | White triangular daymark point up, red rectangular daymark. | Visible 308°45′-315°45′. Reserve light. |
| 19528 G 0935.1 | -Rear, about 327 meters 314°42′ from front, on grain elevator. | 38° 34.3′ S 58° 42.6′ W | **Fl.W.** period 1.5s fl. 0.5s, ec. 1s | 135 **41** | 5 | White triangular daymark point up, red rectangular daymark; 20. | Visible 308°45′-315°45′. Reserve light. |
| 19532 G 0938 | -Espigon Este. | 38° 34.7′ S 58° 42.1′ W | **Fl.R.** period 5s fl. 1s, ec. 4s | 23 **7** | | Red metal structure; 7. | |
| 19536 G 0942 | **Balneario Claromeco.** | 38° 51.5′ S 60° 03.1′ W | **Fl.(2+1)W.** period 30s fl. 0.3s, ec. 3.4s fl. 0.3s, ec. 11s fl. 0.3s, ec. 14.7s | 230 **70** | **26** | White concrete tower, black bands; 177. | Reserve light range 11M. |
| | BAHIA BLANCA: | | | | | | |
| 19540 G 0986 | **-Recalada.** | 38° 59.4′ S 61° 15.6′ W | **Fl.W.** period 9s fl. 0.5s, ec. 8.5s | 240 **73** | **28** | White metal tower, red bands; 220. | **Radiobeacon.** |
| 19547 G 0989 | -Tide gauge. | 39° 08.9′ S 61° 43.3′ W | **Fl.(2)W.** period 10s fl. 1s, ec. 1s fl. 1s, ec. 7s | 46 **14** | 3 | Yellow tube. | Tide gauge. |
| 19550 G 0991 | -Punta Tejada. | 38° 59.1′ S 61° 49.0′ W | **Fl.W.** period 5s fl. 1s, ec. 4s | 52 **16** | 7 | Tower, black and white circular daymark; 33. | |
| 19552 G 0993 | -Chica. | 38° 58.0′ S 61° 53.7′ W | **L.Fl.W.** period 10s fl. 2s, ec. 8s | 52 **16** | 7 | Yellow framework tower, black bands; 49. | |
| 19554 G 0994 | -Tripode. | 38° 57.2′ S 61° 56.3′ W | **Fl.(2)W.** period 10s fl. 0.5s, ec. 1s fl. 0.5s, ec. 8s | 92 **28** | 7 | Red framework tower, white bands; 33. | |
| 19560 G 1000 | --Puerto Rosales breakwater. | 38° 55.8′ S 62° 04.3′ W | **Fl.R.** period 3s fl. 0.3s, ec. 2.7s | | 6 | Red framework tower; 20. | Private light. |
| | -Puerto Belgrano: | | | | | | |
| 19564 G 1004 | --E. mole, head, entrance to outer basin. | 38° 54.0′ S 62° 06.0′ W | **Q.(2)R.** period 5s fl. 0.3s, ec. 0.7s fl. 0.3s, ec. 3.7s | 25 **8** | 6 | Truncated pyramidal tower; 10. | |
| 19568 G 1006 | --S.W. breakwater, extension, head. | 38° 54.3′ S 62° 06.0′ W | **Q.(2)G.** period 5s fl. 0.3s, ec. 0.7s fl. 0.3s, ec. 3.7s | 24 **7** | 7 | White round tower; 13. | |

| (1) No. | (2) Name and Location | (3) Position | (4) Characteristic | (5) Height | (6) Range | (7) Structure | (8) Remarks |
|---|---|---|---|---|---|---|---|

## ARGENTINA

| (1) No. | (2) Name and Location | (3) Position | (4) Characteristic | (5) Height | (6) Range | (7) Structure | (8) Remarks |
|---|---|---|---|---|---|---|---|
| 19572<br>*G 1008* | --W. mole, head, entrance to outer basin. | 38° 54.0´ S<br>62° 08.1´ W | **Iso.G.**<br>period 2s | 26<br>**8** | 6 | Truncated pyramidal tower; 13. | |
| 19572.2<br>*G 1010* | --No. 1. | 38° 48.2´ S<br>62° 14.7´ W | **Oc.R.**<br>period 10s<br>lt. 6s, ec. 4s | 10<br>**3** | 5 | Metal platform. | |
| 19572.4<br>*G 1010.2* | --No. 2. | 38° 48.4´ S<br>62° 15.1´ W | **Oc.G.**<br>period 10s<br>lt. 6s, ec. 4s | 10<br>**3** | 5 | Metal platform. | |
| 19572.6<br>*G 1010.4* | --No. 3. | 38° 48.4´ S<br>62° 14.4´ W | **Iso.R.**<br>period 2s | 10<br>**3** | 5 | Metal platform. | |
| | -Puerto Ingeniero White: | | | | | | |
| 19573<br>*G 1012.4* | --SE. jetty. | 38° 47.9´ S<br>62° 15.3´ W | **Fl.R.**<br>period 1.5s<br>fl. 0.5s, ec. 1s | 20<br>**6** | | Black metal square tower; 7. | Private light. |
| 19573.1<br>*G 1012.6* | --NW. jetty. | 38° 47.8´ S<br>62° 15.5´ W | **Fl.R.**<br>period 1.5s | 30<br>**9** | | Black metal structure on hut; 13. | Private light. |
| 19574<br>*G 1013.4* | --Grain elevator jetty No. 9. | 38° 47.6´ S<br>62° 15.7´ W | **F.R.** | | | Metal post; 3. | Private light. |
| 19575<br>*G 1013.44* | --Central pier, head, No. 3. | 38° 47.6´ S<br>62° 15.8´ W | **F.R.** | | | Metal post; 3. | Tide gauge close N.<br>Private light. |
| 19576<br>*G 1013.46* | ---No. 7. | 38° 47.6´ S<br>62° 15.9´ W | **F.R.** | | | Metal post; 3. | Private light. |
| 19577<br>*G 1013.6* | --Muelle Cargill, E. end. | 38° 47.5´ S<br>62° 16.2´ W | **Q.(2)R.**<br>period 4s | 33<br>**10** | 4 | Red fiberglass tower on truncated pyramid; 10. | |
| 19577.5<br>*G 1013.65* | ---W. end. | 38° 47.5´ S<br>62° 16.3´ W | **Q.(2)R.**<br>period 4s | 33<br>**10** | 4 | Red fiberglass tower on truncated pyramid; 10. | |
| 19578.3<br>*G 1015.3* | --Muelle de Inflamables, SE. end. | 38° 47.1´ S<br>62° 18.2´ W | **F.R.** | 16<br>**5** | | Metal post; 3. | Private light. |
| | -Puerto Belgrano: | | | | | | |
| 19578.4<br>*G 1015.1* | -- Muelle Mega. | 38° 47.3´ S<br>62° 17.2´ W | **VQ(6)+L.Fl.W.**<br>period 10s | 26<br>**8** | 2 | S.CARDINAL YB, Beacon, topmark, points down. | Marks water intake.<br>Private light. |
| 19578.6<br>*G 1015.35* | ---NW. end. | 38° 46.9´ S<br>62° 18.7´ W | **F.R.** | 16<br>**5** | | Metal past; 3. | Private light. |
| 19580<br>*G 1020* | **-El Rincon.** | 39° 23.1´ S<br>62° 00.9´ W | **Fl.(2+1)W.**<br>period 40s<br>fl. 0.2s, ec. 5.4s<br>fl. 0.2s, ec. 17s<br>fl. 0.2s, ec. 17s | 210<br>**64** | **29** | White truncated conical tower, black bands; 203. | |
| 19584<br>*G 1024* | **Segunda Barranca Point.** | 40° 46.5´ S<br>62° 16.4´ W | **Fl.(3)W.**<br>period 22s<br>fl. 0.2s, ec. 9.3s<br>fl. 0.2s, ec. 9.3s<br>fl. 0.2s, ec. 2.8s | 126<br>**38** | **27** | White truncated conical tower, black bands, dwelling; 112. | Reserve light range 23M. |
| 19588<br>*G 1028* | **Rio Negro.** | 41° 03.4´ S<br>62° 50.3´ W | **Fl.(2)W.**<br>period 20s<br>fl. 1s, ec. 4s<br>fl. 1s, ec. 14s | 141<br>**43** | **16** | White round masonry tower, dwelling; 52. | Reserve light range 11M. |
| | SAN ANTONIO OESTE: | | | | | | |
| 19596<br>*G 1031* | -San Matias. | 40° 49.3´ S<br>64° 43.2´ W | **Fl.(2)W.**<br>period 11s<br>fl. 0.5s, ec. 2s<br>fl. 0.5s, ec. 8s | 138<br>**42** | 12 | White pyramidal tower, black bands; 52. | |
| 19598<br>*G 1038* | -Punta Villarino. | 40° 48.7´ S<br>64° 54.2´ W | **Fl.W.**<br>period 6s<br>fl. 0.5s, ec. 5.5s | 112<br>**34** | 6 | Black pyramidal tower, yellow band; 20. | |

| (1) No. | (2) Name and Location | (3) Position | (4) Characteristic | (5) Height | (6) Range | (7) Structure | (8) Remarks |
|---|---|---|---|---|---|---|---|
| | | | **ARGENTINA** | | | | |
| 19599<br>*G 1034* | -Pedro Garcia Range, front. | 40° 49.4´ S<br>64° 53.2´ W | **Fl.W.**<br>period 1.5s<br>fl. 0.5s, ec. 1s | 92<br>**28** | 9 | White rectangular daymark, black stripes; 39. | |
| 19601<br>*G 1035* | --Rear, 1.3 miles 032°23′ from front. | 40° 48.2´ S<br>64° 52.3´ W | **Fl.G.**<br>period 3s<br>fl. 0.5s, ec. 2.5s | 128<br>**39** | 12 | White water tank, black stripes; 79. | |
| 19604<br>*G 1036* | -Banco Reparo Outer Range, front. | 40° 46.8´ S<br>64° 55.5´ W | **Fl.W.**<br>period 2s<br>fl. 0.5s, ec. 1.5s | 49<br>**15** | 9 | Metal framework tower, red triangular daymark point up on three rectangular daymarks; 46. | |
| 19608<br>*G 1037* | --Rear, 1.4 miles 001° from front. | 40° 45.4´ S<br>64° 55.4´ W | **Fl.R.**<br>period 3s<br>fl. 0.5s, ec. 2.5s | 136<br>**41** | 8 | Square tower, white bands; 79. | |
| 19612<br>*G 1042* | -Cangrejal Inner Range, front. | 40° 45.0´ S<br>64° 52.9´ W | **Fl.W.**<br>period 1.5s<br>fl. 0.5s, ec. 1s | 49<br>**15** | 8 | Tower, orange rectangular daymark; 49. | |
| 19616<br>*G 1042.1* | --Rear, 2.5 miles 024° from front. | 40° 42.7´ S<br>64° 51.6´ W | **Fl.R.**<br>period 4s<br>fl. 0.5s, ec. 3.5s | 79<br>**24** | 6 | Two white truncated pyramidal towers, red band. | **Radar reflector.** |
| 19626<br>*G 1045* | Las Grutas. | 40° 47.8´ S<br>65° 04.3´ W | **Iso.W.**<br>period 2s | 233<br>**71** | 10 | Water tank; 98. | |
| 19628<br>*G 1046.3* | Punta Colorada, Hipasam. | 41° 41.8´ S<br>65° 01.5´ W | **L.Fl.(2)W.**<br>period 10s<br>fl. 2s, ec. 2s<br>fl. 2s, ec. 4s | 177<br>**54** | 12 | Building. | |
| 19632<br>*G 1047* | Punta Quiroga. | 42° 14.2´ S<br>64° 28.2´ W | **Fl.W.**<br>period 10s<br>fl. 1s, ec. 9s | 131<br>**40** | 11 | Black tower, white bands, hut; 20. | |
| 19634<br>*G 1048* | -Punta Buenos Aires. | 42° 14.3´ S<br>64° 22.4´ W | **Fl.W.**<br>period 3s<br>fl. 0.5s, ec. 2.5s | 125<br>**38** | 7 | White tower, red stripes, hut; 20. | |
| 19636<br>*G 1048.8* | Punta Tehuelche. | 42° 24.3´ S<br>64° 18.0´ W | **Fl.(3)W.**<br>period 20s<br>fl. 1s, ec. 3s<br>fl. 1s, ec. 3s<br>fl. 1s, ec. 11s | 115<br>**35** | 11 | White tower, black bands, white base; 39. | |
| 19638<br>*G 1048.4* | -Sarmiento. | 42° 14.9´ S<br>64° 10.8´ W | **Fl.(2)W.**<br>period 10s<br>fl. 0.5s, ec. 1.5s<br>fl. 0.5s, ec. 7.5s | 62<br>**19** | 10 | Red round concrete tower, white bands; 16. | |
| | PENINSULA VALDEZ: | | | | | | |
| 19640<br>*G 1049* | **-Almirante Brown.** | 42° 13.0´ S<br>64° 15.3´ W | **Fl.(2)W.**<br>period 16s<br>fl. 1s, ec. 4s<br>fl. 1s, ec. 10s | 249<br>**76** | 10 | White square concrete tower, red bands, red square daymark; 16. | |
| 19652<br>*G 1050* | **-Punta Norte.** | 42° 04.5´ S<br>63° 46.2´ W | **Fl.W.**<br>period 10s<br>fl. 0.2s, ec. 9.8s | 203<br>**62** | 14 | White round tower, black bands; 52. | Intensified 160°-250°. |
| 19656<br>*G 1052* | -Punta Bajos. | 42° 23.2´ S<br>63° 36.8´ W | **Fl.W.**<br>period 3s<br>fl. 1s, ec. 2s | 89<br>**27** | 14 | Black pyramidal tower; 66. | |
| 19660<br>*G 1054* | **-Punta Delgada.** | 42° 45.9´ S<br>63° 38.2´ W | **Fl.(2+1)W.**<br>period 25s<br>fl. 0.3s, ec. 3.2s<br>fl. 0.3s, ec. 10.4s<br>fl. 0.3s, ec. 10.5s | 233<br>**71** | **28** | Brick tower, dwelling; 46. | Emergency light. |
| | GOLFO NUEVO: | | | | | | |
| 19664<br>*G 1058* | -Morro Nuevo. | 42° 52.4´ S<br>64° 08.7´ W | **Fl.W.**<br>period 5s<br>fl. 0.5s, ec. 4.5s | 305<br>**93** | 13 | Red tower, white band; 39. | |

| (1)<br>No. | (2)<br>Name and Location | (3)<br>Position | (4)<br>Characteristic | (5)<br>Height | (6)<br>Range | (7)<br>Structure | (8)<br>Remarks |
|---|---|---|---|---|---|---|---|

**ARGENTINA**

| (1)<br>No. | (2)<br>Name and Location | (3)<br>Position | (4)<br>Characteristic | (5)<br>Height | (6)<br>Range | (7)<br>Structure | (8)<br>Remarks |
|---|---|---|---|---|---|---|---|
| 19668<br>*G 1074* | -Punta Ninfas, S. side of entrance to gulf. | 42° 58.1′ S<br>64° 18.9′ W | **Fl.(2)W.**<br>period 20s<br>fl. 1s, ec. 3s<br>fl. 1s, ec. 15s | 295<br>**90** | 11 | Black metal framework tower, yellow bands; 39. | Obscured between S. shore of Golfo Nuevo and bearing 158°, except in sectors 131°-134° and 148°-152°. |
| 19672<br>*G 1073* | -Bahia Cracker Anchorage Range, front. | 42° 57.0′ S<br>64° 29.2′ W | **Fl.G.**<br>period 4s<br>fl. 1s, ec. 3s | 56<br>**17** | 5 | Metal framework tower, red rectangular daymark, yellow triangular daymark point up; 16. | |
| 19676<br>*G 1073.1* | --Rear, 0.6 mile 181° from front. | 42° 57.7′ S<br>64° 29.2′ W | **Fl.W.**<br>period 3s<br>fl. 0.5s, ec. 2.5s | 171<br>**52** | 6 | Metal framework tower, red rectangular daymark, yellow triangular daymark point down; 23. | |
| 19680<br>*G 1073.4* | -Punta Cracker (Captain Rodriguez). | 42° 56.2′ S<br>64° 30.5′ W | **Fl.W.**<br>period 8s<br>fl. 1s, ec. 7s | 273<br>**83** | 7 | White tower, red bands; 23. | |
| 19684<br>*G 1072* | -Punta Conscriptos. | 42° 53.3′ S<br>64° 42.1′ W | **Fl.(2)W.**<br>period 22s<br>fl. 1s, ec. 6s<br>fl. 1s, ec. 14s | 318<br>**97** | 10 | Black square metal framework tower; 33. | |
| 19688<br>*G 1066* | -Acantilado. | 42° 47.6′ S<br>64° 57.0′ W | **Fl.W.**<br>period 6s<br>fl. 1s, ec. 5s | 187<br>**57** | 8 | Red metal framework tower, white band; 43. | |
| 19696<br>*G 1064* | -Punta Flecha. | 42° 38.7′ S<br>64° 58.1′ W | **Fl.W.**<br>period 9s<br>fl. 0.7s, ec. 8.3s | 138<br>**42** | 7 | White metal framework tower, red stripes; 43. | |
| 19698<br>*G 1067* | -Muelle Madryn, off front of pier head. | 42° 45.7′ S<br>65° 01.4′ W | **V.Q.W.R.** | 33<br>**10** | 1 | Yellow column, white band on dolphin; 10. | |
| 19700<br>*G 1068* | --N. side of pier. | 42° 45.7′ S<br>65° 01.6′ W | **V.Q.R.** | 33<br>**10** | 1 | Yellow column, white band; 10. | Xenon. |
| 19702<br>*G 1069* | --S. side of pier. | 42° 45.7′ S<br>65° 01.5′ W | **V.Q.G.** | 33<br>**10** | 1 | Yellow column, white band; 10. | |
| 19708<br>*G 1070* | -Ore jetty, E. end. | 42° 44.1′ S<br>65° 01.1′ W | **Fl.(3)W.**<br>period 12s<br>fl. 0.5s, ec. 2s<br>fl. 0.5s, ec. 2s<br>fl. 0.5s, ec. 6.5s | 56<br>**17** | 10 | Black fiberglass tower, yellow band; 23. | |
| 19710<br>*G 1070.1* | -Muelle Pesquero. | 42° 44.3′ S<br>65° 01.6′ W | **Q.Y.** | 44<br>**13** | 2 | Black Tower; 16. | |
| 19712<br>*G 1070.4* | -West dolphin. | 42° 44.2′ S<br>65° 01.0′ W | **V.Q.W.** | 33<br>**10** | 1 | Yellow post, white band, yellow base; 7. | |
| 19720<br>*G 1062* | -Cerro Gorro Frigio. | 42° 34.7′ S<br>64° 18.1′ W | **Fl.W.**<br>period 4.5s<br>fl. 0.5s, ec. 4s | 328<br>**100** | 6 | Black tower, white bands, white dwelling; 16. | Obscured 334°-000°. |
| 19724<br>*G 1060* | -Puerto Piramides. | 42° 34.1′ S<br>64° 16.5′ W | **Fl.W.**<br>period 3s<br>fl. 0.5s, ec. 2.5s | 285<br>**87** | 5 | White tower, red bands, red dwelling; 20. | Visible 328°-056°. |
| 19728<br>*G 1076* | Rio Chubut, Punta del Faro. | 43° 22.3′ S<br>65° 02.8′ W | **Fl.W.**<br>period 9s<br>fl. 0.7s, ec. 8.3s | 121<br>**37** | 6 | Black tower, white bands; 36. | |
| 19736<br>*G 1078* | -Escollera Norte. | 43° 20.4′ S<br>65° 02.9′ W | **Iso.R.**<br>period 2s | 26<br>**8** | 5 | Red round tower, white bands. | |
| 19737<br>*G 1078.5* | -Escollera Sur. | 43° 20.6′ S<br>65° 02.8′ W | **Fl.G.**<br>period 5s<br>fl. 0.5s, ec. 4.5s | 26<br>**8** | 5 | White, red and green round tower; 20. | |
| 19740<br>*G 1080* | **Punta Lobos.** | 43° 47.6′ S<br>65° 19.9′ W | **Fl.(2)W.**<br>period 15s<br>fl. 0.5s, ec. 4.5s<br>fl. 0.5s, ec. 9.5s | 476<br>**145** | 14 | White round concrete tower, red bands; 36. | |

| (1) No. | (2) Name and Location | (3) Position | (4) Characteristic | (5) Height | (6) Range | (7) Structure | (8) Remarks |
|---|---|---|---|---|---|---|---|
| | | | **ARGENTINA** | | | | |
| 19744 *G 1084* | Cape Raso. | 44° 20.7´ S 65° 14.0´ W | **Fl.(3)W.R.** period 40s fl. 0.5s, ec. 7s fl. 0.5s, ec. 7s fl. 0.5s, ec. 24.5s | 177 **54** | W. 11 R. 7 | Two pyramidal towers, white base; 75. | W. 140°-290°, R.-310°, W.-020°. |
| 19748 *G 1086* | San Jose, on San Jose Hill. | 44° 30.8´ S 65° 16.9´ W | **Fl.W.R.** period 5s fl. 0.5s, ec. 4.5s | 276 **84** | W. 13 R. 10 | Black pyramidal tower, yellow band; 52. | R. 216°-241°, W. 216°. |
| 19752 *G 1087* | Santa Elena Beacon. | 44° 30.9´ S 65° 21.2´ W | **Fl.W.R.** period 9s fl. 1s, ec. 8s | 69 **21** | W. 5 R. 3 | Black pyramidal tower, white bands; 23. | R. 297°-322°, W.-297°. |
| 19760 *G 1089* | Camarones, close W. of Punta Albatross. | 44° 47.8´ S 65° 42.6´ W | **Fl.W.R.** period 5s fl. 1s, ec. 4s | 72 **22** | W. 9 R. 8 | Red fiberglass tower, yellow base; 13. | R. 297°30′-314°30′, W. 297°30′. |
| 19764 *G 1089.4* | Bahia San Gregorio. | 45° 01.5´ S 65° 37.7´ W | **Fl.W.** period 5.2s fl. 0.2s, ec. 5s | 564 **172** | 13 | Yellow square concrete tower, black diagonal stripes; 30. | |
| 19768 *G 1092* | Isla Rasa Summit. | 45° 06.3´ S 65° 24.1´ W | **Fl.W.** period 8s fl. 1s, ec. 7s | 75 **23** | 9 | Black column; 20. | |
| 19776 *G 1096* | Bahia Bustamante. | 45° 07.9´ S 66° 32.2´ W | **Fl.W.** period 10s fl. 1s, ec. 9s | 335 **102** | 5 | White tower, two red stripes point down, hut at base; 20. | |
| 19784 *G 1095* | Punta Ulloa. | 45° 09.0´ S 66° 28.6´ W | **Fl.(2)W.** period 15s fl. 1s, ec. 4s fl. 1s, ec. 9s | 115 **35** | 6 | Black tower; 23. | |
| 19788 *G 1097* | Cabo Aristazabal. | 45° 13.0´ S 66° 31.6´ W | **Fl.W.** period 5s fl. 1s, ec. 4s | 151 **46** | 11 | Black tower; 52. | |
| 19792 *G 1104* | Cabo San Jorge. | 45° 46.7´ S 67° 22.7´ W | **Fl.(4)W.** period 32s fl. 1s, ec. 5s fl. 1s, ec. 5s fl. 1s, ec. 5s fl. 1s, ec. 13s | 256 **78** | 14 | Masonry tower, black hut; 89. | |
| | CALETA CORDOVA: | | | | | | |
| 19796 *G 1100* | -First Range, Astra, front. | 45° 44.8´ S 67° 22.5´ W | **Q.R.** | 131 **40** | 4 | Black tower, yellow band; 36. | Visible 255°30′-280°30′. |
| 19800 *G 1100.1* | --Rear, Loma Blanca, about 700 meters 268° from front. | 45° 44.8´ S 67° 23.0´ W | **Fl.W.** period 3s fl. 1s, ec. 2s | 180 **55** | 5 | Red truncated pyramidal tower; 36. | Visible 255°30′-280°30′. |
| 19804 *G 1102* | -Second Range, Caleta Cordova, front. | 45° 43.4´ S 67° 21.3´ W | **Q.W.** | 174 **53** | 5 | White truncated pyramidal structure; 36. | |
| 19808 *G 1102.1* | --Rear, Novales, about 260 meters 353°30′ from front. | 45° 43.3´ S 67° 21.3´ W | **Fl.W.** period 3s fl. 1s, ec. 2s | 259 **79** | 3 | Black truncated pyramidal structure, red triangular daymark point up, white bands; 36. | |
| 19810 *G 1103* | -Pilar YPF. | 45° 44.8´ S 67° 21.5´ W | **Q.W.** | | 6 | Concrete column; 33. | |
| 19912 *G 1134* | Cabo Blanco. | 47° 12.1´ S 65° 44.3´ W | **Fl.(5)W.** period 40s fl. 1.5s, ec. 5.5s fl. 1.5s, ec. 5.5s fl. 1.5s, ec. 5.5s fl. 1.5s, ec. 5.5s fl. 1.5s, ec. 10.5s | 220 **67** | 14 | Round brickwork tower, white dwelling; 89. | Reserve light Fl.(3)W. 30s. **Radiobeacon.** |
| 19916 *G 1136* | Punta Guzman. | 47° 20.9´ S 65° 43.2´ W | **Fl.(2)W.** period 15s fl. 1s, ec. 2s fl. 1s, ec. 11s | 85 **26** | 10 | Metal framework tower, black rectangular daymark; 56. | |

| (1) No. | (2) Name and Location | (3) Position | (4) Characteristic | (5) Height | (6) Range | (7) Structure | (8) Remarks |
|---|---|---|---|---|---|---|---|

**ARGENTINA**

| | | | | | | | |
|---|---|---|---|---|---|---|---|
| | PUERTO DESEADO: | | | | | | |
| 19920 *G 1139* | **-Beauvoir.** | 47° 45.2′ S 65° 53.6′ W | **Fl.W.** period 4s fl. 0.5s, ec. 3.5s | 157 **48** | **19** | On top of church; 89. | |
| 19924 *G 1140* | -Estacion, outer Range, front. | 47° 45.4′ S 65° 53.7′ W | **Q.W.** | 89 **27** | 11 | White tower, orange rectangular daymark, black stripes; 59. | Visible 254°-074°. |
| 19928 *G 1140.1* | --Alonso, rear, 852 meters 283°51′ from front. | 47° 45.3′ S 65° 54.4′ W | **Iso.R.** period 2s | 138 **42** | 11 | Black column; 75. | Visible 222°-042°. Intensified 254°-344°. |
| 19932 *G 1146* | -Inner Range, Roca Magallanes, front. | 47° 45.5′ S 65° 55.5′ W | **Fl.R.** period 2s fl. 0.5s, ec. 1.5s | 36 **11** | 6 | Orange truncated tower; 39. | Visible 184°15′-004°15′. |
| 19936 *G 1146.1* | --Rear, De las Barrancas, 1230 meters 274°15′ from front. | 47° 45.5′ S 65° 56.4′ W | **Fl.W.** period 3s fl. 0.9s, ec. 2.1s | 52 **16** | 8 | White pyramidal tower, red stripes; 30. | |
| 19940 *G 1152* | Isla Pinguino, SE. extremity. | 47° 54.8′ S 65° 43.1′ W | **Fl.(2)W.** period 16s fl. 0.5s, ec. 5s fl. 0.5s, ec. 10s | 197 **60** | 12 | White tower, dwelling, red bands near top; 72. | |
| 19944 *G 1153* | Punta Azopardo. | 47° 55.7′ S 65° 47.7′ W | **Fl.W.** period 7s fl. 0.5s, ec. 6.5s | | 5 | Black framework tower, yellow bands; 16. | |
| 19948 *G 1154* | Punta Medanosa. | 48° 06.2′ S 65° 55.8′ W | **Fl.(2)W.** period 11s fl. 1s, ec. 3s fl. 1s, ec. 6s | 95 **29** | 10 | White framework tower, black bands; 39. | |
| 19952 *G 1156* | Cabo Guardian. | 48° 21.4′ S 66° 21.3′ W | **Fl.W.R.** period 7.5s fl. 0.5s, ec. 7s | 157 **48** | W. 14 R. 12 | Black framework tower; 118. | R. 320°-324°, W.320°. |
| 19956 *G 1158* | Campana. | 48° 24.0′ S 66° 28.2′ W | **Fl.(2)W.R.** period 16s fl. 0.5s, ec. 3.5s fl. 0.5s, ec. 11.5s | 164 **50** | W. 11 R. 9 | Black tower, white top; 85. | R. 291°30′-300°30′, W.291°30′. |
| 19960 *G 1160* | Cabo Danoso. | 48° 48.7′ S 67° 12.3′ W | **Fl.(4)W.** period 45s fl. 1s, ec. 5s fl. 1s, ec. 5s fl. 1s, ec. 5s fl. 1s, ec. 26s | 144 **44** | 10 | Red round tower, white bands; 36. | |
| | BAHIA SAN JULIAN: | | | | | | |
| 19964 *G 1162* | -Cabo Curioso. | 49° 11.0′ S 67° 37.1′ W | **Fl.(3)W.** period 45s fl. 1.5s, ec. 9s fl. 1.5s, ec. 9s fl. 1.5s, ec. 22.5s | 302 **92** | 14 | White square tower, black band; 75. | |
| 19984 *G 1174* | -Third Range, Norte, front. | 49° 15.5′ S 67° 41.2′ W | **Q.W.** | 102 **31** | 7 | White column, red bands, red triangular daymark point up; 26. | Visible 227°30′-237°30′. |
| 19988 *G 1174.1* | --Rear, auxiliary, 340 meters 232° from front. | 49° 15.6′ S 67° 41.4′ W | **Fl.R.** period 3s fl. 0.9s, ec. 2.1s | 157 **48** | 6 | White column, red bands, red triangular daymark point down; 43. | Visible 227°30′-237°30′. |
| 19992 *G 1178* | -Fourth Range, Justicia, front. | 49° 17.5′ S 67° 41.5′ W | **Fl.W.** period 2s fl. 0.4s, ec. 1.6s | 49 **15** | 6 | Tower, white bands, red rectangular daymark; 52. | Visible 196°30′-206°30′. |
| 19996 *G 1178.1* | --Rear, Pueblo, 3120 meters 202° from front. | 49° 19.1′ S 67° 42.5′ W | **Iso.W.R.** period 5s | 108 **33** | W. 9 R. 6 | Black tower, black triangular daymark point down in yellow rectangular daymark; 69. | W. 196°30′-020°30′, R.-165°30′-175°30′. |
| 20000 *G 1184* | -Fifth Range, Caldera Baja, front. | 49° 16.5′ S 67° 39.9′ W | **Q.W.** | 52 **16** | 6 | Black triangular daymark point up in yellow rectangular daymark. | Visible 040°-150°. |

| (1) No. | (2) Name and Location | (3) Position | (4) Characteristic | (5) Height | (6) Range | (7) Structure | (8) Remarks |
|---|---|---|---|---|---|---|---|

## ARGENTINA

| (1) No. | (2) Name and Location | (3) Position | (4) Characteristic | (5) Height | (6) Range | (7) Structure | (8) Remarks |
|---|---|---|---|---|---|---|---|
| 20004 *G 1184.1* | --Rear, Caldera Alta, 1333 meters 055° from front. | 49° 16.1′ S 67° 39.0′ W | **Fl.R.** period 3s fl. 0.9s, ec. 2.1s | 108 **33** | 3 | Black triangular daymark point down in yellow rectangular daymark. | Visible 034°-118°. |
| 20008 *G 1190* | -Sixth Range, Canalizo, front. | 49° 16.2′ S 67° 43.4′ W | **Q.R.** | 69 **21** | 6 | White base, red triangular daymark point up; 20. | Visible 331°30′-351°30′. Occasional. |
| 20012 *G 1190.1* | --Rear, Wood, 1292 meters 341°30′ from front. | 49° 15.5′ S 67° 43.7′ W | **Fl.W.** period 3s fl. 0.9s, ec. 2.1s | 121 **37** | 7 | White base, red triangular daymark point down; 20. | Visible 331°30′-351°06′. Occasional. |
| 20016 *G 1196* | **Cape San Francisco de Paula.** | 49° 44.3′ S 67° 43.4′ W | **Fl.(2)W.** period 15s fl. 0.5s, ec. 5.5s fl. 0.5s, ec. 8.5s | 282 **86** | 14 | Black tower; 26. | |
| | PUERTO SANTA CRUZ: | | | | | | |
| 20020 *G 1210.1* | -Santa Cruz, S. side of entrance, 2.2 km. S. of Entrada Point, rear. | 50° 09.2′ S 68° 21.7′ W | **Fl.(4)W.** period 60s fl. 1.5s, ec. 5s fl. 1.5s, ec. 5s fl. 1.5s, ec. 5s fl. 1.5s, ec. 39s | 515 **157** | 13 | Black round metal tower, white bands, white round base; 39. | Visible 062°-018°. |
| 20024 *G 1210* | -Entrada, common front. | 50° 08.2′ S 68° 22.4′ W | **Q.W.** | 112 **34** | 6 | White metal framework tower, red bands; 85. | Visible 151°-161°, 277°-287°. |
| 20028 *G 1209.9* | --Rear, Quilla, 1830 meters 282° from front. | 50° 07.9′ S 68° 23.8′ W | **Fl.W.** period 3s fl. 0.9s, ec. 2.1s | 418 **127** | 6 | Black tower; 39. | Visible 277°-287°. Occasional. |
| 20032 *G 1208* | -Baja, Range, front. | 50° 07.0′ S 68° 18.6′ W | **Q.W.** | 56 **17** | 6 | Black tower, white bands, white triangular daymark point down; 30. | Visible 357.30°-017.30°. **Radar reflector.** |
| 20036 *G 1208.1* | --Rear, Alta, 2116 meters 003° from front. | 50° 05.9′ S 68° 18.5′ W | **Fl.W.** period 3s fl. 0.9s, ec. 2.1s | 115 **35** | 7 | Metal framework tower; 98. | Visible 318.30°-088.30°. |
| 20040 *G 1211* | -Punta Quilla, mole SE. end. | 50° 07.0′ S 68° 24.2′ W | **Fl.R.** period 5s fl. 0.3s, ec. 4.7s | 56 **17** | 3 | Red metal beacon. | |
| 20044 *G 1211.2* | ---Elbow. | 50° 06.9′ S 68° 24.4′ W | **Fl.R.** period 5s fl. 0.3s, ec. 4.7s | 56 **17** | 3 | Red metal beacon. | Fl.G. mark 2 beacons 80 meters WSW. |
| 20048 *G 1212* | -Iribas Range, front. | 50° 03.9′ S 68° 30.2′ W | **Fl.W.** period 2s fl. 0.6s, ec. 1.4s | 46 **14** | 6 | Orange triangular daymark point up in white rectangular daymark; 20. | Visible 298°30′-308°30′. |
| 20052 *G 1212.1* | --Rear, Canadon, 1930 meters 302°45′ from front. | 50° 03.0′ S 68° 31.5′ W | **Fl.W.** period 6s fl. 1.8s, ec. 4.2s | 374 **114** | 6 | Orange triangular daymark point down in white rectangular daymark; 20. | Visible 180°-270°, 298°30′-308°30′. |
| 20068 *G 1222* | Ria Coig. | 50° 53.5′ S 69° 07.9′ W | **Fl.(2)W.** period 25s fl. 1.1s, ec. 3.3s fl. 1.1s, ec. 19.5s | 256 **78** | 13 | Red round tower, white bands; 36. | |
| 20072 *G 1226* | Cabo Buen Tiempo. | 51° 32.7′ S 68° 57.0′ W | **Fl.(3)W.** period 45s fl. 1s, ec. 7s fl. 1s, ec. 7s fl. 1s, ec. 28s | 371 **113** | 14 | Black tower with hut; 30. | Visible 165°-051°. |
| 20152 *G 1260* | **Cabo Virgenes.** | 52° 20.0′ S 68° 21.4′ W | **Fl.W.** period 5s fl. 0.8s, ec. 4.2s | 226 **69** | **24** | White truncated pyramidal tower, black bands; 85. | **Radiobeacon.** |
| | | | **Fl.R.** period 5s fl. 1s, ec. 4s | | 5 | | Visible 296°-316°. |

| (1) No. | (2) Name and Location | (3) Position | (4) Characteristic | (5) Height | (6) Range | (7) Structure | (8) Remarks |
|---|---|---|---|---|---|---|---|
| | | | **ARGENTINA** | | | | |
| 20156<br>*G 1260.5* | Magallanes. | 52° 39.9´ S<br>68° 36.1´ W | **Fl.(3)W.**<br>period 50s<br>fl. 1s, ec. 10s<br>fl. 1s, ec. 10s<br>fl. 1s, ec. 27s | 174<br>**53** | 12 | Yellow metal tower, black bands; 43. | **Radar reflector.** |
| 20157<br>*G 1260.6* | Aries Platform. | 52° 40.9´ S<br>68° 02.4´ W | **Mo.(U)W.**<br>period 15s<br>fl. 0.7s, ec. 0.4s<br>fl. 0.7s, ec. 0.4s<br>fl. 1.8s, ec. 11s | 49<br>**15** | 10 | | **AIS** (MMSI No 701000891).<br>**Horn:** Mo.(U) ev. 30s. (bl. 0.75s, si. 1s, bl. 0.75s, si. 1s, bl. 2.5s, si. 24s). |
| | | | **F.R.** | | 2 | | |
| | RACON | | **D(– • •)** | | | | (3 & 10cm). |
| 20158<br>*G 1260.65* | Carina Platform. | 52° 45.4´ S<br>68° 13.2´ W | **Mo.(U)W.**<br>period 15s<br>fl. 0.7s, ec. 0.4s<br>fl. 0.7s, ec. 0.4s<br>fl. 1.8s, ec. 11s | 49<br>**15** | 10 | | **AIS** (MMSI No 701000890).<br>**Horn:** Mo.(U) ev. 30s. (bl. 0.75s, si. 1s, bl. 0.75s, si. 1s, bl. 2.5s, si. 24s). |
| | | | **F.R.** | | 2 | | |
| | RACON | | **M(– –)** | | | | (3 & 10cm). |
| 20160<br>*G 1261* | Punta de Arenas, Paramo Chico. | 53° 08.5´ S<br>68° 12.4´ W | **Fl.W.**<br>period 7.5s<br>fl. 0.5s, ec. 7s | 75<br>**23** | 10 | Metal truncated pyramidal tower; 56. | |
| 20192<br>*G 1262* | San Sebastian. | 53° 19.5´ S<br>68° 09.5´ W | **Fl.(3)W.**<br>period 40s<br>fl. 1s, ec. 5s<br>fl. 1s, ec. 5s<br>fl. 1s, ec. 27s | 197<br>**60** | 14 | Round concrete tower, blue and yellow diagonal stripes; 36. | |
| 20196<br>*G 1266* | Cabo Domingo. | 53° 40.7´ S<br>67° 51.4´ W | **L.Fl.W.**<br>period 8s<br>fl. 2s, ec. 6s | 295<br>**90** | 7 | White metal framework tower, black bands, hut at base; 20. | |
| | RIO GRANDE: | | | | | | |
| 20216<br>*G 1269* | -Second Range, front. | 53° 45.4´ S<br>67° 44.0´ W | **Fl.G.**<br>period 2s<br>fl. 0.7s, ec. 1.3s | 85<br>**26** | 10 | Black metal framework tower, red diamond daymark, white bands; 52. | |
| 20220<br>*G 1269.1* | --Rear, 400 meters 245° from front. | 53° 47.1´ S<br>67° 42.1´ W | **Iso.W.**<br>period 2s | 121<br>**37** | 11 | Black tower, yellow band, on water tower on building; 75. | |
| 20224<br>*G 1270* | -Third Range, front. | 53° 47.3´ S<br>67° 42.2´ W | **Q.W.** | 23<br>**7** | 11 | Black metal framework tower, red and white bands; 23. | |
| 20228<br>*G 1270.1* | --Rear, 167 meters 212° from front. | 53° 47.5´ S<br>67° 41.6´ W | **Iso.W.**<br>period 3s | 72<br>**22** | 11 | Black metal framework tower, yellow bands; 59. | |
| 20232<br>*G 1271* | -Fourth Range, front. | 53° 47.7´ S<br>67° 41.1´ W | **Q.R.** | 32<br>**10** | 10 | White metal column, black top; 20. | |
| 20236<br>*G 1271.1* | --Rear, 120 meters 163°26′ from front. | 53° 47.7´ S<br>67° 41.1´ W | **Iso.G.**<br>period 5s | 36<br>**11** | 10 | White metal framework tower, orange and black bands; 30. | |
| 20256<br>*G 1274* | Cabo Penas. | 53° 50.8´ S<br>67° 33.5´ W | **Fl.(2)W.**<br>period 20s<br>fl. 0.5s, ec. 4.5s<br>fl. 0.5s, ec. 14.5s | 149<br>**46** | 10 | Black metal framework tower and hut; 43. | |
| 20260<br>*G 1275* | Cabo San Pablo. | 54° 17.1´ S<br>66° 41.8´ W | **Fl.(2)W.**<br>period 20s<br>fl. 0.8s, ec. 6.5s<br>fl. 0.8s, ec. 12s | 449<br>**137** | 11 | Yellow truncated pyramidal tower, black triangular daymark point down; 20. | |
| 20264<br>*G 1276* | Cabo San Diego. | 54° 39.5´ S<br>65° 07.9´ W | **Fl.(3)W.**<br>period 28s | 131<br>**40** | 13 | White square concrete framework tower, black cupola; 43. | Visible 143°-055°. |

| (1) No. | (2) Name and Location | (3) Position | (4) Characteristic | (5) Height | (6) Range | (7) Structure | (8) Remarks |
|---|---|---|---|---|---|---|---|

## ARGENTINA

| (1) No. | (2) Name and Location | (3) Position | (4) Characteristic | (5) Height | (6) Range | (7) Structure | (8) Remarks |
|---|---|---|---|---|---|---|---|
| 20268 *G 1279* | Isla Observatorio (Ano Nuevo). | 54° 39.5´ S 64° 08.8´ W | **Fl.(3)W.** period 32s fl. 1s, ec. 8s fl. 1s, ec. 8s fl. 1s, ec. 13s | 213 **65** | 13 | White round metal tower, black bands; 75. | |
| 20269 *G 1283* | San Juan del Salvamento. | 54° 44.0´ S 63° 52.5´ W | **Fl.(2)W.** period 15s fl. 1s, ec. 3s fl. 1s, ec. 10s | 236 **72** | 10 | Octagonal wooden struture, gray top; 21. | |
| 20272 *G 1280* | Estrecho de Le Maire. | 54° 48.0´ S 64° 42.0´ W | **Fl.(3)W.** period 32s fl. 1s, ec. 5s fl. 1s, ec. 5s fl. 1s, ec. 19s | 154 **47** | 8 | Yellow trapezoidal daymark over black trapezoidal daymark; 13. | Visible 064°-211°. |
| 20276 *G 1281* | -Capitan Zaratiegui. | 54° 48.2´ S 64° 41.8´ W | **Fl.W.** period 3s fl. 0.3s, ec. 2.7s | | 6 | Black tower, five red circles on upper part; 13. | |
| 20280 *G 1282* | -Teniente Palet. | 54° 47.7´ S 64° 40.5´ W | **Fl.W.** period 3s fl. 0.6s, ec. 2.4s | | | Yellow metal tripod, black bands; 20. | |
| 20284 *G 1277* | Buen Suceso. | 54° 49.0´ S 65° 14.1´ W | **Fl.(2)W.** period 16s fl. 0.5s, ec. 2.5s fl. 0.5s, ec. 12.5s | 187 **57** | 9 | White metal framework tower, red bands; 16. | |
| 20288 *G 1278* | -Martins Lopez. | 54° 47.5´ S 65° 16.0´ W | **Fl.W.** period 5s fl. 0.5s, ec. 4.5s | 33 **10** | 8 | Red metal pyramidal tower, white bands; 23. | |
| 20292 *G 1289* | Islote Elizalde. | 54° 54.7´ S 65° 54.7´ W | **Fl.W.** period 3s fl. 0.5s, ec. 2.5s | 249 **76** | 7 | White round tower, red band; 13. | |
| 20296 *G 1290* | Punta Pique. | 54° 54.5´ S 65° 57.1´ W | **Fl.W.** period 6s fl. 1s, ec. 5s | 26 **8** | 7 | White metal framework tower; 10. | |
| 20300 *G 1288* | San Gonzalo. | 54° 57.4´ S 65° 58.4´ W | **Fl.W.** period 10s fl. 0.5s, ec. 9.5s | 125 **38** | 7 | White round tower, green bands; 13. | |
| | BEAGLE CHANNEL: | | | | | | |
| 20304 *G 1292* | -Cabo San Pio. | 55° 03.4´ S 66° 31.4´ W | **Fl.(2)W.** period 16s fl. 0.5s, ec. 4.5s fl. 0.5s, ec. 10.5s | 177 **54** | 9 | White conical stone tower, red bands; 26. | Visible 265°-109°. |

## FALKLAND ISLANDS (ISLAS MALVINAS)

| (1) No. | (2) Name and Location | (3) Position | (4) Characteristic | (5) Height | (6) Range | (7) Structure | (8) Remarks |
|---|---|---|---|---|---|---|---|
| 20335 *G 1341* | Volunteer Point. | 51° 30.8´ S 57° 44.4´ W | **Fl.(4)W.** period 20s | | 10 | | |
| 20335.2 *G 1341.4* | Strike off Point. | 51° 35.2´ S 57° 58.6´ W | **Fl.R.** period 6s | | 2 | | |
| 20335.4 *G 1341.5* | Long Island. | 51° 33.7´ S 58° 02.4´ W | **Fl.W.** period 5s | | 10 | | |
| 20336 *G 1352* | Cape Pembroke. | 51° 40.9´ S 57° 43.2´ W | **Fl.(3)W.** period 20s | 99 **30** | 10 | White fiberglass tower, black bands; 69. | Visible inshore in Berkley Sound, Port William and Harriet as far as the land permits. |
| 20340 *G 1342* | Mengeary (William) Point, N. side of entrance to Port William. | 51° 38.8´ S 57° 43.8´ W | **Fl.(2)W.** period 7s fl. 0.5s, ec. 1s fl. 0.5s, ec. 5s | | 10 | White fiberglass lantern box; 7. | |

| (1) No. | (2) Name and Location | (3) Position | (4) Characteristic | (5) Height | (6) Range | (7) Structure | (8) Remarks |
|---|---|---|---|---|---|---|---|
| | | | **FALKLAND ISLANDS (ISLAS MALVINAS)** | | | | |
| 20344 *G 1344* | Blanco Bay, W. side of bay. | 51° 40.1′ S 57° 50.9′ W | **Fl.W.R.G.** period 2s fl. 0.5s, ec. 1.5s | 30 **9** | W. 7 R. 5 G. 5 | White metal column; 10. | R. 090°-263°, W.-268°, G.-090°. |
| 20345 *G 1345* | Stanley Harbor Range, front. | 51° 41.8′ S 57° 49.9′ W | **F.R.** | 118 **36** | 7 | Pole, red diamond daymark; 20. | Visible 173°44′-197°44′. |
| | | | **F.R.** | 121 **37** | | | Visible 090°-270°. |
| 20346 *G 1345.1* | -Rear, 130 meters 185°44′ from front. | 51° 41.9′ S 57° 49.9′ W | **F.R.** | 138 **42** | 7 | Pole, red diamond daymark; 26. | Visible 176°44′-194°44′. |
| | | | **F.R.** | 138 **42** | | | Visible 090°-270°. |
| 20348 *G 1346* | Navy Point, W. entrance to Port Stanley. | 51° 40.9′ S 57° 49.9′ W | **Fl.R.** period 6s | 16 **5** | 2 | White concrete column, red lantern; 6. | Visible 197°-076°. |
| 20352 *G 1348* | Engineer Point, E. entrance to Port Stanley. | 51° 40.9′ S 57° 49.6′ W | **Fl.G.** period 6s | 20 **6** | 2 | White concrete column, red lantern; 10. | Visible 042°-210°. |
| 20353 *G 1353* | -Fox Point. | 51° 55.3′ S 58° 24.1′ W | **Fl.(2)W.** period 10s | 45 **14** | 10 | White hut. | |
| 20357 *G 1354* | Mare Harbor, beacon J. | 51° 54.0′ S 58° 28.2′ W | **Oc.W.R.G.** period 5s lt. 3s, ec. 2s | 66 **20** | W. 9 R. 6 G. 7 | White and orange triangular daymark point up; 10. | R. 358°-011°, W.-017°, G.-090°, obsc.-358°. |
| 20358 *G 1354.3* | -Beacon I. | 51° 53.5′ S 58° 29.6′ W | **Fl.W.** period 3s fl. 0.4s, ec. 2.6s | 13 **4** | 6 | White and orange triangular daymark point up; 10. | |
| 20358.1 *G 1354.69* | -East Cove, main jetty. | 51° 54.1′ S 58° 26.0′ W | **2 F.G.** | | | Dolphin. | F.G. and F.R. lights on dolphins mark E. and W. end of jetty. |
| 20358.2 *G 1354.7* | --W. jetty. | 51° 54.0′ S 58° 26.7′ W | **2 F.R.** | | | Jetty. | F.G. and F.R. lights mark E. and W. end of jetty. |
| 20359 *G 1355* | -Providence Head, beacon L. | 51° 54.6′ S 58° 26.4′ W | **Fl.W.R.** period 2s fl. 0.4s, ec. 1.6s | 26 **8** | 6 | White and orange triangular daymark point down; 10. | R. shore-105°, W.-109°, R.-shore. |
| 20359.1 *G 1356* | -Kukri Point, beacon K. | 51° 54.3′ S 58° 25.7′ W | **Oc.W.** period 6s lt. 4s, ec. 2s | 26 **8** | 7 | White and orange triangular daymark point up; 10. | |
| | CUMBERLAND BAY: | | | | | | |
| 20361 *G 1359* | -Porpoise Point. | 52° 20.2′ S 59° 18.5′ W | **Fl.W.** period 10s | | 10 | | |
| | SOUTH ORKNEY ISLANDS: | | | | | | |
| 20362 *G 1375* | -Signy Island. | 60° 42.4′ S 45° 35.5′ W | **F.W.** | 80 **24** | | Framework tower; 39. | Occasional. |
| 20363 *G 1378* | -Scotia Bay, Navidad. | 60° 45.4′ S 44° 44.2′ W | **Iso.W.** period 2s | | | White round fiberglass tower, red top; 10. | |
| 20363.1 *G 1379* | --Bordenave, Davis Point. | 60° 45.1′ S 44° 41.2′ W | **Fl.W.** period 5s fl. 1s, ec. 3s | 13 **4** | | Red round fiberglass tower, white band; 13. | |
| 20363.2 *G 1378.5* | -Destacamento. | 60° 44.2′ S 44° 44.3′ W | **Fl.W.** period 3s | | | Lantern on radio mast. | |

| (1) No. | (2) Name and Location | (3) Position | (4) Characteristic | (5) Height | (6) Range | (7) Structure | (8) Remarks |
|---|---|---|---|---|---|---|---|

## CHILE

ESTRECHO DE MAGELLANES (STRAIT OF MAGELLAN):

| | | | | | | | |
|---|---|---|---|---|---|---|---|
| 20364 *G 1402* | **-Punta Dungeness.** | 52° 23.8´ S 68° 25.9´ W | **Fl.W.** period 10s fl. 0.2s, ec. 9.8s | 105 **32** | **22** | White cylindrical iron tower, red band, adjoining white house with red roof; 82. | Visible 223°-144°. |
| | -RACON | | **N(– •)** period 48s fl. 3s, ec. 45s | 105 **32** | **17** | | (10cm). |
| 20368 *G 1404* | **-Cabo Espiritu Santo.** | 52° 39.6´ S 68° 36.4´ W | **Fl.W.** period 15s fl. 0.3s, ec. 14.7s | 230 **70** | **23** | White cylindrical iron tower, red band, concrete base; 30. | Visible 154°-303°. |
| | -RACON | | **T(–)** period 50s fl. 4s, ec. 46s | 220 **67** | **18** | | (10cm). |

# Section 15

## Radiobeacons

| (1) No. | (2) Name | (3) Position | (4) Characteristic | (5) Range | (6) Sequence | (7) Frequency | (8) Remarks |
|---|---|---|---|---|---|---|---|
| | | | **GREENLAND** | | | | |
| 10 | Ittoqqortoormit, Scoresbysund | 70° 29.2′ N<br>21° 58.3′ W | **SC**<br>(• • •  – • – •). | 200 | | 343<br>NON, A2A. | Aeromarine. |
| 20 | Kulusuk | 65° 32.0′ N<br>37° 10.0′ W | **KK**<br>(– • –  – • –). | 50 | | 283<br>NON, A2A. | Aeromarine. |
| 30 | Ikerasassuaq, Prins Christian Sund | 60° 03.5′ N<br>43° 09.9′ W | **OZN**<br>(– – –  – – • •  – •). | 200 | | 372<br>A1A. | Aeromarine. |
| 35 | Nanortalik | 60° 08.7′ N<br>45° 15.3′ W | **NN**<br>(– •  – •). | 20 | | 270<br>NON, A2A. | Aeromarine. |
| 40 | Oaqortoq, Julianehab | 60° 43.4′ N<br>46° 01.5′ W | **JH**<br>(• – – –  • • • •). | 20 | | 265<br>NON, A2A. | Aeromarine. |
| 45 | Narssaq | 60° 54.0′ N<br>46° 01.2′ W | **NS**<br>(– •  • • •). | 20 | | 404<br>NON, A2A. | Aeromarine. |
| 50 | Simiutaq | 60° 41.4′ N<br>46° 35.5′ W | **SI**<br>(• • •  • •). | 100 | | 279<br>NON, A2A. | Aeromarine. |
| 60 | Paamiut, Frederikshaab | 61° 59.8′ N<br>49° 39.1′ W | **FH**<br>(• • – •  • • • •). | 100 | | 331<br>NON, A1A. | Aeromarine. |
| 70 | Kokoerne | 64° 04.2′ N<br>52° 00.7′ W | **KU**<br>(– • –  • • –). | 150 | | 298<br>NON, A2A. | Aeromarine. |
| 72 | Nuuk, Godthab | 64° 10.8′ N<br>51° 44.9′ W | **GH**<br>(– – •  • • • •). | 20 | | 314<br>NON, A2A. | Aeromarine. |
| 75 | Maniitsoq, Sukkertoppen | 65° 25.0′ N<br>52° 54.0′ W | **ST**<br>(• • •  –). | 20 | | 310<br>NON, A2A. | Aeromarine. |
| 80 | Sisimiut, Holsteinsborg | 66° 56.0′ N<br>53° 42.0′ W | **HB**<br>(• • • •  – • • •). | 200 | | 328<br>NON, A2A. | Aeromarine. |
| 90 | Aasiaat, Egedesminde | 68° 42.0′ N<br>52° 50.0′ W | **EM**<br>(•  – –). | 50 | | 215<br>NON, A2A. | Aeromarine. |
| 95 | Oasigiannguit, Christianhab | 68° 50.0′ N<br>51° 13.0′ W | **CH**<br>(– • – •  • • • •). | 20 | | 265<br>NON, A2A. | Aeromarine. |
| 97 | Ilulissat, Jakobshavn | 69° 14.6′ N<br>51° 04.7′ W | **JV**<br>(• – – –  • • • –). | 50 | | 367<br>NON, A2A. | Aeromarine. |
| 100 | Qeqertarsuaq, Godhavn | 69° 15.0′ N<br>53° 32.0′ W | **GN**<br>(– – •  – •). | 150 | | 306<br>A1A. | Aeromarine. |
| 110 | Upernavik | 72° 48.0′ N<br>56° 09.0′ W | **UP**<br>(• • –  • – – •). | 200 | | 399<br>NON, A2A. | Aeromarine. |
| | | | **CANADA - ATLANTIC COAST** | | | | |
| 115 | Clyde, Baffin Island | 70° 20.0′ N<br>68° 35.4′ W | **YCY**<br>(– • – –  – • – •  – • – –<br>). | 80 | | 256 | AERO. |
| 120 | Cape Hooper, Baffin Island | 68° 26.2′ N<br>66° 44.0′ W | **UZ**<br>(• • –  – – • •). | 50 | | 287<br>NON, A2A. | AERO. |
| 130 | Broughton Island, Baffin Island | 67° 33.7′ N<br>64° 01.0′ W | **YJI**<br>(– • – –  • – – –  • •). | 50 | | 237<br>NON, A2A. | AERO. |
| 140 | Cape Dyer, Baffin Island | 66° 39.9′ N<br>61° 21.7′ W | **VN**<br>(• • • –  – •). | 50 | | 248<br>NON, A2A. | AERO. |
| 150 | Koartac, P.Q. (Cape Hope Advance) | 61° 02.7′ N<br>69° 37.9′ W | **UHA**<br>(• • –  • • • •  • –). | 100 | | 285<br>NON, A2A. | AERO. Carrier signal. |

| (1) No. | (2) Name | (3) Position | (4) Characteristic | (5) Range | (6) Sequence | (7) Frequency | (8) Remarks |
|---|---|---|---|---|---|---|---|
| | | | **CANADA - ATLANTIC COAST** | | | | |
| 160 | Coral Harbor, N.W.T. | 64° 09.0′ N<br>83° 22.4′ W | **ZS**<br>(– – • •   • • •). | 300 | | 362<br>A2A. | AERO. Carrier signal. |
| 170 | Chesterfield Inlet Light Station, N.W.T. | 63° 20.5′ N<br>90° 42.5′ W | **YCS**<br>(– • – –   – • – •   • • •). | 60 | | 341<br>A2A. | Carrier signal. |
| 180 | Rankin Inlet, N.W.T. | 62° 48.8′ N<br>92° 06.1′ W | **RT**<br>(• – •   –). | 150 | | 284<br>A2A. | AERO. Carrier signal. |
| 190 | Eskimo Point, N.W.T. | 61° 06.5′ N<br>94° 04.0′ W | **YEK**<br>(– • – –   •   – • –). | 150 | | 329<br>A2A. | Carrier signal. |
| 200 | Churchill, Man. | 58° 46.4′ N<br>94° 10.6′ W | **Q**<br>(– – • –). | 75 | | 356<br>A2A. | AERO. Carrier signal. |
| 210 | Churchill, Man. | 58° 45.7′ N<br>93° 57.2′ W | **YQ**<br>(– • – –   – – • –). | 150 | | 305<br>A2A. | Carrier signal. |
| 220 | Button Islands, N.W.T. | 60° 41.7′ N<br>64° 37.5′ W | **B**<br>(– • • •).<br>period 360s<br>tr 60s<br>si 300s | 180 | | 312<br>A2A. | Seasonal. Carrier signal. |
| 232 | Nameless Point, Nfld. | 51° 18.7′ N<br>56° 44.5′ W | **Y**<br>(– • – –).<br>period 360s<br>tr(3) 60s<br>si 300s | 40 | II | 290<br>NON, A2A. | Carrier signal. |
| 234 | Belle Isle (North Point), Nfld. | 52° 00.0′ N<br>55° 16.8′ W | **R**<br>(• – •).<br>period 360s<br>tr 60s<br>si 300s | 100 | III | 290<br>NON, A2A. | Seasonal. Carrier signal. |
| 240 | Natashquan, Que. | 50° 13.4′ N<br>61° 50.6′ W | **NA**<br>(– •   • –). | 150 | | 385 | AERO. |
| 244 | Sept-Iles, Que. | 50° 11.3′ N<br>66° 06.7′ W | **ZV**<br>(– – • •   • • • –). | 150 | | 273 | |
| 254 | Gull Island, Nfld. | 49° 59.9′ N<br>55° 21.5′ W | **G**<br>(– – •).<br>period 360s<br>tr(3) 60s<br>si 120s<br>repeats(1) 180s | 80 | III, VI | 304<br>NON, A2A. | Seasonal. Carrier signal. Transmits continuously during periods of low visibility. During periods of clear weather, transmits between 00-10 and 30-40 minutes past each hour. |
| 260 | Stephenville, Nfld. | 48° 33.4′ N<br>58° 34.4′ W | **JT**<br>(• – – –   –). | 80 | | 390 | AERO. |
| 290 | Tete de Galantry Light Station, St. Pierre Island (Fr.) | 46° 45.9′ N<br>56° 09.3′ W | **Y**<br>(– • – –). | 100 | | 342<br>A2A. | AERO. |
| 300 | St. Pierre, St. Pierre Island (Fr.) | 46° 46.0′ N<br>56° 11.0′ W | **MQ**<br>(– –   – – • –). | 80 | | 354<br>A2A. | AERO. |
| 332 | East Point Light Station, P.E.I. | 46° 27.2′ N<br>61° 58.0′ W | **N**<br>(– •).<br>period 360s<br>tr(3) 60s<br>si 300s | 50 | II | 318<br>A2A. | Carrier signal. |
| 350 | Blanc Sablon, P.Q. | 51° 25.2′ N<br>57° 10.2′ W | **BX**<br>(– • • •   – • • –). | 100 | | 220<br>A2A. | AERO. |
| 370 | Port Menier, Anticosti Island | 49° 50.2′ N<br>64° 23.4′ W | **PN**<br>(• – – •   – •). | 100 | | 360<br>A2A. | AERO. Carrier signal. |
| 390 | Mont Joli, P.Q. | 48° 34.0′ N<br>68° 15.6′ W | **YY**<br>(– • – –   – • – –). | 150 | | 340 | AERO. |
| 395 | Pointe au Pere | 48° 31.1′ N<br>68° 28.1′ W | **K**<br>(– • –). | | | 290 | Seasonal. Transmits upon request to Mont-Joli Coast Guard Radio/ VCF. |
| 400 | Ile Bicquette Calibration Station, P.Q. | 48° 24.9′ N<br>68° 53.6′ W | **T**<br>(–). | | | 320<br>A2A. | Seasonal. Transmits upon request (24 hours in advance) to Quebec Coast Guard Radio/VCC. |

| (1) No. | (2) Name | (3) Position | (4) Characteristic | (5) Range | (6) Sequence | (7) Frequency | (8) Remarks |
|---|---|---|---|---|---|---|---|

**CANADA - ATLANTIC COAST**

| (1) No. | (2) Name | (3) Position | (4) Characteristic | (5) Range | (6) Sequence | (7) Frequency | (8) Remarks |
|---|---|---|---|---|---|---|---|
| 405 | Ste-Croix, F.P. | 46° 38.5′ N<br>71° 41.7′ W | **N**<br>(– •). | 10 | | 360 | |
| 410 | Quebec Calibration Station, P.Q. | 46° 48.8′ N<br>71° 09.6′ W | **T**<br>(–). | 5 | | 320<br>A2A. | Transmits upon request (6 hours in advance) to Quebec Coast Guard Radio/VCC. |
| 470 | Halifax Calibration Station, N.S. | 44° 41.0′ N<br>63° 36.8′ W | **T**<br>(–). | | | 286<br>NON, A2A. | Transmits upon request (6 hours in advance) to Halifax Marine Radio/ VCS. |
| 518 | Seal Island Light Station, N.S. | 43° 23.5′ N<br>66° 00.9′ W | **H**<br>(• • • •).<br>period 360s<br>tr(3) 60s<br>si 300s | 75 | VI | 322<br>A2A. | Carrier signal. |

**UNITED STATES - ATLANTIC AND GULF COASTS**

| (1) No. | (2) Name | (3) Position | (4) Characteristic | (5) Range | (6) Sequence | (7) Frequency | (8) Remarks |
|---|---|---|---|---|---|---|---|
| 1212 | Nantucket Shoals Lighted Horn Buoy N, Ma. | 40° 30.0′ N<br>69° 26.0′ W | **NS**<br>(– •  • • •).<br>period 360s<br>tr 50s<br>(—) 10s<br>si 300s | 50 | | 285<br>A2A. | |
| 1214 | Montauk Point Light Station, N.Y. | 41° 04.0′ N<br>71° 51.8′ W | **MP**<br>(– –  • – – •).<br>period 360s<br>tr 50s<br>(—) 10s<br>si 300s | 125 | | 293<br>A2A. | |
| 1400 | Kennedy, N.Y. | 40° 35.0′ N<br>73° 48.0′ W | **JF**<br>(• – – –  • • – •). | 25 | | 373<br>NON, A2A. | AERO. |
| 1582 | Charleston Light Station (Sullivan's Island), S.C. | 32° 45.5′ N<br>79° 50.6′ W | **S**<br>(• • •).<br>period 360s<br>tr 50s<br>(—) 10s<br>si 300s | 125 | III | 298<br>A2A. | |
| 1620 | Tybee Light Station, Ga. | 32° 01.3′ N<br>80° 50.7′ W | **TB**<br>(–  – • • •).<br>period 60s<br>tr 50s<br>(—) 10s | 75 | | 317<br>A2A. | |
| 1670 | Palm Beach, Fl. | 26° 41.0′ N<br>80° 13.0′ W | **PB**<br>(• – – •  – • • •). | | | 356<br>A2A. | AERO. |
| 1690 | Miami, Fl. | 25° 44.0′ N<br>80° 09.6′ W | **U**<br>(• • –). | 100 | | 322<br>A2A. | |
| 1700 | Marathon, Fl. | 24° 42.7′ N<br>81° 05.7′ W | **MTH**<br>(– –  –  • • • •). | 50 | | 260<br>NON, A2A. | AERO. |
| 1710 | Fish Hook, Fl. | 24° 33.0′ N<br>81° 47.0′ W | **FIS**<br>(• • – •  • •  • • •). | 100 | | 332<br>NON, A2A. | AERO. |
| 1740 | Yankeetown, Fl. | 28° 58.0′ N<br>82° 41.8′ W | **Y**<br>(– • – –). | 65 | | 290<br>A2A. | |

**BERMUDA**

| (1) No. | (2) Name | (3) Position | (4) Characteristic | (5) Range | (6) Sequence | (7) Frequency | (8) Remarks |
|---|---|---|---|---|---|---|---|
| 1880 | St. Davids Head | 32° 22.0′ N<br>64° 38.9′ W | **BSD**<br>(– • • •  • • •  – • •). | 155 | | 323<br>A2A. | |

| (1) No. | (2) Name | (3) Position | (4) Characteristic | (5) Range | (6) Sequence | (7) Frequency | (8) Remarks |
|---|---|---|---|---|---|---|---|
| | | | **BAHAMA ISLANDS** | | | | |
| 1900 | West End International Airport | 26° 41.3′ N<br>78° 58.7′ W | **ZWE**<br>(– – • • • – – – •). | 100 | | 317<br>A2A. | AERO. |
| 1920 | Naussau International Airport | 25° 02.0′ N<br>77° 28.0′ W | **ZQA**<br>(– – • • – – • – • –). | 240 | | 251<br>A1A. | AERO. |
| 1925 | Great Inagua | 20° 57.6′ N<br>73° 40.5′ W | **ZIN**<br>(– – • • • • – •). | | 50 | 376<br>A2A. | AERO. |
| | | | **CUBA** | | | | |
| 1940 | San Julian | 22° 05.0′ N<br>84° 13.0′ W | **USJ**<br>(• • – • • • • – – –). | 155 | | 402 | AERO. |
| 1950 | Havana | 22° 58.0′ N<br>82° 26.0′ W | **A**<br>(• –). | 256 | | 339 | AERO. |
| 1960 | Varder | 23° 05.0′ N<br>81° 22.0′ W | **UVR**<br>(• • – • • • – • – •). | 216 | | 272<br>A2A. | AERO. |
| 1980 | Cayo Coco | 22° 30.9′ N<br>78° 30.7′ W | **UNC**<br>(• • – – • – • – •). | | | 256<br>A2A. | AERO. |
| 1990 | Guantanamo Bay | 19° 54.0′ N<br>75° 10.0′ W | **NBW**<br>(– • – • • • • – –). | | | 276.2 | AERO. |
| 2000 | Santiago de Cuba | 19° 58.0′ N<br>75° 50.0′ W | **UCU**<br>(• • – – • – • • • –). | 70 | | 339<br>A2A. | AERO. |
| | | | **BELIZE** | | | | |
| 2080 | Belize | 17° 32.0′ N<br>88° 18.0′ W | **BZE**<br>(– • • • – – • • •). | 192 | | 392<br>NON, A2A. | AERO. |
| | | | **COSTA RICA** | | | | |
| 2100 | Limon (TIM) | 10° 00.1′ N<br>83° 01.6′ W | **M**<br>(– –).<br>period 600s | 50<br>100 | | 290<br>A2A. | Transmits upon request through Limon (TIM) at 00 and 30 minutes past the hour requested. |
| | | | **PANAMA - ATLANTIC COAST** | | | | |
| 2130 | Almirante | 9° 17.4′ N<br>82° 23.6′ W | **B**<br>(– • • •). | | | 290<br>A2A. | Transmits continuously between 0500 to 1300. |
| | | | **COLOMBIA** | | | | |
| 2140 | Isla San Andres | 12° 35.1′ N<br>81° 42.3′ W | **SPP**<br>(• • • • – – • • – – •). | 40 | | 387<br>NON, A2A. | AERO. |
| 2160 | Riohacha | 11° 33.0′ N<br>72° 54.0′ W | **RHC**<br>(• – • • • • • – • – •). | 75 | | 295<br>NON, A2A. | AERO. |
| 2165 | Portete | 12° 14.2′ N<br>71° 59.7′ W | **PTE**<br>(• – – • – •). | | | 420 | AERO. |

| (1) No. | (2) Name | (3) Position | (4) Characteristic | (5) Range | (6) Sequence | (7) Frequency | (8) Remarks |
|---|---|---|---|---|---|---|---|
| | | | **VENEZUELA** | | | | |
| 2180 | Maiquetia | 10° 37.0′ N<br>66° 59.0′ W | **MIQ**<br>(– – •• – – • –). | 130 | | 292<br>A2A. | AERO. |
| 2190 | La Orchilla | 11° 48.0′ N<br>66° 07.0′ W | **ORC**<br>(– – – • – • – • – •). | 180 | | 320<br>A2A. | |
| 2200 | Hiquerote | 10° 28.0′ N<br>66° 05.7′ W | **HOT**<br>(•••• – – – –). | 240 | | 353<br>NON, A2A. | AERO. |
| 2210 | Margarita | 10° 55.3′ N<br>63° 57.4′ W | **MTA**<br>(– – – • –). | 100 | | 206<br>A2A. | AERO. |
| | | | **CAYMAN ISLANDS** | | | | |
| 2220 | Grand Cayman | 19° 17.0′ N<br>81° 23.0′ W | **ZIY**<br>(– – •• •• – • – –). | 240 | | 344<br>NON, A2A. | AERO. |
| 2225 | Cayman Brac | 19° 41.4′ N<br>79° 51.4′ W | **CBC**<br>(– • – • – ••• – • – •). | 240 | | 415 | AERO. |
| | | | **JAMAICA** | | | | |
| 2230 | Montego Bay | 18° 30.0′ N<br>77° 55.0′ W | **MBJ**<br>(– – – ••• • – – –). | 150 | | 248<br>NON, A2A. | AERO. |
| 2240 | Kingston | 17° 58.0′ N<br>76° 53.0′ W | **KIN**<br>(– • – •• – •). | 250 | | 360<br>NON, A2A. | AERO. |
| | | | **HAITI** | | | | |
| 2250 | Port-au-Prince | 18° 35.0′ N<br>72° 17.0′ W | **HHP**<br>(•••• •••• • – – •). | 240 | | 270<br>A2A. | AERO. |
| | | | **DOMINICAN REPUBLIC** | | | | |
| 2260 | Punta Caucedo | 18° 27.0′ N<br>69° 40.0′ W | **HIV**<br>(•••• •• ••• –). | 240 | | 400<br>A2A. | AERO. |
| | | | **PUERTO RICO** | | | | |
| 2270 | Dorado | 18° 28.0′ N<br>66° 25.0′ W | **DDP**<br>(– •• – •• • – – •). | 365 | | 391<br>NON, A2A. | AERO. |
| 2290 | Roosevelt Roads | 18° 14.0′ N<br>65° 37.0′ W | **NRR**<br>(– • • – • • – •). | 115 | | 264<br>NON, A2A. | AERO. |
| | | | **LEEWARD ISLANDS** | | | | |
| 2300 | Saint Barthelemy | 17° 54.0′ N<br>62° 51.0′ W | **BY**<br>(– ••• – • – –). | 50 | | 338<br>A1A. | AERO. |
| 2310 | Coolidge (Antiqua) | 17° 07.5′ N<br>61° 47.6′ W | **ZDX**<br>(– – •• – •• – •• –). | 256 | | 369<br>NON, A2A. | AERO. |
| 2330 | Marie-Galante/Grand Bourq, Guadeloupe | 15° 52.0′ N<br>61° 16.0′ W | **MG**<br>(– – – – •). | 50 | | 376<br>A2A. | AERO. |
| 2340 | Dominica. | 15° 32.8′ N<br>61° 18.4′ W | **DOM**<br>(– •• – – – – –). | 100 | | 273 | AERO. |

| (1) No. | (2) Name | (3) Position | (4) Characteristic | (5) Range | (6) Sequence | (7) Frequency | (8) Remarks |
|---|---|---|---|---|---|---|---|
| | | | **WINDWARD ISLANDS** | | | | |
| 2350 | Martinque (Fort de France) | 14° 36.0′ N<br>61° 06.0′ W | **FXF**<br>(• • – • – • • – • • – •). | 100 | | 314<br>A2A. | AERO. |
| 2360 | Hewanorra, Saint Lucia | 13° 44.0′ N<br>60° 59.0′ W | **BNE**<br>(– • • • – • •). | 100 | | 305 | AERO. |
| 2370 | Arnos Vale, Saint Vincent | 13° 09.0′ N<br>61° 13.0′ W | **SV**<br>(• • • • • • –). | 143 | | 403 | AERO. |
| 2380 | Barbados (Seawell Aerodome) | 13° 04.0′ N<br>59° 30.0′ W | **BGI**<br>(– • • • – – • • •). | 256 | | 345<br>NON, A2A. | AERO. |
| 2390 | Grenada | 12° 00.5′ N<br>61° 46.7′ W | **GND**<br>(– – • – • – • •). | 115 | | 362<br>NON, A2A. | AERO. |
| | | | **TRINIDAD AND TOBAGO** | | | | |
| 2400 | Crown Point, Tobago | 11° 09.0′ N<br>60° 51.0′ W | **TAB**<br>(– • – – • • •). | 100 | | 323<br>A2A. | AERO. |
| 2410 | Piarco, Trinidad | 10° 36.0′ N<br>61° 26.0′ W | **POS**<br>(• – – • – – – • • •). | 256 | | 382<br>NON, A2A. | AERO. |
| | | | **GUYANA** | | | | |
| 2420 | Timehri | 6° 30.0′ N<br>58° 14.0′ W | **TIM**<br>(– • • – –). | 150 | | 356<br>A2A. | AERO. |
| 2430 | Georgetown | 6° 49.3′ N<br>58° 08.9′ W | **8RB**<br>(– – – • • • – • – • • •). | 200 | | 300<br>A2A. | |
| 2450 | Skeldon | 5° 53.0′ N<br>57° 09.0′ W | **SKD**<br>(• • • – • – – • •). | 92 | | 378<br>NON, A2A. | AERO. |
| | | | **SURINAME** | | | | |
| 2460 | Paramaribo | 5° 50.9′ N<br>55° 09.4′ W | **PB**<br>(• – – • – • • •). | 400 | | 315<br>A2A. | |
| | | | **BRAZIL** | | | | |
| 2480 | Amapa | 2° 04.0′ N<br>50° 52.0′ W | **AMP**<br>(• – – – • – – •). | 70 | | 275<br>NON, A2A. | AERO. Transmits between the hours of 0800Z- 2200Z. |
| 2485 | Canivete | 0° 30.6′ N<br>50° 24.9′ W | **CN**<br>(– • – • – •). | 200 | | 310<br>A2A. | |
| 2500 | Salinopolis Light Station | 0° 37.0′ S<br>47° 21.3′ W | **BL**<br>(– • • • • – • •). | 300 | | 315<br>A2A. | |
| 2520 | Sao Luis | 2° 35.0′ S<br>44° 14.0′ W | **SLI**<br>(• • • • – • • • •). | 50 | | 280<br>NON, A2A. | AERO. |
| 2525 | Ponta de Sao Marcos | 2° 29.3′ S<br>44° 18.1′ W | **SM**<br>(• • • – –). | 200 | | 300<br>A2A. | |
| 2530 | Parnaiba | 2° 54.0′ S<br>41° 45.0′ W | **PNB**<br>(• – – • – • – • • •). | 100 | | 365<br>NON, A2A. | AERO. |
| 2535 | Mucuripe | 3° 43.6′ S<br>38° 28.3′ W | **MU**<br>(– – • • –). | 300 | | 295<br>A2A. | |
| 2540 | Fortaleza | 3° 47.0′ S<br>38° 32.0′ W | **FLZ**<br>(• • – • • – • • – – • •). | 150 | | 260<br>NON, A2A. | AERO. |

| (1) No. | (2) Name | (3) Position | (4) Characteristic | (5) Range | (6) Sequence | (7) Frequency | (8) Remarks |
|---|---|---|---|---|---|---|---|
| | | | **BRAZIL** | | | | |
| 2550 | Fernando de Noronha | 3° 52.0′ S<br>32° 26.0′ W | **NOR**<br>(– • – – – • – •). | 150 | | 300<br>NON, A2A. | AERO. |
| 2560 | Calcanhar | 5° 09.7′ S<br>35° 29.1′ W | **DA**<br>(– • • • –). | 300 | | 305<br>A2A. | |
| 2580 | Joao Pessoa | 7° 09.0′ S<br>34° 57.0′ W | **JPS**<br>(• – – – • – – • • • •). | 50 | | 320<br>NON, A2A. | AERO. |
| 2600 | Maceio | 9° 31.0′ S<br>35° 47.0′ W | **MCO**<br>(– – – • – • – – –). | 70 | | 340<br>NON, A2A. | AERO. |
| 2610 | Sergipe | 10° 58.2′ S<br>37° 02.2′ W | **AI**<br>(• – • •). | 200 | | 320<br>A2A. | |
| 2620 | Salvador | 12° 55.0′ S<br>38° 20.0′ W | **SVD**<br>(• • • • • • – – • •). | 200 | | 275<br>NON, A2A. | AERO. |
| 2630 | Ilheus | 14° 49.0′ S<br>39° 02.0′ W | **YLH**<br>(– • – – • – • • • • • •). | 70 | | 305<br>NON, A2A. | AERO. |
| 2640 | Caravelas | 17° 39.0′ S<br>39° 15.0′ W | **CVL**<br>(– • – • • • • – • – • •). | 100 | | 365<br>NON, A2A. | AERO. |
| 2650 | Parcel dos Abrolhos | 17° 57.9′ S<br>38° 41.5′ W | **AV**<br>(• – • • • –). | 300 | | 290<br>A2A. | |
| 2670 | Vitoria | 20° 12.0′ S<br>40° 15.0′ W | **VTR**<br>(• • • – – • – •). | 100 | | 350<br>NON, A2A. | AERO. |
| 2680 | Cabo Sao Tome Light Station | 22° 02.5′ S<br>41° 03.2′ W | **SK**<br>(• • • – • –). | 300 | | 300<br>A2A. | |
| 2690 | Aldeia | 22° 49.0′ S<br>42° 06.0′ W | **ADA**<br>(• – – • • • –). | 50 | | 345<br>NON, A2A. | AERO. |
| 2700 | Ilha Rasa Light Station | 23° 03.8′ S<br>43° 08.8′ W | **IH**<br>(• • • • • •). | 300 | | 315<br>A2A. | |
| 2710 | Santa Cruz | 22° 56.0′ S<br>43° 43.0′ W | **SCR**<br>(• • • – • – • • – •). | 60 | | 255<br>NON, A2A. | AERO. |
| 2720 | Ubatuba | 23° 27.0′ S<br>45° 04.0′ W | **UBT**<br>(• • – – • • • –). | 50 | | 295<br>NON, A2A. | AERO. |
| 2730 | Ilha da Moela | 24° 03.1′ S<br>46° 15.8′ W | **NR**<br>(– • • – •). | 300 | | 305<br>A2A. | |
| 2740 | Paranagua (Ilha do Mel) | 25° 30.0′ S<br>48° 19.0′ W | **NX**<br>(– • – • • –). | 300 | | 320<br>A2A. | |
| 2745 | Navegantes | 26° 52.5′ S<br>48° 39.1′ W | **NVG**<br>(– • • • • – – – •). | 50 | | 235<br>NON, A2A. | AERO. |
| 2747 | Ilha de Santa Catarina | 27° 41.7′ S<br>48° 30.0′ W | **FNP**<br>(• • – • – • • – – •). | 50 | | 220<br>NON, A2A. | AERO. |
| 2750 | Cabo Santa Marta Grande Light Station | 28° 36.2′ S<br>48° 48.8′ W | **SW**<br>(• • • • – –). | 300 | | 310<br>A2A. | |
| 2760 | Tramandai Light Station | 30° 00.6′ S<br>50° 08.2′ W | **FB**<br>(• • – • – • • •). | 300 | | 300<br>A2A. | |
| 2770 | Rio Grande | 32° 09.0′ S<br>52° 06.2′ W | **RG**<br>(• – • – – •). | 300 | | 290<br>A2A. | |
| 2780 | Arroio Chui | 33° 44.5′ S<br>53° 22.3′ W | **UI**<br>(• • – • •). | 200 | | 312<br>A2A. | |
| | | | **URUGUAY** | | | | |
| 2800 | Cabo Santa Maria Light Station | 34° 40.3′ S<br>54° 09.1′ W | **LP**<br>(• – • • • – – •). | 80 | | 310<br>A2A. | |

| (1) No. | (2) Name | (3) Position | (4) Characteristic | (5) Range | (6) Sequence | (7) Frequency | (8) Remarks |
|---|---|---|---|---|---|---|---|
| | | | **URUGUAY** | | | | |
| 2810 | Punta del Este | 34° 57.9′ S<br>54° 57.0′ W | **PDE**<br>(• – – •  – • •  •). | 90 | | 320<br>A2A. | |
| | | | **ARGENTINA** | | | | |
| 2840 | Punta Indio | 35° 21.5′ S<br>57° 18.0′ W | **PDI**<br>(• – – •  – • •  • •). | 50 | | 325<br>A2A. | AERO. |
| 2860 | Segunda Barranca | 40° 46.8′ S<br>62° 16.7′ W | **SB**<br>(• • •  – • • •).<br>period 360s<br>tr (interrupted by 2 long dashes) 120s<br>si 240s | 200 | I, II | 310<br>A2A. | Transmits continuously during periods of low visibility. During periods of clear weather, transmits at 00, 06, 30, and 36 minutes past each hour. |
| 2862 | El Rincon | 39° 23.2′ S<br>62° 00.8′ W | **RN**<br>(• – •  – •).<br>period 360s<br>tr (interrupted by 2 long dashes) 120s<br>si 240s | 200 | III, IV | 310<br>A2A. | Transmits continuously during periods of low visibility. During periods of clear weather, transmits at 02, 08, 32, and 38 minutes past each hour. |
| 2864 | Recalada, Bahia Blanca | 38° 59.5′ S<br>61° 15.6′ W | **BB**<br>(– • • •  – • • •).<br>period 360s<br>tr (interrupted by 2 long dashes) 120s<br>si 240s | 200 | V, VI | 310<br>A2A. | Transmits continuously during periods of low visibility. During periods of clear weather, transmits at 04, 10, 34, and 40 minutes past each hour. |
| 2870 | Punta Delgada Light Station | 42° 46.0′ S<br>63° 38.9′ W | **PD**<br>(• – – •  – • •).<br>period 120s | 200 | | 315<br>A2A. | Transmits continuously during periods of low visibility. During periods of clear weather, transmits at 04, 10, 34, and 40 minutes past each hour. |
| 2880 | Cabo Blanco Light Station | 47° 12.2′ S<br>65° 44.5′ W | **CB**<br>(– • – •  – • • •).<br>period 360s<br>tr 9.8s<br>si 2.2s<br>(—) 17.0s<br>si 1.0s<br>(—) 17.0s<br>si 1.0s<br>repeats(1) 48s<br>tr 9.8s<br>si 254.2s | 200 | | 295<br>A2A. | Transmits continuously during periods of low visibility. During periods of clear weather, transmits at 02, 08, 32, and 38 minutes past each hour. |
| 2890 | San Julian | 49° 19.0′ S<br>67° 48.0′ W | **SJU**<br>(• • •  • – – –  • • –). | 150 | | 375<br>A2A. | AERO. Transmits occasionally. |
| 2900 | Rio Gallegos | 51° 37.0′ S<br>69° 17.0′ W | **GAL**<br>(– – •  • –  • – • •). | 350 | | 330<br>A2A. | AERO. Transmits between the hours of 0900- 2400. |
| 2910 | Cabo Virgenes Light Station | 52° 20.0′ S<br>68° 21.0′ W | **CV**<br>(– • – •  • • • –). | 200 | | 300<br>A2A. | Transmits continuously during periods of low visibility. During periods of clear weather, transmits at 10, 16, 40, and 46 minutes past each hour. |

# Section 16

## Differential GPS Stations

| (1) No. | (2) Name | (3) Position | (4) Station ID | (5) Range | (6) Frequency | (7) Transfer Rate | (8) Remarks |
|---|---|---|---|---|---|---|---|
| | | | **CANADA-ATLANTIC COAST** | | | | |
| 100 | Cape Ray (Port aux Basques), Newfoundland | 47° 38.0′ N<br>59° 14.0′ W | T 942<br>R 340<br>R 341 | 189 | 288 | 200 | |
| 110 | Cape Race, Newfoundland | 46° 46.0′ N<br>53° 11.0′ W | T 940<br>R 338<br>R 339 | 283 | 315 | 200 | |
| 115 | Cape Norman, Newfoundland | 51° 30.0′ N<br>54° 49.0′ W | T 944<br>R 342<br>R 343 | 189 | 310 | 200 | Message Types: 3,5,6,7,9,16. |
| 118 | Rigolet, Newfoundland | 54° 15.0′ N<br>58° 30.0′ W | T 946<br>R 344<br>R 345 | 162 | 299 | 200 | |
| 120 | Fox Island, Nova Scotia | 45° 20.0′ N<br>61° 05.0′ W | T 934<br>R 336<br>R 337 | 162 | 307 | 200 | |
| 125 | Western Head, Nova Scotia | 43° 59.0′ N<br>64° 40.0′ W | T 935<br>R 334<br>R 335 | 162 | 312 | 200 | Message Types: 3,5,6,7,9,16. |
| 135 | Point Escuminac, New Brunswick | 47° 04.0′ N<br>64° 48.0′ W | T 936<br>R 332<br>R 333 | 162 | 319 | 200 | |
| 140 | Partridge Island, New Brunswick | 45° 14.0′ N<br>66° 03.0′ W | T 939<br>R 326<br>R 327 | 162 | 295 | 200 | |
| 145 | Riviere-du-Loup, Quebec | 47° 46.0′ N<br>69° 36.0′ W | T 926<br>R 318<br>R 319 | 162 | 300 | 200 | Message Types: 3,5,6,7,9,16. |
| 148 | Moisie, Quebec | 50° 12.0′ N<br>66° 07.0′ W | T 925<br>R 320<br>R 321 | 162 | 313 | 200 | Message Types: 3,5,6,7,9,16. |
| 150 | Lauzon, Quebec | 46° 49.0′ N<br>71° 10.0′ W | T 927<br>R 316<br>R 317 | 178 | 309 | 200 | |
| 155 | Trois-Rivieres, Quebec | 46° 23.0′ N<br>72° 27.0′ W | T 928<br>R 314<br>R 315 | 92 | 321 | 200 | |
| 160 | St. Jean Richelieu, Quebec | 45° 19.0′ N<br>73° 19.0′ W | T 929<br>R 312<br>R 313 | 178 | 296 | 200 | |
| 170 | Cardinal, Ontario | 44° 47.0′ N<br>75° 25.0′ W | T 919<br>R 308<br>R 309 | 162 | 306 | 200 | |
| 180 | Wiarton, Ontario | 44° 45.0′ N<br>81° 07.0′ W | T 918<br>R 310<br>R 311 | 135 | 286 | 200 | |
| | | | **UNITED STATES-ATLANTIC AND GULF COASTS** | | | | |
| 200 | Brunswick, Maine | 43° 53.7′ N<br>69° 56.3′ W | T 800 | 115 | 316 | 100 | |
| 210 | Portsmouth, New Hampshire | 43° 04.2′ N<br>70° 42.6′ W | T 801 | 70 | 288 | 100 | |

| (1) No. | (2) Name | (3) Position | (4) Station ID | (5) Range | (6) Frequency | (7) Transfer Rate | (8) Remarks |
|---|---|---|---|---|---|---|---|
| | | **UNITED STATES-ATLANTIC AND GULF COASTS** | | | | | |
| 220 | Chatham, Massachusetts | 41° 40.3′ N<br>69° 57.0′ W | T 802 | 95 | 325 | 200 | |
| 230 | Montauk Point, New York | 41° 04.0′ N<br>71° 51.4′ W | T 803 | 125 | 293 | 100 | |
| 240 | Sandy Hook, New Jersey | 40° 28.3′ N<br>74° 00.7′ W | T 804 | 100 | 286 | 200 | |
| 250 | Cape Henelopen, Delaware | 38° 46.6′ N<br>75° 05.3′ W | T 805 | 180 | 298 | 200 | |
| 260 | Cape Henry, Virginia | 36° 55.6′ N<br>76° 00.4′ W | T 806 | 130 | 289 | 100 | |
| 270 | Fort Macon, North Carolina | 34° 41.9′ N<br>76° 41.0′ W | T 807 | 130 | 294 | 100 | |
| 280 | Charleston, South Carolina | 32° 45.5′ N<br>79° 50.6′ W | T 808 | 150 | 298 | 100 | |
| 290 | Cape Canaveral, Florida | 28° 27.6′ N<br>80° 32.6′ W | T 809 | 250 | 289 | 100 | |
| 300 | Miami, Florida | 25° 43.9′ N<br>80° 09.6′ W | T 810 | 75 | 322 | 100 | |
| 310 | Key West, Florida | 24° 34.9′ N<br>81° 39.1′ W | T 811 | 110 | 286 | 100 | |
| 320 | Egmont Key, Florida | 27° 36.1′ N<br>82° 45.7′ W | T 812 | 210 | 312 | 200 | |
| 330 | Isabella, Puerto Rico | 18° 30.0′ N<br>67° 02.0′ W | T 817 | 125 | 295 | 100 | |
| 340 | Mobile Point, Alabama | 30° 13.6′ N<br>88° 01.4′ W | T 813 | 180 | 300 | 100 | |
| 350 | English Turn, Louisiana | 29° 52.7′ N<br>89° 56.5′ W | T 814 | 180 | 293 | 200 | |
| 360 | Galveston, Texas | 29° 19.8′ N<br>94° 44.2′ W | T 815 | 180 | 296 | 100 | |
| 370 | Aransas Pass, Texas | 27° 50.3′ N<br>97° 03.5′ W | T 816 | 180 | 304 | 100 | |
| | | **BERMUDA** | | | | | |
| 400 | St. David's Head | 32° 22.0′ N<br>64° 38.0′ W | T 950 | 173 | 323 | 100 | |
| | | **BRAZIL** | | | | | |
| 700 | Canivete | 0° 30.6′ N<br>50° 24.9′ W | R 463 | 200 | 310 | 100 | Message Types: 1,2,3,6,16. |
| 705 | Ponta de Sao Marcos | 2° 29.3′ S<br>44° 18.1′ W | R 460 | 200 | 300 | 100 | Message Types: 1,2,3,6,16. |
| 710 | Ponta de Calcanhar | 5° 09.7′ S<br>35° 29.1′ W | R 467 | 200 | 305 | 100 | Message Types: 1,2,3,6,16. |
| 715 | Sergipe | 10° 58.2′ S<br>37° 02.2′ W | R 468 | 200 | 320 | 100 | Message Types: 1,2,3,6,16. |
| 720 | Canal dos Abrolhos | 17° 57.9′ S<br>38° 41.5′ W | R 461 | 200 | 290 | 100 | Message Types: 1,2,3,6,16. |
| 725 | Cabo Sao Tome | 22° 02.5′ S<br>41° 03.2′ W | R 465 | 200 | 300 | 100 | Message Types: 1,2,3,6,16. |

| (1) No. | (2) Name | (3) Position | (4) Station ID | (5) Range | (6) Frequency | (7) Transfer Rate | (8) Remarks |
|---|---|---|---|---|---|---|---|
| | | | **BRAZIL** | | | | |
| 730 | Ilha Rasa | 23° 03.8´ S<br>48° 08.8´ W | | | | | |
| 735 | Ilha da Moela | 24° 03.1´ S<br>46° 15.8´ W | R 462 | 200 | 305 | 100 | Message Types: 1,2,3,6,16. |
| 740 | Cabo Santa Marta | 28° 36.2´ S<br>48° 48.8´ W | R 466 | 200 | 310 | 100 | Message Types: 1,2,3,6,16. |
| 745 | Rio Grande | 32° 09.0´ S<br>52° 06.2´ W | R 464 | 200 | 290 | 100 | Message Types: 1,2,3,6,16. |
| | | | **ARGENTINA** | | | | |
| 900 | Buenos Aires | 34° 37.4´ S<br>58° 21.2´ W | | | 2570 | | |
| 910 | Rosario | 32° 58.4´ S<br>60° 37.2´ W | | | 2950 | | |

# INDEX – LIGHTS

## A



## B

## C

## H



## I

## M



## N

## Q

## T



## U



## V



## W

## X



## Y



## Z

# INDEX – DIFFERENTIAL GPS STATIONS

| Inter. | U.S. |
|---|---|
| G0000.5 | 17458 |
| G0001 | 17460 |
| G0002 | 17464 |
| G0004 | 17470 |
| G0005 | 17472 |
| G0005.5 | 17474 |
| G0006.5 | 17480 |
| G0006.8 | 17484 |
| G0006.9 | 17488 |
| G0007.4 | 17496 |
| G0007.5 | 17500 |
| G0007.7 | 17504 |
| G0008.4 | 17510 |
| G0008.5 | 17511 |
| G0009 | 17512 |
| G0010.6 | 17528 |
| G0010.7 | 17530 |
| G0011.5 | 17534 |
| G0012 | 17536 |
| G0014 | 17540 |
| G0018 | 17548 |
| G0019 | 17550 |
| G0020 | 17552 |
| G0021 | 17556 |
| G0021.5 | 17560 |
| G0022 | 17562 |
| G0024 | 17564 |
| G0028 | 17568 |
| G0029 | 17572 |
| G0030 | 17576 |
| G0034 | 17584 |
| G0035.2 | 17589 |
| G0035.3 | 17590 |
| G0036 | 17588 |
| G0038 | 17592 |
| G0039 | 17596 |
| G0040 | 17597 |
| G0041 | 17598 |
| G0041.8 | 17598.5 |
| G0042.05 | 17599.3 |
| G0042.08 | 17599.6 |
| G0042.3 | 17599 |
| G0044 | 17604 |
| G0045 | 17608 |
| G0045.4 | 17610 |
| G0046 | 17612 |
| G0047 | 17614 |
| G0048 | 17616 |
| G0050 | 17620 |
| G0052 | 17600 |
| G0053.7 | 17634 |
| G0054 | 17624 |
| G0056 | 17636 |
| G0056.5 | 17640 |
| G0058 | 17648 |
| G0062 | 17652 |
| G0063 | 17656 |
| G0064 | 17660 |
| G0065 | 17662 |
| G0066 | 17664 |
| G0070 | 17668 |
| G0070.5 | 17670 |
| G0071 | 17677 |
| G0072 | 17672 |
| G0073 | 17674 |
| G0074 | 17676 |
| G0078 | 17680 |
| G0079 | 17695 |
| G0080 | 17684 |
| G0084 | 17688 |
| G0087 | 17696 |
| G0087.2 | 17700 |
| G0087.4 | 17704 |
| G0087.5 | 17701 |
| G0087.6 | 17702 |
| G0087.7 | 17703.1 |
| G0088 | 17708 |
| G0090 | 17712 |
| G0091 | 17713 |
| G0092 | 17716 |
| G0093 | 17718 |
| G0094 | 17720 |
| G0097 | 17724 |
| G0098 | 17728 |
| G0102 | 17736 |
| G0103 | 17742 |
| G0104 | 17740 |
| G0105 | 17744 |
| G0108 | 17748 |
| G0110 | 17756 |
| G0114 | 17760 |
| G0116 | 17764 |
| G0117 | 17766 |
| G0119 | 17766.5 |
| G0119.3 | 17766.7 |
| G0119.4 | 17766.71 |
| G0119.5 | 17766.73 |
| G0119.6 | 17766.75 |
| G0119.7 | 17766.77 |
| G0120 | 17784 |
| G0121.4 | 17767 |
| G0121.45 | 17767.3 |
| G0121.5 | 17767.5 |
| G0122 | 17768 |
| G0123 | 17780 |
| G0124 | 17772 |
| G0125 | 17778 |
| G0125.5 | 17802 |
| G0126 | 17804 |
| G0130 | 17786 |
| G0132 | 17788 |
| G0138 | 17796 |
| G0144 | 17792 |
| G0146 | 17800 |
| G0148 | 17808 |
| G0152 | 17812 |
| G0152.5 | 17810 |
| G0154 | 17816 |
| G0156 | 17824 |
| G0157 | 17826 |
| G0158 | 17828 |
| G0162 | 17832 |
| G0164 | 17836 |
| G0166 | 17840 |
| G0168 | 17844 |
| G0170 | 17848 |
| G0172 | 17852 |
| G0177 | 17856 |
| G0178 | 17860 |
| G0180 | 17864 |
| G0180.6 | 17872 |
| G0180.8 | 17876 |
| G0182 | 17880 |
| G0183 | 17882 |
| G0184 | 17884 |
| G0186 | 17888 |
| G0188 | 17892 |
| G0189 | 17900 |
| G0190 | 17904 |
| G0191.5 | 17907.5 |
| G0192 | 17908 |
| G0202 | 17912 |
| G0204 | 17920 |
| G0205 | 17932 |
| G0205.4 | 17936 |
| G0206 | 17948 |
| G0208 | 17944 |
| G0212 | 17960 |
| G0212.4 | 17961 |
| G0212.5 | 17962.5 |
| G0212.6 | 17962 |
| G0212.65 | 17962.3 |
| G0214 | 17964 |
| G0218 | 17968 |
| G0219 | 17980 |
| G0220 | 17972 |
| G0222 | 17976 |
| G0223 | 17984 |
| G0223.4 | 17989 |
| G0224 | 17992 |
| G0226 | 17996 |
| G0227 | 18000 |
| G0229.5 | 18004 |
| G0230 | 18010 |
| G0233 | 18011 |
| G0234.5 | 18013 |
| G0235 | 18014 |
| G0236 | 18016 |
| G0236.2 | 18018 |
| G0237 | 18020 |
| G0238 | 18024 |
| G0242 | 18028 |
| G0244 | 18032 |
| G0244.3 | 18035 |
| G0244.5 | 18034 |
| G0244.6 | 18035.5 |
| G0246 | 18036 |
| G0247 | 18040 |
| G0247.2 | 18044 |
| G0249 | 18048 |
| G0251 | 18064 |
| G0251.3 | 18063 |
| G0251.6 | 18064.5 |
| G0251.7 | 18065 |
| G0252 | 18062 |
| G0252.2 | 18061 |
| G0254 | 18060 |
| G0256 | 18066 |
| G0262 | 18127 |
| G0262.3 | 18126 |
| G0266 | 18132 |
| G0267 | 18128 |
| G0268 | 18136 |
| G0269 | 18140 |
| G0270 | 18144 |
| G0270.2 | 18145 |
| G0274 | 18148 |
| G0279 | 18154 |
| G0282 | 18156 |
| G0286 | 18164 |
| G0287 | 18168 |
| G0288 | 18160 |
| G0290.5 | 18170 |
| G0292 | 18172 |
| G0292.9 | 18173 |
| G0293.1 | 18173.5 |
| G0294 | 18174 |
| G0296 | 18176 |
| G0298 | 18180 |
| G0298.5 | 18182 |
| G0299 | 18184 |
| G0300 | 18188 |
| G0301 | 18192 |
| G0302 | 18196 |
| G0304 | 18204 |
| G0305 | 18206 |
| G0306 | 18200 |
| G0308 | 18208 |
| G0310 | 18210 |
| G0312 | 18213 |
| G0313.5 | 18214 |
| G0314 | 18232 |
| G0315 | 18234 |
| G0315.1 | 18236 |
| G0315.3 | 18237 |
| G0315.4 | 18238 |
| G0316 | 18216 |
| G0316.5 | 18228 |
| G0317 | 18220 |
| G0317.2 | 18224 |
| G0318 | 18256 |
| G0318.5 | 18259 |
| G0320 | 18240 |
| G0320.19 | 18240.5 |
| G0320.2 | 18241 |
| G0320.3 | 18243 |
| G0320.31 | 18244 |
| G0320.4 | 18247 |
| G0320.6 | 18248 |
| G0320.65 | 18249 |
| G0320.7 | 18245 |
| G0320.8 | 18246 |
| G0321 | 18252 |
| G0322 | 18264 |
| G0322.1 | 18268 |
| G0323 | 18272 |
| G0323.1 | 18276 |
| G0324 | 18280 |
| G0324.1 | 18284 |
| G0325 | 18288 |
| G0326 | 18296 |
| G0327 | 18292 |
| G0327.3 | 18300 |
| G0327.6 | 18304 |
| G0327.8 | 18308 |
| G0327.9 | 18310 |
| G0328 | 18312 |
| G0330 | 18316 |
| G0331 | 18320 |
| G0331.2 | 18321 |

| Inter. | U.S. |
|---|---|
| G0331.21 | 18322 |
| G0332 | 18324 |
| G0334 | 18328 |
| G0335 | 18330 |
| G0335.5 | 18330.5 |
| G0336 | 18331 |
| G0338 | 18332 |
| G0340 | 18336 |
| G0342 | 18340 |
| G0343 | 18342 |
| G0346 | 18344 |
| G0348 | 18348 |
| G0349 | 18352 |
| G0350 | 18356 |
| G0352 | 18360 |
| G0352.5 | 18362 |
| G0356 | 18364 |
| G0358 | 18368 |
| G0360 | 18372 |
| G0362 | 18376 |
| G0364 | 18396 |
| G0365 | 18392 |
| G0366 | 18400 |
| G0367 | 18380 |
| G0367.4 | 18374 |
| G0368 | 18384 |
| G0369.5 | 18401 |
| G0372 | 18388 |
| G0374 | 18389 |
| G0376 | 18404 |
| G0380.3 | 18409 |
| G0380.32 | 18410 |
| G0381.8 | 18412 |
| G0382.25 | 18413 |
| G0382.4 | 18414 |
| G0382.5 | 18416 |
| G0384 | 18455 |
| G0385 | 18420 |
| G0385.4 | 18424 |
| G0385.41 | 18425 |
| G0386 | 18432 |
| G0386.4 | 18433 |
| G0387 | 18436 |
| G0388 | 18440 |
| G0388.4 | 18441 |
| G0388.41 | 18441.1 |
| G0388.63 | 18439.4 |
| G0388.7 | 18439.2 |
| G0388.8 | 18439 |
| G0389 | 18434 |
| G0389.1 | 18434.5 |
| G0390 | 18438 |
| G0391 | 18435 |
| G0392 | 18444 |
| G0394 | 18448 |
| G0396 | 18452 |
| G0397 | 18453 |
| G0398 | 18452.5 |
| G0398.5 | 18452.3 |
| G0402 | 18456 |
| G0404 | 18460 |
| G0406 | 18468 |
| G0408 | 18472 |
| G0409 | 18476 |
| G0409.5 | 18478 |
| G0410.9 | 18484 |
| G0411 | 18480 |
| G0411.1 | 18492 |
| G0412 | 18496 |
| G0414 | 18497 |
| G0414.2 | 18498 |
| G0414.6 | 18508 |
| G0414.8 | 18512 |
| G0415 | 18500 |
| G0415.5 | 18506 |
| G0416 | 18504 |
| G0416.3 | 18501 |
| G0416.5 | 18502 |
| G0416.8 | 18503 |
| G0417 | 18503.5 |
| G0417.5 | 18522 |
| G0418 | 18464 |
| G0419 | 18517 |
| G0419.2 | 18518 |
| G0420 | 18516 |
| G0424 | 18520 |
| G0426 | 18524 |
| G0427 | 18525 |
| G0427.5 | 18526 |
| G0428 | 18532 |
| G0429 | 18534 |
| G0430 | 18536 |
| G0431 | 18538 |
| G0431.5 | 18537 |
| G0432 | 18528 |
| G0433.5 | 18542 |
| G0434 | 18540 |
| G0435 | 18539 |
| G0439 | 18543.5 |
| G0439.2 | 18543 |
| G0440 | 18541 |
| G0448 | 18548 |
| G0450 | 18544 |
| G0454 | 18552 |
| G0458 | 18556 |
| G0459 | 18558 |
| G0462 | 18560 |
| G0464 | 18570 |
| G0466 | 18568 |
| G0468 | 18571 |
| G0470 | 18572 |
| G0472 | 18576 |
| G0474 | 18580 |
| G0475 | 18584 |
| G0476 | 18585 |
| G0476.2 | 18585.1 |
| G0476.4 | 18585.2 |
| G0476.6 | 18585.3 |
| G0476.8 | 18585.4 |
| G0477 | 18588 |
| G0478 | 18592 |
| G0479 | 18610 |
| G0480 | 18612 |
| G0484 | 18616 |
| G0486 | 18620 |
| G0490 | 18624 |
| G0492 | 18628 |
| G0495 | 18632 |
| G0496 | 18636 |
| G0497 | 18640 |
| G0498 | 18644 |
| G0498.1 | 18648 |
| G0499.1 | 18656 |
| G0500 | 18668 |
| G0501 | 18660 |
| G0501.1 | 18664 |
| G0502 | 18680 |
| G0502.2 | 18684 |
| G0502.4 | 18676 |
| G0502.5 | 18673 |
| G0502.55 | 18674 |
| G0502.6 | 18688 |
| G0503 | 18689 |
| G0503.2 | 18689.2 |
| G0504 | 18690 |
| G0506 | 18692 |
| G0509 | 18696 |
| G0512 | 18700 |
| G0513.5 | 18702 |
| G0516 | 18704 |
| G0520 | 18724 |
| G0524 | 18726 |
| G0528 | 18748 |
| G0530 | 18752 |
| G0532 | 18753 |
| G0538 | 18756 |
| G0540 | 18760 |
| G0541 | 18761 |
| G0542 | 18762 |
| G0544 | 18763 |
| G0545 | 18764 |
| G0545.4 | 18768 |
| G0545.6 | 18769 |
| G0545.7 | 18770 |
| G0546 | 18772 |
| G0548 | 18776 |
| G0548.5 | 18778 |
| G0550 | 18781 |
| G0551 | 18784 |
| G0552 | 18788 |
| G0552.4 | 18794 |
| G0554 | 18800 |
| G0555 | 18796 |
| G0555.4 | 18812 |
| G0555.45 | 18828 |
| G0555.48 | 18810 |
| G0555.5 | 18804 |
| G0555.6 | 18830 |
| G0555.7 | 18820 |
| G0555.8 | 18808 |
| G0558 | 18848 |
| G0560 | 18852 |
| G0562 | 18856 |
| G0562.5 | 18857 |
| G0563 | 18858 |
| G0564 | 18859 |
| G0566 | 18860 |
| G0570 | 18864 |
| G0572 | 18872 |
| G0578 | 18878 |
| G0580 | 18880 |
| G0582 | 18884 |
| G0584 | 18888 |
| G0588 | 18892 |
| G0591 | 18896 |
| G0592 | 18900 |
| G0594 | 18904 |
| G0596 | 18908 |
| G0598 | 18912 |
| G0599 | 18916 |
| G0600 | 18920 |
| G0602 | 18924 |
| G0604 | 18928 |
| G0605 | 18930 |
| G0606 | 18932 |
| G0607.4 | 18936 |
| G0608 | 18944 |
| G0610 | 18945 |
| G0612 | 18948 |
| G0614 | 18956 |
| G0615 | 18959.7 |
| G0616 | 18960 |
| G0618 | 18962 |
| G0620 | 18964 |
| G0622 | 18972 |
| G0624 | 18968 |
| G0625 | 18975 |
| G0625.2 | 18974 |
| G0625.4 | 18975.5 |
| G0626 | 18980 |
| G0626.2 | 18976 |
| G0626.4 | 18984 |
| G0626.6 | 18988 |
| G0627.2 | 18999 |
| G0627.4 | 18996 |
| G0627.5 | 18998 |
| G0627.6 | 18999.06 |
| G0627.8 | 18999.11 |
| G0628 | 18999.18 |
| G0628.1 | 18999.23 |
| G0628.15 | 18999.25 |
| G0628.2 | 18999.29 |
| G0628.4 | 18999.35 |
| G0628.6 | 18999.42 |
| G0628.8 | 18999.48 |
| G0629 | 18999.53 |
| G0629.1 | 18999.6 |
| G0629.2 | 18999.65 |
| G0629.3 | 18999.72 |
| G0629.4 | 18999.83 |
| G0629.5 | 18999.78 |
| G0629.6 | 18999.89 |
| G0629.7 | 18999.95 |
| G0629.8 | 18999.91 |
| G0630.2 | 18958 |
| G0630.4 | 18958.5 |
| G0630.8 | 18959 |
| G0631 | 18959.5 |
| G0631.2 | 18957 |
| G0631.4 | 18946.9 |
| G0631.6 | 18946.7 |
| G0631.8 | 18946.8 |
| G0632.15 | 18947 |
| G0632.2 | 18946.5 |
| G0632.4 | 18946.6 |
| G0633 | 18946 |
| G0634.5 | 18946.21 |
| G0636 | 19000 |
| G0639 | 19004 |
| G0640 | 19008 |

# CROSS REFERENCE - INTERNATIONAL vs. U.S. LIGHT NUMBER

| Inter. — | U.S. | Inter. — | U.S. | Inter. — | U.S. | Inter. — | U.S. |
|---|---|---|---|---|---|---|---|
| G0644 | 19012 | G0773.4 | 19307.3 | G0928 | 19488 | G1070.1 | 19710 |
| G0658 | 19016 | G0774 | 19307.5 | G0928.19 | 19496 | G1070.4 | 19712 |
| G0660 | 19020 | G0775 | 19307.6 | G0928.2 | 19497 | G1072 | 19684 |
| G0662 | 19024 | G0789 | 19284 | G0930 | 19484 | G1073 | 19672 |
| G0664 | 19028 | G0791 | 19292 | G0932 | 19504 | G1073.1 | 19676 |
| G0667 | 19030 | G0793 | 19402.3 | G0932.1 | 19508 | G1073.4 | 19680 |
| G0668 | 19032 | G0812 | 19308 | G0932.6 | 19501 | G1074 | 19668 |
| G0672 | 19036 | G0826 | 19384.5 | G0934 | 19516 | G1076 | 19728 |
| G0676 | 19040 | G0828 | 19384 | G0934.1 | 19520 | G1078 | 19736 |
| G0682 | 19044 | G0834 | 19380 | G0935 | 19524 | G1078.5 | 19737 |
| G0683 | 19056 | G0836 | 19382 | G0935.1 | 19528 | G1080 | 19740 |
| G0684 | 19048 | G0840 | 19388 | G0938 | 19532 | G1084 | 19744 |
| G0688 | 19068 | G0843 | 19383 | G0942 | 19536 | G1086 | 19748 |
| G0689.1 | 19076 | G0845 | 19401 | G0986 | 19540 | G1087 | 19752 |
| G0689.2 | 19076.5 | G0848.5 | 19402 | G0989 | 19547 | G1089 | 19760 |
| G0690 | 19080 | G0851 | 19401.5 | G0991 | 19550 | G1089.4 | 19764 |
| G0692 | 19084 | G0851.3 | 19401.7 | G0993 | 19552 | G1092 | 19768 |
| G0696 | 19104 | G0851.5 | 19401.8 | G0994 | 19554 | G1095 | 19784 |
| G0698 | 19108 | G0853 | 19402.65 | G1000 | 19560 | G1096 | 19776 |
| G0699 | 19112 | G0854 | 19402.6 | G1004 | 19564 | G1097 | 19788 |
| G0700 | 19124 | G0860 | 19402.7 | G1006 | 19568 | G1100 | 19796 |
| G0702 | 19184 | G0860.2 | 19402.8 | G1008 | 19572 | G1100.1 | 19800 |
| G0704 | 19136 | G0861.6 | 19374 | G1010 | 19572.2 | G1102 | 19804 |
| G0706 | 19140 | G0861.8 | 19375 | G1010.2 | 19572.4 | G1102.1 | 19808 |
| G0707 | 19144 | G0862 | 19376 | G1010.4 | 19572.6 | G1103 | 19810 |
| G0709 | 19152 | G0862.2 | 19377 | G1012.4 | 19573 | G1104 | 19792 |
| G0710 | 19148 | G0864 | 19373 | G1012.6 | 19573.1 | G1134 | 19912 |
| G0712 | 19156 | G0865 | 19372 | G1013.4 | 19574 | G1136 | 19916 |
| G0714 | 19160 | G0871 | 19368 | G1013.44 | 19575 | G1139 | 19920 |
| G0715 | 19164 | G0872 | 19320 | G1013.46 | 19576 | G1140 | 19924 |
| G0717 | 19126 | G0874 | 19324 | G1013.6 | 19577 | G1140.1 | 19928 |
| G0718 | 19168 | G0876 | 19332 | G1013.65 | 19577.5 | G1146 | 19932 |
| G0721 | 19169 | G0877 | 19328 | G1015.1 | 19578.4 | G1146.1 | 19936 |
| G0721.1 | 19169.1 | G0878 | 19336 | G1015.3 | 19578.3 | G1152 | 19940 |
| G0722 | 19172 | G0879 | 19340 | G1015.35 | 19578.6 | G1153 | 19944 |
| G0724 | 19173 | G0880 | 19344 | G1020 | 19580 | G1154 | 19948 |
| G0724.1 | 19174 | G0881 | 19348 | G1024 | 19584 | G1156 | 19952 |
| G0726 | 19190 | G0882 | 19350 | G1028 | 19588 | G1158 | 19956 |
| G0736 | 19196 | G0882.5 | 19351 | G1031 | 19596 | G1160 | 19960 |
| G0740 | 19200 | G0883 | 19361 | G1034 | 19599 | G1162 | 19964 |
| G0743 | 19228 | G0883.2 | 19360 | G1035 | 19601 | G1174 | 19984 |
| G0744 | 19232 | G0896 | 19316 | G1036 | 19604 | G1174.1 | 19988 |
| G0748 | 19240 | G0900 | 19403 | G1037 | 19608 | G1178 | 19992 |
| G0754 | 19257 | G0901 | 19404 | G1038 | 19598 | G1178.1 | 19996 |
| G0754.4 | 19254 | G0902 | 19408 | G1042 | 19612 | G1184 | 20000 |
| G0754.6 | 19253 | G0903 | 19406 | G1042.1 | 19616 | G1184.1 | 20004 |
| G0755 | 19258 | G0904 | 19420 | G1045 | 19626 | G1190 | 20008 |
| G0756 | 19260 | G0904.3 | 19422 | G1046.3 | 19628 | G1190.1 | 20012 |
| G0757 | 19272 | G0905 | 19412 | G1047 | 19632 | G1196 | 20016 |
| G0758 | 19276 | G0905.5 | 19421 | G1048 | 19634 | G1208 | 20032 |
| G0759 | 19268 | G0908 | 19424 | G1048.4 | 19638 | G1208.1 | 20036 |
| G0760 | 19264 | G0910 | 19428 | G1048.8 | 19636 | G1209.9 | 20028 |
| G0762 | 19280 | G0912 | 19430 | G1049 | 19640 | G1210 | 20024 |
| G0763 | 19281 | G0913 | 19472 | G1050 | 19652 | G1210.1 | 20020 |
| G0764 | 19287 | G0915 | 19436 | G1052 | 19656 | G1211 | 20040 |
| G0765 | 19290 | G0916 | 19436.5 | G1054 | 19660 | G1211.2 | 20044 |
| G0766 | 19296 | G0917 | 19437 | G1058 | 19664 | G1212 | 20048 |
| G0767 | 19300 | G0917.4 | 19469 | G1060 | 19724 | G1212.1 | 20052 |
| G0768 | 19304 | G0917.5 | 19470 | G1062 | 19720 | G1222 | 20068 |
| G0768.5 | 19302 | G0917.7 | 19468 | G1064 | 19696 | G1226 | 20072 |
| G0771 | 19305 | G0919 | 19465 | G1066 | 19688 | G1260 | 20152 |
| G0772 | 19306 | G0919.1 | 19466 | G1067 | 19698 | G1260.5 | 20156 |
| G0773 | 19307 | G0920 | 19464 | G1068 | 19700 | G1260.6 | 20157 |
| G0773.2 | 19307.1 | G0922 | 19475 | G1069 | 19702 | G1260.65 | 20158 |
| G0773.3 | 19307.2 | G0926 | 19480 | G1070 | 19708 | G1261 | 20160 |

| Inter. | U.S. |
|---|---|
| G1262 | 20192 |
| G1266 | 20196 |
| G1269 | 20216 |
| G1269.1 | 20220 |
| G1270 | 20224 |
| G1270.1 | 20228 |
| G1271 | 20232 |
| G1271.1 | 20236 |
| G1274 | 20256 |
| G1275 | 20260 |
| G1276 | 20264 |
| G1277 | 20284 |
| G1278 | 20288 |
| G1279 | 20268 |
| G1280 | 20272 |
| G1281 | 20276 |
| G1282 | 20280 |
| G1283 | 20269 |
| G1288 | 20300 |
| G1289 | 20292 |
| G1290 | 20296 |
| G1292 | 20304 |
| G1341 | 20335 |
| G1341.4 | 20335.2 |
| G1341.5 | 20335.4 |
| G1342 | 20340 |
| G1344 | 20344 |
| G1345 | 20345 |
| G1345.1 | 20346 |
| G1346 | 20348 |
| G1348 | 20352 |
| G1352 | 20336 |
| G1353 | 20353 |
| G1354 | 20357 |
| G1354.3 | 20358 |
| G1354.69 | 20358.1 |
| G1354.7 | 20358.2 |
| G1355 | 20359 |
| G1356 | 20359.1 |
| G1359 | 20361 |
| G1375 | 20362 |
| G1378 | 20363 |
| G1378.5 | 20363.2 |
| G1379 | 20363.1 |
| G1402 | 20364 |
| G1404 | 20368 |
| G917.62 | 19470.5 |
| G917.64 | 19470.7 |
| G920.2 | 19471 |
| G920.4 | 19471.2 |
| G920.6 | 19471.4 |
| H0011 | 812 |
| H0012 | 809 |
| H0012.1 | 809.5 |
| H0012.3 | 810 |
| H0012.4 | 810.1 |
| H0012.6 | 811 |
| H0012.7 | 811.5 |
| H0012.8 | 810.5 |
| H0012.81 | 810.6 |
| H0013.3 | 804 |
| H0013.4 | 800 |
| H0013.8 | 779 |
| H0013.81 | 780 |
| H0013.84 | 784 |
| H0013.85 | 788 |
| H0013.87 | 792 |
| H0013.88 | 796 |
| H0014.5 | 768 |
| H0014.51 | 772 |
| H0024 | 740 |
| H0025 | 744 |
| H0025.5 | 746 |
| H0027 | 752 |
| H0027.1 | 756 |
| H0028 | 749 |
| H0028.1 | 750 |
| H0029 | 751 |
| H0029.1 | 751.1 |
| H0032 | 716 |
| H0033 | 720 |
| H0033.4 | 724 |
| H0034 | 728 |
| H0035 | 732 |
| H0035.4 | 736 |
| H0036 | 708 |
| H0036.1 | 712 |
| H0036.4 | 714 |
| H0038 | 704 |
| H0040 | 700 |
| H0041 | 680 |
| H0042 | 676 |
| H0048 | 668 |
| H0052 | 660 |
| H0053.4 | 608 |
| H0053.41 | 612 |
| H0053.5 | 616 |
| H0054 | 620 |
| H0054.2 | 624 |
| H0054.21 | 628 |
| H0054.3 | 632 |
| H0054.31 | 636 |
| H0054.4 | 640 |
| H0054.6 | 644 |
| H0055 | 650 |
| H0055.5 | 657 |
| H0055.51 | 658 |
| H0056 | 659 |
| H0056.2 | 652 |
| H0056.21 | 656 |
| H0056.4 | 648 |
| H0058 | 601 |
| H0058.1 | 601.1 |
| H0058.4 | 602 |
| H0058.41 | 602.1 |
| H0059 | 603 |
| H0059.1 | 603.1 |
| H0059.5 | 822 |
| H0059.7 | 820.1 |
| H0060 | 820 |
| H0060.5 | 821.1 |
| H0061 | 821 |
| H0061.5 | 823 |
| H0062 | 824 |
| H0062.1 | 825 |
| H0062.15 | 825.05 |
| H0062.2 | 825.1 |
| H0062.5 | 826 |
| H0062.6 | 827 |
| H0062.7 | 827.1 |
| H0063.8 | 827.2 |
| H0064 | 828 |
| H0064.3 | 828.2 |
| H0064.4 | 828.1 |
| H0065 | 829 |
| H0066 | 830 |
| H0067 | 831 |
| H0068 | 832 |
| H0068.1 | 842.1 |
| H0068.3 | 841 |
| H0068.4 | 833 |
| H0068.42 | 834 |
| H0068.5 | 836 |
| H0068.51 | 840 |
| H0068.6 | 842 |
| H0068.8 | 843 |
| H0069 | 844 |
| H0070 | 848 |
| H0070.5 | 848.5 |
| H0071 | 849 |
| H0071.2 | 849.1 |
| H0071.24 | 850 |
| H0071.25 | 849.7 |
| H0071.26 | 849.6 |
| H0071.27 | 849.5 |
| H0071.3 | 849.4 |
| H0071.33 | 849.3 |
| H0071.34 | 849.2 |
| H0071.36 | 850.3 |
| H0071.39 | 850.8 |
| H0071.45 | 850.5 |
| H0071.48 | 851.02 |
| H0071.5 | 851 |
| H0071.53 | 851.05 |
| H0071.54 | 851.03 |
| H0071.55 | 851.07 |
| H0071.7 | 851.1 |
| H0071.8 | 854 |
| H0071.9 | 851.2 |
| H0071.91 | 855.2 |
| H0071.95 | 855 |
| H0071.97 | 855.1 |
| H0071.98 | 855.3 |
| H0072 | 852 |
| H0073 | 857 |
| H0074 | 856 |
| H0074.2 | 858 |
| H0074.5 | 860 |
| H0074.7 | 864 |
| H0075 | 868 |
| H0075.5 | 872 |
| H0075.55 | 873 |
| H0075.6 | 876 |
| H0075.65 | 874 |
| H0075.7 | 888 |
| H0075.8 | 884 |
| H0075.9 | 880 |
| H0076 | 892 |
| H0076.2 | 894 |
| H0076.3 | 910 |
| H0076.4 | 896 |
| H0076.5 | 900 |
| H0077 | 904 |
| H0077.1 | 908 |
| H0078 | 912 |
| H0079 | 914 |
| H0079.5 | 915.2 |
| H0079.7 | 913 |
| H0080 | 916 |
| H0081 | 920 |
| H0082 | 924 |
| H0084 | 928 |
| H0085 | 932 |
| H0085.5 | 934 |
| H0085.7 | 933 |
| H0086 | 936 |
| H0086.4 | 940 |
| H0086.6 | 944 |
| H0086.65 | 938 |
| H0086.7 | 945 |
| H0086.8 | 946 |
| H0087 | 948 |
| H0088 | 960 |
| H0088.1 | 964 |
| H0089 | 952 |
| H0089.1 | 956 |
| H0089.5 | 966 |
| H0089.7 | 967 |
| H0089.8 | 967.2 |
| H0090 | 972 |
| H0091 | 967.3 |
| H0092 | 968 |
| H0093 | 974 |
| H0094 | 976 |
| H0096 | 984 |
| H0102 | 988 |
| H0104 | 992 |
| H0108 | 980 |
| H0110 | 1000 |
| H0112.55 | 1009 |
| H0112.6 | 1010 |
| H0114 | 1012 |
| H0116 | 1016 |
| H0117 | 2740.5 |
| H0122 | 1020 |
| H0122.1 | 1024 |
| H0123 | 1028 |
| H0124 | 2752 |
| H0124.1 | 2756 |
| H0132 | 1052 |
| H0135 | 1044 |
| H0135.1 | 1048 |
| H0136 | 1040 |
| H0137 | 1038 |
| H0138 | 1036 |
| H0140 | 1032 |
| H0141 | 2737 |
| H0141.2 | 2739 |
| H0141.7 | 2722 |
| H0142 | 2736 |
| H0143 | 2728 |
| H0143.1 | 2732 |
| H0144 | 2724 |
| H0144.5 | 2720 |
| H0145 | 2716 |
| H0145.7 | 2717 |
| H0145.71 | 2718 |
| H0146.5 | 2714 |
| H0148 | 2704 |
| H0150 | 2700 |

| Inter. | U.S. |
|---|---|
| H0152 | 2688 |
| H0152.5 | 2692 |
| H0152.51 | 2696 |
| H0154 | 2680 |
| H0156 | 2668 |
| H0161 | 2660 |
| H0164 | 2640 |
| H0168 | 2644 |
| H0169 | 2648 |
| H0170 | 2652 |
| H0175 | 2636 |
| H0178 | 2616 |
| H0179 | 2620 |
| H0179.5 | 2634 |
| H0180 | 2632 |
| H0186 | 2628 |
| H0188 | 2624 |
| H0190 | 2608 |
| H0192 | 2604 |
| H0194 | 2600 |
| H0195 | 2596 |
| H0196 | 2568 |
| H0197 | 2572 |
| H0197.2 | 2576 |
| H0198 | 2580 |
| H0201 | 2592 |
| H0202 | 2560 |
| H0205 | 2536 |
| H0205.08 | 2537 |
| H0205.2 | 2548 |
| H0206 | 2540 |
| H0206.1 | 2544 |
| H0208 | 2516 |
| H0210 | 2520 |
| H0214 | 2524 |
| H0214.2 | 2534 |
| H0214.3 | 2535 |
| H0218 | 2504 |
| H0219 | 2496 |
| H0220 | 2492 |
| H0222 | 2468 |
| H0222.4 | 2469 |
| H0222.6 | 2469.5 |
| H0223 | 2484 |
| H0223.1 | 2488 |
| H0224 | 2472 |
| H0226 | 2476 |
| H0227 | 2480 |
| H0230 | 2460 |
| H0232 | 2452 |
| H0232.4 | 2456 |
| H0234 | 2428 |
| H0234.1 | 2432 |
| H0238 | 2436 |
| H0242.5 | 2418 |
| H0244 | 2420 |
| H0250 | 2408 |
| H0252 | 2404 |
| H0254 | 2400 |
| H0258 | 2396 |
| H0259 | 2395 |
| H0260 | 2392 |
| H0262 | 2394 |
| H0263 | 2390 |
| H0264 | 2380 |
| H0264.4 | 2381 |
| H0265 | 2376 |
| H0266 | 2368 |
| H0268 | 2364 |
| H0270 | 2360 |
| H0272 | 2358 |
| H0275 | 2356 |
| H0276 | 2352 |
| H0277 | 2344 |
| H0278 | 2348 |
| H0282 | 2347 |
| H0283 | 2349 |
| H0286 | 2320 |
| H0286.1 | 2324 |
| H0286.5 | 2328 |
| H0287 | 2340 |
| H0288 | 2332 |
| H0289 | 2336 |
| H0290 | 2312 |
| H0294 | 2316 |
| H0296 | 2306 |
| H0298 | 2304 |
| H0300 | 2300 |
| H0302 | 2296 |
| H0304 | 2292 |
| H0308 | 2288 |
| H0309 | 2286 |
| H0310 | 2284 |
| H0312 | 2280 |
| H0313 | 2268 |
| H0314 | 2272 |
| H0318 | 2264 |
| H0318.2 | 2265 |
| H0320 | 2244 |
| H0321 | 2260 |
| H0322 | 2248 |
| H0323..3 | 2240 |
| H0323.4 | 2241 |
| H0324 | 2236 |
| H0325 | 2228 |
| H0328 | 2212 |
| H0329 | 2216 |
| H0330 | 2208 |
| H0332 | 2160 |
| H0338 | 2172 |
| H0341 | 2184 |
| H0341.2 | 2188 |
| H0342 | 2192 |
| H0343 | 2193 |
| H0345 | 2180 |
| H0345.2 | 2181 |
| H0348 | 2156 |
| H0350 | 2140 |
| H0352 | 2144 |
| H0352.1 | 2148 |
| H0356 | 2136 |
| H0360 | 2128 |
| H0362 | 2124 |
| H0364 | 2120 |
| H0367 | 2116 |
| H0368 | 2108 |
| H0370 | 2104 |
| H0372 | 2100 |
| H0372.4 | 2096 |
| H0373 | 2092 |
| H0375 | 2084 |
| H0377 | 2080 |
| H0379.4 | 2076 |
| H0379.7 | 2072 |
| H0380 | 2068 |
| H0381 | 2065 |
| H0382 | 2064 |
| H0383 | 2066 |
| H0384 | 2058 |
| H0386 | 2060 |
| H0387 | 2057 |
| H0388 | 2040 |
| H0390 | 2032 |
| H0392 | 2036 |
| H0394 | 2020 |
| H0394.5 | 2024 |
| H0394.51 | 2028 |
| H0395 | 2022 |
| H0395.2 | 2022.1 |
| H0395.4 | 2021.2 |
| H0395.41 | 2021 |
| H0395.42 | 2021.1 |
| H0395.5 | 2021.3 |
| H0395.51 | 2021.4 |
| H0397 | 2044 |
| H0397.5 | 2042 |
| H0398 | 2048 |
| H0399 | 2052 |
| H0400 | 2056 |
| H0400.4 | 2012 |
| H0410 | 2004 |
| H0410.1 | 2008 |
| H0422 | 1960 |
| H0424 | 1964 |
| H0424.1 | 1968 |
| H0429 | 1954 |
| H0429.5 | 1955 |
| H0430 | 1956 |
| H0432 | 1952 |
| H0433 | 1940 |
| H0434 | 1936 |
| H0435 | 1934 |
| H0436 | 1932 |
| H0438 | 1924 |
| H0440 | 1920 |
| H0442 | 1908 |
| H0443 | 1912 |
| H0443.2 | 1916 |
| H0444 | 1904 |
| H0448 | 1884 |
| H0449 | 1880 |
| H0450 | 1876 |
| H0451 | 1874 |
| H0452 | 1872 |
| H0454 | 1868 |
| H0458 | 1848 |
| H0458.4 | 1852 |
| H0459 | 1860 |
| H0459.1 | 1864 |
| H0460 | 1856 |
| H0462.2 | 1866.5 |
| H0468 | 1844 |
| H0470 | 1836 |
| H0471 | 1840 |
| H0472 | 1824 |
| H0473 | 1828 |
| H0473.1 | 1832 |
| H0474 | 1820 |
| H0474.4 | 1807 |
| H0474.42 | 1806 |
| H0474.7 | 1812 |
| H0474.71 | 1816 |
| H0475 | 1796 |
| H0476 | 1804 |
| H0477 | 1800 |
| H0478 | 1788 |
| H0479 | 1792 |
| H0480.2 | 1786 |
| H0482 | 1784 |
| H0482.5 | 1780 |
| H0483 | 1776 |
| H0484 | 1760 |
| H0486.2 | 1773 |
| H0486.3 | 1774 |
| H0487 | 1768 |
| H0490 | 1752 |
| H0492 | 1756 |
| H0494 | 1744 |
| H0495 | 1749 |
| H0498 | 1736 |
| H0500 | 1740 |
| H0500.5 | 1734 |
| H0501 | 1735 |
| H0502 | 1732 |
| H0503 | 1733 |
| H0503.2 | 1733.1 |
| H0503.3 | 1733.2 |
| H0504 | 1728 |
| H0504.4 | 1730 |
| H0506 | 1724 |
| H0508 | 1720 |
| H0510 | 1716 |
| H0510.5 | 1717 |
| H0511 | 1714 |
| H0511.5 | 1711 |
| H0512 | 1712 |
| H0513 | 1710 |
| H0513.7 | 1705 |
| H0514 | 1704 |
| H0514.5 | 1706 |
| H0515 | 1708 |
| H0516.5 | 1702 |
| H0518 | 1700 |
| H0520 | 1696 |
| H0522 | 1692 |
| H0526 | 1648 |
| H0526.5 | 1652 |
| H0527 | 1660 |
| H0527.1 | 1664 |
| H0528 | 1668 |
| H0530 | 1672 |
| H0530.1 | 1676 |
| H0531 | 1680 |
| H0536 | 1644 |
| H0537 | 1632 |
| H0538 | 1636 |
| H0539 | 1640 |
| H0540 | 1620 |
| H0543 | 1608 |
| H0543.5 | 1594 |

# CROSS REFERENCE - INTERNATIONAL vs. U.S. LIGHT NUMBER

| Inter. | U.S. |
|---|---|
| H0544 | 1610 |
| H0545 | 1612 |
| H0546 | 1595 |
| H0547 | 1604 |
| H0547.4 | 1598 |
| H0548 | 1592 |
| H0549 | 1600 |
| H0554 | 1588 |
| H0554.6 | 1584 |
| H0555 | 1580 |
| H0556 | 1556 |
| H0558 | 1560 |
| H0560 | 1572 |
| H0560.2 | 1576 |
| H0561 | 1564 |
| H0561.1 | 1568 |
| H0562 | 1552 |
| H0563 | 1536 |
| H0563.1 | 1540 |
| H0563.4 | 1544 |
| H0563.6 | 1548 |
| H0566 | 1524 |
| H0567 | 1528 |
| H0570 | 1508 |
| H0576 | 1496 |
| H0578 | 1492 |
| H0580 | 1484 |
| H0582 | 1472 |
| H0582.1 | 1476 |
| H0583 | 1478 |
| H0583.2 | 1479 |
| H0584 | 1440 |
| H0586 | 1444 |
| H0588 | 1464 |
| H0591 | 1452 |
| H0594 | 1460 |
| H0596 | 1448 |
| H0597 | 1436 |
| H0599 | 1424 |
| H0599.1 | 1428 |
| H0600 | 1432 |
| H0601 | 1420 |
| H0605 | 1412 |
| H0606 | 1416 |
| H0606.5 | 1410 |
| H0607 | 1408 |
| H0608 | 1404 |
| H0612 | 1400 |
| H0613 | 1402 |
| H0614 | 1352 |
| H0616 | 1388 |
| H0617 | 1376 |
| H0617.4 | 1380 |
| H0617.5 | 1384 |
| H0617.6 | 1386 |
| H0618 | 1360 |
| H0619 | 1372 |
| H0620 | 1356 |
| H0622 | 1396 |
| H0623 | 1392 |
| H0623.5 | 1390 |
| H0624 | 1336 |
| H0625 | 1326 |
| H0626 | 1332 |
| H0627 | 1333 |
| H0627.1 | 1334 |
| H0628 | 1340 |
| H0629 | 1344 |
| H0629.1 | 1348 |
| H0630 | 1316 |
| H0632 | 1320 |
| H0634 | 1324 |
| H0635 | 1302 |
| H0636 | 1300 |
| H0638 | 1312 |
| H0640 | 1272 |
| H0642 | 1278 |
| H0644 | 1276 |
| H0645 | 1280 |
| H0648 | 1284 |
| H0650 | 1288 |
| H0651 | 1293 |
| H0651.2 | 1294 |
| H0651.6 | 1296 |
| H0652 | 1264 |
| H0654 | 1268 |
| H0654.5 | 1268.1 |
| H0654.9 | 1271 |
| H0655.1 | 1270 |
| H0655.15 | 1269 |
| H0656 | 1240 |
| H0658 | 1244 |
| H0660 | 1248 |
| H0664 | 1252 |
| H0666 | 1256 |
| H0668 | 1260 |
| H0670 | 1236 |
| H0670.5 | 1228 |
| H0671.5 | 1224 |
| H0672 | 1220 |
| H0674 | 1216 |
| H0674.2 | 1186 |
| H0674.4 | 1218 |
| H0675 | 1212 |
| H0677 | 1200 |
| H0677.6 | 1204 |
| H0678 | 1208 |
| H0679 | 1188 |
| H0679.2 | 1192 |
| H0679.3 | 1196 |
| H0679.5 | 1198 |
| H0680 | 1184 |
| H0680.4 | 1206 |
| H0680.7 | 1185 |
| H0681 | 1176 |
| H0682 | 1178 |
| H0682.5 | 1182 |
| H0683 | 1180 |
| H0686 | 1172 |
| H0692 | 1168 |
| H0692.4 | 1169 |
| H0693 | 1156 |
| H0694 | 1160 |
| H0694.5 | 1164 |
| H0696 | 1152 |
| H0697.7 | 1150 |
| H0698 | 1148 |
| H0702 | 1144 |
| H0704 | 1140 |
| H0705 | 1136 |
| H0707 | 1132 |
| H0708 | 1128 |
| H0710 | 1124 |
| H0712 | 1120 |
| H0716 | 1116 |
| H0718 | 1100 |
| H0718.4 | 1104 |
| H0719 | 1108 |
| H0720 | 1112 |
| H0721 | 1092 |
| H0722 | 1096 |
| H0724 | 1084 |
| H0725 | 1080 |
| H0726 | 1088 |
| H0728 | 1076 |
| H0730 | 1068 |
| H0732 | 1064 |
| H0734 | 1072 |
| H0736 | 1060 |
| H0742 | 9164 |
| H0744 | 9168 |
| H0745 | 9172 |
| H0745.4 | 9184 |
| H0745.6 | 9180 |
| H0745.8 | 9182 |
| H0746 | 9160 |
| H0750 | 9156 |
| H0752 | 9148 |
| H0752.1 | 9152 |
| H0756 | 9144 |
| H0757.5 | 9132 |
| H0757.51 | 9136 |
| H0758 | 9100 |
| H0760 | 9112 |
| H0761 | 9104 |
| H0761.1 | 9108 |
| H0762.6 | 9120 |
| H0764 | 9124 |
| H0764.1 | 9128 |
| H0766.2 | 9131 |
| H0767 | 9130 |
| H0770 | 9080 |
| H0772 | 9092 |
| H0772.1 | 9096 |
| H0774 | 9098 |
| H0778 | 8916 |
| H0779 | 8920 |
| H0782 | 8932 |
| H0782.1 | 8936 |
| H0784 | 8948 |
| H0786 | 8952 |
| H0792 | 8981 |
| H0792.1 | 8982 |
| H0796 | 8983 |
| H0796.1 | 8983.1 |
| H0798 | 8984 |
| H0800 | 8996 |
| H0801 | 9000 |
| H0802 | 9020 |
| H0802.1 | 9024 |
| H0803 | 9012 |
| H0803.1 | 9016 |
| H0804.4 | 9028 |
| H0804.41 | 9032 |
| H0806 | 9040 |
| H0818 | 9052 |
| H0822 | 9056 |
| H0832 | 9057 |
| H0833 | 9058 |
| H0838 | 9060 |
| H0839 | 9064 |
| H0842 | 9068 |
| H0843 | 9072 |
| H0856 | 8904 |
| H0857.5 | 8902 |
| H0857.51 | 8903 |
| H0865.1 | 8893 |
| H0866 | 8880 |
| H0870 | 8864 |
| H0870.4 | 8868 |
| H0872 | 8848 |
| H0873 | 8840 |
| H0873.2 | 8844 |
| H0874 | 8832 |
| H0876 | 8852 |
| H0878 | 8856 |
| H0882 | 8432 |
| H0886 | 8424 |
| H0888 | 8444 |
| H0888.1 | 8448 |
| H0896 | 8472 |
| H0902 | 8464 |
| H0903 | 8423 |
| H0903.5 | 8423.5 |
| H0907.5 | 8402 |
| H0909 | 8484 |
| H0910 | 8490 |
| H0913.4 | 8420 |
| H0913.5 | 8422 |
| H0914 | 8470 |
| H0914.1 | 8470.1 |
| H0915 | 8471 |
| H0915.4 | 8469 |
| H0920 | 8072 |
| H0922 | 8084 |
| H0924 | 8088 |
| H0925 | 8100 |
| H0928 | 8092 |
| H0928.1 | 8096 |
| H0930 | 8104 |
| H0931 | 8106 |
| H0932 | 8108 |
| H0936 | 8112 |
| H0936.1 | 8116 |
| H0939 | 8120 |
| H0949 | 8128 |
| H0949.2 | 8132 |
| H0950 | 8156 |
| H0954 | 8140 |
| H0954.1 | 8144 |
| H0956 | 8148 |
| H0962 | 8164 |
| H0978 | 8184 |
| H0978.1 | 8188 |
| H0982 | 8192 |
| H0996 | 8216 |
| H0998 | 8220 |
| H1006 | 8228 |
| H1006.1 | 8232 |
| H1008 | 8236 |

# CROSS REFERENCE - INTERNATIONAL vs. U.S. LIGHT NUMBER

| Inter. | U.S. |
|---|---|
| H1012 | 8240 |
| H1012.1 | 8244 |
| H1016 | 8248 |
| H1016.1 | 8252 |
| H1018 | 8253 |
| H1024 | 8260 |
| H1039 | 8292 |
| H1039.4 | 8306 |
| H1039.5 | 8306.1 |
| H1039.6 | 8306.2 |
| H1039.7 | 8306.3 |
| H1039.8 | 8306.4 |
| H1044 | 8304 |
| H1045 | 8310 |
| H1046 | 8308 |
| H1048 | 8316 |
| H1049 | 8830 |
| H1049.1 | 8831 |
| H1050 | 8320 |
| H1050.1 | 8324 |
| H1054 | 8318 |
| H1056 | 8328 |
| H1057 | 8332 |
| H1057.5 | 8336 |
| H1058 | 8340 |
| H1058.1 | 8344 |
| H1060 | 8356 |
| H1062 | 8360 |
| H1068 | 8376 |
| H1068.1 | 8380 |
| H1072 | 8384 |
| H1072.1 | 8388 |
| H1074 | 7851.5 |
| H1074.4 | 7851 |
| H1076 | 7852 |
| H1078 | 7856 |
| H1081.4 | 7865 |
| H1094 | 7892 |
| H1094.1 | 7896 |
| H1116 | 7912 |
| H1116.1 | 7916 |
| H1124 | 7944 |
| H1129 | 7948 |
| H1130.05 | 7956 |
| H1140 | 7968 |
| H1141 | 7972 |
| H1142 | 7976 |
| H1149 | 7992 |
| H1150 | 7996 |
| H1156 | 8000 |
| H1160 | 8020 |
| H1168 | 8036 |
| H1170.3 | 8052 |
| H1170.4 | 8048 |
| H1173 | 8060 |
| H1173.1 | 8064 |
| H1174 | 8065 |
| H1176.4 | 8825 |
| H1176.5 | 8818 |
| H1182 | 8804 |
| H1182.1 | 8808 |
| H1188 | 8800 |
| H1189 | 8798 |
| H1194 | 8796 |
| H1196 | 8780 |
| H1196.1 | 8784 |
| H1196.5 | 8778 |
| H1197.5 | 8792 |
| H1202 | 8764 |
| H1202.1 | 8768 |
| H1202.3 | 8776 |
| H1202.4 | 8776.1 |
| H1208 | 8760 |
| H1210 | 8752 |
| H1210.1 | 8756 |
| H1210.5 | 8757 |
| H1216.1 | 8748 |
| H1218 | 8736 |
| H1222 | 8720 |
| H1223 | 8740 |
| H1223.2 | 8718 |
| H1224 | 8724 |
| H1228 | 8716 |
| H1230 | 8688 |
| H1230.1 | 8692 |
| H1231 | 8684 |
| H1232 | 8676 |
| H1232.3 | 8672 |
| H1232.35 | 8671 |
| H1232.5 | 8668 |
| H1234 | 8664 |
| H1234.5 | 8662 |
| H1236 | 8652 |
| H1236.3 | 8653 |
| H1236.4 | 8654 |
| H1237 | 8608 |
| H1238 | 8596 |
| H1238.5 | 8600 |
| H1240 | 8604 |
| H1244 | 8612 |
| H1248.05 | 8616 |
| H1248.1 | 8617 |
| H1256 | 8620 |
| H1256.1 | 8624 |
| H1260.5 | 8634 |
| H1264 | 8640 |
| H1264.1 | 8644 |
| H1270 | 8584 |
| H1270.1 | 8588 |
| H1272 | 8576 |
| H1273 | 8568 |
| H1274 | 8560 |
| H1276 | 8564 |
| H1283 | 8554 |
| H1291 | 8536 |
| H1291.1 | 8540 |
| H1292 | 8512 |
| H1292.1 | 8516 |
| H1296 | 8520 |
| H1296.1 | 8524 |
| H1300 | 8528 |
| H1300.1 | 8532 |
| H1304 | 7844 |
| H1308 | 7824 |
| H1313 | 7812 |
| H1314 | 7819 |
| H1316 | 7816 |
| H1319 | 7784 |
| H1319.2 | 7786 |
| H1322 | 7774 |
| H1323 | 7772 |
| H1324 | 7764 |
| H1324.4 | 7768 |
| H1325.1 | 7756 |
| H1326 | 7766 |
| H1328 | 7736 |
| H1328.1 | 7740 |
| H1332 | 7744 |
| H1332.1 | 7748 |
| H1334 | 7750 |
| H1348 | 7728 |
| H1350 | 7724 |
| H1352 | 7720 |
| H1354 | 7708 |
| H1354.1 | 7712 |
| H1359 | 7703 |
| H1360 | 7700 |
| H1362 | 7680 |
| H1368 | 7692 |
| H1368.1 | 7696 |
| H1369 | 7686 |
| H1372 | 7668 |
| H1374 | 7664 |
| H1375 | 7665 |
| H1375.1 | 7666 |
| H1376 | 7660 |
| H1378 | 7656 |
| H1394 | 7632 |
| H1394.1 | 7636 |
| H1400 | 7640 |
| H1400.1 | 7644 |
| H1402 | 7648 |
| H1402.1 | 7652 |
| H1418.2 | 7592 |
| H1418.5 | 7598 |
| H1419 | 7597 |
| H1424 | 7580 |
| H1430 | 7581 |
| H1440 | 7485 |
| H1440.1 | 7486 |
| H1442 | 7469 |
| H1442.1 | 7470 |
| H1446 | 7480 |
| H1446.1 | 7484 |
| H1452 | 7498 |
| H1452.1 | 7499 |
| H1464 | 7496 |
| H1472 | 7500 |
| H1472.1 | 7504 |
| H1477 | 7508 |
| H1477.1 | 7512 |
| H1478 | 7516 |
| H1478.1 | 7520 |
| H1479 | 7521 |
| H1479.1 | 7522 |
| H1491 | 7532 |
| H1491.1 | 7536 |
| H1492 | 7553 |
| H1492.1 | 7554 |
| H1493 | 7540 |
| H1493.1 | 7544 |
| H1494 | 7548 |
| H1494.1 | 7552 |
| H1496 | 7556 |
| H1496.1 | 7560 |
| H1505 | 7564 |
| H1505.2 | 7568 |
| H1507 | 7572 |
| H1507.1 | 7576 |
| H1514 | 7452 |
| H1515 | 7450 |
| H1517 | 7444 |
| H1520.5 | 7428 |
| H1521 | 7424 |
| H1525 | 7436 |
| H1530 | 7392 |
| H1531 | 7396 |
| H1535 | 7335 |
| H1542 | 7380 |
| H1542.5 | 7382 |
| H1550 | 7376 |
| H1551 | 7374 |
| H1552 | 7368 |
| H1556 | 7360 |
| H1559 | 7358 |
| H1562 | 7356 |
| H1564 | 7402 |
| H1564.2 | 7354 |
| H1566 | 7308 |
| H1567 | 7312 |
| H1567.1 | 7316 |
| H1567.3 | 7328 |
| H1567.31 | 7332 |
| H1567.36 | 7400 |
| H1567.37 | 7400.1 |
| H1568 | 7320 |
| H1568.1 | 7324 |
| H1580 | 7276 |
| H1580.1 | 7280 |
| H1581.5 | 7291 |
| H1581.51 | 7291.1 |
| H1581.7 | 7273 |
| H1581.71 | 7274 |
| H1582 | 7284 |
| H1582.4 | 7288 |
| H1583 | 7300 |
| H1584 | 7304 |
| H1585 | 7305 |
| H1585.1 | 7306 |
| H1588 | 7272 |
| H1590 | 7264 |
| H1591.4 | 7256 |
| H1591.41 | 7260 |
| H1591.6 | 7252 |
| H1591.8 | 7254 |
| H1596 | 7240 |
| H1596.2 | 7241 |
| H1600 | 7204 |
| H1600.1 | 7208 |
| H1606 | 7196 |
| H1608 | 7194 |
| H1608.4 | 7192 |
| H1609 | 7184 |
| H1610 | 7188 |
| H1612 | 7176 |
| H1616 | 7164 |
| H1616.1 | 7168 |
| H1618 | 7140 |
| H1619 | 7144 |
| H1619.1 | 7148 |

# CROSS REFERENCE - INTERNATIONAL vs. U.S. LIGHT NUMBER

| Inter. | U.S. |
|---|---|
| H1620 | 7152 |
| H1620.4 | 7156 |
| H1620.41 | 7160 |
| H1633 | 7136 |
| H1638 | 7108 |
| H1640 | 7112 |
| H1655 | 7097 |
| H1655.1 | 7098 |
| H1665 | 7093 |
| H1666 | 7092 |
| H1674 | 7080 |
| H1680 | 7072 |
| H1686 | 7068 |
| H1687 | 7066 |
| H1687.1 | 7067 |
| H1700 | 7060 |
| H1701 | 7052 |
| H1701.1 | 7056 |
| H1703 | 7032 |
| H1704 | 7040 |
| H1704.1 | 7044 |
| H1706 | 7036 |
| H1708 | 7038 |
| H1718 | 7004 |
| H1727 | 6988 |
| H1738 | 6980 |
| H1740 | 6978 |
| H1740.1 | 6979 |
| H1752.2 | 6972 |
| H1752.4 | 6976 |
| H1754 | 6960 |
| H1754.1 | 6964 |
| H1756 | 6956 |
| H1757 | 6953 |
| H1762 | 6944 |
| H1768 | 6936 |
| H1770 | 6940 |
| H1782 | 6914 |
| H1798 | 6906 |
| H1800 | 6900 |
| H1808 | 6884 |
| H1808.1 | 6888 |
| H1811 | 6892 |
| H1826 | 6872 |
| H1828 | 6868 |
| H1830 | 6856 |
| H1830.1 | 6860 |
| H1842 | 6848 |
| H1846 | 6840 |
| H1846.1 | 6844 |
| H1852 | 6836 |
| H1853 | 6838 |
| H1854 | 6837 |
| H1864 | 3132 |
| H1866 | 3136 |
| H1870 | 3144 |
| H1870.1 | 3148 |
| H1878 | 3160 |
| H1882 | 3164 |
| H1884 | 3168 |
| H1886 | 3172 |
| H1887 | 2776 |
| H1887.1 | 2780 |
| H1889.5 | 2800 |
| H1889.7 | 2801 |
| H1889.71 | 2802 |
| H1889.8 | 2804 |
| H1890 | 2772 |
| H1890.1 | 2808 |
| H1890.2 | 2812 |
| H1890.42 | 2816 |
| H1890.44 | 2820 |
| H1890.45 | 2824 |
| H1890.5 | 2828 |
| H1890.6 | 2832 |
| H1890.61 | 2836 |
| H1890.63 | 2829 |
| H1890.7 | 2837 |
| H1890.71 | 2838 |
| H1890.74 | 2839 |
| H1890.75 | 2839.5 |
| H1890.77 | 2830 |
| H1890.8 | 2844 |
| H1891 | 2852 |
| H1891.2 | 2856 |
| H1891.3 | 2860 |
| H1891.5 | 2864 |
| H1891.6 | 2868 |
| H1892 | 2848 |
| H1894 | 2840 |
| H1896 | 2876 |
| H1896.1 | 2880 |
| H1898 | 2872 |
| H1899 | 2884 |
| H1899.1 | 2888 |
| H1899.4 | 2900 |
| H1899.5 | 2904 |
| H1899.7 | 2892 |
| H1899.8 | 2896 |
| H1899.9 | 2908 |
| H1900 | 2916 |
| H1900.4 | 2920 |
| H1901 | 2912 |
| H1902 | 2924 |
| H1902.1 | 2928 |
| H1903 | 2936 |
| H1904 | 2932 |
| H1906 | 2940 |
| H1907 | 2948 |
| H1907.1 | 2952 |
| H1908 | 2988 |
| H1909 | 2956 |
| H1909.1 | 2960 |
| H1909.7 | 2976 |
| H1909.71 | 2980 |
| H1909.8 | 2968 |
| H1909.81 | 2972 |
| H1910 | 2996 |
| H1910.1 | 3000 |
| H1910.4 | 2994 |
| H1911 | 2992 |
| H1914 | 3008 |
| H1918 | 3012 |
| H1918.1 | 3016 |
| H1922 | 3020 |
| H1922.1 | 3024 |
| H1928 | 3028 |
| H1928.1 | 3032 |
| H1930 | 3036 |
| H1930.1 | 3040 |
| H1933 | 3046 |
| H1934 | 3048 |
| H1936 | 3052 |
| H1936.1 | 3056 |
| H1940 | 3088 |
| H1940.1 | 3092 |
| H1943 | 3080 |
| H1943.1 | 3084 |
| H1944 | 3104 |
| H1946 | 3108 |
| H1946.1 | 3112 |
| H1950 | 3116 |
| H1950.1 | 3120 |
| H1958 | 3124 |
| H1974 | 3184 |
| H1974.1 | 3188 |
| H1975 | 3176 |
| H1978 | 3192 |
| H1990 | 3196 |
| H1991 | 3216 |
| H1992 | 3220 |
| H1992.5 | 3224 |
| H1993 | 3228 |
| H1994 | 3200 |
| H1994.1 | 3204 |
| H1994.2 | 3208 |
| H1994.3 | 3209 |
| H1994.34 | 3209.5 |
| H1994.37 | 3211 |
| H1994.4 | 3212 |
| H1994.6 | 3234 |
| H1994.61 | 3234.1 |
| H1997.4 | 3244 |
| H1997.41 | 3248 |
| H1997.5 | 3249 |
| H1997.6 | 3249.5 |
| H1997.8 | 3250 |
| H1997.81 | 3251 |
| H1999 | 3272 |
| H1999.1 | 3276 |
| H2000 | 3264 |
| H2001 | 3268 |
| H2002 | 3256 |
| H2002.1 | 3260 |
| H2010 | 3280 |
| H2027 | 3298 |
| H2031 | 6824 |
| H2032 | 6828 |
| H2041.2 | 6817 |
| H2041.3 | 6818 |
| H2042 | 6816 |
| H2043 | 6812 |
| H2044 | 6820 |
| H2048 | 6800 |
| H2050 | 3304 |
| H2050.5 | 3308 |
| H2050.6 | 3312 |
| H2051 | 3316 |
| H2051.1 | 3320 |
| H2052 | 3321 |
| H2052.1 | 3322 |
| H2054 | 3324 |
| H2055 | 3325 |
| H2056 | 3336 |
| H2063 | 3348 |
| H2064 | 3360 |
| H2066 | 3364 |
| H2066.1 | 3368 |
| H2072 | 6776 |
| H2074 | 6780 |
| H2074.1 | 6784 |
| H2084 | 6768 |
| H2086 | 6764 |
| H2088 | 3380 |
| H2090 | 3388 |
| H2090.1 | 3392 |
| H2093 | 3396 |
| H2096 | 6752 |
| H2098 | 6744 |
| H2098.1 | 6748 |
| H2104 | 3432 |
| H2106 | 3436 |
| H2108 | 3456 |
| H2112 | 3464 |
| H2112.1 | 3468 |
| H2113 | 3472 |
| H2115 | 3460 |
| H2118 | 3480 |
| H2122 | 3484 |
| H2124 | 3488 |
| H2126 | 3500 |
| H2128 | 3496 |
| H2130 | 3492 |
| H2131 | 3504 |
| H2133 | 3508 |
| H2136 | 3516 |
| H2138 | 3520 |
| H2140 | 3524 |
| H2142 | 3532 |
| H2142.2 | 3536 |
| H2142.3 | 3540 |
| H2142.31 | 3544 |
| H2142.8 | 3564 |
| H2143 | 3568 |
| H2143.1 | 3572 |
| H2143.3 | 3584 |
| H2143.31 | 3588 |
| H2143.4 | 3592 |
| H2143.5 | 3596 |
| H2143.6 | 3608 |
| H2143.7 | 3612 |
| H2143.9 | 3616 |
| H2143.91 | 3620 |
| H2144 | 3632 |
| H2144.1 | 3636 |
| H2145 | 3640 |
| H2146 | 6724 |
| H2148 | 6732 |
| H2160 | 6715.1 |
| H2160.1 | 6715.2 |
| H2160.5 | 6714 |
| H2160.6 | 6715 |
| H2162 | 6692 |
| H2164 | 6684 |
| H2166 | 3652 |
| H2167 | 3662 |
| H2168 | 3656 |
| H2172 | 6664 |
| H2174 | 6652 |
| H2182 | 3660 |

# CROSS REFERENCE - INTERNATIONAL vs. U.S. LIGHT NUMBER

| Inter. | U.S. |
|---|---|
| H2186 | 3668 |
| H2187 | 3670 |
| H2194 | 3676 |
| H2202 | 3680 |
| H2204 | 3684 |
| H2206 | 3696 |
| H2208 | 3700 |
| H2218 | 3688 |
| H2218.1 | 3692 |
| H2226 | 6600 |
| H2228 | 6584 |
| H2238.2 | 6546 |
| H2244 | 6552 |
| H2244.1 | 6556 |
| H2246 | 6540 |
| H2250 | 6528 |
| H2250.1 | 6532 |
| H2254 | 3728 |
| H2255 | 3740 |
| H2255.1 | 3744 |
| H2256 | 3756 |
| H2256.1 | 3760 |
| H2259 | 3772 |
| H2261 | 3748 |
| H2261.1 | 3752 |
| H2262 | 3776 |
| H2262.1 | 3780 |
| H2267 | 3801 |
| H2267.1 | 3802 |
| H2272 | 6512 |
| H2274 | 3836 |
| H2274.1 | 3840 |
| H2278 | 3812 |
| H2282 | 3848 |
| H2284 | 3852 |
| H2285 | 3860 |
| H2285.1 | 3864 |
| H2286 | 3868 |
| H2286.1 | 3872 |
| H2288 | 3876 |
| H2290 | 3884 |
| H2290.1 | 3888 |
| H2293 | 3900 |
| H2294 | 3932 |
| H2294.1 | 3936 |
| H2300 | 3924 |
| H2300.1 | 3928 |
| H2310 | 3940 |
| H2310.1 | 3942 |
| H2321 | 3988 |
| H2323 | 4004 |
| H2323.1 | 4008 |
| H2323.3 | 4012 |
| H2323.4 | 4016 |
| H2324 | 4020 |
| H2326 | 4028 |
| H2328 | 4029 |
| H2330 | 4032 |
| H2330.1 | 4036 |
| H2332 | 4048 |
| H2333.2 | 4082 |
| H2333.21 | 4086 |
| H2334 | 4096 |
| H2335.9 | 4104, 4116 |
| H2336 | 4108 |
| H2336.1 | 4112 |
| H2338 | 4130 |
| H2340 | 4124 |
| H2340.1 | 4128 |
| H2342 | 4148 |
| H2343 | 4180 |
| H2346 | 4204 |
| H2346.1 | 4208 |
| H2347 | 4192 |
| H2348 | 4228 |
| H2348.1 | 4232 |
| H2349 | 4244 |
| H2350 | 4236 |
| H2350.1 | 4240 |
| H2354 | 4284 |
| H2356 | 4308 |
| H2356.1 | 4312 |
| H2358 | 4316 |
| H2358.1 | 4320 |
| H2360 | 4332 |
| H2360.1 | 4336 |
| H2361 | 4356 |
| H2362 | 4340 |
| H2362.1 | 4344 |
| H2364 | 4348 |
| H2364.1 | 4352 |
| H2366 | 4424 |
| H2366.1 | 4428 |
| H2366.4 | 4460 |
| H2368 | 4436 |
| H2370 | 4472 |
| H2370.1 | 4476 |
| H2372 | 4480 |
| H2380 | 4528 |
| H2380.1 | 4532 |
| H2382 | 4544 |
| H2384 | 4588 |
| H2384.1 | 4592 |
| H2385 | 4614 |
| H2386 | 4608 |
| H2386.1 | 4612 |
| H2387 | 4560 |
| H2388 | 4624 |
| H2388.1 | 4628 |
| H2389 | 4656 |
| H2390 | 4636 |
| H2390.1 | 4640 |
| H2392 | 4680 |
| H2392.1 | 4684 |
| H2398 | 4732 |
| H2398.1 | 4736 |
| H2398.4 | 4728 |
| H2400 | 4748 |
| H2401 | 4752 |
| H2401.1 | 4756 |
| H2402 | 4804 |
| H2402.1 | 4808 |
| H2404 | 4872 |
| H2405 | 4888 |
| H2405.1 | 4892 |
| H2408 | 4932 |
| H2408.1 | 4936 |
| H2409 | 4940 |
| H2409.1 | 4944 |
| H2410 | 4956 |
| H2411 | 4988 |
| H2414 | 5028 |
| H2414.1 | 5032 |
| H2416 | 5044 |
| H2416.1 | 5046 |
| H2422 | 5072 |
| H2422.1 | 5076 |
| H2424 | 5047 |
| H2424.1 | 5048 |
| H2426 | 5104 |
| H2426.1 | 5108 |
| H2450 | 5136 |
| H2450.1 | 5140 |
| H2451 | 5144 |
| H2451.1 | 5148 |
| H2452 | 5172 |
| H2452.1 | 5176 |
| H2453 | 5206 |
| H2454 | 5192 |
| H2454.1 | 5196 |
| H2456 | 5208 |
| H2458 | 5224 |
| H2458.1 | 5228 |
| H2460 | 5252 |
| H2460.1 | 5256 |
| H2470 | 5300 |
| H2470.1 | 5304 |
| H2472 | 5308 |
| H2472.1 | 5312 |
| H2476 | 5352 |
| H2476.1 | 5356 |
| H2478 | 5364 |
| H2478.1 | 5368 |
| H2480 | 5388 |
| H2480.1 | 5392 |
| H2482 | 5404 |
| H2482.1 | 5408 |
| H2484 | 5448 |
| H2484.1 | 5452 |
| H2486 | 5496 |
| H2486.1 | 5500 |
| H2487 | 5476 |
| H2487.1 | 5480 |
| H2490 | 5512 |
| H2490.1 | 5516 |
| H2496 | 5544 |
| H2496.1 | 5548 |
| H2497 | 5564 |
| H2497.1 | 5568 |
| H2499 | 5572 |
| H2499.1 | 5576 |
| H2506 | 5632 |
| H2517.04 | 5701 |
| H2517.1 | 5704 |
| H2517.11 | 5708 |
| H2517.2 | 5692 |
| H2517.21 | 5696 |
| H2517.5 | 5648 |
| H2518 | 5668 |
| H2518.4 | 5702 |
| H2518.41 | 5703 |
| H2519 | 5646 |
| H2519.1 | 5647 |
| H2522.5 | 5748 |
| H2522.6 | 5788 |
| H2522.61 | 5792 |
| H2528 | 5800 |
| H2528.1 | 5804 |
| H2528.4 | 5796 |
| H2530 | 5816 |
| H2530.1 | 5820 |
| H2531 | 5840 |
| H2531.1 | 5844 |
| H2532 | 5872 |
| H2533 | 5928 |
| H2533.1 | 5932 |
| H2535 | 5888 |
| H2535.1 | 5892 |
| H2536 | 5900 |
| H2537 | 5920 |
| H2537.1 | 5924 |
| H2538 | 5984 |
| H2538.1 | 5988 |
| H2541 | 5992 |
| H2543 | 6064 |
| H2543.1 | 6068 |
| H2543.5 | 6069 |
| H2543.51 | 6071 |
| H2544 | 6088 |
| H2544.1 | 6092 |
| H2545 | 6120 |
| H2545.1 | 6124 |
| H2546 | 6132 |
| H2547 | 6146 |
| H2548 | 6152 |
| H2548.1 | 6156 |
| H2550 | 6096 |
| H2550.1 | 6100 |
| H2551 | 6184 |
| H2551.1 | 6188 |
| H2552 | 6180 |
| H2556 | 6228 |
| H2556.1 | 6232 |
| H2558 | 6256 |
| H2558.1 | 6260 |
| H2560 | 6240 |
| H2560.1 | 6244 |
| H2568 | 6288 |
| H2568.1 | 6292 |
| H2571 | 6316 |
| H2572 | 6324 |
| H2573 | 6332 |
| H2574 | 6336 |
| H2576 | 6372 |
| H2578 | 6412 |
| H2578.1 | 6416 |
| H2601 | 6452 |
| H2601.4 | 6464 |
| H2604 | 6492 |
| H2606 | 6496 |
| H2608 | 6500 |
| H2673 | 6510 |
| H3342 | 9196 |
| H3344 | 9204 |
| H3348 | 9208 |
| H3348.1 | 9212 |
| H3358 | 9224 |
| H3359 | 9226 |
| H3360 | 9232 |
| H3362 | 9236 |

| Inter. | U.S. |
|---|---|
| H3364 | 9240 |
| H3364.1 | 9244 |
| H3368 | 9252 |
| H3372 | 9280 |
| H3376 | 9312 |
| H3380 | 9264 |
| H3384 | 9265 |
| H3386 | 9396 |
| H3388 | 9266 |
| H3392 | 9267 |
| H3396 | 9272 |
| H3398 | 9336 |
| H3398.1 | 9340 |
| H3399 | 9344 |
| H3399.1 | 9348 |
| H3401 | 9352 |
| H3404 | 9356 |
| H3406 | 9364 |
| H3416 | 9380 |
| H3419 | 9424 |
| H3419.1 | 9428 |
| H3421 | 9416 |
| H3421.1 | 9420 |
| H3422 | 9432 |
| H3423 | 9400 |
| H3423.1 | 9404 |
| H3425 | 9436 |
| H3425.1 | 9440 |
| H3426 | 9444 |
| H3426.1 | 9448 |
| H3427 | 9452 |
| H3427.1 | 9456 |
| H3430 | 9472 |
| H3432 | 8712 |
| H3433 | 8700 |
| H3434 | 9476 |
| H3434.1 | 9480 |
| H3436 | 8704 |
| H3436.1 | 8708 |
| H3440 | 8696 |
| H3456 | 9492 |
| H3458 | 9540 |
| H3460 | 9528 |
| H3460.1 | 9532 |
| H3462 | 9520 |
| H3462.1 | 9524 |
| H3464 | 9516 |
| H3464.5 | 9514 |
| H3465 | 9508 |
| H3465.1 | 9512 |
| H3468 | 9506 |
| H3471 | 9558 |
| H3472 | 9556 |
| H3474 | 9584 |
| H3476 | 9588 |
| H3478 | 9596 |
| H3484 | 9628 |
| H3497 | 9624 |
| H3500 | 9632 |
| H3502 | 9636 |
| H3504 | 9648 |
| H3508 | 9656 |
| H3512 | 9664 |
| H3514 | 9684 |
| H3515 | 9708 |
| H3516 | 9692 |
| H3516.1 | 9696 |
| H3516.3 | 9688 |
| H3516.4 | 9700 |
| H3526 | 9736 |
| H3530 | 9748 |
| H3534 | 9772 |
| H3541 | 9778 |
| H3542 | 9784 |
| H3542.1 | 9788 |
| H3557 | 9814 |
| H3560 | 9816 |
| H3564 | 9820 |
| H3566 | 9824 |
| H3568 | 9836 |
| H3570 | 9848 |
| H3578 | 9872 |
| H3579 | 9852 |
| H3596 | 9892 |
| H3600 | 9904 |
| H3602 | 9916 |
| H3602.1 | 9920 |
| H3604 | 9908 |
| H3605 | 9912 |
| H3606 | 9924 |
| H3606.1 | 9928 |
| H3607 | 9932 |
| H3609 | 9896 |
| H3618 | 9944 |
| H3618.1 | 9948 |
| H3630 | 9952 |
| H3631 | 9966 |
| H3632 | 9968 |
| H3644 | 9980 |
| H3646 | 9996 |
| H3650 | 10004 |
| H3651 | 10008 |
| H3651.4 | 10012 |
| H3652 | 10016 |
| H3655 | 10024 |
| H3657 | 10036 |
| H3658 | 10028 |
| H3659 | 10032 |
| H3660 | 10040 |
| H3661 | 10044 |
| H3663 | 10060 |
| H3664 | 10064 |
| H3665 | 10068 |
| H3667 | 10076 |
| H3670 | 10088 |
| H3672 | 10092 |
| H3674 | 10112 |
| H3676 | 10100 |
| H3677 | 10104 |
| H3680 | 10120 |
| H3682 | 10128 |
| H3682.1 | 10132 |
| H3683 | 10133 |
| H3683.2 | 10134 |
| H3688 | 10136 |
| H3694 | 10148 |
| H3698 | 10160 |
| H3699 | 10152 |
| H3700 | 10168 |
| H3702 | 10172 |
| H3708 | 10184 |
| H3710 | 10192 |
| H3710.5 | 10196 |
| H3711 | 10200 |
| H3718 | 10212 |
| H3721 | 10226 |
| H3722 | 10224 |
| H3725 | 10228 |
| H3730 | 10256 |
| H3736 | 10248 |
| H3740 | 10244 |
| H3742 | 10268 |
| H3742.04 | 10272 |
| H3742.5 | 10274 |
| H3742.6 | 10276 |
| H3746 | 10320 |
| H3748 | 10336 |
| H3750 | 10344 |
| H3753 | 10348 |
| H3754 | 10352 |
| H3755 | 10356 |
| H3758 | 10376 |
| H3759.4 | 10388 |
| H3762 | 10404 |
| H3763 | 10412 |
| H3765 | 10416 |
| H3774 | 10436 |
| H3776 | 10440 |
| H3778 | 10452 |
| H3779 | 10460 |
| H3780 | 10464 |
| H3781 | 10468 |
| H3782 | 10484 |
| H3784 | 10508 |
| H3784.4 | 10496 |
| H3785 | 10528 |
| H3785.4 | 10524 |
| H3785.6 | 10520 |
| H3786 | 10532 |
| H3786.2 | 10536 |
| H3787.41 | 10494 |
| H3787.5 | 10492 |
| H3788 | 10540 |
| H3790 | 10560 |
| H3793 | 10548 |
| H3793.6 | 10544 |
| H3794 | 10588 |
| H3795 | 10584 |
| H3796 | 10576 |
| H3796.2 | 10572 |
| H3797 | 10582 |
| H3798.4 | 10608 |
| H3800 | 10632 |
| H3803.4 | 10633 |
| H3804 | 10636 |
| H3805 | 10640 |
| H3805.4 | 10640.5 |
| H3805.5 | 10641 |
| H3805.7 | 10634 |
| H3806 | 10668 |
| H3812 | 10596 |
| H3814 | 10672 |
| H3815 | 10648 |
| H3816 | 10644 |
| H3817 | 10652 |
| H3817.02 | 10670 |
| H3817.4 | 10684 |
| H3817.5 | 10688 |
| H3818 | 10700 |
| H3819 | 10692 |
| H3819.5 | 10640.1 |
| H3820 | 10728 |
| H3822 | 10732 |
| H3826 | 10736 |
| H3834 | 10740 |
| H3837 | 10742 |
| H3838 | 10765 |
| H3840 | 10776 |
| H3846 | 10796 |
| H3848 | 10792 |
| H3851 | 10804 |
| H3852 | 10808 |
| H3855 | 10810 |
| H3858 | 10816 |
| H3864 | 10832 |
| H3864.5 | 10828 |
| H3865 | 10834 |
| H3872 | 10844 |
| H3874 | 10852 |
| H3875 | 10864 |
| H3876 | 10860 |
| H3878 | 10872 |
| H3880 | 10868 |
| H3884 | 10880 |
| H3885 | 10884 |
| H3887 | 10892 |
| H3888 | 10896 |
| H3889 | 10904 |
| H3890 | 10908 |
| H3892 | 10916 |
| H3894 | 10920 |
| H3896 | 10936 |
| H3906 | 10940 |
| H3908 | 10944 |
| H3914 | 10946 |
| H3916 | 10948 |
| H3918 | 10952 |
| H3920 | 10956 |
| H3926 | 10964 |
| H3928 | 10968 |
| H3930 | 10972 |
| H3932 | 10976 |
| H3934 | 10984 |
| H3938 | 10980 |
| H3942 | 10988 |
| H3950 | 11004 |
| H3952 | 11044 |
| H3954 | 11048 |
| H3956 | 11008 |
| H3957 | 11010 |
| H4032 | 11052 |
| H4034 | 11056 |
| H4060 | 11064 |
| H4064 | 11068 |
| H4074 | 11076 |
| H4076 | 11080 |
| H4077 | 11084 |
| H4078 | 11088 |
| H4080 | 11096 |
| H4082 | 11100 |

| Inter. | U.S. |
|---|---|
| H4083 | 11112 |
| H4083.4 | 11116 |
| H4083.41 | 11120 |
| H4083.6 | 11114 |
| H4085.5 | 11128 |
| H4089 | 11104 |
| H4089.1 | 11108 |
| H4090 | 11132 |
| H4092 | 11140 |
| H4096 | 11148 |
| H4098 | 11150 |
| H4100 | 11152 |
| H4104 | 11156 |
| H4108 | 11160 |
| H4110 | 11172 |
| H4112 | 11184 |
| H4113 | 11188 |
| H4114 | 11192 |
| H4115 | 11196 |
| H4116.4 | 11191 |
| H4118 | 11200 |
| H4119 | 11204 |
| H4120 | 11208 |
| H4120.4 | 11212 |
| H4122 | 11220 |
| H4123 | 11225 |
| H4126 | 11232 |
| H4127 | 11230 |
| H4130 | 11244 |
| H4134 | 11248 |
| H4138 | 11260 |
| H4138.6 | 11304 |
| H4139 | 11308 |
| H4140 | 11310 |
| H4144 | 11280 |
| H4145 | 11276 |
| H4146 | 11264 |
| H4146.4 | 11272 |
| H4147 | 11316 |
| H4148 | 11312 |
| H4150 | 11324 |
| H4152 | 11328 |
| H4154 | 11332 |
| H4155 | 11334 |
| H4156 | 11336 |
| H4157.4 | 11344 |
| H4161 | 11356 |
| H4166 | 11360 |
| H4168 | 11364 |
| H4170 | 11376 |
| H4170.4 | 11380 |
| H4171 | 11372 |
| H4172 | 11392 |
| H4174 | 11384 |
| H4175 | 11388 |
| H4178 | 11400 |
| H4178.3 | 11398 |
| H4180 | 11424 |
| H4181.5 | 11420 |
| H4184 | 11428 |
| H4186 | 11436 |
| H4188 | 11416 |
| H4192 | 11444 |
| J3060 | 11608 |
| J4229.5 | 15203 |
| J4229.55 | 15203.2 |
| J4230 | 15203.1 |
| J4230.2 | 15203.15 |
| J4230.4 | 15206 |
| J4230.5 | 15207 |
| J4231 | 15208 |
| J4231.5 | 15209.1 |
| J4231.6 | 15209.2 |
| J4231.9 | 15211 |
| J4232 | 15212 |
| J4232.5 | 15213 |
| J4233 | 15214 |
| J4233.2 | 15214.2 |
| J4233.25 | 15214.3 |
| J4233.4 | 15214.4 |
| J4233.41 | 15214.45 |
| J4233.5 | 15214.5 |
| J4233.6 | 15214.6 |
| J4233.62 | 15215 |
| J4233.63 | 15215.1 |
| J4234 | 15216 |
| J4235 | 15215.5 |
| J4235.1 | 15215.51 |
| J4236 | 15220 |
| J4238 | 15224 |
| J4238.1 | 15228 |
| J4240 | 15232 |
| J4241 | 15236 |
| J4241.4 | 15240 |
| J4242 | 15244 |
| J4243 | 15248 |
| J4244 | 15252 |
| J4244.4 | 15256 |
| J4245 | 15260 |
| J4246 | 15264 |
| J4246.1 | 15264.1 |
| J4247 | 15266 |
| J4247.6 | 15267.1 |
| J4249 | 15280 |
| J4249.5 | 15284 |
| J4250 | 15276 |
| J4253 | 15288 |
| J4253.2 | 15290 |
| J4254 | 15292 |
| J4255 | 15304 |
| J4256 | 15296 |
| J4256.4 | 15297 |
| J4257 | 15300 |
| J4257.4 | 15301 |
| J4258 | 15305 |
| J4258.1 | 15306 |
| J4259 | 15308 |
| J4259.1 | 15312 |
| J4259.2 | 15316 |
| J4259.21 | 15316.1 |
| J4259.3 | 15317 |
| J4259.32 | 15318 |
| J4259.4 | 15331 |
| J4259.5 | 15332 |
| J4260 | 15336 |
| J4261 | 15340 |
| J4261.2 | 15344 |
| J4262 | 15348 |
| J4266 | 15352 |
| J4268 | 15354 |
| J4270 | 15360 |
| J4270.2 | 15364 |
| J4271 | 15356 |
| J4271.5 | 15356.1 |
| J4272 | 15368 |
| J4273 | 15368.1 |
| J4273.5 | 15372.2 |
| J4274 | 15372 |
| J4275 | 15376.1 |
| J4276 | 15376 |
| J4277 | 15380.2 |
| J4278 | 15380 |
| J4279 | 15382 |
| J4279.55 | 15382.2 |
| J4279.7 | 15382.5 |
| J4282 | 15388 |
| J4284 | 15384 |
| J4286 | 15392 |
| J4286.1 | 15392.1 |
| J4286.31 | 15395 |
| J4286.4 | 15392.5 |
| J4286.41 | 15392.6 |
| J4297 | 15396 |
| J4297.2 | 15397 |
| J4298 | 15393 |
| J4298.1 | 15394 |
| J4299.5 | 15395.6 |
| J4299.6 | 15395.5 |
| J4300 | 15406 |
| J4300.5 | 15407 |
| J4308 | 15412 |
| J4310 | 15408 |
| J4311 | 15415 |
| J4312 | 15418 |
| J4313 | 15420.2 |
| J4314 | 15420 |
| J4315.5 | 15424.2 |
| J4316 | 15424 |
| J4317 | 15428 |
| J4317.2 | 15432 |
| J4317.6 | 15437 |
| J4318 | 15436 |
| J4318.5 | 15439 |
| J4319 | 15440 |
| J4324 | 15444 |
| J4325 | 15445 |
| J4325.5 | 15446 |
| J4326 | 15452 |
| J4330 | 15456 |
| J4332 | 15460 |
| J4336 | 15464 |
| J4337 | 15480 |
| J4338 | 15476 |
| J4339 | 15468 |
| J4339.1 | 15472 |
| J4340 | 15484 |
| J4340.1 | 15488 |
| J4341.8 | 15489.3 |
| J4341.82 | 15489.4 |
| J4348 | 15492 |
| J4352 | 15496 |
| J4353 | 15500 |
| J4354 | 15504 |
| J4355.5 | 15505 |
| J4356.2 | 15505.5 |
| J4358 | 15571 |
| J4358.1 | 15572 |
| J4358.3 | 15506.5 |
| J4358.6 | 15506 |
| J4358.7 | 15507 |
| J4358.9 | 15508 |
| J4358.95 | 15510 |
| J4364 | 15576 |
| J4368 | 15580 |
| J4372 | 15512 |
| J4372.1 | 15516 |
| J4372.7 | 15517 |
| J4372.8 | 15517.5 |
| J4373 | 15518 |
| J4373.05 | 15519 |
| J4374 | 15520 |
| J4378 | 15528 |
| J4384 | 15536 |
| J4384.1 | 15540 |
| J4385 | 15532 |
| J4386 | 15544 |
| J4386.2 | 15544.6 |
| J4386.3 | 15544.3 |
| J4388 | 15548 |
| J4390 | 15554 |
| J4390.5 | 15554.1 |
| J4392 | 15552 |
| J4395 | 15562.25 |
| J4395.2 | 15562.4 |
| J4395.3 | 15562.3 |
| J4396 | 15556 |
| J4396.1 | 15560 |
| J4397 | 15562.2 |
| J4397.2 | 15562.1 |
| J4400 | 15564 |
| J4403 | 15584 |
| J4403.1 | 15585 |
| J4404 | 15588 |
| J4404.2 | 15588.3, 15588.4 |
| J4404.4 | 15588.2 |
| J4404.5 | 15588.1 |
| J4406 | 15592 |
| J4409 | 15604 |
| J4409.4 | 15635.5 |
| J4409.6 | 15635 |
| J4410 | 15610 |
| J4410.5 | 15611 |
| J4411 | 15617 |
| J4411.1 | 15617.1 |
| J4411.3 | 15618 |
| J4411.5 | 15619 |
| J4412 | 15600 |
| J4414 | 15596 |
| J4416 | 15620 |
| J4416.1 | 15630 |
| J4416.15 | 15629 |
| J4416.16 | 15629.1 |
| J4416.5 | 15623.01 |
| J4416.55 | 15623.02 |
| J4416.6 | 15623.03 |
| J4416.65 | 15623.04 |
| J4417.01 | 15623.05 |
| J4417.02 | 15623.06 |
| J4417.03 | 15623.07 |

| Inter. | U.S. | Inter. | U.S. | Inter. | U.S. | Inter. | U.S. |
|---|---|---|---|---|---|---|---|
| J4417.04 | 15623.08 | J4450 | 15752 | J4570 | 11792 | J4642.25 | 12001.5 |
| J4417.05 | 15623.09 | J4450.5 | 15756 | J4572 | 11800 | J4642.3 | 12016 |
| J4417.07 | 15623.1 | J4450.7 | 15760 | J4575 | 11804 | J4642.32 | 12020 |
| J4417.082 | 15625 | J4450.9 | 15764 | J4576 | 11808 | J4642.34 | 12024 |
| J4417.09 | 15627 | J4451 | 15768 | J4578 | 11812 | J4642.4 | 12028 |
| J4417.1 | 15627.1 | J4452 | 15776 | J4580 | 11816 | J4642.5 | 12026 |
| J4418 | 15632 | J4453 | 15772 | J4581 | 11820 | J4642.6 | 12030 |
| J4418.2 | 15632.3 | J4454 | 15778 | J4582 | 11824 | J4643.4 | 12012 |
| J4418.21 | 15632.4 | J4455 | 15782 | J4583 | 11828 | J4644 | 12036 |
| J4418.3 | 15632.2 | J4456 | 15780 | J4584 | 11832 | J4644.1 | 12040 |
| J4418.4 | 15632.1 | J4456.5 | 15784 | J4585 | 11832.1 | J4644.3 | 12044 |
| J4418.7 | 15634 | J4456.7 | 15792 | J4586 | 11833 | J4644.4 | 12044.4 |
| J4419 | 15636 | J4457 | 15788 | J4586.1 | 11833.1 | J4644.5 | 12044.8 |
| J4419.2 | 15636.3 | J4462 | 15796 | J4587.6 | 11834 | J4644.6 | 12045 |
| J4419.21 | 15636.4 | J4466 | 15797 | J4588 | 11835 | J4644.7 | 12045.2 |
| J4419.3 | 15636.2 | J4469 | 15800 | J4589 | 11836 | J4644.8 | 12045.6 |
| J4419.4 | 15636.1 | J4471 | 11684 | J4589.4 | 11837 | J4644.9 | 12046 |
| J4420 | 15640 | J4471.3 | 11620 | J4589.8 | 11837.1 | J4645 | 12048 |
| J4421 | 15644 | J4471.5 | 11624 | J4590.4 | 11837.2 | J4645.1 | 12048.4 |
| J4421.5 | 15644.1 | J4472 | 11616 | J4591 | 11838 | J4645.2 | 12048.8 |
| J4421.6 | 15644.2 | J4476 | 11640 | J4591.1 | 11838.1 | J4645.3 | 12049 |
| J4421.9 | 15645 | J4476.5 | 11644 | J4593 | 11841 | J4645.4 | 12049.4 |
| J4422 | 15648 | J4477 | 11632 | J4593.2 | 11841.1 | J4646 | 12032 |
| J4422.5 | 15650 | J4478 | 11636 | J4593.5 | 11844 | J4647 | 12052 |
| J4422.51 | 15650.1 | J4479 | 11646 | J4594.4 | 11852 | J4648 | 12056 |
| J4422.7 | 15649.1 | J4481 | 11648 | J4594.44 | 11856 | J4648.2 | 12056.1 |
| J4422.8 | 15649 | J4482 | 11664 | J4595 | 11880 | J4648.22 | 12056.4 |
| J4424.5 | 15661 | J4489 | 11688 | J4595.1 | 11884 | J4648.25 | 12056.2 |
| J4424.51 | 15661.1 | J4490 | 11680 | J4596 | 11864 | J4648.27 | 12056.6 |
| J4426 | 15652 | J4491 | 11712 | J4596.6 | 11872 | J4648.3 | 12060.2 |
| J4427 | 15656 | J4492 | 11696 | J4596.8 | 11868 | J4648.31 | 12060.4 |
| J4427.3 | 15657 | J4493 | 11700 | J4598 | 11888 | J4648.32 | 12060.6 |
| J4427.31 | 15657.1 | J4493.5 | 11698 | J4600 | 11892 | J4648.321 | 12060.8 |
| J4428 | 15664 | J4494 | 11704 | J4602 | 11896 | J4648.322 | 12061 |
| J4430 | 15668 | J4495 | 11708 | J4604 | 11924 | J4648.323 | 12061.2 |
| J4431 | 15670 | J4498 | 11760 | J4606 | 11928 | J4648.324 | 12061.4 |
| J4431.5 | 15684 | J4499 | 11761 | J4608 | 11920 | J4648.325 | 12061.6 |
| J4432 | 15672 | J4501 | 11755 | J4610 | 11916 | J4648.326 | 12061.8 |
| J4433 | 15676 | J4501.1 | 11755.2 | J4613 | 11912 | J4648.327 | 12062 |
| J4433.1 | 15680 | J4503 | 11753 | J4616 | 11904 | J4648.328 | 12062.2 |
| J4435 | 15688 | J4506 | 11752 | J4618 | 11908 | J4648.329 | 12062.4 |
| J4436 | 15692 | J4508 | 11748 | J4620 | 11900 | J4648.33 | 12062.6 |
| J4436.1 | 15692.1 | J4509 | 11768 | J4624 | 11940 | J4648.331 | 12062.8 |
| J4436.3 | 15694 | J4514 | 11732 | J4624.2 | 11944 | J4648.5 | 12064 |
| J4436.5 | 15696 | J4518 | 11729 | J4624.5 | 11936 | J4648.7 | 12068 |
| J4437 | 15700 | J4520 | 11728 | J4625 | 11948 | J4648.75 | 12068.2 |
| J4438 | 15704 | J4524 | 11716 | J4626 | 11952 | J4648.751 | 12068.4 |
| J4440 | 15708 | J4531 | 11743 | J4627 | 11956 | J4648.752 | 12068.6 |
| J4440.5 | 15712 | J4532 | 11744 | J4628 | 11960 | J4648.753 | 12068.8 |
| J4441 | 15716 | J4537 | 11750 | J4628,5 | 11960.5 | J4648.754 | 12069 |
| J4441.5 | 15717 | J4539 | 11676 | J4629 | 11964 | J4648.755 | 12069.2 |
| J4441.55 | 15718 | J4540 | 11672 | J4630 | 11933 | J4648.756 | 12069.4 |
| J4441.56 | 15718.5 | J4542 | 11764 | J4632 | 12072 | J4649 | 12060 |
| J4441.6 | 15719 | J4542.5 | 11733 | J4634 | 11976 | J4650 | 12076 |
| J4441.62 | 15719.5 | J4543 | 11740 | J4635 | 11968 | J4654 | 12080 |
| J4441.7 | 15720 | J4544 | 11736 | J4635.1 | 11972 | J4655 | 12084 |
| J4442 | 15724 | J4545 | 11741 | J4636 | 11980 | J4656 | 12088 |
| J4443.1 | 15732 | J4546 | 11742 | J4636.1 | 11984 | J4656.1 | 12092 |
| J4445 | 15728 | J4547 | 11686 | J4639 | 11992 | J4657.4 | 12086 |
| J4445.2 | 15735 | J4550 | 11668 | J4640 | 11988 | J4658 | 12096 |
| J4445.25 | 15735.5 | J4560 | 11776 | J4641.3 | 12001 | J4662 | 12108 |
| J4446 | 15744 | J4562 | 11780 | J4641.4 | 12002 | J4664 | 12100 |
| J4447 | 15736 | J4565 | 11784 | J4642 | 12000.5 | J4668 | 12104 |
| J4447.2 | 15740 | J4566 | 11788 | J4642.2 | 12004 | J4669 | 12112 |
| J4448 | 15748 | J4568 | 11796 | J4642.21 | 12008 | J4669.4 | 12112.5 |

# CROSS REFERENCE - INTERNATIONAL vs. U.S. LIGHT NUMBER

| Inter. | U.S. |
|---|---|
| J4669.6 | 12112.7 |
| J4669.7 | 12112.9 |
| J4670.8 | 12114 |
| J4674 | 12172 |
| J4675 | 12176 |
| J4675.5 | 12188 |
| J4676 | 12180 |
| J4677 | 12184 |
| J4678 | 12200 |
| J4680 | 12192 |
| J4681 | 12196 |
| J4682 | 12204 |
| J4686 | 12168 |
| J4688 | 12164 |
| J4691 | 12162 |
| J4692 | 12160 |
| J4694 | 12136 |
| J4696 | 12144 |
| J4698 | 12148 |
| J4700 | 12140 |
| J4701 | 12152 |
| J4702 | 12156 |
| J4704 | 12208 |
| J4705 | 12158 |
| J4708 | 12212 |
| J4712 | 12220 |
| J4716 | 12228 |
| J4718 | 12236 |
| J4722 | 12116 |
| J4724 | 12120 |
| J4726 | 12128 |
| J4728 | 12124 |
| J4730 | 12132 |
| J4732 | 12248 |
| J4734 | 12244 |
| J4736 | 12256 |
| J4737 | 12252 |
| J4738 | 12288 |
| J4740 | 12292 |
| J4744 | 12284 |
| J4745 | 12285 |
| J4748 | 12240 |
| J4750 | 12260 |
| J4752 | 12264 |
| J4753 | 12268 |
| J4754 | 12272 |
| J4758 | 12280 |
| J4760 | 12276 |
| J4764 | 12328 |
| J4766 | 12332 |
| J4768 | 12336 |
| J4772 | 12340 |
| J4774 | 12344 |
| J4778 | 12304 |
| J4779 | 12308 |
| J4780 | 12312 |
| J4782 | 12324 |
| J4786 | 12316 |
| J4788 | 12320 |
| J4792 | 12296 |
| J4794 | 12300 |
| J4798 | 12352 |
| J4800 | 12348 |
| J4802 | 12356 |
| J4804 | 12360 |
| J4806.6 | 12384 |
| J4806.8 | 12380 |
| J4807 | 12388 |
| J4808 | 12392 |
| J4809 | 12396 |
| J4809.4 | 12400 |
| J4810 | 12404 |
| J4811 | 12405 |
| J4811.5 | 12406 |
| J4812 | 12408 |
| J4814 | 12420 |
| J4816 | 12428 |
| J4818 | 12432 |
| J4819 | 13712 |
| J4820 | 12436 |
| J4822 | 12440 |
| J4823 | 12448 |
| J4823.5 | 12452 |
| J4824 | 12456 |
| J4824.5 | 12464 |
| J4826 | 12460 |
| J4827 | 12472 |
| J4827.5 | 12468 |
| J4827.8 | 12476 |
| J4827.9 | 12480 |
| J4828 | 12484 |
| J4830 | 12500 |
| J4830.2 | 12490 |
| J4830.4 | 12492 |
| J4832 | 12504 |
| J4833 | 12505 |
| J4833.1 | 12505.2 |
| J4836 | 12512 |
| J4838 | 12516 |
| J4840 | 12542 |
| J4841 | 12542.5 |
| J4842 | 12528 |
| J4842.5 | 12540 |
| J4843 | 12536 |
| J4843.5 | 12544 |
| J4845 | 12561 |
| J4845.1 | 12561.5 |
| J4846 | 12552 |
| J4847 | 12556 |
| J4847.1 | 12560 |
| J4847.6 | 12562 |
| J4848 | 12564 |
| J4849 | 12565 |
| J4849.4 | 12565.6 |
| J4854 | 12572 |
| J4855 | 12576 |
| J4857 | 12580 |
| J4858 | 12585 |
| J4859 | 12597 |
| J4859.1 | 12598 |
| J4860 | 12590 |
| J4860.1 | 12592 |
| J4862 | 12600 |
| J4867 | 12612 |
| J4867.5 | 12613 |
| J4868 | 12616 |
| J4872 | 12620 |
| J4875 | 12628 |
| J4875.2 | 12632 |
| J4875.4 | 12636 |
| J4875.41 | 12640 |
| J4875.6 | 12641 |
| J4875.7 | 12642 |
| J4875.8 | 12643 |
| J4875.9 | 12644.5 |
| J4876.2 | 12645 |
| J4876.3 | 12646 |
| J4877 | 12647 |
| J4877.2 | 12647.5 |
| J4879 | 12648 |
| J4880 | 12656 |
| J4881 | 12660 |
| J4881.1 | 12660.5 |
| J4881.3 | 12661 |
| J4882 | 12664 |
| J4883 | 12668 |
| J4883.7 | 12668.1 |
| J4886 | 12672 |
| J4888 | 12676 |
| J4894 | 12684 |
| J4896 | 12688 |
| J4896.6 | 12689 |
| J4897.3 | 12696 |
| J4897.4 | 12700 |
| J4897.6 | 12712 |
| J4899 | 12720 |
| J4899.3 | 12728 |
| J4899.5 | 12732 |
| J4900 | 12716 |
| J4902 | 12736 |
| J4904 | 12746 |
| J4905 | 12748 |
| J4906 | 12752 |
| J4908 | 12756 |
| J4908.08 | 12758.2 |
| J4909 | 12759 |
| J4913 | 12772 |
| J4914 | 12784 |
| J4915 | 12776 |
| J4916 | 12780 |
| J4917 | 12788 |
| J4918 | 12800 |
| J4920 | 12792 |
| J4922 | 12804 |
| J4923 | 12806 |
| J4923.5 | 12806.5 |
| J4924 | 12807 |
| J4926 | 12808 |
| J4928 | 12812 |
| J4930 | 12816 |
| J4930.1 | 12820 |
| J4931 | 12824 |
| J4932 | 12828 |
| J4933 | 12832 |
| J4933.1 | 12836 |
| J4934 | 12840 |
| J4934.1 | 12844 |
| J4936 | 12848 |
| J4936.1 | 12852 |
| J4938.9 | 12860 |
| J4939 | 12856 |
| J4939.1 | 12864 |
| J4942 | 12872 |
| J4944 | 12884 |
| J4945 | 12886 |
| J4946 | 12892 |
| J4948 | 12894 |
| J4950 | 12896 |
| J4952 | 12900 |
| J4954 | 12904 |
| J4956 | 12908 |
| J4958 | 12912 |
| J4960 | 12916 |
| J4962 | 12920 |
| J4964 | 12924 |
| J4964.1 | 12928 |
| J4964.6 | 12940 |
| J4965 | 12942 |
| J4966 | 12944 |
| J4967 | 12945 |
| J4968 | 12945.2 |
| J4969 | 12946 |
| J4969.4 | 12946.2 |
| J4970 | 12947 |
| J4971 | 12947.2 |
| J4972 | 12947.4 |
| J4975 | 12948 |
| J4980.53 | 12948.52 |
| J4980.6 | 12948.54 |
| J4980.63 | 12948.56 |
| J4981 | 12948.62 |
| J4981.2 | 12948.64 |
| J4984 | 12948.7 |
| J4988 | 12952 |
| J4990 | 12956 |
| J4990.1 | 12960 |
| J4992 | 12964 |
| J4993 | 12968 |
| J4994 | 12972 |
| J4995 | 12976 |
| J4996 | 12978 |
| J5012 | 12980 |
| J5013 | 12988 |
| J5013.1 | 12992 |
| J5015.5 | 12996 |
| J5016 | 13000 |
| J5018 | 13008 |
| J5020 | 13012 |
| J5021 | 13016 |
| J5022.5 | 13017 |
| J5024 | 13020 |
| J5025 | 13032 |
| J5026.1 | 13028 |
| J5029 | 13033.4 |
| J5032 | 13036 |
| J5032.2 | 13040 |
| J5033 | 13044 |
| J5034 | 13048 |
| J5034.1 | 13052 |
| J5034.3 | 13056 |
| J5035 | 13064 |
| J5035.2 | 13068 |
| J5035.4 | 13072 |
| J5035.6 | 13076 |
| J5035.8 | 13080 |
| J5035.9 | 13082 |
| J5036 | 13084 |
| J5036.3 | 13088 |
| J5036.6 | 13100 |
| J5037 | 13104 |

| Inter. | U.S. |
|---|---|
| J5038 | 13096 |
| J5039 | 13092 |
| J5041 | 13108 |
| J5043 | 13110 |
| J5046 | 13112 |
| J5048 | 13154 |
| J5052 | 13164 |
| J5052.1 | 13168 |
| J5052.4 | 13169 |
| J5052.8 | 13170 |
| J5054 | 13172 |
| J5055 | 13176 |
| J5055.3 | 13177 |
| J5055.35 | 13178 |
| J5055.5 | 13194 |
| J5056 | 13178.2 |
| J5057 | 13178.4 |
| J5059 | 13179 |
| J5060.4 | 13180 |
| J5061 | 13184 |
| J5062 | 13192 |
| J5062.4 | 13196 |
| J5063 | 13204 |
| J5064 | 13212 |
| J5066.3 | 13208 |
| J5066.6 | 13216 |
| J5068 | 13220 |
| J5068.6 | 13222 |
| J5068.8 | 13224 |
| J5069 | 13228 |
| J5069.4 | 13249 |
| J5069.5 | 13250 |
| J5069.6 | 13251 |
| J5070 | 13244 |
| J5071 | 13248 |
| J5071.5 | 13248.5 |
| J5072 | 13264 |
| J5072.2 | 13242, 13265 |
| J5072.4 | 13272 |
| J5072.6 | 13276 |
| J5072.8 | 13280 |
| J5073.2 | 13240 |
| J5073.4 | 13236 |
| J5073.5 | 13236.5 |
| J5073.6 | 13237 |
| J5073.65 | 13237.5 |
| J5073.7 | 13238 |
| J5074.12 | 13254 |
| J5074.22 | 13255 |
| J5076 | 13284 |
| J5077 | 13340 |
| J5078 | 13284.5 |
| J5078.2 | 13284.6 |
| J5078.6 | 13288 |
| J5078.7 | 13286 |
| J5078.8 | 13292 |
| J5079 | 13296 |
| J5080 | 13300 |
| J5080.2 | 13304 |
| J5081.6 | 13328 |
| J5081.8 | 13316 |
| J5082 | 13332 |
| J5082.4 | 13336 |
| J5082.45 | 13336.5 |
| J5082.6 | 13306 |
| J5082.7 | 13308 |
| J5083 | 13312 |
| J5083.2 | 13314 |
| J5083.3 | 13334 |
| J5083.7 | 13338 |
| J5084 | 13344 |
| J5084.5 | 13356 |
| J5084.6 | 13358 |
| J5084.65 | 13359 |
| J5084.7 | 13359.5 |
| J5084.8 | 13364 |
| J5090 | 13380 |
| J5090.05 | 13382 |
| J5090.09 | 13383 |
| J5090.2 | 13388 |
| J5090.25 | 13392 |
| J5090.3 | 13396 |
| J5090.35 | 13398 |
| J5090.4 | 13400 |
| J5090.45 | 13404 |
| J5090.5 | 13406 |
| J5090.55 | 13420 |
| J5090.6 | 13424 |
| J5091 | 13428 |
| J5091.2 | 13432 |
| J5091.5 | 13436 |
| J5092 | 13440 |
| J5092.2 | 13444 |
| J5092.3 | 13448 |
| J5092.4 | 13452 |
| J5092.6 | 13456 |
| J5092.8 | 13460 |
| J5093 | 13464 |
| J5094 | 13468 |
| J5095 | 13488 |
| J5096 | 13492 |
| J5097 | 13472 |
| J5097.1 | 13476 |
| J5097.2 | 13480 |
| J5097.21 | 13484 |
| J5097.3 | 13496 |
| J5097.31 | 13500 |
| J5097.4 | 13508 |
| J5097.41 | 13512 |
| J5097.5 | 13470 |
| J5097.6 | 13512.3 |
| J5097.65 | 13512.32 |
| J5097.7 | 13512.34 |
| J5097.75 | 13512.36 |
| J5098 | 13513 |
| J5099 | 13518 |
| J5099.2 | 13518.2 |
| J5099.4 | 13518.4 |
| J5099.6 | 13518.6 |
| J5102 | 13536 |
| J5103 | 13538 |
| J5104 | 13524 |
| J5104.2 | 13532 |
| J5105 | 13540 |
| J5106 | 13544 |
| J5106.2 | 13544.1 |
| J5106.5 | 13545 |
| J5106.6 | 13546 |
| J5106.65 | 13547 |
| J5107 | 13548 |
| J5108 | 13552 |
| J5114 | 13556 |
| J5116 | 13560 |
| J5120 | 13566 |
| J5121 | 13569 |
| J5121.5 | 13570 |
| J5122 | 13571 |
| J5122.5 | 13571.1 |
| J5123 | 13571.2 |
| J5125.05 | 13575.7 |
| J5128 | 13568 |
| J5128.1 | 13573 |
| J5128.2 | 13573.1 |
| J5128.3 | 13573.2 |
| J5128.4 | 13573.3 |
| J5128.5 | 13573.4 |
| J5128.6 | 13573.5 |
| J5128.7 | 13573.6 |
| J5128.8 | 13573.7 |
| J5128.9 | 13573.8 |
| J5129 | 13575.5 |
| J5130 | 13572 |
| J5130.5 | 13574 |
| J5130.6 | 13575 |
| J5136 | 13576 |
| J5138 | 13580 |
| J5143 | 13622 |
| J5144 | 13616 |
| J5145 | 13608 |
| J5145.2 | 13612 |
| J5146 | 13604 |
| J5148 | 13600 |
| J5156 | 13592 |
| J5157 | 13596 |
| J5160 | 13656 |
| J5161 | 13652 |
| J5162 | 13660 |
| J5164 | 13664 |
| J5166 | 13647 |
| J5167 | 13647.1 |
| J5168 | 13648 |
| J5169 | 13649 |
| J5174 | 13672 |
| J5176 | 13676 |
| J5190 | 13618 |
| J5191 | 13619 |
| J5192 | 13623 |
| J5192.6 | 13628 |
| J5192.8 | 13632 |
| J5193 | 13634 |
| J5193.2 | 13635 |
| J5193.5 | 13630 |
| J5194 | 13636 |
| J5197 | 13638 |
| J5200 | 13644 |
| J5202 | 13678 |
| J5203 | 13680 |
| J5203.4 | 13684 |
| J5204 | 13688 |
| J5204.4 | 13692 |
| J5204.6 | 13696 |
| J5204.8 | 13700 |
| J5210 | 13708 |
| J5222 | 13720 |
| J5226 | 13724 |
| J5231 | 13728 |
| J5232 | 13716 |
| J5233 | 13733 |
| J5233.1 | 13734 |
| J5236 | 13736 |
| J5237 | 13740 |
| J5238 | 13744 |
| J5240 | 13748 |
| J5244 | 14144 |
| J5249 | 13772 |
| J5250 | 13756 |
| J5250.1 | 13760 |
| J5250.4 | 13764 |
| J5250.41 | 13768 |
| J5251 | 13770 |
| J5251.1 | 13771 |
| J5252 | 13775.5 |
| J5252.4 | 13775 |
| J5253 | 13776 |
| J5254.1 | 13782.2 |
| J5254.2 | 13782.4 |
| J5254.3 | 13782.6 |
| J5255 | 13778 |
| J5255.1 | 13778.1 |
| J5256 | 13784 |
| J5256.1 | 13788 |
| J5260 | 13804 |
| J5260.1 | 13808 |
| J5260.4 | 13809 |
| J5260.5 | 13810 |
| J5266 | 13828 |
| J5272 | 13832 |
| J5275 | 13844 |
| J5275.1 | 13848 |
| J5276 | 13836 |
| J5276.1 | 13840 |
| J5278 | 13856 |
| J5282 | 13860 |
| J5292 | 13912 |
| J5294 | 13908 |
| J5295 | 14060 |
| J5295.95 | 13928 |
| J5296 | 13932 |
| J5296.1 | 13933 |
| J5296.4 | 13934 |
| J5297 | 13924 |
| J5300 | 13940 |
| J5301.4 | 13948 |
| J5302 | 13956 |
| J5304 | 13952 |
| J5306 | 13960 |
| J5307 | 13964 |
| J5307.5 | 13962 |
| J5308 | 13976 |
| J5309 | 13984 |
| J5310 | 13992 |
| J5312 | 13980 |
| J5313 | 13988 |
| J5314 | 13996 |
| J5316 | 14004 |
| J5317 | 14000 |
| J5318 | 14040 |
| J5325 | 14044 |
| J5325.3 | 14048 |
| J5325.5 | 14052 |

# CROSS REFERENCE - INTERNATIONAL vs. U.S. LIGHT NUMBER

| Inter. | U.S. |
|---|---|
| J5325.82 | 14054 |
| J5326 | 14056 |
| J5327 | 14112 |
| J5327.9 | 14080 |
| J5328 | 14072 |
| J5329 | 14084 |
| J5332 | 14088 |
| J5332.1 | 14092 |
| J5340 | 14116 |
| J5340.1 | 14120 |
| J5341 | 14124 |
| J5347 | 14149 |
| J5352 | 14148 |
| J5356 | 13864 |
| J5368 | 14156 |
| J5370 | 14158 |
| J5376 | 14160 |
| J5380 | 14164 |
| J5382 | 14168 |
| J5384 | 14184 |
| J5386 | 14172 |
| J5388 | 14182 |
| J5390 | 14192 |
| J5392 | 14204 |
| J5392.1 | 14208 |
| J5399 | 14212 |
| J5399.1 | 14216 |
| J5402 | 14220 |
| J5404 | 14224 |
| J5406 | 14228 |
| J5408 | 14230 |
| J5411.4 | 14231.9 |
| J5412 | 14234 |
| J5414 | 14232 |
| J5422 | 14240 |
| J5424 | 14244 |
| J5426 | 14248 |
| J5430 | 14260 |
| J5431.1 | 14265 |
| J5432 | 14270 |
| J5434 | 14272 |
| J5438 | 14280 |
| J5440 | 14284 |
| J5440.5 | 14288 |
| J5442 | 14292 |
| J5444 | 14296 |
| J5444.5 | 14298 |
| J5445 | 14300 |
| J5446 | 14304 |
| J5447 | 14308 |
| J5448 | 14312 |
| J5454 | 14324 |
| J5456.8 | 14333 |
| J5457 | 14336 |
| J5458 | 14344 |
| J5458.1 | 14348 |
| J5463 | 14352 |
| J5466 | 14360 |
| J5468 | 14364 |
| J5470 | 14368 |
| J5480 | 14392 |
| J5482 | 14388 |
| J5482.5 | 14396 |
| J5484 | 14404 |
| J5486 | 14412 |
| J5488 | 14416 |
| J5490 | 14420 |
| J5491 | 14424 |
| J5492 | 14432 |
| J5492.6 | 14428 |
| J5494 | 14436 |
| J5496 | 14440 |
| J5496.1 | 14444 |
| J5518 | 14456 |
| J5518.1 | 14460 |
| J5520 | 14452 |
| J5524 | 14468 |
| J5528 | 14464 |
| J5532 | 14509 |
| J5533 | 14510 |
| J5540.8 | 14508 |
| J5542 | 14513 |
| J5542.01 | 14514 |
| J5545 | 14512 |
| J5552 | 14520 |
| J5556 | 14524 |
| J5560 | 14536 |
| J5564 | 14540 |
| J5564.1 | 14544 |
| J5569.8 | 14548 |
| J5569.9 | 14550 |
| J5569.91 | 14551 |
| J5574 | 14564 |
| J5574.1 | 14568 |
| J5578 | 14572 |
| J5582 | 14596 |
| J5582.1 | 14600 |
| J5592 | 14497 |
| J5594 | 14496 |
| J5601 | 14472 |
| J5604 | 14488 |
| J5608 | 14480 |
| J5610 | 14604 |
| J5618 | 14624 |
| J5618.1 | 14628 |
| J5628 | 14632 |
| J5629 | 14636 |
| J5630 | 14644 |
| J5631 | 14648 |
| J5632 | 14652 |
| J5632.5 | 14702 |
| J5633 | 14700 |
| J5634 | 14694 |
| J5635 | 14696 |
| J5635.1 | 14696.1 |
| J5635.3 | 14697.5 |
| J5635.4 | 14697 |
| J5635.7 | 14698 |
| J5636 | 14708 |
| J5636.5 | 14699 |
| J5637 | 14704 |
| J5638 | 14688 |
| J5639.2 | 14660 |
| J5640 | 14656 |
| J5642 | 14664 |
| J5642.1 | 14668 |
| J5646 | 14672 |
| J5647.17 | 14674 |
| J5647.5 | 14673 |
| J5649 | 14692 |
| J5650 | 14712 |
| J5656 | 14716 |
| J5656.5 | 14720 |
| J5656.8 | 14722 |
| J5657.5 | 14730 |
| J5657.6 | 14731 |
| J5657.7 | 14731.5 |
| J5658 | 14732 |
| J5659 | 14728 |
| J5662.3 | 14727 |
| J5662.5 | 14727.5 |
| J5664 | 14736 |
| J5666 | 14737.5 |
| J5667.3 | 14738 |
| J5667.38 | 14739.3 |
| J5667.4 | 14739.6 |
| J5668 | 14740 |
| J5668.5 | 14742 |
| J5672 | 14752 |
| J5673.13 | 14755.4 |
| J5673.14 | 14755.6 |
| J5673.21 | 14754 |
| J5674 | 14756 |
| J5675 | 14745 |
| J5678 | 14760 |
| J5678.4 | 14761 |
| J5686 | 14765 |
| J5687.5 | 14766.5 |
| J5688 | 14767 |
| J5688.2 | 14767.2 |
| J5690 | 14768 |
| J5694 | 14772 |
| J5695 | 14774 |
| J5695.1 | 14776 |
| J5696 | 14784 |
| J5698 | 14792 |
| J5698.1 | 14796 |
| J5698.5 | 14800 |
| J5698.51 | 14804 |
| J5699.5 | 14798 |
| J5700 | 16851 |
| J5702 | 14880 |
| J5704 | 14888 |
| J5705 | 14882 |
| J5705.2 | 14882.5 |
| J5706 | 14884 |
| J5710 | 14896 |
| J5712 | 14892 |
| J5715 | 14834 |
| J5716 | 14836 |
| J5718 | 14840 |
| J5722 | 14844 |
| J5723 | 14848 |
| J5723.5 | 14850 |
| J5724 | 14812 |
| J5725 | 14816 |
| J5725.1 | 14820 |
| J5727 | 14828 |
| J5728 | 14825 |
| J5730 | 14832 |
| J5731 | 14852 |
| J5734 | 14860 |
| J5736 | 14864 |
| J5736.1 | 14868 |
| J5736.2 | 14868.5 |
| J5736.3 | 14869 |
| J5736.4 | 14870 |
| J5736.45 | 14871 |
| J5736.5 | 14872 |
| J5738.5 | 14862 |
| J5739 | 14873 |
| J5739.5 | 14874 |
| J5743 | 14878 |
| J5746 | 14904 |
| J5748 | 14908 |
| J5750 | 14912 |
| J5752 | 14916 |
| J5752.1 | 14920 |
| J5760.4 | 14926 |
| J5770 | 14929 |
| J5772 | 14932 |
| J5772.23 | 14932.3 |
| J5772.25 | 14932.6 |
| J5772.3 | 14933 |
| J5772.31 | 14933.1 |
| J5772.5 | 14934 |
| J5773 | 14936 |
| J5773.5 | 14937 |
| J5774 | 14937.1 |
| J5775 | 14937.05 |
| J5776 | 14940 |
| J5777 | 14944 |
| J5780 | 14948 |
| J5782 | 14984 |
| J5784 | 14960 |
| J5784.1 | 14964 |
| J5785.6 | 14981 |
| J5785.8 | 14980 |
| J5787 | 14983 |
| J5787.4 | 14983.5 |
| J5789 | 14988 |
| J5790 | 14992 |
| J5790.5 | 14996 |
| J5790.6 | 15060 |
| J5790.8 | 15062 |
| J5790.85 | 15063 |
| J5790.86 | 15063.1 |
| J5790.9 | 15062.4 |
| J5790.95 | 15062.6 |
| J5791 | 15000 |
| J5792 | 15004 |
| J5793 | 15016 |
| J5793.1 | 15020 |
| J5793.5 | 15021 |
| J5794 | 15008 |
| J5795 | 15024 |
| J5795.1 | 15024.5 |
| J5795.3 | 15026 |
| J5795.31 | 15026.1 |
| J5795.5 | 15028 |
| J5798 | 15048 |
| J5799 | 15036 |
| J5800 | 15040 |
| J5800.1 | 15044 |
| J5800.2 | 15044.5 |
| J5800.4 | 15045 |
| J5800.6 | 15045.5 |
| J5800.7 | 15046 |
| J5801 | 15052 |
| J5802 | 15056 |

| Inter. | U.S. |
|---|---|
| J5804 | 15096 |
| J5805 | 15104 |
| J5806 | 15100 |
| J5806.5 | 15102 |
| J5807 | 15108 |
| J5809.2 | 15116 |
| J5809.4 | 15116.4 |
| J5809.6 | 15116.6 |
| J5811 | 15120 |
| J5812.5 | 15125 |
| J5812.54 | 15122 |
| J5812.56 | 15122.1 |
| J5812.6 | 15125.2 |
| J5812.65 | 15125.4 |
| J5813.8 | 15126 |
| J5813.82 | 15127 |
| J5814 | 15128 |
| J5815 | 15076 |
| J5815.4 | 15072 |
| J5816 | 15068 |
| J5816.2 | 15068.2 |
| J5816.4 | 15068.4 |
| J5816.6 | 15068.6 |
| J5817 | 15064 |
| J5817.1 | 15082 |
| J5817.15 | 15084 |
| J5817.2 | 15092 |
| J5817.4 | 15088 |
| J5817.5 | 15093 |
| J5818 | 15080 |
| J5819 | 15160 |
| J5819.1 | 15158 |
| J5819.2 | 15156 |
| J5819.4 | 15152 |
| J5819.5 | 15154 |
| J5819.6 | 15140 |
| J5820 | 15149 |
| J5820.1 | 15150 |
| J5820.4 | 15148.2 |
| J5820.5 | 15148.4 |
| J5821 | 15144 |
| J5821.1 | 15148 |
| J5821.3 | 15151 |
| J5821.8 | 15136 |
| J5821.85 | 15137 |
| J5822 | 15151.6 |
| J5822.1 | 15151.65 |
| J5822.4 | 15151.7 |
| J5823 | 15151.8 |
| J5824 | 15150.1 |
| J5824.2 | 15150.2 |
| J5825 | 15150.3 |
| J5825.2 | 15150.4 |
| J5827 | 15132 |
| J5830.2 | 15174 |
| J5830.3 | 15161 |
| J5830.5 | 15162 |
| J5830.7 | 15164 |
| J5834 | 15176 |
| J5834.2 | 15177 |
| J5834.3 | 15177.1 |
| J5834.4 | 15178 |
| J5834.5 | 15178.1 |
| J5837 | 15180 |
| J5837.2 | 15182 |
| J5837.4 | 15183 |
| J5838 | 15184 |
| J5839 | 15196 |
| J5839.1 | 15196.1 |
| J5839.8 | 15197 |
| J5839.9 | 15197.2 |
| J5840.1 | 15197.4 |
| J5840.3 | 15197.8 |
| J5840.4 | 15198 |
| J5841.5 | 15200 |
| J5841.54 | 15200.05 |
| J5841.58 | 15200.1 |
| J5841.6 | 15201 |
| J5841.7 | 15202 |
| J5841.8 | 15202.5 |
| J5842 | 16266 |
| J5842.5 | 16265 |
| J5843 | 16264.7 |
| J5843.5 | 16264.5 |
| J5844 | 16264 |
| J5844.5 | 16267.5 |
| J5845 | 16267 |
| J5846 | 16256 |
| J5846.1 | 16260 |
| J5848 | 16252 |
| J5848.5 | 16250 |
| J5850 | 16248 |
| J5851 | 16244 |
| J5852 | 16240 |
| J5856 | 16236 |
| J5858 | 16225 |
| J5859.4 | 16230 |
| J5861 | 16228 |
| J5866 | 16220 |
| J5868 | 16208 |
| J5872 | 16212 |
| J5872.1 | 16216 |
| J5882 | 16197 |
| J5882.1 | 16197.1 |
| J5882.4 | 16196.2 |
| J5882.42 | 16196.1 |
| J5882.44 | 16196.4 |
| J5882.46 | 16196.3 |
| J5882.48 | 16196.6 |
| J5882.51 | 16196.5 |
| J5882.52 | 16196.8 |
| J5882.54 | 16196.7 |
| J5882.56 | 16196.91 |
| J5882.58 | 16196.9 |
| J5882.6 | 16196.93 |
| J5882.62 | 16196.94 |
| J5884.24 | 16190 |
| J5884.25 | 16190.1 |
| J5884.43 | 16191.94 |
| J5884.9 | 16191.8 |
| J5885 | 16191.7 |
| J5885.2 | 16191.91 |
| J5885.3 | 16191.9 |
| J5885.4 | 16191.92 |
| J5888 | 16192 |
| J5891 | 16180 |
| J5891.1 | 16184 |
| J5892 | 16164 |
| J5892.1 | 16168 |
| J5892.4 | 16172 |
| J5892.5 | 16176 |
| J5894.3 | 16169 |
| J5894.31 | 16169.5 |
| J5895 | 16152 |
| J5896 | 16156 |
| J5897 | 16157 |
| J5900 | 16148 |
| J5903 | 16140 |
| J5903.1 | 16144 |
| J5908 | 16132 |
| J5908.5 | 16133 |
| J5908.6 | 16133.5 |
| J5908.7 | 16134 |
| J5908.71 | 16134.5 |
| J5909.5 | 16118 |
| J5911 | 16117 |
| J5912 | 16116 |
| J5912.5 | 17230 |
| J5913 | 16112 |
| J5913.4 | 16111 |
| J5913.5 | 16110 |
| J5914 | 16109 |
| J5915 | 16108 |
| J5930 | 16268 |
| J5934 | 16288 |
| J5936 | 16292 |
| J5937 | 16296 |
| J5937.5 | 16300 |
| J5940 | 16280 |
| J5942 | 16284 |
| J5943 | 16304 |
| J5943.1 | 16308 |
| J5943.2 | 16312 |
| J5944 | 16316 |
| J5945 | 16320 |
| J5946 | 16324 |
| J5947 | 16328 |
| J5948 | 16332 |
| J5948.4 | 16336 |
| J5950 | 16340 |
| J5950.2 | 16344 |
| J5950.4 | 16348 |
| J5950.6 | 16352 |
| J5950.7 | 16356 |
| J5952 | 16364 |
| J5954 | 16368 |
| J5954.5 | 16369 |
| J5955 | 16372 |
| J5957 | 16374 |
| J5958 | 16376 |
| J5964 | 16380 |
| J5968 | 16384 |
| J5970 | 16388 |
| J5972 | 16392 |
| J5974 | 16396 |
| J5976 | 16400 |
| J5982 | 16420 |
| J5984 | 16419 |
| J5985 | 16418 |
| J5986 | 16404 |
| J5989 | 16412 |
| J5989.1 | 16416 |
| J5990 | 16410 |
| J5990.1 | 16411 |
| J5992 | 16424 |
| J5994 | 16428 |
| J5994.1 | 16431 |
| j5994.11 | 16431.5 |
| J5997 | 16432 |
| J5999 | 16440 |
| J6002 | 16447 |
| J6003 | 16448 |
| J6006 | 16445 |
| J6006.1 | 16446 |
| J6007 | 16460 |
| J6008.2 | 16461 |
| J6009.6 | 16473 |
| J6009.7 | 16457 |
| J6010 | 16476 |
| J6010.5 | 16477 |
| J6012 | 16478 |
| J6013 | 16479 |
| J6014 | 16483 |
| J6016 | 16480 |
| J6018 | 16481 |
| J6020 | 15818, 16482 |
| J6024 | 15816 |
| J6028 | 15820 |
| J6030 | 15821 |
| J6034 | 15824 |
| J6038 | 15828 |
| J6041 | 15832.7 |
| J6041.5 | 15832.5 |
| J6041.8 | 15832.3 |
| J6042 | 15832 |
| J6043 | 15833 |
| J6043.5 | 15834 |
| J6043.6 | 15835 |
| J6043.7 | 15835.5 |
| J6043.8 | 15835.7 |
| J6044 | 15840 |
| J6045 | 15844 |
| J6048 | 16484 |
| J6052 | 16488 |
| J6052.1 | 16492 |
| J6064 | 16500 |
| J6065 | 16502 |
| J6067 | 16516 |
| J6067.2 | 16520 |
| J6067.21 | 16524 |
| J6068 | 16504 |
| J6069 | 16508 |
| J6072 | 16527 |
| J6081 | 16528 |
| J6081.2 | 16530 |
| J6085 | 16532 |
| J6085.2 | 16544 |
| J6086 | 16564 |
| J6088 | 16568 |
| J6089 | 16570 |
| J6090 | 16572 |
| J6090.3 | 16576 |
| J6090.5 | 16580 |
| J6090.51 | 16584 |
| J6091 | 16588 |
| J6092 | 16592 |
| J6098 | 16604 |
| J6102 | 16600 |
| J6112 | 16605 |
| J6121 | 16606 |

| Inter. | U.S. |
|---|---|
| J6123 | 16606.1 |
| J6124 | 16606.2 |
| J6124.5 | 16606.3 |
| J6125 | 16606.4 |
| J6126 | 16606.5 |
| J6127 | 16606.6 |
| J6129 | 16606.7 |
| J6130 | 16606.8 |
| J6132 | 16612 |
| J6132.1 | 16616 |
| J6132.2 | 16620 |
| J6134 | 16621 |
| J6134.1 | 16621.1 |
| J6134.2 | 16622 |
| J6134.21 | 16622.1 |
| J6134.3 | 16622.5 |
| J6134.36 | 16622.7 |
| J6134.38 | 16622.8 |
| J6134.6 | 16623 |
| J6134.8 | 16623.1 |
| J6136 | 16624 |
| J6138 | 16628 |
| J6143 | 16630 |
| J6144 | 16632 |
| J6144.2 | 16633 |
| J6144.21 | 16634 |
| J6144.5 | 16635 |
| J6145 | 16660 |
| J6146 | 16656 |
| J6146.5 | 16652 |
| J6147 | 16636 |
| J6147.5 | 16638 |
| J6147.8 | 16639 |
| J6148.5 | 16650 |
| J6149 | 16648 |
| J6149.2 | 16649 |
| J6151 | 16662 |
| J6152 | 16664 |
| J6153.6 | 16674 |
| J6154.5 | 16678 |
| J6156 | 16679 |
| J6157 | 16680 |
| J6159 | 16684 |
| J6159.7 | 16687.1 |
| J6160 | 16688 |
| J6164 | 16728 |
| J6166 | 16700 |
| J6166.5 | 16701 |
| J6166.7 | 16702 |
| J6167.6 | 16726 |
| J6167.65 | 16725.5 |
| J6167.66 | 16725.51 |
| J6172 | 16732 |
| J6174 | 16736 |
| J6176 | 16740 |
| J6180 | 16744 |
| J6188 | 16748 |
| J6190 | 16747 |
| J6191 | 16756 |
| J6191.1 | 16760 |
| J6191.2 | 16761 |
| J6191.9 | 16784 |
| J6191.91 | 16788 |
| J6192.1 | 16790.5 |
| J6193 | 16790 |
| J6193.5 | 16763 |
| J6194 | 16764 |
| J6196 | 16768 |
| J6198 | 16772 |
| J6200 | 16776 |
| J6202 | 16780 |
| J6204 | 16792 |
| J6206 | 16804 |
| J6207 | 16808 |
| J6208 | 16810 |
| J6214 | 16812 |
| J6216 | 16806 |
| J6218 | 16807 |
| J6222.5 | 16811 |
| J6222.8 | 16813 |
| J6223 | 16813.5 |
| J6226 | 16814 |
| J6229 | 16815 |
| J6229.2 | 16819 |
| J6229.5 | 16817 |
| J6229.51 | 16818 |
| J6236 | 16821 |
| J6236.1 | 16822 |
| J6254 | 16828 |
| J6255.3 | 16831 |
| J6256 | 16832 |
| J6260 | 16840 |
| J6261.2 | 16841 |
| J6261.3 | 16842 |
| J6262 | 16836 |
| J6265 | 16835 |
| J6266 | 16844 |
| J6266.2 | 16846 |
| J6266.3 | 16846.6 |
| J6266.33 | 16846.8 |
| J6266.4 | 16846.3 |
| J6266.5 | 16847 |
| J6266.51 | 16847.5 |
| J6267 | 16848 |
| J6267.3 | 16848.2 |
| J6267.4 | 16848.3 |
| J6267.6 | 16848.4 |
| J6267.8 | 16849 |
| J6268 | 16850 |
| J6269 | 16856 |
| J6270 | 16852 |
| J6274 | 16860 |
| J6275 | 16860.2 |
| J6279.9 | 16872 |
| J6280 | 16872.1 |
| J6283 | 16873 |
| J6283.1 | 16873.1 |
| J6285.4 | 16873.82 |
| J6285.6 | 16873.81 |
| J6287 | 16873.83 |
| J6288 | 16873.84 |
| J6288.2 | 16873.85 |
| J6294 | 16875.5 |
| J6297 | 16875 |
| J6299 | 16879.7 |
| J6299.6 | 16879.8 |
| J6299.7 | 16879.9 |
| J6300.4 | 16890 |
| J6301 | 16892 |
| J6310 | 16880 |
| J6310.1 | 16884 |
| J6312 | 16896 |
| J6314 | 16900 |
| J6330 | 15850 |
| J6336 | 15880 |
| J6336.5 | 15876 |
| J6337 | 15884 |
| J6338 | 15888 |
| J6339 | 15892 |
| J6339.4 | 15896 |
| J6340 | 15868 |
| J6340.1 | 15872 |
| J6342 | 15864 |
| J6343 | 15852 |
| J6343.5 | 15853 |
| J6346 | 15900 |
| J6346.6 | 15901 |
| J6346.61 | 15902 |
| J6347.2 | 15903 |
| J6352 | 15912 |
| J6352.1 | 15916 |
| J6352.5 | 15918 |
| J6352.51 | 15919 |
| J6352.52 | 15921 |
| J6352.53 | 15923 |
| J6352.54 | 15925 |
| J6352.55 | 15926 |
| J6356 | 15932 |
| J6356.1 | 15936 |
| J6357 | 15938 |
| J6357.5 | 15940 |
| J6358.2 | 15941 |
| J6358.21 | 15942 |
| J6358.45 | 15957 |
| J6358.451 | 15957.1 |
| J6358.6 | 15954 |
| J6359 | 15952 |
| J6359.2 | 15950 |
| J6365 | 15958 |
| J6366 | 15959 |
| J6366.1 | 15959.1 |
| J6368 | 15960 |
| J6372 | 15964 |
| J6374 | 15968 |
| J6375.4 | 15976 |
| J6375.41 | 15980 |
| J6376 | 15972 |
| J6376.4 | 15992 |
| J6376.41 | 15996 |
| J6376.6 | 15984 |
| J6376.61 | 15988 |
| J6377 | 16024 |
| J6377.1 | 16028 |
| J6378 | 16012 |
| J6380 | 16008 |
| J6381 | 16013 |
| J6381.1 | 16014 |
| J6382 | 16020 |
| J6384 | 16016 |
| J6386 | 16032 |
| J6389 | 16036 |
| J6393 | 16037 |
| J6393.5 | 16038 |
| J6393.7 | 16040 |
| J6394.4 | 16049 |
| J6394.41 | 16050 |
| J6395 | 16050.5 |
| J6395.1 | 16051 |
| J6396 | 16053 |
| J6398 | 16044 |
| J6399 | 16054 |
| J6403 | 16060 |
| J6404 | 16080 |
| J6404.1 | 16084 |
| J6404.31 | 16077 |
| J6406 | 16088 |
| J6408.3 | 16093 |
| J6408.8 | 16094 |
| J6409 | 16096 |
| J6411 | 16100 |
| J6414 | 16064 |
| J6416 | 16056 |
| J6419 | 17004 |
| J6420 | 17000 |
| J6424 | 17008 |
| J6425 | 17012 |
| J6425.4 | 17016 |
| J6426 | 17024 |
| J6427 | 17020 |
| J6427.5 | 17025 |
| J6427.51 | 17025.5 |
| J6428 | 16904 |
| J6431 | 16906 |
| J6433 | 16910 |
| J6434 | 16912 |
| J6438 | 16920 |
| J6440 | 16924 |
| J6441 | 16928 |
| J6442 | 16932 |
| J6444 | 16936 |
| J6446 | 16952 |
| J6446.5 | 16950 |
| J6447 | 16976 |
| J6448 | 16964 |
| J6448.4 | 16956 |
| J6448.7 | 16959, 16973.5 |
| J6448.9 | 16962 |
| J6449 | 16961 |
| J6449.5 | 16961.3 |
| J6449.7 | 16961.7 |
| J6452 | 16960 |
| J6452.6 | 16988 |
| J6453 | 16992 |
| J6453.2 | 16993 |
| J6453.4 | 16996 |
| J6453.5 | 17037 |
| J6453.8 | 17039 |
| J6455 | 17049 |
| J6455.1 | 17049.5 |
| J6457 | 17052 |
| J6458.5 | 17058 |
| J6459 | 17068 |
| J6459.5 | 17064 |
| J6460.3 | 17069 |
| J6461.5 | 17073 |
| J6461.52 | 17074 |
| J6461.6 | 17076 |
| J6461.85 | 17077 |
| J6461.95 | 17082 |
| J6462 | 17036 |

# CROSS REFERENCE - INTERNATIONAL vs. U.S. LIGHT NUMBER

| Inter. | U.S. |
|---|---|
| J6469 | 17084 |
| J6470 | 17085 |
| J6472 | 17028 |
| J6474 | 17032 |
| J6476 | 17014 |
| J6477 | 17100 |
| J6477.5 | 17087 |
| J6478 | 17088 |
| J6478.2 | 17088.5 |
| J6479 | 17089 |
| J6479.5 | 17090 |
| J6480.36 | 17106 |
| J6480.37 | 17107 |
| J6480.4 | 17108 |
| J6480.42 | 17112 |
| J6480.44 | 17116 |
| J6481 | 17140 |
| J6483 | 17128 |
| J6483.2 | 17132 |
| J6483.4 | 17136 |
| J6484 | 17138 |
| J6485 | 17139 |
| J6487 | 17142 |
| J6488 | 17141 |
| J6489 | 17144 |
| J6490 | 17148 |
| J6492 | 17168 |
| J6494 | 17172 |
| J6499 | 17162.3 |
| J6500 | 17164 |
| J6500.1 | 17163 |
| J6500.6 | 17162.5 |
| J6500.8 | 17162.1 |
| J6501 | 17162 |
| J6502 | 17160 |
| J6502.1 | 17161 |
| J6502.25 | 17155.5 |
| J6502.5 | 17155 |
| J6503 | 17154 |
| J6504 | 17156 |
| J6508 | 17152 |
| J6508.5 | 17153 |
| J6508.8 | 17153.6 |
| J6509 | 17192 |
| J6509.1 | 17192.5 |
| J6509.2 | 17193 |
| J6509.8 | 17190 |
| J6510 | 17184 |
| J6512 | 17188 |
| J6514 | 17194 |
| J6515 | 17195 |
| J6516 | 17195.5 |
| J6517 | 17200 |
| J6518 | 17196 |
| J6521 | 17204 |
| J6524 | 17210 |
| J6525 | 17212 |

| Inter. | U.S. |
|---|---|
| J6526 | 17216 |
| J6530.3 | 17224 |
| J6615 | 17227 |
| J6800 | 17242 |
| J6810 | 17244 |
| J6836 | 17278 |
| J6841 | 17292 |
| J6843 | 17296 |
| J6843.1 | 17300 |
| J6847 | 17309 |
| J6847.1 | 17310 |
| J6858 | 17324 |
| J6858.1 | 17328 |
| J6858.5 | 17329 |
| J6858.51 | 17330 |
| J6862 | 17332 |
| J6864.4 | 17352 |
| J6866 | 17353 |
| J6866.5 | 17355 |
| J6867.2 | 17358 |
| J6868 | 17360 |
| J6870 | 17364 |
| J6870.6 | 17368 |
| J6870.7 | 17370 |
| J6873 | 17388 |
| J6873.1 | 17392 |
| J6878.9 | 17376 |
| J6879.4 | 17399.6 |
| J6879.9 | 17399.4 |
| J6880 | 17399.8 |
| J6894 | 17416 |
| J6895 | 17420 |
| J6895.1 | 17424 |
| J6901 | 17428 |
| J6902 | 17436 |
| J6904 | 17440 |
| J6907.3 | 17455.5 |
| J7000 | 17456.5 |
| J7000.1 | 17456.6 |
| J7000.8 | 17456.7 |
| J7000.9 | 17456.8 |
| L5000 | 4 |
| L5100 | 8 |
| L5200 | 12 |
| L5200.1 | 16 |
| L5204 | 20 |
| L5204.1 | 24 |
| L5212 | 28 |
| L5212.1 | 32 |
| L5214 | 36 |
| L5215 | 48 |
| L5215.1 | 52 |
| L5216 | 40 |
| L5216.1 | 44 |
| L5217 | 72 |
| L5221 | 56 |
| L5221.1 | 60 |

| Inter. | U.S. |
|---|---|
| L5222 | 64 |
| L5222.1 | 68 |
| L5226 | 92 |
| L5228 | 96 |
| L5230 | 100 |
| L5232 | 104 |
| L5234 | 108 |
| L5235 | 137 |
| L5235.1 | 138 |
| L5238 | 116 |
| L5238.1 | 120 |
| L5242 | 132 |
| L5242.1 | 136 |
| L5244 | 112 |
| L5246 | 124 |
| L5246.1 | 128 |
| L5260 | 140 |
| L5260.1 | 144 |
| L5264 | 148 |
| L5264.1 | 152 |
| L5266 | 156 |
| L5270 | 160 |
| L5273.9 | 164 |
| L5281.9 | 216 |
| L5281.91 | 220 |
| L5282.1 | 224 |
| L5284 | 212 |
| L5346 | 228 |
| L5348 | 232 |
| L5348.1 | 236 |
| L5400 | 248 |
| L5500 | 252 |
| L5504 | 256 |
| L5508 | 260 |
| L5508.1 | 264 |
| L5512 | 282 |
| L5520 | 284 |
| L5520.1 | 288 |
| L5525 | 292 |
| L5530 | 296 |
| L5531 | 294 |
| L5531.1 | 294.1 |
| L5535 | 300 |
| L5550 | 304 |
| L5552 | 308 |
| L5554 | 312 |
| L5554.1 | 316 |
| L5558 | 320 |
| L5572 | 326 |
| L5572.1 | 326.1 |
| L5575 | 328 |
| L5580 | 332 |
| L5590 | 336 |
| L5594 | 340 |
| L5596 | 344 |
| L5596.1 | 348 |
| L5598 | 352 |

| Inter. | U.S. |
|---|---|
| L5598.1 | 356 |
| L5620 | 364 |
| L5620.1 | 368 |
| L5625 | 372 |
| L5625.1 | 376 |
| L5640 | 380 |
| L5660 | 384 |
| L5680 | 388 |
| L5680.1 | 392 |
| L5696 | 396 |
| L5696.1 | 400 |
| L5706 | 408 |
| L5706.1 | 412 |
| L5712 | 404 |
| L5718 | 424 |
| L5719.1 | 425 |
| L5719.11 | 425.1 |
| L5720 | 426 |
| L5720.1 | 426.1 |
| L5790 | 428 |
| L5791 | 432 |
| L5800 | 436 |
| L5840 | 440 |
| L5860 | 444 |
| L5860.1 | 448 |
| L5870 | 468 |
| L5870.1 | 472 |
| L5884 | 476 |
| L5884.1 | 480 |
| L5890 | 460 |
| L5890.1 | 464 |
| L5891 | 457 |
| L5891.1 | 457.1 |
| L5891.4 | 458 |
| L5891.41 | 458.1 |
| L5892 | 456 |
| L5918 | 508 |
| L5920 | 512 |
| L5920.1 | 516 |
| L5928 | 520 |
| L5928.1 | 524 |
| L5932 | 535 |
| L5932.1 | 536 |
| L5936 | 560 |
| L5940 | 540 |
| L5940.1 | 544 |
| L5942 | 548 |
| L5942.1 | 552 |
| L5944 | 556 |
| L5951 | 562 |
| L5951.1 | 566 |
| L5970 | 580 |
| L5970.1 | 584 |
| L5990 | 596 |

L5990 ................596

www.ingramcontent.com/pod-product-compliance
Lightning Source LLC
Chambersburg PA
CBHW081538300426
44116CB00015B/2670